OXFORD ENG[...]

General editor: MI[...]
Associate General Editors: PETER [...]

FOUR RESTORATION LIBERTINE PLAYS

THE court of Charles II (1660–85) adopted libertinism as a lifestyle, pursuing pleasure with an abandon that shocked and titillated onlookers. Seventeenth-century intellectuals saw libertinism as a body of thought that might underwrite changes in philosophy, politics, and science. These two aspects of libertinism, the lubricious and the learned, found expression in the sex comedies written during the 1670s and early 1680s, a time when London theatre was unfettered by morality. The four plays in this volume capture the gamut of contemporary reactions to libertinism, from the outraged disapproval of Thomas Shadwell's sprawling, experimental *The Libertine* (1675), to the cool acquiescence of Sir George Etherege's brilliant comedy, *The Man of Mode* (1676), the cheerful assent of Thomas Durfey's rollicking farce, *A Fond Husband* (1677), and the moody forebodings of Thomas Otway's darkly comic tale of marital warfare, *Friendship in Fashion* (1678).

DEBORAH PAYNE FISK is an Associate Professor in the Department of Literature and an Affiliate Professor in the Department of Performing Arts at American University, Washington, DC. The editor of *The Cambridge Companion to English Restoration Theatre*, she has published extensively on seventeenth- and eighteenth-century theatre. Currently Professor Payne Fisk is working on *A History of World Theatre* for Laurence King Press. She also does dramaturgical work for theatre companies in Washington, DC.

MICHAEL CORDNER is Reader in the Department of English and Related Literature at the University of York. He has edited George Farquhar's *The Beaux' Stratagem*, the *Complete Plays* of Sir George Etherege, and, for Oxford English Drama, *Four Restoration Marriage Plays* and Sheridan's *The School for Scandal and Other Plays*. He is writing books on *The Comedy of Marriage* and *Shakespeare and the Actor*.

PETER HOLLAND is Professor of English at the University of Notre Dame, Indiana.

MARTIN WIGGINS is a fellow of the Shakespeare Institute and Lecturer in English at the University of Birmingham.

OXFORD ENGLISH DRAMA

J. M. Barrie
Peter Pan and Other Plays

Aphra Behn
The Rover and Other Plays

John Ford
'Tis Pity She's a Whore and Other Plays

Ben Jonson
The Alchemist and Other Plays

Ben Jonson
The Devil is an Ass and Other Plays

D. H. Lawrence
*The Widowing of Mrs Holroyd and
Other Plays*

Christopher Marlowe
Doctor Faustus and Other Plays

John Marston
The Malcontent and Other Plays

Thomas Middleton
Women Beware Women and Other Plays

*A Mad World, My Masters, and Other
Plays*

Richard Brinsley Sheridan
The School for Scandal and Other Plays

J. M. Synge
*The Playboy of the Western World and
Other Plays*

John Vanbrugh
The Relapse and Other Plays

John Webster
The Duchess of Malfi and Other Plays

Oscar Wilde
*The Importance of Being Earnest and
Other Plays*

William Wycherley
The Country Wife and Other Plays

Court Masques
ed. David Lindley

Eighteenth-Century Women Dramatists
ed. Melinda Finberg

Five Romantic Plays
ed. Paul Baines and Edward Burns

Four Jacobean Sex Tragedies
ed. Martin Wiggins

Four Restoration Marriage Plays
ed. Michael Cordner

Four Revenge Tragedies
ed. Katharine Maus

*London Assurance and Other Victorian
Comedies*
ed. Klaus Stierstorfer

*The New Woman and Other
Emancipated Woman Plays*
ed. Jean Chothia

*The Roaring Girl and Other City
Comedies*
ed. James Knowles and Eugene
Giddens

OXFORD WORLD'S CLASSICS

Four Restoration Libertine Plays

THOMAS SHADWELL
The Libertine

SIR GEORGE ETHEREGE
The Man of Mode; or, Sir Fopling Flutter

THOMAS DURFEY
A Fond Husband; or, The Plotting Sisters

THOMAS OTWAY
Friendship in Fashion

Edited with an Introduction and Notes by
DEBORAH PAYNE FISK

OXFORD

UNIVERSITY PRESS

Great Clarendon Street, Oxford OX2 6DP

Oxford University Press is a department of the University of Oxford.
It furthers the University's objective of excellence in research, scholarship,
and education by publishing worldwide in

Oxford New York

Auckland Cape Town Dar es Salaam Hong Kong Karachi
Kuala Lumpur Madrid Melbourne Mexico City Nairobi
New Delhi Shanghai Taipei Toronto

With offices in

Argentina Austria Brazil Chile Czech Republic France Greece
Guatemala Hungary Italy Japan South Korea Poland Portugal
Singapore Switzerland Thailand Turkey Ukraine Vietnam

Oxford is a registered trade mark of Oxford University Press
in the UK and in certain other countries

Published in the United States
by Oxford University Press Inc., New York

First published as an Oxford World's Classics paperback 2005
Reissued 2009

British Library Cataloguing in Publication Data

Data available

Library of Congress Cataloging in Publication Data

Four Restoration libertine plays / edited with an introduction and notes by Deborah Payne Fisk
p. cm. — (Oxford English drama)
Includes bibliographical references.
1. English drama — Restoration, 1660–1700. 2. Libertinism — Drama. I. Payne Fisk, Deborah.
II. Shadwell, Thomas, 1642?–1692. Libertine. III. Etherege, George, Sir, 1635?–1691. Man of mode.
IV. D'Urfey, Thomas, 1653–1723. Fond husband. V. Otway, Thomas, 1652–1685. Friendship in fashion.
VI. Series.
PR1266.F675 2005 822'.408 — dc22 — 2004027977

ISBN 978-0-19-955594-9

1

Typeset in Ehrhardt
by RefineCatch Limited, Bungay, Suffolk
Printed in Great Britain by
Clays Ltd, St Ives plc

TO
RODNEY HARALD FISK

CONTENTS

ACKNOWLEDGEMENTS

I am grateful for the expert advice Michael Cordner offered through the various stages of preparing this edition. His experience and knowledge saved me from committing more mistakes than I care to admit. Mary Partridge did an expert job with the collations, Edwin Pritchard did the same with copy-editing, and Martin Wiggins answered several anxious last-minute queries with calm and wisdom. Throughout the project, Judith Luna at OUP has proved to be a bastion of strength and patience. I want to thank her especially for seeing the project through. I also want to thank Peter Holland for first suggesting that I undertake *Four Restoration Libertine Plays*. Christopher Wheatley, Richard Sha, and Kathleen Lesko read the introduction and suggested invaluable improvements. Any remaining errors are, of course, my responsibility. The Henry E. Huntington Library in the summer of 1998 and the William Andrews Clark Memorial Library in the autumn of 1999 provided short-term fellowships that allowed me to produce copy texts from their first editions. The Folger Shakespeare Library, as always, has been a haven and a refuge. I drew heavily upon the collections of all three libraries to write the notes and the introduction. A memorable Folger Institute seminar with Barbara Mowat and Paul Werstine in the spring of 1998 introduced me to the basic principles of textual editing and abated my initial terror. A sabbatical from American University for 1999–2000 allowed me to draft the notes and introduction.

Finally, I want to acknowledge my husband, Rodney Harald Fisk, who courted me that summer of 1998, when I first began work on the copy texts. His bimonthly trips from Washington, DC, to the West Coast resulted in a romantic outcome more typical of Jane Austen than Sir George Etherege. Then again, we do not necessarily want to live first hand what we study.

INTRODUCTION

AT one time, calling four comedies from the Restoration (1660–1714) 'libertine' would have been an exercise in redundancy. Everyone knew, so the reasoning went, that these comedies advocated sexual pleasure and were therefore essentially 'libertine' in nature. That so many Restoration scripts dropped out of the performance repertory by the mid-eighteenth century, not to resurface until the 1920s, supplied further proof of their licentious nature. These views, standard in critical assessments from Samuel Johnson through to the 1950s, were occasionally challenged by critics hoping to rescue the plays from the slag heap of time. Ironically, while the moralists may have banned Restoration comedies from the library and the stage, the advocates tacitly admitted to the same concern by inventing adroit arguments that deflected attention away from sex to—well, practically anything else.

The Romantic critic Charles Lamb made one of the first note-worthy defences along these lines, arguing that Restoration comedies 'are a world of themselves almost as much as fairy-land. . . . The Fainalls and the Mirabels, the Dorimants and the Lady Touchwoods, in their own sphere, do not offend my moral sense; in fact they do not appeal to it at all.'[1] In the 1960s Aubrey Williams put forth an ingenious variation on the 'they aren't *really* about sex' thesis. Instead Williams condemned the 'scholars and critics [who] apparently have become both captives and abettors of a mythic Restoration sexuality'.[2] Of the plays, Williams asserted that behind the 'fallen world' of Restoration comedies 'there is usually implied, or explicitly affirmed, both an immanent and a transcendent order of Providence',[3] a perhaps startling statement given the cheerful immorality of any number of plays. The historical interpretations of the last two decades have again shifted attention away from sex, this time to politics. Historicists, by the very nature of their enterprise, read sexual behaviour as symptomatic of larger social forces, such as class tensions or royalist ideology; thus, sexual desire can never be 'about' itself but something else. For

[1] Charles Lamb, 'On the Artificial Comedy of the Last Century', in Percy Fitzgerald (ed.), *The Art of the Stage as set out in Lamb's Dramatic Essays* (London, 1885), 74.

[2] Aubrey L. Williams, *An Approach to Congreve* (New Haven, 1979), 12.

[3] Ibid. 18.

Laura Brown 'the formal centrality of libertine philosophy for the Restoration dramatists results from its direct implication of the essential social contradictions of their time and class'.[4] For J. Douglas Canfield 'Restoration comedy . . . is part of this same *official discourse*, to borrow a concept central to the work of the great Russian critic Mikhail Bakhtin. That is, it underwrites the same ideology, the same natural right of the English aristocracy—from peers to the gentry—to rule because they are superior in intelligence (wit) and natural parts, and because they have been bred to rule'.[5]

Recently Maximillian E. Novak has argued against the tendency to explain away the sexual content of Restoration comedies: 'I think, however, that at this juncture we should be willing to admit what common sense would seem to dictate. Almost all of these plays are indeed about sex to a degree, and some of them are almost exclusively about sex.'[6] While Novak is right to assert the obvious here, one hesitates to use 'sex' and 'libertine' as interchangeable adjectives. To do so assumes that any comedy in which sex features prominently is somehow libertine in nature. This is not the case. As Robert D. Hume demonstrated some years ago, the Restoration stage featured a wide variety of comic forms, including Spanish romance, reform comedy, wit comedy, sex comedy, sentiment-tinged comedy, French farce, and Augustan intrigue comedy.[7] Sex, directly or indirectly, drives the plots of these comedies, whether manifesting itself in the banter-as-foreplay exchanges of the 'gay couple', the swaggering masculine energy of the hero in a Spanish-style comedy, or the teasing insouciance of a heroine in a comedy of wit. While these plays may be sexy, they are not necessarily libertine.

This is not to agree with those critics who dismiss libertinism outright, maintaining that it never existed as an 'organized philosophy' in Restoration England and therefore had little to do with the drama.[8] Libertinism *did* exist in the late seventeenth century, but like all intellectual movements, it does not easily yield a consistent body of

---

[4] Laura Brown, *English Dramatic Form, 1660–1760* (New Haven, 1981), 41.

[5] J. Douglas Canfield, *Tricksters & Estates: On the Ideology of Restoration Comedy* (Lexington, Ky., 1997), 1.

[6] Maximillian E. Novak, 'Libertinism and Sexuality', in Susan J. Owen (ed.), *A Companion to Restoration Drama* (Oxford, 2001), 54.

[7] See Robert D. Hume, *The Development of English Drama in the Late Seventeenth Century* (Oxford, 1976).

[8] See Robert D. Hume, 'The Myth of the Rake in "Restoration" Comedy', *Studies in the Literary Imagination*, 10 (1977), 28.

thought or a single point of origin. There are differences too between French and English libertinism, as several scholars have observed. Philosophical libertinism, which merged scepticism with materialism, typified continental thinking, whereas sexual libertinism, as James Grantham Turner points out, coloured English thought from Shakespeare to the eighteenth century.[9] To complicate matters further, people reacted differently to libertinism, some expressing laconic bemusement, others a cool advocacy, and still others outraged condemnation. As the plays in this volume reveal, writers in the seventeenth century were hardly uniform in their thinking, any more than we are today: Shadwell's take differs markedly from Durfey and Etherege. All of these dramatists do register its effects, suggesting that libertinism, however untidy a concept, was a social and intellectual force in late seventeenth-century English life.

To arrive at some notion of what libertinism meant to the four dramatists included herein, we might consider briefly some of the strands of thought that, interwoven, produced this movement. Maximillian E. Novak looks to Théophile de Viau (1590–1626), who first articulated several of the major tenets of libertinism: ignore social conventions (which are merely artificial constructs); question social institutions, such as marriage or the church; and elevate physical sensation over formal learning.[10] While de Viau influenced a circle of like-minded thinkers in France, the writings of Pierre Gassendi (1592–1655) did far more to popularize ideas that ultimately would prove useful to the advocates of libertine thought. Gassendi is credited with introducing the atomistic theories of the ancient philosopher Epicurus (341–270 BC) into the mainstream of European intellectual life. Gassendi, a Catholic priest, attempted to purge Epicurus' writings of the atheism and materialism that had been associated with it since the classical period. Most controversial was Epicurus' belief that pleasure (whether it be the pleasure of motion, as in copulation, or the pleasure of rest, as in the tranquillity of the soul) is the highest good; he also taught that 'we must release ourselves from the prison of affairs and politics'.[11] While Gassendi retreated from the more lubricious implications of neo-Epicurean doctrine, he nevertheless 'joined his libertine friends in believing that philosophy could flourish only if it

---

[9] James G. Turner, 'The Properties of Libertinism', *Eighteenth-Century Life*, 9 (1985), 79.

[10] Novak, 'Libertinism and Sexuality', 55.

[11] Epicurus, *The Extant Remains*, trans. Cyril Bailey (Oxford, 1926), 98–9.

were free from the restraints of both the world and authority'.[12] There was also a keen interest in epistemology in this intellectual circle. Richard Popkin has shown how the scepticism of Pierre Charron (1541–1603), which questioned whether human beings could possess true knowledge of things, affected Gassendi and other *libertins érudits*.[13] By the 1640s Gassendi was associated with François Luillier, one of the more notorious freethinkers and libertines in Paris; indeed, some historians maintain that Gassendi by this period was himself a 'secret libertine'.[14]

Epicurus filtered through French intellectual circles in the sixteenth and seventeenth centuries; a century earlier, the Italian humanists rediscovered Lucretius (*c.*94–55 BC), another ancient writer whose thought would influence Restoration libertinism. Poggio Bracciolini (1380–1459), who periodically scoured French and German monasteries for ancient manuscripts, turned up a copy of Lucretius' *De rerum natura* in 1417. This six-book poem, composed in dactylic hexameters, extended several key neo-Epicurean notions, among them the concept of pleasure. *De rerum natura* quickly made its presence felt in humanist circles. In 1431 Lorenzo Valla (1405–57) circulated a dialogue *De voluptate* (*On Pleasure*), an attempt, in the words of Maristella de P. Lorch, 'to render through language a deeply felt conviction (*persuasio*) that life as we live it first and foremost with our senses is good (*bonum*)—in fact, the only good (*unicum bonum*)—because of the continuous successful encounter (*connubium*, or marriage) of the senses with the object of their desire (*natura*)'.[15] Valla's personal association with notorious *roués* further kindled the already inflammatory reputation of *De voluptate*. He studied Latin with Pietro Aretino (1492–1556), whose pornographic *Sonnetti lussuriosi* (*Lewd Sonnets*) accompanied drawings of sixteen sexual positions by Giuliano Romano, the 25-year-old pupil of Raphael. In 1433 Valla became

---

[12] Lisa Tunick Sarasohn, 'Epicureanism and the Creation of a Privatist Ethic in Early Seventeenth-Century France', in Margaret J. Osler (ed.), *Atoms, Pneuma, and Tranquillity* (Cambridge, 1991), 175.

[13] Richard H. Popkin, *The History of Scepticism from Erasmus to Descartes* (New York, 1964), 67–112, *passim*.

[14] See Réne Pintard's still seminal study of French libertine thought, *Le Libertinage érudit* (Paris, 1943), 127–8. Richard W. F. Kroll takes issue with the view 'that the political significance of neo-Epicureanism is primarily royalist and libertine'. See *The Material Word* (Baltimore, 1991), 18. Scholars continue, though, to stress the connection between Gassendi, neo-Epicureanism, and libertine 'freethinking'.

[15] Maristella de P. Lorch, 'The Epicurean in Lorenzo Valla's *On Pleasure*', in Osler (ed.), *Atoms, Pneuma, and Tranquillity*, 92.

secretary to Alfonso of Aragon, whose court was known throughout Europe for its licentiousness.

Works by Italian humanists, such as Valla, or French *libertins érudits*, such as Gassendi, established the philosophical basis for libertinism. By the mid-seventeenth century, translations made available the writings of Epicurus and Lucretius to English readers. Richard Kroll speculates that Lucy Hutchinson, wife of the regicide, 'probably made the first complete translation of Lucretius into English'.[16] Certainly by 1656 interest was evident: that year the scientist Walter Charleton published a translation of *Epicurus's Morals*, and the polyglot John Evelyn produced a translation of the first book of *De rerum natura*. These would be followed by the publication during the Restoration of Thomas Creech's 1682 translation, as well as John Dryden's *Miscellany Poems* (London, 1692), which also made the verse of Lucretius available to English readers. Neo-Epicureanism complemented the more popular notions of a libertine like Théophile de Viau. The retreat from political service advocated by Epicurus (via Gassendi) allowed for the independence of thought that led ultimately to questioning social institutions, such as marriage. Epistemological scepticism shed further doubt on received knowledge and social norms. Scepticism could also lead to atheism, a charge frequently levelled against libertines. And the emphasis on sensation in the atomistic theories of Lucretius was taken to justify the libertine pursuit of pleasure.

Criticism that purports to detect the fingerprint of philosophy on popular art risks scorn. Nonetheless, scholars have for the past fifty years drawn upon the history of ideas to contextualize Restoration comedy. Dale Underwood, for one, chronicled the impact of neo-Epicurean philosophy on the libertine dramatist, Sir George Etherege. He describes how classical and medieval thought contributed to the Restoration cult of pleasure: the 'hedonistic tendencies' of the Greek Cynics (such as Diogenes) could be used to bolster libertinism, while the anti-rationalism of the Christian sceptic 'presented one more source of attack upon the traditional structure of orthodox thought'. More recently, Warren Chernaik documented the impact of Hobbes upon Restoration libertinism, maintaining that 'Hobbes and Lucretius were essentially alike in their appeal. Both were perceived as radical, anti-establishment figures . . .'[17] In part, the demonizing of Hobbes

---

[16] Kroll, *The Material Word*, 96.
[17] Warren Chernaik, *Sexual Freedom in Restoration Literature* (Cambridge, 1995), 22.

was due to a flagrant misreading of his masterpiece *The Leviathan* (1651). Rochester and others appropriated from Hobbes his philosophical scepticism and tendency to question traditional morality while rejecting other strands of his thought that were less compatible with a fashionable libertinism. Because of this sort of appropriation, Hobbes's name by the Restoration became synonymous with godlessness.

Suffice it to say that the humanist revival of classical thought, the philosophical movements of the 1640s and 1650s, and the availability of affordable translations combined to produce an intellectual climate that—in some circles at least—made possible the scepticism, defiance, and sensuality characteristic of seventeenth-century libertinism.[18] In 1656, the same year that saw translations of Epicurus and Lucretius published by Charleton and Evelyn respectively, Francis Osborne printed his *Advice to a Son*, a sort of libertine conduct book for offspring sufficiently benighted to think marriage a good thing. Even within 'popular culture' libertinism was felt: Ned Ward, that scribbler of cheap print, invokes 'Great Lucretius' in *The Libertine's Choice*.[19] While the allusion to Lucretius in an otherwise negligible poem might have given pause to Gassendi or Charleton, the very gesture reveals the extent to which libertinism had infiltrated popular culture. The 'well-defined starting-point' and 'very rapid development' of erotic literature from 1650 onwards, beginning with *La puttana errante*, provides further evidence that libertinism, in the words of David Foxon, had emerged by the mid-seventeenth century 'as a fashionable and pervasive mode of thought whose freedom related to religion, politics, and society as well as to sexual life'.[20]

The history of the word 'libertine' parallels its social evolution. Latinate in origin (*libertinus*), in Roman antiquity it applied to a freedman, someone manumitted from slavery. By 1542, the word lost its original function of social classification; instead, the French *libertin* designated, according to the *Oxford English Dictionary*, 'certain

---

[18] Elizabeth L. Eisenstein observes that 'the impact of printing points in two quite opposite directions—toward tolerant "Erasmian" trends and ultimately higher criticism and modernism, and toward more rigid dogmatism, culminating in literal fundamentalism and Bible Belts'. See *The Printing Revolution in Early Modern Europe* (Cambridge, 1983), 169.

[19] Edward Ward, *The Libertine's Choice; or, The Mistaken Happiness of the Fool in Fashion* (London, 1704), 11.

[20] David Foxon, *Libertine Literature in England, 1660–1745* (New Hyde Park, NY, 1965), 49.

antinomian sects of the early sixteenth century' (2a). By the early seventeenth century 'libertine', both in France and England, connoted a freethinker, someone who held 'loose' opinions about religion. Concurrent with this meaning is Shakespeare's use of the word to describe someone of dissolute, licentious character. This latter meaning is the one that made its way into popular literature, eventually, by the end of the seventeenth century, extinguishing all prior religious and philosophical associations. As a point of comparison, one might think of the evolution of the term 'deconstruction' in our own time. Originally a series of philosophical and aesthetic propositions entertained by a handful of French and American intellectuals, deconstruction has some thirty years later—about the time it took terms like 'libertine' and 'epicure' to go from the heights of Walter Charleton to the depths of Ned Ward—come to mean something like 'interpretation' in the jargon of everyday film reviews. Thus to point, as have some scholars, to the more debased uses of the word 'libertine' during the Restoration is hardly to vitiate its impact; rather, it suggests that libertinism was sufficiently potent to filter into the popular realm of lampoons, ballads, and drama without yet losing—at least not entirely—its philosophical underpinnings.

Concepts like libertinism require more than intellectual force for their dissemination: social conditions must also be amenable. Deconstruction required the political tumult of the 1960s and 1970s to provide the cultural fecundity necessary for its growth. Certainly the same can be argued for Restoration England, that libertinism's purchase on intellectual and popular culture—especially the drama—was partly due to the historical moment. Standard treatments of the Restoration stress the 'relief' felt by citizens oppressed by the puritan strictures of the Interregnum (1649–60). After years of deprivation, so the argument goes, people were eager for more self-expression (including sexual freedom) and welcomed the restoration of a monarch known for his easy, sensual nature. As with any generalization, there are exceptions. John Milton, whose writings straddle the Interregnum and the Restoration, is a notable instance of someone whose views were clearly at odds with the new official culture of hedonism. As ongoing persecution of Quakers, Anabaptists, and Presbyterians in the period indicates, many people shared Milton's religious and political principles. Not everyone lit bonfires or danced deliriously in the streets of London upon the eve of the Restoration in 1660.

Nonetheless, there is little question that the court of Charles II became infamous for what onlookers styled its 'libertine' or 'epicure' qualities. The diarist Samuel Pepys, no stranger to the demands of the flesh, grumbled early in the monarch's reign that the 'King and his new Queene minding their pleasures at Hampton Court' were neglecting more princely duties.[21] For the duration of his diary, Pepys noted faithfully every alteration in Charles II's love life, as one mistress displaced another. Keeping track of the monarch's numerous sexual conquests became something of a national pastime, as did chronicling the health of the royal 'member'.[22] Equally of note were the more dissolute escapades of court wits like John Wilmot, the earl of Rochester, George Villiers, the duke of Buckingham, or Sir Charles Sedley. Not only did they give free rein to their sexual appetites but they also defied basic standards of decency. Sedley, dead drunk on a balcony, dipped his penis in a glass of wine, emptied the glass, and then urinated on the outraged crowd that had gathered below. Buckingham killed the husband of his mistress in a duel. Rochester, the most notorious libertine of all, engaged in a host of outrageous acts: he kidnapped his future wife (her father had had the good sense to question Rochester's suitability as a prospective mate); he wrote scatological and pornographic lyrics; he tipped over a sundial in the king's garden; he disguised himself as a mountebank and sold medicines to gullible citizens; and he involved the king in a whorehouse caper that included the dramatist George Etherege. Rochester also happened to be the wittiest poet of the period, capable of penning verses at once heartbreakingly tender and arrestingly coarse.

The close connection between the court and libertinism rendered the latter a peculiarly urban phenomenon, one moreover confined to the up-market neighbourhoods, such as Westminster, preferred by the cognoscenti. Several pamphlets published during the 1670s not only specified fashionable London but, more particularly, the London playhouse as the site of libertine values such as wit, promiscuity, and irreverence. *Gallantry-A-La-Mode* (1674), a long poem in couplets, describes in one memorable section a rake taking a young woman to a performance of Dryden's *Marriage A-la-Mode*, fully expecting that the performance will arouse her sufficiently to make seduction easy later that evening.[23] If London and the court were associated with

[21] *The Diary of Samuel Pepys*, ed. Robert Latham and William Matthews, 11 vols. (Berkeley, 1970–83), iii. 127.

[22] See ch. 3 in Harold Weber's *Paper Bullets: Print and Kingship under Charles II* (Lexington, Ky., 1996).

[23] *Gallantry-A-La-Mode* (Scholars' Facsimiles & Reprints 342), ed. Maximillian E. Novak and David S. Rodes (Delmar, NY, 1980).

libertine practices, the country, as Maximillian E. Novak observes, was by this time known for all things 'stupid, barbaric, and dull'.[24] The exasperated author of *Remarques on the Humours and Conversations of the Town* (1673) objected strongly to what had become the standard stage representation of the country gentlemen: '*thou hast there seen us brought in with a high-crown'd Hat, a Sword put through the wast-band of our Breeches, and a pair of antick tops; where we tamely stand, whilst the learned man of Humours practices upon us with his sleights, and intrigues.*'[25] The libertine wit, by contrast, is as a kind of 'hero' who extols an atheism grounded in the writings of Aristotle and Epicurus while mocking marriage and conventional morality. Interestingly, the author attributes this phenomenon to a superfluity of gentlemen dramatists. Claiming affinity with the court, they embrace what 'will pass for a wit in the Town'. Moreover, unlike a 'mercenary Poet, who ventures for his gain', the gentleman dramatist need not worry about box-office failure; thus freed from the constraints of the market, he can 'hazard his abilities' and write whatever he wants, even offensive libertine fare.[26]

As argued previously, plays that feature sex are not necessarily 'libertine'. What characterizes the libertine plays written during the period is the persistence of a set of attitudes: scepticism about received knowledge; defiance against social sanctions and institutions; and a professed commitment to a life of hedonism (as opposed to a professed desire for a particular man or woman). James Grantham Turner also detects an ethos of *grands esprits*; he argues that the heroic ideology informing the tragicomedies and heroic dramas of the 1660s transmuted into a 'erotic heroism'. While Turner sees everywhere in Restoration literature 'the attempt to heroize sexuality', he admits that 'the stage, particularly the tragedy, was evidently the means of transmission'.[27] Several factors coalesced to produce the 'libertine offensive', to use the phrase coined by Maximillian E. Novak, in the drama of the 1670s, the decade represented in this volume. Advocates of libertinism, men like the earl of Rochester, the duke of Buckingham, or Sir Charles Sedley, had especially close ties to the theatre. Some

---

[24] Maximillian E. Novak, 'Margery Pinchwife's "London Disease": Restoration Comedy and the Libertine Offensive of the 1670s', *Studies in the Literary Imagination*, 10 (1977), 1.

[25] *Remarques on the Humours and Conversations of the Town* (London, 1673), A2ʳ⁻ᵛ.

[26] Ibid. 108–9.

[27] James G. Turner, 'The Libertine Sublime: Love and Death in Restoration England', *Studies in Eighteenth-Century Culture*, 19 (1989), 102.

wrote or translated plays themselves; others functioned as important patrons to dramatists. All of them exercised aesthetic power, commenting on scripts, revising passages, and making recommendations to the managers who ran the companies. The 'transmission' of their influence can be seen in the career of a playwright like John Dryden. Concerned with entrée into court circles, Dryden ingratiated himself with a series of increasingly important patrons. In 1671, at work on the comedy *Marriage A-la-Mode*, Dryden gave the manuscript to Rochester for correction, who in turn showed it to Charles II. Their influence shows not only in the polished repartee of the court characters—indeed Dryden in the dedication pays homage to Rochester's stylistic authority—but also in the subject matter. It is, as Novak observes, one of the first plays to register fully the impact of libertine thought.[28] Libertinism also shaped authorial behaviour. James Anderson Winn points out that contemporaries were quick to mock Dryden's affectation of the rakish speech typical of the court libertines once he had ingratiated himself with the Rochester circle.[29]

Changes within the companies also smoothed the way for the transmission of libertine values. In 1668 Sir William Davenant died, and management of the Duke's Company devolved to his widow Mary and the superb actor Thomas Betterton. Davenant, a product of the Caroline period, frequently waxed nostalgic about the older drama: it was through him, for instance, that Dryden claimed to have acquired a love of Shakespeare. During Davenant's tenure, the Duke's Company staged tragicomedies modelled on earlier plays written by Fletcher and other Caroline playwrights.[30] Betterton, who played three of the libertine rakes in this volume, appears more willing in his capacity as manager to consider licentious fare. Indeed, his own comedy *The Amorous Widow*, an adaptation from Molière, showcases what Robert D. Hume calls 'titillative sex'.[31] Then too professional dramatists by 1670 increasingly vied with the gentlemen writers who had dominated—in the case of the King's Company, almost exclusively—the restored theatre. Dependent upon bread, they were, as the author of *Remarques on the Humours and Conversations of the Town* noted, far more subject to the pressures of the market place, which included not merely the audience but also patrons and critics. If arbiters of taste,

[28] Novak, 'Libertinism and Sexuality', 60–1.

[29] James Anderson Winn, *John Dryden and his World* (New Haven, 1987), 225.

[30] See chapter 2 in Nancy Klein Maguire, *Regicide and Restoration: English Tragicomedy, 1660–1671* (Cambridge, 1992).

[31] Hume, *The Development of English Drama*, 265.

such as Rochester and Buckingham, promoted libertine values, then the professional dramatists had at the very least to respond to this phenomenon.

This is not to suggest that dramatists embraced wholeheartedly the 'libertine values' debated in the pamphlet wars of the 1670s or expressed in the erotic verse of Rochester or Sir John Oldham. Because drama is a public art form, it is subject to constraints that do not otherwise govern private poems. Although manuscript circulation could, according to Harold Love, 'bring a new poem to as many readers as might have encountered it as a printed broadside', that very mode of transmission was intended to circumvent the sort of censorship typically visited upon the press or the stage.[32] Moreover, frequent complaints by women in the audience suggest strongly that even during these more relaxed times there were limits to what could be represented, as the outcry occasioned by *The Country Wife* (1675) or *The Kind Keeper* (1678) indicates.[33] Given the public nature of the theatre, it would have been impossible for a dramatist to express the sort of views voiced by a speaker in a Rochester lyric. And while professional dramatists, whether out of pressure or sheer curiosity, may have been drawn to explore libertinism in a succession of plays, their views were hardly of a piece. Sometimes in our eagerness to sketch the outline of an intellectual movement, we detect uniformly its major themes, forgetting how individual temperament and various social determinations shape response, as the ensuing discussion shows.

The Libertine

Thomas Shadwell's *The Libertine* premièred at Dorset Garden in early June 1675, the same month in which Rochester, drunk and obstreperous, toppled the king's sundial. We know from the prompter John Downes that Thomas Betterton, the most renowned actor of the Restoration stage, played the role of Don John, the eponymous libertine. Downes does not mention the rest of the cast, nor is a cast list printed with the first or subsequent editions. A copy of the 1676 quarto in the Boston Public Library includes a manuscript cast 'which is compatible with the company at this time' (Van Lennep, 368). It

---

[32] *The Works of John Wilmot, Earl of Rochester*, ed. Harold Love (Oxford, 1999), p. xxiv.

[33] See David Roberts, *The Ladies: Female Patronage of Restoration Drama, 1660–1700* (Oxford, 1989).

confirms that Betterton played Don John and lists William Mountfort as Don Lopez and Joseph Williams as Don Antonio. Susanna Percival Mountfort played Maria; Frances Maria Knight personated Leonora; while Charlotte Butler and Mrs Twyford performed the sisters Flavia and Clara. The inimitable Anthony Leigh was given the role of Jacomo, a part well suited to his comic genius. The play was by all accounts a great hit. John Downes mentions it along with *The Virtuoso*, the other play Shadwell wrote during this period, as 'both very well Acted, and got the Company great Reputation. The *Libertine* perform'd by Mr. *Betterton* Crown'd the Play' (p. 78). Shadwell in the preface acknowledged its acclaim: 'I have no reason to complain of the success of this play since it pleased those whom, of all the world, I would please most. Nor was the town unkind to it, for which reason I must applaud my good fortune to have pleased with so little pains . . .' (ll. 22–5).

If Shadwell's claim in the prefatory essay is true, he wrote the play in a little over three weeks, there being 'no act in it which cost me above five days writing; and the last two, the playhouse having great occasion for a play, were both written in four days, as several can testify' (ll. 25–8). The preface also makes evident Shadwell's interest in theatrical innovation. As several critics have noted,[34] *The Libertine* departs markedly from earlier plays about Don Juan in showcasing a villain so repulsive as to be almost unrecognizable, a departure Shadwell freely admitted: 'I hope the readers will excuse the irregularities of the play when they consider that the extravagance of the subject forced me to it. And I had rather try new ways to please than to write on in the same road, as too many do' (ll. 11–14). Even the prologue advertised *The Libertine* as 'The most irregular play upon the stage' (line 15). In searching for a dramatic form that might answer 'the extravagance of the subject', Shadwell wedded music and spectacle to a plot that veers from slapstick humour to chilling scenes of violence and degradation. Precisely because of what Michael Neill calls 'its furiously unstable tone',[35] critics remain uncertain whether to consider *The Libertine* a 'sober-faced burlesque' or a 'morally instructive mock-tragedy'.[36] A critical practice that focuses solely on the action—on a

[34] See e.g. the brief discussion in Novak, 'Libertinism and Sexuality', 62.

[35] Michael Neill, 'Heroic Heads and Humble Tails: Sex, Politics, and the Restoration Comic Rake', *The Eighteenth Century: Theory and Interpretation*, 24 (1983), 128.

[36] For the former view, see Hume, *Development of English Drama*, 312; for the latter, see Aaron Jaffe, 'Seditious Appetites and Creeds: Shadwell's Libertine and Hobbes's Foole', *Restoration*, 24 (2000), 57.

reading rather than a consideration of performance—will no doubt register these sorts of 'tonal' difficulties and therefore see ambiguities in Shadwell's attitude toward libertinism. *The Libertine* defies our expectations of the neoclassicism shaping plays from this period: it violates the unities, and it ignores genre. Juxtaposing scenes of rape and murder with moments of humour, provided mainly by the servant Jacomo, *The Libertine* careers from philosophy to comedy to outright horror.

The rapid shifts in mood, however, do not preclude a carefully crafted dramatic structure nor do they obviate Shadwell's ultimate repudiation of libertine values. The play was often advertised as *The Libertine Destroy'd*,[37] and this alternative title underscores the intent of dismantling not merely the practitioner but the practice itself. Aaron Jaffe argues that *The Libertine* stands 'outside the immediate purview of most examinations of Restoration libertinism' in excoriating 'both the social implications of libertine doctrines and practices and their misappropriation of Hobbesian ideas and language'.[38] Jaffe demonstrates how the three Dons in the play bear a marked resemblance to Hobbes's 'Foole' in *The Leviathan*, a figure who 'thinks that the most reasonable actions are those that are most instrumental to his own desires'; moreover, Shadwell's use of humours, in which dramatic character is reduced to one overriding trait, shows the Dons to be little more than automatons, less than human.[39]

Of the four plays in this volume, *The Libertine* is by far the most overtly philosophical: Act 1 opens with Don John stringing together a series of propositions that establish his libertine credentials. The Dons laugh at law and morality, maintaining that conscience is an instrument of oppression, a way 'to make men cowards'. Education is another form of 'dull slavery'. Don John advocates that men should rely on 'infallible nature' and 'natural appetites', seizing what they desire with impunity. Even sensationalist theory is pressed—albeit illogically—into service: 'By nature's order, sense should guide our reason, | Since to the mind all objects sense conveys' (lines 30–1). While the more educated members of the audience would have detected the allusions to various threads of libertine thought, one need not have read this body of literature to divine Shadwell's ethical bent in

---

[37] See e.g. the performances listed in Part 2 of *The London Stage*; by the eighteenth century, the play was advertised regularly as *Don John; or, The Libertine Destroy'd*.

[38] Jaffe, 'Seditious Appetites and Creeds', 56.

[39] Ibid. 64.

this play.[40] 'Extravagance' indicates that Shadwell self-consciously ventured beyond standard dramatic forms, but it also refers to the play's 'subject' (or content): someone who has strayed into moral and theological error, another contemporary meaning of the word. Thus in the figure of Don John, Shadwell encompasses *all* of libertinism's dangerous associations: the rake, the freethinker, the atheist. To realize its ambitious scope, *The Libertine* demanded an excessive dramatic form, one that distorts genre, space, and time to reveal the disease at the core of this fashionable intellectual movement.[41] A 'pure' genre like tragedy, precisely because its classical form was thought to derive from nature, would have elevated Don John, giving his actions a stature and inevitability at odds with the mission here to debunk libertinism.

Over the course of five acts, the story moves from Seville, to a storm at sea, to a country setting, and then, full circle, back to Seville. Against these varied settings are foregrounded Don John's claims about libertinism. The urban setting of Seville in Act 1 provides the backdrop to the first major speech in which Don John advocates a life of unfettered indulgence. Seville, home to artifice and convention, is implicitly contrasted to the 'natural' behaviour of the libertines. Yet, when confronted with the bald power of a storm in Act 3, Don John retorts petulantly, as if the thunderbolts were simply another recalcitrant being blocking his immediate gratification: 'You paltry, foolish, bugbear thunder! Am I the mark of your senseless rage?' (ll. 50–1). Ironically, for someone wedded to the natural, Don John does not see the power of nature, just as he fails to recognize the intrinsic claims of morality, culture, or religion. When the three Dons happen upon shepherds and nymphs in 'a delightful grove' in 4.2, neither pastoral beauty nor innocence moves them; again, blind to nature, they ignore the pleas of Jacomo to spare the women. Don John justifies the impending rapes—which are likened to those visited upon the Sabine women—by retorting, 'I am not in love but in lust; and to such a one a bellyful's a bellyful, and there's an end on't' (ll. 133–4).

[40] Christopher J. Wheatley argues that Shadwell's ethical beliefs, which were grounded in contemporary thought, were recognized as such by his peers. See especially the 'Introduction: The Complexity of Restoration Ethics', in *Without God or Reason: The Plays of Thomas Shadwell and Secular Ethics in the Restoration* (Lewisburg, Pa., 1993).

[41] Rose Zimbardo sees *The Libertine* as a failed tragedy because 'the scenes do not juxtapose ideas or figures in conceptual configurations, nor do they develop or explore character' (124). Although Shadwell eschews the form and characterization of tragedy, he nonetheless sequences the play carefully. See Rose A. Zimbardo, *A Mirror to Nature: Transformations in Drama and Aesthetics 1660–1732* (Lexington, Ky., 1986).

These two different manifestations of the natural, the one sublime, the other bucolic, normally elicit awe and delight. Don John proves incapable of a natural response to nature, a perverse reaction adumbrated in the weird configuration of temporality in the play. Time, as a progressive sequence of causal events, does not occur in *The Libertine*. There is some sense of the events that transpired before the onset of the action, such as Don John's act of parricide or his murder of Don Pedro, the governor of Seville. Once the play begins, the Dons make their way from Seville through a shipwreck to some unnamed coast and then back to Seville; but the sequencing of these scenes defies any natural progression. They just happen, arbitrarily and suddenly, as in a dream, and even the sense of place is vague. Shadwell, normally careful about stage directions, does not specify the location of the scenes in which the Dons commit their most heinous crimes, as if to situate their grotesque behaviour in a nether region that defies the logic of place. By contrast, Shadwell specifies natural and religious settings: the 'delightful grove' of 4.2 and the church of 4.3 and 5.2, thus giving substance—a sense of place—to those locales at odds with the libertinism of the Dons.

Shadwell's 'extravagant' design also shows in the music. *The Libertine* has an unusually high percentage of songs for a Restoration play: as Ian Spink notes, 'originally . . . there was vocal music in each act, including masque-like episodes in Acts IV and V'.[42] These pieces run the gamut of musical styles, ranging from serenades to epithalamia to 'rustic music'. Two of the original songs were reprinted in William Turner's *New Ayres and Dialogues* (1678) and *Choice Ayres and Songs* (1679). Henry Purcell later wrote several new numbers for a revival in 1692. Certainly the play was considered sufficiently musical to inspire Isaac Pocock to use it as the basis of a two-act opera, also called *The Libertine*, which premièred at Covent Garden on 20 May 1817.[43] Given the surfeit of music in the play, Shadwell possibly conceived of *The Libertine* as an opera. Shadwell was by this point in his career skilful at 'weaving music into the plot and in structuring the musical scenes'.[44] Brian Corman and Todd S. Gilman point out that he 'was a trained (though not professional) musician with a thorough familiarity with musical idiom from the most traditional English ballad to the

[42] Ian Spink, 'Purcell's Music for "The Libertine" ', *Music & Letters*, 81 (2000), 522.

[43] Isaac Pocock, *The Libertine*, MS No. 1973 in the Larpent Collection, Huntington Library, San Marino, California.

[44] Margaret Laurie, 'Music for the Stage II: From 1650', in *The Seventeenth Century* (Music in Britain), ed. Ian Spink (Oxford, 1992), 320.

latest French opera'.[45] It was during this period that the patent companies, hoping to compete with foreign imports, began mounting their own productions of semi-operas, an endeavour with which Shadwell was closely involved. In 1674 appeared an operatic version of the Davenant/Dryden *Tempest*, most likely adapted by Shadwell. The following year the Duke's Company staged Shadwell's *Psyche*, an expensive production that failed at the box office and soured the company's appetite for more opera.

Shadwell turned almost immediately from *Psyche* to *The Libertine*, if we accept the time frame he outlines in the preface. While *The Libertine* does not formally qualify as an opera, or even a semi-opera, it nonetheless shows that Shadwell had learned to use music dramatically and even ironically. The mélange of musical styles, like the diffuse sense of temporality and place in *The Libertine*, violates decorum and further creates the sense of 'extravagance' Shadwell sought in this script. The songs, originally set by William Turner, function in much the same manner as the comic interludes featuring Jacomo: to lull spectators temporarily into smiling at some manifestation of the libertine code, only to shock them at its perniciousness. Don John's serenade to Maria in 1.1, in which he advertises himself as 'a faithful, young, vigorous lover' (l. 318) is succeeded by Octavio's paean to Maria's divine beauty: she is 'so bright a miracle' (l. 356) and 'so sweet, so powerful a grace' (l. 362). Typically, Don John celebrates himself, while Octavio rejoices in his beloved. Shadwell juxtaposes these two songs to comment slyly on Don John's solipsism; the murder of Octavio moments later shifts the tone from irony to horror. The mock epithalamium sung at Don John's behest by his 'minstrels' unmercifully ridicules the six women who have just discovered themselves to be his 'wives'. The 'wanton song' performed by Clara and Flavia in 3.2 that asserts woman's 'nature wild' is followed by the murder of their father and injuring of their fiancés. The 'symphony of rustic music' sung by the shepherds and nymphs of 4.2 is followed by rape and pillage. And the final 'Song of Devils' in 5.2, one of two extant pieces of music from the original production, precedes the ultimate horror: the descent of an unrepentant Don John to hell.

Because *The Libertine* departs from dramatic and theatrical conventions, its larger design is not readily apparent: most critics are arrested by the 'tonal ambiguities'. Taken sequentially, however, the musical

---

[45] Brian Corman and Todd S. Gilman, 'The Musical Life of Thomas Shadwell', *Restoration*, 20 (1996), 150.

interludes parallel a larger progression in the play as we move from the formal enunciation of libertine precepts at the outset to the grotesque outcome of libertine practice at the conclusion. Similarly, the music evolves from light-hearted serenades to the dirge-like 'Song of Devils' in C minor.[46] As Curtis Price points out, 'Turner creates a feeling of sombre awe largely through a distinctive tonal plan. . . . A cloud of "eternal dreadful doom" thus hangs heavy in the air' (Price, 114). Systematically, music and action work hand-in-hand to discredit libertinism's favourite themes: the pleasure of romantic love, the freedom to choose lovers, the perfection of a Golden Age of unfettered natural desires. Every act showcases some aspect of 'benign' libertinism and then pushes its premiss to the most extreme degree. Christopher J. Wheatley observes that Coleridge in the *Biographia Literaria* thought that Shadwell's purpose was not to 'dramatize a divine justice, but to take libertine philosophy to its logical conclusion and show that it is horrific'.[47] For instance, the light-hearted exchange between the sisters Clara and Flavia in 3.2, in which they contrast their lack of freedom to the imagined liberty of Englishwomen, transmutes rapidly from an implicit plea for choice in marriage to an act of gross misjudgement that costs the life of their father. Moments such as these unsettle precisely because they subject unexamined propositions— naive girls should have complete freedom—to scrutiny.

The play consistently reveals the futility of secular stances in the face of evil. Marriage, friendship, romantic love, kinship ties, even nature, whether sublime or bucolic, cannot withstand the onslaught of rape, pillage, murder, incest, and desecration visited by the Dons on their hapless victims. The religious hermit who appears in 3.2 and Jacomo, himself a kind of religious fool, are the only characters who escape the mayhem; significantly, both simply walk away. Their respective exits constitute the only sane response to someone who mouths a philosophy as illogical as it is pernicious. One cannot debate rationally with Don

---

[46] As Ian Spink notes, Purcell reset Turner's original music for the 'Song of Devils' in Act 5. The 'Symphony for Flat Trumpets', which preceded the 'Song of Devils', is virtually the same march Purcell wrote for the procession carrying Queen Mary's body to Westminster Abbey in March 1695 ('Purcell's Music for "The Libertine" ', 520). The 'Song of Devils' follows in the same key and uses the same instruments to create an atmosphere of sombre horror moments before the unrepentant Don John descends into hell. A purely textual reading of the play that ignores the musical interludes or spatial relationships will invariably, like Laura Brown, conclude that 'Shadwell's play is an exaggeration of the Don John story so outrageous as to be almost ridiculous'. See *English Dramatic Form, 1660–1760: An Essay in Generic History* (New Haven, 1981), 105.

[47] Wheatley, *Without God or Reason*, 90.

John—indeed, he derides reason throughout the play—and one cannot vanquish him, as the bodies strewn in his wake testify. The embodiment of Christianity, the hermit is unwavering in his response to evil: he offers charity to the shipwrecked Dons and then, realizing their wicked aims, departs immediately. Jacomo, the reluctant servant to Don John, functions more as an everyman in the play. Tempted himself, he briefly emulates Don John in contemplating raping the unconscious Leonora in Act 1. A coward, he fails initially to protect any of his master's victims. As the play progresses, however, Jacomo's protests shift from sarcastic asides—he is the only character to speak directly to the audience—to pleading on behalf of others. By the final act, he has grown sufficiently in moral stature to leave, even if doing so results in his death, as Don John has threatened throughout the play.

If production values are overlooked, it is far easier to conclude that *The Libertine* represents 'the last extreme, where satire is indistinguishable from bleak, unredeemed irony'.[48] While Don John remains unrepentant and therefore unredeemed—as the story dictates—the staging of the final scene conveys an atmosphere far removed from irony. It opens in a church and '*on each side*' we see '*the ghosts of Don John [senior], Maria, Don Francisco, Leonora, Flora, Maria's Brother, and others, with torches in their hands*'. They remain on stage throughout, silent reminders of the carnage wrought by Don John's libertinism. The C minor march that follows provides a suitably sombre musical accompaniment to this tableau of shades. Don John's final defiant speech, if imagined against this staging, appears far less ironic and far more repulsive. Modern readers, accustomed to the Nietzschean patter of Shaw's Don Juan, the ultimate ironist, might perhaps find it difficult to recapture the stark morality of Shadwell's *The Libertine*. The play, however, remained overwhelmingly popular until the middle of the eighteenth century, a time when audiences were far less receptive to libertine fare on the stage, a good indication of the enduring appeal of Shadwell's ethical stance.

The Man of Mode

Sir George Etherege's coolly brilliant rebuttal to *The Libertine*, *The Man of Mode*, premièred at Dorset Garden some nine months later, on 11 March 1676. Part of the court circle of wits, Etherege emulated their excesses, enjoying a series of affairs—one with two sisters con-

---

[48] Zimbardo, *A Mirror to Nature*, 123.

currently—and propounding fashionable libertine principles in a poem entitled, appropriately enough, 'The Libertine'.[49] We know from the correspondence Etherege penned years later when he was British 'Resident' in Ratisbon that he admired Shadwell as a dramatist. Although Etherege no longer wrote plays himself, he nonetheless admitted to William Jephson his desire 'to read a good one, wherefore pray lett Will: Richards send me Mr. Shadwells when it is printed'.[50] Certainly, *The Man of Mode*, if indeed a deliberate response, smacks of the sort of rivalry accorded a worthy competitor. It is as crafted, stylish, and witty as *The Libertine* is sprawling, experimental, and earnest. To audiences the connection between the two plays would have been apparent: Thomas Betterton, who had played Don John to critical acclaim, followed his *tour de force* with another turn as a libertine, this time as the glorious monster Dorimant. Michael Neill notes the similarity between the two characters, observing that 'Etherege's protagonist . . . is in his way, as those around him frequently remark, as "wild," "barbarous," "extravagant," and "irregular" as any Don John. . . . Dorimant exhibits an appetite for power and a degree of perverse cruelty beside which Don John's carnal gusto seems positively good natured'.[51]

One might hesitate to call Don John's carnal appetite 'good natured'; Neill, however, exercises keen insight into both characters. *The Man of Mode* showcases a libertine who indulges not mere brutish appetite but the erotics of power. While Dorimant refrains from contorting sensationalist theory into a justification for his action, he nonetheless subscribes to a libertine ethos.[52] A sensualist, he juggles three

---

[49] 'The Libertine', in *Miscellaneous Works, Written by His Grace, George, Late Duke of Buckingham* (London, 1704), 120–1. This volume, despite the title, included several poems by other writers.

[50] Frederick Bracher thinks it likely the play in question is Shadwell's *The Squire of Alsatia*, which was produced in May 1688. See *Letters of Sir George Etherege*, ed. Frederick Bracher (Berkeley, 1974), 186.

[51] Michael Neill, 'Heroic Heads and Humble Tails', 132.

[52] Some critics argue quite the opposite, that ultimately *The Man of Mode* repudiates libertine language and values. Lisa Berglund, for instance, maintains that Harriet and Young Bellair 'counter rakish antagonism to constancy, affection, and honor by demonstrating that conventional morality may be, like Harriet herself, "wild, witty, lovesome, beautiful" '. J. Douglas Canfield avers that Harriet socializes 'the great sexual energy of the highly desirable Don Juan figure,' an alteration registered in Dorimant's shift from libertine to religious language. See Lisa Berglund, 'The Language of the Libertines: Subversive Morality in *The Man of Mode*', SEL 30 (1990), 369–86, at 37; and J. Douglas Canfield, *Word as Bond in English Literature from the Middle Ages to the Restoration* (Philadelphia, 1989), 114.

women in the play who represent past, present, and future affairs: Mrs Loveit, his cast-off mistress; Bellinda, his one-night stand; and Emilia, a prospective amour even though she is intended for Young Bellair, supposedly a close 'friend'. Of Emilia, Dorimant cynically remarks, 'She's a discreet maid, and I believe nothing can corrupt her but a husband' (1.1.406–7). A pragmatist as well as a hedonist, Dorimant's genius resides in detecting the 'passion that lies panting under' the mask of social artifice, as well as divining the individual psychology behind the façade of good manners (3.3.317–18). He suspects that Emilia veils desire with discretion, but he will bide his time patiently until her marriage to a romantic young fool makes possible a future assignation.

Dorimant is a libertine in other respects: he flouts social mores. A freethinker, he dissects publicly the social commonplaces others uphold. To Young Bellair, who woos the penniless Emilia, he observes coldly that 'The wise will find a difference in our fate: | You wed a woman, I a good estate' (4.2.181–2). To the enraged Mrs Loveit, who thunders against his chronic infidelity, he brutally asserts his right to frankness, while simultaneously using that 'right' to humiliate her: 'Good nature and good manners corrupt me. I am honest in my inclinations and would not, wert not to avoid offence, make a lady a little in years believe I think her young, wilfully mistake art for nature, and seem as fond of a thing I am weary of, as when I doted on't in earnest' (2.2.181–5). To Medley, who remarks the growing friendship between Dorimant and Bellair, he states impassively: 'It is our mutual interest to be so. It makes the women think the better of his understanding, and judge more favourably of my reputation. It makes him pass upon some for a man of very good sense, and I upon others for a very civil person' (1.1.394–7). In the same spirit of social insurgency, Dorimant parades the libertine's preference for nature over artifice. Refusing the orange-flower water proffered by his valet, Dorimant declares his intention to 'smell as I do today, no offence to the ladies' noses' (1.1.326).

Nevertheless, *The Man of Mode*, like *The Libertine*, goes to some length to expose several of the contradictions at the heart of libertinism. As James G. Turner points out, Restoration libertines were 'particularly fascinated by the oxymoronic conjunction of the civil and the rude'. Their rebellion, like that of adolescents, is 'deeply in need of the law to guarantee their privileges and to fuel their emotional rebellion'.[53] Outrageous behaviour, whether sexual or social, derives its

---

[53] Turner, 'The Properties of Libertinism', 81.

efficacy from the very morality it seeks to overturn, and, in that sense, libertines require the existence of standards without which their transgressions would be meaningless. Consistently in *The Man of Mode* we are reminded of the conventions that make possible Dorimant's fashionable pose. His partiality for the 'natural' human body, as exemplified by his choice of human musk over orange-flower water, is thrown into question by Bellair's observation moments later that 'no man in town has a better fancy in his clothes'. By comparison to Sir Fopling Flutter, the original fashion victim, Dorimant does indeed appear 'natural', but he requires the presence of a fop to frame his more refined fashion sensibilities, just as he needs the naivety of Bellair, the prissiness of Lady Woodvill, or the jealousy of Mrs Loveit to set off his blunt pronouncements against social forms.

While the play never falters in its unblinking appraisal of libertinism, its coolly ironic and analytical tone should not be mistaken for a rejection of libertine values.[54] Detachment differs from repudiation, and the alternative to libertinism, embodied in Bellair's naive romanticism, hardly represents a viable option. Etherege's sleight of hand here is to demystify libertinism while retaining its allure. In that sense, the play is rather like Dorimant himself: showing its teeth while reeling us in. Like Dorimant's women, we should know better—in some instances, we *do* know better—but we submit anyway. Such, *The Man of Mode* suggests, is the power of libertinism. Similarly, Dorimant's desire for Harriet should not be taken as evidence that he has by the play's conclusion become a 'reformed rake' or a 'socialized' Don Juan. Admittedly, in several asides, Dorimant confesses to a precipitate passion and worries that Harriet may have 'an ascendant o'er me and may revenge the wrongs I have done her sex' (4.1.139–40). He courts her in the religious language of the Petrarchan lover, rather than the witty rejoinder of the libertine, taken by some critics as evidence of a change in his character. And in the final scene he pledges to undertake a 'Lenten' sojourn to the 'great rambling lone house' in the country where Harriet resides with 'an old lame aunt' and her mother, a true test of resolution for this otherwise urban creature. Etherege, however, qualifies these moments. Dorimant may be wooing Harriet assiduously, but moments before the play concludes, he pulls aside

---

[54] Robert Markley points out that Etherege, 'more deliberately than any of his contemporaries . . . explores the ironies and tensions inherent in the Cavalier ideals of wit and carriage'. See *Two-Edg'd Weapons: Style and Ideology in the Comedies of Etherege, Wycherley, and Congreve* (Oxford, 1988), 100.

Mrs Loveit, claiming had she been 'reasonable', he could have continued to see her *and* still marry his rich heiress. He also attempts another assignation with Bellinda. Earlier in the scene, Dorimant addresses Emilia in an aside with the ambiguous title of 'Mistress Bride', perhaps an allusion to the dual role she will soon play as wife to Bellair and eventual mistress to Dorimant. Emilia responds with the equally ambiguous command to 'Defer the formal joy you are to give me, and mind your business with her', which can, of course, be construed as an innocuous or suggestive statement (5.2.104–5).

Dorimant's earlier proclamations about the evanescent nature of love also haunt this climactic scene of courtship. 'Love', as he reminds Mrs Loveit, 'gilds us over and makes us show fine things to one another for a time, but soon the gold wears off, and then again the native brass appears' (2.2.189–91), or 'What we swear at such a time may be a certain proof of a present passion; but, to say truth, in love there is no security to be given for the future' (2.2.196–8). In a reading of the play, it is easy to dwell on the glories of the language—the exchanges between Dorimant and Harriet are truly brilliant—and to forget the complications created by the presence of other characters on stage. Emilia, soon to be 'corrupted' by a husband, stands silent witness to Dorimant's pleas for marriage; moments later Mrs Loveit, the abandoned mistress, and Bellinda, the recently discarded quick fling, enter the drawing room of Mrs Townley. The spectacle of these three women and the stages of passion they represent—past, present, and, possibly, the future—throw into relief Dorimant's declaration of steadfast love. Their entry into the scene reminds us of Dorimant's flippant response to Mrs Loveit, that vows sworn in the heat of the moment will invariably melt.

The three scenes immediately preceding 5.2 also argue for a sceptical interpretation of *The Man of Mode*: 4.2 shows us a post-coital Dorimant and Bellinda; 4.3 presents Bellinda hurrying away anxiously in a chair; and 5.1 gives us Dorimant tormenting Mrs Loveit for the sheer cussedness of it—and horrifying Bellinda who, in watching him emotionally dismember his former mistress, realizes her fate. Had these scenes occurred earlier in the play, it might be easier to posit Dorimant as a reformed libertine; however, Etherege's comic design, which places these scenes immediately prior to his courtship of Harriet, suggests a continuity of behaviour, rather than a transformation. The ending withholds the marriage celebration that traditionally concludes romantic comedy; instead, Harriet tells her mother that while she 'never will do, anything against my duty' (5.2.255–6), she nonetheless 'never will marry any other man' (5.2.311–12). The ending *implies* marriage—but we are never entirely certain. *The Man of Mode* defers indefinitely the narrative pleasure accruing from the spectacle of a permanent union, and thereby re-enacts the central paradox confronting the libertine, that the very appetite spurring him to 'heroic' conquests must perforce render inadequate every woman, every sexual experience.[55] Never can the libertine (or the spectators of this play, for that matter) enjoy 'the sense of an ending' that underwrites the Western aesthetic, and it is precisely this teasing deferral of satisfaction that makes this comic masterpiece and its central figure so compelling.[56]

We might note too that while Harriet may be rich enough to render less constricting the shackles of marriage, there is no evidence that Dorimant, *if* they wed, will 'dwindle' into a monogamous husband. Harriet's wit ensures that she will exercise the same discretion towards Dorimant's extramarital escapades as he has towards his mistresses' honour.[57] Unlike Mrs Loveit, at whom Harriet publicly 'jeers' for her emotional displays, she will never throw tantrums or tear fans. Perhaps it is for this reason that Dorimant seeks to establish from the outset Harriet's social acumen. Having learned from the Orange-Woman of Harriet's wealth and beauty, he immediately enquires after her wit— her ability socially and linguistically to navigate the rocky shoals of their competitive, fiercely inbred milieu. Dorimant also discerns that Harriet, for all her protestations against artifice, is like himself acutely aware of social forms, and she will never give cause for embarrassment. Urged to pledge herself to Dorimant against her mother's wishes, Harriet declares, 'May he hate me—a curse that frights me when I speak it—if ever I do a thing against the rules of decency and honour' (5.2.159–60).

[55] The compulsive sexuality of the libertine is often viewed through the lens of psychoanalysis. Warren Chernaik summarizes well this line of thought: 'Psychoanalytically, it can be seen as Oedipal, with the unattainable mother as origin of a series of unsatisfactory surrogates, "while the adversaries, deceived, fought and eventually even killed, represent the unconquerable mortal enemy, the father" '. See *Sexual Freedom in Restoration Literature*, 3.

[56] See Frank Kermode, *The Sense of an Ending: Studies in the Theory of Fiction* (Oxford, 1966).

[57] My reading of Harriet and her relationship to Dorimant differs markedly from the very good interpretation put forth by Pat Gill, who thinks that Harriet 'functions as a mirror, reflecting Dorimant and refracting the women he seduced'; she thus provides 'a way out of the monotonous cycle of corruption in which Dorimant finds himself'. See *Interpreting Ladies: Women, Wit, and Morality in the Restoration Comedy of Manners* (Athens, Ga., 1994), 48.

What might possibly ensue between Dorimant and Harriet—we have no way of knowing, of course—is the Restoration equivalent of a 'political marriage'. The couple in question have undoubtedly fallen in love, but their attraction, as Harriet frequently reminds Dorimant, should not cloud the true nature of their union. Though she would wish him 'devout', she would not have him 'turn fanatic'. We might recall that the earl of Rochester, often mentioned as the model for Dorimant, wrote tender love letters to his wife alongside missives to pals detailing the latest benders, brawls, or noxious 'cures' for syphilis. The whores and willing women were a foregone conclusion, as was Rochester's assumption of a libertine privilege underwritten by an aristocratic ethos. Dorimant, if he passes his test in the country, will have a rich estate and a wife sufficiently equipped with 'wit' and 'malice', not to mention respect for 'decency and honour', to smile graciously amidst the whispers and, when necessary, to 'jeer' at her rivals. Harriet, for her part, secures residence in London, a city to her so magical that even the 'worst cry' of the street-traders yields 'music'. It is the consummate libertine union, a mating of leopards.

A Fond Husband

Some fifteen months separate *The Man of Mode* from Thomas Durfey's *A Fond Husband; or, The Plotting Sisters*. The first known performance for Durfey's rollicking comedy is 31 May 1677. From the start, *A Fond Husband* was a smash hit—Charles II was said to have attended three of the first five nights—and it enjoyed frequent revivals throughout the Restoration and well into the eighteenth century (Van Lennep, i. 257). The prompter John Downes attributed its success to the efforts of the Duke's Company: *A Fond Husband* 'took extraordinary well, and being perfectly Acted; got the Company great Reputation and Profit' (77). Given the pattern of casting in the play, there is good evidence that Durfey, by this period very much a company writer, tailored parts for specific actors. The role of Old Fumble, a doddering roué, showcased the comic radiance of Anthony Leigh (who also specialized in licentious prelates). James Nokes, the other brilliant comedian in the company—Colley Cibber years later would recall in detail the respective talents of these men—played Peregrine Bubble, the foolish cuckold, again a role suited to his particular talents. William Smith, who took a wide range of roles over his career, performed Rashley, and Henry Harris, an excellent character actor, played the part of Ranger.

The choice of Elizabeth Barry and Rebecca Marshall as the 'plotting' sisters of the title also drew upon a pattern of casting much in evidence during this period, 'the angel and the she-devil'.[58] From 1670 on, tragedies and heroic dramas frequently juxtaposed 'good' and 'bad' female characters. The King's Company usually cast Rebecca Marshall, who specialized in passionate and sadistic women, against Elizabeth Bowtell, who, given her girlish looks and voice, tended toward virtuous heroines. Marshall, long a mainstay of the King's Company, defected to the rival Duke's Company several months before the première of *A Fond Husband*. Durfey drew upon Marshall's reputation for playing wily, 'bad' women in fashioning for her the role of Maria, the jealous, vengeful sister determined to expose the sexual shenanigans of her sister-in-law Emilia. Although the Duke's Company lacked Bowtell, they had an equally promising ingénue in Elizabeth Barry, who was two years into an illustrious stage career. Barry had already proved herself in a range of roles and would have been more than capable of personating the winsome adulteress Emilia. Durfey handed these two talented actresses a comic gem in 2.4, a scene that spoofs 'the angel and she-devil' convention almost to the point of high camp. Their characters disgorge vitriol as they battle each other for Rashley, Maria threatening to 'trample' Emilia into 'ashes' and Emilia warning that she will 'forge a plot shall blow thee into air'.

As that scene indicates, *A Fond Husband* is a far cry from the philosophical musings of *The Libertine* or the ironic detachment of *The Man of Mode*. Durfey's script is far closer in spirit to Ned Ward than Walter Charleton. For the cheerfully licentious characters who dot the landscape of this play, libertinism is more a lifestyle than a philosophy, a 'roving and uncontrolled way of love' (1.1.16) as Rashley announces at the outset. One still detects, albeit in popular form, aspects of the libertine credo. The play opens with Emilia's maid Betty singing about sexual passion and vigour; and the double entendre on 'sceptre' no doubt would have brought to mind the many contemporary jokes about the king's own 'rod' of state. The ensuing dialogue between the illicit lovers Rashley and Emilia frames their amour as the love of angels, 'a second-rate innocence where affection, not duty, bears prerogative'. Rashley thus promulgates the libertine preference for sensation over custom—for satisfying the demands of the flesh, not the demands of society. The word 'sense' (or 'senses') appears some fifteen

---

[58] Elizabeth Howe, *The First English Actresses: Women and Drama 1660–1700* (Cambridge, 1992), 152.

times in the script, denoting both the physical and practical realms of life. Libertine philosophy subsumes both meanings: ideally one should base actions on the common sense that derives from emotions and appetites, not from social conventions or rules. Emilia's foolish husband Bubble, her sister-in-law Maria, and her unsuccessful suitor Ranger are all said to lack 'sense', nor do any of them exhibit the healthy animal lust—the other sense of 'sense'—so enjoyed by Emilia and Rashley.

The striking line from Rochester's poem *A Ramble in St. James's Park*—'There's something gen'rous in meer Lust'[59]—could very well function as the motto for *A Fond Husband*. If *The Man of Mode* seduces us, then *A Fond Husband* takes a different tack, cajoling us into agreeing that the life of 'angels' led by those two cheerfully unrepentant adulterers Rashley and Emilia is far more wholesome than the malice displayed by other characters. Durfey is closer in spirit to a dramatist like Aphra Behn, whose plays also showcase wholesome animal lust, than he is to an ironist like Etherege. He also shares with Behn a partiality for the discoveries, trapdoors, and descents of which a playhouse like Dorset Garden was fully capable. Durfey's plays revel in the farcical business of bodies careering out of control, and his plots show what happens when obsessive characters resort to ludicrous devices to realize their aims. In the main plot, Emilia and Rashley want to enjoy as much sex as possible while eluding the suspicions of her foolish old husband Bubble. That Emilia and Rashley are desired respectively by Ranger, a rival to Rashley, and Maria, sister to Bubble, intensifies the lovers' need for subterfuge. The subplot similarly juxtaposes characters with rival objectives: Sir Roger Petulant hopes to marry his son Sneak, an idiotic Cambridge undergraduate, to the witty Cordelia. The ancient lecher Old Fumble also wants her, while Cordelia seemingly wants little more than to cast a bemused eye on the frantic machinations unfolding around her.

Like most farce, *A Fond Husband* relies on repetitive episodes, physical business, and running sight gags, including two bed tricks. Rashley hides under tables, disappears through trapdoors, and conceals himself in closets. Sneak frantically eludes his uncle and pregnant mistress. In 5.3, Emilia and Rashley triumphantly 'sink in the trap' that secures their quick escape from the outraged Maria, who tries to expose the lovers to the credulous Bubble. In 5.4, Emilia and Rashley dress the servants Betty and Jeremy in their bedclothes, fully

[59] *The Works of John Wilmot, Earl of Rochester*, ed. Harold Love (Oxford, 1999), 78.

expecting to prove Maria and Ranger fools yet again. Cordelia substitutes an eager governess for herself in Fumble's bed, betting the success of her ruse on the old man's vain refusal to wear his spectacles. The comedy throughout these scenes depends upon the repeated failure of the old, the foolish, and the malevolent to thwart youthful high spirits; in particular, the plot contrasts the petty meanness of Ranger and Maria against the generous desires of Rashley and Emilia. Physical humour also signifies sexual vigour in *A Fond Husband*. The agility of Rashley and Emilia, as they wriggle (literally) out of successive calamities, points to a similar nimbleness in sex, an analogy the script secures by opening and ending their story with amorous scenes in Emilia's bedchamber.

Durfey's comedy upholds the natural in another regard. Attempts by various characters to paper over the visible signs of their appetites fail (albeit humorously). Their desires, no matter how skilfully disguised, come to the surface, perhaps another comment on the futility of denying nature. The plot discloses Sir Roger's youthful peccadilloes despite his pretension of middle-aged probity, and it reveals Sneak's pregnant mistress despite his affectation of a naive undergraduate persona. Durfey, who habitually in his plays exploits the spatial potential of the baroque stage, also makes good use of the shutter-and-groove technology of Dorset Garden for comic discoveries that bring yet more hidden desires to light. In 5.2, for instance, a scene opens upstage to reveal Sneak's 'sweating-chair' for the cure of venereal disease to a horrified Sir Roger and bemused Cordelia. Even those grand tricksters Rashley and Emilia are discovered *in flagrante*, as the assembled cast rush into Emilia's bedroom to find them descending into pleasure yet again. Much has been made of this final 'discovery' (the word Sir Roger uses) by literary critics who, variously, find it 'sublime', 'humorous', or 'absurd'.[60] At first glance, it seems an odd conclusion to the preceding action. Bubble tries to wound Emilia with his sword; Rashley proffers a duel, should Bubble think it necessary, and then exits abruptly; Emilia stammers excuses until, tongue-tied, she realizes that 'absence is most necessary' (5.5.45) and then flees offstage; Cordelia marvels delightedly at the wacky proceedings; and Bubble declares his intentions to secure a divorce immediately and

---

[60] See Christopher J. Wheatley, 'Thomas Durfey's *A Fond Husband*, Sex Comedies of the Late 1670s, and the Comic Sublime', *Studies in Philology*, 90 (1993), 376; John McVeagh, *Thomas Durfey and Restoration Drama: The Work of a Forgotten Writer* (Aldershot, 2000), 64; and J. Douglas Canfield, *Tricksters and Estates: On the Ideology of Restoration Comedy* (Lexington, Ky., 1997), 237.

then 'spend the remainder of my life in penning a satire against women' (5.5.56–7). Maria admits that 'chance' rather than her own attempts at 'wit' overthrew 'the mighty sophistress' Emilia; and Ranger addresses the audience with the larger 'moral'.

The precipitous nature of the conclusion probably 'plays' better than it reads, as is true of most farce. In this kind of comedy, timing is all, and the design of the play hints strongly at the kind of pacing Durfey intended for the cast. The first three acts contain between one and three scenes; Acts 1 and 3 are long and unbroken. As the plot accelerates, and the accompanying shenanigans of Rashley and Emilia intensify, the fourth and fifth acts break down into four and five short scenes respectively. The final act has an especially frenetic pace, as Rashley and Emilia career wildly from one near miss to another; and the ending, in which one event rapidly eclipses the next, concludes nicely the mounting comic hysteria. While Christopher J. Wheatley is correct to note the 'sublime' nature of the lovers' language (which parodies Longinus), in a staging of this play it is not the language of love but the comic grammar of bodies that impresses the audience. And the ending only appears 'absurd' if one concludes, as does J. Douglas Canfield, that 'the apparent satire on libertinism is undercut at the end by Ranger's surprising declaration'.[61] 'Satire' seems far too harsh a sobriquet for such a comic romp; moreover, the abrupt exits of Emilia and Rashley, far from being 'absurd', are perfectly suited to the repetitive, almost mechanical, nature of farce whereby an action recurs endlessly until someone pulls the plug.

Arguably, if *A Fond Husband* satirizes anyone, it is those who would stop the fun: the spoilsports, the foolish, the malevolent. Ranger's final speech to the audience admits as much when he vows never 'from this hour' to 'baulk a love-intrigue' (5.5.75). Instead, Ranger resolves to conform to the fashionably libertine tastes of the time, as well he might, given the sour consequences of his and Maria's efforts. Emilia, 'the mighty sophistress', has been 'o'erthrown', but through 'no wit of our own', as Maria reminds Ranger (5.5.64). Their interference has ruined a marriage, destroyed the illusions of a doting foolish husband, and halted the hilarious proceedings for the audience. If anything, *A Fond Husband* is something of a cautionary tale directed against the self-righteous: the plot suggests that moral crusades result from thwarted desire, not ethical convictions. In Durfey's genial farce, libertines are a far cry from the murderers and rapists who inhabit

[61] *Tricksters and Estates*, 236.

Shadwell's extravagant experiment, or the brilliant sadist who resides in Etherege's world of ironic posturing, a point underscored by the original casting. Revealingly, Durfey wrote the part of Rashley not for Thomas Betterton, who had played the ruthless libertines Don John and Dorimant to such acclaim, but for William Smith. As an actor, Smith was far better known for portraying heroic figures from classical antiquity or good-natured lovers than he was for personating villains or ill-natured rakes. As the choice of Smith and the young Elizabeth Barry might suggest, the libertines here are lusty youths chafing against social convention. In *A Fond Husband*, they have been airbrushed almost to the point of wholesomeness: they amuse, they titillate, but they certainly do not offend.

Friendship in Fashion

The final play in this volume has a scant history in the theatre: one performance of *Friendship in Fashion* occurred at Dorset Garden on 5 April 1678 and perhaps another on the 25th. The play was licensed on 31 May (Van Lennep, i.269). Thereafter it disappears from sight: not a single performance is known after the première. Thomas Otway framed the role of Goodvile for Betterton, thereby returning the famous actor to one of his well-known 'lines', that of the dissolute and ill-tempered libertine. In so doing, Otway suggested a tonal affinity between Goodvile, the ghastly husband in *Friendship in Fashion*, and Don John and Dorimant. William Smith, who had played Rashley the previous year in *A Fond Husband*, was cast as Truman, a doting young blade similar to his previous role. Elizabeth Barry played Mrs Goodvile, while Mrs Gibbs performed Victoria, Mrs Price the part of Camilla, and Anne Marshall Quin the part of Lady Squeamish. Cave Underhill, always skilled in comic roles, played the dull-witted Sir Noble Clumsy, while the redoubtable Anthony Leigh personated the fop Malagene. The versatile actors John Bowman and Thomas Jevon acted those musical followers of fashion, Saunter and Caper.

Despite this abundance of talent, the play appears to have failed with audiences. The anxiety-ridden dedication to the earl of Dorset, who was usually munificent in matters of patronage, hints that something went badly amiss. Otway mentions 'the unlucky censures some have passed upon me for this play' (ll. 14–15), as well as being 'accused of the thing by some people of the world, who had perhaps as little reason to think I could be guilty of it as to believe themselves deserved it' (ll. 17–19). While Otway never specifies 'the thing' that so offended his enemies, the oblique language suggests that some 'people of the world' thought themselves personated in the play and therefore killed the production, the same problem that had bedevilled John Dryden the previous month with *The Kind Keeper; or Mr. Limberham*. Otway had neither Dryden's literary reputation nor the social capital to withstand such an assault, and the play vanished from repertory. Despite its obscurity, *Friendship in Fashion* warrants our consideration. In recent years, scholarship has resuscitated Aphra Behn's *The Rover* (1677) and Thomas Southerne's *The Wives' Excuse* (1695): both plays are readily available in well-edited, inexpensive editions and, as often happens in modern theatre, dissemination in print has in turn inspired theatrical production. The same has not occurred with *Friendship in Fashion*. Twenty-five years ago, Robert D. Hume complained that 'this great play has attracted no critical attention at all', further maintaining that '*Friendship in Fashion* is brilliant, but not fun. Neglect of it is astonishing . . .'[62] Since then, critics undertaking large-scale thematic or historical studies of Restoration drama have cast a cursory eye on *Friendship in Fashion*; typically, it garners a page or two of discussion.[63] Jessica Munns in her monograph on Otway provides one of the few serious considerations of the play, as does Harold Weber in his study of Restoration rakes.[64] In part, neglect of *Friendship in Fashion* can be attributed to Otway's well-deserved reputation for tragedy: simply put, even in his own time, Otway's serious plays eclipsed his three forays into comedy.

Robert D. Hume's incisive remark that the play is 'not fun' also explains the relative obscurity of *Friendship in Fashion*. It is that most uncomfortable of entertainments, a comedy that depresses. While Otway shares Etherege's fascination with the erotics of power, his marginal position within Restoration society, in addition to his troubled personality, destined him to a far bleaker outlook. *The Man of Mode*, with its crafted cadences and witty rejoinders, boasts the self-assured virtuosity of the *cognoscenti*. By contrast, *Friendship in Fashion*, with its rough humour, acrid plot, and unsavoury imagery, reveals a man at odds with his culture, including its embrace of libertinism. In tone, the play is much closer to harsh satires like William Wycherley's *The Plain Dealer* (1676) or Thomas Southerne's *The Wives' Excuse*

[62] *The Development of English Drama in the Late Seventeenth Century*, 331, 332.

[63] See, for instance, Derek Hughes's discussion in *English Drama 1660–1700*, 225–7.

[64] See *Restoration Politics and Drama: The Plays of Thomas Otway 1675–1683* (Newark, Del., 1995), and *The Restoration Rake-Hero: Transformations in Sexual Understanding in Seventeenth-Century England* (Madison, 1986).

(1691/2) than it is to any of the other plays in this volume. In form, *Friendship in Fashion* follows the outline of what Michael Cordner calls the 'marriage play'. Unlike the courtship plot of romantic comedy, the marriage play 'centres on a marriage in crisis or balances a courtship action against a detailed anatomy of an irretrievably failed union'.[65]

Given the desolate subject matter and the abrasive humour, it should not surprise that *Friendship in Fashion* quickly fell out of repertory. Restoration audiences, accustomed as they were to libertine fare by the late 1670s, nonetheless baulked at plays that were too ill natured or coarse. Wycherley in *The Plain Dealer* makes apparent his disappointment in the audience, especially the women, who cried down his portrait of the randy female hypocrites in *The Country Wife*. Dryden exudes a tone of bewilderment in the preface to *The Kind Keeper; or Mr Limberham*, marvelling that his play sufficiently offended the 'keeping' part of the town to warrant suppression. As the popularity of *The Man of Mode* or *A Fond Husband* might indicate, Restoration audiences wanted their libertine comedy edged with gilt, in the manner of Etherege, or trimmed with sequins, as with Durfey. Otway's play is far plainer garb: its plot focuses on a husband and wife at war, rather than the seductions of a smooth-talking rake or the escapades of good-natured adulterers. Their domestic war poisons surrounding principalities: relations, friends, even hangers-on are pulled into the spiralling dispute.

In terms of plot, *Friendship in Fashion* satisfies the basic tenets of libertine comedy. Early exposition establishes Goodvile's libertine character: within ten days of marriage, as Truman relates, 'he debauched me with two vizards in a hackney to supper' (1.1.25–6). In the ensuing interval—mere months—Goodvile has seduced his kinswoman Victoria, in addition to frequenting whores. As the play opens, Goodvile, suspecting that Victoria is pregnant, attempts to fob her off on Truman, his 'friend'; he then turns his attentions to Camilla, the love interest of another 'friend' Valentine. In the words of Derek Hughes, 'Goodvile (Betterton) is an uglier version of Dorimant . . .'[66] Like Etherege's creation, or even Horner in Wycherley's *The Country Wife*, Goodvile withholds secrets from his male 'friends', and thinks nothing of debauching their fiancées or wives. Appetitive and self-interested, he satisfies instinctual desires and ignores societal conventions. Unlike Dorimant, however, Goodvile is sufficiently repulsive as

[65] *Four Restoration Marriage Plays*, ed. Michael Cordner (Oxford, 1995), p. xii.
[66] *English Drama 1660–1700*, 225.

to banish any questions about Otway's attitude toward libertinism. The 'good nature' associated with the cultivated libertine—Dorimant uses the phrase several times, as do the speakers in several Rochester poems—is nowhere here apparent, quite the opposite. For instance, despite a professed dislike for his wife, Goodvile watches her jealously, hoping to catch her *in flagrante* with Truman. He torments Saunter and Caper, the harmless fops who want only to sing and dance, and he humiliates the pompous Lady Squeamish and abuses the pretentious Malagene far beyond their just deserts.

If anything, the character of Goodvile can be seen as a rebuke to the commonplace of the agreeable rake, he of the witty rejoinder and becoming negligence. Otway instead gives us a libertine who is drunk and obnoxious throughout much of the play, and, in place of droll quips, descends to name-calling, invective, and curses. Goodvile's outburst against Caper and Saunter in Act 4 typifies his loutish behaviour. Exasperated, he calls the fops an 'ill-ordered, addle-pated, waddling brace of puppies!' (4.1.344). He orders Saunter to 'sing and be safe' and Caper, that 'slight grasshopper', to 'dance and divert me'. When they refuse, Goodvile shoves the two men at his wife and exits the scene, as the stage directions specify. Similarly, his sole attempt at romantic language is undercut by another infantile gesture. When he glimpses Victoria, Goodvile steps aside and 'makes mouths' at his former mistress, declaring, 'farewell, fubb' (3.1.594). His enraptured imagining of Camilla ('Now for the lovely, kind, yielding Camilla . . . Swelling burning breasts, dying eyes, balmy lips, trembling joints, millions of kisses, and unspeakable joys wait for me'), uttered immediately after this childish display, reveals the slavering appetite of a glutton, someone whose desires and impulses are both undisguised and uncontrolled (3.1.595–7).

Good nature in this play belongs not to the rake but to those who are normally marginalized or even scorned in libertine comedies: the fops, the put-upon wife, the abandoned mistress. Victoria, the Mrs Loveit of *Friendship in Fashion*, does not exact revenge against Mrs Goodvile or Camilla, who has just gained ascendancy in Goodvile's heart. Rather, in an extraordinary monologue at the beginning of Act 5, she asks herself whether 'Goodvile's wife ever wronged me?' and then, having concluded 'never', decides to 'let my revenge light wholly on that false, perjured man. As he has deceived and ruined me, I'll play false with him, make myself privy to his whole design of surprising Truman and his wife together' (5.1.3–8). True to her declaration, Victoria assists Mrs Goodvile, even generously ignoring a pointed rebuke from the wronged wife: "Tis true she reproached me, but 'twas done so handsomely that I had doubly deserved it to have taken notice of it.' Just as the character of Victoria departs from the standard depiction of the abandoned, vengeful mistress, so do the characters of Saunter and Caper deviate from the usual treatment of the fop. Unlike Sir Fopling Flutter in *The Man of Mode*, who desires only to make a ballet to himself, these gentlemen want to sing and dance for the ladies, even vowing to protect their honour when necessary. Caper, hearing of Sir Noble Clumsy's drunken affront to Victoria and Lady Squeamish, asks 'how durst you treat ladies so rudely as we saw you but now?' (5.1.226–7). Dissatisfied with the inebriated response, he asks Sir Noble Clumsy to fight. The sound of fiddles interrupts this challenge and Caper, overcome as always by music, enthuses to Lady Squeamish that 'we'll dance forever', Saunter adding, 'And sing', until they both in unison cry 'And love'. The prospect of pleasure—a pleasure grounded in art, not malevolence—quickly vanquishes the possibility of violence.

Throughout the play, Goodvile's persecution of Caper and Saunter seems out of proportion to their 'crime'—which is to enjoy innocent diversions and entertain ladies. Infuriated by their sweet-natured (if somewhat inane) courtliness, Goodvile tries repeatedly to humiliate them before his wife or guests. Enraged by their devotion to song and dance, he orders a servant to tie up one of Caper's legs and to gag Saunter, a symbolic annihilation of art. Otway, like Shadwell before him, envisions libertinism as a destructive force, one that ruins the social bonds and activities that sustain human beings. Goodvile, possessed by the same insurgency that grips Don John, destroys a marriage to a clever, beautiful woman, ruins the reputation of a devoted mistress, and betrays two close friends. Otway also focuses attention on the superfluous cruelty of the libertine. Not content with betraying his wife, Goodvile brings home in Act 5 the two whores he intends to set up as surrogate partners, a grotesque parody of marriage. Goodvile's every action exceeds the precipitate cause and therefore asks us, whether as readers or spectators, to contemplate the motives of a man so wantonly vicious in temperament.

Otway's choice to channel his condemnation through a more conventional comic form—rather than experiment with the sort of grand design undertaken by Shadwell—may account for the failure of *Friendship in Fashion* in the seventeenth and eighteenth centuries. Audiences accustomed to the plays of Etherege, Behn, Durfey, or Ravenscroft would have come to the theatre expecting a verbal or physical romp. Instead, they were presented with a grim depiction of a society that makes marriage or friendship impossible. Even the alliances forged between Mrs Goodvile and Victoria, or Truman and Valentine, depend for their efficacy on a mutually realized goal: the thwarting of Goodvile. A play like *The Libertine*, half poised between spoken drama and opera, 'extravagant' in its design, defied audience expectations whereas *Friendship in Fashion* merely disappointed them. Then too the moral abyss in Otway's dramatic world may have proved too much for audiences who expected an implied ethical stance, as in Shadwell, or, at the very least, the compensatory sheen of Etherege's verbal pyrotechnics. Otway, however, refuses to temper his harsh vision: rough and blunt, the play forces us to see, in a comic vein no less, the worst of human behaviour. *Friendship in Fashion* indicts savagely a fashionable libertinism that renders untenable any human motive other than self-interest.

In certain respects, Otway is closer to modern dramatists like Jean Genet, Peter Weiss, or Edward Albee than he is to his contemporaries; indeed, some of the exchanges between the Goodviles are worthy of George and Martha in *Who's Afraid of Virginia Woolf?*. That quality of seeing things differently pitted Otway against his peers and his audiences throughout his brief, tragic career. While *Friendship in Fashion* deserves our attention because of its sheer craft, it also speaks to us in a way that perhaps eluded the seventeenth century. Modern drama, if nothing else, has accustomed us to scrutinizing closely the internal dynamics of marriage and friendship; we are similarly used to situating the failure of human relationships against the backdrop of larger social forces. In its compassion for marginalized characters, especially women, *Friendship in Fashion* also seems peculiarly modern. The revival of interest these past twenty years in Aphra Behn should pave the way for an appreciation of male dramatists like Otway who shared her interest in the plight of women during the Restoration. This edition goes some modest way toward making this neglected masterpiece available; hopefully, future scholarship and productions will further enlarge Otway's reputation as a comic dramatist.

NOTE ON THE TEXTS

ALL the plays in this volume were published within months of their stage première: *The Libertine*, which opened in June of 1675, was licensed for publication on 10 February 1676; *The Man of Mode*, which opened in March of 1676, was licensed on 22 November 1676; *A Fond Husband*, which probably opened in May of 1677, was licensed on 26 November 1677; and *Friendship in Fashion*, which most likely opened in April of 1678, was licensed on 22 June 1678. The lag between production and print follows a pattern typical for the 1670s. Judith Milhous and Robert D. Hume, in surveying the publication of plays during this period, note that by the middle of the decade, the normal time lapse had shortened to six months (by the 1680s it would shorten again, to three months).[1] Interestingly, the least popular of the plays, *Friendship in Fashion*, was the one most rapidly hurried into print, suggesting, perhaps, that Thomas Otway hoped to realize from copyright what he had not earned at the box office. With the exception of *Friendship in Fashion*, the remaining three plays enjoyed frequent revivals and printings through the Restoration and the early eighteenth century. None of the plays has been significantly altered, nor is there evidence of authorial corrections in later editions.

That being the case, I have used the first quarto for my copy text. Substantive departures from the first quarto, whether editorial or derived from later seventeenth- or early eighteenth-century editions, are explained in the notes. Square brackets identify a reading imported from a later printing. I have modernized spelling and punctuation throughout. In keeping with series practice, standard forms have been adopted for characters' names in entries and exits, as well as speech prefixes. All necessary alterations have been silently introduced. Latin forms in stage directions and speech prefixes have been silently translated: 'solus' or 'sola' as 'alone', 'manet' as 'remains', and 'omnes' as 'all'. 'Exit' and 'exeunt' have been retained. When the first quartos have vague or problematic stage directions ('exit' for a multiple departure), I have made silent corrections. Again, in keeping with the editorial principles of this series, I have expanded stage directions to

---

[1] Judith Milhous and Robert D. Hume, 'Dating Play Premières from Publication Data, 1660–1700', *Harvard Library Bulletin*, 22 (1974), 374–405.

help the reader visualize the action. Restoration plays tend to use stage directions lightly, and occasionally those provided are confusing. For clarity, I have placed editorial stage directions and changes to original stage directions in square brackets. Series conventions dictate the silent emendation of some stage directions; for instance, concluding directions to a scene are indicated by 'exit' or 'exeunt', regardless of whether or not the first quarto specifies the characters' names.

The 1676 quarto of *The Libertine* lays out some passages as verse that appear to be prose. I have experimented with both versions and relied heavily on Michael Cordner's expert advice in this matter. Initially, I retained these speeches as verse, a practice Gillian Manning follows in her recent edition; however, Michael Cordner persuaded me to change them to prose. Upon reflection, I ultimately agreed with his reasoning, but readers, actors, and directors should be aware of the possibility of verse, especially at moments of high pathos. As with so much else relating to seventeenth-century printing, there is not a definitive solution to this problem.

Of the four plays included herein, it should not surprise that the most canonical, *The Man of Mode*, has appeared in several notable single-play editions: a modern-spelling text by W. B. Carnochan for the Regents Restoration Drama Series (Lincoln: University of Nebraska, 1966), an old-spelling text by John Conaghan for The Fountainwell Drama Texts (Edinburgh: Oliver & Boyd, 1973), and a modern-spelling text by John Barnard for The New Mermaids (London: Ernest Benn, 1979). A. Wilson Verity edited the first modern collection of Etherege's *Works* in 1888 (London: John C. Nimmo), but he used for his copy text the first collected edition of 1704, not the first quarto, thus importing numerous errors. Additionally, Verity's Victorian sensibilities frequently dictated changes to 'offensive' language. H. F. B. Brett-Smith corrected these errors in his old-spelling *Dramatic Works* (Oxford: Basil Blackwell, 1927). To date, the most authoritative collection is Michael Cordner's *The Plays of Sir George Etherege* (Cambridge: Cambridge University Press, 1982), which modernizes spelling but retains, as much as possible, original punctuation and phrasing.

The modern publication history of the remaining three plays is sketchy at best. Recently, Gillian Manning prepared *The Libertine* for her modern-spelling collection, *Libertine Plays of the Restoration* (London: J. M. Dent, 2001). Previously, it had appeared in 1927 as part of *The Complete Works of Thomas Shadwell*, an old-spelling edition put together by Montague Summers (London: Fortune Press,

1927). Durfey's *A Fond Husband* has been edited by Jack A. Vaughn and included in his volume, *Two Comedies* (Rutherford, Pa.: Fairleigh Dickinson, 1976). *Friendship in Fashion* has been included in two old-spelling editions, *The Complete Works of Thomas Otway*, edited by Montague Summers (Bloomsbury: Nonesuch, 1926), and *The Works of Thomas Otway*, edited by J. C. Ghosh (Oxford: Clarendon, 1932).

THE RESTORATION PLAYHOUSE

THE Restoration playhouse retained from its Elizabethan predecessor a deep 'thrust' or forestage that extended well beyond a proscenium borrowed from continental design. The auditorium, in a manner typical of continental theatres, was divided into pit, boxes, and galleries, although the English pit, unlike its French equivalent, was slanted to improve sightlines. Spatial divisions within the auditorium corresponded roughly to social divisions: the pit was frequented by the *beau monde* and young men of fashion, who frequently made loud (and, according to the dramatists, obnoxious) pronouncements on the play or actors; the boxes were occupied by courtiers and nobility; and the galleries were used by frugal-minded citizens.

The earliest theatres were quite small. When William Davenant converted Lisle's Tennis Court into the Lincoln's Inn Fields Theatre for the Duke's Company in 1661, it measured roughly 30 by 75 feet. The popularity of semi-operas and audience taste for spectacle necessitated larger playhouses that could accommodate more complicated stage machinery. In 1671 Dorset Garden Theatre replaced Lincoln's Inn Fields; at 57 by 140 feet, it was nearly twice the size of the earlier structure. It is in this theatre that all of the four plays in this volume were originally staged. The rival King's Company hurried to build an equally impressive edifice, producing the Drury Lane Theatre in 1674, which measured a nearly equivalent 58 by 140 feet. Despite almost doubling its size in one decade, the Restoration playhouse remained a cosy playing space. Audiences could see the smallest gesture and hear subtle changes in pitch and tone; according to Colley Cibber, one of the best contemporary sources on staging, vocal projection for the actors was effortless.

The open platform forward of the proscenium created an atmosphere of intimacy and, in all likelihood, promoted audience identification with the stage action. Drury Lane in 1674 had a stage that was roughly 34 feet deep; *half* of that space was forward of the proscenium. Doors in the proscenium walls, topped by balconies, opened onto this forestage from both ends. Some scholars conjecture that these doors were used for most entrances, especially in comedy (which is thought to have been played 'downstage', almost exclusively on the forestage forward of the proscenium). While a tempting explanation, it remains conjectural. The balconies surmounting the doors in the proscenium walls could be used for stage business (for instance, the window that 'opens' in 1.1 of *The Libertine*, allowing Maria to fling down a note). As in the Elizabethan period, an exit through one door and re-entry through another could indicate a change of place. The floor of the stage was 'raked' (i.e. slanted upward toward the back stage wall), making for improved sightlines for the audience.

Behind the proscenium, grooves in the stage floor accommodated wings and shutters. A particular setting (i.e. Lady Townley's house in *The Man of Mode*) could be produced by sliding from the wings a pair of matching shutters (with the scene painted on them) towards each other until they met to create a unified stage picture. 'Wings' (side scenes) framed the shutters, adding depth and ornamentation. Although we do not know conclusively the number of shutter positions available on the Restoration stage, most scholars estimate two. Three different sets of shutters could be sequentially displayed at these two different positions, making for frequent scene changes during a performance.

Audiences first saw the scenic (i.e. 'inner') stage after the prologue was spoken and the curtain drawn. All scenery changes took place in front of the audience, and the shutter-and-groove technology available to playhouses like Dorset Garden ensured that scene changes were both fluid and rapid. It also permitted the playing of the 'discovery scenes' so beloved by Restoration dramatists. Enough space existed between the grooves to allow for the 'discovery' of actors or stage properties when one set of shutters opened to reveal another set. Such a moment occurs in *A Fond Husband* in 5.2 when a scene opens to reveal Sneak's sweating-chair for venereal disease. *The Man of Mode* affords another example, as we move from the public space of Lady Townley's house in 4.1 to the privacy of Dorimant's dwelling in 4.2, where he has just enjoyed sex with Bellinda, as the famous stage direction ('*Handy tying up linen*') indicates. Normally, these scenic transitions occurred within a given act. At the conclusion of an act, all of the players exited and instrumental music would be played by theatre musicians, thus allowing the stage-hands to set up the shutters and wings for the next act.

The reader is encouraged to keep these staging conventions in mind while reading. Plays invariably are written for a specific space; playhouse space also shapes dramatic convention. Asides to the audience, one of the hallmarks of Restoration comedy, would be impossible in a playhouse without a pronounced forestage. Topical allusions to specific locales would seem odd without painted scenery that made them manifest. Above all, the reader is encouraged to imagine the intimacy and camaraderie of the Restoration playhouse, an environment where actors and the audience often knew each other and shared a common cultural and theatrical vocabulary.

SELECT BIBLIOGRAPHY

THE best general introduction to the staging and production of Restoration plays is found in the preface to Part 1 of *The London Stage*, ed. William Van Lennep (Carbondale, Ill., 1965). Peter Holland's *The Ornament of Action* (Cambridge, 1979) discusses the staging of the drama and advances some intriguing hypotheses about the use of performance space in the Restoration playhouse. Jocelyn Powell, in *Restoration Theatre Production* (London, 1984), looks more closely at the technical features of the Restoration playhouse and scenic design. J. L. Styan's *Restoration Comedy in Performance* (Cambridge, 1986), uses contemporary materials, such as conduct books and illustrations, to recreate staging conditions. For information about performers and personnel, readers are advised to consult Philip H. Highfill, Jr., Kalman A. Burnim, and Edward A. Langhans's *A Biographical Dictionary of Actors, Actresses, Musicians, Dancers, Managers and Other Stage Personnel in London, 1660–1800* (16 vols.; Carbondale, Ill., 1973–93). Pierre Danchin's *The Prologues and Epilogues of the Restoration, 1660–1700* (7 vols.; Nancy, 1981–8) gathers together all of the known prologues and epilogues in the period, as well as providing a good overview of this theatrical convention.

A number of useful collections of essays on Restoration drama have been published, especially in the last few years: John Russell Brown and Bernard Harris (eds.), *Restoration Theatre* (London, 1965); John Loftis (ed.), *Restoration Drama: Modern Essays in Criticism* (New York, 1966); Earl Miner (ed.), *Restoration Dramatists: A Collection of Critical Essays* (Englewood Cliffs, NJ, 1966); Robert D. Hume (ed.), *The London Theatre World, 1660–1800* (Carbondale, Ill., 1980); Richard W. Bevis (ed.), *English Drama: Restoration and Eighteenth Century, 1660–1789* (London, 1988); J. Douglas Canfield and Deborah C. Payne (eds.), *Cultural Readings of Restoration and Eighteenth-Century English Theatre* (Athens, Ga., 1995); Katherine M. Quinsey (ed.), *Broken Boundaries: Women and Feminism in Restoration Drama* (Lexington, Ky., 1996); Deborah Payne Fisk (ed.), *The Cambridge Companion to English Restoration Theatre* (Cambridge, 2000); Susan J. Owen (ed.), *A Companion to Restoration Drama* (Oxford, 2001).

Robert D. Hume's *The Development of English Drama in the Late Seventeenth Century* (Oxford, 1976) remains the best general overview of dramatic genre in the period. His sections on the various types of comedy are helpful, and he includes brief considerations of the four plays in this volume. Laura Brown's *English Dramatic Form, 1660–1760: An Essay in Generic History* (New Haven, 1981), considers genre change from a Marxist perspective. Eric Rothstein and Frances M. Kavenik, *The Designs of Carolean Comedy* (Carbondale, Ill., 1988), locates generic change in audience taste and the box office. Brian Corman's *Genre and Generic Change in English Comedy, 1660–1710* (Toronto, 1993) follows closely on the heels of Hume's formalist approach.

Most studies of Restoration comedy focus on the canonical dramatists; invariably, they include a discussion of Sir George Etherege's *The Man of Mode*, but they tend to overlook the other plays in this volume. The more influential of these canonical studies include Thomas H. Fujimura, *The Restoration Comedy of Wit* (Princeton, 1952); Norman Holland, *The First Modern Comedies* (Cambridge, Mass., 1959); Virginia Ogden Birdsall, *Wild Civility: The English Comic Spirit on the Restoration Stage* (Bloomington, Ind., 1970); Robert Markley, *Two-Edg'd Weapons: Style and Ideology in the Comedies of Etherege, Wycherley, and Congreve* (Oxford, 1988); and Pat Gill, *Interpreting Ladies: Women, Wit, and Morality in the Restoration Comedy of Manners* (Athens, Ga., 1994). J. Douglas Canfield's *Tricksters and Estates: On the Ideology of Restoration Comedy* (Lexington, Ky., 1997) is one of the few studies to consider Shadwell, Durfey, and Otway, as well as Etherege.

Nonetheless, Shadwell has begun to attract more critical attention. Christopher J. Wheatley wrote the first full-length monograph, *Without God or Reason* (Lewisburg, Pa., 1993), which includes a very good discussion of *The Libertine*. Following soon after in 1996 was a special issue of the journal *Restoration* devoted solely to Shadwell's dramatic works. Barbara A. Simerka considers *The Libertine* at length in her recent monograph, *Eros and Atheism: Providential Ideology in the Don Juan Plays of Tirso de Molina and Thomas Shadwell* (Lewisburg, Pa., 2000). J. M. Armistead's *Four Restoration Playwrights: A Reference Guide to Thomas Shadwell, Aphra Behn, Nathaniel Lee, and Thomas Otway* (Boston, 1984) provides readers with a useful bibliography of writings by and about Shadwell; it also covers Otway.

As might be expected, Etherege, because of his canonical status, has been the subject of several individual studies. David D. Mann published a major bibliography, *Sir George Etherege: A Reference Guide* (Boston, 1981); he has also produced the eminently useful *A*

Concordance to the Plays and Poems of Sir George Etherege (Westport, Conn., 1985). Long ago Bonamy Dobrée included a biographical sketch of Etherege in his *Essays in Biography, 1680–1726* (London, 1925); interestingly, no one to date has written a critical biography of this compelling figure. Frederick Bracher compiled Etherege's amusing letters in a nicely annotated edition, *Letters of Sir George Etherege* (Berkeley, 1973). Dale Underwood's *Etherege and the Seventeenth-Century Comedy of Manners* (New Haven, 1957) remains the single best intellectual study of Etherege's plays, while Arthur R. Huseboe's *Sir George Etherege* (Boston, 1987) provides readers with a general overview. Numerous articles and individual book chapters have been devoted to *The Man of Mode*, and there is little sign of cessation in the near future.

Until recently, Durfey was accorded little more than a passing glance in large thematic or generic treatments of Restoration comedy (see above). J. Douglas Canfield and Christopher Wheatley paved the way for serious consideration of this very good dramatist. Canfield discusses several of Durfey's comedies in *Tricksters and Estates*, while Wheatley takes up *A Fond Husband* in an important article, 'Thomas Durfey's *A Fond Husband*, Sex Comedies of the 1670s and Early 1680s, and the Comic Sublime', *SP* 90 (1993), 371–90. More recently, two book-length studies have appeared: Garry Sherbert's *Menippean Satire and the Poetics of Wit: Ideologies of Self-Consciousness in Dunton, D'Urfey, and Sterne* (New York, 1996) and John McVeagh's *Thomas Durfey and Restoration Drama: The Work of a Forgotten Writer* (Aldershot, 2000).

Otway's comedies have received far less attention than his tragedies; to date, most scholarship continues to focus on *Venice Preserv'd* to the exclusion of his other, very good plays. Fortunately, Jessica Munns devotes several incisive pages to *Friendship in Fashion* in *Restoration Politics and Drama: The Plays of Thomas Otway, 1675–1683* (Newark, Del., 1995), as does Harold Weber in *The Restoration Rake-Hero: Transformations in Sexual Understanding in Seventeenth-Century England* (Madison, 1986). Robert D. Hume first drew attention to the play in *The Development of English Drama in the Late Seventeenth Century*. Roswell Ham sketched Otway's life in *Otway and Lee: Biography from a Baroque Age* (New Haven, 1931). That biography has been superseded by J. Douglas Canfield's entry in the *Dictionary of Literary Biography*, lxxx: *Restoration and Eighteenth-Century Dramatists*, ed. Paula Backscheider (Detroit, 1989).

A CHRONOLOGY OF LIBERTINE PLAYS

THE following is a selective and no doubt highly idiosyncratic list of plays written between 1660 and 1700, in which at least one plot features a major character who espouses libertine philosophy or enacts a libertine lifestyle (which is not necessarily the same as the philandering present in the farces, intrigue, or city comedies of the period). The dates are of the first known performance.

John Dryden, *Marriage A-la-Mode* (1671)
Thomas Shadwell, *Epsom-Wells* (1672)
Joseph Arrowsmith, *The Reformation* (c.1673)
Edward Ravenscroft, *The Careless Lovers* (1673)
John Dover, *The Mall; or, The Modish Lovers* (c.1674)
John Crowne, *The Country Wit* (1675)
Sir Francis Fane, *Love in the Dark* (1675)
William Wycherley, *The Country-Wife* (1675)
Thomas Shadwell, *The Libertine* (1675)
Sir George Etherege, *The Man of Mode* (1676)
William Wycherley, *The Plain Dealer* (1676)
Thomas Shadwell, *The Virtuoso* (1676)
Aphra Behn, *The Rover* (1677)
Thomas Durfey, *A Fond Husband* (1677)
Thomas Otway, *Friendship in Fashion* (1678)
Thomas Shadwell, *A True Widow* (1678)
Aphra Behn, *Sir Patient Fancy* (1678)
John Dryden, *The Kind Keeper; or, Mr Limberham* (1678)
Nathaniel Lee, *The Princess of Cleve* (c.1680)
Edward Ravenscroft, *The London Cuckolds* (1681)
Aphra Behn, *The City Heiress; or, Sir Timothy Treat-all* (1682)
John Crowne, *City Politiques* (banned 1682; performed 1683)
Thomas Otway, *The Atheist* (1683)
Sir Charles Sedley, *Bellamira* (1687)
Thomas Southerne, *Sir Anthony Love* (1690)
Thomas Southerne, *The Wives' Excuse; or, Cuckolds make Themselves* (1691)
Thomas Durfey, *The Marriage-Hater Match'd* (1692)
William Congreve, *The Old Batchelour* (1693)
William Congreve, *The Double-Dealer* (1693)
Sir John Vanbrugh, *The Relapse* (1696)

THE LIBERTINE

THOMAS SHADWELL

To the most Illustrious Prince William, Duke, Marquis, and Earl of Newcastle, etc.°

May it please your grace,
The favours have been so many and so great, which your grace's unwearied bounty° has conferred upon me, that I cannot omit this opportunity of telling the world how much I have been obliged and by whom. My gratitude will not suffer me to smother the favours in silence, nor the pride they have raised me to, let me conceal the name of so excellent a patron. The honour of being favoured by the great Newcastle is equal with any real merit, I am sure infinitely above mine. Yet the encouragement I receive from your grace is the certain way to make the world believe I have some desert, or to create in me the most favourable thoughts of myself. My name may thus, when otherwise it would perish, live in after ages under the protection of your grace's, which is famous abroad and will be eternized in this nation for your wit, beyond all poets; judgement and prudence, before all statesmen; courage and conduct, above all generals; constancy and loyalty, beyond all subjects; virtue and temperance, above all philosophers; for skill in weapons and horsemanship and all other arts befitting your quality,° excelling all noblemen; and, lastly, for those eminent services in defence of your king and country, with an interest and power much exceeding all, and with loyalty equalling any nobleman. And, indeed, the first was so great, that it might justly have made the greatest prince afraid of it, had it not been so strongly secured by the latter.

All these heroic qualities I admired and worshipped at a distance before I had the honour to wait upon your grace° at your house. For so vast was your bounty to me as to find me out in my obscurity and oblige me several years before you saw me at Welbeck,° where, when I arrived, I found a respect so extremely above the meanness of my condition, that I still received it with blushes, having had nothing to recommend me but the birth and education without the fortune of a gentleman, besides some writings of mine which your grace was pleased to like. Then was soon added to my former worship° and admiration, infinite love and infinite gratitude, and a pride of being favoured by one in whom I observed a majesty equal with greatest princes, yet affability exceeding ordinary gentlemen, a greatness that none e'er approached without awe or parted from without satisfaction.

Then, by the great honour I had to be daily admitted into your grace's public and private conversation, I observed that admirable

experience and judgement surmounting all the old, and that vigorous- 40
ness of wit and smartness of expression exceeding all the young I ever
knew; and not only in sharp and apt replies, the most excellent way of
pursuing a discourse, but, which is much more difficult, by giving easy
and unforced occasions, the most admirable way of beginning one; and
all this adapted to men of all circumstances and conditions, your grace 45
being able to discourse with every man in his own way, which, as it
shows you to be a most accurate observer of all men's tempers, so it
shows your excellency in all their arts. But when I had the favour daily
to be admitted to your grace's more retired conversation, when I alone
enjoyed the honour, I must declare I never spent my hours with that 50
pleasure or improvement, nor shall I ever enough acknowledge that
and the rest of the honours done me by your grace, as much above my
condition as my merit.

And now, my lord, after all this, imagine not I intend this small
present of a play, though favoured here by those I most wish it should 55
be, as any return;° for all the services of my life cannot make a sufficient one. I only lay hold on this occasion to publish to the world
your great favours and the grateful acknowledgments of

My most noble lord, your grace's
most obliged, humble, and obedient servant, 60
Thomas Shadwell

THE CHARACTERS OF THE PLAY°

Don John, *the libertine; a rash, fearless man, guilty of all vice*

Don Antonio
Don Lopez } *his two friends*

Don Octavio, *Maria's lover*
[Maria's Brother]
Jacomo, *Don John's man*
Leonora, *Don John's mistress, abused by him, yet follows him for love*
Maria, *abused by Don John and following him for revenge*
[Flora], *maid to Maria*
Don Francisco, *father to Clara and Flavia*

Clara
Flavia } *his daughters*

Six Women, *all wives to Don John*
Hermit
Two gentlemen, *intended for husbands to Clara and Flavia*
Ghosts
Shepherds and shepherdesses
Old woman
Office and soldiers
Singers, servants, attendants

SCENE: SEVILLE

4

PREFACE

The story from which I took the hint of this play is famous all over Spain, Italy, and France.° It was first put into a Spanish play, as I have been told, the Spaniards having a tradition, which they believe, of such a vicious Spaniard as is represented in this play. From them the Italian comedians took it, and from them the French took it, and four several French plays were made upon the story.°

The character of the libertine and, consequently, those of his friends, are borrowed, but all the plot, till the latter end of the fourth act, is new. And all the rest is very much varied from anything which has been done upon the subject.°

I hope the readers will excuse the irregularities of the play° when they consider that the extravagance of the subject forced me to it. And I had rather try new ways to please than to write on in the same road, as too many do. I hope that the severest reader will not be offended at the representation of those vices on which they will see a dreadful punishment inflicted. And I have been told by a worthy gentleman that many years ago,° when first a play was made upon this story in Italy, he has seen it acted there by the name of *Atheisto Fulminato* in churches on Sundays as a part of devotion,° and some, not of the least judgement and piety here, have thought it rather an useful moral than an encouragement to vice.

I have no reason to complain of the success of this play° since it pleased those whom, of all the world, I would please most. Nor was the town° unkind to it, for which reason I must applaud my good fortune to have pleased with so little pains, there being no act in it which cost me above five days writing;° and the last two, the playhouse having great occasion for a play, were both written in four days, as several can testify. And this I dare declare, notwithstanding the foul, coarse, and ill-mannered censure passed upon them who write plays in three, four, or five weeks time, by a rough, hobbling rhymer in his postscript to another man's play, which he spoiled and called *Love and Revenge*,° I having before publicly owned the writing two plays in so short a time.° He ought not to have measured any man's abilities who writes for the stage with his own, for some may write that in three weeks which he cannot in three years. But he is angry that any man should write sense so easily when he finds it so laborious a thing to write even fustian, that he is believed to have been three years drudging upon *The Conquest of China*.° But he ought not to be called a poet who cannot write ten times a better in three weeks.

I cannot here pass by his saucy epistle to this *Conquest* which, instead of expressions of just respect due to the birth and merit of his patron, is stuffed with railing against others. And, first, he begins with the vanity of his tribe. What tribe that really is, it is not hard to guess. But all the poets will bear me witness it is not theirs, who are sufficiently satisfied that he is no more a poet than servant to his majesty,° as he presumes to write himself, which I wonder he will do since protections are taken off. I know not what place he is sworn into in Extraordinary,° but I am sure there is no such thing as Poet in Extraordinary.

But I wonder, after all his railing, he will call these poets his brethren. If they were, methinks he might have more natural affection than to abuse his brethren. But he might have spared that title, for we can find no manner of relation betwixt him and them; for they are all gentlemen that will not own him° or keep him company. And that, perhaps, is the cause which makes him so angry with them, to tax them° in his ill-mannered epistle with impudence, which he, having a particular affection for his own vice, calls by the name of frailty. Impudence indeed is a very pretty frailty.

But, whatever the poets are guilty of, I wish he had as much of poetry in him as he has of that frailty, for the good of the Duke's Theatre.° They might then have hopes of gaining as much by his good sense as they have lost by his fustian.

Thus much I thought fit to say in vindication of the poets, though I think he has not authority enough with men of sense to fix any calumny upon the tribe, as he calls it. For which reason, I shall never trouble myself to take notice of him hereafter, since all men of wit will think that he can do the poets no greater injury than pretending to be one. Nor had I said so much in answer to his coarse railing but to reprehend his arrogance and lead him to a little better knowledge of himself, nor does his base language in his postscript deserve a better return.

Prologue

Our author sent me hither for a scout,
To spy what bloody critics were come out;°
Those picaroons in wit, who infest this road,°
And snap both friend and foe that come abroad.°
This savage party crueller appears,   5
Than in the channel Ostend privateers.°
You in this road, or sink or plunder all;
Remorseless as a storm on us you fall.
But, as a merchant, when by storms distressed,
Flings out his bulky goods to save the rest   10
(Hoping a calm may come, he keeps the best),
In this black tempest which o'er us impends,
Near rocks and quick sands, and no ports of friends,
Our poet gives this over to your rage,
The most irregular play upon the stage,°   15
As wild and as extravagant as the age.
Now, angry men, to all your spleens give vent;
When all your fury has on this been spent,
Elsewhere you with much worse shall be content.
The poet has no hopes you'll be appeased,   20
Who come on purpose but to be displeased.
Such corrupt judges should excepted be,
Who can condemn before they hear or see.
Ne'er were such bloody critics yet in fashion;
You damn by absolute predestination.°   25
But why so many to run one man down?
It were a mighty triumph when y' have done.
Our scarcity of plays you should not blame,°
When by foul poaching you destroy the game.
Let him but have fair play, and he may then   30
Write himself into favour once again.
If after this your anger you'll reveal,
To Caesar he must make his just appeal;°
There mercy and judgement equally do meet,
To pardon faults and to encourage wit.   35

1.1

[*A street in Seville*]°

Enter Don John, Don Lopez, Don Antonio, Jacomo, Don John's valet

DON JOHN Thus far without a bound we have enjoyed
Our prosp'rous pleasures, which dull fools call sins;
Laughed at old feeble judges and weak laws;
And at the fond, fantastic thing called conscience,°
Which serves for nothing but to make men cowards;   5
An idle fear of future misery,
And is yet worse than all that we can fear.

DON LOPEZ Conscience made up of dark and horrid thoughts,
Raised from the fumes of a distempered spleen.

DON ANTONIO A senseless fear, would make us contradict   10
The only certain guide, infallible nature;°
And, at the call of melancholy fools,
Who style all actions which they like not, sins,
To silence all our natural appetites.

DON JOHN Yet those conscientious fools that would persuade us   15
To I know not what, which they call piety,
Have in reserve private, delicious sins,
Great as the happy libertine enjoys,
With which, in corners, wantonly they roll.°

DON LOPEZ Don John, thou art our oracle; thou hast   20
Dispelled the fumes which once clouded our brains.

DON ANTONIO By thee, we have got loose from education,
And the dull slavery of pupillage,°
Recovered all the liberty of nature;
Our own strong reason now can go alone,   25
Without the feeble props of splenetic fools,
Who contradict our common mother, nature.

DON JOHN Nature gave us our senses, which we please,
Nor does our reason war against our sense.
By nature's order, sense should guide our reason,   30
Since to the mind all objects sense conveys.°
But fools for shadows lose substantial pleasures,
For idle tales abandon true delight,
And solid joys of days for empty dreams at night.

Away, thou foolish thing, thou cholic of the mind,°   35
Thou worm by ill-digesting stomachs bred.
In spite of thee, we'll surfeit in delights,
And never think ought can be ill that's pleasant.

JACOMO A most excellent sermon and, no doubt, gentlemen, you
have edified much by it.   40

DON JOHN Away, thou formal, phlegmatic coxcomb; thou°
Hast neither courage nor yet wit enough
To sin thus. Thou art my dull, conscientious pimp.
And when I am wanton with my whore within,
Thou, with thy beads and prayer-book, keep'st the door.°   45

JACOMO Sir, I find your worship is no more afraid to be damned than
other fashionable gentlemen of the age. But, methinks, halters and
axes° should terrify you. With reverence to your worships, I've
seen civiller men hanged, and men of as pretty parts° too. There's
scarce a city in Spain but is too hot for you, you have committed   50
such outrages wheresoe'er you come.

DON LOPEZ Come, for diversion, pray let's hear your fool preach a
little.

JACOMO For my part, I cannot but be troubled that I shall lose my
honour by you, sir; for people will be apt to say, like master, like   55
man.°

DON JOHN Your honour, rascal? A sow-gelder may better pretend
to it.

JACOMO But I have another scruple, sir.

DON JOHN What's that?   60

JACOMO I fear I shall be hanged in your company.

DON JOHN That's an honour you will ne'er have courage to deserve.

JACOMO It is an honour I am not ambitious of.

DON LOPEZ Why does the fool talk of hanging? We scorn all laws.

JACOMO It seems so, or you would not have cut your elder brother's   65
throat, Don Lopez.

DON LOPEZ Why, you coxcomb, he kept a good estate from me, and I
could not whore and revel sufficiently without it.

DON ANTONIO Look you, Jacomo, had he not reason?

JACOMO Yes, Antonio, so had you to get both your sisters with child.   70
'Twas very civil, I take it.

DON ANTONIO Yes, you fool, they were lusty, young, handsome
wenches and pleased my appetite. Besides, I saved the honour of
the family by it, for if I had not, somebody else would.

JACOMO O horrid villainy! But you are both saints to my hopeful   75

9

master.° I'll turn° him loose to Beelzebub° himself; he shall outdo him at his own weapons.

DON JOHN I, you rascal?°

JACOMO O no, sir, you are as innocent. To cause your good old father to be killed was nothing.   80

DON JOHN It was something and a good thing too, sirrah. His whole design was to debar me of my pleasures. He kept his purse from me and could not be content with that, but still would preach his senseless morals to me, his old, dull, foolish stuff against my pleasure. I caused him to be sent I know not whither.° But he believed he   85 was to go to heaven. I care not where he is since I am rid of him.

JACOMO Cutting his throat was a very good return for his begetting of you.

DON JOHN That was before he was aware on't. 'Twas for his own sake; he ne'er thought of me in the business.   90

JACOMO [crosses himself] Heaven bless us!

DON JOHN You dog, I shall beat out your brains if you dare be so impudent as to pray in my company.

JACOMO Good sir, I have done, I have done—

DON LOPEZ Prithee let the insipid° fool go on.   95

DON ANTONIO Let's hear the coxcomb number up your crimes, the patterns we intend to imitate.

JACOMO Sir, let me lay your horrid crimes before you. The unhappy minute may perhaps arrive, when the sense of 'em may make you penitent.   100

DON ANTONIO 'Twere better thou wert hanged.

DON LOPEZ Repent! Cowards and fools do that.

DON JOHN Your valiant, well-bred gentlemen never repent. But what should I repent of?

JACOMO After the murder of your father, the brave Don Pedro,   105 Governor of Seville, for whom the town are still in grief, was in his own house barbarously killed by you.

DON JOHN Barbarously! You lie, you rascal: 'twas finely done. I run him through the lungs as handsomely, and killed him as decently,° and as like a gentleman as could be. The jealous coxcomb° deserved   110 death; he kept his sister from me. Her eyes would have killed me if I had not enjoyed her, which I could not do without killing him. Besides, I was alone and killed him hand to fist.

JACOMO I never knew you go to church but to take sanctuary for a murder, or to rob churches of their plate.   115

DON JOHN Heaven needs not be served in plate, but I had use on't.

JACOMO How often have you scaled the walls of monasteries? Two nuns, I know, you ravished, and a third you dangerously wounded for her violent resistance.

DON JOHN The perverse jades were uncivil and deserved such usage.   120

JACOMO Some thirty murders, rapes innumerable, frequent sacrilege, parricide; in short, not one in all the catalogue of sins have 'scaped you.

DON JOHN My business is my pleasure: that end I will always compass without scrupling the means. There is no right or wrong but   125
what conduces to or hinders pleasure. But, you tedious, insipid rascal, if I hear more of your morality, I will carbonado° you.

DON ANTONIO We live the life of sense, which no fantastic thing, called reason, shall control.

DON LOPEZ My reason tells me I must please my sense.   130

DON JOHN My appetites are all I'm sure I have from heaven, since they are natural; and them I always will obey.

JACOMO I doubt it not, sir; therefore, I desire to shake hands and part.

DON JOHN D'ye hear, dog? Talk once more of parting, and I will saw your windpipe. I could find in my heart to cut your rascal's nose off   135
and save the pox a labour.° [*Reaches for his sword*] I'll do't, sirrah.° [*Lunges*] Have at you!

JACOMO [*kneeling*] Good sir, be not so transported. I will live, sir, and will serve you in anything. I'll fetch a wench or anything in the world, sir. (*Aside*) O, how I tremble at this tyrant's rage.   140

DON ANTONIO Come, 'tis night. We lose time to our adventures.

DON LOPEZ I have bespoke music for our serenading.

DON JOHN Let's on and live the noble life of sense.
  To all the powers of love and mighty lust,
  In spite of formal fops I will be just.°   145
  What ways soe'er conduce to my delight,
  My sense instructs me, I must think 'em right.
  On, on, my soul, and make no stop in pleasure,
  They're dull, insipid fools that live by measure.
       Exeunt all but Jacomo

JACOMO What will become of me? If I should leave him, he's so   150
revengeful, he would travel o'er all Spain to find me out and cut my throat. I cannot live long with him neither. I shall be hanged, or knocked o' th' head, or share some dreadful fate or other with him. 'Tis just between him and me, as between the devil and the witch° who repents her bargain and would be free from future ills, but, for   155
the fear of present, durst not venture.°

Enter Leonora

Here comes Leonora, one of those multitudes of ladies he has sworn, lied to, and betrayed.

LEONORA Jacomo, where is Don John? I could not live to endure a longer absence from him. I have sighed and wept myself away. I 160 move but have no life left in me. His coldness and his absence have given me fearful and killing apprehensions. Where is my dear?

JACOMO Your *dear*, madam? He's yours no more.

LEONORA Heaven! What do I hear? Speak, is he dead?

JACOMO To you he is.   165

LEONORA Ah, me. Has he forgot his vows and oaths? Has he no conscience, faith, or honour left?

JACOMO Left, madam? He ne'er had any.

LEONORA It is impossible. You speak this out of malice sure.

JACOMO There's no man knows him better than I do. I have a greater 170 respect for you than for any he has betrayed and will undeceive you. He is the most perfidious wretch alive.

LEONORA Has he forgot the sacred contract, which was made privately betwixt us and confirmed before the altar during the time of holy mass?   175

JACOMO All times and places are alike to him.

LEONORA O how assiduous was he in his passion! How many thousand vows and sighs he breathed! What tears he wept, seeming to suffer all the cruel pangs which lovers e'er endured! How eloquent were all his words and actions!   180

JACOMO His person and his parts are excellent, but his base vices are beyond all measure. Why would you believe him?

LEONORA My own love bribed me to believe him. I saw the man I loved more than the world. Oft on his knees, with his eyes up to heaven, kissing my hand with such an amorous heat and with such 185 ardour, breathing fervent vows of loyal love, and venting sad complaints of extreme sufferings. I, poor, easy soul, flattering myself to think he meant as I did, lost all my sex's faculty, dissembling; and in a month must I be thus betrayed?

JACOMO Poor lady! I cannot but have bowels for you;° your sad 190 narration makes me weep in sadness. But you are better used than others. I ne'er knew him constant a fortnight before.

LEONORA Then, then he promised he would marry me.

JACOMO If he were to live here one month longer, he would marry half the town, ugly and handsome, old and young. Nothing that's 195 female comes amiss to him.

LEONORA Does he not fear a thunderbolt from heaven?

JACOMO No, nor a devil from hell. He owns no deity but his voluptuous appetite, whose satisfaction he will compass by murders, rapes,
treasons, or ought else. But pray let me ask you one civil question: 200
did you not give him earnest° of your body, madam?

LEONORA Mock not my misery. O, that confounds me! Ah, I thought
him true and loved him so, I could deny him nothing.

JACOMO Why, there 'tis. I fear you have, or else he would have married
you. He has married six within this month and promised fifteen   205
more, all whom he has enjoyed and left, and is this night gone on
some new adventure, some rape or murder, some such petty thing.

LEONORA O monster of impiety! O false Don John! Wonder of
cruelty! (*She swoons*)

JACOMO What a pox! Does she swoon at the news? Alas, poor soul,   210
she has moved me now to pity, as she did to love. [*Looks around*] Ha!
The place is private. If I should make use of a natural receipt° to
refresh her and bring her to life again, 'twould be a great pleasure
to me and no trouble to her. [*Looks around again*] Hum! 'Tis very
private, and I dare sin in private. [*Leonora stirs*] A deuce° take her!   215
She revives and prevents me.

LEONORA Where is the cruel tyrant? Inhuman° monster? But I will
strive to fortify myself. But O my misfortune! O my misery! Under
what strange enchantments am I bound? Could he be yet a thousand
times more impious, I could not choose but love his person still.   220

JACOMO Be not so passionate. If you could be discreet and love yourself, I'd put you in a way to ease your grief now and all your cares
hereafter.

LEONORA If you can now ease an afflicted woman, who else must
shortly rid herself of life, employ your charity. 'Twas never placed   225
yet on a wretch needed it more than I.

JACOMO If loyalty in a lover be a jewel, say no more. I can tell you
where you may have it.

LEONORA Speak not of truth in man; it is impossible.

JACOMO Pardon me. I speak on my own knowledge.   230

LEONORA Is your master true then? And have you happily deceived
me? Speak.

JACOMO As true as all the power of hell can make him.

LEONORA If he be false, let all the world be so.

JACOMO There's another-guess man° than he, madam.   235

LEONORA Another! Who can that be? (*Aside*) No, no, there's no truth
found in the sex.

JACOMO He is a civil, virtuous, and discreet sober person.

LEONORA Can there be such a man? What does he mean?

JACOMO There is, madam, a man of goodly presence too. Something 240
inclining to be fat, of a round, plump face, with quick and sparkling
eyes, and mouth of cheerful overture. His nose, which is the only
fault, is somewhat short,° but that's no matter, his hair and
eyebrows black, and so forth.

LEONORA [aside] How? He may perhaps be bribed by some other 245
man, and what he said of his master may be false.

JACOMO [aside] How she surveys me! (Sings and struts about) Fa, la, la.

LEONORA Who is this you speak of?

JACOMO A man who, envy must confess, has excellent parts, but those
are gifts, gifts—mere gifts—thanks be to heaven for them. 250

LEONORA But shall I never know his name?

JACOMO He's one whom many ladies have honoured with their affection, but no more of that. They have met disdain and so forth. But
he'll be content to marry you. (Sings) Fa, la, la, la.

LEONORA Again, I ask you who he is. 255

JACOMO [aside] Lord, how inapprehensive she is! Can you not guess?

LEONORA No.

JACOMO [bows] Your humble servant, madam.

LEONORA [curtsies] Yours, sir.

JACOMO It is myself in person and, upon my honour, I will be true 260
and constant to you.

LEONORA Insolent varlet! Am I fallen so low to be thy scorn?

JACOMO Scorn! As I am a Christian soul, I am in earnest.

LEONORA Audacious villain! Impudence itself!

JACOMO Ah, madam! Your servant, your true lover must endure a 265
thousand such bobs from his mistress. I can bear, madam, I can.

LEONORA Because thy master has betrayed me, am I become so
infamous?

JACOMO 'Tis something hard, madam, to preserve a good reputation
in his company. I can scarce do't myself. 270

LEONORA Am I so miserable to descend to his man?

JACOMO Descend, say you? Ha, ha, ha.

LEONORA Now I perceive all's false which you have said of him.
Farewell, you base, ungrateful fellow. [Begins to leave]

JACOMO [stops her] Hold, madam. Come in the morning, and I will 275
place you in the next room where you shall overhear our discourse.
You'll soon discover the mistake and find who 'tis that loves you.
Retire, madam; I hear somebody coming.

Exeunt

[*Enter Don John*]

DON JOHN Let me see, here lives a lady. I have seen Don Octavio haunting about this house and making private signs to her. I never saw her face, but am resolved to enjoy her because he likes her. Besides, she's another woman.° 280

Enter [Don] Antonio

Antonio, welcome to our place of rendezvous. Well, what game! What adventure.

Enter [Don] Lopez

Come, dear Lopez. 285

DON ANTONIO I have had a rare adventure.

DON LOPEZ What, dear Antonio?

DON ANTONIO I saw at a villa not far off a grave, mighty, bearded fool drinking lemonade with his mistress. I misliked his face, plucked him by the whiskers, pulled all one side of his beard off, fought 290 with him, run him through the thigh, carried away his mistress, served her in her kind,° and then let her go.

DON JOHN Gallantly performed, like a brave soldier in an enemy's country. When they will not pay contribution, you fight for forage.

DON LOPEZ Pox on't, I have been damnably unfortunate. I have 295 neither beat man nor lain with woman tonight, but fallen in love most furiously. I dogged my new mistress to her lodging; she's Don Bernardo's sister and shall be my punk.

DON JOHN I could meet with no willing dame but was fain to commit a rape to pass away the time. 300

DON ANTONIO O, a rape is the joy of my heart. I love a rape, upon my clavis,° exceedingly.

DON JOHN But mine, my lads, was such a rape it ought to be registered, a noble and heroic rape.

DON LOPEZ Ah, dear Don John! 305

DON ANTONIO How was it?

DON JOHN 'Twas in a church, boys.

DON ANTONIO Ah, gallant leader!

DON LOPEZ Renowned Don John!

DON ANTONIO Come, let's retire; you have done enough for once. 310

DON JOHN Not yet, Antonio. I have an intrigue here.

Enter fiddlers [and a singer]

Here are my fiddlers. Rank yourselves close under this window and sing the song I prepared.

[*The fiddlers accompany singer*]

SONG

Thou joy of all hearts, and delight of all eyes,   315
Nature's chief treasure, and beauty's chief prize,
     Look down, you'll discover
Here's a faithful, young, vigorous lover.
     With a heart full as true
     As e'er languished for you;   320
Here's a faithful, young, vigorous lover.

The heart that was once a monarch in's breast
Is now your poor Captive, and can have no rest,
     'Twill never give over,
     But about your sweet bosom will hover.   325
     Dear Miss, let it in,
     By heaven, 'tis no sin;
Here's a faithful, young, vigorous, vigorous lover.

DON JOHN Now fiddlers, be gone.
     [*Exeunt fiddlers and singer.*] *Window opens.*° *Maria looks out*
     and flings a paper down

MARIA Retire, my dear Octavio. Read that note. Adieu.   330
     Exit Maria

DON JOHN Good, she takes me for Octavio. I warrant you, boys, I
shall succeed in this adventure. Now my false light assist me. (*Reads
by a dark lantern*)° 'Go from this window. Within eight minutes,
you shall be admitted to the garden door. You know the sign.' Ha,
the sign! Gad, she lies; I know not the sign.   335

DON ANTONIO What will you do? You know not the sign. Let's away
and be contented this night.

DON JOHN My friends, if you love me, retire. I'll venture, though
thunderbolts should fall upon my head.

DON LOPEZ Are you mad? As soon as she discovers the deceit, she'll   340
raise the house upon you, and you'll be murdered.

DON JOHN She'll not raise the house for her own sake, but, rather,
grant me all I ask to keep her counsel.

DON ANTONIO 'Tis very dangerous. Be careful of yourself.

DON JOHN The more danger, the more delight. I hate the common   345
road of pleasure. What, can I fear at such a time as this? The
cowardly deer are valiant in their rutting time. I say, be gone.

DON ANTONIO We'll not dispute your commands. Good luck to you.
  Exeunt Don Antonio, Don Lopez
DON JOHN How shall I know this devilish sign?
  Enter Octavio with fiddlers [and singer] and stands under
  Maria's window
 Ha! Whom have we here? Some serenading coxcomb. Now shall we   350
have some damned song or other, a Cloris or a Phyllis° at least.
  [*The fiddlers accompany singer*]

     SONG

  Cloris, when you disperse your influence,
   Your dazzling beams are quick and clear,°
   You so surprise and wound the sense,   355
   So bright a miracle y' appear.
  Admiring mortals you astonish so,
    No other deity they know,
  But think that all divinity's below.

  One charming look from your illustrious face   360
   Were able to subdue mankind,
   So sweet, so powerful a grace
   Makes all men lovers but the blind.
  Nor can they freedom by resistance gain,
    For each embraces the soft chain,
  And never struggles with the pleasant pain.   365

OCTAVIO [*to the singer and fiddlers*] Be gone, be gone! The window
opens.
  [*Exeunt singer and fiddlers*]
DON JOHN 'Sdeath! This is Octavio. I must dispatch him, or he'll
spoil all; but I would fain hear the sign first.
MARIA [*leaning out the window*] What strange mistake is this? Sure he   370
did not receive my note, and then I am ruined.
OCTAVIO She expects the sign. [*Searches*] Where's my whistle? O
here. (*Whistles*)
DON JOHN I have found it; that must be the sign.
MARIA I dare not speak aloud. [*To Octavio*] Go to the garden door.   375
  Don John rushes upon Octavio and snatches the whistle out of his
  hand
OCTAVIO 'Sdeath, what ruffian's this?
DON JOHN One that will be sure to cut your throat.

OCTAVIO Make not a promise to yourself of what you can't perform.
    Octavio and Don John fight
DON JOHN I warrant you. [*Lunges*] Have at you!
MARIA O heaven! Octavio's fighting. O my heart!   380
OCTAVIO O, I am slain!
    [*Octavio*] *falls*
DON JOHN I knew I should be as good as my word. I think you have
    it, sir. Ha! He's dying. Now for the lady. I'll draw him further off,
    that his groans may not disturb our pleasure. Stay. By your leave,
    sir, I'll change hat and cloak with you; it may help me in my   385
    design.
OCTAVIO O, barbarous villain!
    [*Octavio*] *dies*
MARIA They have done fighting, and I hear no noise. O unfortunate
    woman! My dear Octavio killed!
FLORA Perhaps, madam, he has killed the other. I'll down to the gar-   390
    den door. If he be well, he'll come thither, as well to satisfy his
    appointment, as to take refuge. Your brother's safe; he may come in
    securely.
    Exit Flora to the door
MARIA Haste, haste! Fly, fly! O Octavio! I'll follow her.
    Maria follows
DON JOHN Now for the garden door. This whistle will do me excellent   395
    service. Now good luck.
    Don John goes to the door and whistles
FLORA Octavio?
DON JOHN The same.
FLORA Heaven be praised. My lady thought you had been killed.
DON JOHN I am unhurt. Let's quickly to her.   400
FLORA O, she'll° be overjoyed to see you alive.
DON JOHN I'll make her more overjoyed before I have done with her.
    This is a rare adventure!
    Enter Maria at the garden door
FLORA Here's your jewel, madam. Speak softly.
MARIA O my dear Octavio! Have I got you within these arms?   405
DON JOHN Ay, my dear, unpierced by anything but your eyes.
MARIA Those will do you no hurt. But are you sure you are not
    wounded?
DON JOHN I am. Let me embrace my pretty dear. [*Aside*] And yet she
    may be a blackamoor° for ought I know.   410

MARIA We'll retire to my chamber. Flora, go out and prepare us a collation.

DON JOHN O admirable adventure! Come, my delight.

Exeunt Don John, Maria, and Flora.

Enter Don Lopez, [Don] Antonio, Jacomo

JACOMO Where's my pious master?

DON ANTONIO We left him hereabouts. I wonder what he has done in his adventure. I believe he has had some bustle.°   415

DON LOPEZ I thought I heard fighting hereabout.

JACOMO Gad forgive me! Fighting! Where, where?

DON ANTONIO O thou incorrigible coward!

DON LOPEZ [*notices Octavio*] See, here's some of his handy work; here's a man killed.   420

JACOMO Another murder. Heaven, what will become of me? I shall be hanged, yet dare not run away from him.

Enter an Officer with a guard, going the round°

OFFICER Stand! Who are there?

DON LOPEZ We do stand, rascal; we never use to run.   425

JACOMO [*aside*] Now shall I be taken and hanged for my master's murder.

Offers to run°

DON ANTONIO Stand, you dog! Offer once more to run, and I'll put bilbow° in your guts.

JACOMO Gad forgive me! What will become of me?   430

OFFICER What's here? A man murdered? Yield, you are my prisoners.

JACOMO With all my heart. But, as I hope to be saved, we did not kill him, sir.

OFFICER These must be the murderers. Disarm 'em.

DON ANTONIO How now, rascal! Disarm us!   435

DON LOPEZ We are not used to part with our swords.

JACOMO I care not a farthing for my sword. [*Offers sword to Antonio*] 'Tis at your service.

DON ANTONIO Do you hear, rascal? Keep it and fight, or I'll swear the murder against you.°   440

DON LOPEZ Offer to flinch, and I'll run you through.

OFFICER Take their swords, or knock 'em down.

They fight. Jacomo offers to run; some of the guards stop him

JACOMO A pox on't. I had as good fight and die, as be taken and be hanged.

Guards are beaten off

DON LOPEZ Are you gone, you dogs? I have pinked° some of you.   445
JACOMO Ah, rogues! Villains! I have met with you.
DON ANTONIO O brave Jacomo! You fought like an imprisoned rat.
  The rogue had concealed courage and did not know it.
JACOMO O cowards! Rascals! A man can get no honour by fighting
  with such poltroons! But for all that, I will prudently withdraw;   450
  this place will suddenly be too hot for us.
DON LOPEZ Once in your life, you are in the right, Jacomo.
JACOMO O good sir, there is as much to be ascribed to conduct as to
  courage, I assure you.
      Exeunt

[1.2]°

Maria's chamber
Enter Don John and Maria

MARIA Speak softly, my dear. Should my brother hear us, we are
  ruined.
DON JOHN Though I can scarce contain my joy, I will. [*Aside*] O she's
  a rare creature in the dark. Pray heaven she be so in the light.
      Enter Flora with a candle; as soon as they discover Don John,
      they shriek out
MARIA O heaven! I am ruined and betrayed.   5
FLORA He has Octavio's clothes on.
MARIA O he has murdered him. My brother shall revenge it.
DON JOHN I will cut his throat if he offers it.
MARIA AND FLORA Thieves! Murder! Murder! Thieves!
DON JOHN I will stop your shrill windpipes.   10
      Enter Maria's brother with his sword drawn
BROTHER 'Sdeath! A man in my sister's chamber! Have at you,
  villain!
DON JOHN [*drawing his sword*] Come on, villain.
      Don John kills the brother
FLORA Murder, murder!
MARIA O villain, thou hast killed my brother and dishonoured me.   15
      Enter five or six servants with drawn swords
  O your master's murdered!
DON JOHN So many of you, 'tis no matter. Your heroes in plays beat
  five times as many.° Have at you, rogues.

Maria runs away shrieking, and Don John beats the servants off
and stops Flora

Now give me the key of the garden, or I'll murder thee.

FLORA Murder! Murder! [*Throws down key*] There, take it.   20

Flora runs away

DON JOHN So, thus far it is well; this was a brave adventure.

'Mongst all the joys which in the world are sought,

None are so great as those by dangers bought.

Exit

2.1

[Don John's lodging in Seville]°

Enter Jacomo

JACOMO What will this lewd master of mine do? This town of Seville will not much care for his company after his last night's achievements. He must now either fly or hang for't. Ha! Methinks my blood grows chill at the naming of that dreadful word, 'hang'. What will become of me? I dare not leave him, and yet I fear that I shall   5
perish with him. He's certainly the first that ever set up a religion to the devil.

Enter Leonora

LEONORA I come to claim your promise. Is Don John within?

JACOMO No, madam, but I expect him every minute. You see, madam, what honour I have for you, for I venture my ears to do   10
this.

LEONORA You oblige me extremely.° So great is the present pain of doubt that we desire to lose it, though in exchange of certainty that° must afflict us more.

JACOMO I hear him coming; withdraw quickly.   15

Leonora withdraws

Enter Don John

DON JOHN How now, sir, what wise thoughts have you in your noodle?

JACOMO Why, sir, I was considering how well I could endure to be hanged.

DON JOHN And why so, buffle?°   20

JACOMO Why, you will force me to wait upon you in all your fortunes, and you are making what haste you can to the gallows.

DON JOHN Again at your reproofs. You insipid rascal. I shall cut your ears off, dog.

JACOMO Good sir, I have done; yet I cannot but admire, since you are   25
resolved to go to the devil, that you cannot be content with the common way of travelling but must ride post° to him.

DON JOHN Leave off your idle tales, found out by priests to keep the rabble in awe.

JACOMO O horrid wickedness! If I may be bold to ask, what noble   30
exploits did your chivalry perform last night?

DON JOHN Why, sir, I committed a rape upon my father's monument.

JACOMO O horror!

DON JOHN Do you start, you villain? Ha!

JACOMO I, sir? Who I, sir? Not I, sir.   35

DON JOHN D' hear, rascal, let me not see a frown upon your face. If I do, I will cut your throat, you rogue.

JACOMO No, sir, no, sir, I warrant you. I am in a very good humour, I assure you. [*Aside*] Heaven deliver me!

DON JOHN Now listen and learn. I killed a lady's lover and supplied   40
his place, by stratagem enjoyed her. In came her foolish brother and surprised me, but perished by my hand, and I doubt not but I mauled three or four of his servants.

>   *Jacomo starts*

JACOMO (*aside*) O horrid fact!

DON JOHN Again, villain, are you frowning?   45

JACOMO No, sir, no, sir, don't think so ill of me, sir. [*Aside*] Heaven send me from this wicked wretch! [*To Don John*] What will become of us, sir? We shall be apprehended.

DON JOHN Can you fear your rascally carcass when I venture mine? I observe always, those that have the most despicable persons, are   50
most careful to preserve 'em.

JACOMO Sir, I beg your pardon; but I have an odd humour, makes me something unfit for your worship's service.

DON JOHN What's that, sirrah?

JACOMO 'Tis a very odd one; I am almost ashamed to tell it to you.   55

DON JOHN Out with it, fool.

JACOMO Why, sir, I cannot tell what is the reason, but I have a most unconquerable antipathy to hemp.° I could never endure a bell-rope. Hanging is a kind of death I cannot abide; I am not able to endure it.   60

DON JOHN I have taken care to avoid that. My friends are gone to hire a vessel, and we'll to sea together to seek a refuge and a new scene of pleasure.

JACOMO All three, sir?

DON JOHN Yes, sir.   65

JACOMO Three as civil, discreet, sober persons as a man would wish to drink with.

>   *Enter Leonora*

LEONORA I can hold no longer!°

DON JOHN 'Sdeath, you dog. How came she here?

JACOMO I don't know, sir; she stole in—   70

LEONORA What witchcraft do I suffer under? That when I abhor his
vices, I still love his person. Ah, Don John! Have I deserved that
you should fly me? Are all your oaths and vows forgotten by you?
[*Jacomo sneaks away*]

DON JOHN No, no. In these cases, I always remember my oaths and
never forget to break them.   75

LEONORA O impiety! Did I, for this, yield up my honour to you?
After you had sighed and languished many months and showed all
signs of a sincere affection, I trusted in your truth and constancy;
without the bond of marriage, yielded up a virgin's treasure, all my
innocence; believed your solemn contract when you invoked all the   80
powers above to testify your vows.

DON JOHN They think much of us; why don't they witness 'em for
you? Pish, 'tis nothing but a way of speaking which young, amorous
fellows have gotten.

LEONORA Did you not love me then? What injury had I e'er done   85
you, that you should feign affection to betray me?

DON JOHN Yes, faith, I did love you and showed you as frequent and
as hearty signs of it as I could, and, egad, y'are an ungrateful
woman if you say the contrary.

LEONORA O heaven! Did you—and do not now? What crime have I   90
committed that could make you break your vows and oaths and
banish all your passion? Ah, with what tenderness have I received
your feigned affection, and ne'er thought I lived but in your
presence. My love was too fervent to be counterfeit.

DON JOHN That I know not, for since your sex are such dissemblers, 95
they can hold out against and seem to hate the men they love. Why
may they not seem to love the men they hate?

LEONORA O cruel man! Could I dissemble? Had I a thousand lives, I
ventured all each time I saw your face. Nay, were I now discovered,
I should instantly be sacrificed to my raging brother's fury—and   100
can I dissemble?

DON JOHN I do not know whether you do or no. You see I don't; I am
something free with you.

LEONORA And do you not love me then?

DON JOHN Faith, madam, I loved you as long as I could for the heart 105
and blood of me, and there's an end of it. What a devil would you
have more?°

LEONORA O cruel man! How miserable have you made me!

DON JOHN Miserable! Use variety as I do, and you'll not be miserable.
Ah, there's nothing so sweet to frail human flesh as variety.   110

LEONORA Inhuman creature! What have I been guilty of, that thou shouldst thus remove thy affections from me?

DON JOHN Guilty, no. But I have had enough of you, and I have done what I can for you, and there's no more to be said.

LEONORA Tigers would have more pity than thou hast.   115

DON JOHN Unreasonable woman! Would you have a man love after enjoyment? I think the devil's in you.

LEONORA Do you upbraid me with the rash effects of love which you caused in me? And do you hate me for what you ought to love me for? Were you not many months with vows and oaths betraying me   120
to that weakness? Ungrateful monster!

DON JOHN Why the devil did you not yield before? You women always rook° in love; you'll never play upon the square° with us.

LEONORA False man! I yielded but too soon. Unfortunate woman!

DON JOHN Your dissembling arts and jilting tricks, taught you by   125
your mothers, and the phlegmatic coldness of your constitutions make you so long in yielding, that we love out almost all our love before you begin; and yet you would have our love last as long as yours. I got the start of you a long way and have reason to reach the goal before you.   130

LEONORA Did you not swear you would forever love me?

DON JOHN Why, there 'tis. Why did you put me to the trouble to swear it? If you women would be honest and follow the dictates of sense and nature, we should agree about the business presently and never be forsworn for the matter.   135

LEONORA Are oaths so slighted by you? Perfidious man!

DON JOHN Oaths? Snares to catch conceited women with. I would have sworn all the oaths under the sun. Why, I would have committed treason for you, and yet I knew I should be weary of you.

LEONORA I thought such love as mine might have deserved your   140
constancy, false and ungrateful man!

DON JOHN Thus your own vanity, not we, betray you. Each woman thinks, though men are false to others, that she is so fine a person, none can be so to her. You should not take our words of course° in earnest.   145

LEONORA Thus devils do in hell, who cruelly upbraid whom they have tempted thither.

DON JOHN In short, my constitution will not let me love you longer. And, whatever some hypocrites pretend, all mankind obey their constitutions and cannot do otherwise.   150

LEONORA Heaven, sure, will punish this vile treachery.

DON JOHN Do you then leave it to heaven, and trouble yourself no
   farther about it.

LEONORA Ye sacred powers, who take care of injured innocence,
   assist me.   155

   Enter Jacomo

JACOMO Sir, sir! Stand upon your guard.

DON JOHN How now! What's the matter?

JACOMO Here's a whole battalion of courageous women come to
   charge you.

   Enter six Women°

DON JOHN Keep 'em out, you villain.   160

JACOMO I cannot; they overrun me.

DON JOHN What an inundation of strumpets is here?

LEONORA O heaven! I can stay no longer to be a witness of his
   falsehood.

   Exit Leonora

FIRST WOMAN My dear, I desire a word in private with you.   165

DON JOHN 'Faith, my dear I am something busy, but I love thee
   dearly. (*Aside*) A pox on thee!

SECOND WOMAN Don John, a word. 'Tis time now we should declare
   our marriage; 'tis now above three weeks.

DON JOHN Ay, we will do it suddenly.   170

THIRD WOMAN Prithee honey, what business can these idle women
   have? Send them packing, that we may confer about our affairs.

FOURTH WOMAN Lord! How am I amazed at the confidence of some
   women! Who are these that will not let one converse with one's own
   husband? [*Takes Don John's arm*] By your leave, ladies.   175

JACOMO Now it works! Tease him, ladies, worry him soundly.

FIFTH WOMAN [*to the Fourth Woman*] Nay, by your leave, good
   madam. (*Pulls Don John from the Fourth Woman*) If you go to
   that°—

SIXTH WOMAN Ladies, by all your leaves. Sure none of you will have   180
   the confidence to pretend an interest in this gentleman?

DON JOHN [*aside*] I shall be torn in pieces.—Jacomo, stand by me.

FIRST WOMAN Lord, madam, what's your meaning? None ought to
   claim a right to another woman's husband, let me tell you that.

SECOND WOMAN You are in the right, madam. [*To Don John*] There-   185
   fore prithee dear, let's withdraw and leave them. I do not like their
   company.

DON JOHN Ay, presently, my dear. [*Aside*] What an excellent thing is a
   woman before enjoyment and how insipid after it!

FOURTH WOMAN Come, prithee, put these women out of doubt and   190
let them know our marriage.

DON JOHN Tomorrow we'll declare and celebrate our nuptials.

SIXTH WOMAN Ladies, the short and long on't is you are very uncivil
to press upon this gentleman. [*To Don John*] Come, love, e'en tell
'em the truth of the story.   195

FOURTH WOMAN Uncivil, madam! Pardon me; one cannot be so in
speaking to one's own.

THIRD WOMAN That's true. She little thinks who that is.

SIXTH WOMAN To their own! Ha, ha, ha, that's true. [*To Don John*]
Come, honey, keep 'em no longer in ignorance.   200

FOURTH WOMAN Come, ladies, I will undeceive you all. Think no
further of this gentleman, I say, think no further of him.

FIRST WOMAN What can this mean?

DON JOHN Hold, for heaven's sake! You know not what you do.

FOURTH WOMAN Yes, yes, I do. It shall all out! I'll send 'em away   205
with fleas in their ears.° Poor silly creatures!

DON JOHN [*aside*] Now will civil wars arise.

FOURTH WOMAN Trouble yourselves no longer about Don John. He
is mine. He is mine, ladies.

ALL Yours!   210

DON JOHN [*aside*] Pox on't. I must set a good face upon the business;
I see murder will out.

SIXTH WOMAN Yours! That's pleasant; he's mine.

FIFTH WOMAN I have been too long patient. He is my husband.

FIRST WOMAN Yours? How can that be? I am sure I am his wife.   215

THIRD WOMAN Are you not ashamed, ladies, to claim my husband?

SECOND WOMAN Are you all mad? I am sure I am married to
him.

ALL You!

DON JOHN Look you, ladies, a man's but a man. Here's my body; take   220
't among you as far as 'twill go. The devil can't please you all.

JACOMO Pray, ladies, will you dispatch? For there are a matter of
fifteen more that are ready to put in their claims and must be heard
in their order.

DON JOHN How now, rogue? This is your fault, sirrah.   225

JACOMO My fault? Sir, no. The ladies shall see I am no traitor. Look
you, ladies—

DON JOHN Peace, villain, or I will cut your throat. Well, ladies, know,
then, I am married to one in this company; and tomorrow morning,
if you will repair° to this place, I will declare my marriage, which   230

27

now, for some secret reasons, I am obliged to conceal. [*Aside*] Now
will each strumpet think 'tis her I mean.

FIRST WOMAN That's well enough.

FOURTH WOMAN I knew he would own me at last.

THIRD WOMAN Now they will soon see their errors.   235

FIFTH WOMAN [*to Don John*] Now we'll conceal it no longer, dearest.

DON JOHN No, no, I warrant you.

SIXTH WOMAN Lord, how blank these ladies will look.

SECOND WOMAN Poor ladies.

JACOMO Ladies, pray let me ask a question. Which of you is really   240
married to him?

ALL I, I, I.

DON JOHN 'Sdeath, you son of a baboon. Come, pox on't, why should
I dally any longer? Why should I conceal my good actions? In one
word, I am married to every one of you and have above fourscore   245
more, nor will I ever give over till I have as many wives and
concubines as the *Grand Signior*.°

JACOMO A very modest, civil person, truly.

FOURTH WOMAN O horrid villain!

SIXTH WOMAN Perfidious monster!   250

  Enter Don Lopez and [*Don*] *Antonio*

DON ANTONIO How now, Don John. [*Sees the Women*] Ha! You are a
ravenous bird of prey indeed. Do you fly at no less than a whole
covey of whores at once? You scorn a single strumpet for your
quarry.

DON LOPEZ° What, in tears too? Fie, Don John, thou art the most   255
ungentle knight alive. Use your ladies civilly, for shame.

DON JOHN Ay, before the victory, I grant you. But after it, they
should wear chains and follow the conqueror's chariot.

DON LOPEZ Alas, poor harlots!

DON JOHN Peace, peace, good words. These are certain animals called 260
wives, and all of 'em are my wives. Do you call a man of honour's
wives harlots? Out on't.

FIRST WOMAN Perfidious monster!

DON ANTONIO Excellent!

DON JOHN Come on, you are come very opportunely to help to cele-   265
brate my several and respective° weddings. Come, my dears. 'Faith,
we will have a ballad at our weddings. Where are my fiddlers?

SIXTH WOMAN O savage beast!

FOURTH WOMAN Inhuman villain! Revenge shall follow.

DON JOHN Pox on revenge. Call in my minstrels.   270

Enter fiddlers [and singer]
Come, sing my epithalamium.°
[The fiddlers accompany singer]

SONG

Since liberty nature for all has designed,
A pox on the fool who to one is confined.
   All creatures besides,   275
  When they please, change their brides.
All females they get when they can.
 Whilst they nothing but nature obey,
  How happy, how happy are they?
But the silly, fond animal, man,   280
Makes laws 'gainst himself, which his appetites sway;
   Poor fools, how unhappy are they?

CHORUS *Since liberty nature for all has designed,*
    A pox on the fool who to one is confined.

At the first going down, a woman is good; 285
But whene'er she comes up, I'll n'er chew the cud,°
   But out she shall go,
  And I'll serve 'em all so.
 When with one my stomach is cloyed,°
 Another shall soon be enjoyed.   290
  Then how happy, how happy are we?
 Let the coxcomb, when weary, drudge on,
And foolishly stay when he would fain be gone.
   Poor fool! How unhappy is he?

CHORUS *At the first going down, etc.*   295

Let the rabble obey; I'll live like a man,
Who, by nature, is free to enjoy all he can.
   Wise nature does teach
  More truth than fools preach;
 They bind us, but she gives us ease.   300
I'll revel and love where I please.
She, she's my infallible guide.
 But were the bless'd freedom denied
Of variety in the things we love best,
  Dull man were the slavishest beast. 305

CHORUS *Let the rabble obey, etc.*

DON JOHN Come, how do you like this? Let's be merry, my brides.

FOURTH WOMAN O monstrous traitor! Do you mock our misery?

DON JOHN Good spouse, be not so passionate. 'Faith, we'll have a
dance. [*To the fiddlers*] Strike up.   310
    Dance°

DON LOPEZ Be comforted, good ladies; you have companions in your
misfortunes.

DON ANTONIO He has been married in all the cities of Spain. What a
breed of Don Johns shall we have!

DON JOHN Come, sweethearts, you must be civil to these gentlemen.   315
They are my friends and men of honour.

SIXTH WOMAN Men of honour! They are devils if they be your
friends.

DON JOHN I hate unreasonable, unconscionable fellows who, when
they are weary of their wives, will still keep 'em from other men.   320
Gentlemen, ye shall command mine.

FOURTH WOMAN Think'st thou I will outlive this affront?

DON JOHN I'll trust you for that. There's ne'er a Lucrece° nowadays;
the sex has learnt more wit since. Let me see, Antonio, thou shalt
have for thy present use, let me see, my sixth wife. 'Faith, she's a   325
pretty, buxom wench and deserves hearty usage from thee.

SIXTH WOMAN Traitor, I'll be revenged on all thy treachery.

DON ANTONIO A mettled girl. I like her well. She'll endure a rape
gallantly. I love resistance: it endears the pleasure.

DON JOHN And, Lopez, thou shalt have, let me see, ay, my fourth   330
spouse. She's a brave virago; and, gad, if I had not been something
familiar with her already, I would venture my life for her.

FOURTH WOMAN Vile wretch! Think'st thou I will outlive this
affront? Impious villain! Though thou hast no sense of virtue or
honour left, thou shalt find I have.   335

DON JOHN Virtue and honour! There's nothing good or ill but as it
seems to each man's natural appetite, if they will consent freely. [*To
Don Antonio and Don Lopez*] You must ravish, friends. That's all I
know; you must ravish.

FIRST WOMAN Unheard-of villainy! Fly from this hellish place.   340

DON ANTONIO Ladies, you shall fly; but we must ravish first.

DON LOPEZ Yes, I assure you we must ravish.

FOURTH WOMAN No, monster: I'll prevent you. (*Stabs herself*)

DON ANTONIO 'Sdeath, she's as good as her word. The first time I
e'er knew a woman so.   345

DON LOPEZ Pox on't! She has prevented me; she's dead.

DON JOHN Say you so? Well, go thy ways. Thou wert a girl of pretty parts, that's the truth on't; but I ne'er thought this had been in thee.

SECOND WOMAN These, sure, are devils in the shape of men.   350

DON JOHN Now see my providence.° If I had been married to none but her, I had been a widower.

FIRST WOMAN O horror! Horror! Fly! Fly!

SIXTH WOMAN No, I'll be revenged first on this barbarous wretch.

DON JOHN Why, look you, here's a wench of mettle for you. Go   355
ravish quickly.

SIXTH WOMAN Let's fly and call for help. Some in the street may help us.

The Women all run off, crying 'Help! Murder! Murder!'

DON ANTONIO Let 'em go. They are confined; they can't get out.

DON JOHN It shall ne'er be said that a woman went out of this house   360
re infecta.° But after that, 'twill be time for us to fly.

DON LOPEZ We have hired a vessel. The master is a brave rogue of my acquaintance; he has been a bandit.

DON ANTONIO A brave, honest, wicked fellow, as heart can wish. I have ravished, robbed, and murdered with him.   365

DON JOHN That's well. Hey, where are my rogues? Hey!

Enter Servant and Jacomo

Here, sirrah, do you send my goods on board.

DON ANTONIO My man will direct you.

Exit Servant

DON JOHN Come, sirrah, do you remove this body to another room.

JACOMO O horrid fact!° What, another murder? What shall I do?   370

DON JOHN Leave your complaints, you dog. I'll send you after her.

JACOMO O! I shall be hanged; I shall be hanged!

DON JOHN Take her up, rascal, or I'll cut your throat.

JACOMO I will, sir. O mercy upon me! I shall be hanged.

DON JOHN Now, sirrah, do you run into the streets and force in the   375
next woman you meet, or I'll cut your windpipe; and let nobody out.

JACOMO What hellish fact will he now commit?

DON JOHN Take her up, you hen-hearted, compassionate rascal.

JACOMO Heaven! What will become of me? Oh-h!   380

Jacomo carries the Fourth Woman off

DON JOHN Now gentlemen, you shall see I'll be civil to you; you shall not ravish alone. Indeed, I am loathe to meddle° with mine old acquaintance. But if my man can meet with a woman I have not lain

withal, I'll keep you company, let her be old or young, ugly or
handsome, no matter.   385

DON LOPEZ 'Faith, I will ever say you are a well-bred man.

DON ANTONIO A very civil person, a man of honour.

Enter Servant, forcing in an ugly old woman, who cries out

DON JOHN This unlucky rogue has made but a scurvy choice, but I'll
keep my word. Come bawd, you must be ravished, bawd.

OLD WOMAN O murder! Murder! Help! Help! I was never ravished in   390
my life.

DON JOHN That I dare swear; but to show I am a very vigorous man,
I'll begin with you. [*To Servant*] But you rascal, jackal, I'll make
you cater better next time.

SERVANT Indeed sir, this was the first I met.   395

DON JOHN Come on, beldam,° thy face shall not protect thee.

OLD WOMAN O my honour! My honour! Help, help, my honour!

DON JOHN Come to our business.

Enter Jacomo

JACOMO O sir! Sir! Shift for yourself;° we shall all be hanged. The
house is beset. O what shall we do?   400

DON JOHN Away, coward. Were the king of Spain's army beleaguering
us, it should not divert me from this exploit.

DON ANTONIO Nor me.

DON LOPEZ Nor me. Let's on.

DON JOHN [*to Jacomo*] Keep the doors fast,° sirrah. Come on.   405

JACOMO O what will become of me! O heaven! Mercy on me! O! O!

Exeunt

[2.2]°

[*Maria's chamber*]

Enter Maria and her Maid Flora, in man's habit°

MARIA Thus I have abandoned all my fortune and laid by my sex,
revenge, for thee.° Assist me now, you instruments of blood, for my
dear brother's, and for my much more dear Octavio's, sake. Where
are my bravos?°

FLORA They have beset° the villain's house, and he shall ne'er come   5
out alive.

MARIA O let 'em show no more remorse than hungry lions o'er their
prey will. How miserable am I made by that inhuman monster! No
savage beast wild deserts e'er brought forth, provoked by all its

hunger and its natural rage, could yet have been so cruel. O my   10
Octavio, whither art thou fled, from the most loving and most
wretched creature of her sex? What ages of delight each hour with
thee brought forth! How much, when I had thee, was all the world
unenvied by me! Nay, I pitied all my sex, that could have nothing
worth their care since all the treasure of mankind was mine.   15
Methought I could look down on queens when he was with me. But
now, compared to me, how happy is the wretched, whose sinews
crack upon the merciless engine° of his torture! I live with greater
torments than he dies.

FLORA   Leave your complaints. Tears are no sacrifice for blood.   20

MARIA   Now my just grief to just revenge give place. I am ashamed of
these soft tears, till I've revenged thy horrid murder. O that I could
make the villain linger out an age in torments! But I will revel in his
blood. O I could suck the last drop that warms the monster's heart,
that might inspire me with such cruelty as vile man, with all his   25
horrid arts of power, is yet a stranger to; then I might root out all
his cursed race.

FLORA   I'll follow all your fortunes, my dear lady. Had I ten thousand
lives, in this cause I'd venture one by one to my last stake.

MARIA   Thou art my dear and faithful creature; let not thy fortunes   30
thus be wracked° with mine. Be gone and leave thy most unhappy
mistress, one that has miseries enow° to sink the sex.

FLORA   I will not leave you till death takes me from you.

MARIA   O that I had been some poor lost mountain girl, nursed up by
goats, or suckled by wild beasts, exposed to all the rage of heats and   35
killing colds, I ne'er could have been abandoned to such fury. More
savage cruelty reigns in cities than ever yet in deserts among
the most venomous serpents and remorseless ravenous beasts
could once be found. So much has barbarous art debauched man's
innocent nature.°   40

FLORA   Lay by your tears till your revenge be finished; then, then you
may have leisure to complain.°

MARIA   I will. 'Tis blood I now must spill, or lose my own in the
attempt. But if I can have the fortune, with my own hand, to reach
the dog's vile heart, I then shall die contented, and in the other   45
world I'll torture him so, devils shall learn of me to use the damned.

FLORA   Let's to our sacred instruments of revenge.

MARIA   Come on. So just a cause would turn the vilest ruffian to a
saint.

    Exeunt

[2.3]

Bravos watch at Don John's house°
Enter Maria and Flora

MARIA Come, friends, let once a woman preach courage to you. Inspired by my just rage this arm shall teach you wonders. I'll show you now what love with just revenge can do.

FIRST BRAVO We are so practised in the trade of death, we need no teaching.   5

MARIA There's gold, good store. If you dispatch the dog, I'll give you yet much more. If not, if all the wealth I have can buy your lives, I'll have 'em instead of his.

FIRST BRAVO For half the sum, I'd kill a bishop at the altar.

Maria and Flora retire

Enter Don John, Don Antonio, Don Lopez, Jacomo

DON JOHN Now we have finished our design; let's make a sally and   10
raise the siege.

DON ANTONIO Jacomo, do you lead the van.°

DON LOPEZ Lead on, Jacomo, or we are sure to lose you. You are not good at bringing up the rear.

JACOMO Nay, good gentlemen, I know myself better than to take   15
place of° men of quality, especially upon this occasion.

DON JOHN Sirrah, go on. [*Drawing his sword*] I'll prick him forward. Remember, if you do not fight, I am behind you.

JACOMO O heaven! O Jacomo! What will become of thy dear person? Is this your courage to put me forward to what you dare not meet   20
yourselves?

DON JOHN No words, rogue. On, on, I say!

JACOMO O I shall be murdered! Murdered! Oh-h.

DON JOHN On, on, you dog.

JACOMO Inhuman master! It must be so! Heaven have mercy on my   25
better part.

Enter Maria [and Flora, armed]

MARIA [*to the Bravos*] Fall on, fall on.° That's the villain! [*Lunges at Don John*] Have at you, dog.

DON JOHN Courage, Jacomo.

The Dons drive the Bravos offstage. Maria and Flora remain°

JACOMO Oh-h!   30

MARIA O cowardly villains! The traitor will escape their hands. O dogs! More feeble than the feeblest of our sex. [*To Flora*] Let's after him and try our strength.

Enter Don John

He is returned. Fall on.

DON JOHN Ha! Must I encounter boys?   35

    Don John kills Flora

FLORA O I am slain.

MARIA [*lunging at Don John*] At thy heart, base villain.

    Don John disarms Maria

DON JOHN There, take your sword. I'll not nip roguery in the bud.
    Thou may'st live to be as wicked as myself.

MARIA Poor Flora! But, dog, I'll be revenged on thee yet ere I die.   40

    Exit Maria. Enter Don Lopez, Don Antonio, Jacomo

JACOMO What! No thanks? No reward?

DON JOHN What's the matter, sirrah?

JACOMO What, no acknowledgement? You are but an ungrateful man,
    let me tell you that, to treat a man of my prowess thus.

DON JOHN What has your valour done?   45

JACOMO Nothing, nothing; saved your life only, that's all. But men of
    valour are nothing nowadays. 'Tis an ungrateful age. I fought like a
    hero.

DON ANTONIO Called a stag at bay.°

DON LOPEZ You can fight, when there's no way of escape, without   50
    it.

JACOMO [*sees Flora's body*] O! What's here! Another murder! Fly, fly,
    we shall be hanged.

DON JOHN Come on! Let's now to sea to try our fortunes.

JACOMO Ay, make haste. I've laid horses° and will shift by land.
    Farewell, sir; a good voyage.   55

    [*Jacomo begins to leave*]

DON JOHN I will murder you, if you refuse to go to sea.

JACOMO O good sir, consider, do but consider. I am so sea-sick
    always. That wicked element does not agree with me.

DON JOHN Dare you dispute! Go on, I say.

JACOMO O good sir, think, think a little. The merciless waves will   60
    never consider a man of parts. Besides, sir, I can swim no more than
    I can fly.

DON JOHN I'll leave you dead upon the place, if you refuse.

JACOMO O sir, on my knees I beg you'll let me stay. I am the last of all
    my family; my race will fail, if I should fail.   65

DON JOHN Damn your race.

DON ANTONIO Do not we venture with you?

JACOMO You have nothing but your lives to venture, but I have a

whole family to save; I think upon posterity. Besides, gentlemen, I
can look for no safety in such wicked company.   70

DON JOHN I'll kill the villain. His fear will else betray us.

JACOMO O hold, hold! For heaven's sake hold.

   Ghost of Don John's father rises°

GHOST Hold, hold!

JACOMO Ay, hold, hold. O heaven! Your father's ghost! (*Falls down
and roars*) A ghost! A ghost! Oh-h!   75

DON JOHN 'Sdeath! What's here? My father alive!

GHOST No, no; inhuman murderer, I am dead.

DON JOHN That's well. I was afraid the old gentleman had come
for his estate again. If you would have that, 'tis too late: 'tis
spent.

GHOST Monster, behold these wounds.   80

DON JOHN I do. They were well meant and well performed, I see.

DON ANTONIO This is strange! How I am amazed!

DON LOPEZ Unheard-of wonder!

GHOST Repent, repent of all thy villainies;
 My clamorous blood to heaven for vengeance cries.   85
 Heaven will pour out his judgements on you all;
 Hell gapes for you; for you each fiend does call,
 And hourly waits your unrepenting fall.
 You with eternal horrors they'll torment,
 Except of all your crimes you suddenly repent.   90

   Ghost sinks

JACOMO Oh-h! Heaven deliver me from these monsters.

DON JOHN Farewell; thou art a foolish ghost. Repent, quoth he. What
could this mean? Our senses are all in a mist sure.

DON ANTONIO They are not; 'twas a ghost.

DON LOPEZ I ne'er believed those foolish tales before.   95

DON JOHN Come, 'tis no matter. Let it be what it will; it must be
natural.

DON ANTONIO And nature is unalterable in us too.

DON JOHN 'Tis true. The nature of a ghost cannot change ours.

DON LOPEZ It was a silly ghost, and I'll no sooner take his word than a   100
whore's.

DON JOHN Thou art in the right. [*To Jacomo*] Come, fool. Fool, rise.
The ghost is gone.

JACOMO O I die, I die! Pray let me die in quiet.

DON ANTONIO O if he be dying, take him up; we'll give him burial in   105
the sea. Come on.

JACOMO Hold, hold, gentlemen. Bury me not till I am dead, I beseech
   you.

DON JOHN If you be not, sirrah, I'll run you through.

JACOMO Hold, hold, sir. I'll go, I'll go.   110

DON LOPEZ AND DON ANTONIO Let's on.

DON JOHN   Should all the bugbears cowards feign appear,°
              I would urge on without one thought of fear.°

DON ANTONIO And I.

DON LOPEZ And I.   115

     Exeunt

3.1

[The ship]

Enter Don John, Don Lopez, Don Antonio, Jacomo, Captain of the Ship, Masters and Sailors

MASTER Mercy upon us! What sudden dreadful storm is this? We are all lost; we shall split upon the rocks. Luff, luff°—

JACOMO O, O! Mercy! O I was afraid of this! See what your wickedness has brought me to? Mercy, mercy!

DON JOHN Take away thy cowardly face. It offends me, rascal. 5

CAPTAIN Such dreadful claps of thunder I never yet remembered.

DON JOHN Let the clouds roar on and vomit all their sulphur out. They ne'er shall fright me.

DON ANTONIO These are the squibs and crackers° of the sky.

DON LOPEZ Fire on, fire on. We are unmoved. 10

CAPTAIN The heavens are all on fire. These unheard-of prodigies amaze me.

DON JOHN Can you, that have stood so many cannons, be frightened at the farting and the belching of a cloud?

MASTER Bless me, captain! Six of our foremast men are even now 15 struck dead with lightning.

SAILOR O that clap has rent our masts in sunder.

JACOMO O we are lost! *[To Don John]* You can swim, sir. Pray save me, sir, for my own and family's sake.

DON JOHN Toss these cowardly rogues overboard. Captain, courage! 20 Let the heavens do their worst, 'tis but drowning at last.

JACOMO But, in the name of heaven, but drowning, quoth he! Your drowning will prepare you for burning,° though oh-h-h—

SAILOR Captain, captain, the ship's on fire in the forecastle°—

CAPTAIN All hands to work upon the forecastle. Heaven! How it 25 blazes already.

Exit Captain

JACOMO Oh-h! We burn, we drown, we sink! O, we perish; we are lost; we are lost. Oh-h-h—

MASTER O horrid apparitions! Devils stand and guard the fire and will not suffer us to quench it. We are lost. 30

Enter Captain

CAPTAIN In all the dangers I have been, such horrors I never knew. I am quite unmanned.°

DON LOPEZ A man, and fear? 'Tis but dying at last.

DON JOHN I never yet could know what that foolish thing fear is.

CAPTAIN Help, help, the fire increases. What horrid sights are these?   35
Where'er I turn me, fearful spirits appear.

    Exeunt Captain and Sailors

DON JOHN Let's into the boat and with our swords keep out all
others.

DON ANTONIO While they are busy 'bout the fire, we may 'scape.

DON LOPEZ If we get from hence, we certainly shall perish on the   40
rocks.

DON JOHN I warrant you.

JACOMO O good gentlemen, let us shift for ourselves, and let the rest
burn, or drown, and be damned and they will.

DON JOHN No, you have been often leaving me. Now shall be the time   45
we'll part. Farewell.

JACOMO O! I'll stand by you while I live.

    A thunderclap strikes Don John and Jacomo down

O the devil, the devil! What horrors do I feel? O I am killed; I am
dead!

DON JOHN 'Sdeath! Why this to me? You paltry, foolish, bugbear   50
thunder! Am I the mark of your senseless rage?

DON LOPEZ Nothing but accident. Let's leap into the boat.

    [*Enter Captain and Sailors*]

DON ANTONIO The sailors all make towards us; they'll in and sink it.

DON JOHN [*to Jacomo*] Sirrah, if you come on, you run upon my
sword.   55

    [*The Dons climb into the lifeboat*]

JACOMO O cruel tyrant! I burn, I drown, I sink! O I die. I am lost.

CAPTAIN All shift aboard. We perish. We are lost.

MASTER All lost, all lost.

    A great shriek; [*the Captain and Sailors*] *all leap overboard°*

claps of thunder never were in my remembrance. Yon ship is all on   5
fire, and the poor, miserable wretches must all perish. The dreadful
object melts my heart and brings a flood of tears into my eyes. It is
prodigious, for on the sudden, all the heavens are clear again, and
the enraged sea is become more patient.

Enter Don Francisco

DON FRANCISCO O father, have you not been frighted at this   10
prodigious storm and at yon dreadful spectacle?

HERMIT No man that has an apprehension but would have been
moved with horror.

DON FRANCISCO 'Twas the most violent tempest I ever saw. Hold—
yonder are some coming in a small vessel and must necessarily split   15
upon the rock. I'll go and help to succour 'em.

HERMIT Here are some this way, just come in a small boat. Go you to
those, and these I will assist.

DON FRANCISCO I'll haste to their relief.

Exit Don Francisco

HERMIT Ha, these are come safe to land. Three men, goodly men they   20
seem to be. I am bound in charity to serve them. They come
towards me.

Enter Don John, Don Antonio, and Don Lopez

DON JOHN Much ado, we are safe, but my man's lost. Pox on him! I
shall miss the fool; it° was a necessary blockhead.

DON ANTONIO But you have lost your goods, which were more   25
necessary.

DON LOPEZ Our jewels and money we have all about us.

DON JOHN It makes me laugh to think how the fools we left behind
were puzzled which death to choose, burning or drowning.

DON ANTONIO But how shall we dispose of ourselves? We are plaguy   30
wet and cold. Ha! What old fool is that?

DON LOPEZ It is an hermit, a fellow of mighty beard and sanctity.

DON JOHN I know not what sanctity he may have, but he has beard
enough to make an owl's nest or stuff a saddle with.

HERMIT Gentlemen, I see you are shipwrecked and in distress; and   35
my function obliges me in charity to succour you in what I may.

DON ANTONIO Alas, what canst thou help us to? Dost thou know of
ever a° house near hand, where we may be furnished with some
necessaries?

HERMIT On the other side of this vast rock, there is a fertile and   40
pleasant valley where one Don Francisco, a rich and hospitable

man, has a sweet dwelling. He will entertain you nobly. He's
gone to assist some shipwrecked persons and will be here presently.
In the meantime, what my poor cave can afford, you shall be
welcome to.   45

DON LOPEZ What can that afford? You oblige yourself to fasting and
abstinence.

HERMIT I have studied physic° for the relief of needy people, and I
have some cordials° which will refresh you. I'll bring one to you.
     Exit Hermit

DON JOHN A good, civil, old hypocrite. But this is a pleasant kind of   50
religion that obliges 'em to nastiness° and want of meat. I'll ha'
none on't.

DON ANTONIO No, nor of any other, to my knowledge.
     Enter Hermit with a cordial

HERMIT Gentlemen, pray taste of this vial. It will comfort your cold
stomachs.   55

DON JOHN Ha, 'tis excellent, 'faith. Let it go round.

HERMIT Heaven bless it to you.

DON LOPEZ Ha, it warms.

DON ANTONIO Thank thee. Thou art a very honest old fellow, i' faith.

DON JOHN I see thou art very civil, but you must supply us with one   60
necessary more, a very necessary thing and very refreshing.

HERMIT What's that, sir?

DON JOHN It is a whore, a fine, young, buxom whore.

DON ANTONIO AND DON LOPEZ A whore, old man, a whore.

HERMIT Bless me! Are you men or devils?   65

DON JOHN Men, men, and men of lust and vigour. Prithee old sot,
leave thy prating and help me to a strumpet, a fine salacious°
strumpet. I know you zealots have enough of 'em. Women love
your godly whoremasters.

HERMIT O monsters of impiety! Are you so lately 'scaped the wrath   70
of heaven thus to provoke it?

DON ANTONIO How! By following the dictates of nature, who can do
otherwise?

DON LOPEZ All our actions are necessitated;° none command their
own wills.   75

HERMIT O horrid blasphemy! Would you lay your dreadful and
unheard-of vices upon heaven? No, ill men, that° has given you free
will to good.

DON JOHN I find thou retir'st here and never read'st or think'st.
Can that blind faculty, the will, be free,   80

When it depends upon the understanding,
Which argues first before the will can choose?
And the last dictate of the judgement sways
The will, as in a balance the last weight
Put in the scale, lifts up the other end,   85
And with the same necessity.

HERMIT But foolish men and sinners act against
Their understandings, which inform 'em better.

DON ANTONIO None willingly do anything against the last
Dictates of their judgements; whatsoe'er men do,   90
Their present opinions lead 'em to.

DON LOPEZ As fools that are afraid of sin are, by the thought
Of present pleasure or some other reason,
Necessarily biased to pursue
The opinion they are of at that moment.   95

HERMIT The understanding yet is free and might persuade 'em better.

DON JOHN The understanding never can be free;
For what we understand, spite of ourselves we do.
All objects are ready formed and placed
To our hands; and these the senses to the mind convey,   100
And as those represent them, this must judge.°
How can the will be free when the understanding,
On which the will depends, cannot be so?

HERMIT Lay by your devilish philosophy and change the dangerous
and destructive course of your lewd lives.   105

DON ANTONIO Change our natures? Go bid a blackamoor be white.
We follow our constitutions, which we did not give ourselves.

DON LOPEZ What we are, we are by nature. Our reason tells us we
must follow that.

DON JOHN Our constitutions tell us one thing and yours another; and   110
which must we obey? If we be bad, 'tis nature's fault that made us
so.

HERMIT Farewell. I dare no longer hear your impious discourse. Such
hardened wretches I ne'er heard of yet.
          Exit Hermit

DON ANTONIO Farewell, old fool.   115

DON JOHN Thus sots condemn what they can never answer.
          Enter Don Francisco
This, I believe, is Francisco, whom he spoke of. If he has but a
handsome wife or daughters, we are happy.

DON LOPEZ Sir, we are shipwrecked men; and if you can direct us to a

place where we may be furnished with some necessaries, you will   120
oblige us.

DON FRANCISCO Gentlemen, I have a house hard by; you shall be
welcome to it. I even now endeavoured to succour a youth and
beauteous woman who, with two sailors in a boat, were driven
towards these rocks, but were forced back again and, I fear, are lost   125
by this time. I desire nothing more than to assist men in extremes
and am o'erjoyed at the opportunity of serving you.

DON JOHN We thank you.

DON FRANCISCO You shall command my house as long as you
please. I see you are cavaliers° and hope you will bear with some   130
inconvenience. I have two young and, though I say it, handsome
daughters, who are tomorrow morning to be married. The solemnity
will bring much company together, which, I fear, may incommode
my house and you.

DON ANTONIO You pose us with this kindness.°   135

DON JOHN Whatever pleases you cannot be inconvenient to us.

DON LOPEZ On the contrary, we shall be glad to assist you at the
ceremony and help to make up the joyful chorus.

DON FRANCISCO You shall command my house and me; I'll show you
the way to it.   140

DON JOHN [bows] Your humble servant. We'll follow you.
    Exit Don Francisco
This is an admirable adventure.° He has daughters, boys, and to be
married too. If they have been so foolish to preserve those toys°
they call maidenheads, their senseless husbands shall not be
troubled with them. I'll ease them of those. Pox, what should those   145
dull drudging animals, called husbands, do with such treasures?
No, they are for honest whoremasters, boys.

DON ANTONIO Well said, Don. We will not be wanting in our
endeavours to succeed you.

DON LOPEZ To you alone we must give place. *Allons.*   150
    *Exeunt Don John, Don Antonio, and Don Lopez. Enter Hermit,
    Maria in man's habit,° and Leonora*

HERMIT Heaven be praised. You are safely now on land.

MARIA We thank you, reverend father, for your assistance.

LEONORA We never shall forget the obligation.

HERMIT I am happy to be so good an instrument.

LEONORA We followed a vessel which we saw fired with lightning,   155
and we fear that none of 'em escaped.

MARIA I hope the villain I pursue has 'scaped. I would not be

43

revenged by heaven, but my own hand; or, if not by that, by the hangman's.

LEONORA Did anyone come to land? For I most nearly am concerned 160
for one, the grief for whom, if he be lost, will soon, I fear, destroy
me.

HERMIT Here were three of that company came safe to land, but such
impious wretches as did not deserve to escape, and such as no
virtuous person can be concerned for, sure. I was stiff with fear and 165
horror when I heard 'em talk.

MARIA Three, say you?

LEONORA [aside] By this sad description it must be Don John and his
two wicked associates; I am ashamed to confess the tenderness I
have for him. Why should I love that wretch? O my too violent 170
passion hurries me I know not whither! Into what fearful dangerous
labyrinths of misery will it conduct me?

MARIA Were they gentlemen?

HERMIT By their outsides they seemed so, but their insides declared
them devils. 175

MARIA [aside] Heaven, it must be the villain and his barbarous companions. They are reserved for my revenge. Assist me, heaven, in
that just cause. O villain, villain, inhuman villain! Each minute is,
methinks, a tedious age, till I have dipped my hands in thy heart's
blood. 180

HERMIT You seem o'erjoyed at the news of their safe arrival. Can any
have a kindness for such dissolute abandoned atheists?

MARIA No. 'Tis revenge that I pursue against the basest of all villains.

HERMIT Have a care. Revenge is heaven's, and must not be usurped
by mortals. 185

MARIA Mine is revenge for rapes and cruel murders, and those heaven
leaves to earth to punish.

HERMIT They are horrid crimes, but magistrates must punish
them.

LEONORA [aside] What do I hear? Were he the basest of all men, my 190
love is so headstrong and so wild within me, I must endeavour to
preserve him or destroy myself. To what deplorable condition am I
fallen? What chains are these that hold me? O that I could break
them! And yet, I would not if I could. O my heart!

HERMIT They are gone to one Don Francisco's house; that road will 195
bring you to it. 'Tis on the other side of this rock, in a pleasant
valley. I have not stirred these forty years from these small bounds,

or I would give him notice what devils he harbours in his house.
You will do well to do it.

JACOMO (*offstage*) Help, help, murder! I am drowned; I am dead.   200
Help, help!

HERMIT Ha, what voice is that? I must assist him.

MARIA Father, farewell. Come, madam, will you go to this house?
Now, monster, for my revenge.

LEONORA I will. [*Aside*] But for different ends we go;   205
'Tis love conducts me, but revenge brings you.

    Exeunt Maria, Leonora

JACOMO [*extends a hand through the stage floor*]° O help, help! I sink, I
sink!

HERMIT Poor man, sure he is almost drowned.

JACOMO No, not yet. I have only drunk something too much of a   210
scurvy, unpleasant liquor.

HERMIT Reach me your hand. (*Pulls him out*)

JACOMO Ay, and my heart too. Oh-h! Sir, a thousand thanks to you. I
vow to Gad, y'are a very civil person, and, as I am an honest man,
have done me the greatest kindness in the world, next to the piece   215
of the mast which I floated upon, which I must ever love and
honour. I am sorry it swam away. I would have preserved it, and
hung it up in the seat of our ancient family.

HERMIT Thank heaven for your deliverance and leave such vain
thoughts.   220

JACOMO I do with all my heart, but I am not settled enough to say my
prayers yet. Pray, father, do you for me. 'Tis nothing with you. You
are used to it; it is your trade.

HERMIT Away, vain man. You speak as if you had drunk too deeply of
another liquor than seawater.   225

JACOMO No, I have not, but I would fain. Where may a man light of a
good glass of wine? I would gladly have an antidote to my poison.
Methinks [*spits*]—pah!—these fishes have but a scurvy time; I am
sure they have very ill drinking.

HERMIT Farewell, and learn more devotion and thankfulness to   230
heaven.

    Exit Hermit

JACOMO Ha, 'tis uncivilly done to leave a man in a strange country.
But these hermits have no breeding. Poor Jacomo, dear Jacomo,
how I love thy person; how glad am I to see thee safe! For I swear, I
think thou art as honest a fellow as e'er I met with. Well, farewell,   235

thou wicked element. If ever I trust thee again—well, haddocks, I
defy you. You shall have none of me, no, not a collop. No, no, I will
be eaten by worms, as all my ancestors have been. If heaven will but
preserve me from the monsters of the land—my master and his two
companions who, I hope, are drowned—I'll preserve myself from   240
those of the sea. [*Looks around*] Let me see, here is a path. This
must lead to some house. I'll go, for I am plaguy sick with this salt
water. [*Spits*] Pah!

    Exit Jacomo. Enter Clara, and Flavia with her two Maids

CLARA O Flavia, this will be our last happy night. Tomorrow is our
execution day: we must marry.   245

FLAVIA Ay, Clara, we are condemned without reprieve. 'Tis better to
live as we have done, kept from all men, than for each to be confined to one whom yet we never saw and, a thousand to one, shall
never like.

CLARA Out on't. A Spanish wife° has a worse life than a cooped   250
chicken.

FLAVIA A singing bird in a cage is a princely creature compared to
that poor animal called a wife here.

CLARA Birds are made tame by being caged, but women grow wild by
confinement; and that, I fear, my husband will find to his cost.   255

FLAVIA None live pleasantly here, but those who should be
miserable—strumpets. They can choose their mates, but we must
be like slaves condemned to the galleys. We have not liberty to sell
ourselves, or venture one throw° for our freedom.

CLARA O that we were in England! There, they say, a lady may choose   260
a footman and run away with him if she likes him, and no dishonour
to the family.

FLAVIA That's because the families are so very honourable, that
nothing can touch them. There, wives run and ramble° whither and
with whom they please and defy all censure.   265

CLARA Ay, and a jealous husband is a more monstrous creature there
than a wittol° here, and would be more pointed at. They say, if a
man be jealous there, the women will all join and pull him to pieces.

FLAVIA O happy country! We ne'er touch money; there, the wives
can spend their husbands' estates for 'em. O blessed   270
country!

CLARA Ay, there, they say the husbands are the prettiest, civil, easy,
good-natured, indifferent° persons in the whole world. They ne'er
mind what their wives do, not they.

FLAVIA Nay, they say they love those men best that are kindest to their 275 wives. Good men; poor hearts! And here, if an honest gentleman offers a wife a civility by the by, our bloody, butcherly husbands are cutting of throats presently.

CLARA O that we had those frank civil Englishmen instead of our grave, dull, surly Spanish blockheads, whose greatest honour lies in 280 preserving their beards and foreheads inviolable.

FLAVIA In England, if a husband and wife like not one another, they draw two several ways and make no bones on't. While the husband treats° his mistress openly in his glass-coach,° the wife, for decency's sake, puts on her vizard and whips away in a hackney° with a 285 gallant,° and no harm done.

CLARA Though, of late, 'tis as unfashionable for a husband to love his wife there as 'tis here. Yet 'tis fashionable for her to love somebody else, and that's something.

FLAVIA Nay, they say, gentlemen will keep company with a cuckold 290 there as soon as another man, and ne'er wonder at him.

CLARA O happy country! There a woman may choose for herself, and none will into° the trap of matrimony unless she likes the bait; but here we are tumbled headlong and blindfold into it.

FLAVIA We are used as they use hawks: never unhooded or whistled 295 off till they are just upon the quarry.°

CLARA And 'tis for others, not ourselves, we fly too.

FLAVIA No more. This does but put us in mind of our misery.

CLARA It does so; but prithee let's be merry one night. Tomorrow is our last. Farewell all happiness! 300

FLAVIA O that this happy day would last our lives' time. But prithee, my dear, let's have thy song and divert ourselves as well as we can in the meantime.

CLARA 'Tis a little too wanton.

FLAVIA Prithee let's be a little wanton this evening; tomorrow we 305 must take our leaves on't.

CLARA Come on then. Our maids shall join in the chorus. [*The Maids come forward*] Here they are.

FLAVIA AND CLARA (*sing*)

SONG 310

> *Woman who is by nature wild*
> *Dull bearded man encloses;*
> *Of nature's freedom we're beguiled*
> *By laws which man imposes,*

   Who still himself continues free;   315
   Yet we poor slaves must fettered be.

CHORUS *A shame on the curse*
    Of 'for better, for worse';°
 'Tis a vile imposition on nature.
    For women should change,   320
    And have freedom to range,
 Like to every other wild creature.

 So gay a thing was ne'er designed
  To be restrained from roving;
 Heaven meant so changeable a mind   325
   Should have its change in loving.
 By cunning we could make men smart,
 But they by strength o'ercome our art.

CHORUS *A shame on the curse*
    Of 'for, etc.'   330

 How happy is the village maid,
  Whom only love can fetter;
 By foolish honour ne'er betrayed,
  She serves a power much greater.
 That lawful prince the wisest rules;   335
 Th' usurper honour rules but fools.

CHORUS *A shame on the curse*
    Of 'for, etc.'

 Let us resume our ancient right,
  Make man at distance wonder;   340
 Though he victorious be in fight,
  In love we'll keep him under.
 War and ambition hence be hurled,
 Let love and beauty rule the world.

CHORUS *A shame on the curse,*   345
    Of 'for, etc.'

FLAVIA O dear Clara, that this were true! But now let's home; our
 father will miss us.

CLARA No, he's walked abroad with the three shipwrecked gentlemen.

FLAVIA They're proper° handsome gentlemen. But the chief, whom   350
they call Don John, exceeds the rest.

CLARA I never saw a finer person. Pray heaven either of our husbands
prove as good.

FLAVIA Do not name 'em. Let the maids go home. [*To the Maids*]
And, if my father be there, let him know we are here.   355

    Exit Maids

CLARA In the meantime, if he be thereabouts, do you go down that
walk, and I'll go this way, and perhaps one of us shall light on him.

FLAVIA Agreed.

    *Exeunt Flavia and Clara [in different directions]. Enter Don
    John, Don Lopez, Don Antonio*

DON JOHN Where have you left the old man, Don Francisco?

DON LOPEZ He's very busy at home, seeing all things prepared for his   360
daughters' weddings tomorrow.

DON JOHN His daughters are gone this way. If you have any friendship for me, go and watch the old man. And if he offers to come
towards us, divert him that I may have freedom to attack his
daughters.   365

DON ANTONIO You may be sure of us that have served you with our
lives; besides, the justice of this cause will make us serve you.
Adieu.

    Exeunt Don Lopez, Don Antonio

DON JOHN Now for my virgins. Assist me, Love. Fools, you shall have
no maidenheads tomorrow night. Husbands have maidenheads!   370
No, no, poor sneaking° fools.

    Enter Jacomo

JACOMO I have lost my way. I think I shall never find this house. But I
shall never think myself out of my way unless I meet my impious
master. Heaven grant he be drowned.

DON JOHN How now, rascal. Are you alive?   375

JACOMO O heaven! He's here. Why was this lewd creature saved? I am
in a worse condition than ever. Now I have 'scaped drowning, he
brings hanging fresh into my memory.

DON JOHN What? Mute, sirrah?

JACOMO Sir, I am no more your servant; you parted with me. I thank   380
you, sir. I am beholding to you. Farewell, good sir. I am my own
man now. [*Begins to leave*]

DON JOHN [*stops him*] No. Though you are a rogue, you are a necessary
rogue, and I'll not part with you.

49

JACOMO I must be gone. I dare not venture further with you.   385

DON JOHN Sirrah, do you know me, and dare you say this to me?
  [*Pulls out his sword*] Have at your guts! I will rip you from the navel
  to the chin.

JACOMO O good sir, hold, hold. [*Aside*] He has got me in his clutches;
  I shall never get loose. Oh-h!   390

DON JOHN Come, dog. Follow me close, stinking rascal.

JACOMO I am too well pickled in the salt water to stink, I thank you. I
  shall keep a great while. [*Aside*] But you were a very generous° man
  to leave a gentleman, your friend, in danger, as you did me. I have
  reason to follow you. But if I serve you not in your kind,° then am I   395
  a soused sturgeon.

DON JOHN Follow me, sirrah. I see a lady.

JACOMO Are you so fierce already?

    Enter Clara, singing 'A shame on the curse, etc.'

CLARA [*aside*] Ha! This is the stranger. What makes him here?°

DON JOHN [*aside*] A delicate creature. Ha! This is the lady.—How   400
  happy am I to meet you here.

CLARA What mean you, sir?

DON JOHN I was undone enough before with seeing your picture in
  the gallery, but I see you have more excellencies than beauty. Your
  voice needed not have conspired with that to ruin me.   405

CLARA Have you seen my picture?

DON JOHN And loved it above all things I ever saw, but the original. I
  am lost beyond redemption unless you can pity me.

JACOMO (*aside*) He has been lost a hundred times, but he always finds
  himself again—and me too, a pox on him!   410

DON JOHN When love had taken too fast hold on me ever to let me go,
  I too late found you were tomorrow to be married.

CLARA Yes, I am condemned to one I never saw, and you are come to
  rally me and my misfortunes.

JACOMO Ah, madam, say not so. My master is always in earnest.   415

DON JOHN So much I am in earnest now, that if you have no way to
  break this marriage off and pity me, I soon shall repent I ever came
  to land. I shall suffer a worse wreck upon the shore. Here, I shall
  linger out my life in the worst of pains, despairing love; there, I
  should have perished quickly.   420

JACOMO Ah poor man! He's in a desperate condition. I pity him with
  all my heart.

DON JOHN Peace, rascal. Madam, this is the only opportunity I am
  like to have. Give me leave to improve° it.

CLARA Sure, sir, you cannot be in earnest.   425

DON JOHN If all the oaths under the sun can convince you, madam, I
swear—

JACOMO O sir, sir, have a care of swearing for fear you should, once in
your life, be forsworn.

DON JOHN Peace, dog, or I shall slit your windpipe.   430

JACOMO Nay, I know if he be forsworn, 'tis the first time, that's
certain.

CLARA But, sir, if you be in earnest, and I had an inclination, 'tis
impossible to bring it about. My father has disposed of me.

DON JOHN Dispose of yourself. I'll do well enough with him, and my   435
fortune and quality are too great for him, for whom you are
intended, to dispute with me.

CLARA If this be true, would you win a woman at first sight?

DON JOHN Madam, this is like to be the first and last. Tomorrow is
the fatal day that will undo me.   440

JACOMO Courage, Don, matters go well.

CLARA (aside) Nay, I had rather have a peasant of my own choosing
than an emperor of another's. He is a handsome gentleman, and
seems to be of quality. O that he could rid me of my intended
slavery! [To Don John] Sir, talk not of impossible things; for could I   445
wish this, my father's honour will not suffer him to dispense with°
his promise.

DON JOHN I'll carry you beyond his power and your intended
husband's too.

CLARA It cannot be. But I must leave you; I dare not be seen with   450
you.

DON JOHN Remember the short time you have to think on this. Will
you let me perish without relief? If you will have pity on a wretched
man, I have a priest in my company. I'll marry you, and we'll find
means to fly early in the morning before the house are stirring.   455

CLARA I confess I am to be condemned to a slavery, that nothing can
be worse; yet this were a rash attempt.

DON JOHN If you will not consent to my just desires, I am resolved to
kill myself and fall a sacrifice to your disdain. Speak! Speak my
doom. (Holds his sword to his breast)   460

CLARA Hold, hold!

JACOMO [aside] Ay, hold, hold. Poor foolish woman, she should not
need to bid him hold.

CLARA I'll find a means this night to speak with you alone; but I fear
this is but for your diversion.   465

JACOMO [*aside*] Yes, 'tis for diversion indeed, the common diversion of all the world.

DON JOHN By all that's great and good, my intentions are honourable.

CLARA Farewell, sir. I dare not stay longer.

DON JOHN Will you keep your word, madam?   470

JACOMO [*aside*] You'll keep yours, no doubt.

CLARA I will. Anything rather than marry one I cannot love, as I can no man of another's choosing.

DON JOHN Remember, madam, I perish if you do not. I have only one thing to say: keep this secret from your sister till we have effected it.   475 I'll give you sufficient reason for what I say.
      Exit Clara
Victoria, victoria!° I have her fast; she's my own.

JACOMO You are a hopeful° man. You may come to good in time.
      Enter Flavia

DON JOHN Here is the other sister. Have at her.

JACOMO Why, sir, sir! Have you no conscience? Will not one at once   480 serve your turn?

DON JOHN Stand by, fool.— Let me see, you are the lady.

FLAVIA What say you, sir?

DON JOHN You have lately taken up a stray heart of mine. I hope you do not intend to detain it without giving me your own in   485 exchange.

FLAVIA I, a heart of yours? Since when, good sir? You were but this day shipwrecked on this coast and never saw my face before.

DON JOHN I saw your picture, and I saw your motion, both so charming I could not resist them. But now I have a nearer view, I   490 see plainly I am lost.

FLAVIA [*aside*] A goodly handsome man! But what can this mean?

DON JOHN Such killing beauties I ne'er saw before. My heart is irrevocably gone.

FLAVIA Whither is it gone, sir? I assure you I have no such thing about   495 me that I know of.

DON JOHN Ah, madam, if you would give me leave to search you, I should find it in some little corner about you that shall be nameless.

FLAVIA It cannot be about me. I have none but my own, and that I must part with tomorrow to I know not whom.   500

DON JOHN If the most violent love that man e'er knew can e'er deserve that treasure, it is mine. If you give that away, you lose the truest lover that e'er languished yet.

JACOMO [*aside*] What can be the end of this? Sure blood must follow

this dishonour of the family; and I, unfortunate, shall have my   505
throat cut for company.

FLAVIA Do you know where you are?

DON JOHN Yes, madam, in Spain, where opportunities are very
scarce, and those that are wise make use of 'em as soon as they have
'em.   510

FLAVIA You have a mind to divert yourself, but I must leave you. I am
disposed to be more serious.

DON JOHN Madam, I swear by all—

JACOMO Hold, hold! Will you be forsworn again?

DON JOHN Peace, villain. I shall cut that tongue out.   515

FLAVIA Farewell. I cannot stay.

Exit Flavia

DON JOHN I'll not leave her. I'll thaw her, if she were ice, before I have
done with her.

JACOMO There is no end of this lewdness. Well, I must be killed or
hanged, once for all, and there's an end on't.   520

Exeunt Don John and Jacomo. Enter Maria and Leonora

LEONORA I am faint with what I suffered at sea and with my wandering
since. Let us repose a little. We shall not find this house tonight.

MARIA I ne'er shall rest till I have found Don Francisco's house, but
I'll sit down a while.

LEONORA [*aside*] I hope he will not find it till I have found means to   525
give Don John warning of his cruel intentions. I would save his life,
who, I fear, would not do that for me. But in the miserable case that
I am in, if he denies his love, death would be the welcomest thing
on earth to me.

MARIA [*aside*] O my Octavio! How does the loss of thee perplex me   530
with despair! The honour of mankind is gone with thee. Why do I
whine? Grief shall no longer usurp the place of my revenge. How
could I gnaw the monster's heart! Villain, I'll be with you! When I
have revenged my dear Octavio's loss, I then shall die contented.

Enter Don Lopez and Don Antonio

DON LOPEZ The old man's safe. I long to know Don John's success.   535

DON ANTONIO He's engaged upon a noble cause. If he succeeds,
'twill be a victory worth the owning.

DON LOPEZ [*sees Maria and Leonora*] Ha, whom have we here? A
young man well habited, with a lady too. They seem to be strangers.

DON ANTONIO A mischief comes into my head that's worth the   540
doing.

DON LOPEZ What's that, dear Antonio?

DON ANTONIO We are in a strange country and may want money. I
would rob that young fellow. We have not robbed a good while;
methinks 'tis a new wickedness to me.   545

DON LOPEZ Thou art in the right. I hate to commit the same dull sin
over and over again, as if I were married to it. Variety makes all
things pleasant.

DON ANTONIO But there's one thing we'll ne'er omit. When we have
robbed the man, we'll ravish the woman.   550

DON LOPEZ Agreed. Let's to't, man.—Come on, young gentleman,
we must see what riches you have about you.

MARIA O villains! Thieves, thieves! These are the inhuman
companions of that bloody monster.

LEONORA Have pity on poor miserable strangers.   555

DON ANTONIO Peace. We'll use you kindly,° very kindly.

DON LOPEZ Do you carry that young gentleman, bind him to a tree,
and bring the money, while I wait upon the lady.

DON ANTONIO Will you play me no foul play in the meantime then?
For we must cast lots about the business you wot of.   560

DON LOPEZ No, upon my honour.

MARIA Honour, you villain?

DON ANTONIO Come, young gentleman. I'll tame you.

MARIA Help, help!

> *Exit Don Antonio, haling Maria*

LEONORA [*to Don Lopez*] Have you no humanity in you? Take our   565
money, but leave us liberty. Be not so barbarously cruel.

> [*Enter Don Antonio*]

DON ANTONIO Come. I have made haste with him; now let us draw
cuts who enjoys the lady first.

LEONORA O heaven assist me! What do I hear? Help, help!

> *Enter four or five Country Fellows, coming from work*

FIRST COUNTRY FELLOW What, two men a robbing of a lady!   570
Begone and let her alone, or we have sower cudgels° shall wasler°
your bones, I tell you that.

DON ANTONIO How now, rogues?

> *Don Lopez and Don Antonio fight the Country Fellows off*
> *the stage*

LEONORA Thanks to heaven. I fly, I fly! Where shall I hide myself?

> *Exit Leonora. Enter Don John and Jacomo*

DON JOHN I shall conquer 'em both. Now, sirrah, what think you?   575

JACOMO Why, I think you manage your business as discreetly, and
take as much pains to have your throat cut, as any man in Spain.

DON JOHN Your fear o'er-rules your sense. Mine is a life monarchs
might envy.

JACOMO 'Tis like to be a very short one at this rate.   580

DON JOHN Away, fool. 'Tis dark; I must be gone. I shall scarce find
the way home.

    Enter Leonora

LEONORA Heaven guard me from these wicked wretches. Help, help!
They are here.

DON JOHN How now, madam? What, afraid of a man?   585

LEONORA Don John, no, not of you. You are the man i' th' world I
would have met.

DON JOHN Leonora, you are the woman i' th' world I would have
avoided. [*Aside*] 'Sdeath! She will spoil my new designs, but I have a
trick for her. [*To Leonora*] What miracle brought you hither?   590

LEONORA Love, that works the greatest miracles, made me follow
you, and the same storm drove me on this shore on which you were
thrown, and thus far I've wandered till I have found you.

DON JOHN [*aside*] This is the most unreasonable, insatiable loving
lady that ever was abused by man. She has a kind of spaniel love:°   595
the worse you use her, the more loving she is. Pox on her, I must be
rid of her.

LEONORA I am very faint and weary, yet I was resolved not to rest till
I had found you.

DON JOHN Your unwearied love has o'ercome and convinced me   600
there is not such a woman° breathing.

LEONORA This is a sovereign medicine for all my sorrows. I now,
methinks, am happier than ever, but I am faint and ill.

DON JOHN Here, madam, I have an excellent cordial; 'twill refresh
you. And I'll conduct you where you shall never be unhappy more.   605

LEONORA From that dear hand 'tis welcome. To your health. (*Drinks*)

DON JOHN And to your own destruction. You have drunk your last.

LEONORA What means my love?

DON JOHN Y' have drunk the subtlest° poison that art e'er yet
invented.   610

JACOMO O murder! Murder! What have you done?

DON JOHN Peace, villain. Leave your unseasonable pity. [*To Leonora*]
You cannot live two minutes.

LEONORA O ungrateful tyrant! Thou hast murdered the only creature
living that could love thee. Heaven will revenge it, though to me 'tis   615
kindness. Here all my sorrows shall forever cease.

DON JOHN Why would you persecute me with your love?

LEONORA I could not help it. I came to preserve you and am
destroyed for't.

JACOMO O horrid fact! 620

DON JOHN To preserve me! [*Indicates his sword*] I wear my safety by
my side.

LEONORA [*staggers*] O I faint! Guard yourself. There's a young
gentleman pursues your life. Have a care. I came to tell you this,
and thus I am rewarded. Heaven pardon you. Farewell. I can no 625
more. (*Dies*)

JACOMO This object° sure will strike your heart! Tigers would melt
at this. O the earth will open and swallow you up, and me for
company. There's no end of your murders.

DON JOHN This is the first time I ever knew compassion. Poor fool, I 630
pity her, but 'tis too late.

> Farewell all senseless thoughts of a remorse;
> I would remove whate'er would stop my course.

Exeunt

4.1

[The house of Don Francisco]

Enter Don John, Don Lopez, Don Antonio, Jacomo

DON JOHN This night's success exceeded all my hopes. I had admittance to their several° chambers, and I have been contracted to both the sisters and this day resolve to marry 'em and at several times enjoy them. And, in my opinion, I shall have a brace of as pretty wives as any man in Spain.   5

DON ANTONIO Brave Don John, you are master of your art. Not a woman in Spain can stand before you.

DON LOPEZ We can but envy you and at a distance imitate, but both their maids shall to pot,° I assure you.

JACOMO How far will the devil hurry you?   10

DON JOHN 'Tis not the devil; 'tis the flesh, fool.

JACOMO Here will be fine cutting of throats. Poor Jacomo, must thou be cut off in the flower of thy age?

Enter Don Francisco

DON FRANCISCO *[bowing]* Gentlemen, your servant. I hope you rested well this night.   15

DON LOPEZ We thank you, sir; never better.

DON ANTONIO We never shall requite this obligation.

JACOMO I warrant you, my master will. He's a very grateful civil person indeed.

DON JOHN The favour is too great to be suddenly requited, but I shall   20
study to deserve it.

JACOMO Good man, you will deserve it.

Enter two Bridegrooms

DON FRANCISCO Gentlemen, you are come. You are early.

FIRST BRIDEGROOM This joyful occasion made us think it late.

SECOND BRIDEGROOM The expectation of so great a blessing as   25
we this day hope to enjoy would let us have but little rest last night.

FIRST BRIDEGROOM And the fruition will afford us less tonight.

DON JOHN *[aside]* Poor fools! You shall be bobbed. How it tickles my spleen° to think on't.   30

DON FRANCISCO These are to be my sons-in-law.

DON JOHN *[aside]* And my cuckolds beforehand.

DON FRANCISCO Pray know 'em, gentlemen; they are men of honour.

DON JOHN I shall be glad to serve them. (*Aside*) But first I'll serve their ladies.   35

DON FRANCISCO [*to the Bridegrooms*] Come, gentlemen, I'll now conduct you to my daughters—and [*to Don John, Don Lopez, and Don Antonio*] beg your pardon for the moment. I'll wait on you again.
            Exit Don Francisco and Bridegrooms

DON ANTONIO These fools will spoil your design.

DON JOHN No, poor sots. I have persuaded the ladies to feign sickness   40
and put off their marriage till tomorrow morning to gain time; in the meanwhile, I have 'em safe, boys.

DON LOPEZ But will not the sisters betray you to one another?

DON JOHN No, I have wheedled each into a jealousy of the other, and each believes that, if the other knows it, she in honour will reveal it   45
to the father.

JACOMO Sir, if you be so very weary of your life, why don't you make use of a convenient beam?° 'Tis the easier way so you may die without the filthy pother you keep about it.

DON JOHN Away, coward. 'Tis a sign I am not weary of my life that I   50
make so much use on't.

JACOMO O Jacomo! Thou art lost. 'Tis pity a fellow of thy neat spruce parts should be destroyed.
            Enter Don Francisco

DON FRANCISCO Come, gentlemen, will you not refresh yourselves with some cool wines this morning?   55

DON LOPEZ We thank you, sir. We have already.
            Enter a Servant

SERVANT Sir, here's a young gentleman, a stranger, desires to speak with you.

DON FRANCISCO Admit him.
            Enter Maria in man's habit
Your humble servant.   60

MARIA Sir, when I've told you what I come for, I doubt not but I shall deserve your thanks. I come to do you service.

DON FRANCISCO You have 'em, sir, already.

MARIA You have lodged within your house some shipwrecked men who are greater villains than the earth e'er bore. I come to give you   65
warning of 'em and to beg your power to revenge such horrid actions as heart could never yet conceive, or tongue could utter.
[*Sees Don John and others*] Ha! They are these! Revenge, revenge cruel unnatural rapes and murders! They are devils in the shapes of men.   70

DON FRANCISCO What say you, sir?

JACOMO [*aside*] Now the snare is fallen upon me. Methinks I feel cold steel already in my body. Too well I know that face.

DON JOHN [*aside*] I know that face. Now, impudence, assist me. [*To Don Francisco*] What mad young man is that?   75

DON FRANCISCO These, by their habits and their miens, are gentlemen and seem to be men of honour.

MARIA [*pointing to Don Antonio and Don Lopez*] By these two, last night I was robbed and bound to a tree, and there have been all night, and but this morning was relieved by peasants. I had a lady   80
with me, whom they said they would ravish, and this morning I saw her dead. They must have murdered her.

DON FRANCISCO Heaven! What do I hear?

JACOMO [*aside*] Oh! I am noosed already; I feel the knot, methinks, under my left ear.   85

DON ANTONIO The youth raves. We never saw his face; we never stirred from the bounds of this house since we came hither.

DON LOPEZ 'Sdeath, let me kill the villain. Shall he thus affront men of our quality and honour?

DON FRANCISCO Hold! Consider I am a magistrate.   90

DON JOHN The youth was robbed and with the fright has lost his wits. Poor fool! Let him be bound in's bed.

DON FRANCISCO Do not persist in this, but have a care. These injuries to men of honour shall not go unpunished.

MARIA Whither shall injured innocence fly for succour if you so soon   95
can be corrupted? Monster, I'll revenge myself! [*Draws her sword*] Have at thy heart!

DON FRANCISCO What means the youth? Put up your sword.
        [*Don Antonio and Don Lopez seize Maria*]

DON ANTONIO We told you, sir, he was mad.

MARIA O impudent villains! [*To Don Francisco*] I ask your pardon, sir.   100
My griefs and injuries transport me so, I scarce can utter them. That villain is Don John, who basely murdered the governor of Seville in his house and then dishonoured his fair sister.

DON JOHN Death and hell! This injury is beyond all sufferance. [*Reaches for his sword*]   105

DON FRANCISCO Hold, sir! Think in whose house you are.

JACOMO O Lord, what will this come to? Ah, Jacomo! Thy line of life is short.

MARIA This is the villain who killed the lover of Antonio's sister, deflowered her, and murdered her brother in his own house.   110

DON JOHN I'll have no longer patience.

DON ANTONIO Such a villain should have his throat cut, though in a church.

DON LOPEZ No man of honour will protect those who offer such injuries.   115

DON JOHN [*draws against Maria*] Have at you, villain.

DON FRANCISCO Nay then. [*Calling offstage*] Within there. Ho! [*Interposes himself between Don John and Maria*] I will protect him, or perish with him.

      Enter two Bridegrooms

FIRST BRIDEGROOM What's the matter?   120

DON JOHN (*to [Don] Antonio and [Don] Lopez*) This rashness will spoil my design upon the daughters. If I had perfected° that, I would have owned all this for half a duccatoon.° [*To Don Francisco*] I ask your pardon for my ill manners. I was provoked too far; indeed, the accusations are so extravagant and odd, I rather should   125 have laughed at 'em. Let the young fool have a vein opened.° He's stark staring mad.

DON ANTONIO A foolish impostor.° We ne'er saw Seville till last night.

MARIA O impudence!   130

JACOMO No, not we. We never were there till yesterday. Pray, sir, lay that young fellow by the heels° for lying on us, men of honour.

DON FRANCISCO What is the matter, friend, you tremble so?

DON LOPEZ [*aside*] 'Sdeath! The dog's fear will betray us.

JACOMO I tremble, sir? No, no, sir. I tremble! Though it would make   135 anyone tremble to hear one lie as that young gentleman does. [*To Maria*] Have you no conscience in you?

MARIA Heaven can witness for me, I speak not false. Octavio, my dear Octavio, being dearest to me of all the world, I would in Seville have revenged his murder; but the villain there escaped me. I followed   140 him to sea and, in the same storm in which their ship perished, I was thrown on shore. O my Octavio! If this foul, unnatural murder be not revenged, there is no justice left among mankind. His ghost, and all the rest whom he has barbarously murdered, will interrupt your quiet. They'll haunt you in your sleep. Revenge, revenge!   145

SECOND BRIDEGROOM This is wonderful.°

DON FRANCISCO There must be something in this. His passion cannot be counterfeited, nor your man's fear.

JACOMO My fear? I scorn your words; I fear nothing under the sun. I fear? Ha, ha, ha.   150

DON JOHN Will you believe this one false villain against three who are gentlemen and men of honour?

JACOMO Nay, against four who are gentlemen and men of honour?

MARIA O villain, that I had my sword imbrued in thy heart's blood. O my dear Octavio! Do justice, sir, or heaven will punish you.   155

Enter Clara

DON FRANCISCO Gentlemen, he is too earnest in his grief and anger to be what you would have him, an imposter. My house has been your sanctuary, and I am obliged in honour not to act as a magistrate, but your host. No violence shall here be offered to you, but you must instantly leave this house, and if you would have safety,   160 find it somewhere else. Be gone.

DON JOHN This is very well.

MARIA O, will you let 'em go unpunished? Whither shall I fly for vengeance?

DON FRANCISCO Pray leave this place immediately.   165

JACOMO [*to Don John*] Ah, good sir, let's be gone. [*Bowing to Don Francisco*] Sir, your most humble servant.

CLARA O sir, consider what you do. Do not banish Don John from hence.

FIRST BRIDEGROOM Ha, what means she?   170

DON FRANCISCO What say you?

CLARA O sir, he is my husband; we were last night contracted.

DON FRANCISCO O heaven! What do I hear?

FIRST BRIDEGROOM I am dishonoured, abused. Villain, thou diest.

DON JOHN Villain, you lie. I will cut your throat first.   175

DON FRANCISCO [*calling out*] Hey! Where are my people here?

Enter servants and Flavia

FLAVIA O, sir, hold. If you banish Don John, I am lost forever.

DON FRANCISCO O devil! What do I hear?

FLAVIA He is my husband, sir; we were last night contracted.

CLARA Your husband! Heaven, what's this?   180

SECOND BRIDEGROOM Hell and damnation!

DON FRANCISCO O, I have lost my senses.

MARIA O monster! Now am I to be believed?

JACOMO [*kneeling*] O spare my life! I am innocent, as I hope to live and breathe.   185

DON JOHN Dog, you shall fight for your life, if you have it.

DON FRANCISCO First, I'll revenge myself on these.

[*Draws on his daughters*]

DON JOHN Hold, hold. They are both my wives, and I will have them.

Don John runs at Flavia and Clara. They run out

DON FRANCISCO O devil! Fall on.

MARIA Fall on. I will assist you. (*Fight*)   190

Maria and Don Francisco are killed. The two Bridegrooms are hurt. Jacomo runs away.

DON JOHN Now we've done their business.

Enter Jacomo

Ah, cowardly rogue! Are not you a son of a whore?

JACOMO Ay, sir, what you please. A man had better be a living son of a whore than a dead hero, by your favour.°

DON JOHN I could find in my heart to kill the rascal. His fear, some   195
time or other, will undo us.

JACOMO Hold, sir. I went, sir, to provide for your escape. Let's take horses out of the stable and fly. Abundance of company are coming, expecting the wedding; and we are irreparably lost if we take not this time. I think my fear will now preserve you.   200

DON ANTONIO I think he counsels well. Let's fly to a new place of pleasure.

DON JOHN But I shall leave my business undone with the two women.

DON LOPEZ 'Tis now scarce feasible. Let's fly. You'll light on others as handsome where we come next.   205

DON JOHN Well, dispose of me as you please, and yet it troubles me.

JACOMO Haste, haste, or we shall be apprehended.

Exeunt Don John, Don Antonio, Don Lopez, and Jacomo.
Enter Clara and Flavia

FLAVIA O that I ever lived to see this day, this fatal day! 'Twas our vile disobedience caused our poor father's death, which heaven will revenge on us. So lewd a villain as Don John was never heard   210
of yet.

CLARA That we should be so credulous! O dreadful accident! Dear father, what expiation can we make? Our crime's too foul for tears to wash away, and all our lives will be too short to spend in penitence for this, our levity and disobedience. He was the best of   215
fathers and of men.

FLAVIA What will become of us, poor miserable maids lost in our fortunes and our reputations? Our intended husbands, if they recover of their wounds, will murder us; and 'tis but justice. Our lives too now cannot be worth the keeping. Those devils in the   220
shapes of men are fled.

CLARA Let us not waste our time in fruitless grief; let us employ

some to pursue the murderers. And, for ourselves, let's to the next
monastery, and there spend all our weary life in penitence.

FLAVIA Let's fly to our last sanctuary in this world, and try, by a   225
religious life, to expiate this crime. There is no safety, or no hope
but there. Let's go and bid a long farewell to all the world, a thing
too vain and little worth our care.

CLARA Agreed; farewell to all the vanity on earth,
    Where wretched mortals, tossed 'twixt hope and fear,   230
    Must of all fixed and solid joy despair.
    Exeunt

4.2

A delightful grove

Enter two Shepherds and two Nymphs

FIRST SHEPHERD Come, nymphs and shepherds, haste away
    To th'happy sports within these shady groves.
    In pleasant lives time slides away apace,
    But with the wretched seems to creep too slow.

FIRST NYMPH Our happy leisure we employ in joys,   5
    As innocent as they are pleasant. We,
    Strangers to strife and to tumultuous noise,
    To baneful envy, and to wretched cares,
    In rural pleasures spend our happy days,
    And our soft nights in calm and quiet sleeps.   10

SECOND SHEPHERD No rude ambition interrupts our rest,
    Nor base and guilty thoughts how to be great.

SECOND NYMPH In humble cottages we have such contents
    As uncorrupted nature does afford,
    Which the great, that surfeit under gilded roofs   15
    And wanton in down beds, can never know.

FIRST SHEPHERD Nature is here not yet debauched by art;
    'Tis as it was in Saturn's happy days.°
    Minds are not here by luxury invaded;°
    A homely plenty, with sharp appetite,°   20
    Does lightsome health and vigorous strength impart.

FIRST NYMPH A chaste-cold spring does here refresh our thirst,
    Which by no feverish surfeit is increased;
    Our food is such as nature meant for men,
    Ere with the vicious eating was an art.   25

SECOND NYMPH In noisy cities riot is pursued,°
    And lewd luxurious living softens men,
    Effeminates fools in body and in mind,
    Weakens their appetites, and decays their nerves.
SECOND SHEPHERD With filthy steams from their excess of meat   30
    And cloudy vapours raised from dangerous wine,
    Their heads are never clear or free to think;
    They waste their lives in a continual mist.
FIRST SHEPHERD Some subtle and ill men choose temperance,
    Not as a virtue, but a bawd to vice,   35
    And vigilantly wait to ruin those,
    Whom luxury and ease have lulled asleep.
SECOND SHEPHERD Yes, in the clamorous courts of tedious law,
    Where what is meant for a relief's a grievance;°
    Or in king's palaces, where cunning strives,   40
    Not to advance king's interests, but its own.
FIRST NYMPH There they in a continual hurry live,
    And seldom can, for all their subtle arts,
    Lay their foundations sure; but some
    Are undermined, others blown down by storms.   45
SECOND NYMPH Their subtlety is but a common road
    Of flattering great men, and oppressing little,
    Smiling on all they meet, and loving none.
FIRST SHEPHERD In populous cities, life is all a storm;
    But we enjoy a sweet perpetual calm.   50
    Here our own flocks we keep, and here
    I and my Phyllis can embrace unenvied.
SECOND SHEPHERD And I and Celia without jealousy.
    But hark, the pipes begin; now for our sports.
       A symphony of rustic music

SONG   55

Nymphs and shepherds come away;
In these groves let's sport and play,
Where each day is a holiday,
Sacred to ease and happy love,
To dancing, music, poetry.   60
Your flocks may now securely rove,
Whilst you express your jollity.

Enter Shepherds and Shepherdesses, singing in chorus

     We come, we come; no joy like this.
     Now let us sing, rejoice, and kiss.
     The great can never know such bliss.   65
1   *As this.*
2   *As this.*
3   *As this.*
ALL   *As this.*
     The great can never know such bliss.   70

     1 *All th' inhabitants o' th'wood*
       Now celebrate the spring
     That gives fresh vigour to the blood
       Of every living thing.
CHORUS   *The birds have been singing and billing before us,*   75
     And all the sweet choristers join in the chorus.

     2 *The nightingales with jugging throats°*
       Warble out their pretty notes,
       So sweet, so sweet, so sweet.
     And thus our loves and pleasures greet.   80
CHORUS   *Then let our pipes sound, let us dance, let us sing,*
     Till the murmuring groves with loud echoes shall ring.

   Dance begins

     3   *How happy are we,*
         From all jealousy free;
     No dangers or cares can annoy us.   85
         We toy and we kiss,
         And love's our chief bliss—
     A pleasure that never can cloy us.
CHORUS   *Our days we consume in unenvied delights,*
     And in love and soft rest our happy long nights.   90

     4   *Each nymph does impart*
         Her love without art
     To her swain, who thinks that his chief treasure.
         No envy is feared,
         No sighs are e'er heard,   95
     But those which are caused by our pleasure.
CHORUS   *When we feel the blessed raptures of innocent love,*
     No joys exceed ours but the pleasures above.

GENERAL CHORUS   *In these delightful fragrant groves,*
     Let's celebrate our happy loves.   100

> *Let's pipe, and dance, and laugh, and sing;*
> *Thus every happy living thing*
> *Revels in the cheerful spring.*

Dance continues. Enter Don John, Don Lopez, Don Antonio,
Jacomo

DON JOHN So, thus far we are safe. We have almost killed our horses
with riding cross out of all roads.   105

JACOMO Nay, you have had as little mercy on them as if they had been
men or women. But yet we are not safe; let us fly farther.

DON JOHN The house I lighted at was mine during my life, which I
sold to that fellow. He, since he holds by that tenure, will carefully
conceal us.   110

JACOMO 'Tis a tenure I will not give him two months' purchase for.

DON JOHN Besides, our swords are used to conquest.

DON ANTONIO At worst, there is a church hard by. We'll put it to its
proper use—take refuge in't.

DON LOPEZ Look here. Here are shepherds and young pretty   115
wenches. Shall we be idle, Don?

DON ANTONIO By no means. 'Tis a long time, methinks, since we
were vicious.

DON JOHN We'll serve 'em as the Romans did the Sabines.° We'll rob
'em of their women, only we'll return the punks again when we   120
have used them.

JACOMO For heaven's sake, hold.

DON JOHN Sirrah, no more. Do as we do: ravish, rascal, or, by my
sword, I'll cut thee into so many pieces, it shall pose an arithmetician
to sum up the fractions of thy body.   125

JACOMO I ravish! O good sir! My courage lies not that way. Alas, I—I
am almost famished. I have not eat today.

DON JOHN Sirrah, by heaven do as I bid thee, or thou shalt never eat
again. Shall I keep a rascal for a cipher?°

JACOMO O what will become of me? I must do it.   130

DON JOHN Come on, rogue, fall on.

DON ANTONIO Which are you for?

DON JOHN 'Tis all one. I am not in love but in lust, and to such a one
a bellyful's a bellyful, and there's an end on't.

FIRST SHEPHERDESS What means this violence?   135

SECOND SHEPHERDESS O! Heaven protect us.

JACOMO Well, I must have one too. If I be hanged, I had as good be
hanged for something.

[Shepherds advance menacingly]

DON LOPEZ Rogues, come not on; we'll be in your guts.

> *Don John, Don Lopez, Don Antonio, and Jacomo run off with
> a woman. [Three or four Shepherds follow, brandishing
> weapons]*

ALL SHEPHERDESSES (*cry out*) Help, help.   140

> *Exeunt Shepherdesses*

FIRST SHEPHERD [*looking after the retreating figures*] What devils are
these?

> *Three or four Shepherds return with Jacomo*

Here's one rogue. Have we caught you, sir? We'll cool your courage.

JACOMO Am I taken prisoner? I shall be kept as an honourable
hostage, at least.   145

SECOND SHEPHERD Where are these villains, these ravishers?

JACOMO Why, you need not keep such a stir, gentlemen. You will have
all your women again, and no harm done. Let me go; I'll fetch 'em
to you.

FIRST SHEPHERD No, you libidinous swine. We'll revenge the rapes   150
on you.

JACOMO Good, kind, civil people, pass this by. 'Tis true, my master's
a very Tarquin,° but I ne'er attempted to ravish before.

SECOND SHEPHERD I'll secure you from ever doing of it again.
Where's your knife?   155

JACOMO Heaven! What do you mean? O spare me! I am unprepared;
let me be confessed.

FIRST SHEPHERD We will not kill you; we'll but geld you. Are you so
hot,° sir?

JACOMO O bloody villains! Have a care. 'Tis not the season for that— 160
the sign's in Scorpio.°

SECOND SHEPHERD Down with him.

JACOMO O help, help! Murder, murder! Have a care what you do; I
am the last of all my race. Will you destroy a whole stock and take
away my representers° of my family?   165

FIRST SHEPHERD There shall be no more of the breed of you.

JACOMO I am of an ancient family. Will you cut off all hopes of a son
and heir? Help, help! Master, Don John! Oh-h-h!

> *Enter Don John, Don Lopez, and Don Antonio*

DON JOHN How now, rogues? Do you abuse my man?

> [*Shepherds flee*]

JACOMO O sir, this is the first good thing you ever did. If you had not   170
come just in the nick, I had lost my manhood.

DON ANTONIO 'Tis no matter, for the use you make on't.

DON LOPEZ But come; let's now to supper.

JACOMO Come on. I am almost starved.

> *Exeunt Don John, Don Antonio, Don Lopez, and Jacomo.*
> *Shepherds return*

FIRST SHEPHERD Let's not complain, but dog the rogues, and, when   175
we have housed 'em,° we will to the next magistrate and beg his
power to apprehend 'em.

> *Exeunt*

4.3

> *A church, with the statue of Don Pedro on horseback in it*

> [*Enter Don John, Jacomo, Don Antonio, and Don Lopez*]

DON JOHN Let's in and see this church.

JACOMO Is this a time to see churches? But let me see, whose statue's
this? O heaven! This is Don Pedro's, whom you murdered at Seville.

DON JOHN Say you so? Read the inscription.

JACOMO [*reads*] 'Here lies Don Pedro, governor of Seville, barbar-   5
ously murdered by that impious villain, Don John, 'gainst whom
his innocent blood cries still for vengeance'.

DON JOHN Let it cry on. [*To the statue*] Art thou there i' faith? Yes, I
killed thee, and would do't again upon the same occasion. Jacomo,
invite him to supper.   10

JACOMO What, a statue! Invite a statue to supper? Ha, ha. Can marble
eat?

DON JOHN I say, rascal, tell him I would have him sup with me.

JACOMO Ha, ha, ha! Who the devil put this whimsy into your head?
Ha, ha, ha! Invite a statue to supper?   15

DON JOHN I shall spoil your mirth, sirrah. I will have it done.

JACOMO Why, 'tis impossible. Would you have me such a coxcomb—
invite marble to eat? Ha, ha, ha.

> *Jacomo goes several times towards the statue and returns*
> *laughing*

Good Mr Statue, if it shall please your worship, my master desires
you to make collation with him presently.   20

> *The statue nods his head. Jacomo falls down and roars*

O I am dead! Oh-h-h!

DON JOHN The statue nods its head. 'Tis odd.

DON ANTONIO 'Tis wonderful.

DON LOPEZ I am amazed.

JACOMO O I cannot stir! Help, help.   25

DON JOHN Well, governor, come take part of a collation with me. 'Tis
    by this time ready. Make haste; 'tis I invite you.

> *The statue nods again*

    Say you so? Come on, let's set all things in order quickly.

JACOMO O fly, fly.

DON ANTONIO This is prodigious.   30

> *Exeunt*

4.4

*A dining-room. A table spread, Servants setting on wine
and meat*

[*Enter Don John, Don Antonio, Don Lopez, and
Jacomo*]

DON JOHN Come, our meat is ready; let's sit. Pox on this foolish
    statue. It puzzles me to know the reason on't. [*To Jacomo*] Sirrah,
    I'll give you leave to sit.

DON ANTONIO Let's eat. Ne'er think on't.

JACOMO Ay, come, let's eat. I am too hungry now to think on the   5
    fright.

> *Jacomo eats greedily*

DON JOHN This is excellent meat. How the rogue eats. You'll choke
    yourself.

JACOMO I warrant you, look to yourself.°

DON ANTONIO Why, Jacomo, is the devil in you?   10

JACOMO No, no. If he be, 'tis a hungry devil.

DON LOPEZ Will you not drink?

JACOMO I'll lay a good foundation first.

DON JOHN The rascal eats like a cannibal.

JACOMO Ay, 'tis no matter for that.   15

DON JOHN Some wine, sirrah.

JACOMO [*pushes bottle back*] There, sir, take it; I am in haste.

DON ANTONIO 'Sdeath, the fool will be strangled.

JACOMO The fool knows what he does.

DON JOHN [*raising a glass*] Here's to Don Pedro's ghost; he should   20
    have been welcome.

JACOMO O name him not.

DON LOPEZ The rascal is afraid of you after death.

JACOMO (*almost choked*) Oh-h! Some wine; give me some wine.

DON ANTONIO Take it.   25

JACOMO So, now 'tis down.

DON ANTONIO Are you not satisfied yet?

JACOMO Peace, peace, I have but just begun.
> *One knocks hard at the door*

Who's there? Come in; I am very busy.

DON JOHN [*to Jacomo*] Rise and do your duty.   30
> *Knocks again*

JACOMO But one morsel more; I come. [*Hears more knocking*] What a
pox, are you mad?
> *Enter the Ghost* [*of Don Pedro*]

O the devil, the devil.

DON JOHN Ha! It is the ghost; let's rise and receive him.

DON ANTONIO I am amazed.   35

DON LOPEZ Not frighted, are you?

DON ANTONIO I scorn the thoughts of fear.
> *They salute° the Ghost*

DON JOHN Come governor, you are welcome. Sit there. If we had
thought you would have come, we would have stayed for you.
> *The Ghost sits*

[*To Jacomo*] But come on, sirrah, give me some wine.   40

JACOMO O, I am dead! What shall I do? I dare not come near you.

DON JOHN Come rascal, or I'll cut your throat.

JACOMO I come, I come. (*Fills wine. His hand trembles*) Oh-h!

DON JOHN Why do you tremble, rascal? Hold it steadily.

JACOMO O! I cannot.   45
> *Jacomo snatches meat from the table and runs aside*

DON JOHN [*raises glass*] Here, governor; your health. [*Drinks*]
Friends, put it about.° Here's excellent meat; taste of this ragout. If
you had had a body of flesh, I would have given you *cher entire*,° but
the women care not for marble. Come, I'll help you. Come, eat and
let old quarrels be forgotten.   50

GHOST I come not here to take repast with you;
Heaven has permitted me to animate
This marble body, and I come to warn
You of that vengeance is in store for you,
If you amend not your pernicious lives.   55

JACOMO O heaven!

DON ANTONIO What? Are you come to preach to us?

DON LOPEZ Keep your harangues for fools that will believe 'em.

DON JOHN We are too much confirmed. Pox o' this dry discourse;
    give me some wine. Come, here's to your mistress. You had one   60
    when you were living, not forgetting your sweet sister. [*To Jacomo*]
    Sirrah, more wine.

JACOMO Ay, sir. Good sir, do not provoke the ghost. His marble fists
    may fly about your ears and knock your brains out.

DON JOHN Peace, fool.   65

GHOST Tremble, you impious wretches and repent.
    Behold, the powers of hell wait for you.
       Devils rise°

JACOMO O! I will steal from hence. O the devil!

DON JOHN Sirrah, stir not. By heaven, I'll use thee worse than devils
    can do. Come near, coward.   70

JACOMO O I dare not stir. What will become of me?

DON JOHN Come sirrah, eat.

JACOMO O sir, my appetite is satisfied.

DON JOHN Drink, dog, the ghost's health. Rogue, do't, or I'll run my
    sword down your throat.   75

JACOMO Oh-h! Here, Mr Statue, your health. [*Drinks*]

DON JOHN Now, rascal, sing to entertain him.

JACOMO Sing, quoth he! O I have lost my voice; I cannot be merry in
    such company. Sing?

DON ANTONIO Who are these with ugly shapes?   80

DON LOPEZ Their manner of appearing is something strange.

GHOST They're devils that wait for such hard impious men. They're
    heaven's instruments of eternal vengeance.

DON JOHN Are they some of your retinue? Devils, say you? I am sorry
    I have no burnt brandy to treat 'em with; that's drink fit for devils.°   85
       The devils sink
    Ha! They vanish.

GHOST Cannot the fear of hell's eternal tortures
    Change the horrid course of your abandoned lives?
    Think on those fires, those everlasting fires,
    That shall, without consuming, burn you ever.   90

DON JOHN Dreams, dreams too slight to lose my pleasure for.
    In spite of all you say, I will go on
    Till I have surfeited on all delights.
    Youth is a fruit that can but once be gathered,
    And I'll enjoy it to the full.   95

DON ANTONIO Let's push it on; nature chalks out the way that we should follow.

DON LOPEZ 'Tis her fault if we do what we should not. Let's on. Here's a brimmer to our leader's health.

JACOMO [*aside*] What hellish fiends are these! 100

DON JOHN Let me tell you, 'tis something ill-bred to rail at your host that treats you civilly. You have not yet forgot your quarrel to me.

GHOST 'Tis for your good. By me, heaven warns you of its wrath and gives you a longer time for your repentance. I invite you this night to a repast of mine. 105

DON JOHN Where?

GHOST At my tomb.

DON ANTONIO What time?

GHOST At dead of night.

DON JOHN We'll come. 110

GHOST Fail not.

DON LOPEZ I warrant you.

GHOST Farewell, and think upon your lost condition.

DON JOHN Farewell, governor. I'll see what treat you'll give us.

DON ANTONIO AND DON LOPEZ And I. 115

JACOMO That will not I. Pox on him, I have had enough of his company; I shall not recover it this week. If I eat with such a host, I'll be hanged.

DON JOHN If you do not, by heaven you shall be hanged.

JACOMO Whither will your lewdness carry me? I do not care for having 120 a ghost for my landlord. Will not these miracles do good upon you?

DON JOHN There's nothing happens but by natural causes,
Which in unusual things fools cannot find,
And then they style 'em miracles. But no accident
Can alter me from what I am by nature. 125
Were there—
　　　　Legions of ghosts and devils in my way,
　　　　One moment in my course of pleasure I'd not stay.
Exeunt

5.1

[A street in Seville]

Enter Jacomo, with back, breast, and headpiece°

JACOMO Well, this damned master of mine will not part with me; and
we must fight five or six times a day, one day with another,° that's
certain. Therefore thou art wise, honest Jacomo, to arm thyself, I
take it. Sa-sa-sa! Methinks I am very valiant on the sudden. Sa-sa-
sa! Hah! There I have you! Paph—have at you. Hah! There I have   5
you through. That was a fine thrust in tierce.° Hah! Death! What
noise is that?

Enter Don John

DON JOHN How now, sirrah, what are you doing?

JACOMO Nothing but practising to run people through the bodies,
that's all. For I know somebody's throat must be cut before   10
midnight.

DON JOHN In armour too! Why, that cannot help you, you are such a
cowardly fool. Fear will betray you faster within, than that can
defend you without.

JACOMO I fear nobody breathing, I. Nothing can terrify me but the   15
devilish ghost. Ha! Who's that coming? O heaven!

DON JOHN Is this your courage? You are preparing for flight before an
enemy appears.

JACOMO No, no, Sir, not I. I only leapt back to put myself upon my
guard. [*Sings*] *Fa, la, la—*   20

Enter Don Lopez and Don Antonio

DON JOHN Whom have we here?

JACOMO O where, where! Who are they?

DON JOHN O my friends! Where have you been?

DON ANTONIO We went to view the stately nunnery hard by and have
been chatting with the poor sanctified fools till it's dark. We have 25
been chaffering for nun's flesh.

DON LOPEZ There I made such a discovery. If you do not assist me, I
am ruined forever. Don Bernardo's sister, whom I fell in love with
in Seville, is this day placed there for probation;° and if you cannot
advise me to some way or other of getting her out for some present   30
occasion I have for her, I am a lost man, that's certain.

DON ANTONIO The business is difficult, and we resolve to manage it
in council.

JACOMO [*aside*] Now will they bring me into some wicked occasion or
other of showing my prowess. A pox on 'em.   35

DON JOHN Have you so long followed my fortunes to boggle at difficulty upon so honourable an occasion? Besides, here is no
difficulty.

DON LOPEZ No? The walls are so high and the nunnery so strongly
fortified, 'twill be impossible to do it by force. We must find some   40
stratagem.

DON JOHN The stratagem is soon found out.

DON ANTONIO As how, Don John?

DON JOHN Why, I will set fire on the nunnery: fire the hive and the
drones must out, or be burnt within. Then may you with ease,   45
under pretence of succour, take whom you will.

DON LOPEZ 'Tis a gallant design.

DON ANTONIO I long to be about it. Well, Don, thou art the bravest
fellow breathing.

JACOMO Gentlemen, pray what became of that brave fellow that fired   50
the temple at Ephesus?° Was he not hanged, gentlemen? Hum?

DON ANTONIO We are his rivals, fool; and who would not suffer for
so brave an action?

DON JOHN He's a scoundrel and a poltroon that would not have his
death for his fame.   55

DON LOPEZ That he is, a damned son of a whore and not fit to drink
with.

JACOMO 'Tis a rare thing to be a martyr for the devil. But what good
will infamy do you when you are dead? When honour is nothing
but a vapour to you while you are living? For my part, I'd not be   60
hanged to be Alexander the Great.°

DON ANTONIO What a phlegmatic dull rascal is that, who has no
ambition in him.

JACOMO Ambition! What, to be hanged? Besides, what's the intrinsic
value of honour when a man is underground? Let 'em but call me   65
honest Jacomo, as I am while I live; and let 'em call me, when I am
dead, Don John, if they will.

DON JOHN Villain, dare you profane my name?

JACOMO Hold, sir; think what you do. You cannot hurt me; my arms
are pistol-proof.   70

    Enter a Servant

SERVANT I come to give you notice of an approaching danger. You
must fly. An officer with some shepherds have found you were at
our house, and are come to apprehend you for some outrage you

have committed. I came to give you notice, knowing our family has
a great respect for you.   75

DON JOHN Yes, I know your family has a great respect for me, for I
have lain with everyone in it but thee and thy master.

JACOMO Why, look you now, I thought what 'twould come to. Fly, sir,
fly. The darkness of the night will help us. Come, I'll lead the way.

DON JOHN Stay, sirrah. You shall have one occasion more of showing 80
your valour.

DON ANTONIO Did ever any knight errant fly that was so well
appointed?

DON LOPEZ No. You shall stay and get honour, Jacomo.

JACOMO Pox of honour. I am content with the stock I have already.   85

DON JOHN You are easily satisfied. But now let's fire the nunnery.

DON ANTONIO Come on.

DON LOPEZ I long to be at it.

JACOMO O Jacomo! Thy life is not worth a piece of eight.° 'Tis in
vain to dissuade 'em, sir. I will never trouble you with another   90
request if you'll be graciously pleased to leave me out of this
adventure.

DON JOHN Well, you have your desire.

JACOMO A thousand thanks. And when I see you again, I will be
humbly content with a halter.   95

DON JOHN But, do you hear, fool? Stand sentinel here, and if
anything happens extraordinary, give us notice of it.

JACOMO O good sir! What do you mean? That's as bad as going with
you.

DON JOHN Let me find you here when I come again, or you are a dead   100
man.

    Exeunt Don John, Don Lopez, and Don Antonio

JACOMO I am sure I am a dead man if you find me here. But would
my armour were off now, that I might run the lighter. Night assist
me. Heaven! What noise is that? To be left alone in the dark and
fear ghosts and devils is very horrible.   105

    Enter Officer, Guards, and Shepherds

But, O, who are these?

FIRST SHEPHERD We are thus far right. The ravishers went this way.

SECOND SHEPHERD For heaven's sake, take 'em dead or alive. Such
desperate villains ne'er were seen.

JACOMO [*aside*] So, if I be catched, I shall be hanged; if not, I shall be 110
killed. 'Tis very fine. These are the shepherds. I'll hide myself.

    [*He stands close against the wall*]

FIRST SHEPHERD If we catch the rogues, we will broil 'em alive. No death can be painful enough for such wretches.

JACOMO [*aside*] O bloody-minded men!

SECOND SHEPHERD O impious vile wretches! That we had you in our clutches! Open your dark-lantern,° and let's search for 'em.

JACOMO [*aside*] What will become of me? My armour will not do now.

FIRST SHEPHERD Thus far we hunted them upon a good scent, but now we are at a fault.°

JACOMO [*aside*] Let me see. I have one trick left. I have a disguise will fright the devil.

SECOND SHEPHERD They must be hereabouts.

JACOMO I'll in amongst them, and certainly this will fright 'em.

FIRST SHEPHERD O heaven! What horrid object's this?

JACOMO The devil.

SECOND SHEPHERD O fly, fly! The devil, the devil. Fly—
 Exeunt Shepherds, [Officer, and Guards], frighted

JACOMO Farewell, good gentlemen. This is the first time my face e'er did me good. But I'll not stay, I take it. Yet whither shall I fly? O! What noise is that? I am in the dark, in a strange place too; what will follow? There lie.° O my arms! Ha! Who's there? Let me go this way—O the ghost! The ghost! Gad forgive me, 'twas nothing but my fear.
 A noise within: 'Fire, fire! The nunnery's on fire!'
O vile wretches! They have done the deed. There is no flying. Now the place will be full of people and wicked lights that will discover me if I fly.

WITHIN Fire, fire, fire! The nunnery's on fire! Help, help.
 Several people cross the stage crying 'fire'

JACOMO What shall I do? There's no way but one: I'll go with the crowd. Fire, fire! Murder! Help, help! Fire, fire—
 More people cross the stage. Jacomo runs with them. Enter Don John, Don Antonio, Don Lopez, four Nuns

DON JOHN Fear not, ladies; we'll protect you.

FIRST NUN Our sex and habits will protect us.

DON LOPEZ Not enough. We will protect you better.

FIRST NUN Pray leave us. We must not consort with men.

DON ANTONIO What? Would you run into the fire to avoid mankind? You are zealous, ladies, indeed.

DON JOHN Come, ladies, walk with us. We'll put you in a place of safety.

FIRST NUN We'll go no further. We are safe enough. Be gone and help
  to quench the fire.

DON JOHN We have another fire to quench; come along with us.

DON LOPEZ Ay, come; you must go.   150

DON ANTONIO Come along; we know what's good for you. [*Handles
  the Nuns roughly*] You must go with us.

FIRST NUN Heaven! What violence is this? What impious men are
  these? Help, help!

> *All the Nuns cry, 'Help!' Enter Flavia and Clara, [dressed as]*
> *probationers°*

FLAVIA Here are the bloody villains, the causes of our misery.   155

CLARA Inhuman butchers! Now we'll have your lives.

DON JOHN [*noticing them*] Ha! Here are a brace of my wives. If you
  have a mind to this fool, take her betwixt you. For my part, I'll have
  my own. Come, wives, along with me. We must consummate, my
  spouses, we must consummate.   160

CLARA What monsters are these?

ALL NUNS Help, help!

DON ANTONIO 'Sdeath! These foolish women are their own enemies.

DON LOPEZ Here are so many people, if they cry out more, they'll
  interrupt us in our brave design.   165

DON JOHN I warrant you, when they cry out, let us out-noise 'em.
  Come, women, you must go along with us.

FIRST NUN Heaven! What shall we do? Help, help!

DON JOHN Help, help! Fire, fire, fire!

DON LOPEZ AND DON ANTONIO Help, help!   170

> *Don John, Don Antonio, and Don Lopez hale the women by the*
> *hands, who still cry out. Enter several people, crying out 'Fire!',*
> *Jacomo in the rear*

JACOMO Fire, fire, fire! Help, help! 'Sdeath! Here's my master.

DON JOHN Sirrah, come along with me. I have use of you.

JACOMO I am caught.

DON JOHN Here sirrah, take one of my wives and force her after me.
  Do you refuse, villain?   175

> *Enter Shepherds, with Officer and Guards*

NUNS Help, help! Good people, help! Rescue us from these villains.

FIRST SHEPHERD Who are you, committing violence on women?

SECOND SHEPHERD Heavens! They are the villains we seek for.

JACOMO Where is my armour now? O my armour.

OFFICER Fall on.   180

*Don John, Don Antonio, Don Lopez, and Jacomo fight with the
Officer, Guards, and Shepherds. The women fly. Jacomo falls
down as killed. Two Shepherds and the Officer are killed.*

DON JOHN Say you so, rogues?

DON LOPEZ So, the field's our own.

DON JOHN But a pox on't. We have bought a victory too dear—we
have lost the women.

DON ANTONIO We'll find 'em again. But poor Jacomo's killed. 185

JACOMO (*aside*) That's a lie.

DON LOPEZ 'Faith, let's carry off our dead.

DON JOHN Agreed. We'll bury him in the church. While the ghost
treats us, we'll treat the worms with the body of a rascal.

JACOMO (*aside*) Not yet a while. 190

DON LOPEZ Come, let's take away the fool.

JACOMO [*rising*] No, the fool can take up himself. 'Sdeath, you resolve
not to let me alone, dead or alive. [*Sees the bodies*] Here are more
murders. O!

DON LOPEZ O counterfeiting rascal! Are you alive? 195
          The clock strikes twelve

DON ANTONIO The clock strikes twelve.

DON JOHN 'Slife, our time's come; we must to the tomb. I would not
break my word with the ghost for a thousand doubloons.

JACOMO Nor I keep it for ten times the money.

DON JOHN But you shall keep your word, sir. 200

JACOMO Sir, I am resolved to fast tonight; 'tis a vigil. Besides, I care
not for eating in such base company.

OFFSTAGE Follow, follow, follow.

DON LOPEZ D'hear that noise? The remaining rogues have raised the
mobile° and are coming upon us. 205

JACOMO Oh! Let's fly, fly! What will become of me?

DON ANTONIO Let's to the church and give the rogues the go-by.

DON JOHN Come on. Since 'tis my time, and I have promised the
governor, I'll go. You had best stay, sirrah, and be taken.

JACOMO No. Now I must go to the church whether I will or no. Away, 210
away, fly!

          *Exeunt Don John, Don Antonio, Don Lopez, and Jacomo. Enter
          two Shepherds with a great rabble*

ALL Here they went. Follow, follow.
          Exeunt

5.2

The church. The statue of Don Pedro on horseback

*On each side of the church, the ghosts of Don John [senior],
Maria, Don Francisco, Leonora, Flora, Maria's Brother, and
others, with torches in their hands*

Enter Don John, Don Antonio, Don Lopez, and Jacomo

JACOMO Good sir, let's go no farther. Look what horrid attendants
are here. This wicked ghost has no good meaning in him.

DON JOHN He resolves to treat us in state. I think he has robbed all
the graves hereabouts of their dead to wait upon us.

DON ANTONIO I see no entertainment prepared.   5

DON LOPEZ He has had the manners to light off his horse and
entertain us.

DON JOHN He would not sure be so ill-bred to make us wait on him
on foot.

JACOMO Pox on his breeding. I shall die with fear. I had as good have   10
been taken and hanged. What horror seizes me!

DON JOHN Well, governor, you see we are as good as our words.

DON ANTONIO Where's your collation?

DON LOPEZ Bid some of your attendants give us some wine.
    Ghost descends°

STATUE Have you not yet thought on your lost condition?   15
Here are the ghosts of some whom you have murdered,
That cry for vengeance on you.

DON JOHN[SENIOR'S] GHOST Repent, repent of all your horrid crimes.
Monsters, repent, or hell will swallow you.

DON JOHN That's my old man's voice. D'hear old gentleman, you   20
talk idly.

JACOMO I do repent. O spare me! (*Kneels*) I do repent of all my sins,
but especially of following this wicked wretch.

DON ANTONIO (*kicks him*) Away, fool.

DON FRANCISCO'S GHOST My blood cries out upon thee, barbarous   25
wretch.

DON JOHN That's my host, Francisco. 'Faith, thou wert a good
honest blockhead, that's the truth on't.

FLORA'S GHOST Thou shalt not escape vengeance for all thy crimes.

DON JOHN What fool's that? I am not acquainted with her.   30

LEONORA'S GHOST In time lay hold on mercy and repent.

DON JOHN That was Leonora, a good-natured, silly wench, something too loving, that was all her fault.

MARIA'S GHOST Villain, this is the last moment of thy life,
And thou in flames eternally shalt howl. 35

DON JOHN Thou liest. This is the young, hot-headed fool we killed at Francisco's. Pox on him, he disappointed me in my design upon the daughters. Would thou wert alive again, that I might kill thee once more.

DON LOPEZ No more of this old foolish stuff. Give us some wine to begin with. 40

DON ANTONIO Ay, give us some wine, governor.

DON JOHN What, do you think to treat us thus? I offered you a better entertainment. Prithee trouble us no more, but bid some of your attendants give us some wine. I'll drink to you and all the good company. 45

STATUE Give 'em the liquor they have most delighted in.

Two of the ghosts go out and bring four glasses full of blood, then give 'em to Don John, Don Antonio, and Don Lopez

DON LOPEZ This is something.

DON JOHN This is civil.

DON LOPEZ I hope a good dessert will follow. 50

Ghost offers a glass to Jacomo, who runs around Don John, Don Antonio, and Don Lopez, roaring

JACOMO Are you stark distracted? Will you drink of that liquor? Oh-h! What d'you mean? Good sweet ghost, forbear your civility. O I am not dry, I thank you.

DON JOHN Give it me. Here, take it, sirrah.

JACOMO By no means, sir. I never drink between meals. O, sir— 55

DON JOHN Take it, rascal.

JACOMO O heavens!

DON JOHN Now governor, your health. 'Tis the reddest drink I ever saw.

DON LOPEZ [*spits*] Ha! Pah! 'Tis blood. 60

DON ANTONIO [*spits*] Pah! It is.

JACOMO O I'll have none of it.

Don Lopez and Don Antonio throw the glasses down

DON JOHN 'Sdeath, do you mean to affront us?

STATUE 'Tis fit for such bloodthirsty wretches.

DON JOHN Do you upbraid me with my killing of you? I did it and would do it again. I'd fight with all your family one by one, and cut 65

off root and branch to enjoy your sister. But will you treat us yet no
otherwise?

STATUE Yes, I will, ye impious wretches.

    A flourish°

DON LOPEZ What's here? Music to treat us with? 70

DON ANTONIO There is some pleasure in this.

SONG OF DEVILS

FIRST DEVIL   *Prepare, prepare, new guests draw near,*
        And on the brink of hell appear.

SECOND DEVIL   *Kindle fresh flames of sulphur there.* 75
        Assemble all ye fiends,
        Wait for the dreadful ends
    Of impious men, who far excel
        All th' inhabitants of hell.

CHORUS OF DEVILS 80

    Let 'em come, let 'em come,
    To an eternal dreadful doom,
    Let 'em come, let 'em come.

THIRD DEVIL   *In mischiefs they have all the damned outdone;*
    Here they shall weep, and shall unpitied groan, 85
    Here they shall howl, and make eternal moan.

FIRST DEVIL   *By blood and lust they have deserved so well,*
    That they shall feel the hottest flames of hell.

SECOND DEVIL   *In vain they shall here their past mischiefs bewail,*
    In exquisite torments that never shall fail. 90

THIRD DEVIL   *Eternal darkness they shall find,*
        And them eternal chains shall bind
        To infinite pain of sense and mind.

CHORUS OF ALL

    Let 'em come, etc. 95

STATUE Will you not relent and feel remorse?

DON JOHN Couldst thou bestow another heart on me, I might; but
with this heart I have, I cannot.

DON LOPEZ These things are prodigious.

DON ANTONIO I have a kind of grudging to relent, but something 100
holds me back.

DON LOPEZ If we could, 'tis now too late. I will not.

DON ANTONIO We defy thee.

STATUE Perish, ye impious wretches; go and find
    The punishments laid up in store for you.   105
        It thunders. Don Lopez and Don Antonio are swallowed up
    Behold their dreadful fates, and know that thy last moment's come.

DON JOHN Think not to fright me, foolish ghost. I'll break your
    marble body in pieces and pull down your horse.

JACOMO If fear has left me my strength, I'll steal away.
        Exit Jacomo

DON JOHN These things I see with wonder, but no fear.   110
    Were all the elements to be confounded,
    And shuffled all into their former chaos;°
    Were seas of sulphur flaming round about me,
    And all mankind roaring within those fires,
    I could not fear or feel the least remorse.   115
    To the last instant, I would dare thy power.
    Here I stand firm, and all thy threats contemn;
    Thy murderer stands here; now do thy worst.
        It thunders and lightens. The devils descend and sink with Don
        John, who is covered with a cloud of fire as he sinks

STATUE Thus perish all
    Those men, who by their words and actions dare   120
    Against the will and power of heaven declare.
    Scene shuts°

Epilogue

Spoken by Jacomo

Through all the perils of the play I've run,
But know not how your fury I may shun;
I'm in new dangers now to be undone.
I had but one fierce master there,
But I have many cruel tyrants here,   5
Who do most bloodily my life pursue;
Who takes my livelihood, may take that too.
'Gainst little players you great factions raise,
Make solemn leagues and covenants against plays.°
We, who by no allies assisted are,   10
Against the great confederates must make war.
You need not strive our province to o'er-run;
By our own stratagems we are undone.
We've laid out all our pains, nay wealth, for you,
And yet, hard-hearted men, all will not do.   15
'Tis not your judgements sway, for you can be
Pleased with damned plays (as heart can wish to see).
'Oons, we do what we can; what would you more?
Why do you come, and rant, and damn, and roar?
'Sdeath, what a devil would you have us do?   20
Each take a prison, and there humbly sue,
Angling for single money with a shoe.°
What, will you be Don Johns? Have you no remorse?
Farewell, then, bloody men, and take your course.
Yet stay: 25
If you'll be civil, we will treat of peace,
And th' articles o' th' treaty shall be these.
'First, to the men of wit we all submit;
The rest shall swagger too within the pit,°
And may roar out their little or no wit.   30
But do not swear so loud to fright the city,°
Who neither care for wicked men, nor witty;
They start at ills they do not like to do,
But shall in shops be wickeder than you.
Next, you'll no more be troubled with machines.°   35

Item, you shall appear behind our scenes,°
And there make love with the sweet chink of guineas,°
The unresisted eloquence of ninnies.
Some of our women shall be kind to you,
And promise free ingress and egress too.°   40
But if the faces which we have won't do,
We will find out some of sixteen for you.
We will be civil when nought else will win ye;
We will new bait our Trap, and that will bring ye.'
Come, faith, let all old breaches now be healed,   45
And the said articles shall be signed and sealed.

THE MAN OF MODE; OR, SIR FOPLING FLUTTER

SIR GEORGE ETHEREGE

To Her Royal Highness the Duchess°

Madam,

Poets, however they may be modest otherwise, have always too good an opinion of what they write. The world, when it sees this play dedicated to your royal highness, will conclude I have more than my 5 share of that vanity. But I hope the honour I have of belonging to you will excuse my presumption. 'Tis the first thing I have produced in your service, and my duty obliges me to what my choice durst not else have aspired.

I am very sensible, madam, how much it is beholding to your indul- 10 gence for the success it had in the acting,° and your protection will be no less fortunate to it in the printing; for all are so ambitious of making their court to you, that none can be severe to what you are pleased to favour.

This universal submission and respect is due to the greatness of 15 your rank and birth, but you have other illustrious qualities which are much more engaging. Those would but dazzle, did not these really charm the eyes and understandings of all who have the happiness to approach you.

Authors on these occasions are never wanting to publish a particu- 20 lar° of their patron's virtues and perfections, but your Royal High-ness's are so eminently known, that did I follow their examples, I should but paint those wonders here of which every one already has the idea in his mind. Besides, I do not think it proper to aim at that in prose which is so glorious a subject for verse; in which hereafter if I 25 show more zeal than skill, it will not grieve me much, since I less passionately desire to be esteemed a poet than to be thought,

> Madam,
>   Your royal highness's most humble,
>   most obedient, and most faithful servant, 30
>   George Etherege

THE CHARACTERS OF THE PLAY°

Mr Dorimant
Mr Medley
Old Bellair ⎱ Gentlemen
Bellair
Sir Fopling Flutter

Lady Townley
Emilia
Mrs Loveit ⎱ Gentlewomen
Bellinda
Lady Woodvill and Harriet, her daughter

Pert and Busy   Waiting Women

A Shoemaker
An Orange-Woman
Three Slovenly Bullies
Two Chairmen
Mr Smirk, a parson
Handy, a *valet de chambre*
Pages, footmen, &c.

Prologue

by Sir Car Scroope,° Baronet

Like dancers on the ropes, poor poets fare:°
Most perish young, the rest in danger are.
This, one would think, should make our author wary,
But gamester-like the giddy fools miscarry.
A lucky hand or two so tempts 'em on,   5
They cannot leave off play till they're undone.°
With modest fears a muse does first begin,
Like a young wench newly enticed to sin;
But, tickled once with praise by her good will,°
The wanton fool would never more lie still.   10
'Tis an old mistress you'll meet here tonight,
Whose charms you once have looked on with delight.
But now of late such dirty drabs have known ye,°
A muse o' th' better sort's ashamed to own you.
Nature well drawn and wit must now give place   15
To gaudy nonsense and to dull grimace;
Nor is it strange that you should like so much
That kind of wit, for most of yours is such.
But I'm afraid that while to France we go,°
To bring you home fine dresses, dance, and show,   20
The stage like you will but more foppish grow.
Of foreign wares why should we fetch the scum,
When we can be so richly served at home?
For heaven be thanked 'tis not so wise an age,
But your own follies may supply the stage.°   25
Though often ploughed, there's no great fear the soil
Should barren grow by the too frequent toil,
While at your doors are to be daily found
Such loads of dunghill to manure the ground.
'Tis by your follies that we players thrive,   30
As the physicians by diseases live.
And as each year some new distemper reigns,
Whose friendly poison helps to increase their gains,
So among you, there starts up every day
Some new unheard of fool for us to play.   35

Then for your own sakes be not too severe,
Nor what you all admire at home, damn here.
Since each is fond of his own ugly face,
Why should you, when we hold it, break the glass?

1.1

A dressing room, a table covered with a toilet, clothes laid ready.°

Enter Dorimant in his gown and slippers, with a note in his hand made up, repeating verses.

DORIMANT 'Now for some ages had the pride of Spain,
      Made the Sun shine on half the world in vain.'°

(*Then looking on the note*) 'For Mrs Loveit.' What a dull, insipid thing is a billet-doux written in cold blood after the heat of the business is over! It is a tax upon good nature which I have here been labouring to pay and have done it, but with as much regret as ever 5
fanatic° paid the Royal Aid or church duties.° 'Twill have the same fate I know that all my notes to her have had of late—'twill not be thought kind enough. Faith, women are i' the right when they jealously examine our letters, for in them we always first discover 10
our decay of passion. Hey! Who waits?°

    Enter Handy

HANDY Sir.

DORIMANT Call a footman.

HANDY None of 'em are come yet.

DORIMANT Dogs! Will they ever lie snoring abed till noon. 15

HANDY 'Tis all one, sir. If they're up, you indulge 'em so, they're ever poaching° after whores all the morning.

DORIMANT Take notice henceforward who's wanting in his duty. The next clap he gets, he shall rot for an example. What vermin are those chattering without? 20

HANDY Foggy° Nan, the orange-woman, and swearing Tom, the shoemaker.

DORIMANT Go, call in that overgrown jade with the flasket° of guts before her. Fruit is refreshing in a morning.

    Exit Handy

        'It is not that I love you less 25
        Than when before your feet I lay.'°

    Enter Orange-Woman [and Handy]

How now double-tripe!° What news do you bring?

ORANGE-WOMAN News! Here's the best fruit has come to town t' year. Gad, I was up before four a clock this morning and bought all the choice i' the market. 30

DORIMANT The nasty refuse of your shop.

ORANGE-WOMAN You need not make mouths at it, I assure you. 'Tis all culled° ware.

DORIMANT The citizens buy better on a holiday in their walk to Tottenham.°

ORANGE-WOMAN Good or bad, 'tis all one. I never knew you commend anything. Lord, would the ladies had heard you talk of 'em as I have done. (*Sets down the fruit*) Here, bid your man give me an angel.°

DORIMANT [*to Handy*] Give the bawd her fruit again.

ORANGE-WOMAN Well, on my conscience, there never was the like of you. God's my life, I had almost forgot to tell you, there is a young gentlewoman lately come to town with her mother that is so taken with you.

DORIMANT Is she handsome?

ORANGE-WOMAN Nay, Gad, there are few finer women, I tell you but so, and a hugeous fortune they say. Here, eat this peach; it comes from the stone.° 'Tis better than any Newington° y' have tasted.

DORIMANT (*taking the peach*) This fine woman, I'll lay my life, is some awkward, ill-fashioned country toad, who, not having above four dozen of black hairs on her head, has adorned her baldness with a large white fruz,° that she may look sparkishly° in the forefront of the King's box at an old play.°

ORANGE-WOMAN Gad, you'd change your note quickly if you did but see her.

DORIMANT How came she to know me?

ORANGE-WOMAN She saw you yesterday at the Change.° She told me you came and fooled with the woman at the next shop.

DORIMANT I remember there was a mask° observed me indeed. Fooled, did she say?

ORANGE-WOMAN Ay, I vow she told me twenty things you said too, and acted with head and with her body so like you.

            Enter Medley

MEDLEY Dorimant, my life, my joy, my darling sin! How dost thou?

ORANGE-WOMAN Lord, what a filthy trick these men have got of kissing one another!° (*She spits*)

MEDLEY Why do you suffer this cart-load of scandal to come near you and make your neighbours think you so improvident to need a bawd?

ORANGE-WOMAN [*to Dorimant*] Good now,° we shall have it! You did but want him to help you. [*Offers her basket again*] Come, pay me for my fruit.

MEDLEY Make us thankful for it, huswife. Bawds are as much out of
fashion as gentlemen ushers.° None but old formal ladies use the
one, and none but foppish old stagers° employ the other. Go, you
are an insignificant brandy bottle.°   75

DORIMANT Nay, there you wrong her; three quarts of canary° is her
business.

ORANGE-WOMAN What you please, gentlemen.

DORIMANT To him; give him as good as he brings.

ORANGE-WOMAN Hang him, there is not such another heathen in the   80
town again, except it be the shoemaker without.

MEDLEY I shall see you hold up your hand at the bar next sessions for
murder, huswife. That shoemaker can take his oath you are in fee
with the doctors to sell green fruit to the gentry, that the crudities
may breed diseases.°   85

ORANGE-WOMAN Pray give me my money.

DORIMANT Not a penny. When you bring the gentlewoman hither
you spoke of, you shall be paid.

ORANGE-WOMAN The gentlewoman! The gentlewoman may be as
honest° as your sisters, for ought I know. Pray pay me, Mr Dorimant,   90
and do not abuse me so. I have an honester way of living; you
know it.

MEDLEY Was there ever such a resty° bawd?

DORIMANT Some jade's° tricks she has, but she makes amends when
she's in good humour. Come, tell me the lady's name, and Handy   95
shall pay you.

ORANGE-WOMAN I must not; she forbid me.

DORIMANT That's a sure sign she would have you.

MEDLEY Where does she live?

ORANGE-WOMAN They lodge at my house.   100

MEDLEY Nay, then she's in a hopeful way.°

ORANGE-WOMAN Good Mr Medley, say your pleasure of me, but
take heed how you affront my house. God's my life, in a hopeful
way!

DORIMANT Prithee peace. What kind of woman's the mother?   105

ORANGE-WOMAN A goodly grave gentlewoman. Lord, how she talks
against the wild young men o' the town! As for your part, she
thinks you an arrant devil; should she see you, on my conscience,
she would look if you had not a cloven foot.

DORIMANT Does she know me?   110

ORANGE-WOMAN Only by hearsay. A thousand horrid stories have
been told her of you, and she believes 'em all.

MEDLEY By the character, this should be the famous Lady Woodvill and her daughter Harriet.

ORANGE-WOMAN The devil's in him for guessing, I think. 115

DORIMANT Do you know 'em?

MEDLEY Both very well. The mother's a great admirer of the forms and civility of the last age.

DORIMANT An antiquated beauty may be allowed to be out of humour at the freedoms of the present. This is a good account of 120 the mother; pray, what is the daughter?

MEDLEY Why, first, she's an heiress, vastly rich.

DORIMANT And handsome?

MEDLEY What alteration a twelve-month may have bred in her, I know not, but a year ago she was the beautifullest creature I ever 125 saw: a fine, easy, clean shape;° light brown hair in abundance; her features regular; her complexion clear and lively; large, wanton eyes; but, above all, a mouth that has made me kiss it a thousand times in imagination; teeth white and even; and pretty, pouting lips, with a little moisture ever hanging on them, that look like the 130 Provence rose° fresh on the bush ere the morning sun has quite drawn up the dew.

DORIMANT Rapture, mere rapture!

ORANGE-WOMAN Nay, gad, he tells you true. She's a delicate° creature. 135

DORIMANT Has she wit?

MEDLEY More than is usual in her sex, and as much malice. Then, she's as wild as you would wish her, and has a demureness in her looks that makes it so surprising.

DORIMANT Flesh and blood cannot hear this and not long to know 140 her.

MEDLEY I wonder what makes her mother bring her up to town; an old, doting keeper cannot be more jealous of his mistress.

ORANGE-WOMAN She made me laugh yesterday. There was a judge came to visit 'em, and the old man she told me did so stare upon 145 her, and, when he saluted° her, smacked° so heartily. Who would think it of 'em?

MEDLEY God-a-mercy, judge!

DORIMANT Do 'em right. The gentlemen of the long robe have not been wanting by their good examples to countenance the crying sin 150 o' the nation.

MEDLEY Come, on with your trappings.° 'Tis later than you imagine.

DORIMANT Call in the shoemaker, Handy.

ORANGE-WOMAN Good Mr Dorimant, pay me. Gad, I had rather give you my fruit than stay to be abused by that foul-mouthed rogue. What you gentlemen say, it matters not much; but such a dirty fellow does one more disgrace.

DORIMANT [*to Handy*] Give her ten shillings. [*To Orange-Woman*] And be sure you tell the young gentlewoman I must be acquainted with her.

ORANGE-WOMAN Now do you long to be tempting this pretty creature. Well, heavens mend you!

MEDLEY Farewell, bog!°

Exeunt Orange-Woman and Handy

Dorimant, when did you see your *pis aller*,° as you call her, Mrs Loveit?

DORIMANT Not these two days.

MEDLEY And how stand affairs between you?

DORIMANT There has been great patching of late, much ado. We make a shift to hang together.

MEDLEY I wonder how her mighty spirit bears it.

DORIMANT Ill enough on all conscience. I never knew so violent a creature.

MEDLEY She's the most passionate in her love and the most extravagant in her jealousy of any woman I ever heard of. What note is that?

DORIMANT An excuse I am going to send her for the neglect I am guilty of.

MEDLEY Prithee read it.

DORIMANT No, but if you will take the pains, you may.

MEDLEY (*reads*) 'I never was a lover of business, but now I have a just reason to hate it, since it has kept me these two days from seeing you. I intend to wait upon you in the afternoon, and, in the pleasure of your conversation, forget all I have suffered during this tedious absence.' This business of yours, Dorimant, has been with a vizard° at the playhouse. I have had an eye on you. If some malicious body should betray you, this kind note would hardly make your peace with her.

DORIMANT I desire no better.

MEDLEY Why, would her knowledge of it oblige you?

DORIMANT Most infinitely. Next to the coming to a good understanding with a new mistress, I love a quarrel with an old one. But the devil's in't, there has been such a calm in my affairs of late, I have not had the pleasure of making a woman so much as break her fan, to be sullen, or forswear herself these three days.

MEDLEY A very great misfortune! Let me see, I love mischief well
enough to forward this business myself. I'll about it presently, and,   195
though I know the truth of what y'ave done will set her a-raving,
I'll heighten it a little with invention, leave her in a fit o' the
mother,° and be here again before y'are ready.

DORIMANT Pray stay. You may spare yourself the labour. The business is undertaken already by one who will manage it with as much   200
address,° and, I think, with a little more malice than you can.

MEDLEY Who i' the devil's name can this be?

DORIMANT Why, the vizard, the very vizard you saw me with.

MEDLEY Does she love mischief so well as to betray herself to spite
another?   205

DORIMANT Not so neither, Medley. I will make you comprehend the
mystery. This mask, for a farther confirmation of what I have been
these two days swearing to her, made me yesterday at the playhouse
make her a promise before her face, utterly to break off with Loveit,
and, because she tenders° my reputation and would not have me do   210
a barbarous thing, has contrived a way to give me a handsome
occasion.

MEDLEY Very good.

DORIMANT She intends, about an hour before me, this afternoon
to make Loveit a visit, and, having the privilege by reason of a   215
professed friendship between 'em, to talk of her concerns—

MEDLEY Is she a friend?

DORIMANT O, an intimate friend!

MEDLEY Better and better. Pray proceed.

DORIMANT —she means insensibly to insinuate a discourse of me   220
and artificially raise her jealousy to such a height that, transported with the first motions of her passion, she shall fly upon
me with all the fury imaginable as soon as ever I enter. The
quarrel being thus happily begun, I am to play my part: confess
and justify all my roguery, swear her impertinence and ill humour   225
makes her intolerable, tax her with the next fop° that comes
into my head, and, in a huff, march away, slight her, and leave her
to be taken by whosoever thinks it worth his time to lie down
before her.

MEDLEY This vizard is a spark and has a genius that makes her   230
worthy of yourself, Dorimant.

Enter Handy, Shoemaker, and Footman

DORIMANT [*to the Footman*] You rogue there, who sneak like a dog
that has flung down a dish, if you do not mend your waiting, I'll

uncase° you and turn you loose to the wheel of fortune. [*Gives note
to Handy*] Handy, seal this, and let him run with it presently.   235
　　Exeunt Handy and Footman°

MEDLEY Since y'are resolved on a quarrel, why do you send her this
kind note?

DORIMANT To keep her at home in order to the business. (*To the
Shoemaker*) How, now, you drunken sot?

SHOEMAKER 'Sbud, you have no reason to talk. I have not had a bottle   240
of sack° of yours in my belly this fortnight.

MEDLEY The orange-woman says your neighbours take notice what a
heathen you are, and design to inform the bishop and have you
burned for an atheist.

SHOEMAKER Damn her, dunghill! If her husband does not remove   245
her, she stinks so, the parish intend to indict him for a nuisance.

MEDLEY I advise you like a friend: reform your life. You have brought
the envy of the world upon you by living above yourself. Whoring
and swearing are vices too genteel for a shoemaker.

SHOEMAKER 'Sbud, I think you men of quality will grow as   250
unreasonable as the women. You would engross° the sins o' the
nation. Poor folks can no sooner be wicked, but th' are railed at by
their betters.

DORIMANT Sirrah, I'll have you stand i' the pillory for this libel.

SHOEMAKER Some of you deserve it, I'm sure. There are so many of   255
'em, that our journeymen nowadays, instead of harmless ballads,
sing nothing but your damned lampoons.°

DORIMANT Our lampoons, you rogue?

SHOEMAKER Nay, good master, why should not you write your own
commentaries as well as Caesar?°   260

MEDLEY The rascal's read, I perceive.
　　[*Handy enters*]

SHOEMAKER You know the old proverb, ale and history.°

DORIMANT [*to Handy*] Draw on my shoes, sirrah.

SHOEMAKER Here's a shoe.

DORIMANT Sits with more wrinkles than there are in an angry bully's   265
forehead.

SHOEMAKER 'Sbud, as smooth as your mistress's skin does upon her;
so, strike your foot in home. 'Sbud, if e'er a monsieur of 'em all
make more fashionable ware, I'll be content to have my ears
whipped off with my own paring knife.   270

MEDLEY And served up in a ragout instead of coxcombs° to a company of French shoemakers for a collation.

SHOEMAKER Hold, hold! Damn 'em caterpillars;° let 'em feed upon
cabbage. Come, master, your health this morning next my heart
now.°   275

DORIMANT Go, get you home and govern your family better. Do not
let your wife follow you to the alehouse, beat your whore, and lead
you home in triumph.

SHOEMAKER 'Sbud, there's never a man i' the town lives more like a
gentleman with his wife than I do. I never mind her motions; she   280
never inquires into mine. We speak to one another civilly, hate one
another heartily, and, because 'tis vulgar to lie and soak together,°
we have each of us our several° settle-bed.°

DORIMANT [to Handy] Give him half a crown.

MEDLEY Not without he will promise to be bloody drunk.   285

SHOEMAKER Tope's the word° i' the eye of the world. For my
master's honour, Robin!

DORIMANT Do not debauch my servants, sirrah.

SHOEMAKER I only tip him the wink. He knows an alehouse from a
hovel.   290

Exit Shoemaker

DORIMANT [to Handy] My clothes, quickly.

MEDLEY Where shall we dine today?

Enter Bellair

DORIMANT Where you will. Here comes a good third man.

BELLAIR Your servant, gentlemen.

MEDLEY Gentle sir, how will you answer° this visit to your honour-   295
able mistress? 'Tis not her interest you should keep company with
men of sense,° who will be talking reason.

BELLAIR I do not fear her pardon, do you but grant me yours for my
neglect of late.

MEDLEY Though y'ave made us miserable by the want of your good   300
company, to show you I am free from all resentment, may the
beautiful cause of our misfortune give you all the joys happy lovers
have shared ever since the world began.

BELLAIR You wish me in heaven, but you believe me on my journey to
hell.   305

MEDLEY You have a good strong faith, and that may contribute much
towards your salvation. I confess I am but of an untoward constitution, apt to have doubts and scruples; and in love they are no less
distracting than in religion. Were I so near marriage, I should cry
out by fits as I ride in my coach, 'Cuckold, cuckold!', with no less   310
fury than the mad fanatic does 'Glory' in Bethlem.°

BELLAIR Because religion makes some run mad, must I live an atheist?

MEDLEY Is it not great indiscretion for a man of credit, who may have money enough on his word, to go and deal with Jews, who for little sums make men enter into bonds and give judgements?° 315

BELLAIR Preach no more on this text. I am determined, and there is no hope of my conversion.

DORIMANT (*to Handy, who is fiddling about him*) Leave your unnecessary fiddling! A wasp that's buzzing about a man's nose at dinner is not more troublesome than thou art. 320

HANDY You love to have your clothes hang just,° sir.

DORIMANT I love to be well dressed, sir, and think it no scandal to my understanding.

HANDY Will you use the essence° or orange-flower water?° 325

DORIMANT I will smell as I do today, no offence to the ladies' noses.

HANDY Your pleasure, sir.
      [*Exit Handy*]

DORIMANT That a man's excellency should lie in neatly tying of a ribbon or a cravat! How careful's nature in furnishing the world with necessary coxcombs!° 330

BELLAIR That's a mighty pretty suit of yours, Dorimant.

DORIMANT I am glad 't has your approbation.

BELLAIR No man in town has a better fancy° in his clothes than you have.

DORIMANT You will make me have an opinion of my genius. 335

MEDLEY There is a great critic, I hear, in these matters lately arrived piping hot from Paris.

BELLAIR Sir Fopling Flutter, you mean.

MEDLEY The same.

BELLAIR He thinks himself the pattern of modern gallantry. 340

DORIMANT He is indeed the pattern of modern foppery.

MEDLEY He was yesterday at the play, with a pair of gloves up to his elbows and a periwig more exactly curled than a lady's head newly-dressed for a ball.

BELLAIR What a pretty lisp he has! 345

DORIMANT Ho, that he affects in imitation of the people of quality of France.

MEDLEY His head stands for the most part on one side; and his looks are more languishing than a lady's when she lolls at stretch in her coach, or leans her head carelessly against the side of a box i' the 350 playhouse.

DORIMANT He is a person indeed of great acquired follies.

MEDLEY He is like many others: beholding to his education for making him so eminent a coxcomb. Many a fool had been lost to the world, had their indulgent parents wisely bestowed neither learning nor good breeding on 'em.   355

BELLAIR He has been, as the sparkish word is, brisk upon the ladies already. He was yesterday at my Aunt Townley's and gave Mrs Loveit a catalogue of his good qualities, under the character of a complete gentleman, who, according to Sir Fopling, ought to dress well, dance well, fence well, have a genius for love letters, an agreeable voice for a chamber,° be very amorous, something discreet, but not over-constant.   360

MEDLEY Pretty ingredients to make an accomplished person.

DORIMANT I am glad he pitched upon Loveit.   365

BELLAIR How so?

DORIMANT I wanted a fop to lay to her charge, and this is as pat as may be.

BELLAIR I am confident she loves no man but you.

DORIMANT The good fortune were enough to make me vain, but that I am in my nature modest.   370

BELLAIR Hark you, Dorimant. With your leave, Mr Medley, 'tis only a secret concerning a fair lady.

MEDLEY Your good breeding, sir, gives you too much trouble. You might have whispered without all this ceremony.   375

BELLAIR (to Dorimant) How stand your affairs with Bellinda of late?

DORIMANT She's a little jilting baggage.°

BELLAIR Nay, I believe her false enough, but she's ne'er the worse for your purpose. She was with you yesterday in a disguise at the play.

DORIMANT There we fell out and resolved never to speak to one another more.   380

BELLAIR The occasion?

DORIMANT Want of courage to meet me at the place appointed. These young women apprehend loving as much as the young men do fighting at first; but, once entered, like them too, they all turn bullies straight.   385

Enter Handy to Bellair

HANDY Sir, your man without desires to speak with you.

BELLAIR Gentlemen, I'll return immediately.

Exit Bellair

MEDLEY A very pretty fellow, this.

DORIMANT He's handsome, well-bred, and by much the most tolerable of all the young men that do not abound in wit.   390

MEDLEY Ever well-dressed, always complaisant,° and seldom impertinent. You and he are grown very intimate, I see.

DORIMANT It is our mutual interest to be so. It makes the women think the better of his understanding, and judge more favourably of 395 my reputation. It makes him pass upon some for a man of very good sense, and I upon others for a very civil person.

MEDLEY What was that whisper?

DORIMANT A thing which he would fain have known, but I did not think it fit to tell him. It might have frighted him from his honourable 400 intentions of marrying.

MEDLEY Emilia, give her her due, has the best reputation of any young woman about the town who has beauty enough to provoke detraction. Her carriage is unaffected, her discourse modest, not at all censorious nor pretending like the counterfeits of the age. 405

DORIMANT She's a discreet maid, and I believe nothing can corrupt her but a husband.

MEDLEY A husband?

DORIMANT Yes, a husband. I have known many women make a difficulty of losing a maidenhead, who have afterwards made none of 410 making a cuckold.

MEDLEY This prudent consideration, I am apt to think, has made you confirm poor Bellair in the desperate resolution he has taken.

DORIMANT Indeed, the little hope I found there was of her in the state she was in, has made me by my advice contribute something 415 towards the changing of her condition.

Enter Bellair

Dear Bellair! By heavens, I thought we had lost thee. Men in love are never to be reckoned on when we would form a company.

BELLAIR Dorimant, I am undone. My man has brought the most surprising news i' the world. 420

DORIMANT Some strange misfortune is befallen your love.

BELLAIR My father came to town last night and lodges i' the very house where Emilia lies.

MEDLEY Does he know it is with her you are in love?

BELLAIR He knows I love but knows not whom, without some 425 officious sot has betrayed me.

DORIMANT Your Aunt Townley is your confidante and favours the business.

BELLAIR I do not apprehend any ill office from her. I have received a letter, in which I am commanded by my father to meet him at my 430 aunt's this afternoon. He tells me farther he has made a match for

me, and bids me resolve to be obedient to his will or expect to be
disinherited.

MEDLEY Now's your time, Bellair. Never had lover such an opportunity of giving a generous proof of his passion.   435

BELLAIR As how, I pray?

MEDLEY Why, hang an estate, marry Emilia out of hand, and provoke
your father to do what he threatens. 'Tis but despising a coach,
humbling yourself to a pair of galoshes,° being out of countenance
when you meet your friends, pointed at and pitied wherever you go   440
by all the amorous fops that know you, and your fame will be
immortal.

BELLAIR I could find in my heart to resolve not to marry at all.

DORIMANT Fie, fie, that would spoil a good jest and disappoint the
well-natured town of an occasion of laughing at you.   445

BELLAIR The storm I have so long expected, hangs o'er my head and
begins to pour down upon me. I am on the rack and can have no
rest till I'm satisfied in what I fear. Where do you dine?

DORIMANT At Long's or Lockett's.°

MEDLEY At Long's, let it be.   450

BELLAIR I'll run and see Emilia and inform myself how matters
stand. If my misfortunes are not so great as to make me unfit for
company, I'll be with you.

  Exit Bellair. Enter a Footman with a letter

FOOTMAN (*to Dorimant*) Here's a letter, sir.

DORIMANT The superscription's right: 'For Mr Dorimant'.   455

MEDLEY Let's see the very scrawl and spelling of a true-bred whore.

DORIMANT I know the hand; the style is admirable, I assure you.

MEDLEY Prithee read it.

DORIMANT (*reads*) 'I told a you, you dud not love me; if you dud, you
would have seen me again ere now. I have no money and am very   460
mallicolly. Pray, send me a guynie to see the operies. Your servant to
command, Molly.'

MEDLEY Pray, let the whore have a favourable answer, that she may
spark it in a box and do honour to her profession.

DORIMANT She shall—and perk up° i' the face of quality! [*To Handy*] 465
Is the coach at door?

HANDY You did not bid me send for it.

DORIMANT Eternal blockhead!

  Handy offers to go

Hey, sot!

HANDY Did you call me, sir?   470

DORIMANT I hope you have no just exception to the name, sir?

HANDY I have sense, sir.

DORIMANT Not so much as a fly in winter. How did you come, Medley?

MEDLEY In a chair.°   475

FOOTMAN You may have a hackney coach, if you please, sir.

DORIMANT I may ride the elephant,° if I please, sir. Call another chair, and let my coach follow to Long's.

    Exeunt, Dorimant singing 'Be calm ye great parents, etc.'°

2.1

[*Lady Townley's house*]°

Enter Lady Townley and Emilia

LADY TOWNLEY I was afraid, Emilia, all had been discovered.

EMILIA I tremble with the apprehension still.

LADY TOWNLEY That my brother should take lodgings i' the very house where you lie.

EMILIA 'Twas lucky we had timely notice to warn the people to be   5
secret. He seems to be a mighty good-humoured old man.

LADY TOWNLEY He ever had a notable smirking way with him.

EMILIA He calls me rogue, tells me he can't abide me, and does so bepat me!

LADY TOWNLEY On my word, you are much in his favour then.   10

EMILIA He has been very inquisitive, I am told, about my family, my reputation, and my fortune.

LADY TOWNLEY I am confident he does not i' the least suspect you are the woman his son's in love with.

EMILIA What should make him then inform himself so particularly of   15
me?

LADY TOWNLEY He was always of a very loving temper himself. It may be he has a doting fit upon him. Who knows?

EMILIA It cannot be.

Enter Bellair

LADY TOWNLEY Here comes my nephew. Where did you leave your   20
father?

BELLAIR Writing a note within. Emilia, this early visit looks as if some kind jealousy would not let you rest at home.

EMILIA The knowledge I have of my rival gives me a little cause to fear your constancy.   25

BELLAIR My constancy! I vow—

EMILIA Do not vow. Our love is frail as is our life, and full as little in our power; and are you sure you shall outlive this day?

BELLAIR I am not, but when we are in perfect health, 'twere an idle thing to fright ourselves with the thoughts of sudden death.   30

LADY TOWNLEY Pray, what has passed between you and your father i' the garden?

BELLAIR He's firm in his resolution. Tells me I must marry Mrs Harriet, or swears he'll marry himself and disinherit me. When I

saw I could not prevail with him to be more indulgent, I dissembled 35
an obedience to his will, which has composed his passion and will
give us time, and, I hope, opportunity to deceive him.

Enter Old Bellair, with a note in his hand

LADY TOWNLEY Peace, here he comes.

OLD BELLAIR *[to Bellair]* Harry, take this and let your man carry it for
me to Mr Fourbe's° chamber, my lawyer i' the Temple.° 40

[Exit Bellair]

(*To Emilia*) Neighbour, adod, I am glad to see thee here. [*To Lady
Townley*] Make much of her, sister, she's one of the best of your
acquaintance. I like her countenance and her behaviour well. She
has a modesty that is not common i' this age, adod, she has.

LADY TOWNLEY I know her value, brother, and esteem her 45
accordingly.

OLD BELLAIR Advise her to wear a little more mirth in her face.
Adod, she's too serious.

LADY TOWNLEY The fault is very excusable in a young woman.

OLD BELLAIR Nay, adod, I like her ne'er the worse. A melancholy 50
beauty has her charms. I love a pretty sadness in a face which varies
now and then, like changeable colours,° into a smile.

LADY TOWNLEY Methinks you speak very feelingly, brother.

OLD BELLAIR I am but five-and-fifty, sister, you know—an age not
altogether unsensible! (*To Emilia*) Cheer up, sweetheart. I have a 55
secret to tell thee may chance to make thee merry. We three will
make collation together anon; i' the meantime, mum.°

Enter Bellair

I can't abide you; go, I can't abide you. [*To Bellair*] Harry, come.
You must along with me to my Lady Woodvill's. I am going to slip°
the boy at a mistress. 60

BELLAIR At a wife, sir, you would say.

OLD BELLAIR You need not look so glum, sir. A wife is no curse when
she brings the blessing of a good estate with her. But an idle town
flirt,° with a painted face, a rotten reputation, and a crazy° fortune,
adod, is the devil and all, and such a one I hear you are in league 65
with.

BELLAIR I cannot help detraction, sir.

OLD BELLAIR Out, a pize° o' their breeches! There are keeping fools°
enough for such flaunting baggages, and they are e'en too good
for 'em. (*To Emilia*) Remember night. Go, y'are a rogue, y'are a 70
rogue. Fare you well, fare you well. [*To Bellair*] Come, come, come
along, sir.

Exeunt Old Bellair and Bellair

LADY TOWNLEY On my word, the old man comes on apace. I'll lay my life he's smitten.

EMILIA This is nothing but the pleasantness of his humour.   75

LADY TOWNLEY I know him better than you. Let it work; it may prove lucky.

Enter a Page

PAGE Madam, Mr Medley has sent to know whether a visit will not be troublesome this afternoon?

LADY TOWNLEY Send him word his visits never are so.   80

[*Exit Page*]

EMILIA He's a very pleasant° man.

LADY TOWNLEY He's a very necessary man among us women. He's not scandalous i' the least,° perpetually contriving to bring good company together, and always ready to stop up a gap at ombre;° then, he knows all the little news o' the town.   85

EMILIA I love to hear him talk o' the intrigues.° Let 'em be never so dull in themselves, he'll make 'em pleasant i' the relation.

LADY TOWNLEY But he improves things so much one can take no measure of the truth from him. Mr Dorimant swears a flea or maggot is not made more monstrous by a magnifying glass than a   90
story is by his telling it.

Enter Medley

EMILIA Hold, here he comes.

LADY TOWNLEY Mr Medley.

MEDLEY [*bowing*] Your servant, madam.

LADY TOWNLEY You have made yourself a stranger of late.   95

EMILIA I believe you took a surfeit of ombre last time you were here.

MEDLEY Indeed, I had my bellyful of that termagant lady dealer. There never was so insatiable a carder, an old gleeker° never lov'd to sit to't like her! I have played with her now at least a dozen times, till she 'as worn out all her fine complexion and her tour° would   100
keep in curl no longer.

LADY TOWNLEY Blame her not, poor woman. She loves nothing so well as a black ace.

MEDLEY The pleasure I have seen her in when she has had hope in drawing for a matador!°   105

EMILIA 'Tis as pretty sport to her as persuading masks off is to you to make discoveries.

LADY TOWNLEY Pray, where's your friend, Mr Dorimant?

MEDLEY Soliciting his affairs.° He's a man of great employment—

has more mistresses now depending° than the most eminent lawyer   110
in England has causes.°

EMILIA Here has been Mrs Loveit so uneasy and out of humour these
two days.

LADY TOWNLEY How strangely love and jealousy rage in that poor
woman!   115

MEDLEY She could not have picked out a devil upon earth so proper
to torment her: has made her break a dozen or two of fans already,
tear half-a-score points° in pieces, and destroy hoods and knots°
without number.

LADY TOWNLEY We heard of a pleasant serenade he gave her t' other   120
night.

MEDLEY A Danish serenade,° with kettledrums and trumpets.

EMILIA O barbarous!

MEDLEY What? You are of the number of the ladies whose ears are
grown so delicate since our operas, you can be charmed with noth-   125
ing but *flûtes douces*° and French hautboys?°

EMILIA Leave your raillery and tell us, is there any new wit come
forth—songs or novels?

MEDLEY A very pretty piece of gallantry, by an eminent author, called
The Diversions of Bruxelles,° very necessary to be read by all old   130
ladies who are desirous to improve themselves at questions and
commands,° blindman's buff, and the like fashionable recreations.

EMILIA O ridiculous!

MEDLEY Then there is *The Art of Affectation*,° written by a late
beauty of quality, teaching you how to draw up your breasts, stretch   135
up your neck, to thrust out your breech, to play with your head, to
toss up your nose, to bite your lips, to turn up your eyes, to speak in
a silly, soft tone of a voice, and use all the foolish French words that
will infallibly make your person and conversation charming; with a
short apology at the latter end, in the behalf of young ladies who   140
notoriously wash and paint,° though they have naturally good
complexions.

EMILIA What a deal of stuff you tell us!

MEDLEY Such as the town affords, madam. The Russians, hearing the
great respect we have for foreign dancing, have lately sent over   145
some of their best baladines,° who are now practising a famous
ballet which will be suddenly danced at the Bear Garden.°

LADY TOWNLEY Pray forbear your idle stories and give us an account
of the state of love, as it now stands.

MEDLEY Truly, there has been some revolutions in those affairs, great   150

chopping and changing° among the old, and some new lovers,
whom malice, indiscretion, and misfortune, have luckily brought
into play.

LADY TOWNLEY What think you of walking into the next room and
sitting down before you engage in this business?   155

MEDLEY I wait upon you, and I hope—though women are commonly
unreasonable—by the plenty of scandal I shall discover, to give you
very good content, ladies.

    Exeunt

2.2

    [*A room in Mrs Loveit's house*]°

    [*Enter*] *Mrs Loveit putting up a letter, then pulling out her
    pocket glass and looking in it*

MRS LOVEIT Pert.

    [*Enter Pert*]

PERT Madam.

MRS LOVEIT I hate myself. I look so ill today.

PERT Hate the wicked cause on't, that base man Mr Dorimant, who
makes you torment and vex yourself continually.   5

MRS LOVEIT He is to blame indeed.

PERT To blame to be two days without sending, writing, or coming
near you, contrary to his oath and covenant! 'Twas to much purpose to make him swear. I'll lay my life there's not an article but he
has broken: talked to the vizards i' the pit, waited upon the ladies   10
from the boxes to their coaches, gone behind the scenes, and
fawned upon those little insignificant creatures, the players. 'Tis
impossible for a man of his inconstant temper to forbear, I'm sure.

MRS LOVEIT I know he is a devil; but he has something of the angel
yet undefaced in him, which makes him so charming and agreeable,   15
that I must love him, be he never so wicked.°

PERT I little thought, madam, to see your spirit tamed to this degree,
who banished poor Mr Lackwit but for taking up another lady's fan
in your presence.

MRS LOVEIT My knowing of such odious fools contributes to the   20
making of me love Dorimant the better.

PERT Your knowing of Mr Dorimant, in my mind, should rather
make you hate all mankind.

MRS LOVEIT So it does, besides himself.

PERT Pray, what excuse does he make in his letter?   25

MRS LOVEIT He has had business.

PERT Business in general terms would not have been a current excuse
for another. A modish man is always very busy when he is in pursuit of a new mistress.

MRS LOVEIT Some fop has bribed you to rail at him. He had business.   30
I will believe it and will forgive him.

PERT You may forgive him anything, but I shall never forgive him his
turning me into ridicule, as I hear he does.

MRS LOVEIT I perceive you are of the number of those fools his wit
had made his enemies.   35

PERT I am of the number of those he's pleased to rally, madam; and, if
we may believe Mr Wagfan and Mr Caperwell,° he sometimes
makes merry with yourself too among his laughing companions.

MRS LOVEIT Blockheads are as malicious to witty men as ugly women
are to the handsome. 'Tis their interest, and they make it their   40
business to defame 'em.

PERT I wish Mr Dorimant would not make it his business to defame
you.

MRS LOVEIT Should he, I had rather be made infamous by him than
owe my reputation to the dull discretion of those fops you talk of.   45
        Enter Bellinda
    (*Running to her*) Bellinda!

BELLINDA My dear.

MRS LOVEIT You have been unkind of late.

BELLINDA Do not say unkind, say unhappy!

MRS LOVEIT I could chide you. Where have you been these two days?   50

BELLINDA Pity me rather, my dear, where I have been so tired with
two or three country gentlewomen, whose conversation has been
more unsufferable than a country fiddle.

MRS LOVEIT Are they relations?

BELLINDA No, Welsh acquaintance I made when I was last year at   55
St Winifred's.° They have asked me a thousand questions of the
modes and intrigues of the town, and I have told 'em almost as
many things for news that hardly were so when their gowns were in
fashion.

MRS LOVEIT Provoking creatures, how could you endure 'em?   60

BELLINDA (*aside*) Now to carry on my plot; nothing but love could
make me capable of so much falsehood. 'Tis time to begin lest
Dorimant should come before her jealousy has stung her. (*Laughs*

and then speaks on) I was yesterday at a play with 'em, where I was
fain to show 'em the living as the man at Westminster does the 65
dead.° That is Mrs Such-a-one admired for her beauty; this is
Mr Such-a-one cried up for a wit; that is sparkish Mr Such-a-one
who keeps reverend Mrs Such-a-one; and there sits fine Mrs
Such-a-one who was lately cast off by my Lord Such-a-one.

MRS LOVEIT Did you see Dorimant there? 70

BELLINDA I did, and imagine you were there with him and have no
mind to own it.

MRS LOVEIT What should make you think so?

BELLINDA A lady masked in a pretty *déshabillé*,° whom Dorimant
entertained with more respect than the gallants do a common 75
vizard.

MRS LOVEIT (*aside*) Dorimant at the play entertaining a mask! O
heavens!

BELLINDA (*aside*) Good.

MRS LOVEIT Did he stay all the while? 80

BELLINDA Till the play was done, and then led her out, which
confirms me it was you.

MRS LOVEIT Traitor!

PERT Now you may believe he had business, and you may forgive him
too. 85

MRS LOVEIT Ungrateful, perjured man!

BELLINDA You seem so much concerned, my dear. I fear I have told
you unawares what I had better have concealed for your quiet.

MRS LOVEIT What manner of shape had she?

BELLINDA Tall and slender; her motions were very genteel. Certainly 90
she must be some person of condition.°

MRS LOVEIT Shame and confusion be ever in her face when she
shows it.

BELLINDA I should blame your discretion for loving that wild man,
my dear; but they say he has a way so bewitching, that few can 95
defend their hearts who know him.

MRS LOVEIT I will tear him from mine, or die i' the attempt.

BELLINDA Be more moderate.

MRS LOVEIT Would I had daggers, darts, or poisoned arrows in my
breast, so I could but remove the thoughts of him from thence. 100

BELLINDA Fie, fie, your transports are too violent, my dear. This may
be but an accidental gallantry, and 'tis likely ended at her coach.

PERT Should it proceed farther, let your comfort be, the conduct
Mr Dorimant affects will quickly make you know your rival. Ten to

one, let you see her ruined, her reputation exposed to the town, a   105
happiness none will envy her but yourself, madam.

MRS LOVEIT Whoe'er she be, all the harm I wish her is, may she love
him as well as I do, and may he give her as much cause to hate him.

PERT Never doubt the latter end of your curse, madam!

MRS LOVEIT May all the passions that are raised by neglected love,   110
jealousy, indignation, spite, and thirst of revenge eternally rage
in her soul, as they do now in mine. (*Walks up and down with a
distracted air*)

    Enter a Page

PAGE Madam, Mr Dorimant—

MRS LOVEIT I will not see him.   115

PAGE I told him you were within, madam.

MRS LOVEIT Say you lied, say I'm busy, shut the door. Say anything.

PAGE He's here, madam.

    Enter Dorimant

DORIMANT 'They taste of death who do at heaven arrive,
      But we this paradise approach alive.'°   120

    (*To Mrs Loveit*) What? Dancing the galloping nag without a fiddle?°
    *Dorimant offers to catch Mrs Loveit by the hand. She flings
    away and walks on*

    (*Pursuing her*) I fear this restlessness of the body, madam, proceeds
from an unquietness of the mind. What unlucky accident puts you
out of humour? A point ill-washed, knots spoiled i' the making up,
hair shaded awry, or some other little mistake in setting you in   125
order?

PERT A trifle in my opinion, sir, more inconsiderable than any you
mention.

DORIMANT O Mrs Pert, I never knew you sullen enough to be silent.
Come, let me know the business.   130

PERT The business, sir, is the business that has taken you up these two
days. How have I seen you laugh at men of business, and now to
become a man of business yourself!

DORIMANT We are not masters of our own affections; our inclinations
daily alter. Now we love pleasure, and anon we shall dote on business.   135
Human frailty will have it so, and who can help it?

MRS LOVEIT Faithless, inhuman, barbarous man—

DORIMANT [*aside*] Good. Now the alarm° strikes.

MRS LOVEIT Without sense of love, of honour, or of gratitude. Tell
me, for I will know, what devil masked she was you were with at the   140
play yesterday?

DORIMANT Faith, I resolved as much as you, but the devil was obstinate and would not tell me.

MRS LOVEIT False in this as in your vows to me! You do know!

DORIMANT The truth is, I did all I could to know.   145

MRS LOVEIT And dare you own it to my face? (*Tears her fan in pieces*)
Hell and furies!

DORIMANT Spare your fan, madam. You are growing hot and will
want it to cool you.

MRS LOVEIT Horror and distraction seize you! Sorrow and remorse   150
gnaw your soul and punish all your perjuries to me—(*Weeps*)

DORIMANT (*turning to Bellinda*)
            'So thunder breaks the cloud in twain,
            And makes a passage for the rain.'°
Bellinda, you are the devil that have raised this storm. You were   155
at the play yesterday and have been making discoveries to your
dear.

BELLINDA Y'are the most mistaken man i' the world.

DORIMANT It must be so, and here I vow revenge: resolve to pursue
and persecute you more impertinently than ever any loving fop did   160
his mistress; hunt you i' the park, trace you i' the Mall;° dog you in
every visit you make; haunt you at the plays; and, i' the drawing
room,° hang my nose in your neck and talk to you whether you will
or no; and ever look upon you with such dying eyes till your friends
grow jealous of me, send you out of town, and the world suspect   165
your reputation. (*In a lower voice*) At my Lady Townley's when we
go from hence.

        Dorimant looks kindly on Bellinda

BELLINDA I'll meet you there.

DORIMANT Enough.

MRS LOVEIT Stand off! (*Pushing Dorimant away*) You sha' not stare   170
upon her so.

DORIMANT [*aside*] Good! There's one made jealous already.°

MRS LOVEIT Is this the constancy you vowed?

DORIMANT Constancy at my years? 'Tis not a virtue in season; you
might as well expect the fruit the autumn ripens i' the spring.   175

MRS LOVEIT Monstrous principle!

DORIMANT Youth has a long journey to go, madam. Should I have set
up my rest° at the first inn I lodged at, I should never have arrived
at the happiness I now enjoy.

MRS LOVEIT Dissembler, damned dissembler!   180

DORIMANT I am so, I confess. Good nature and good manners

corrupt me. I am honest in my inclinations and would not, wert not to avoid offence, make a lady a little in years believe I think her young, wilfully mistake art for nature, and seem as fond of a thing I am weary of, as when I doted on't in earnest.   185

MRS LOVEIT False man.

DORIMANT True woman.

MRS LOVEIT Now you begin to show yourself.

DORIMANT Love gilds us over and makes us show fine things to one another for a time, but soon the gold wears off, and then again the   190 native brass appears.

MRS LOVEIT Think on your oaths, your vows and protestations, perjured man.

DORIMANT I made 'em when I was in love.

MRS LOVEIT And therefore ought they not to bind? O impious!   195

DORIMANT What we swear at such a time may be a certain proof of a present passion; but, to say truth, in love there is no security to be given for the future.

MRS LOVEIT Horrid and ungrateful, begone; and never see me more!

DORIMANT I am not one of those troublesome coxcombs who,   200 because they were once well-received, take the privilege to plague a woman with their love ever after. I shall obey you, madam, though I do myself some violence.

   Dorimant offers to go, and Loveit pulls him back

MRS LOVEIT Come back; you sha' not go. Could you have the ill nature to offer it?   205

DORIMANT When love grows diseased, the best thing we can do is to put it to a violent death. I cannot endure the torture of a lingering and consumptive passion.

MRS LOVEIT Can you think mine sickly?

DORIMANT O, 'tis desperately ill! What worse symptoms are there   210 than your being always uneasy when I visit you, your picking quarrels with me on slight occasions, and, in my absence, kindly listening to the impertinences of every fashionable fool that talks to you?

MRS LOVEIT What fashionable fool can you lay to my charge?   215

DORIMANT Why, the very cock-fool° of all those fools, Sir Fopling Flutter.

MRS LOVEIT I never saw him in my life but once.

DORIMANT The worse woman you, at first sight to put on all your charms, to entertain him with that softness in your voice and all   220 that wanton kindness in your eyes you so notoriously affect when you design a conquest.

MRS LOVEIT So damned a lie did never malice yet invent! Who told
  you this?

DORIMANT No matter. That ever I should love a woman that can dote   225
  on a senseless caper, a tawdry French ribbon, and a formal cravat!

MRS LOVEIT You make me mad.

DORIMANT A guilty conscience may do much. Go on! Be the game-
  mistress o' the town and enter° all our young fops, as fast as they
  come from travel.   230

MRS LOVEIT Base and scurrilous!

DORIMANT A fine mortifying reputation 'twill be for a woman of
  your pride, wit, and quality!

MRS LOVEIT This jealousy's a mere pretence, a cursed trick of your
  own devising. I know you.   235

DORIMANT Believe it and all the ill of me you can. I would not have a
  woman have the least good thought of me that can think well of
  Fopling. Farewell. Fall to—and much good may do you° with your
  coxcomb.

MRS LOVEIT Stay, O stay, and I will tell you all.   240

DORIMANT I have been told too much already.
        Exit Dorimant

MRS LOVEIT Call him again.

PERT E'en let him go, a fair riddance.

MRS LOVEIT Run, I say, call him again. I will have him called!

PERT The devil should carry him away first, were it my concern.   245
        Exit Pert

BELLINDA H'as frighted me from the very thoughts of loving men.
  For heaven's sake, my dear, do not discover what I told you. I dread
  his tongue as much as you ought to have done his friendship.
        Enter Pert

PERT He's gone, madam.

MRS LOVEIT Lightning blast him!   250

PERT When I told him you desired him to come back, he smiled,
  made a mouth at me, flung into his coach, and said—

MRS LOVEIT What did he say?

PERT Drive away, and then repeated verses.

MRS LOVEIT Would I had made a contract to be a witch when first I   255
  entertained this greater devil. Monster, barbarian! I could tear
  myself in pieces. Revenge, nothing but revenge, can ease me.
  Plague, war, famine, fire, all that can bring universal ruin and misery on mankind! With joy I'd perish to have you in my power but
  this moment.   260
        Exit Mrs Loveit

PERT Follow, madam. Leave her not in this outrageous passion.
    Pert gathers up the things
BELLINDA [*aside*] H'as given me the proof which I desired of his love,
    but 'tis a proof of his ill nature too. I wish I had not seen him use
    her so.

        I sigh to think that Dorimant may be,   265
        One day as faithless, and unkind to me.
    Exeunt

3.1

Lady Woodvill's lodgings.

Enter Harriet and Busy, her woman

BUSY [*pleading*] Dear madam, let me set that curl in order.

HARRIET Let me alone! I will shake 'em all out of order.

BUSY Will you never leave this wildness?

HARRIET Torment me not.

BUSY Look, there's a knot falling off. 5

HARRIET Let it drop.

BUSY But one pin, dear madam.

HARRIET How do I daily suffer under thy officious fingers!

BUSY Ah, the difference that is between you and my Lady Dapper!
How uneasy she is if the least thing be amiss about her. 10

HARRIET She is indeed most exact. Nothing is ever wanting to make
her ugliness remarkable!

BUSY Jeering people say so.

HARRIET Her powdering, painting, and her patching° never fail in
public to draw the tongues and eyes of all the men upon her. 15

BUSY She is indeed a little too pretending.

HARRIET That women should set up for beauty as much in spite of
nature as some men have done for wit.

BUSY I hope without offence one may endeavour to make oneself
agreeable. 20

HARRIET Not when 'tis impossible. Women then ought to be no more
fond of dressing than fools should be of talking. Hoods and
modesty, masks and silence, things that shadow and conceal—they
should think of nothing else.

BUSY Jesu! Madam, what will your mother think is become of you? 25
For heaven's sake, go in again.

HARRIET I won't!

BUSY This is the extravagant'st thing that ever you did in your life, to
leave her and a gentleman who is to be your husband.

HARRIET My husband! Hast thou so little wit to think I spoke what I 30
meant when I overjoyed her in the country with a low curtsy and
'what you please, madam; I shall ever be obedient'.

BUSY Nay, I know not. You have so many fetches.°

HARRIET And this was one: to get her up to London! Nothing else, I
assure thee. 35

BUSY Well, the man, in my mind, is a fine man.

HARRIET The man indeed wears his clothes fashionably and has a pretty, negligent way with him, very courtly and much affected. He bows, and talks, and smiles so agreeably as he thinks.

BUSY I never saw anything so genteel.   40

HARRIET Varnished over with good breeding, many a blockhead makes a tolerable show.

BUSY I wonder you do not like him.

HARRIET I think I might be brought to endure him, and that is all a reasonable woman should expect in a husband; but there is duty i'   45
the case and, like the haughty Merab,° I

       Find much aversion in my stubborn mind,
which°

       Is bred by being promised and designed.°

BUSY I wish you do not design your own ruin. I partly guess your   50
inclinations, madam. That Mr Dorimant—

HARRIET Leave your prating and sing some foolish song or other.

BUSY I will—the song you love so well ever since you saw Mr Dorimant. [Sings]

SONG   55

When first Amintas charmed my heart,
  My heedless sheep began to stray;
The wolves soon stole the greatest part,
  And all will now be made a prey.

Ah, let not love your thoughts possess,   60
  'Tis fatal to a shepherdess;
The dang'rous passion you must shun,
  Or else like me be quite undone.

HARRIET Shall I be paid down by a covetous parent for a purchase?° I need no land. No, I'll lay myself out all in love. It is decreed.   65
   Enter Bellair

BELLAIR What generous resolution are you making, madam?

HARRIET Only to be disobedient, sir.

BELLAIR Let me join hands with you in that.

HARRIET With all my heart! I never thought I should have given you mine so willingly. Here. [*They join hands*] I, Harriet—   70

BELLAIR And I, Harry—

HARRIET Do solemnly protest—

BELLAIR And vow—

HARRIET That I with you—
BELLAIR And I with you—   75
BOTH Will never marry!
HARRIET A match—
BELLAIR And no match! How do you like this indifference now?
HARRIET You expect I should take it ill, I see.
BELLAIR 'Tis not unnatural for you women to be a little angry. You   80
    miss a conquest, though you would slight the poor man were he in
    your power.
HARRIET There are some, it may be, have an eye like Bart'lomew,° big
    enough for the whole fair, but I am not of the number, and you may
    keep your gingerbread.° 'Twill be more acceptable to the lady   85
    whose dear image it wears, sir.
BELLAIR I must confess, madam, you came a day after the fair.°
HARRIET You own then you are in love.
BELLAIR I do.
HARRIET The confidence° is generous, and, in return, I could almost   90
    find in my heart to let you know my inclinations.
BELLAIR Are you in love?
HARRIET Yes—with this dear town, to that degree I can scarce endure
    the country in landscapes and in hangings.°
BELLAIR What a dreadful thing 'twould be to be hurried back to   95
    Hampshire!°
HARRIET Ah, name it not!
BELLAIR As for us, I find we shall agree well enough. Would we could
    do something to deceive the grave people!
HARRIET Could we delay their quick proceedings, 'twere well. A   100
    reprieve is a good step towards the getting of a pardon.
BELLAIR If we give over the game, we are undone. What think you of
    playing it on booty?°
HARRIET What do you mean?
BELLAIR Pretend to be in love with one another. 'Twill make some   105
    dilatory excuses we may feign pass the better.
HARRIET Let us do't, if it be but for the dear pleasure of dissembling.
BELLAIR Can you play your part?
HARRIET I know not what it is to love, but I have made pretty°
    remarks by being now and then where lovers meet. Where did you   110
    leave their gravities?
BELLAIR I' th' next room. Your mother was censuring our modern
    gallant.
        Enter Old Bellair and Lady Woodvill

HARRIET Peace! Here they come. I will lean against this wall and look
bashfully down upon my fan, while you, like an amorous spark,   115
modishly entertain me.

LADY WOODVILL [*to Old Bellair*] Never go about to excuse 'em.
Come, come, it was not so when I was a young woman.

OLD BELLAIR Adod, they're something disrespectful.

LADY WOODVILL Quality° was then considered and not rallied by   120
every fleering fellow.

OLD BELLAIR Youth will have its jest, adod it will.

LADY WOODVILL 'Tis good breeding now to be civil to none but
players and Exchange women;° they are treated by 'em as much
above their condition as others are below theirs.   125

OLD BELLAIR Out, a pize on 'em! Talk no more. The rogues ha' got
an ill habit of preferring beauty, no matter where they find it.

LADY WOODVILL See your son and my daughter. They have
improved their acquaintance since they were within.

OLD BELLAIR Adod, methinks they have! Let's keep back and   130
observe.

BELLAIR Now for a look and gestures that may persuade 'em I am
saying all the passionate things imaginable.

HARRIET Your head a little more on one side; ease yourself on your
left leg, and play with your right hand.   135

BELLAIR Thus, is it not?

HARRIET Now set your right leg firm on the ground, adjust your belt,
then look about you.

BELLAIR A little exercising will make me perfect.

HARRIET Smile and turn to me again very sparkish.   140

BELLAIR Will you take your turn and be instructed?

HARRIET With all my heart.

BELLAIR At one motion play your fan, roll your eyes, and then settle a
kind look upon me.

HARRIET So.   145

BELLAIR Now spread your fan, look down upon it, and tell° the sticks
with a finger.

HARRIET Very modish.

BELLAIR Clap your hand up to your bosom, hold down your gown,
shrug a little, draw up your breasts, and let 'em fall. Again, gently,   150
with a sigh or two, etc.°

HARRIET By the good instructions you give, I suspect you for one
of those malicious observers who watch people's eyes and, from
innocent looks, made scandalous conclusions.

BELLAIR I know some indeed who out of mere love to mischief are as   155
    vigilant as jealousy itself, and will give you an account of every
    glance that passes at a play and i' th' Circle.°

HARRIET 'Twill not be amiss now to seem a little pleasant.

BELLAIR Clap your fan then in both your hands, snatch it to your
    mouth, smile, and with a lively motion fling your body a little   160
    forwards. So—now spread it, fall back on the sudden, cover your
    face with it, and break out into a loud laughter. Take up!° Look
    grave and fall a-fanning of yourself. Admirably well acted.

HARRIET I think I am pretty apt at these matters!

OLD BELLAIR Adod, I like this well.   165

LADY WOODVILL This promises something.

OLD BELLAIR Come, there is love i' th' case, adod there is, or will be.
    [*To Harriet*] What say you, young lady?

HARRIET All in good time, sir. You expect we should fall to and love as
    game-cocks° fight as soon as we are set together. Adod, y'are   170
    unreasonable!

OLD BELLAIR Adod, sirrah,° I like thy wit well.

      Enter a Servant

SERVANT The coach is at the door, madam.

OLD BELLAIR Go, get you and take the air together.

LADY WOODVILL Will not you go with us?   175

OLD BELLAIR Out a pize. Adod, I ha' business and cannot. We shall
    meet at night at my sister Townley's.

BELLAIR (*aside* [*to Harriet*]) He's going to Emilia. I overheard him
    talk of a collation.

      Exeunt

3.2

    [*Lady Townley's house*]°

    Enter Lady Townley, Emilia, and Mr Medley

LADY TOWNLEY I pity the young lovers we last talked of, though, to
    say truth, their conduct has been so indiscreet, they deserve to be
    unfortunate.

MEDLEY Y' have had an exact account, from the great lady i' th' box
    down to the little orange wench.   5

EMILIA Y' are a living libel, a breathing lampoon!° I wonder you are
    not torn in pieces.

MEDLEY What think you of setting up an office of intelligence for these matters? The project may get money.

LADY TOWNLEY You would have great dealings with country ladies.   10

Enter Bellinda

MEDLEY More than Muddiman° has with their husbands.

LADY TOWNLEY Bellinda, what has become of you? We have not seen you here of late with your friend Mrs Loveit.

BELLINDA Dear creature! I left her but now so sadly afflicted.

LADY TOWNLEY With her old distemper, jealousy!   15

MEDLEY Dorimant has played her some new prank.

BELLINDA Well, that Dorimant is certainly the worst man breathing.

EMILIA I once thought so.

BELLINDA And do you not think so still?

EMILIA No, indeed.   20

BELLINDA O Jesu!

EMILIA The town does him a great deal of injury, and I will never believe what it says of a man I do not know again, for his sake!

BELLINDA You make me wonder.

LADY TOWNLEY He's a very well-bred man.   25

BELLINDA But strangely ill-natured.

EMILIA Then he's a very witty man.

BELLINDA But a man of no principles.

MEDLEY Your man of principles is a very fine thing indeed.

BELLINDA To be preferred to men of parts by women who have   30
regard to their reputation and quiet. Well, were I minded to play the fool, he should be the last man I'd think of.

MEDLEY He has been the first in many ladies' favours, though you are so severe, madam.

LADY TOWNLEY What he may be for a lover, I know not; but he's a   35
very pleasant acquaintance, I am sure.

BELLINDA Had you seen him use Mrs Loveit as I have done, you would never endure him more.

EMILIA What, he has quarrelled with her again?

BELLINDA Upon the slightest occasion. He's jealous of Sir Fopling.   40

LADY TOWNLEY She never saw him in her life but yesterday, and that was here.

EMILIA On my conscience, he's the only man in town that's her aversion. How horribly out of humour she was all the while he talked to her!   45

BELLINDA And somebody has wickedly told him—

Enter Dorimant

EMILIA Here he comes.

MEDLEY Dorimant, you are luckily come to justify yourself. Here's a
lady—

BELLINDA Has a word or two to say to you from a disconsolate   50
person.

DORIMANT You tender your reputation too much, I know, madam, to
whisper with me before this good company.

BELLINDA To serve Mrs Loveit, I'll make a bold venture.

DORIMANT Here's Medley, the very spirit of scandal.   55

BELLINDA No matter!

EMILIA 'Tis something you are unwilling to hear, Mr Dorimant.

LADY TOWNLEY Tell him, Bellinda, whether he will or no!

BELLINDA (aloud) Mrs Loveit—

DORIMANT Softly, these are laughers. You do not know 'em.   60

BELLINDA (to Dorimant apart) In a word, y' have made me hate you,
which I thought you never could have done.

DORIMANT In obeying your commands.

BELLINDA 'Twas a cruel part you played! How could you act it?

DORIMANT Nothing is cruel to a man who could kill himself to please   65
you. Remember five o'clock tomorrow morning.

BELLINDA I tremble when you name it.

DORIMANT Be sure you come.

BELLINDA I sha' not.

DORIMANT Swear you will!   70

BELLINDA I dare not.

DORIMANT Swear, I say.

BELLINDA By my life, by all the happiness I hope for—

DORIMANT You will.

BELLINDA I will.   75

DORIMANT Kind.

BELLINDA I am glad I've sworn. I vow, I think I should ha' failed you
else!

DORIMANT Surprisingly kind! In what temper did you leave Loveit?

BELLINDA Her raving was prettily over,° and she began to be in a   80
brave way of defying you and all your works.° Where have you been
since you went from thence?

DORIMANT I looked in at the play.

BELLINDA I have promised and must return to her again.

DORIMANT Persuade her to walk in the Mall this evening.   85

BELLINDA She hates the place and will not come.

DORIMANT Do all you can to prevail with her.

BELLINDA For what purpose?

DORIMANT Sir Fopling will be here anon. I'll prepare him to set upon
her there before me.   90

BELLINDA You persecute her too much, but I'll do all you'll ha' me.

DORIMANT (*aloud*) Tell her plainly, 'tis grown so dull a business, I can
drudge on no longer.

EMILIA There are afflictions in love, Mr Dorimant.

DORIMANT You women make 'em, who are commonly as unreason-   95
able in that as you are at play;° without the advantage be on your
side, a man can never quietly give over when he's weary.

MEDLEY If you would play without being obliged to complaisance,
Dorimant, you should play in public places.°

DORIMANT Ordinaries° were a very good thing for that, but gentle-   100
men do not of late frequent 'em. The deep play is now in private
houses.°

    Bellinda offering to steal away

LADY TOWNLEY Bellinda, are you leaving us so soon?

BELLINDA I am to go to the Park° with Mrs Loveit, Madam.

    Exit Bellinda

LADY TOWNLEY This confidence° will go nigh to spoil this young   105
creature.

MEDLEY 'Twill do her good, madam. Young men who are brought up
under practising lawyers prove the abler counsel when they come to
be called to the bar themselves.

DORIMANT The town has been very favourable to you this afternoon,   110
my Lady Townley. You use to have an *embarras*° of chairs and
coaches at your door, an uproar of footmen in your hall, and a noise
of fools above here.

LADY TOWNLEY Indeed, my house is the general rendezvous and,
next to the playhouse, is the common refuge of all the young idle   115
people.

EMILIA Company is a very good thing, madam, but I wonder you do
not love it a little more chosen.

LADY TOWNLEY 'Tis good to have an universal taste. We should love
wit, but for variety be able to divert ourselves with the extravagancies   120
of those who want it.

MEDLEY Fools will make you laugh.

EMILIA For once or twice; but the repetition of their folly after a visit
or two grows tedious and insufferable.

LADY TOWNLEY You are a little too delicate,° Emilia.   125

    Enter a Page

PAGE Sir Fopling Flutter, madam, desires to know if you are to be
seen.

LADY TOWNLEY Here's the freshest fool in town, and one who has
not cloyed you yet. Page!

PAGE Madam.   130

LADY TOWNLEY Desire him to walk up.

[*Exit Page*]

DORIMANT Do not you fall on him, Medley, and snub him. Soothe
him up in his extravagance. He will show the better.

MEDLEY You know I have a natural indulgence for fools and need not
this caution, sir.   135

Enter Sir Fopling Flutter, with his Page after him

SIR FOPLING Page, wait without.

[*Exit Page*]

(*To Lady Townley*) Madam, I kiss your hands. I see yesterday was
nothing of chance; the *belles assemblees*° form themselves here every
day. (*To Emilia*) Lady, your servant. Dorimant, let me embrace
thee. Without lying, I have not met with any of my acquaintance   140
who retain so much of Paris as thou dost: the very air thou hadst
when the marquise mistook thee i' th' Tuileries° and cried, 'Hey,
Chevalier,'° and then begged thy pardon.

DORIMANT I would fain wear in fashion as long as I can, sir. 'Tis a
thing to be valued in men as well as baubles.   145

SIR FOPLING Thou art a man of wit and understands the town. Prithee
let thee and I be intimate. There is no living without making some
good man the confidant of our pleasures.

DORIMANT 'Tis true, but there is no man so improper for such a
business as I am.   150

SIR FOPLING Prithee, why hast thou so modest an opinion of thyself?

DORIMANT Why, first, I could never keep a secret in my life;
and, then, there is no charm so infallibly makes me fall in love
with a woman as my knowing a friend loves her. I deal honestly
with you.   155

SIR FOPLING Thy humour's very gallant, or let me perish. I knew a
French count so like thee.

LADY TOWNLEY Wit, I perceive, has more power over you than
beauty, Sir Fopling. Else you would not have let this lady stand so
long neglected.   160

SIR FOPLING (*to Emilia*) A thousand pardons, madam. Some civility's
due of course° upon the meeting a long absent friend. The *éclat* of
so much beauty, I confess, ought to have charmed me sooner.

EMILIA The *brillant*° of so much good language, sir, has much more power than the little beauty I can boast.   165

SIR FOPLING I never saw anything prettier than this high work° on your *point d'Espagne.*°

EMILIA 'Tis not so rich as *point de Venise.*°

SIR FOPLING Not altogether, but looks cooler and is more proper for the season. Dorimant, is not that Medley?   170

DORIMANT The same, sir.

SIR FOPLING [*to Medley*] Forgive me, sir, in this *embarras* of civilities, I could not come to have you in my arms sooner. You understand an equipage° the best of any man in town, I hear.

MEDLEY By my own, you would not guess it.   175

SIR FOPLING There are critics who do not write, sir.

MEDLEY Our peevish poets will scarce allow it.

SIR FOPLING Damn 'em! They'll allow no man wit who does not play the fool like themselves and show it. Have you taken notice of the gallesh° I brought over?   180

MEDLEY O yes. 'T has quite another air than th' English makes.

SIR FOPLING 'Tis as easily known from an English tumbril° as an Inns of Court man° is from one of us.

DORIMANT Truly there is a *bel air*° in galleshes as well as men.

MEDLEY But there are few so delicate to observe it.   185

SIR FOPLING The world is generally very *grossier*° here indeed.

LADY TOWNLEY (*to Emilia*) He's very fine.

EMILIA Extreme proper.°

SIR FOPLING A slight suit I made to appear in at my first arrival—not worthy your consideration, ladies.   190

DORIMANT The pantaloon° is very well mounted.

SIR FOPLING The tassels are new and pretty.

MEDLEY I never saw a coat better cut.

SIR FOPLING It makes me show long-waisted and, I think, slender.

DORIMANT That's the shape our ladies dote on.   195

MEDLEY Your breech, though, is a handful too high in my eye, Sir Fopling.

SIR FOPLING Peace, Medley. I have wished it lower a thousand times, but, a pox on't, 'twill not be.

LADY TOWNLEY His gloves are well fringed, large, and graceful.   200

SIR FOPLING I was always eminent for being *bien ganté.*°

EMILIA He wears nothing but what are originals of the most famous hands in Paris.

SIR FOPLING You are in the right, madam.

LADY TOWNLEY The suit?   205
SIR FOPLING Barroy.°
EMILIA The garniture?°
SIR FOPLING Le Gras.
MEDLEY The shoes?
SIR FOPLING Piccar.   210
DORIMANT The periwig?
SIR FOPLING Chedreux.
LADY TOWNLEY AND EMILIA The gloves?
SIR FOPLING Orangerie.° You know the smell, ladies. Dorimant, I
    could find in my heart for an amusement to have a gallantry with   215
    some of our English ladies.
DORIMANT 'Tis a thing no less necessary to confirm the reputation of
    your wit than a duel will be to satisfy the town of your courage.
SIR FOPLING Here was a woman yesterday—
DORIMANT Mistress Loveit.   220
SIR FOPLING You have named her!
DORIMANT You cannot pitch on a better for your purpose.
SIR FOPLING Prithee, what is she?
DORIMANT A person of quality, and one who has a rest of reputation
    enough° to make the conquest considerable. Besides, I hear she   225
    likes you too.
SIR FOPLING Methoughts she seemed, though, very reserved and
    uneasy all the time I entertained her.
DORIMANT Grimace and affectation! You will see her i' th' Mall
    tonight.   230
SIR FOPLING Prithee, let thee and I take the air together.
DORIMANT I am engaged to Medley, but I'll meet you at St James's°
    and give you some information, upon the which you may regulate
    your proceedings.
SIR FOPLING All the world will be in the Park tonight. Ladies, 'twere   235
    pity to keep so much beauty longer within doors, and rob the Ring°
    of all those charms that should adorn it. [Calling] Hey, Page!
        Enter Page
    See that all my people be ready.
        [Page] goes out again
    Dorimant, à revoir.°
        [Exit Sir Fopling]
MEDLEY A fine mettled° coxcomb.   240
DORIMANT Brisk and insipid.
MEDLEY Pert and dull.

EMILIA However you despise him, gentleman, I'll lay my life he passes for a wit with many.

DORIMANT That may very well be. Nature has her cheats, stums° a   245
brain, and puts sophisticate° dullness often on the tasteless multitude for true wit and good humour. Medley, come.

MEDLEY I must go a little way. I will meet you i' the Mall.

DORIMANT I'll walk through the garden thither. (*To Lady Townley and Emilia*) We shall meet anon and bow.   250

LADY TOWNLEY Not tonight. We are engaged about a business, the knowledge of which may make you laugh hereafter.

MEDLEY Your servant, ladies.

DORIMANT *A revoir*, as Sir Fopling says.
    Exeunt Medley and Dorimant

LADY TOWNLEY The old man will be here immediately.   255

EMILIA Let's expect him i' th' garden.

LADY TOWNLEY [*mimicking Old Bellair*] Go, you are a rogue.

EMILIA I can't abide you.
    Exeunt

3.3

The Mall°

Enter Harriet, Bellair, she pulling him

HARRIET Come along.

BELLAIR And leave your mother?

HARRIET Busy will be sent with a hue and cry after us, but that's no matter.

BELLAIR 'Twill look strangely in me.   5

HARRIET She'll believe it a freak° of mine and never blame your manners.

BELLAIR What reverend acquaintance is that she has met?

HARRIET A fellow beauty of the last king's time,° though by the ruins you would hardly guess it.   10
    Exeunt Bellair and Harriet. Enter Dorimant and crosses the stage. Enter Bellair and Harriet

BELLAIR By this time, your mother is in a fine taking.°

HARRIET If your friend Mr Dorimant were but here now, that she might find me talking with him.

BELLAIR She does not know him, but dreads him, I hear, of all
mankind.   15

HARRIET She concludes if he does but speak to a woman, she's
undone—is on her knees every day to pray heaven defend me
from him.

BELLAIR You do not apprehend him so much as she does.

HARRIET I never saw anything in him that was frightful.   20

BELLAIR On the contrary, have you not observed something extreme
delightful in his wit and person?

HARRIET He's agreeable and pleasant, I must own, but he does so
much affect being so, he displeases me.

BELLAIR Lord, madam, all he does and says is so easy and so natural. 25

HARRIET Some men's verses seem so to the unskilful, but labour i'
the one and affectation in the other to the judicious plainly
appear.

BELLAIR I never heard him accused of affectation before.

Enter Dorimant and stares upon her

HARRIET It passes on the easy town, who are favourably pleased in 30
him to call it humour.

Exeunt Bellair and Harriet

DORIMANT 'Tis she! It must be she—that lovely hair, that easy shape,
those wanton eyes, and all those melting charms about her mouth
which Medley spoke of. I'll follow the lottery° and put in for a prize
with my friend Bellair.   35

Exit Dorimant repeating

'In love the victors from the vanquished fly;
They fly that wound, and they pursue that die.'°

*Enter Bellair and Harriet and, after them, Dorimant standing at
a distance*

BELLAIR Most people prefer High Park° to this place.

HARRIET It has the better reputation, I confess, but I abominate the
dull diversions there: the formal bows, the affected smiles, the silly 40
by-words, and amorous tweers in passing. Here one meets with a
little conversation now and then.

BELLAIR These conversations have been fatal to some of your sex,
madam.

HARRIET It may be so. Because some who want temper° have been 45
undone by gaming, must others who have it wholly deny themselves
the pleasure of play?

DORIMANT (*coming up gently and bowing to her*) Trust me, it were
unreasonable, madam.

HARRIET (*starts and looks grave*) Lord! Who's this?   50

BELLAIR Dorimant.

DORIMANT Is this the woman your father would have you marry?

BELLAIR It is.

DORIMANT Her name.

BELLAIR Harriet.   55

DORIMANT I am not mistaken; she's handsome.°

BELLAIR Talk to her; her wit is better than her face. We were wishing
for you but now.

DORIMANT (*to Harriet*) Overcast with seriousness o' the sudden! A
thousand smiles were shining in that face but now. I never saw so   60
quick a change of weather.

HARRIET (*aside*) I feel as great a change within, but he shall never
know it.

DORIMANT You were talking of play, madam. Pray, what may be your
stint?°   65

HARRIET A little harmless discourse in public walks, or, at most, an
appointment in a box, barefaced, at the playhouse. You are for
masks and private meetings where women engage for all they are
worth, I hear.

DORIMANT I have been used to deep play, but I can make one at°   70
small game when I like my gamester well.

HARRIET And be so unconcerned you'll ha' no pleasure in't.

DORIMANT Where there is a considerable sum to be won, the hope of
drawing people in makes every trifle considerable.

HARRIET The sordidness of men's natures, I know, makes 'em willing   75
to flatter and comply with the rich, though they are sure never to be
the better for 'em.

DORIMANT 'Tis in their power to do us good, and we despair not but
at some time or other they may be willing.

HARRIET To men who have fared in this town like you, 'twould be a   80
great mortification to live on hope. Could you keep a Lent for a
mistress?

DORIMANT In expectation of a happy Easter; and, though time be
very precious, think forty days well lost to gain your favour.

HARRIET Mr Bellair, let us walk; 'tis time to leave him. Men grow dull 85
when they begin to be particular.°

DORIMANT Y' are mistaken. Flattery will not ensue, though I know y'
are greedy of the praises of the whole Mall.

HARRIET You do me wrong.

DORIMANT I do not. As I followed you, I observed how you were   95 pleased when the fops cried 'She's handsome, very handsome; by God she is' and whispered aloud your name—the thousand several forms you put your face into; then, to make yourself more agreeable, how wantonly you played with your head, flung back your locks, and looked smilingly over your shoulder at 'em.

HARRIET I do not go begging the men's as you do the ladies' good liking, with a sly softness in your looks and a gentle slowness in your bows as you pass by 'em. As thus, sir. (*Acts him*) Is not this like you?

Enter Lady Woodvill and Busy

BELLAIR Your mother, madam!

Bellair pulls Harriet. She composes herself

LADY WOODVILL Ah, my dear child Harriet.

BUSY Now is she so pleased with finding her again, she cannot chide her!

LADY WOODVILL Come away.

DORIMANT 'Tis now but high Mall,° madam, the most entertaining time of all the evening.

HARRIET I would fain see that Dorimant, mother, you so cry out of for° a monster. He's in the Mall, I hear.

LADY WOODVILL Come away then! The plague is here, and you should dread the infection.

BELLAIR You may be misinformed of the gentleman.

LADY WOODVILL O no! I hope you do not know him. He is the prince of all the devils in the town, delights in nothing but in rapes and riots.

DORIMANT If you did but hear him speak, madam.

LADY WOODVILL O he has a tongue, they say, would tempt the angels to a second fall.

Enter Sir Fopling with his equipage,° six Footmen, and a Page

SIR FOPLING Hey, Champagne, Norman, La Rose, La Fleur, La Tour, La Verdure!° Dorimant.

LADY WOODVILL Here, here he is among this rout. He names him! Come away, Harriet, come away.

Exeunt Lady Woodvill, Harriet, Busy, and Bellair

DORIMANT This fool's coming has spoiled all. She's gone, but she has left a pleasing image of herself behind that wanders in my soul. It must not settle there.

SIR FOPLING What reverie is this? Speak, man.

DORIMANT 'Snatched from myself, how far behind
Already I behold the shore!'°

Enter Medley

MEDLEY Dorimant, a discovery! I met with Bellair.

DORIMANT You can tell me no news, sir. I know all.

MEDLEY How do you like the daughter?   135

DORIMANT You never came so near truth in your life as you did in her
description.

MEDLEY What think you of the mother?

DORIMANT Whatever I think of her, she thinks very well of me, I find.

MEDLEY Did she know you?   140

DORIMANT She did not. Whether she does now or no, I know not.
Here was a pleasant scene towards, when in came Sir Fopling,
mustering up his equipage, and at the latter end named me and
frighted her away.

MEDLEY Loveit and Bellinda are not far off. I saw 'em alight at   145
St James's.°

DORIMANT Sir Fopling, hark you, a word or two. (*Whispers*) Look you
do not want assurance.

SIR FOPLING I never do on these occasions.

DORIMANT Walk on; we must not be seen together. Make your   150
advantage of what I have told you. The next turn° you will meet the
lady.

SIR FOPLING [*to his Footmen and Page*] Hey! Follow me all.

Exeunt Sir Fopling and his equipage

DORIMANT Medley, you shall see good sport anon between Loveit
and this Fopling.   155

MEDLEY I thought there was something toward by that whisper.

DORIMANT You know a worthy principle of hers?

MEDLEY Not to be so much as civil to a man who speaks to her in the
presence of him she professes to love.

DORIMANT I have encouraged Fopling to talk to her tonight.   160

MEDLEY Now you are here, she will go nigh to beat him.

DORIMANT In the humour she's in, her love will make her do some
very extravagant thing, doubtless.

MEDLEY What was Bellinda's business with you at my Lady
Townley's?   165

DORIMANT To get me to meet Loveit here in order to an *éclaircissement*. I made some difficulty of it and have prepared this rencounter°
to make good my jealousy.

Enter Mrs Loveit, Bellinda, and Pert

MEDLEY Here they come.

DORIMANT I'll meet her and provoke her with a deal of dumb civility   170

in passing by, then turn short and be behind her when Sir Fopling
sets upon her. [*Bows to Mrs Loveit*]

       'See how unregarded now
       That piece of Beauty passes'°

    Exeunt Dorimant and Medley

BELLINDA How wonderful respectfully he bowed!   175

PERT He's always over-mannerly when he has done a mischief.

BELLINDA Methoughts indeed at the same time he had a strange
despising countenance.

PERT The unlucky° look he thinks becomes him.

BELLINDA I was afraid you would have spoke to him, my dear.   180

MRS LOVEIT I would have died first. He shall no more find me the
loving fool he has done.

BELLINDA You love him still!

MRS LOVEIT No.

PERT I wish you did not.   185

MRS LOVEIT I do not, and I will have you think so. What made you
hale me to this odious place, Bellinda?

BELLINDA I hate to be hulched up° in a coach. Walking is much
better.

MRS LOVEIT Would we could meet Sir Fopling now.   190

BELLINDA Lord, would you not avoid him?

MRS LOVEIT I would make him all the advances that may be.

BELLINDA That would confirm Dorimant's suspicion, my dear.

MRS LOVEIT He is not jealous, but I will make him so and be revenged
a way he little thinks on.   195

BELLINDA (*aside*) If she should make him jealous, that may make him
fond of her again. I must dissuade her from it. [*To Mrs Loveit*]
Lord, my dear, this will certainly make him hate you.

MRS LOVEIT 'Twill make him uneasy, though he does not care for me.
I know the effects of jealousy on men of his proud temper.°   200

BELLINDA 'Tis a fantastic remedy: its operations are dangerous and
uncertain.

MRS LOVEIT 'Tis the strongest cordial we can give to dying love; it
often brings it back when there's no sign of life remaining. But I
design not so much the reviving his, as my revenge.   205

    Enter Sir Fopling and his equipage

SIR FOPLING Hey! Bid the coachman send home four of his horses
and bring the coach to Whitehall.°

    Exit Servant

I'll walk over the park. Madam, the honour of kissing your

fair hands is a happiness I missed this afternoon at my Lady
Townley's.   210

MRS LOVEIT You were very obliging, Sir Fopling, the last time I saw
you there.

SIR FOPLING The preference was due to your wit and beauty. [*Bows*]
Madam, your servant. There never was so sweet an evening.

BELLINDA 'T has drawn all the rabble of the town hither.   215

SIR FOPLING 'Tis pity there's not an order made that none but the
beau monde° should walk here.

MRS LOVEIT 'Twould add much to the beauty of the place. See what a
sort of nasty fellows are coming.

> *Enter four*° *ill-fashioned Fellows, singing ' 'Tis not for kisses*
> *alone, etc.'*°

MRS LOVEIT Foh! Their periwigs are scented with tobacco so   220
strong—

SIR FOPLING —It overcomes our pulvilio. Methinks I smell the
coffeehouse they come from.

FIRST MAN Dorimant's convenient,° Madam Loveit.

SECOND MAN I like the oily buttock° with her.   225

THIRD MAN What spruce prig° is that?

FIRST MAN A caravan° lately come from Paris.

SECOND MAN Peace, they smoke.°

> *Exeunt Fellows, singing 'There's something else to be done, etc.'*°
> *Enter Dorimant and Medley*

DORIMANT They're engaged.

MEDLEY She entertains him as if she liked him.   230

DORIMANT Let us go forward, seem earnest in discourse, and show
ourselves. Then you shall see how she'll use him.

BELLINDA Yonder's Dorimant, my dear.

MRS LOVEIT I see him. (*Aside*) He comes insulting,° but I will disappoint him in his expectation. (*To Sir Fopling*) I like this pretty, nice   235
humour of yours, Sir Fopling. [*To Bellinda*] With what a loathing
eye he looked upon those fellows!

SIR FOPLING I sat near one of 'em at a play today and was almost
poisoned with a pair of cordovan gloves° he wears.

MRS LOVEIT O filthy cordovan! How I hate the smell! (*Laughs in a*   240
loud, affected way)

SIR FOPLING Did you observe, madam, how their cravats hung loose
an inch from their neck and what a frightful air it gave 'em?

MRS LOVEIT O I took particular notice of one that is always spruced
up with a deal of dirty, sky-coloured ribbon.   245

BELLINDA That's one of the walking flageolets° who haunt the Mall o' nights.

MRS LOVEIT O, I remember him! H' has a hollow tooth,° enough to spoil the sweetness of an evening.

SIR FOPLING I have seen the tallest walk the streets with a dainty pair   250
of boxes,° neatly buckled on.

MRS LOVEIT And a little footboy at his heels, pocket-high, with a flat cap—a dirty face—

SIR FOPLING And a snotty nose.

MRS LOVEIT O, odious! There's many of my own sex with that Holborn   255
equipage° trig to Gray's Inn Walks,° and now and then travel hither on a Sunday.

MEDLEY She takes no notice of you.

DORIMANT Damn her! I am jealous° of a counter-plot!

MRS LOVEIT Your liveries are the finest, Sir Fopling. O, that page!   260
That page is prettily'st dressed. They are all Frenchmen?

SIR FOPLING There's one damned English blockhead among 'em; you may know him by his mien.

MRS LOVEIT [pointing] O, that's he, that's he! What do you call him?

SIR FOPLING [calls to a Footman] Hey! [To Mrs Loveit] I know not what to call him.   265

MRS LOVEIT What's your name?

FOOTMAN John Trott, madam!

SIR FOPLING O insufferable! Trott, Trott, Trott! There's nothing so barbarous as the names of our English servants. What countryman   270
are you,° sirrah?

FOOTMAN Hampshire, sir.

SIR FOPLING Then Hampshire be your name.° [Hails him] Hey, Hampshire!

MRS LOVEIT O that sound! That sound becomes the mouth of a man   275
of quality.

MEDLEY Dorimant, you look a little bashful on the matter.

DORIMANT She dissembles better than I thought she could have done.

MEDLEY You have tempted her with too luscious a bait. She bites at   280
the coxcomb.

DORIMANT She cannot fall from loving me to that?

MEDLEY You begin to be jealous in earnest.

DORIMANT Of one I do not love.

MEDLEY You did love her.   285

DORIMANT The fit has long been over.

MEDLEY But I have known men fall into dangerous relapses when they have found a woman inclining to another.

DORIMANT (*to himself*) He guesses the secret of my heart! I am concerned but dare not show it, lest Bellinda should mistrust all I have done to gain her. 290

BELLINDA (*aside*) I have watched his look and find no alteration there. Did he love her, some signs of jealousy would have appeared.

DORIMANT I hope this happy evening, madam, has reconciled you to the scandalous Mall. We shall have you now hankering° here again. 295

MRS LOVEIT Sir Fopling, will you walk?

SIR FOPLING I am all obedience, madam.

MRS LOVEIT Come along then; and let's agree to be malicious on all the ill-fashioned things we meet.

SIR FOPLING We'll make a critique on the whole Mall, Madam. 300

MRS LOVEIT Bellinda, you shall engage.°

BELLINDA To the reserve of our friends, my dear.

MRS LOVEIT No, no! Exceptions°—

SIR FOPLING We'll sacrifice all to our diversion.

MRS LOVEIT All, all. 305

SIR FOPLING All.

BELLINDA All? Then let it be.

Exeunt Sir Fopling, Loveit, Bellinda, and Pert, laughing

MEDLEY Would you had brought some more of your friends, Dorimant, to have been witnesses of Sir Fopling's disgrace and your triumph. 310

DORIMANT 'Twere unreasonable to desire you not to laugh at me, but pray do not expose me to the town this day or two.

MEDLEY By that time you hope to have regained your credit.

DORIMANT I know she hates Fopling, and only makes use of him in hope to work on me again. Had it not been for some powerful 315 considerations which will be removed tomorrow morning, I had made her pluck off this mask and show the passion that lies panting under.

Enter a Footman

MEDLEY Here comes a man from Bellair, with news of your last° adventure. 320

DORIMANT I am glad he sent him. I long to know the consequence of our parting.

FOOTMAN Sir, my master desires you to come to my Lady Townley's presently and bring Mr Medley with you. My Lady Woodvill and her daughter are there. 325

MEDLEY Then all's well, Dorimant.

FOOTMAN They have sent for the fiddles and mean to dance. He bid
me tell you, sir, the old lady does not know you, and would have you
own yourself to be Mr Courtage. They are all prepared to receive
you by that name.   330

DORIMANT That foppish admirer of quality, who flatters the very
meat at honourable tables and never offers love to a woman below a
lady-grandmother.

MEDLEY You know the character you are to act, I see.

DORIMANT This is Harriet's contrivance—wild, witty, lovesome,   335
beautiful, and young. Come along, Medley.

MEDLEY This new woman would well supply the loss of Loveit.

DORIMANT That business must not end so. Before tomorrow sun is
set, I will revenge and clear it.
>   'And you and Loveit to her cost shall find,
>   I fathom all the depths of Womankind.'°

Exeunt

4.1

[*Lady Townley's house*]

The scene opens° with the fiddles playing a country dance.

Enter Dorimant, Lady Woodvill, Bellair and Harriet, Old Bellair and Emilia, Medley and Lady Townley, as having just ended the dance.

OLD BELLAIR So, so so! A smart bout,° a very smart bout, adod!

LADY TOWNLEY How do you like Emilia's dancing, brother?

OLD BELLAIR Not at all, not at all.

LADY TOWNLEY You speak not what you think, I am sure.

OLD BELLAIR No matter for that. Go, bid her dance no more. It don't   5
become her, it don't become her. Tell her I say so. (*Aside*) Adod, I love her.

DORIMANT (*to Lady Woodvill*) All people mingle nowadays, madam; and in public places women of quality have the least respect showed 'em.   10

LADY WOODVILL I protest, you say the truth, Mr Courtage.

DORIMANT Forms and ceremonies, the only things that uphold quality and greatness, are now shamefully laid aside and neglected.

LADY WOODVILL Well, this is not the women's age, let 'em think what they will. Lewdness is the business now; love was the business   15
in my time.

DORIMANT The women indeed are little beholding to the young men of this age. They're generally only dull admirers of themselves, and make their court to nothing but their periwigs and their cravats, and would be more concerned for the disordering of 'em, though   20
on a good occasion, than a young maid would be for the tumbling° of her head or handkercher.°

LADY WOODVILL I protest, you hit 'em.

DORIMANT They are very assiduous to show themselves at court, well dressed to the women of quality; but their business is with the stale   25
mistresses of the town, who are prepared to receive their lazy addresses by industrious old lovers who have cast 'em off and made 'em easy.

HARRIET He fits my mother's humour so well, a little more and she'll dance a kissing dance° with him anon.   30

MEDLEY Dutifully observed, madam.

DORIMANT They pretend to be great critics in beauty. By their talk, you would think they liked no face and yet can dote on an ill one, if it belong to a laundress or a tailor's daughter. They cry a woman's past her prime at twenty, decayed at four-and-twenty, old and   35
insufferable at thirty.

LADY WOODVILL Insufferable at thirty! That they are in the wrong, Mr Courtage, at five-and-thirty, there are living proofs enough to convince 'em.

DORIMANT Ay, madam. There's Mrs Setlooks, Mrs Droplip, and my   40
Lady Loud. Show me among all our opening buds, a face that promises so much beauty as the remains of theirs.

LADY WOODVILL The depraved appetite of this vicious age tastes° nothing but green fruit, and loathes it when 'tis kindly° ripened.   45

DORIMANT Else so many deserving women, madam, would not be so untimely neglected.

LADY WOODVILL I protest, Mr Courtage, a dozen such good men as you would be enough to atone for that wicked Dorimant and all the under-debauchees of the town.   50

    Harriet, Emilia, Bellair, Medley, Lady Townley break out into
    a laughter

What's the matter there?

MEDLEY A pleasant mistake, madam, that a lady has made occasions a little laughter.

OLD BELLAIR Come, come, you keep 'em idle! They are impatient till the fiddles play again.   55

DORIMANT You are not weary, madam?

LADY WOODVILL One dance more! I cannot refuse you, Mr Courtage.

    They dance. After the dance, Old Bellair, singing and dancing, up
    to Emilia.

EMILIA You are very active, sir.

OLD BELLAIR Adod, sirrah. When I was a young fellow, I could ha' capered up to my woman's gorget.°   60

DORIMANT [*to Lady Woodvill*] You are willing to rest yourself, madam?

LADY TOWNLEY [*to Lady Woodvill and Dorimant*] We'll walk into my chamber and sit down.

MEDLEY Leave us Mr Courtage. He's a dancer, and the young ladies   65
are not weary yet.

LADY WOODVILL We'll send him out again.

HARRIET If you do not quickly, I know where to send for Mr Dorimant.

LADY WOODVILL This girl's head, Mr Courtage, is ever running on
that wild fellow.   70

DORIMANT 'Tis well you have got her a good husband, madam. That
will settle it.

Exeunt Lady Townley, Lady Woodvill, and Dorimant

OLD BELLAIR (*to Emilia*) Adod, sweetheart, be advised and do not
throw thyself away on a young, idle fellow.

EMILIA I have no such intention, sir.   75

OLD BELLAIR Have a little patience! Thou shalt have the man I spake
of. Adod, he loves thee and will make a good husband. But no
words.

EMILIA But, sir—

OLD BELLAIR No answer. Out a pize! Peace, and think on' t.   80

Enter Dorimant

DORIMANT Your company is desired within, sir.

OLD BELLAIR I go, I go! Good Mr Courtage, fare you well! (*To
Emilia*) Go! I'll see you no more.

EMILIA What have I done, sir?

OLD BELLAIR You are ugly, you are ugly! Is she not, Mr Courtage?   85

EMILIA Better words, or I shan't abide you.

OLD BELLAIR Out a pize! Adod, what does she say? Hit her a pat for
me there.

Exit Old Bellair

MEDLEY You have charms for the whole family.

DORIMANT You'll spoil all with some unseasonable jest, Medley.   90

MEDLEY You see I confine my tongue and am content to be a bare°
spectator, much contrary to my nature.

EMILIA Methinks, Mr Dorimant, my Lady Woodvill is a little fond of
you.

DORIMANT Would her daughter were.   95

MEDLEY It may be you may find her so. Try her: you have an
opportunity.

DORIMANT And I will not lose it. Bellair, here's a lady has something
to say to you.

BELLAIR I will wait upon her. Mr Medley, we have both business with 100
you.

DORIMANT Get you altogether then. (*To Harriet*) That demure curt-
sey is not amiss in jest, but do not think in earnest it becomes you.

HARRIET Affectation is catching, I find; from your grave bow I got it.

DORIMANT Where had you all that scorn and coldness in your look?   105

HARRIET From nature, sir. Pardon my want of art. I have not learnt those softnesses and languishings which now in faces are so much in fashion.

DORIMANT You need 'em not. You have a sweetness of your own, if you would but calm your frowns and let it settle. 110

HARRIET My eyes are wild and wandering like my passions and cannot yet be tied to rules of charming.

DORIMANT Women indeed have commonly a method of managing those messengers of love. Now they will look as if they would kill, and anon they will look as if they were dying. They point and 115 rebate° their glances, the better to invite us.

HARRIET I like this variety well enough, but hate the set face that always looks as if it would say, 'Come love me'—a woman who at plays makes the *doux yeux*° to a whole audience and at home cannot forbear 'em to her monkey.° 120

DORIMANT Put on a gentle smile and let me see how well it will become you.

HARRIET I am sorry my face does not please you as it is, but I shall not be complaisant and change it.

DORIMANT Though you are obstinate, I know 'tis capable of 125 improvement and shall do you justice, madam, if I chance to be at court when the critics of the circle° pass their judgement, for thither you must come.

HARRIET And expect to be taken in pieces, have all my features examined, every motion censured, and on the whole be condemned to be 130 but pretty or a beauty of the lowest rate. What think you?

DORIMANT The women, nay, the very lovers who belong to the drawing room, will maliciously allow you more than that. They always grant what is apparent, that they may the better be believed when they name concealed faults they cannot easily be disproved in. 135

HARRIET Beauty runs as great a risk° exposed at court as wit does on the stage, where the ugly and the foolish all are free to censure.

DORIMANT (*aside*) I love her, and dare not let her know it. I fear she has an ascendant° o'er me and may revenge the wrongs I have done her sex. (*To Harriet*) Think of making a party,° madam. Love will 140 engage.

HARRIET You make me start! I did not think to have heard of love from you.

DORIMANT I never knew what 'twas to have a settled ague° yet, but now and then have had irregular fits. 145

HARRIET Take heed. Sickness after long health is commonly more violent and dangerous.

DORIMANT (*aside*) I have took the infection from her and feel the disease now spreading in me. (*To her*) Is the name of love so frightful that you dare not stand it?   150

HARRIET 'Twill do little execution out of your mouth on me, I am sure.

DORIMANT It has been fatal—

HARRIET To some easy women, but we are not all born to one destiny. I was informed you use to° laugh at love and not make it.   155

DORIMANT The time has been, but now I must speak—

HARRIET If it be on that idle subject, I will put on my serious look, turn my head carelessly from you, drop my lip, let my eyelids fall, and hang half o'er my eyes—thus, while you buzz a speech of an hour long in my ear, and I answer never a word! Why do you not   160
begin?

DORIMANT That the company may take notice how passionately I make advances of love, and how disdainfully you receive 'em.

HARRIET When your love's grown strong enough to make you bear being laughed at, I'll give you leave to trouble me with it. Till when,   165
pray forbear, sir.

Enter Sir Fopling and others in masks

DORIMANT What's here? Masquerades?°

HARRIET I thought that foppery had been left off, and people might have been in private with a fiddle.

DORIMANT 'Tis endeavoured to be kept on foot still by some who   170
find themselves the more acceptable the less they are known.

BELLAIR This must be Sir Fopling.

MEDLEY That extraordinary habit shows it.

BELLAIR What are the rest?

MEDLEY A company of French rascals whom he picked up in Paris   175
and has brought over to be his dancing equipage on these occasions.
Make him own himself: a fool is very troublesome when he presumes
he is incognito.

SIR FOPLING (*to Harriet*) Do you know me?

HARRIET Ten to one but I guess at you.   180

SIR FOPLING Are you women as fond of a vizard as we men are?

HARRIET I am very fond of a vizard that covers a face I do not like, sir.

BELLAIR Here are no masks, you see, sir, but those which came with you. This was intended a private meeting, but because you look like a gentleman, if you will discover yourself and we know you to be   185
such, you shall be welcome.

SIR FOPLING (*pulling off his mask*) Dear Bellair!

MEDLEY Sir Fopling! How came you hither?

SIR FOPLING Faith, as I was coming late from Whitehall, after the
king's *couchée*,° one of my people told me he had heard fiddles at   190
my Lady Townley's and—

DORIMANT You need not say any more, sir.

SIR FOPLING Dorimant, let me kiss thee.

DORIMANT Hark you, Sir Fopling. (*Whispers*)

SIR FOPLING Enough, enough, Courtage. [*Sees Harriet*] A pretty   195
kind of young woman that, Medley. I observed her in the Mall
more *éveillée* than our English women commonly are. Prithee what
is she?

MEDLEY The most noted coquette in town; beware of her.

SIR FOPLING Let her be what she will, I know how to take my meas-   200
ures.° In Paris the mode is to flatter the *prude*, laugh at the *faux-
prude*,° make serious love to the *demi-prude*,° and only rally with the
coquette. Medley, what think you?

MEDLEY That, for all this smattering of the mathematics, you may be
out in your judgement at tennis.   205

SIR FOPLING What a *coq-à-l'âne*° is this? I talk of women and thou
answer'st tennis.

MEDLEY Mistakes will be for want of apprehension.

SIR FOPLING I am very glad of the acquaintance I have with this
family.   210

MEDLEY My lady truly is a good woman.

SIR FOPLING Ah, Dorimant!—Courtage, I would say—would thou
hadst spent the last winter in Paris with me. When thou wert there,
La Corneus and Sallyes° were the only habitudes° we had. A
comedian would have been a *bonne fortune*.° No stranger ever   215
passed his time so well as I did some months before I came over. I
was well received in a dozen families, where all the women of
quality used to visit. I have intrigues to tell thee more pleasant than
ever thou read'st in a novel.

HARRIET Write 'em, sir, and oblige us women. Our language wants   220
such little stories.

SIR FOPLING Writing, madam, 's a mechanic° part of wit. A gentleman
should never go beyond a song or a billet.

HARRIET Bussy was a gentleman.

SIR FOPLING Who? D'Ambois?   225

MEDLEY [*aside*] Was there ever such a brisk blockhead?

HARRIET Not D'Ambois, sir, but Rabutin.° He who writ the *Loves of
France*.

SIR FOPLING That may be, madam. Many gentlemen do things that are below 'em. Damn your authors, Courtage. Women are the prettiest things we can fool away our time with. 230

HARRIET I hope ye have wearied yourself tonight at court, sir, and will not think of fooling with anybody here.

SIR FOPLING I cannot complain of my fortune there, madam. Dorimant— 235

DORIMANT Again!

SIR FOPLING Courtage, a pox on't! I have something to tell thee. When I had made my court within°, I came out and flung myself upon the mat under the state° i' th' outward room, i' th' midst of half a dozen beauties who were withdrawn to jeèr° among 240 themselves, as they called it.

DORIMANT Did you know 'em?

SIR FOPLING Not one of 'em, by heavens, not I! But they were all your friends.

DORIMANT How are you sure of that? 245

SIR FOPLING Why, we laughed at all the town, spared nobody but yourself. They found me a man for their purpose.

DORIMANT I know you are malicious to your power.°

SIR FOPLING And, faith, I had occasion to show it, for I never saw more gaping fools at a ball or on a birthday.° 250

DORIMANT You learned who the women were.

SIR FOPLING No matter! They frequent the drawing room.

DORIMANT And entertain themselves pleasantly at the expense of all the fops who come there.

SIR FOPLING That's their business. Faith, I sifted 'em° and find they 255 have a sort of wit among them. (*Pinches a tallow candle*) Ah, filthy!°

DORIMANT Look, he has been pinching the tallow candle.

SIR FOPLING How can you breathe in a room where there's grease frying? Dorimant, thou art intimate with my lady: advise her for her own sake and the good company that comes hither to burn wax 260 lights.

HARRIET What are these masquerades who stand so obsequiously at a distance?

SIR FOPLING A set of baladines, whom I picked out of the best in France and brought over, with a *flûte douce* or two. My servants; 265 they shall entertain you.

HARRIET I had rather see you dance yourself, Sir Fopling.

SIR FOPLING And I had rather do it—all the company knows it—but, madam—

MEDLEY Come, come! No excuses, Sir Fopling.   270

SIR FOPLING By heavens, Medley—

MEDLEY Like a woman, I find you must be struggled with before one brings you what you desire.

HARRIET (*aside*) Can he dance?

EMILIA And fence and sing too, if you believe him.   275

DORIMANT He has no more excellence in his heels than in his head. He went to Paris a plain, bashful English blockhead and is returned a fine, undertaking French fop.

MEDLEY I cannot prevail.

SIR FOPLING Do not think it want of complaisance, madam.   280

HARRIET You are too well bred to want that, Sir Fopling. I believe it want of power.

SIR FOPLING By heavens, and so it is. I have sat up so damned late and drunk so cursed hard since I came to this lewd town that I am fit for nothing but low dancing now—a *courante*, a *bourrée*, or a   285
menuet°—but St André° tells me, if I will but be regular, in one month I shall rise again. (*Endeavours at a caper*) Pox on this debauchery!

EMILIA I have heard your dancing much commended.

SIR FOPLING It had the good fortune to please in Paris. I was judged to   290
rise within an inch as high as the Basque° in an entry° I danced there.

HARRIET I am mightily taken with this fool. Let us sit. Here's a seat, Sir Fopling.

SIR FOPLING At your feet, madam. I can be nowhere so much at ease. By your leave, gown.   295

HARRIET AND EMILIA Ah, you'll spoil it!

SIR FOPLING No matter!° My clothes are my creatures. I make 'em to make my court to you ladies. [*To the musicians*] Hey! *Qu'on commence!*°

> [*Dorimant and Harriet, Bellair and Emilia, and Sir Fopling, by himself, dance*]

To an English dancer, English motions. I was forced to entertain°   300
this fellow, one of my set miscarrying. O horrid! Leave your damned manner of dancing and put on the French air. Have you not a° pattern before you? Pretty well! Imitation in time may bring him to something.

> *After the dance enter Old Bellair, Lady Woodvill, and Lady Townley*

OLD BELLAIR Hey, adod! What have we here, a mumming?°   305

LADY WOODVILL Where's my daughter? Harriet?

DORIMANT Here, here, madam. I know not but under these disguises there may be dangerous sparks. I gave the young lady warning!

LADY WOODVILL Lord, I am so obliged to you, Mr Courtage.

HARRIET Lord, how you admire this man!   310

LADY WOODVILL What have you to except against him?

HARRIET He's a fop.

LADY WOODVILL He's not a Dorimant, a wild, extravagant fellow of the times.

HARRIET He's a man made up of forms and commonplaces, sucked   315
out of the remaining lees of the last age.

LADY WOODVILL He's so good a man that, were you not engaged—

LADY TOWNLEY You'll have but little night to sleep in.

LADY WOODVILL Lord, 'tis perfect day.°

DORIMANT (aside) The hour is almost come I appointed Bellinda; and   320
I am not so foppishly in love here to forget. I am flesh and blood
yet.

LADY TOWNLEY I am very sensible,° madam.

LADY WOODVILL Lord, madam!

HARRIET Look in what a struggle is my poor mother yonder!   325

BELLAIR She has much ado to bring out the compliment.

DORIMANT She strains hard for it.

HARRIET See, see! Her head tottering, her eyes staring, and her underlip trembling.

DORIMANT Now, now, she's in the very convulsions of her civility.   330
(Aside) 'Sdeath, I shall lose Bellinda. I must fright her hence. She'll
be an hour in this fit of good manners else. (To Lady Woodvill) Do
you not know Sir Fopling, madam?

LADY WOODVILL I have seen that face. Oh heaven! 'Tis the same we
met in the Mall. How came he here?   335

DORIMANT A fiddle in this town is a kind of fop-call. No sooner it strikes up, but the house is besieged with an army of masquerades straight.

LADY WOODVILL Lord, I tremble, Mr Courtage! For certain Dorimant is in the company.   340

DORIMANT I cannot confidently say he is not. You had best begone. I will wait upon you; your daughter is in the hands of Mr Bellair.

LADY WOODVILL I'll see her before me. Harriet, come away.

          [Exeunt Lady Woodvill and Harriet]

BELLAIR [calling to servants offstage] Lights, lights!

LADY TOWNLEY Light down there.   345

          [Exeunt Bellair, Lady Townley, and Emilia]

OLD BELLAIR Adod, it needs not.

DORIMANT [*to servants*] Call my Lady Woodvill's coach to the door quickly.

    [*Exit Dorimant. Medley begins to follow him*]

OLD BELLAIR Stay, Mr Medley. Let the young fellows do that duty. We will drink a glass of wine together. 'Tis good after dancing! 350
    [*Sees Sir Fopling*] What mumming spark is that?

MEDLEY He is not to be comprehended in few words.

SIR FOPLING [*to one of his servants*] Hey, La Tour!

MEDLEY Whither away, Sir Fopling?

SIR FOPLING I have business with Courtage. 355

MEDLEY He'll but put the ladies into their coach and come up again.

OLD BELLAIR In the meantime, I'll call for a bottle.

    Exit Old Bellair. Enter Bellair

MEDLEY Where's Dorimant?

BELLAIR Stolen home. He has had business waiting for him there all this night, I believe, by an impatience I observed in him. 360

MEDLEY Very likely, 'tis but dissembling drunkenness, railing at his friends, and the kind soul will embrace the blessing and forget the tedious expectation.

SIR FOPLING I must speak with him before I sleep!

BELLAIR Emilia and I are resolved on that business. 365

MEDLEY Peace. Here's your father.

    [*Enter*] *Old Bellair, and Butler with a bottle of wine*

OLD BELLAIR The women are all gone to bed. [*To Butler*] Fill, boy! Mr Medley, begin a health.

MEDLEY (*whispers*) To Emilia!

OLD BELLAIR Out a pize! She's a rogue, and I'll not pledge you. 370

MEDLEY I know you well.°

OLD BELLAIR Adod, drink it then.

SIR FOPLING Let us have the new bachique.°

OLD BELLAIR Adod, that is a hard° word! What does it mean, sir?

MEDLEY A catch or drinking song. 375

OLD BELLAIR Let us have it then.

SIR FOPLING Fill the glasses round and draw up in a body. [*To Musicians*] Hey! Music!

    Musicians sing°

    The pleasures of love and the joys of good wine,°
    To perfect our happiness, wisely we join. 380
      We to beauty all day

> *Give the sovereign sway,*
> *And her favourite nymphs devoutly obey.*
> *At the plays we are constantly making our court;*
> *And when they are ended, we follow the sport*   385
> *To the Mall and the Park,*
> *Where we love till 'tis dark.*
> *Then sparkling champagne°*
> *Puts an end to their reign;*
> *It quickly recovers*   390
> *Poor languishing lovers,*
> *Makes us frolic and gay, and drowns all our sorrow.*
> *But, alas, we relapse again on the morrow.*
> *Let every man stand*
> *With his glass in his hand,*   395
> *And briskly discharge at the word of command.*
> *Here's a health to all those*
> *Whom tonight we depose.*
> *Wine and beauty by turns great souls should inspire.*
> *Present all together; and now, boys, give fire!°*   400

OLD BELLAIR Adod, a pretty business and very merry.

SIR FOPLING Hark you, Medley. Let you and I take the fiddles and go waken Dorimant.

MEDLEY We shall do him a courtesy, if it be as I guess. For after the fatigue of this night, he'll quickly have his belly full and be glad of 405
an occasion to cry, 'Take away, Handy'!

BELLAIR I'll go with you, and there we'll consult about affairs, Medley.

OLD BELLAIR (*looks on his watch*) Adod, 'tis six o'clock!

SIR FOPLING Let's away then.   410

OLD BELLAIR Mr Medley, my sister tells me you are an honest man. And, adod, I love you. Few words and hearty, that's the way with old Harry, old Harry.

SIR FOPLING [*to his servants*] Light your *flambeaux*.° Hey!

OLD BELLAIR What does the man mean?   415

MEDLEY 'Tis day, Sir Fopling.

SIR FOPLING No matter! Our serenade will look the greater.

> *Exeunt*

4.2

Dorimant's lodging.° A table, a candle, a toilet, etc. Handy tying up linen.

Enter Dorimant in his gown and Bellinda

DORIMANT Why will you be gone so soon?

BELLINDA Why did you stay out so late?

DORIMANT Call a chair, Handy!

[*Exit Handy*]

What makes you tremble so?

BELLINDA I have a thousand fears about me. Have I not been seen,   5
think you?

DORIMANT By nobody but myself and trusty Handy.

BELLINDA Where are all your people?

DORIMANT I have dispersed 'em on sleeveless errands.° What does
that sigh mean?   10

BELLINDA Can you be so unkind to ask me? Well (*sighs*), were it to do
again—

DORIMANT We should do it, should we not?

BELLINDA I think we should. The wickeder man you to make me love
so well. Will you be discreet now?   15

DORIMANT I will.

BELLINDA You cannot.

DORIMANT Never doubt it.

BELLINDA I will not expect it.

DORIMANT You do me wrong.   20

BELLINDA You have no more power to keep the secret than I had not
to trust you with it.

DORIMANT By all the joys I have had and those you keep in store—

BELLINDA —You'll do for my sake what you never did before.°

DORIMANT By that truth thou hast spoken, a wife shall sooner betray   25
herself to her husband.

BELLINDA Yet I had rather you should be false in this than in another
thing you promised me.

DORIMANT What's that?

BELLINDA That you would never see Loveit more but in public   30
places: in the park, at court, and plays.

DORIMANT 'Tis not likely a man should be fond of seeing a damned
old play when there is a new one acted.

BELLINDA I dare not trust your promise.

DORIMANT You may.   35

BELLINDA This does not satisfy me. You shall swear you never will
see her more.

DORIMANT I will: a thousand oaths. By all—

BELLINDA Hold! You shall not, now I think on 't better.

DORIMANT I will swear.   40

BELLINDA I shall grow jealous of the oath and think I owe your truth
to that, not to your love.

DORIMANT Then, by my love! No other oath I'll swear.

>*Enter Handy*

HANDY Here's a chair.

BELLINDA Let me go.   45

DORIMANT I cannot.

BELLINDA Too willingly, I fear.

DORIMANT Too unkindly feared. When will you promise me again?

BELLINDA Not this fortnight.

DORIMANT You will be better than your word.   50

BELLINDA I think I shall. Will it not make you love me less?

>*Fiddles offstage*

(*Starting*) Hark! What fiddles are these?

DORIMANT Look out, Handy.

>*Exit Handy and returns*

HANDY Mr Medley, Mr Bellair, and Sir Fopling. They are coming up.

DORIMANT How got they in?   55

HANDY The door was open for the chair.

BELLINDA Lord, let me fly.

DORIMANT Here, here, down the back stairs. I'll see you into your
chair.

BELLINDA No, no! Stay and receive 'em. And be sure you keep your   60
word and never see Loveit more. Let it be a proof of your kindness.

DORIMANT It shall. Handy, direct her. (*Kissing her hand*) Everlasting
love go along with thee.

>*Exeunt Bellinda and Handy. Enter Bellair, Medley, and Sir*
>*Fopling Flutter*

BELLAIR Not abed yet?

MEDLEY You have had an irregular fit,° Dorimant.   65

DORIMANT I have.

BELLAIR And is it off already?

DORIMANT Nature has done her part, gentlemen. When she falls
kindly to work, great cures are effected in little time, you know.

SIR FOPLING We thought there was a wench in the case by the chair   70
that waited. Prithee make us a *confidence*.°

DORIMANT Excuse me.

SIR FOPLING *Le sage*° Dorimant. Was she pretty?

DORIMANT So pretty she may come to keep her coach and pay parish duties° if the good humour of the age continue.

MEDLEY And be of the number of the ladies kept by public-spirited men for the good of the whole town.

SIR FOPLING Well said, Medley.

Sir Fopling dancing by himself

BELLAIR See Sir Fopling dancing.

DORIMANT You are practising and have a mind to recover, I see.

SIR FOPLING Prithee, Dorimant, why hast not thou a glass hung up here? A room is the dullest thing without one.

BELLAIR Here is company to entertain you.

SIR FOPLING But I mean in case of being alone. In a glass, a man may entertain himself—

DORIMANT The shadow of himself indeed.

SIR FOPLING —Correct the errors of his motions and his dress.

MEDLEY I find, Sir Fopling, in your solitude, you remember the saying of the wise man and study yourself.°

SIR FOPLING 'Tis the best diversion in our retirements. Dorimant, thou art a pretty fellow and wear'st thy clothes well, but I never saw thee have a handsome cravat. Were they made up like mine, they'd give another air to thy face. Prithee let me send my man to dress thee but one day. By heavens, an Englishman cannot tie a ribbon!

DORIMANT They are something clumsy-fisted.

SIR FOPLING I have brought over the prettiest fellow that ever spread a toilet. He served some time under Mérille,° the greatest genie° in the world for a *valet de chambre*.

DORIMANT What? He who formerly belonged to the Duke of Candale?°

SIR FOPLING The same, and got him his immortal reputation.

DORIMANT Y' have a very fine brandenburgh° on, Sir Fopling.

SIR FOPLING It serves to wrap me up after the fatigue of a ball.

MEDLEY I see you often in it, with your periwig tied up.°

SIR FOPLING We should not always be in a set dress. 'Tis more *en cavalier*° to appear now and then in a *déshabillé*.°

MEDLEY Pray, how goes your business with Loveit?

SIR FOPLING You might have answered yourself in the Mall last night. Dorimant, did you not see the advances she made me? I have been endeavouring at a song.

DORIMANT Already?

SIR FOPLING 'Tis my *coup d'essai*° in English. I would fain have thy opinion of it.

DORIMANT Let's see it.   115

SIR FOPLING Hey, page! Give me my song. Bellair, here thou hast a pretty voice; sing it.

BELLAIR Sing it yourself, Sir Fopling.

SIR FOPLING Excuse me.

BELLAIR You learnt to sing in Paris.   120

SIR FOPLING I did of Lambert,° the greatest master in the world; but I have his own fault, a weak voice, and care not to sing out of a ruelle.°

DORIMANT [*aside*] A ruelle is a pretty cage for a singing fop indeed.

BELLAIR (*reads the song*)   125

       How charming Phyllis is, how fair!
         Ah, that she were as willing
       To ease my wounded heart of care,
         And make her eyes less killing.
       I sigh! I sigh! I languish now,   130
         And love will not let me rest;
       I drive about the park and bow
         Still as I meet my dearest.°

SIR FOPLING Sing it, sing it, man. It goes to a pretty new tune which I am confident was made by Baptiste.°   135

MEDLEY Sing it yourself, Sir Fopling; he does not know the tune.

SIR FOPLING I'll venture.

      Sir Fopling sings

DORIMANT Ay, marry! Now 'tis something. I shall not flatter you, Sir Fopling, there is not much thought in't; but 'tis passionate and well turned.   140

MEDLEY After the French way.

SIR FOPLING That I aimed at. Does it not give you a lively image of the thing? Slap down goes the glass,° and thus we are at it.

DORIMANT It does indeed, I perceive, Sir Fopling. You'll be the very head of the sparks, who are lucky in compositions of this nature.   145

      Enter Sir Fopling's Footman

SIR FOPLING La Tour,° is the bath ready?

FOOTMAN Yes, sir.

SIR FOPLING *Adieu donc, mes chers.*°

      Exit Sir Fopling [*and his Footman*]

MEDLEY When have you your revenge on Loveit, Dorimant?

DORIMANT I will but change my linen° and about it.   150

MEDLEY The powerful considerations which hindered have been removed then?

DORIMANT Most luckily, this morning. You must along with me; my reputation lies at stake there.

MEDLEY I am engaged to Bellair.   155

DORIMANT What's your business?

MEDLEY Ma-tri-money, an't° like you.

DORIMANT It does not, sir.

BELLAIR It may in time, Dorimant. What think you of Mrs Harriet?

DORIMANT What does she think of me?   160

BELLAIR I am confident she loves you.

DORIMANT How does it appear?

BELLAIR Why, she's never well but when she's talking of you, but then she finds all the faults in you she can. She laughs at all who commend you, but then she speaks ill of all who do not.   165

DORIMANT Women of her temper betray themselves by their over-cunning. I had once a growing love with a lady who would always quarrel with me when I came to see her; and yet was never quiet if I stayed a day from her.

BELLAIR My father is in love with Emilia.   170

DORIMANT That is a good warrant for your proceedings. Go on and prosper; I must to Loveit. Medley, I am sorry you cannot be a witness.

MEDLEY Make her meet Sir Fopling again in the same place, and use him ill before me.   175

DORIMANT That may be brought about, I think. I'll be at your aunt's anon and give you joy,° Mr Bellair.

BELLAIR You had not best think of Mrs Harriet too much. Without church security,° there's no taking up there.°

DORIMANT I may fall into the snare too. But—   180
    The wise will find a difference in our fate:
    You wed a woman, I a good estate.
Exeunt

4.3

[*The Mall, near Mrs Loveit's lodging*]°
Enter the chair with Bellinda. The Chairmen set it down and open it. Bellinda starting

BELLINDA (*surprised*) Lord, where am I? In the Mall! [*To the Chairmen*]
Whither have you brought me?

FIRST CHAIRMAN You gave us no directions, madam.

BELLINDA (*aside*) The fright I was in made me forget it.

FIRST CHAIRMAN We use to carry a lady from the squire's hither.   5

BELLINDA (*aside*) This is Loveit! I am undone if she sees me. [*To the
Chairmen*] Quickly carry me away.

FIRST CHAIRMAN Whither, an't like, your honour?

BELLINDA Ask no questions.

  Enter [Mrs] Loveit's Footman

FOOTMAN Have you seen my lady, madam?   10

BELLINDA I am just come to wait upon her.

FOOTMAN She will be glad to see you, madam. She sent me to you
this morning to desire your company, and I was told you went out
by five o'clock.

BELLINDA (*aside*) More and more unlucky!   15

FOOTMAN Will you walk in, madam?

BELLINDA I'll discharge my chair and follow. Tell your mistress I am
here.

  Exit Mrs Loveit's Footman. Bellinda gives the Chairmen money
Take this; and if ever you should be examined, be sure you say you
took me up in the Strand° over against the Exchange, as you will   20
answer it to Mr Dorimant.

CHAIRMEN We will, an't like your honour.

  Exeunt Chairmen

BELLINDA Now, to come off, I must on.

    In confidence and lies some hope is left;
        'Twere hard to be found out in the first theft.   25

  Exit

5.1

[*Mrs Loveit's lodging*]

Enter Mrs Loveit and Pert

PERT Well, in my eyes Sir Fopling is no such despicable person.

MRS LOVEIT You are an excellent judge.

PERT He's as handsome a man as Mr Dorimant, and as great a gallant.

MRS LOVEIT Intolerable! Is't not enough I submit to his impertinences, but must I be plagued with yours too?   5

PERT Indeed, Madam—

MRS LOVEIT 'Tis false, mercenary malice.

Enter Mrs Loveit's Footman

FOOTMAN Mrs Bellinda, madam.

MRS LOVEIT What of her?

FOOTMAN She's below.   10

MRS LOVEIT How came she?

FOOTMAN In a chair; ambling Harry brought her.

MRS LOVEIT He bring her! His chair stands near Dorimant's door and
always brings me from thence. Run and ask him where he took her
up. Go.   15

[*Exit Mrs Loveit's Footman*]

There is no truth in friendship neither. Women, as well as men, are
all false, or all are so to me at least.

PERT You are jealous of her too?

MRS LOVEIT You had best tell her I am. 'Twill become the liberty you
take of late. This fellow's bringing of her—her going out by five   20
o'clock—I know not what to think.

Enter Bellinda

Bellinda, you are grown an early riser, I hear.

BELLINDA Do you not wonder, my dear, what made me abroad so
soon?

MRS LOVEIT You do not use to be so.   25

BELLINDA The country gentlewomen I told you of—Lord, they have
the oddest diversions!—would never let me rest till I promised to
go with them to the markets this morning to eat fruit and buy
nosegays.°

MRS LOVEIT Are they so fond of a filthy nosegay?   30

BELLINDA They complain of the stinks of the town and are never well
but when they have their noses in one.

MRS LOVEIT There are essences and sweet waters.°

BELLINDA O they cry out upon perfumes they are unwholesome; one
of 'em was falling into a fit with the smell of these narolii.°

MRS LOVEIT Methinks in complaisance you should have had a
nosegay too.

BELLINDA Do you think, my dear, I could be so loathsome to trick
myself up with carnations and stock-gillyflowers?° I begged their
pardon and told them I never wore anything but orange flowers and
tuberose.° That which made me willing to go was a strange desire I
had to eat some fresh nectarines.

MRS LOVEIT And had you any?

BELLINDA The best I ever tasted.

MRS LOVEIT Whence came you now?

BELLINDA From their lodgings, where I crowded out° of a coach and
took a chair to come and see you, my dear.

MRS LOVEIT Whither did you send for that chair?

BELLINDA 'Twas going by empty.

MRS LOVEIT Where do these country gentlewomen lodge, I pray?

BELLINDA In the Strand, over against the Exchange.

PERT That place is never without a nest of 'em. They are always as
one goes by fleering in balconies or staring out of windows.

Enter Mrs Loveit's Footman

MRS LOVEIT (*to the Footman*) Come hither. (*Whispers*)

BELLINDA (*aside*) This fellow by her order has been questioning the
chairmen! I threatened 'em with the name of Dorimant. If they
should have told truth, I am lost forever.

MRS LOVEIT In the Strand, said you?

FOOTMAN Yes, madam, over against the Exchange.

Exit Mrs Loveit's Footman

MRS LOVEIT She's innocent, and I am much to blame.

BELLINDA (*aside*) I am so frighted, my countenance will betray me.

MRS LOVEIT Bellinda, what makes you look so pale?

BELLINDA Want of my usual rest and jolting up and down so long in
an odious hackney.

Footman returns

FOOTMAN Madam, Mr Dorimant.

MRS LOVEIT What makes him here?°

BELLINDA (*aside*) Then I am betrayed indeed. H' has broke his word,
and I love a man that does not care for me.

MRS LOVEIT Lord! You faint, Bellinda!

BELLINDA I think I shall! Such an oppression° here on the sudden.   70
PERT She has eaten too much fruit, I warrant you.
MRS LOVEIT Not unlikely.
PERT 'Tis that lies heavy on her stomach.
MRS LOVEIT Have her into my chamber, give her some surfeit water,°
and let her lie down a little.   75
PERT Come, madam. I was a strange° devourer of fruit when I was
young, so ravenous.
    Exeunt Bellinda and Pert, leading her off
MRS LOVEIT O that my love would be but calm awhile, that I might
receive this man with all the scorn and indignation he deserves.
    Enter Dorimant
DORIMANT Now for a touch of Sir Fopling to begin with. [*Mimicking*   80
Sir Fopling] Hey, page! Give positive order that none of my people
stir. Let the *canaille*° wait, as they should do. Since noise and
nonsense have such powerful charms—
       'I that I may successful prove,
       Transform myself to what you love'.°   85
MRS LOVEIT If that would do, you need not change from what you
are. You can be vain and loud enough.
DORIMANT But not with so good a grace as Sir Fopling: 'Hey,
Hampshire!' O that sound! That sound becomes the mouth of a
man of quality.   90
MRS LOVEIT Is there a thing so hateful as a senseless mimic?
DORIMANT He's a great grievance indeed to all who, like yourself,
madam, love to play the fool in quiet.
MRS LOVEIT A ridiculous animal, who has more of the ape than the
ape has of the man in him.   95
DORIMANT I have as mean an opinion of a sheer mimic as yourself;
yet, were he all ape, I should prefer him to the gay, the giddy,
brisk-insipid,° noisy fool you dote on.
MRS LOVEIT Those noisy fools, however you despise 'em, have good
qualities which weigh more—or ought, at least—with us women   100
than all the pernicious wit you have to boast of.
DORIMANT That I may hereafter have a just value for their merit,
pray do me the favour to name 'em.
MRS LOVEIT You'll despise 'em as the dull effects of ignorance and
vanity, yet I care not if I mention some. First, they really admire us,   105
while you at best but flatter us well.
DORIMANT Take heed: fools can dissemble too.

MRS LOVEIT They may, but not so artificially as you. There is no fear
they should deceive us. Then they are assiduous, sir; they are ever
offering us their service, and always waiting on our will.   110

DORIMANT You owe that to their excessive idleness! They know not
how to entertain themselves at home and find so little welcome
abroad, they are fain to fly to you who countenance 'em, as a refuge
against the solitude they would be otherwise condemned to.

MRS LOVEIT Their conversation too diverts us better.   115

DORIMANT Playing with your fan, smelling to your gloves, commend-
ing your hair, and taking notice how 'tis cut and shaded after the
new way.

MRS LOVEIT Were it sillier than you can make it, you must allow 'tis
pleasanter to laugh at others than to be laughed at ourselves,   120
though never so wittily. Then, though they want skill to flatter us,
they flatter themselves so well, they save us the labour! We need not
take that care and pains to satisfy 'em of our love which we so often
lose on you.

DORIMANT They commonly indeed believe too well of themselves,   125
and always better of you than you deserve.

MRS LOVEIT You are in the right. They have an implicit faith° in us,
which keeps 'em from prying narrowly into our secrets, and saves
us the vexatious trouble of clearing doubts which your subtle and
causeless jealousies every moment raise.   130

DORIMANT There is an inbred falsehood in women which inclines
'em still to them, whom they may most easily deceive.

MRS LOVEIT The man who loves above his quality, does not suffer
more from the insolent impertinence of his mistress than the
woman who loves above her understanding does from the arrogant   135
presumptions of her friend.

DORIMANT You mistake the use of fools: they are designed for prop-
erties° and not for friends. You have an indifferent° stock of reputation left yet. Lose it all like a frank° gamester on the square;° 'twill
then be time enough to turn rook° and cheat it up again on a good   140
substantial bubble.°

MRS LOVEIT The old and the ill-favoured are only fit for properties
indeed, but young and handsome fools have met with kinder
fortunes.

DORIMANT They have, to the shame of your sex be it spoken. 'Twas   145
this, the thought of this, made me by a timely jealousy endeavour to
prevent the good fortune you are providing for Sir Fopling; but
against a woman's frailty, all our care is vain.

MRS LOVEIT Had I not with a dear experience bought the knowledge of your falsehood, you might have fooled me yet. This is not the first jealousy you have feigned to make a quarrel with me and get a week to throw away on some such unknown, inconsiderable slut, as you have been lately lurking with at plays.

DORIMANT Women, when they would break off with a man, never want th' address to turn the fault on him.

MRS LOVEIT You take a pride of late in using of me ill, that the town may know the power you have over me, which now (as unreasonably as yourself) expects that I—do me all the injuries you can—must love you still.

DORIMANT I am so far from expecting that you should, I begin to think you never did love me.

MRS LOVEIT Would the memory of it were so wholly worn out in me that I did doubt it too! What made you come to disturb my growing quiet?

DORIMANT To give you joy of your growing infamy.

MRS LOVEIT Insupportable! Insulting devil! This from you, the only author of my shame! This from another had been but justice, but from you, 'tis a hellish and inhuman outrage. What have I done?

DORIMANT A thing that puts you below my scorn and makes my anger as ridiculous as you have made my love.

MRS LOVEIT I walked last night with Sir Fopling.

DORIMANT You did, madam, and you talked and laughed aloud, 'Ha, ha, ha'. O that laugh—that laugh becomes the confidence of a woman of quality.

MRS LOVEIT You who have more pleasure in the ruin of a woman's reputation than in the endearments of her love, reproach me not with yourself; and I defy you to name the man can lay a blemish on my fame.

DORIMANT To be seen publicly so transported with the vain follies of that notorious fop to me is an infamy below the sin of prostitution with another man.

MRS LOVEIT Rail on! I am satisfied in the justice of what I did: you had provoked me to 't.

DORIMANT What I did was the effect of a passion whose extravagancies you have been willing to forgive.

MRS LOVEIT And what I did was the effect of a passion you may forgive if you think fit.

DORIMANT Are you so indifferent grown?

MRS LOVEIT I am.   190

DORIMANT Nay, then 'tis time to part. I'll send you back your letters
   you have so often asked for. I have two or three of 'em about me.
   [*Produces letters*]

MRS LOVEIT Give 'em me!

DORIMANT You snatch as if you thought I would not. There. [*Hands*   195
   over letters] And may the perjuries in 'em be mine if ere I see you
   more.

>   *Dorimant offers to go. Mrs Loveit catches him*

MRS LOVEIT Stay!

DORIMANT I will not.

MRS LOVEIT You shall.   200

DORIMANT What have you to say?

MRS LOVEIT I cannot speak it yet.

DORIMANT Something more in the commendation of the fool. Death!
   I want patience; let me go.

MRS LOVEIT I cannot. (*Aside*) I can sooner part with the limbs that   205
   hold him. [*To Dorimant*] I hate that nauseous fool, you know I do.

DORIMANT Was it the scandal you were fond of then?

MRS LOVEIT Y' had raised my anger equal to my love, a thing you
   ne'er could do before; and in revenge, I did—I know not what I did.
   Would you would not think on't anymore.   210

DORIMANT Should I be willing to forget it, I shall be daily minded of
   it. 'Twill be a commonplace for all the town to laugh at me; and
   Medley, when he is rhetorically drunk, will ever be declaiming on it
   in my ears.

MRS LOVEIT 'Twill be believed a jealous spite. Come forget it.   215

DORIMANT Let me consult my reputation; you are too careless of it.
   (*Pauses*) You shall meet Sir Fopling in the Mall again tonight.

MRS LOVEIT What mean you?

DORIMANT I have thought on it, and you must. 'Tis necessary to
   justify my love to the world. You can handle a coxcomb as he   220
   deserves when you are not out of humour, madam!

MRS LOVEIT Public satisfaction for the wrong I have done you? This
   is some new device to make me more ridiculous.

DORIMANT Hear me.

MRS LOVEIT I will not!   225

DORIMANT You will be persuaded.

MRS LOVEIT Never.

DORIMANT Are you so obstinate?

MRS LOVEIT Are you so base?

DORIMANT You will not satisfy my love?   230

MRS LOVEIT I would die to satisfy that; but I will not, to save you
from a thousand racks, do a shameless thing to please your vanity.

DORIMANT Farewell, false woman.

MRS LOVEIT Do! Go!

DORIMANT You will call me back again.   235

MRS LOVEIT Exquisite fiend! I knew you came but to torment me.
        Enter Bellinda and Pert

DORIMANT (*surprised*) Bellinda here!

BELLINDA (*aside*) He starts and looks pale! The sight of me has
touched his guilty soul.

PERT 'Twas but a qualm, as I said, a little indigestion. The surfeit   240
water did it, madam, mixed with a little mirabilis.°

DORIMANT (*aside*) I am confounded and cannot guess how she came
hither!

MRS LOVEIT 'Tis your fortune, Bellinda, ever to be here when I am
abused by this prodigy of ill nature.   245

BELLINDA I am amazed to find him here. How has he the face to come
near you?

DORIMANT (*aside*) Here is fine work towards! I never was at such a
loss before.

BELLINDA One who makes a public profession of breach of faith and   250
ingratitude. I loathe the sight of him.

DORIMANT [*aside*] There is no remedy. I must submit to their tongues
now and some other time bring myself off as well as I can.

BELLINDA Other men are wicked, but then they have some sense of
shame. He is never well but when he triumphs—nay, glories—to a   255
woman's face in his villainies.

MRS LOVEIT You are in the right, Bellinda, but methinks your kindness
for me makes you concern yourself too much with him.

BELLINDA It does indeed, my dear. His barbarous carriage to you
yesterday made me hope you ne'er would see him more, and the   260
very next day to find him here again provokes me strangely. But
because I know you love him, I have done.

DORIMANT You have reproached me handsomely, and I deserve it for
coming hither, but—

PERT You must expect it, sir! All women will hate you for my lady's   265
sake.

DORIMANT [*aside*] Nay, if she begins too, 'tis time to fly. I shall be
scolded to death else! (*Aside to Bellinda*) I am to blame in some
circumstances, I confess, but as to the main, I am not so guilty as

you imagine. [*Aloud*] I shall seek a more convenient time to clear   270
    myself.

MRS LOVEIT Do it now! What impediments are here?

DORIMANT I want time, and you want temper.

MRS LOVEIT These are weak pretences.

DORIMANT You were never more mistaken in your life, and so farewell.   275
    Dorimant flings off

MRS LOVEIT Call a footman, Pert, quickly! I will have him dogged.

PERT I wish you would not for my quiet and your own.

MRS LOVEIT I'll find out the infamous cause of all our quarrels, pluck
    her mask off, and expose her bare-faced to the world.

BELLINDA (*aside*) Let me but escape this time, I'll never venture   280
    more.

MRS LOVEIT Bellinda, you shall go with me.

BELLINDA I have such a heaviness° hangs on me with what I did this
    morning, I would fain go home and sleep, my dear.

MRS LOVEIT Death and eternal darkness! I shall never sleep again.   285
    Raging fevers seize the world and make mankind as restless all as I
    am.
    Exit Mrs Loveit

BELLINDA I knew him false and helped to make him so. Was not her
    ruin enough to fright me from the danger? It should have been, but
    love can take no warning.   290
    Exit

5.2

Lady Townley's house

Enter Medley, Bellair, Lady Townley, Emilia, and Smirk

MEDLEY Bear up, Bellair, and do not let us see that repentance in
    thine we daily do in married faces.

LADY TOWNLEY This wedding will strangely surprise my brother
    when he knows it.

MEDLEY Your nephew ought to conceal it for a time, madam. Since   5
    marriage has lost its good name, prudent men seldom expose their
    own reputations till 'tis convenient to justify their wives.

OLD BELLAIR (*offstage*) Where are you all there? Out, adod, will
    nobody hear?

LADY TOWNLEY My brother! Quickly, Mr Smirk, into this closet.°   10
You must not be seen yet.

  Smirk goes into the closet. Enter Old Bellair and Lady Townley's
  Page

OLD BELLAIR Desire Mr Fourbe to walk into the lower parlour; I will
be with him presently. (*To Bellair*) Where have you been, sir, you
could not wait on me today?

BELLAIR About a business.   15

OLD BELLAIR Are you so good at business? Adod, I have a business
too you shall dispatch out of hand, sir. Send for a parson, sister; my
Lady Woodvill and her daughter are coming.

LADY TOWNLEY What need you huddle up° things thus?

OLD BELLAIR Out a pize! Youth is apt to play the fool, and 'tis not   20
good it should be in their power.

LADY TOWNLEY You need not fear your son.

OLD BELLAIR H' has been idling this morning and, adod, I do not like
him. (*To Emilia*) How dost thou do, sweetheart?

EMILIA You are very severe, sir. Married in such haste!   25

OLD BELLAIR Go to;° thou art a rogue, and I will talk with thee anon.
Here's my Lady Woodvill come.

  Enter Lady Woodvill, Harriet, and Busy

Welcome, madam. Mr Fourbe's below with the writings.°

LADY WOODVILL Let us down and make an end then.

OLD BELLAIR Sister, show the way. (*To Bellair, who is talking to*   30
Harriet) Harry, your business lies not there yet! Excuse him till we
have done, lady, and then, adod, he shall be for thee. Mr Medley, we
must trouble you to be a witness.

MEDLEY I luckily came for that purpose, sir.

  Exeunt Old Bellair, Medley, Bellair, Lady Townley, and Lady
  Woodvill

BUSY What will you do, madam?   35

HARRIET Be carried back and mewed up in the country again, run
away here, anything, rather than be married to a man I do not care
for! Dear Emilia, do thou advise me.

EMILIA Mr Bellair is engaged, you know.

HARRIET I do, but know not what the fear of losing an estate may   40
fright him to.

EMILIA In the desperate condition you are in, you should consult
with some judicious man. What think you of Mr Dorimant?

HARRIET I do not think of him at all.

BUSY She thinks of nothing else, I am sure.   45

EMILIA How fond your mother was of Mr Courtage!

HARRIET Because I contrived the mistake to make a little mirth, you
    believe I like the man.

EMILIA Mr Bellair believes you love him.

HARRIET Men are seldom in the right when they guess at a woman's   50
    mind. Would she whom he loves, loved him no better.

BUSY (aside) That's e'en well enough, on all conscience.

EMILIA Mr Dorimant has a great deal of wit.

HARRIET And takes a great deal of pains to show it.

EMILIA He's extremely well-fashioned.°   55

HARRIET Affectedly grave or ridiculously wild and apish.°

BUSY You defend him still against your mother.

HARRIET I would not were he justly rallied,° but I cannot hear anyone
    undeservedly railed at.

EMILIA Has your woman learnt the song you were so taken with?   60

HARRIET I was fond of a new thing; 'tis dull at second hearing.

EMILIA Mr Dorimant made it.

BUSY She knows it, madam, and has made me sing it at least a dozen
    times this morning.

HARRIET Thy tongue is as impertinent as thy fingers.   65

EMILIA You have provoked her.

BUSY 'Tis but singing the song, and I shall appease her.

EMILIA Prithee do.

HARRIET She has a voice will grate your ears worse than a cat-call,°
    and dresses so ill she's scarce fit to trick up a yeoman's daughter on   70
    a holiday.

    Busy sings°

SONG

As Amoret with Phyllis sat
    One evening on the plain,
And saw the charming Strephon wait   75
    To tell the nymph his pain,

The threat'ning danger to remove
    She whispered in her ear,
'Ah, Phyllis, if you would not love,
    This shepherd do not hear.   80

None ever had so strange an art
    His passion to convey

Into a list'ning virgin's heart
And steal her soul away.

Fly, fly betimes, for fear you give   85
Occasion for your fate.'
'In vain,' said she, 'in vain I strive,
Alas, 'tis now too late!'

Enter Dorimant

DORIMANT 'Music so softens and disarms the mind—
HARRIET That not one arrow does resistance find'.°   90
DORIMANT Let us make use of the lucky minute then.
HARRIET (*aside, turning from Dorimant*) My love springs with my
blood into my face. I dare not look upon him yet.
DORIMANT What have we here: the picture of celebrated Beauty°
giving audience in public to a declared lover?   95
HARRIET Play the dying fop and make the piece complete, sir.
DORIMANT What think you if the hint were well improved? The
whole mystery of making love pleasantly designed and wrought in a
suit of hangings?°
HARRIET 'Twere needless to execute fools in effigy who suffer daily in 100
their own persons.
DORIMANT (*to Emilia aside*) Mrs Bride, for such I know this happy
day has made you—
EMILIA Defer the formal joy you are to give me, and mind your
business with her. (*Aloud*) Here are dreadful preparations,   105
Mr Dorimant: writings sealing and a parson sent for—
DORIMANT —to marry this lady.
BUSY Condemned she is, and what will become of her I know not,
without you generously engage in a rescue.
DORIMANT In this sad condition, madam, I can do no less than offer   110
you my service.
HARRIET The obligation is not great. You are the common sanctuary
for all young women who run from their relations.
DORIMANT I have always my arms open to receive the distressed. But
I will open my heart and receive you where none yet did ever enter.   115
You have filled it with a secret, might I but let you know it.
HARRIET Do not speak it if you would have me believe it. Your tongue
is so famed for falsehood, 'twill do the truth an injury. (*Turns away*
her head)
DORIMANT Turn not away then, but look on me and guess it.   120
HARRIET Did you not tell me there was no credit to be given to faces?

That women nowadays have their passions as much at will as they have their complexions, and put on joy and sadness, scorn and kindness, with the same ease they do their paint and patches? Are they the only counterfeits?   125

DORIMANT You wrong your own while you suspect my eyes. By all the hope I have in you, the inimitable colour in your cheeks is not more free from art than are the sighs I offer.

HARRIET In men who have been long hardened in sin, we have reason to mistrust the first signs of repentance.   130

DORIMANT The prospect of such a heaven will make me persevere and give you marks that are infallible.

HARRIET What are those?

DORIMANT I will renounce all the joys I have in friendship and in wine, sacrifice to you all the interest I have in other women—   135

HARRIET Hold! Though I wish you devout, I would not have you turn fanatic. Could you neglect these a while and make a journey into the country?

DORIMANT To be with you, I could live there and never send one thought to London.   140

HARRIET Whate'er you say, I know all beyond Hyde Park's a desert to you, and that no gallantry can draw you farther.

DORIMANT That has been the utmost limit of my love. But now my passion knows no bounds, and there's no measure to be taken of what I'll do for you from anything I ever did before.   145

HARRIET When I hear you talk thus in Hampshire,° I shall begin to think there may be some little° truth enlarged upon.°

DORIMANT Is this all? Will you not promise me—

HARRIET I hate to promise! What we do then is expected from us and wants much of the welcome it finds when it surprises.   150

DORIMANT May I not hope?

HARRIET That depends on you, and not on me; and 'tis to no purpose to forbid it. (*Turns to Busy*)

BUSY Faith, madam, now I perceive the gentleman loves you too, e'en let him know your mind and torment yourselves no longer.   155

HARRIET Dost think I have no sense of modesty?

BUSY Think: if you lose this, you may never have another opportunity.

HARRIET May he hate me—a curse that frights me when I speak it— if ever I do a thing against the rules of decency and honour.   160

DORIMANT (*to Emilia*) I am beholding to you for your good intentions, madam.

EMILIA I thought the concealing of our marriage from her might have
  done you better service.

DORIMANT Try her again.   165

EMILIA What have you resolved, madam? The time draws near.

HARRIET To be obstinate and protest against this marriage.

        Enter Lady Townley in haste

LADY TOWNLEY (*to Emilia*) Quickly, quickly! Let Mr Smirk out of
  the closet.

        Smirk comes out of the closet

HARRIET A parson! Had you laid him in here?   170

DORIMANT I knew nothing of him.

HARRIET Should it appear you did, your opinion of my easiness may
  cost you dear.

        Enter Old Bellair, Bellair, Medley, and Lady Woodvill

OLD BELLAIR Out a pize! The canonical hour° is almost past. Sister,
  is the man of God come?   175

LADY TOWNLEY He waits your leisure.

OLD BELLAIR [*to Smirk*] By your favour, sir. Adod, a pretty, spruce
  fellow! What may we call him?

LADY TOWNLEY Mr Smirk, my Lady Bigot's chaplain.

OLD BELLAIR A wise woman, adod she is. The man will serve for the   180
  flesh as well as the spirit. Please you, sir, to commission a young
  couple to go to bed together a God's name? Harry?

BELLAIR Here, sir.

OLD BELLAIR Out a pize, without your mistress in your hand!

SMIRK Is this the gentleman?   185

OLD BELLAIR Yes, sir.

SMIRK Are you not mistaken, sir?

OLD BELLAIR Adod, I think not, sir.

SMIRK Sure you are, sir?

OLD BELLAIR You look as if you would forbid the banns, Mr Smirk. I   190
  hope you have no pretension to the lady!

SMIRK Wish him joy, sir. I have done him the good office today
  already.

OLD BELLAIR Out a pize, what do I hear?

LADY TOWNLEY Never storm, brother. The truth is out.   195

OLD BELLAIR How say you, sir? Is this your wedding day?

BELLAIR It is, sir.

OLD BELLAIR And, adod, it shall be mine too. (*To Emilia*) Give me
  thy hand, sweetheart. What dost thou mean? Give me thy hand, I
  say.   200

Emilia and Bellair kneel

LADY TOWNLEY Come, come, give her your blessing. This is the woman your son loved and is married to.

OLD BELLAIR Ha! Cheated! Cozened! And by your contrivance, sister!

LADY TOWNLEY What would you do with her? She's a rogue and you   205
can't abide her.

MEDLEY Shall I hit her a pat for you, sir?

OLD BELLAIR Adod, you are all rogues, and I never will forgive you.

LADY TOWNLEY Whither? Whither away?

MEDLEY Let him go and cool awhile.   210

LADY WOODVILL (*to Dorimant*) Here's a business broke out now, Mr Courtage. I am made a fine fool of.

DORIMANT You see the old gentleman knew nothing of it.

LADY WOODVILL I find he did not. I shall have some trick put upon me if I stay in this wicked town any longer. Harriet, dear child!   215
Where art thou? I'll into the country straight.

OLD BELLAIR Adod, madam, you shall hear me first—
Enter Mrs Loveit and Bellinda

MRS LOVEIT Hither my man dogged him!

BELLINDA Yonder he stands, my dear.

MRS LOVEIT I see him. (*Aside*) And with him the face that has undone   220
me! O that I were but where I might throw out the anguish of my heart! Here it must rage within and break it.

LADY TOWNLEY Mrs Loveit! Are you afraid to come forward?

MRS LOVEIT I was amazed to see so much company here in a morning. The occasion sure is extraordinary.   225

DORIMANT (*aside*) Loveit and Bellinda! The devil owes me a shame today, and I think never will have done paying it.°

MRS LOVEIT Married! Dear Emilia, how am I transported with the news.

HARRIET (*to Dorimant*) I little thought Emilia was the woman   230
Mr Bellair was in love with. I'll chide her for not trusting me with the secret.

DORIMANT How do you like Mrs Loveit?

HARRIET She's a famed mistress of yours, I hear.

DORIMANT She has been, on occasion.   235

OLD BELLAIR (*to Lady Woodvill*) Adod, madam, I cannot help it.

LADY WOODVILL You need make no more apologies, sir.

EMILIA (*to Mrs Loveit*) The old gentleman's excusing himself to my Lady Woodvill.

MRS LOVEIT Ha, ha, ha! I never heard of anything so pleasant.   240

HARRIET (*to Dorimant*) She's extremely overjoyed at something.

DORIMANT At nothing. She is one of those hoiting ladies who gaily fling themselves about and force a laugh when their aching hearts are full of discontent and malice.

MRS LOVEIT O heaven! I was never so near killing myself with laugh-   245
ing. Mr Dorimant, are you a brideman?

LADY WOODVILL Mr Dorimant! Is this Mr Dorimant, madam?

MRS LOVEIT If you doubt it, your daughter can resolve you, I suppose.

LADY WOODVILL I am cheated too, basely cheated.   250

OLD BELLAIR Out a pize, what's here? More knavery yet?

LADY WOODVILL Harriet, on my blessing, come away, I charge you.

HARRIET Dear mother, do but stay and hear me.

LADY WOODVILL I am betrayed and thou art undone, I fear.

HARRIET Do not fear it. I have not, nor never will do, anything against   255
my duty. Believe me, dear mother, do.

DORIMANT (*to Mrs Loveit*) I had trusted you with this secret, but that I knew the violence of your nature would ruin my fortune, as now unluckily it has. I thank you, madam.

MRS LOVEIT She's an heiress, I know, and very rich.   260

DORIMANT To satisfy you, I must give up my interest wholly to my love. Had you been a reasonable woman, I might have secured 'em both and been happy.

MRS LOVEIT You might have trusted me with anything of this kind, you know you might. Why did you go under a wrong name?   265

DORIMANT The story is too long to tell you now. Be satisfied: this is the business, this is the mask has kept me from you.

BELLINDA (*aside*) He's tender of my honour, though he's cruel to my love.

MRS LOVEIT Was it no idle mistress then?   270

DORIMANT Believe me, a wife to repair the ruins of my estate that needs it.

MRS LOVEIT The knowledge of this makes my grief hang lighter on my soul; but I shall never more be happy.

DORIMANT Bellinda!   275

BELLINDA Do not think of clearing yourself with me; it is impossible. Do all men break their words thus?

DORIMANT Th' extravagant words they speak in love. 'Tis as unreasonable to expect we should perform all we promise then, as do all we threaten when we are angry.   280

When I see you next—

BELLINDA Take no notice of me, and I shall not hate you.

DORIMANT How came you to Mrs Loveit?

BELLINDA By a mistake the chairmen made for want of my giving
them directions.   285

DORIMANT 'Twas a pleasant one. We must meet again.

BELLINDA Never.

DORIMANT Never?

BELLINDA When we do, may I be as infamous as you are false.

LADY TOWNLEY Men of Mr Dorimant's character always suffer in   290
the general opinion of the world.

MEDLEY You can make no judgement of a witty man from common
fame, considering the prevailing faction,° madam.

OLD BELLAIR Adod, he's in the right.

MEDLEY Besides, 'tis a common error among women to believe too   295
well of them they know and too ill of them they don't.

OLD BELLAIR Adod, he observes well.

LADY TOWNLEY Believe me, madam, you will find Mr Dorimant as
civil a gentleman as you thought Mr Courtage.

HARRIET If you would but know him better—   300

LADY WOODVILL You have a mind to know him better? Come away!
You shall never see him more.

HARRIET Dear mother, stay!

LADY WOODVILL I won't be consenting to your ruin.

HARRIET Were my fortune in your power—   305

LADY WOODVILL Your person is.

HARRIET Could I be disobedient, I might take it out of yours and put
it into his.

LADY WOODVILL 'Tis that you would be at: you would marry this
Dorimant?   310

HARRIET I cannot deny it. I would and never will marry any other
man.

LADY WOODVILL Is this the duty that you promised?

HARRIET But I will never marry him against your will.

LADY WOODVILL (aside) She knows the way to melt my heart. (To   315
Harriet) Upon yourself light your undoing.

MEDLEY (to Old Bellair) Come, sir, you have not the heart any longer
to refuse your blessing.

OLD BELLAIR Adod, I ha' not. Rise and God bless you both. Make
much of her, Harry; she deserves thy kindness. (To Emilia) Adod,   320
sirrah, I did not think it had been in thee.

Enter Sir Fopling and his Page

SIR FOPLING 'Tis a damned windy day. Hey, page! Is my periwig
   right?

PAGE A little out of order, sir.

SIR FOPLING Pox o' this apartment; it wants an antechamber° to   325
   adjust oneself in. (*To Mrs Loveit*) Madam, I came from your house,
   and your servants directed me hither.

MRS LOVEIT I will give order hereafter they shall direct you better.

SIR FOPLING The great satisfaction I had in the Mall last night has
   given me much disquiet since.   330

MRS LOVEIT 'Tis likely to give me more than I desire.

SIR FOPLING What the devil makes her so reserved? Am I guilty of an
   indiscretion, madam?

MRS LOVEIT You will be of a great one if you continue your mistake,
   sir.   335

SIR FOPLING Something puts you out of humour.

MRS LOVEIT The most foolish, inconsiderable thing that ever did.

SIR FOPLING Is it in my power?

MRS LOVEIT To hang or drown it. Do one of 'em and trouble me no
   more.   340

SIR FOPLING So *fière*?° *Serviteur*,° madam. Medley, where's
   Dorimant?

MEDLEY Methinks the lady has not made you those advances today
   she did last night, Sir Fopling.

SIR FOPLING Prithee do not talk of her.   345

MEDLEY She would be a *bonne fortune*.

SIR FOPLING Not to me at present.

MEDLEY How so?

SIR FOPLING An intrigue now would be but a temptation to me to
   throw away that vigour on one, which I mean shall shortly make my   350
   court to the whole sex in a ballet.

MEDLEY Wisely considered, Sir Fopling.

SIR FOPLING No one woman is worth the loss of a cut° in a
   caper.

MEDLEY Not when 'tis so universally designed.   355

LADY WOODVILL Mr Dorimant, everyone has spoke so much in your
   behalf that I can no longer doubt but I was in the wrong.

MRS LOVEIT There's nothing but falsehood and impertinence in this
   world! All men are villains or fools: take example from my misfortunes. Bellinda, if thou wouldst be happy, give thyself wholly up   360
   to goodness.

HARRIET (*to Mrs Loveit*) Mr Dorimant has been your God almighty long enough. 'Tis time to think of another.

MRS LOVEIT Jeered by her! I will lock myself up in my house and never see the world again.   365

HARRIET A nunnery is the more fashionable place for such a retreat and has been the fatal consequence of many a *belle passion*.

MRS LOVEIT Hold heart till I get home! Should I answer, 'twould make her triumph greater. (*Is going out*)

DORIMANT Your hand, Sir Fopling.   370

SIR FOPLING [*to Mrs Loveit*] Shall I wait upon you, madam?

MRS LOVEIT Legions of fools, as many devils take thee!
        Exit Mrs Loveit

MEDLEY Dorimant, I pronounce thy reputation clear; and henceforward, when I would know anything of woman, I will consult no other oracle.   375

SIR FOPLING Stark mad, by all that's handsome! Dorimant, thou hast engaged me in a pretty business.

DORIMANT I have not leisure now to talk about it.

OLD BELLAIR Out a pize, what does this man of mode do here again?

LADY TOWNLEY He'll be an excellent entertainment within, brother,   380
and is luckily come to raise the mirth of the company.

LADY WOODVILL Madam, I take my leave of you.

LADY TOWNLEY What do you mean, madam?

LADY WOODVILL To go this afternoon part of my way to Hartley.°

OLD BELLAIR Adod, you shall stay and dine first. Come, we will all be   385
good friends, and you shall give Mr Dorimant leave to wait upon you and your daughter in the country.

LADY WOODVILL If his occasions bring him that way, I have now so good an opinion of him, he shall be welcome.

HARRIET To a great rambling lone house that looks as it were not   390
inhabited, the family's so small. There you'll find my mother, an old, lame aunt, and myself, sir, perched up on chairs at a distance in a large parlour, sitting moping like three or four melancholy birds in a spacious volary. Does not this stagger your resolution?

DORIMANT Not at all, madam. The first time I saw you, you left me   395
with the pangs of love upon me; and this day my soul has quite given up her liberty.

HARRIET This is more dismal than the country! Emilia, pity me who am going to that sad place. Methinks I hear the hateful noise of rooks already: kaw, kaw, kaw. There's music in the worst cry in   400
London, 'My dill and cucumbers to pickle'.

OLD BELLAIR Sister, knowing of this matter, I hope you have provided us some good cheer.

LADY TOWNLEY I have brother, and the fiddles too.

OLD BELLAIR Let 'em strike up then. The young lady shall have a   405
dance before she departs.

> *Harriet, Dorimant, Bellair, Emilia, Lady Townley, and Old
> Bellair dance°*

(*After the dance*) So now we'll in and make this an arrant wedding
day.

(*To the pit*) And if these honest gentlemen rejoice,

> Adod, the boy has made a happy choice.

> *Exeunt*

The Epilogue

By Mr Dryden°

Most modern wits such monstrous fools have shown,
They seemed not of heaven's making, but their own.
Those nauseous harlequins in farce may pass,°
But there goes more to a substantial ass!
Something of man must be exposed to view,   5
That, gallants, they may more resemble you.
Sir Fopling is a fool so nicely writ,
The ladies would mistake him for a wit,
And when he sings, talks loud, and cocks, would cry:°
'I vow methinks he's pretty company,   10
So brisk, so gay, so travelled, so refined!'
As he took pains to graft upon his kind.
True fops help nature's work and go to school
To file and finish God A'mighty's fool.
Yet none Sir Fopling him, or him, can call;   15
He's knight o' th' shire, and represents ye all.°
From each he meets, he culls whate'er he can,
Legion's his name, a people in a man.
His bulky folly gathers as it goes,
And, rolling o'er you, like a snowball grows.   20
His various modes from various fathers follow:
One taught the toss, and one the new French wallow.°
His sword knot, this; his cravat, this designed,°
And this, the yard-long snake he twirls behind.°
From one the sacred periwig he gained,   25
Which wind ne'er blew, nor touch of hat profaned.
Another's diving bow he did adore,
Which with a shog casts all the hair before,°
Till he with full decorum brings it back,
And rises with a water spaniel shake.   30
As for his songs, the ladies' dear delight,
Those sure he took from most of you who write.
Yet every man is safe from what he feared,
For no one fool is hunted from the herd.

A FOND HUSBAND; OR,
THE PLOTTING SISTERS

THOMAS DURFEY

Hæc, dum incipias, gravia sunt,
dumque ignores, ubi cognôris, facilia.°
[Terence]

To His Grace, the Duke of Ormond,° Lord Steward of His
Majesty's Household, Knight of the Noble Order of the Garter,
One of His Majesty's most Honourable Privy Council, etc.

May it please your grace,

The arrogance a poet may be guilty of in a dedication often brings
him more terror than his fear for the success of his play; and I always
thought the frowns of an offended patron a greater punishment than
the censures of the partial critics. But the sin of confidence is so
natural to a young poet and so suitable to his character and business,
that an excuse, or reproof, as it would be extremely unnecessary, so it
might perhaps be a hindrance to his fortune. My sense of this has
encouraged me to present this comedy to your grace with this humble
suit: that as it has indifferently passed° in the opinion of the town, it
may have the honour to stand as neuter in your grace's favour. The
greatest confidence of a poet can ask no more, nor can you, my lord,
governed by your excellent temper, grant less. This I know I need not
repeat, nor urge a second time. For whoever yet made an humble
address° to your grace that went away unsatisfied? You are so far from
singularity, so nobly just, and so unwearied in doing good, that to pen
your applause were as impossible a work as to pen the actions of your
life, every hour producing some memorable thing as an addition to the
volume. My lord, 'tis not only my particular grief, but everyone's, for
your grace's departure from England.° And though the great place of
trust conferred upon you by his sacred majesty—and which none can
be more worthy of—gives us proof as well of your pious loyalty as
unequalled grandeur, yet such an influence you have gained on all
hearts, that they had rather the kingdom of Ireland should lose its
preserver than they so good a patron. This, I confess, I am most
sensible of, perhaps having as much cause as any, which relation° I'll
smother lest it is thought interest more than gratitude makes me
resent it.

If I have presumed too much, I have this excuse: that a dedication to
such a person cannot be writ without it, and 'tis the only honour a poet
is ambitious of—to have a great name before his play. I confess I was
guilty of this and have only this excuse for the arrogance of a dedication:
that your grace was pleased to favour my last, and that this was writ
with the same integrity. For the play I can say nothing, only that it was
my own,° though some are pleased to doubt the contrary (the Scotch
song excepted, a part of which was not mine, nor do I desire any

reputation from it). Be pleased, my lord, to forgive this prolixity; and   40
believe my sense of the honour I have in addressing to your grace
almost equals the ambition I shall ever own in styling myself,

        My lord,
           Your grace's most humble
             and most obedient servant,   45
            Thomas Durfey

THE CHARACTERS OF THE PLAY

Rashley,° *a gentleman, friend to Emilia*   Mr Smith
Ranger,° *his rival*   Mr Harris
Peregrine Bubble,° *a credulous fond° cuckold,*
 husband to Emilia   Mr Nokes
Old Fumble,° *a superannuated alderman° that*
 dotes on black women;° he's very deaf and almost
 blind and, seeking to cover his imperfection
 of not hearing what is said to him, answers quite
 contrary   Mr Leigh
Sir Roger Petulant, *a jolly old knight of the last age* Mr Sandford
Sneak, *nephew to Sir Roger, a young raw student* Mr Jevon°
Spatterdash, *servant to Fumble* ⎱
Jeremy, *servant to Rashley* ⎰ Mr Richards
Apothecary   Mr Percival
Emilia,° *wife to Bubble*   Mrs Barry°
Maria, *sister to Bubble*   Mrs Marshall
Cordelia, *niece to Bubble*   Mrs Hughes
Betty, *woman to Emilia*   Mrs Knapper°
Governess   Mrs Norris°
Mrs Snare°
Servants and attendants

SCENE: LONDON

Prologue

If plot and business, comical and new,
Could please the critics that sit here to view,°
The poet might have thought this play would do.
But in this age, design no praise can get;
You cry it conversation wants and wit,   5
As if the obvious rules of comedy
Were only dull grimace and repartee.°
Such, sirs, have been your darlings proved of late;
The author, therefore, careless of his fate,
And knowing wit a chattel hardly got,°   10
Has ventured his whole stock upon a plot.
He says a mock-song, or a smutty tale
Can please the town; and why not this prevail?
I friendly told him, all that I could say,
Was, that your fancies leaned the other way,   15
And you loved wenching better than his play.
For the body still you luxury prepare,
But let the mind be desolate and bare;
Thus lose yourselves in the world's prudent thought,
Then strive to get reprieve by finding fault.   20
A critic is a monster that can sway
Only o'er ignorance, and yet dares prey
Upon that power that formed him out of clay.
Adulterate age, where prudence is a vice,
And wit's as scandalous as avarice;   25
Yet, in despite of this, you're poets too,
And what two fops rail at, a third shall do.
Upon our privileges you encroach,
And with dull rhymes the noble art debauch.
For writing plays you scorn a poet's name;   30
A bawdy song's enough to get you fame,
Where, 'midst the reputation that is due,
You will be sure no man shall censure you.
Yet though your faction does infest the town,

There is a wise cabal dares judge and own
Desert and wit, and our endeavours crown.°
To these we humbly dedicate our plays,
Whilst at their feet our poets throw their bays.°

1.1

A dining room [in Bubble's house]. A table, shuttlecock, and battledores°

Rashley and Emilia, sitting; Betty

BETTY (*sings*)°

SONG

> *In vain, cruel nymph, you my passion despise,*
> *And slight a poor lover that languishing dies.*
> *Though fortune my name with no titles endowed,*   5
> *Yet fierce is my passion and warm is my blood.*
> *Delay in affection exalts an amour,°*
> *For he that loves often will soonest give o'er.*
>
> *But, vigorous and young, I'll flee to thy arms,*
> *Infusing my soul in Elysium of charms.°*   10
> *A monarch I'll be when I lie by thy side,*
> *And thy pretty hand my sceptre shall guide;°*
> *Till, cloyed with delight, you confess with a joy,*
> *No monarch so happy, so pleasant as I.*

[*Exit Betty*]

RASHLEY By heaven, there's nothing so dear to a free and generous   15
spirit as this roving and uncontrolled way of love. Methinks we live
like angels, and every kiss brings a new life of pleasure.

EMILIA You have reason to believe I think so for suffering this early
visit from you in my husband's absence, who, poor man, went from
me by break of day to see a horse race a mile beyond Highgate.°   20

RASHLEY Nay, I confess, 'tis a sign of your kind resentment° of my
passion. O heaven, that happy thought has made me all rapture. I'll
cherish it, madam, as I would my youth or, the best of all my senses,
the sense of feeling.

EMILIA Cherish it rather as the means of keeping our love from my   25
husband's knowledge. Well, I swear the thought of my indirect°
plot sometimes makes me very melancholy.

RASHLEY Melancholy? Fie, Madam, banish such thoughts forever
from your breast. If you are melancholy now, what would you have
done if I had not known you? When the clog° of your conscience—   30

I mean your husband—would have been your perpetual plague,
and given you cause for more melancholy than the contrivance of
the plots you speak of?

EMILIA Ay, but to break a vow, sir, a vow. Little do you think what 'tis
to break a vow.   35

RASHLEY Little do I think? Madam, I thought you had known me so
much a gentleman to imagine I know what belongs to the breaking
a vow as well as another man. To undeceive you, I have broke
twenty vows, that is, unnecessary vows—such as yours are—nay,
and without a scruple of conscience. I thank my stars I'm of a   40
tougher constitution.

EMILIA Besides, you consider not the other inconveniences; you
know my husband's sister, Maria, loves you and is of that untamed,
malicious nature that she'll revenge my invading her propriety in
your heart° by discovering our love to my husband. I know she   45
plots it hourly, and though her pretence is the honour of our family,
her real design° is through her love to you.

RASHLEY Never doubt your husband, madam; he has so strange a
confidence in my fidelity that to possess him° otherwise were
utterly to take away the little sense is left him. You know he brought   50
me to lodge in his house, which prudently I refused at first, and
seemingly fled from the heaven I desired, to make him more
importunate. Since I came here, you know how he has caressed me;
and to colour my design and divert you,° have feigned° a mistress
in this quarter of the town, and then, as if I spoke of her, have told 55
him all that has passed betwixt myself and you, at which the
good-natured creature has laughed extremely and wished me good
luck a thousand times; and can we now doubt further success? By
heaven, we cannot, Madam.

EMILIA Then you know there's another great obstacle; Ned Ranger   60
has long professed a passion for me and doubtless is not ignorant
that my love for you is the cause of his no better success. A jealous
man sees more than twenty others, and 'twill be very necessary for
us to be careful of so dangerous an enemy.

RASHLEY Dangerous? Not at all, madam. Never think him so. Success,   65
which animates the hero and leads him on to greater enterprises
than before he durst attempt, has cherished hopes in me. Let me
alone with him; and, for thy part, egad I'll turn thee loose to any
female-devil on this side Lapland,° either for plot or repartee.

EMILIA Yet still I fear the worst.   70

RASHLEY Fear nothing, madam. Fear is the worst of passions and incident to base, not noble, hearts; besides, our love, considered rightly, is a second-rate innocence where affection, not duty, bears prerogative. 'Tis the great and primitive business of our souls; suspicion and fear came in by the by.°   75

    Enter Betty

BETTY Madam, Mr Ranger, in spite of my resistance, has rudely pressed into the house and is just coming hither.

EMILIA Call up the footmen. Lock the door.

    Enter Ranger

RANGER (*to Betty*) Stand still, Mrs Jilt,° or I shall spoil your door-keeping° hereafter.   80

    [*Exit Betty*]

Jack Rashley—here? Hell and the devil!

EMILIA What insolence is this? Pray, sir, your business?

RANGER Only my zeal, Madam, to give you notice of an approaching danger. Your husband has so entangled his horns° yonder in a hawthorn-bush° that 'tis to be feared without immediate help he   85
will lose the decent and commodious° ornament of his forehead.

EMILIA Most impudent of men! How dare you talk thus?

RANGER Most infamous of women! How dare you do thus?

RASHLEY [*moves threateningly towards Ranger*] Do what, sir?

EMILIA [*to Rashley*] Hold, and as you love me, move no farther. [*To   90
Ranger*] Basest of men! Have you the folly to believe this way can prove beneficial to your love? No, I hate thee mortally, nor shall thy malice from henceforth be successful; I'll disarm it, and when thou thinkest thy plots are surest laid, be sure of a surprise.°

RANGER O infamy! 'Sdeath, is your forehead steel? And is your skin   95
of that obdurate temper you cannot force a blush into your cheeks at the confession of your obscene crime? How great a friend to hell is impudence!

EMILIA [*to Rashley*] Pray, sir, forgive him. 'Tis an insipid fellow that I am often troubled with and believe his insolence for the future shall   100
be prevented. In the meantime, to express my gratitude, give me leave to present you with this necklace. This ring too will fit your finger, nay, and swear you shan't refuse 'em. My husband gives me often such as these; 'tis all the good I get by him.

RANGER Very well. The blessing of a wife let all men judge. What   105
envious fiend to plague me makes me love this creature?

RASHLEY [*to Emilia*] I will preserve your favours as my life. Your memory shall possess my soul and all your charms live ever in my sight. (*Kisses her hand*) My kindest, sweetest, dearest—

RANGER Death and damnation! Must I stay and see this? Madam, this   110
modest carriage before a jealous lover makes—

EMILIA Little for your contentment, I doubt not, sir. But 'tis a fate
proper enough for such busy and inquisitive persons.

RASHLEY (*sings*) *Fa, la, la, la, la.*

RANGER [*to Emilia*] Go. You are a devil—so far from being a woman,   115
that I begin to doubt whether nature had any hand in your creation.
Is't not enough, vile creature, that I know you abuse your husband,
but that you dare give me an ocular proof? Dispense your favours to
the man that horns him before my face? O, unparalleled impudence!

EMILIA Incorrigible fool. Think'st thou to daunt my will? The little ill   120
I do can raise no infamy, nor will I ever doubt it.

RASHLEY [*sings*] *Fa, la, la, la.*
                    The joys of a lover in passion remains,
                    In passion that's fervent and free, etc.
            Enter Betty

BETTY O Madam, my master's just come home and coming up.   125
            [*Exit Betty*]

RANGER Blessed minute! Now I hope his eyes will be unsealed and,
through the right end of the perspective,° see you. Madam, assure
yourself: there shall want nothing in me.

EMILIA I know, sir, and am prepared for the worst of thy malice. [*To
Rashley*] Here, take this battledore, and let us play.   130
            Emilia and Rashley play

RASHLEY Out, out, Madam—you're out.
            Enter Bubble

BUBBLE Ha, ha, ha. [*To Emilia*] Chicken; good morrow, chicken. [*To
Rashley*] Morrow, Tom. [*To Emilia*] Chick, prithee let me kiss thee.
What, in the mumps?° This morning, pop,° no more of that. [*Sees
Ranger*] Ho! What, my old friend Ranger too? Morrow, Ned. Faith,   135
would you had been with me this morning; I have had the rarest
sport yonder at Highgate with two or three country fellows. [*To
Emilia*] Harkee, chick, I have invited 'em all to dinner one day this
week, good, blunt, coarse fellows, faith, but damnable rich. As Gad
jidge me, I passed for a brave° fellow amongst 'em.   140

EMILIA You need boast of applause from such clowns?°

BUBBLE Clowns? What, honest, tough, hard-fisted, plain-dealing
farmers—clowns? Pop, I say, you are an inconsiderable varlet,
chicken, and know not what belongs to such good company.

RANGER She is so well diverted at home, sir, that all rural society is   145
distasteful to her.

EMILIA I guess 'em to be much of your humour, sir: owners of a great
deal of dull, insipid noise and very little or no sense.

BUBBLE Well said, chicken. [*To Ranger*] Ned, to her. To her again,
Ned; 'tis a raging Turk at repartee.° Invent,° invent; strike her   150
home.° Prithee try her wit. Thou art a scholar. For my part, I dare
not. As Gad jidge me, she's always too hard for me.

RANGER And me too, I assure you, sir. But there's a gentleman that
has the good fortune to be more intimate. His address is far more
pleasing than mine.   155

BUBBLE Who, Tom? Come, I'll hold° a guinea° she's too hard for him
too; why, 'tis the readi'st, witti'st, jeering'st, fleering'st quean.°
'Sbud, she's one of the pearls of eloquence. And, pop, by the way,
let me tell you there's ne'er an orator in Christendom has more
tropes and figures;° take her when her hand's in°—   160

RANGER Nor knows the art of wheedling better, I'll say that for her.

BUBBLE Gad, thou art in the right; she's a *non parelio*° at it. But now
you talk of wheedling, prithee, Tom, how goes thy love affairs?
Thou look'st but ill upon't. Any plots, adventures of late? Ha!

RASHLEY None that can make me frown, sir. My stars have allotted   165
me so mild a destiny, that I can caress° my friend with my wonted
air without being discouraged by my success in love affairs.

BUBBLE I'm glad on't, faith. Come, prithee let me be partaker of thy
good fortune. When wert thou with her?

EMILIA Tell him, tell him, sir. Lord, you never used to be so cautious   170
in these matters. Pray, tell him and tremble. (*To Ranger aside*) Now
observe.

RASHLEY Why, sir, I was with her this morning.

BUBBLE So! And what success, prithee?

RASHLEY Why, at my first coming she entertained me with a song,   175
softly expressing the delights of love in an excellent air, and added
to it a thousand kind words and kisses. I had all the privilege
imaginable, and 'twas my good luck to come at a very happy hour;
for her husband went out early i' th' morning a-fowling° as far as
Holloway.°   180

BUBBLE Holloway? A pox on't. What damned luck had I? If it had
been Highgate, I should have met the fool; for I have been there all
this morning.

RASHLEY Ah, 'tis no matter, sir. His company can add little to
anyone's credit; for he is but a kind of a soft-headed, a half-witted   185
fellow.

BUBBLE A ninny, a fool. Ha, ha, ha.

RASHLEY Ay, and the most credulous of all the cuckolds I ever met
with.

BUBBLE Poor animal! Faith, I pity him, but there's a number of 'em   190
about town i'faith. We men of wit should want diversion else.

RANGER [*aside*] We men of wit, quoth a! Damn him. He's duller than
a justice's clerk. To be made a property all this while and not
discern it! O insufferable stupidity!

EMILIA Observe, sir, observe.   195

RANGER Yes, devil, I do observe. I doubt not but my observation shall
add little to your quiet. O curse of—

BUBBLE Why, how now, Ned? What, grinning like a monkey eating of
chestnuts?° Prithee what art thou thinking on? As Gad jidge me, I
think thou art grown insipid, as my wife says. How dost like Tom's   200
intrigue? Ha! Is it not pleasant?

RANGER Very pleasant, sir; and, faith, in my judgement represents as
nearly as any character I ever saw—

BUBBLE Represents? Who, pox! You're at your quirks and quiddits,°
your Cambridge puns and Westminster quibbles,° are you?   205

EMILIA Pray, forward, sir. Methinks 'tis very divertive.

RANGER Very divertive! [*Aside*] Damn her. She was sure the offspring
of Beelzebub.°

RASHLEY After a thousand other caresses, intermixed with kisses, and
smiles, and a world of happy thoughts and fancies extravagantly   210
rendered upon so happy an occasion, she obliged me in a new and
most sensible° way, presenting me, with a sweet and incomparable
grace, this gold watch and this diamond ring.

Ranger looks amazedly

BUBBLE Prithee observe Ned there. He's grown a strange whimsical
fellow. Ha, ha, ha. Look how he stares.   215

RANGER Was ever such an impudence? Sure I dream—and this is all
delusion! Harkee, sir, are you irrecoverably blind?

BUBBLE Blind? What, I blind?

RANGER Methinks that watch looks very like one I have seen your
wife wear often.   220

BUBBLE Ha! As Gad jidge me, and so it does; but much good do thy
heart, Tom, I'll warrant it right.°

RANGER Methinks that ring too much resembles yours.

BUBBLE The square° is right, but I think my stones were a little
bigger.   225

RANGER (*aside*) Now the devil take thee for a dull rogue.

RASHLEY But the best jest was, before she gave me these, there

happened to come rudely into the room a wild, young fellow that I
found afterwards to be my rival, and one she hated for his ill nature
and impertinence; but to see how pitiful he looked to see me so   230
presented before his face would have made you die with laughing.
Ha, ha, ha.

BUBBLE Ha, ha, ha.

EMILIA Ha, ha, ha.

RANGER [*aside*] Hell and furies, what's this I hear? Am I made a   235
property too? If I bear this, may I be posted° for a coward and my
infamy known to all nations. [*Takes Rashley aside*] Harkee, sir.

RASHLEY Well, sir.

RANGER By your ridiculous, fleering behaviour, I guess I was
concerned in your last description, an affront that requires instant   240
satisfaction;° and believe, sir, you shall not carry it off so clearly° as
you imagined. Though he is such a fool to be bubbled out of his
reason, I am not. Follow me, sir, if you dare.

RASHLEY Dare! Lead on, sir. You shall see how much I dare!

EMILIA Hold, sir. You shall not go.   245

RASHLEY Dare follow you?

RANGER Ay, sir. (*Points to Emilia*) 'Twould be a doubtful question if
your protection there were out of the way.

RASHLEY What's that? Protection?

BUBBLE How now? What jokes? Hard° words? What's the matter,   250
Tom? I must have no quarrels here.

EMILIA 'Tis Mr Ranger's ill humour. Prithee, love, speak to him; he's
always disturbing good company. Tell him he's impertinent.

BUBBLE Gad, and so I will. What a pox, a man cannot be a little jocose
in his own house, but he must disturb him; you shall see me go and   255
huff° him.

RANGER His horns, I am sure, are large enough; horns of sufficient
growth, substantial horns; horns visible, large, craggy-branched,
rough horns—and yet he may not believe it.

BUBBLE Believe what, Ned? Ha, ha, ha. He's mad. Downright out of   260
his wits. 'Tis a thick-skulled fellow, God knows, but we were not all
born to be wits. What dost believe, Ned?

RANGER Why, sir, I believe you are mad.

BUBBLE I mad? Damn me, Ned, you're an impertinent fellow. [*To
Emilia*] Now observe, chicken.   265

RANGER How, sir?

BUBBLE I say, sir, an impertinent fellow, sir, and deserve to be
crammed into a powdering-tub.°

185

RANGER [*aside*] Damn this fool. How he tortures me! But my revenge
    lies another way; I'll instantly go to his sister, Maria, who I know   270
    loves Rashley and will willingly join with me in my revenge. This
    must do, and I'll about it instantly.
        Exit Ranger

BUBBLE Ah, he's gone. I thought when I began to roar once, he would
    quickly vanish. I warrant I have frighted him into an ague. Poor
    fool, he'll hardly trouble us again this good while.   275

RASHLEY An uncivil person, first to intrude into our company, and
    then to hinder our discourse, especially of so pleasant a narration.
    Gad, 'twas too much.

BUBBLE Too much? Why, 'twas the devil and all; and, as Gad jidge
    me, he's the son of a whore, and I'll make him an example.   280
        Enter Footman

FOOTMAN Sir Roger Petulant with his nephew and old Mr Fumble
    are come to visit you.

BUBBLE Gadso! Sirrah, wait on 'em up° and call my niece down.
        [*Exit Footman*]
    [*To Emilia*] This is the man, chicken, I told thee that I intend for
    Cordelia's husband. He's very rich, I am told, and his father's a   285
    knight and sheriff of the county.

EMILIA But who is the other, sir?

BUBBLE Why, dost not know him? 'Tis old Alderman Fumble. He's a
    little deaf, but, i'faith, very good company and will so fumble about
    the women. You shall see he's a very jolly fellow, and repartees, and   290
    talks, and chats at all rates; but the devil a word he hears, for he
    always answers quite contrary. He'll make us all laugh, i'faith.

EMILIA I've heard he dotes on all the women he sees and is as
    passionate and inconstant at his age of seventy-three as the brisk
    sparks of our times are at five-and-twenty.   295

RASHLEY He says—the devil take him that believes him—nothing
    fails him but his eyes, which defect he has lately amended by a pair
    of Venetian spectacles.°

BUBBLE Ha, ha. 'Tis a pleasant old fellow. But here they come.
        Enter Sir Roger, Sneak, and Fumble

SIR ROGER [*to Sneak*] Cob!° Come, Cob, come! Along, I say, and   300
    hold up thy head. Fie, fie. Be not so bashful, child. Nay, Cob, what,
    dost think I'll forsake thee? Pish, in verity I will not. Wipe thy eyes,
    I say.
        Enter Cordelia

BUBBLE He's a little moody-hearted, that's the worst on't. But the

young man will show his parts by and by, I warrant ye. Come   305
hither, niece. Sir Roger, your most humble servant.

    Old Fumble pulls out his spectacles and looks on Cordelia

SIR ROGER Yours, good Mr Peregrine.° You see, sir, I am as good as
    my word: I have brought my nephew. [*To Sneak*] Cob, here's your
    Mrs Cob. Look, look up, and go and salute her.° I'll show thee the
    way. Nay, Cob, still in thy dumps? Look upon me, man! I'll do't first.   310

SNEAK Well, well! I'll follow you, uncle. I am a little bashful at present,
    but I shall come to't anon.

SIR ROGER Well said. [*To Cordelia*] Madam, I am your humble servant.
    (*Kisses her*)

SNEAK And I likewise, Madam.   315

FUMBLE I'fack, i'fack! A pretty, well-favoured woman, that there! A
    good eye, good hair, and, i'fack, I think everything good. Ha. Hem.
    [*Aside to Bubble*] Mr Peregrine, prithee who is that there? That
    woman there?

BUBBLE Who, she yonder?   320

FUMBLE Ha!

BUBBLE Why, she's a near friend of mine, sir. (*Aloud*) What an ignorant
    old fellow 'tis, not to know my niece!

FUMBLE A friend? Well, I could have heard you; I could have heard
    you without this exclamation. What, i'fack, I am not deaf; I could   325
    have heard you. But if she be a friend, I hope an old friend may
    salute her; 'tis a civility well paid. By your leave, sweet lady.

    Goes to kiss Cordelia and kisses Sneak

SNEAK What the devil does this old fellow mean? Uncle! Did you ever
    see the like?

SIR ROGER Ha, ha, ha! A pleasant mistake, i'faith.   330

FUMBLE Ha! I'fack, I think I was mistaken, was I not, gentlemen?
    Was I not? I doubt my false light guided me to the wrong person.
    Ha! But come, no matter; I meant it right, madam, I meant it right.
    Never the older for a mistake, i'fack! I meant it right.

CORDELIA I am glad I missed it for all that.   335

SIR ROGER Mr Rashley, you are not merry; in troth, I fear I have
    disturbed you. Ha!

RASHLEY Not at all, sir. 'Tis impossible your free humour can be
    troublesome to anyone.

SIR ROGER You know my old way, sir, jovial and inoffensive. Pray let   340
    me commend my nephew to you. Cob, come hither. He's a little too
    modest, sir, but else I think I may say, a youth of notable parts.
    Come hither, Cob.

RASHLEY I can believe no less. [*To Sneak*] Sir, your humble servant.
SNEAK With all my heart, sir; and I am your servant in like manner.   345
CORDELIA Bless me! What a figure of a husband shall I have?
SIR ROGER You know, sir, when I was a bachelor, I delighted much in
    merry songs and catches.° Ah! Sawny Brome,° rare fellow, and
    when a dozen of us Royalists° were met at the Mitre under the rose°
    there, the leveller° went round, round, i'faith. I hold out still, sir, as   350
    well as I can, and though I cannot sing myself, I keep those that can.
BUBBLE Ay, and so do I.
    [*Enter Betty*]
    My wife's maid shall sing you a Scotch song.° Come, sing it, Betty.
BETTY (*sings*)

— A SCOTCH SONG   355

In January last on Munnonday at morn,°
As along the fields I passed to view the winter corn,
I leaked me behind and saw come o'er the knough°
Yen glenting in an apron with a bonny brent brow.°

I bid, 'Gud morrow, fair maid,' and she right courteously,   360
Bekt lew and sine, 'Kind sir,' she said, 'Gud day agen to ye.'°
I speard o her, 'Fair maid,' quo I, 'How far intend you now?'°
Quo she, 'I mean a mile or twa to yonder bonny brough.'°

'Fair maid, I'm weel contented to ha sike company;°
For I am ganging out the gate that you intend to be.'°   365
When we had walked a mile or twa, I said to her, 'My dow,°
May I not light your apron sine kiss your bonny brow?'°

'Nea, gud sir, you are far mistean, for I am nean o those,°
I hope you ha more breeding than o light a woman's cloths;
For I've a better chosen than any sike as you,   370
Who boldly may my apron light and kiss my bonny brow.'°

'Nay, gif you are contracted, I have no more to say;°
Rather than be rejected, I will give o'er the play.
And I will choose yen o my own that shall not on me rew,°
Will boldly let me light her apron, kiss her bonny brow.'   375

'Sir, I see you are proud-hearted and leath to be said nay;°
You need not tall ha started for eaght that I did say.°
You knaw wemun for modesty no at the first time boo;°
But gif we like your company, we are as kind as you.'

BUBBLE How d'ee like it?   380

SIR ROGER O, I have a hundred such as this, sir.

FUMBLE A pretty matter, i'fack, a very pretty matter.

RASHLEY I doubt, sir, you heard it not.

FUMBLE Ay, is it not, Mr Rashley, is it not? I'fack, I like it well.

RASHLEY With all my heart, sir.   385

FUMBLE Right, i'fack. It was sung well indeed.

EVERYONE Ha, ha, ha.

BUBBLE Well said, Grandsire Fumble. Come, Sir Roger, now let's in
and toss a bumper about.

SIR ROGER I wait upon you, sir. Cob, lead in your mistress.   390

Exeunt

Rashley and Emilia remain

RASHLEY So! Thus far all is well. But what's next to be done? For I
know Ranger and Maria are plotting mischief.

EMILIA To prevent 'em, we must counterfeit a falling-out by railing at
you to my husband. I'll soon confirm it in his opinion, but be sure
you are melancholy enough; and by this means, their designs are   395
frustrated and we still safe in our intrigue.

RASHLEY Excellent! And I'll warrant you, sweet, I'll play my part well.

EMILIA The better will be the success. But let's go in for fear we are
seen.

RASHLEY Thus whilst we're equally involved in thought,   400
That side fares best that lays the wisest plot.

Exeunt Rashley and Emilia

2.[1]

[Another room in Bubble's house]

Enter Ranger and Maria

RANGER Never was an intrigue carried with so much confidence. Every word they spoke retained a double meaning, but so evident that any animal but a dull husband could not fail to understand it. For they were so far from hiding their amour that they openly confessed all, only speaking in a third person for a slender security. 5 He stood and heard it and often would laugh heartily to hear himself notoriously abused.

MARIA An insipid fool! O that I had been there to have changed the scene a little! But, sir, could you be idle on such an occasion? Why did not you play your part cunningly and discover 10 'em?

RANGER Faith, I did what I could. But the cunning devil your sister, still as I was speaking something towards the discovery, would interrupt me and in a minute dash all my hopes by turning what was said into raillery. 15

MARIA Is she so politic? 'Tis very well. I once imagined I could best design, and thought my talent of wit equal with any. But are they so intimate, say ye, sir?

RANGER As man and wife.

MARIA Impudent fellow! Dares he insult over my love? Baffle 20 my passion with a sly pretence? I am not fair enough, but he shall find my brain has wit enough to ruin his design, fool as I am.

RANGER (*aside*) Now the devil in her is working hard for me. We shall have it anon. 25

MARIA Fooled by a brother's wife! A creature that the law makes kin to me! No, 'twas tamely thought, and I, as tamely now, should suffer wrongs had I a dastard spirit. But in me nature has shown her masterpiece; and to a masculine person providence has bestowed an active soul so sensible of wrongs, that to forgive would argue me 30 as base as is their treachery.

RANGER (*aside*) Now she thunders; the devil has been priming her all this while, and now she scatters like a hand-granado.°

MARIA My love refused! 'Tis death to the dull fool! Death, double-death—damnation too, 'tis likely. But why did I name it love? 35

There's no such word; for with this breath I banish it forever, and
in my breast receive obscure° revenge, my heart's delightful darling.
O, the pleasure in that slender word, revenge! I'll plague the fool
her husband with a story shall make his gall flow upwards.°

RANGER Plague him with doubts and make his jealousy break into   40
violent fits of rage and passion. I'll further all, madam; by heaven, I
will not fail you.

MARIA Enough; and doubt not we'll soon turn the current.

RANGER We'll catch 'em in his lodging.

MARIA Entrap 'em there, and bring him in to see it.   45

RANGER Right. What else? We'll shame 'em.

MARIA Slight 'em.

RANGER Laugh at 'em.

MARIA Vex 'em.

RANGER Ruin 'em.   50

MARIA Damn 'em.

RANGER Hey, by Heaven, 'tis excellent, and now I see the sense of
wrongs can arm a female spirit and make it vigorous. O, I adore thy
temper!

MARIA I'll instantly go to her and first charge her with the fact, then 55
upbraid her. For I am resolved never to let her rest till she deserts
his passion.

> And whilst she suffers that base wretch to woo her,
> I'll plot and counterplot, but I'll undo her.

Exit Maria

RANGER (*alone*) I am glad I met with her; for of all the persons I am   60
acquainted with, she only has enough of the devil to follow such a
business closely. For she'll never rest till she has betrayed 'em,
which still will further my revenge; and I am resolved to enjoy her
sister, if it be but only for the dear pleasure of boasting it hereafter.
I'll straight to Bubble and once more infect him with my poison.   65
Maria is my pilot, and her being thus slighted by Rashley will still
augment her desire of revenge: 'tis natural to the sex.

> For baulk a woman once and love rebate,
> Not all the devils shall reclaim her hate.

Exit

2.2

[A room in Bubble's house]
Enter Rashley, Emilia

EMILIA Manage it but carefully; you need not doubt the consequence.
I have already possessed my husband with a belief of our variance,
and I know he's coming up with an intent to reconcile us. I'll not be
seen. The rest is your part; carry it but handsomely, and Ranger's
plots are fruitless. Maria has sent also to speak with him; I guess the   5
business, and I am accordingly provided. But remember you are not
tardy.

RASHLEY Never doubt me, madam; I am more a lover than to be idle in
a business that so nearly concerns us. Besides, 'tis so well contrived
and so easy to be followed that to fail now would demonstrate me as   10
defective in sense as your husband is. But what business can your
sister have with you? The devil and she have been plotting together
about this intrigue.

EMILIA Let 'em plot. I am so much her sister that my part shall never
be wanting to furnish the comedy. I'll go to her straight. In the   15
meantime, be you sure to play your part with him. (*Noise offstage*)
Hark! I hear him coming.
    Exit Emilia

RASHLEY [*alone*] Well, I never thought a woman till now so necessary
a creature. Intrigues are their masterpieces, and as readily they
undertake 'em as a country lawyer a bad cause from a half-witted   20
client. 'Twould be excellent sport to hear the two she-wolves bark
one at another. But since I cannot be there, I'll divert myself with
entertaining the fool, her husband. Here he comes! Now to my
studied posture.
    Enter Bubble

BUBBLE Why, how now, Tom? What, all a-mort? In verity, this is   25
foppery, as Sir Roger says. Come, cheer up, cheer up, man, and hold
up thy head. In troth, thou makes me sad to see thee° look so like—
so like a—gammon° of bacon. There! I was sharp upon him. Ha,
ha! A good jest, a'faith.

RASHLEY (*aside*) Damn him! What a simile the fool has found out! [*To*   30
Bubble] Sir, it lies not in any man's power to banish serious
thoughts at all times. Besides, I have some cause for my present
melancholy.

BUBBLE The cause? Come, come, Tom. I know the cause. Ha, ha. You

thought, I warrant, to have carried matters so privately; but if I   35
once go about such a business, there's ne'er a man in Christendom,
though I say it, can find out a cause° sooner than I.

RASHLEY You may be mistaken in mine, sir, for all that.

BUBBLE Mistaken? Ha, ha! I see, Tom, thou knowest not what 'tis to
be ingenious. I tell thee once more, I do know the cause, the very   40
cause, ay, and more than that, the cause of that cause. 'Sbud,
there's ne'er an attorney in the Inns of Court knows more causes
than I do.

RASHLEY I doubt not, but in the end you'll be brought to confess
yourself too positive° in this particular. But since you have such an   45
excellent faculty and imagine yourself so well skilled in finding out
secrets, come, what is't? What is't?

BUBBLE What is't? Why, ha, ha, ha! My wife. My wife, Tom, and
you're fallen out, ha, ha, ha! Have I mumped you now, i'faith?

RASHLEY I must confess you are in the right, sir.   50

BUBBLE O must you so, sir? What a pox, I warrant you thought we
husbands had no wit but what our wives lend us. But I would have
you to know, Tom, that I am a Leviathan at these matters: to be
plain, that is as much to say, a whale.°

RASHLEY I am sufficiently convinced of your excellent judgement,   55
sir; and, as I have confessed to you freely the cause of my sadness to
be your wife's ill usage of me, so I am continually tortured to guess
the reason. For I am confident, sir, you know I always honoured her
and loved her.

BUBBLE Faith, so thou didst! I'll say that for thee; and, by the Lord   60
Harry, she shall love and honour thee too, or I'll be very sharp upon
her. I'll pinch her severely, faith, for all she's my chicken. Nay, if
she'll be still refractory, rather than fail, thou shalt pinch her too,
Tom. I am not like your surly-burly-waspish-cross-grained fellows
that fall out and fight about their wives. 'Sbud, I'll give my friend   65
leave at any time to chastise my wife if she don't behave herself
civilly.

RASHLEY You ever load me with your kind expressions, dear friend.

BUBBLE Dear Tom,° faith, thou'rt an honest fellow.
          Bubble embraces Rashley

RASHLEY (*aside*) This ever is the fate of cuckolds.   70

BUBBLE Never doubt. I'll bring you together again with a vengeance.°
Nay, I can tell you the reason of her anger too, if I thought 'twere
convenient.

RASHLEY Convenient! Why, sir, 'tis the only thing that conduces to

my contentment; for I have long studies in vain and could never yet   75
so much as guess at it. Let me beg it of you, sit. Come, I'm sure you
cannot deny so near a friend.

BUBBLE I'faith, I cannot, that's the truth on't, and thou shalt have it.
Why, you must know, Tom, one night—when I was examining her
about you—she told me very seriously that the cause of her anger   80
was that you promised to give her a squirrel that night, and never
kept your word, and she loves squirrels passionately.°

RASHLEY 'Tis true, I confess I did promise her; but as the devil would
have it, I was disappointed utterly of my squirrel that night myself,
for I got very drunk and from thence sprung this fatal consequence.°   85

BUBBLE Puh! No matter. I'll warrant thee I'll bring all about again.

RASHLEY O 'tis impossible. I am sure she'll ne'er° be brought to't.

BUBBLE Not brought to't? Yes, I'll lay my commands upon her, and
I'll have you know she shall be brought to't. I'll lay a wager I'll
reconcile you both before night.   90

RASHLEY Done. Any wager.

BUBBLE What shall it be?

RASHLEY Why, five guineas to be spent in a treat of venison and
champagne.

BUBBLE Agreed, i'faith, and we'll drink and sing tory-rory. Not   95
reconcile you! You shall be all one before tomorow morning. I have
a spell for that. I'll do't, I say. Come along, boy.
        Exit Bubble

RASHLEY A petty friend for pimping we applaud,°
        But, of all men, a husband's the best bawd.
        Exit

2.3

[A room in Bubble's house]

Enter Sir Roger, Cordelia, Sneak

SIR ROGER Madam, you, as being the niece to Mr Peregrine, truly
deserve the favour I intend you by this alliance. You are a handsome
woman and, in verity, were I a young man, none should be more
forward than I for a place in your affection. I like your air well; and,
upon my faith, you have the right way on't. Ah, madam, I once saw   5
the days when such an eye as yours—well, I say no more on't. 'Tis

for my nephew now I make addresses. You see what he is, madam: his face is none of the worst, nor his person I think any way defective. In brief, madam, I present him to you, nor shall he want an estate to make him worthy. 10

CORDELIA [*aside*] 'Tis well he named an estate to candy over his bitter pill; my squeamish stomach would else have hardly digested it. Lord, how he looks!

SIR ROGER Cob, go! Prithee go and make your address to the lady. He's newly come from the college,° madam, and is, as the rest of 'em are, 15 a little bashful at first, but by that time h'as seen a play or two—

CORDELIA Methinks this silence becomes him very well, sir. A student should always be contemplative; 'tis a great sign of learning.

SIR ROGER 'Tis a sign he thinks the more. But, madam, ladies of this age are not to be won with imaginary courtship; 'tis the practic part 20 they love, and he that can sing well, dance well, talk well, rhyme modishly, swear decently, and lie confoundedly is certainly the happy man, whilst others pass unregarded.

CORDELIA I see, sir, you are well skilled in modish address;° but give me leave to tell ye—perhaps few other ladies are of my humour—I 25 love words considerately spoken.

SIR ROGER And I too, faith madam. [*To Sneak*] Cob, d'ee hear that, Cob?

SNEAK Ay, ay, 'tis a fine woman, by Jericho,° and now I begin to be a little in heart. I shall put up well enough anon, uncle. 30

SIR ROGER Well said. Why, now I love thee. [*To Cordelia*] And, madam, as to his interior virtues, I dare speak for 'em. His wit is hereditary. Ah, his father, old Sir Jeremy Sneak, had a notable head-piece, and, troth, Cob comes very near him. You'll find it, madam, when he talks with you. 35

CORDELIA Your character of him, sir, gives me the satisfaction I should receive in his discourse. I imagine him to be one of those that hoard up wit for Plato's great year° and are very shy of using their talent for fear of diminishing the value in making it too common. 40

SIR ROGER In verity, madam, I always held him so. Cob!

SNEAK Ay, madam, you may say of me what you please. I am your slave, your vassal, your pig, madam. But as for wit, as my nuncle says, I think I may compare with another, take the court-cabal° away. 'Tis a blessing thrown upon me. Besides, mine is none of 45 your wheedling wits that cheat for a livelihood. I am no parasite, madam. I am a scholar, I!

SIR ROGER In troth, he's in the right. Did not I tell you, madam, he would speak notably? Ah, 'tis a wag.

CORDELIA His disputes in the college have added extremely to his 50 rhetoric. He speaks with good emphasis and gives a delightful period° to every jest, of which I see he has many. But I would fain have the gentleman speak himself: a little talk, I am sure, would become him.

SIR ROGER He shall do't, madam. [*Aside to Sneak*] Cob, now's your 55 time—she's wrought finely. Madam, I'll take my leave for a minute. I know his temper, madam; he'll speak the better for my absence.

    Exit Sir Roger

CORDELIA Pray, sir, what university was blessed with your presence?

SNEAK Cambridge, madam.

CORDELIA Will you not be angry if I ask you one question more? 60

SNEAK O Lord, angry, madam? You do not know me. Angry! You mistake me clearly. We of the round cap° are not given to't; 'tis your graduates are the angry people.

CORDELIA Pray, what have you learned at Cambridge?

SNEAK Learned! What a plaguy question's that? Where's my uncle 65 now? Learned, madam?

CORDELIA Yes, sir. Learned.

SNEAK Why, Madam—I learned nothing.

CORDELIA Nothing, sir!

SNEAK No, but to wear a daggled gown, as the rest do, and eat dry 70 chops of rotten mutton.° We fellow-commoners° don't go thither to learn. Madam, we go for diversion; we—

CORDELIA I thought you had gone to learn the sciences.

SNEAK Right, madam, but not gentlemen. Your green, half-witted pupils, I confess, come thither for some such business; that is, 75 madam, your prigs° that would be parsons. But the sciences of your persons of quality, I'll give you a description. Hum. 'Tis to wench immoderately, to be drunk hourly, to wear their clothes slovenly, to abuse the proctor° damnably, and so be expelled the college triumphantly. There are seven, but I contented myself with these. 80

CORDELIA [*aside*] This is ever sound. Your sly fool is in his nature more impudent than the greatest professors of debauchery.° I must shift him off.°

    Enter Fumble

FUMBLE O, here she is! And, i'fack, I'll put up to her° now I have found her. How dost thou do, girl? Ha! How dost thou do? Give me 85 thy hand. Ah, little rogue! Well, I have been with my goldsmith about the ring I promised thee; thou shalt have it, bird, thou shalt have it. How now, who is that there?

SNEAK [*aside*] O, the devil! Now will the old doting fellow disturb us before I have told her half my mind. [*To Fumble*] Who am I, sir? Why, sir, I am one that cares as little—

FUMBLE Thank you heartily, sir, i'fack. I am very well, only cold weather, cold weather. 'Tis Sir Roger's nephew! A pretty fellow, a very pretty fellow.

SNEAK Very well, sir. [*Aside*] Would you were very sick, sir. 'Oons, I must beat this fellow.

CORDELIA [*aside*] Here's like to be rare sport.

SNEAK Pray, old philosopher, depart in silence for fear of further damage. This lady and I have business.

FUMBLE I'fack, and so she is, sir, very pretty, very pretty, *bona fide*. Ah, that black o' th' top there!° Well, I'll say no more. But, i'fack, black hair, black eyes, and a black—Gad, forgive me, what was I going to say?—patch or two further generation more than tissues and embroideries.°

SNEAK [*aside*] Generation? O Lord! Was ever such an impudence? An old, doting, impotent fellow, one that was rotten in his minority° and now has lost three of his five senses—to talk of generation! I am impatient. [*To Fumble*] Will you be gone, sir? 'Sbud, I will so swinge you else.

CORDELIA Hold, sir, and pray forbear this rudeness; I like his company very well.

SNEAK How! Like him? Why, he has nothing, madam. A lady can like no hearing, no smelling, no tasting, no teeth, no strength, no— nothing I say that a man should have? Besides, he's above fourscore and, by being a stallion in his youth, has acquired to be a baboon in his age,° by Jericho. 'Sbud, like him, quotha?

FUMBLE What does the wag say? Ha! What does he say? He's a pretty, spruce fellow, madam, and, i'fack, knows a hawk from a handsaw,° as the saying is. But here are those not far off that, i'fack, know as much as he, if that were all. What think'st thou, bird? Do they not? Do they not, rogue? Well, still I say that hair of thine—ah, rascal!

CORDELIA I am glad it pleases you, sir.

SNEAK But, madam, when shall I begin? 'Sbud, methinks we lose time.

CORDELIA Begin what, sir?

SNEAK Why, my courtship. Pox o' this old, chattering fellow; if he had not come, I had been out of my pain before now. [*To Fumble*] Hark

ye, reverend° sir. 'Bud! What d'ee do prating here? Why don't you go
and chat to your granddaughter at home, if you love women so well?

FUMBLE Ha! What does the wag say, madam?

CORDELIA He says, sir, he's extremely in love with your   130
granddaughter.

FUMBLE My granddaughter? And, i'fack, she deserves it, madam.
She's a juicy, spritely girl; she'll make a pottle of water of a pint of
ale!° A chip o' the old block, *bona fide*, and shall turn her back to°
ne'er a one in Christendom of her inches,° I'll say that for her.   135

    Enter Betty

BETTY Sir, there's one Mrs Snare below desires to speak with you.

SNEAK Snare! O Lord, what shall I do? How the devil came she to
know I was here? [*To Betty*] Hark; prithee, sweetheart, tell her I am
gone. O, I would not see her for the world!

BETTY Sir, she says she dogged you hither and swears and rants   140
yonder strangely.

SNEAK O damned quean! What shall I do?

BETTY And vows if you come not instantly, she'll go into the parlour
to Sir Roger and discover something to him, I know not what; but I
saw she was a big-bellied woman, and I was loath to discourage her.   145

SNEAK Well, well. Tell her I'll come.

    [*Exit Betty*]

Why, how the devil could she get from Cambridge already?

CORDELIA What's the matter, sir? Not well?

SNEAK Yes, I thank you, madam, very well—only thinking of a little
business I have. I must about it presently. Madam, your servant. I'll   150
wait on you some other time. [*Aside*] I must go and pacify this
quean. This comes of learning the sciences with a pox.

    Exit Sneak

CORDELIA Come, sir, shall we go in?

FUMBLE I'fack, and so he is, madam, but the fellow has some pretty
parts and will grow better in time. But, come; let's go in and see   155
Sir Roger.

CORDELIA 'Twas that I asked you.

FUMBLE Ha! Dost like me, say'st thou, i'fack? I'm glad on't. Shall we
not have a word or two in private, my little queen of fairies? We
must, I say, we must. Ah, rogue! I'll warrant thou art a swinger.°   160
But come, let's go.

    Exeunt

2.4

Emilia's bedchamber

Enter Maria and Emilia severally°

EMILIA [*aside*] Now for my talent of women! I see by her looks I shall have occasion for it.

MARIA Sister!

EMILIA Sister!

MARIA The natural love I bear you, and my desire to prevent your growing infamy, has brought me hither to give you counsel.   5

EMILIA The sense I have of your ill nature, and my knowledge of the little good it will do you, has brought me hither to give you advice.

MARIA Your reputation is loudly branded by all tongues, and I only, as   10
a sister, have power to speak indifferently of your life in hopes of your reformation.

EMILIA Your malice and unexampled envy is mortally hated by all people, I only, as a sister, retaining so much pity as to desire its utter dissolution.   15

MARIA Why do you echo me?

EMILIA Why do you question me? What have I done deserves it?

MARIA Done! Recollect your thoughts and then confess. For my part, shame ties up my tongue. I dare not speak it.

EMILIA Dare not! Nay, that I am sure is false. You dare speak anything.   20
Come, prithee don't fright me; what is't you mean?

MARIA (*aside*) Excellent cunning! She has fitted me.° [*To Emilia*] Why would you seem ignorant? I confess to a stranger you might be cautious of a nice confession, but this artifice to your sister—fie, Emilia!   25

EMILIA Now I'll lay my life your design is to wheedle something out of me to make yourself merry withal.

MARIA Rare° still! No, madam, this is no such merry matter; the infamy of a family is not so to be jested with.

EMILIA Infamy! Nay, then I see 'tis time to be serious. Come, express   30
it. I suppose 'tis the invention of your envy, some new stratagem to affront me with; I am no stranger to your temper.

MARIA This is an impudence beyond a prostitute. Do I not know you are false?

EMILIA False! How?   35

MARIA False to your husband; false with Rashley. I need not tell you
how; you best know that.

EMILIA I know you love him and am sensible of the intrigues and
assignations which you have had, which makes your meaning
visible. But methinks this is so strange a design.°   40

MARIA Design! What is't she means? I hope you can tax me with no
such crime with him.

EMILIA Not I; 'tis not my business. I have only liberty to guess. Yet
indeed your often private meetings were a little suspicious, and I
suppose your late raillery was only a design; but you might have   45
took a better way with your sister. I am not so talkative.

MARIA Exquisite devil! Death, I am incensed beyond all bounds
of reason. I private with him? An intrigue with me? Fury, thou
know'st—

EMILIA I do. And to exasperate thy rage, will now confess all. I do   50
love Rashley more than I love fame. Nay, more than you could do,
could you die for him. But why should that offend you?

MARIA O confusion! I am all o'er fire. Dare you be such a devil? Dare
you love him?

EMILIA Yes; and to vex you more, dare make you of my counsel.   55

MARIA Can I endure this? O, for a look now of a basilisk° that I might
kill thee.

EMILIA Thou art worse.

MARIA Expect to find me so; for if there be a stratagem of malice in all
hell, I'll have it thence. Ah, I'll be a tender sister to thee.   60

EMILIA As ever woman yet was blessed withal.

MARIA Not all the infernals clad in the secret darkest robes of malice
did ever watch a soul they meant to ruin, as I will thee. Thy very
sleeps shall be discovered to me, and every dream I'll trace with so
much care that if thou scapest, thou art the wiser sister and I a poor, 65
unthinking creature, good for nothing.

EMILIA I slight thy threats and dare thee to persevere. Manage thy
hate with such dexterity, the world may wonder at thee and confess
thou hadst the practic part of policy.° Design thy plots so subtly,
that the devil should own himself outdone in his own mystery. Yet,   70
in the arms of him I love, I'd laugh to see my wit out-do 'em.

MARIA Thy wit! Thy wit compare with mine, insipid fool?

EMILIA Yes; and my prosperous fate shall mount me far above thy
shallow stratagems.

MARIA I'll pull thee down from that ambitious height and trample   75
thee in ashes.

EMILIA Do.

MARIA Expect it.

EMILIA And from that low recess, I'll forge a plot shall blow thee
    into air. 80

        I'll make that devil in thy envy tame.

MARIA   And if I fail thee, may I sink and damn.

        Exeunt

3.[1]

[A room in Bubble's house]

Enter Sneak and Mrs Snare

SNEAK Nay, prithee, Peg, have patience.

MRS SNARE Tell not me of patience, sir. For my part, I can stay no longer. You see my condition. If you will consider, so; if not, Sir Roger shall know that the abuse of so innocent a person as I was deserves better satisfaction.　　　　　　　　　　　　　　　5

SNEAK *[aside]* Innocent! 'Sbud, she was a strumpet to the whole college before I knew her. Innocent, with a pox!

MRS SNARE Sir, do not grumble, nor say your devil's *pater noster*° to me, but give me money. Fifty pounds I demand, which I think is reasonable enough, considering the charge° of my journey.　　　10

SNEAK You might have stayed till I came back again. I was not running away.

MRS SNARE But I was, sir, and so might you for anything I know. Come, come, sir. I am to be baffled no more. I am grown older now, make me thankful.°　　　　　　　　　　　　　　　　　15

SNEAK *[aside]* Ay, in impudence, by Jericho. She has been snapped,° it seems, formerly but has now learned cunning. Ah, plague o' these sciences, I say still! *[To Mrs Snare]* Come, wilt thou be civil? Wilt thou take twenty pounds? Pox, use a little conscience in thy dealings. Thou wilt thrive the better for't.　　　　　　　　　20

MRS SNARE I'll abate not a farthing, sir. Don't tell me of conscience.

SNEAK *[aside]* 'Sbud, would she were i' th' sea and a millstone about her neck. I must give it, for if my uncle comes and sees her, I am undone.

　　　　Enter Betty

BETTY O, sir, what shall we do? Sir Roger and my master are just　25
coming.

SNEAK O unhappy minute! If he sees me, I am lost forever. No hole nor corner to hide us in, my little rogue? 'Sbud, here's a guinea for thee; do but contrive handsomely.

BETTY Well, sir, I see you are a gentleman; therefore, I'll help you. This　30
door opens to my lady's chamber. There you may hide yourselves; and, at night, when it begins to grow dark, I'll come and let you out.

SNEAK With all my heart! O, I've an ague on me.

　　　　Exeunt Betty, Sneak, and Mrs Snare. Enter Ranger and Emilia

202

RANGER Are you still resolved?

EMILIA Assure yourself I am and shall be ever.   35

RANGER Give me but hopes, and I'll forget all injuries and ask your
pardon.

EMILIA Fie, this from a man of wit? One that can plot so well? 'Tis
impossible: what would you have me do?

RANGER Desert young Rashley. Come, I beg thee do it.   40

EMILIA Not for the world! O, heaven! Desert him! I love him, sir.

RANGER Go on then, devil, and if I don't plague thee—
         Enter Bubble, Sir Roger, Rashley, Fumble

BUBBLE Now for the venison, Tom. You'll stand to your bargain?

RASHLEY Firmly, sir. Win it, and 'tis yours. Ha, what a devil makes
Ranger here?°   45

SIR ROGER Madam, I hope you'll excuse my last abrupt departure.
My nature, madam, is merry and, in verity, careless sometimes. I
have not since I came to England achieved the polite method of
courtship and address; but if blunt actions, kind behaviour, and
merry songs can do it, I think I have shown an example, have I not,   50
old signor?

FUMBLE I'fack, sir, and 'tis right, let who will say the contrary. What
does he say now? Madam, you may believe him.

EMILIA Anything, sir, rather than put you to the trouble of an apology.
         Emilia frowns on Rashley

RASHLEY What think you now, sir? Do you observe her angry look?   55
Do but see what an eye of indignation she casts upon me!

BUBBLE Ay, ay. I'll put out her eye of indignation presently. I'll fetch
her down with her haughty looks in a moment; I'll make her look as
I'd have her, or I'll put her head into a pudding-bag.

RANGER [*aside*] 'Sdeath, how she looks! Here's another plot a-   60
hatching.

BUBBLE Wife! I have brought honest Tom here to be reconciled to
thee and, to take away all manner of distastes,° he says he will give
thee a squirrel at any time. Would thou not, Tom?

RASHLEY Sir, and my heart into the bargain, if she please to pardon   65
me.

BUBBLE Why, look ye now, he's as honest a fellow as lives, I'll say that
for him.

EMILIA Sir, the affront he offered me was so contrary to my nature,
and his behaviour so opposite to his duty and character, that to   70
forgive him would argue my spirit as mean as by his late deportment
one might guess his breeding.

BUBBLE What! Dare you be refractory? Ho! Do it or, by the Lord
Harry, I shall be very sharp upon you, that's in short.

RANGER Now all the fiends that dwell beneath the centre, and hourly   75
study deeds subtle and horrid, to sooth and snare the souls ye mean
to damn, in favour of your commonwealth appear, and to be still
more devilish, copy her.

BUBBLE Still refractory? Then, thus, I break the truce and sally out
with my full power.   80

RANGER Sir, do you not see her artifice? This is nothing what she
intends; 'tis all feigned, and you are abused, by heaven. Sir, there's
nothing of this real.

BUBBLE Ah, would it were not. But, Ned, thou canst talk well; prithee
go and try if thou canst reconcile 'em. Faith, I'll do as much for   85
thee. Prithee try.

RANGER [aside] Insufferable ignorance! No brains! No sense of feeling!
[To Bubble] Sir, this is all dissimulation and to carry on their design
of abusing you.

BUBBLE Why, peace, I say, not a word of this. 'Sbud, I shall lose   90
my venison by this fool's prating, if I let him alone a little longer.
Wife, I command you once more, and instantly obey upon this
summons, or I'll turn you away like a vagabond for contempt of
my government.° Sir Roger, try you to persuade her. 'Sbud, this
Ned here had liked to have spoiled° all; but what says Scoggin?°   95

EMILIA 'Tis hard to force lost friendship to the blood when once
'tis banished.

RANGER [aside] Had she been bred a witch, she had lost half her
character.

SIR ROGER Come, madam, forget and forgive; 'tis necessary your   100
husband should be obeyed. Mr Rashley, I am sorry to see you so
deserted by the ladies you used to be most in favour withal.

RASHLEY Not I. But you weigh my merits in your own scale, Sir Roger.

SIR ROGER No, faith. I am old now, but, about some thirty years ago, I
could have said something. I could have fetched 'em about with a   105
horse-pox,° i'faith. I never flinched. I was a true knight-errant, I.

FUMBLE What is the meaning of all this? I'fack, I cannot guess the
matter, but mum, I must not discover my failing.

EMILIA Well, sir, rather than be thought disobedient, I will submit,
but heaven knows with what an ill will.   110

BUBBLE Why, so, now all's well, and the venison's mine. Ha, ha, ha. I
thought I should have it. Faith, Tom, be civil and kiss her; 'tis no
confirmation else.

RANGER O, damn him, damn him! Was ever such a coxcomb!

RASHLEY [*aside to Emilia*] 'Tis now about five; at seven, I will not fail   115
ye. Madam, you have given me new life with this favour.

RANGER (*overhearing*) At seven? Good! Thanks to my ear for that
discovery. I shall go near to spoil your assignation.

BUBBLE Go now; get you in and begin a set at ombre, and I'll come
and make one presently.° By the Lord Harry, I am glad they are   120
friends with all my heart.

> *Exeunt Sir Roger, Fumble, Rashley, Emilia smiling. Enter Maria*

RANGER So Paris stole the wife of Menelaus and Troy grew bright
with fire.°

BUBBLE Hey-day! Troy! Why, what hast thou to do with Troy? Ned,
prithee let us talk of our own affairs.   125

MARIA And wisely too, for your reputation suspended one hour will
grow nauseous;° the rabble will shout at ye and point their fingers,
and by your name you will grow infamous.

> *Enter Betty at door*

BUBBLE My name, sister! What dost mean? What name?

MARIA A cuckold. Can you bear it, sir? A cuckold-buzz.°   130

BUBBLE By the Lord Harry, 'tis but a scurvy name for a man of
honour, that's the truth on't; but what is't to me?

RANGER Nothing, sir, nothing—only you are the man, that's all.

BUBBLE That's all, quotha? What a pox does he mean?

MARIA Dull man! I blush to call ye brother; that kind name your want   135
of sense has taken from you.° Can you see the guilty love 'twixt
Rashley and your wife, the melting touches and the glancing eyes,
the often pressings, sighs, and kind caresses and all the signs of
shame and burning lust—and yet be patient? O, the insipid dullness
of a husband! A husband!   140

BUBBLE Rashley and my wife! Pish. Why, I reconciled 'em but just
now; she has been angry with him this week for not giving her a
squirrel he promised her.

RANGER A squirrel? Ha! A very fine present that, if you understood
all.   145

BETTY [*aside*] Happy discovery! This shall to my lady immediately.

> *Exit Betty*

MARIA That anger was designed.° You are abused, and I, that have a
share in all your ignominy, have now resolved prevention. O, that
ever I should live to be a witness of this shame! (*Weeps*) Heaven
knows how I have loved her, instructed her, and told her the duty of   150
a wife was to obey and be constant—yet all would not do. Therefore,

I am resolved to right myself and you in the discovery, nor shall our race in future times be branded with any spurious offspring.

RANGER I could not be believed—I was impertinent—but if you knew what I have seen, sir.   155

BUBBLE Seen! Why, prithee what hast thou seen, Ned?

RANGER Faith, 'twill be no secret long; therefore, I'll tell you. I have seen her lie in Rashley's arms and kiss him; play with his nose, and clap° his cheeks, and laugh till her whole frame was shook with titillation. I guess, sir, 'twas at you, but will not swear it. She'd sing   160 and breathe upon him, and, with her hand locked fast in his and eyes with rapture gazing on his face, she'd tell him wanton stories of her love and of her easy husband. He, to requite her, would display her charms and betwixt every word imprint a kiss to prove his amorous argument.   165

BUBBLE And you have seen this?

RANGER More than this, sir, I have seen—but to tell you is to be called impertinent—such things, such monstrous things.

BUBBLE My head begins to ache. All is not well. Prithee, Ned, out with 'em. Come, I am thy friend and, 'sbud, if I thought anything   170 were done in hugger mugger—

MARIA What would you do then?

BUBBLE Do! Why, I'd ask him civilly whether his meaning were good or no.

RANGER His meaning?   175

BUBBLE Ay. You know 'tis best to begin mildly, that afterwards, if occasion be, a man may cut his throat with greater assurance.

    [Enter Betty, unseen]

MARIA Stare on your infamy with eagle-aspect!° Behold the evidence of shame writ in her eyes and actions! See every glance, each touch, each kind embrace; and when you have seen 'em in the very fact,   180 stand coldly unconcerned and ask the meaning. Ah! Curse upon all dullness.

RANGER Let Rashley smile and point his fingers at ye, tell you a story of a *quondam* mistress—which is indeed your wife—how oft he has lain with her and pleasantly deceived the easy cuckold; yet, as a   185 precedent of excellent nature,° I could advise you still to ask his meaning, his meaning.

MARIA Watch all his actions; and when some kind genius has, to undeceive you, made you a spectator of Rashley—full of hopes and all undressed, entering your bed with a glad lover's haste—step in,   190 and pull him back, and ask his meaning, his meaning!

BUBBLE My bed! My bed is my castle; and, by the Lord Harry, he that
violates it but with a look, my fist shall crush him into mummy.°

RANGER (*aside*) So! Now he begins to take fire.

BUBBLE He's a son of a whore, a dog, a bitch, a succubus;° and, if I   195
find this true, I'll cut him piece-meal, though he were sword-proof
and had a witch to his mother.

MARIA Ay, this is meaning now! Go on and prosper.

RANGER These words display a revived sense of honour, nor shall you
want encouragement to forward it; and since I see your eyes and   200
understanding are opened, I, as your friend, will give this secret to
you. 'Twas my good fortune to hear an assignation appointed
between 'em this night at seven o'clock; I guess 'tis now very near
the hour. You have a key to the chamber: go thither at the time
appointed, and then never trust your friend if you find her not the   205
falsest of women.

   [*Exit Betty*]

BUBBLE If I do, I'll make her the ugliest in Christendom. For I'll cut
off her nose° and send her to the devil for a New Year's gift.

MARIA Here she comes. We must not be seen; 'twill spoil all. Talk of
going abroad and carry it handsomely,° for fear she mistrusts.   210

BUBBLE But where shall we meet?

RANGER At my lodging in the Strand,° about half an hour hence.

   Exeunt Maria and Ranger. Enter Emilia

EMILIA What, studying, my dear? Come, come; indeed, you must not
be so thoughtful. Did you not promise to come and make one at
ombre?   215

BUBBLE [*aside*] Now, if I might be hanged, cannot I speak an angry
word. [*To Emilia*] No, I won't play; I am busy. I am going abroad for
two or three hours. Farewell.

   Exit Bubble

EMILIA 'Tis so. Our intrigue tonight is discovered to him, I find by
his actions. The infernal colleagues, Ranger and Maria, have been   220
possessing him with some strange resolutions. But since 'tis but
what I expected, it gives me the less trouble; and 'tis ten to one but I
have a counterplot left that shall undo their policies, though the
devil made one in the invention.

   Enter Rashley

Did you meet my husband?   225

RASHLEY Yes, but in a strange humour. He looked with so dull an
aspect, and returned my salute so coldly and so far from his usual
manner, that I more than half fear our intrigue is discovered.

EMILIA Without doubt it is. They have played their parts to discover, and it now belongs to us to study to repel. Come, summon your wits   230
together and advise what's to be done in so critical a conjuncture. You had a contriving genius once.

RASHLEY Ay, 'tis true, madam, I had once. But this damned champagne has so dulled it that, egad, 'tis now worth little or nothing. Madam, you know my talent in plot is insignificant, but if   235
a rencounter or cutting Ranger's throat may do the business, I'll thrust my hand as far as any man. I'll spoil his plotting, by heaven, say you but the word.

EMILIA No! Fighting will do in any other business better than this. For instead of defending, it blasts my reputation.   240

RASHLEY The devil take me if I had not like to have forgot that too. Well, I am a dull rogue, madam, that's the truth on't.
    Enter Betty

BETTY O, madam, you are betrayed! Mr Ranger, by what means heaven knows, has been informed of your assignation. I accidentally overheard him telling it to my master, and Madam Maria, coming   245
in, seconded his story with an extravagant fury; and, in conclusion, 'twas designed that he should pretend business abroad but privately return home and surprise ye.

EMILIA 'Tis as I imagined, and I am glad of this caution. Now we may take breath again.   250

RASHLEY Gad, and so am I. But is there no way to keep on the plot and deceive 'em still?

EMILIA 'Tis in my head and will have birth presently. Betty, you have Sneak still fast in my chamber?

BETTY Yes, madam, he's securely locked in, and here's the key.   255

EMILIA Follow me, then, and do as I directed you. In the meantime, sir, go you to your chamber and put on your gown and nightcap as if you had been in bed; and when you hear me stamp, come out and wonder.° Let me alone° for the rest. I'll plague 'em with an after-plot.° Away, the minute's near.   260
    Exeunt Emilia and Betty

RASHLEY What she intends I know not, but am certain of the success by the assurance she does it with. Ha, 'tis a rare creature and, by heaven, is mistress of the sweetest nature, and noblest trust, and most substantial good English principles of any woman in Europe. Well, if cuckolding be a crime, 'tis the sweetest crime in Christendom   265
and has certainly the most practisers. But let that pass; now to my gown and nightcap.
    Exit Rashley. Enter Sir Roger, Fumble, Cordelia, and Servant

SIR ROGER 'Sdeath, I have had confounded luck tonight; not a good
chance since I begun, nor no mirth neither, there's the plague on't.
Had I had the liberty to have sung two or three merry catches and   270
have lost my money with a *trolly lolly lo*, it had been nothing. [*To
Servant*] Here. Hey. Where's Cob? Call him hither quickly, and let
us go.

SERVANT Sir, I have not seen him these two hours; I believe he's gone
home.   275

SIR ROGER How! What, without taking leave of his mistress? 'Tis
impossible.
      [*Exit Servant*]

FUMBLE Sir Roger, you are disturbed, methinks; what is the matter?
Ha! Your behaviour seems to publish that—

SIR ROGER No great matter, sir. [*Aside*] Pox o' this old fool.   280

CORDELIA Sir, it ill becomes a person of your gravity to be angry on
so small an occasion.

SIR ROGER Small! By heaven, madam, 'tis a matter of moment. What,
run away without taking leave? In verity, 'tis barbarous and derogates
from his birth and breeding, nor can I, though his kinsman, excuse—   285

FUMBLE What does Sir Roger say, madam? Does he rally? Ha! He's a
merry man and a good fellow and, i'fack, I love mirth. For my part,
I hate your drowsy, insipid, phlegmatic fellows that sleep over a
glass and talk of nothing but state politics. But Sir Roger is a man
for the purpose, a merry, jolly man he.   290

SIR ROGER Sir, you may spare your commendations for them that
delight in 'em. [*Aside*] What an impertinent old fellow 'tis. [*To
Fumble*] Pray, sir, no more of this. I am not pleased with it.

FUMBLE Your song of Sir Thomas Fairfax and the rest of the brave
old fellows° was very fine, Sir Roger. Well! I'll not be positive, but   295
there was certainly a great deal of judgement and sheer wit in some
of those Rump songs.°

SIR ROGER [*aside*] 'Sdeath, this is the most insufferable old fellow. [*To
Fumble*] Pox, tell not me of Rump songs. Sir, in verity, would you
had been hanged up instead of the Rump° that I might have been   300
free from the noise. But, madam, as I was saying, upon my honour,
I never knew Cob in such an error.

FUMBLE Then, Sir Roger, 'Chevy Chase'° and 'The Hunting of the
Hare'° is finely penned! Finely penned! I'fack it was.

SIR ROGER Oh, the devil! Is there no riddance of this clack? Because   305
he can hear nothing, he would speak all.

FUMBLE Ay, so it was, sir, so it was. But i'fack that 'Hunting' was
most excellently contrived. Ah, he makes the dogs speak notably,

'icod, and the hare repartees again very well for an animal of her
magnitude.°   310

SIR ROGER 'Sbud, I shall grow as deaf as he if I stay longer. I must go
seek my nephew. Come, madam, let's go away and leave him. I am
sure his eyes are so defective, he can't miss us presently.

  Exeunt Sir Roger and Cordelia

FUMBLE And though some petulant, insignificant, and disaffected
persons° have raised calumnies by calling it doggerel and fustian   315
and such like, yet, i'fack, the thing is really a witty, facetious, nay,
and, as some think, a moral satire. For mark me, Sir Roger, and
madam, pray give your attention, for the dogs were hieroglyphic
characters of fanatics, as the hare was of the Quakers;° and i'fack I
have often heard the sisters° sing it instead of an hymn or an   320
anthem for the conversion of unbelievers; and, nay, and as a greater
rarity I have heard it acted to the life betwixt a dog-fanatic and a
cony-Quaker.° But, i'fack, I think you mind me not. Ha, Sir Roger?
Madam? Sir Roger? Madam? What, a vacuity?° Gone? Well. (*Pulls
out spectacles*) I'll after and redeem all, but, 'icod, this was a little   325
uncivil.

  *Exit Fumble. Enter Ranger, Betty with a candle. She sets it on
  the table*

BETTY Come, sir, and with as little noise as you can for fear of
discovery. I swear, were you not a man to whom I am sensibly
obliged,° I should not be drawn to this infidelity.

RANGER I will reward thy care. Are they together?   330

BETTY (*pointing to the little door*) Yes, sir, in that room there.

RANGER [*hands money to Betty*] Take this and begone. I have no
further service for thee, and I would have her ignorant that this is
thy discovery. Away.

BETTY (*aside*) The discovery will add little to your content. But since   335
I have the profit, I care not.

  Exit Betty. Enter Bubble and Maria

BUBBLE Ned! What says she? Are they met?

RANGER Securely and with a great deal of content; they are in that
room in the dark—met! Ah, sir, they are both better practised than
ever to be tardy in a love intrigue.   340

MARIA (*aside*) Now I think I have trapped her finely. O, my joy! I shall
not be able to contain myself.

BUBBLE A man of wit and honour thus abused! 'Tis horrible! A
cuckold! 'Sbud, 'tis a worse name than a conjurer and has more of
the devil in't. But I'll be so revenged, the world shall tremble at it.   345

I'll first cut off her hair to affront her family; then the want of a
nose shall proclaim her bawd, and the penny-pot poets° shall make
ballads on her.

    Exit Bubble

RANGER So! This thrives as I would have it, and we have snapped 'em
finely in the nick, just when the intrigue was at its best perfection!   350
O revenge!

MARIA Ha, ha, ha! Nay, and at such a time when all help is denied
'em: when her blushes, sighs, and entreaties are all fruitless; when
her exasperated husband's rage flows high; and, best of all, when
Rashley is defenceless. O wit, I love thee for this stratagem!   355

RANGER She dared us to persevere, slighted our plots, and had the
confidence to make descriptions of her kind intrigue before her
husband's face, then laughed at us.

MARIA 'Tis now our time. Ha, ha, ha! I thought I could not fail.

RANGER No, and this happy minute brings me more perfect pleasure   360
and more true delight than pristine ages.° For she's one whom hell
designed for its chief instrument; she will out-lie a siren, cheat the
devil, and damn more souls to further her intrigue than Charon's
boat° has room for. (*Aside*) Yet I own a kind of mongrel love° and
must enjoy her, though legions were her guard.   365

    A shriek offstage

MARIA Hark! He's as good as his word. Now I hope she'll own her
sister's wit above her. Well, this was rarely plotted!

RANGER By heaven, it was, and fit to be chronicled, madam. Your wit
surpasses human thought and should be spoken of with wonder.
You plot with such assurance that—   370

    Enter Emilia

Hell! Death and confusion! Can I believe my eyes? She here!

MARIA I am confounded and have lost my senses. Sure, sir, we dream.
Are we awake, think you?

EMILIA [*to Maria*] No, nor shall never wake when I design to raise
my wit above the poor, weak creatures. I could laugh now, but I   375
swear I pity ye. Wear out your tedious nights in dull design, and
then, i' th' morning, hatch the abortive brood which ere night turns
to nothing—slender encouragement, heaven knows, for wit. [*To
Ranger*] And you, sir, plot and sweat and plot again for moonshine
in the water°—poor reward, sir, for one so well skilled in intrigue as   380
you are!

MARIA O that I had thy heart here in my hand! How pleasant were the
diet!° Fate and death! Was ever such a devil?

RANGER No, never! (*Kneels*) Therefore, since thou art a devil, as I now
am sure thou art, have mercy on me and do not take my soul for my   385
first crime, and I will plot no more. Thou art my conqueror. I'll
honour thee. Good devil, do not hurt me.
  Shrieking offstage. Enter Bubble, dragging in Mrs Snare
BUBBLE Strumpet! Whore! Witch! I'll spoil your curls, by the Lord
Harry. [*Spies Emilia*] O Lord, my wife! [*Looks upon Mrs Snare,
aghast*] And she that I have beaten, a stranger!   390
MRS SNARE O heaven! (*Weeps*) Was ever poor sinner so abused?
  Bubble looks amazedly at his wife, then at Mrs Snare, then at a
  lock of black hair in his hand
BUBBLE Madam, I beg your pardon and am ashamed of my fault, but
I'll make you amends presently.
RANGER (*to Emilia, kneeling*) Well, nothing but the greatest devil could
have brought this woman hither for this intrigue; and, therefore,   395
once more I acknowledge thy power.
BUBBLE Ay! You had need ask her pardon. 'Tis you have betrayed us.
[*To Emilia*] Chicken, dear chicken, don't frown so. I confess I was a
fool; but forgive me but this once, and if ever I offend again, I'll
give thee leave to cuckold me indeed.   400
EMILIA Indeed, sir, your jealousy is a little severe. I wonder what I
have done to deserve it.
BUBBLE Nothing. I know thou hast not. Prithee forgive me.
EMILIA But to be disturbed thus when I was at my devotion.°
BUBBLE Prithee forget it. Come, Tom, you may come out now; here's   405
none but friends.
EMILIA (*stamps with her foot*) Who do you mean, sir?
BUBBLE Tom Rashley. Poor fellow, I warrant now he'll be so bashful.
RANGER So, that's something yet, and I'll fetch him out or bleed
for't.   410
  Exit Ranger. Enter Rashley at the other side
EMILIA Look, yonder he is!
MARIA I find it now, and this is all designed. O devil, devil!
  Enter Sir Roger after Rashley
SIR ROGER What's the matter, Mr Rashley? What's the matter?
BUBBLE Rashley here? Hey day! Who the devil is that yonder then?
  Enter Ranger, dragging out Sneak
RANGER Come, sir, appear; I find you are now no Hercules.° Ha!   415
Death, more miracles, Sneak!
SIR ROGER 'Sdeath, my Cob—and taken with a wench! Why, how
now, sirrah?

EMILIA [*aside to Rashley*] Now it works to my wish. Prithee observe
  how they look.   420

RASHLEY Hush. I do.

SNEAK O Lord, uncle, your mercy. I was betrayed, seduced, as a man
  may say. (*To Mrs Snare*) Go, go. Begone; I'll speak with you tomorrow. [*To Sir Roger*] I say, uncle, I was seduced, choused, cheated.

SIR ROGER Catched with a wench? Come, sir, I'll talk with you. O   425
  disgrace to the family! With a wench? A lewd wench? Come along,
  sir. I'll watch you henceforth.
        Exeunt Sir Roger and Sneak

RASHLEY Ha, ha! Why, here has been a great deal of intrigue tonight I
  see, ha, sir? (*Gapes*)° I am sorry now I went to bed so soon, but I
  have been in the sweetest dream yonder.   430

BUBBLE Here has, in troth, been a great deal of intrigue, as thou
  say'st, Tom, but, no matter, now all's well. And since it has happened
  so well, a day of jubilee shall crown it. Tomorrow is my wedding
  day,° and, in memory of that happy hour that conjoined me and my
  sweet chicken there together, we'll have a feast, and I'll sing, and   435
  roar, and drink *cum privilegio*. Go, wait on her in, Tom. [*To Emilia*]
  Chicken, remember we are friends. Go; I'll be with you presently.
        Exeunt Rashley and Emilia, Rashley bowing scornfully to
        Ranger and Maria

RANGER Never was such a day, nor such a deed.

BUBBLE Ned! Let me have no more of your doubts nor counsels. D'ee
  hear? 'Sbud, I say once more my wife is the honestest woman in   440
  Christendom, and you shall hear from me.°
        Exit Bubble

MARIA Was ever the like known?

RANGER Never since Adam, but she was a devil before the creation.

MARIA I'll not give over thus.

RANGER Nor I.   445

MARIA Your hand on't.

RANGER [*clasps her hand*] Here. And may all the demons that have
  power in subtle plots help now, though never more.

MARIA I'll die, but I'll perform it.
        My slights shall with immortal wit be wrought,   450
        And all my senses shall convert to thought.
        Exeunt

4.[1]

[A room in Sir Roger's house]

Enter Sir Roger and Sneak

SIR ROGER Sirrah, haunt me no more; I know thee not.

SNEAK Nay, uncle.

SIR ROGER Go to your wench and let her entertain you; then stock
Sir Jeremy's manor-house at home with bastards—birds of
night°—and teach 'em all to know their father when you ha' done.   5

SNEAK Good uncle, let me speak.

SIR ROGER No place to bring your cattle to but thither, under your
mistress's nose, thou most notorious ass? Mercy o' me, what will
this world come to? Who could imagine that sheep's face of
thine; that mouth, whence ne'er came anything that had sense; that   10
person, that has as oft been thought a Puritan as thou hast been a
fool; then that hanging-dog look? I'll say no more, but the devil is
subtle.

SNEAK Uncle, you know 'tis an old saying: we cannot appoint our
own destinies,° nor did I foresee this. Besides, sir, if you knew her   15
as well as I do, you'd find the woman has some parts that are not
contemptible. 'Sbud, I know what's what. I am not such a fool.

SIR ROGER Not such a fool! In verity, if thou were but a grain nearer
to a natural,° I'd beg thee of the king and adopt another to inherit
thy estate.° Not such a fool!   20

SNEAK No, so I say, sir, since you go to that.° Whoop! What a pox!
You have forgot since you were young yourself?

SIR ROGER I, young? Why, sir, I hope I got no bastards.

SNEAK No. But you kept whores, that you did, and that's all one, *bona
fide*.   25

SIR ROGER *[aside]* This rogue has heard all; I must stop his mouth.
[To Sneak] How, sirrah, I kept whores?

SNEAK It has been thought so, sir, since you go to that. Nay, 'tis no
such miracle nowadays; there's many an old badger about town
does the like. 'Tis grown a custom now.   30

SIR ROGER But 'tis not so customary with your uncle, sir. But, come,
pray express yourself. What women do the infamous world lay to
my charge?

SNEAK What women! 'Bud, are you ignorant? Hum. Nan, Peg, Joan
of the dairy, Sara, Jenny, Dorothy, Mary, Bridget.   35

SIR ROGER Hold, hold, I say! [*Aside*] 'Sdeath, he'll reckon the whole country° presently. I must quiet him; the rogue has me upon the hip.° [*To Sneak*] Harkee, Cob.

SNEAK Then the parson's wife, sir, and the old hostess at the town's end. You see the fool has a good memory.   40

SIR ROGER A waggish one I see thou hast. Ha, if thou couldst remember law cases as well, thou wouldst be a brave fellow. Why, Cob, thou think'st thou hast paid me off now, dost not?

SNEAK I know not. If my wit flow too fast, sir, I cannot help it. 'Tis a good that's thrown upon me; 'tis not my seeking. 'Tis true, I have   45 an unhappy way with me sometimes, but 'tis over presently; it never lasts long, that's one comfort.

SIR ROGER In verity, I see thou hast wit, and now I'll cherish it. Why, Cob, my instruction is for thy good, child. What will thy mistress think when she hears of it? Come, come, in verity, Cob, 'twas ill   50 done, 'twas i'faith. But mum, no more words on't. I'll make all well again.

SNEAK [*aside*] So, so. I have brought him about finely. 'Sbud, I did not think I had so much wit, but I see a man may be mistaken in his own parts.   55

SIR ROGER But d'ee hear, Cob, not a word more of these wenches, let the foolish world say what it will. Thou art a good boy in verity; I like thy wit well. Thou know'st I have no heir, and when I die, Cob, I will not say I'll give thee anything lest I should make thee proud, but expect—expect wonders may fall. Who knows?   60

SNEAK By Jericho, I would not have spoke on't now, but that I had nothing else to say, and you know 'tis a disgrace to a scholar to be silent in company.

SIR ROGER 'Tis no matter; 'tis no matter. Prithee how cam'st thou to know that Peg and I were so intimate?   65

SNEAK Ah, you'll be angry if I should tell you.

SIR ROGER In verity, not I. Angry? Come, come, out with it, Cob, out with't.

SNEAK Why, the truth is, I lay with her one night, and the quean told me all.   70

SIR ROGER Didst thou! God a mercy! [*Aside*] Damn him! What a snake have I fostered? [*To Sneak*] Done like a cock o' th' game° in verity. Ah, when I was of thy years, I could have done as much myself.

SNEAK Yes, she told me you had done as much. But mum, sir, not a   75 word more; I know my cue.

SIR ROGER [*aside*] 'Sdeath, I shall be a by-word to th' town.°
        Enter a Servant
    How now?
SERVANT Sir Roger, I was just coming to your house for you; my
    master desires yours and Mr Sneak's company immediately.   80
SIR ROGER What, the solemnity holds? This is his wedding-day?
SERVANT Yes, sir.
SIR ROGER Tell him I am coming.
        Exit Servant
    Come, Cob, let us go; and mum, d'ee hear? You understand me?
SNEAK I warrant you, sir.   85
        Exeunt

4.2

        [*Dining room in Bubble's house*]
        Bubble, Emilia, Maria, Rashley, Ranger, Cordelia, Fumble
        sitting at a table
BUBBLE Come, come, another bumper about. My chicken's health!
    Here, I am not wet through° yet. Tom, what say'st thou?
RASHLEY With all my heart, sir! O, here comes Sir Roger and his
    nephew.
        Enter Sir Roger and Sneak
SIR ROGER Mr Bubble and gentlemen. [*Bows*] Your most humble   5
    servant.
BUBBLE Yours, good Sir Roger. I am glad to see you, i'faith, and
    you, sweet Mr Sneak. Well, faith, Sir Roger, we have been bumping
    it° it about here; we have been dipped,° as the saying is. Tom
    Rashley, send it round. Come, Sir Roger's a freshman; he'll drink   10
    an ocean.
RASHLEY Fill every man's glass there. Mr Ranger, you want it. 'Tis
    Madam Emilia's health.
RANGER I'll do you reason, sir.
        All drink
    (*Aside*) And ten to one but I have a stratagem shall dash this mirth.   15
    [*To Maria*] Are they ready?
MARIA Hush! We are observed. They are.
BUBBLE So, so. Come, now the song and then the dance.
        [*Enter Musicians*]
    Look ye, gentlemen, you must know—

FUMBLE Come, come, Mr Bubble, let's have t'other soop,° I say.   20
I'fack, we lose time. Ah, sirrah, are you there? Gad, I'll be with you
presently; dust° it about once more, I say. The wine has a pretty
smack with't. It cherishes;° I like it well. Come, another soop, and
then do what you will.

BUBBLE Fill wine there! Gentlemen, as I was saying, I got this song   25
made purposely. 'Tis in praise of marriage, and there was not one
ready-made of 'em in town.° I searched it all over.

RANGER Were you at the poets' lodging?°

BUBBLE Yes, but they had none, for they told me 'twas a song would
not take.° Besides, they were so busy getting plays up for the next   30
term,° that I could hardly get one made.

SIR ROGER Sir, you needed not have troubled 'em; you once had a
very good vein that way° yourself.

BUBBLE Yes, I was mightily given to rapture and flame once. I writ
'Tom Farthing'.° I had a hand too in 'Colly my Cow,'° a song that   35
took well, I can assure you. But this is of another kind, in praise of
marriage, sir; and they told me the town loved nothing but satires
against marriage, and the reason was because they were afraid of
being cuckolded, when, alas, poor, silly rogues, there's no such
thing in nature.   40

RANGER (aside) Well, of all stupid animals, a drowsy° husband is the
most notorious. [To Bubble] But I shall change your note presently,
I doubt not, sir.

BUBBLE You shall hear, gentlemen. [To the Musicians] Hey, the song
there and the dance.   45

MUSICIANS [sing]

SONG°

Under the branches of a spreading tree
Silvander sat, from care and danger free,
And his inconstant, roving humour shows   50
To his dear nymph, that sung of marriage vows.
But she with flowing graces, charming air,
Cried, 'Fie, fie, my dear, give o'er,
Ah, tempt the gods no more,
But thy offence with penitence repair.   55
For though vice in a beauty seem sweet in thy arms,
An innocent virtue has always more charms.'

      'Ah, Phillida,' the angry swain replied,
      'Is not a mistress better than a bride?
      What man that universal yoke retains,   60
      But meets an hour to sigh and curse his chains?'
      She, smiling, cried, 'Change, change that impious mind;
      Without it we could prove not half the joys of love.
      'Tis marriage makes the feeling joys divine;
      For all our life long we from scandal remove,   65
      And at last fall the trophies of honour and love.'

BUBBLE Well sung, i'faith. Look'ee, gentlemen, is it not as I told you?
SIR ROGER In verity, very well, very well, sir.
BUBBLE Come, now the dance.
      Enter Servant
SERVANT Sir, here's a letter for you. It was left by a porter, who said it   70
  required no answer and is gone.
RANGER [*aside to Maria*] So, now for a change of countenance. I think
  this will do.
MARIA If not, I've writ a letter that will; but let's observe.
      Bubble, Emilia, Ranger, Maria, Sir Roger, and Cordelia dance
BUBBLE What the devil has this fellow given me here? A letter? Pray   75
heaven it be no challenge. How? What's here? (*Reads*) 'Sir, That
you are blind, I have heard; that you are a fool, I know; and that you
are a cuckold, I believe. However, as a friend, though unknown, I
am bound in conscience to give you this information: your wife is
false, you are abused. The author of your wrong you know as well   80
as yourself, if you know yourself as well as you know Rashley.'
[*Aside*] O, heaven! Was ever such fate? But, hush, I'll smother my
resentment till they are gone. Come, Sir Roger and gentlemen.
There's a tongue° in the next room. Pray go and eat. I'll be with
you presently.   85
      Exeunt Sir Roger, Sneak, Cordelia, Fumble, Rashley, and
      Emilia
RANGER [*aside*] So, I see by this behaviour it takes, and I'll away lest
he should suspect me. Now for my t'other plot.
      Exit Ranger
BUBBLE O sister, here's a new discovery. The devil is come abroad
again.
MARIA How? The devil?   90
BUBBLE Ay, in the likeness of a letter. Here, prithee read it; 'tis his
character.° I am sure it looks as if 'twere writ with a cloven hoof.
Ha! What think'st thou?

MARIA Sir, he calls you fool here.

BUBBLE Ay, he's a little uncivil, that's the truth on't; but what's to be   95
done, sister?

MARIA A cuckold too.

BUBBLE Ay. Was ever such an impudence?

MARIA I never heard of any, but 'tis no more, sir, than I expected.
Alas, 'tis nothing to be a cuckold now.   100

BUBBLE O, unfortunate estate of marriage! By the Lord Harry, if this
be true, I have praised it to fine purpose. But sister, thou wert wont
to be kind: prithee advise me.

MARIA 'Tis to no purpose, sir. You know I am envious: my words have
double meaning. I did my sister wrong in my last story; pray let me   105
offend no more.

BUBBLE Well, I confess I was to blame, but who the devil could have
mistrusted her when the plot was carried so handsomely?

MARIA O, you will find, sir, she has still more plots; and I find you so
credulous and so wedded to your infamy that, for my part, I am   110
afraid to have anything to do with it.

BUBBLE Help me but this once and, if I fail thee again, may I be proved
a cuckold to the whole county and my case tried in Westminster
Hall.°

MARIA Well, once more then I'll assist you and, to confirm what   115
that letter has informed, know, sir, she is false. And though she
frustrated our last plot by her waiting-woman's means, she certainly
met Rashley that night. I am glad you credit a stranger's letter. For
my part, I love her so well, I should have hardly caused a second
breach between ye else. But since 'tis out and you desire my assist-   120
ance, follow me, and ere night I doubt not but to give you sufficient
proof of your misfortune.

BUBBLE With all my heart, dear sister. 'Sbud, a cuckold? 'Tis
impossible. I ha' no cuckold's face. But I'll be resolved immediately.
Exeunt Bubble and Maria. Enter Ranger and Governess

RANGER Do this; thou shalt command me.   125

GOVERNESS In truth, sir, I am afraid 'twill be discovered, and I would
not have my lady know it for the world.

RANGER I swear she never shall. What, dost thou doubt me? Besides,
I'll be so grateful to thee, thou shalt never have cause to repent this
courtesy.   130

GOVERNESS Sir, you know you always might command me in any reasonable thing. Pray speak it again, sir. What would you have me do?

RANGER Why, only plant me in or near her chamber for a design I

have; she shall be ignorant why or by what means I got thither. I'll still
be careful of thy reputation. Come, take this purse and prithee do it   135
willingly.

GOVERNESS Well, sir, what you mean I know not; but heaven direct all
for the best. I can deny you nothing, sir; I lie in a closet° that joins
to her chamber, where you may both overhear and speak to her.

RANGER That above all things! Prithee let's go.   140

GOVERNESS But for heaven's sake, take care she knows not that I
brought ye thither; I would not be seen in such a business for the
world.

RANGER Ne 'er doubt. I warrant thee I'll be careful.

GOVERNESS Follow me then, sir.

Exeunt

4.3

[*A room in Fumble's house*]

Enter Fumble and Spatterdash

FUMBLE Spat. Sirrah!

SPATTERDASH Here, sir, here.

FUMBLE Whither is this rascal gone? Well, i'fack, I am too full of
clemency. I must swinge this rogue, or he'll never be good for
anything. He's at nine-holes° now, I'll lay my life. A damned villain   5
that spends me three-pence a day,° I know not how.

SPATTERDASH O Lord. Who? I, sir?

FUMBLE Who's within there? What, will nobody hear me? Am I left
desolate?° I have not the plague, I think.° Ha!

SPATTERDASH Why, here am I, sir. I have been here all this while.   10

FUMBLE O, sirrah, are you come? Where have you been, ha? I say,
where have you been, rogue?

SPATTERDASH Nowhere, sir, not I.

FUMBLE Sirrah! I must be left alone, must I? And when I have a
message to send, go myself? Ha! Sirrah, Mr Little-Pox° has a boy   15
that, though he was stinted at nurse° and is not above pocket-high,
can run, and frisk, and jump upon occasion, sirrah; know a bailey
by his nose and a wench by her buttocks,° ye rogue; and a good
linguist, and a pretty pimp, sirrah; and can hold the door with a
steady hand,° ye rogue. But thou, a rascal, a drone, art good for   20
nothing.

SPATTERDASH Anything, sir, I warrant you. Try me, and you shall find I can hold a door as well as he.

FUMBLE Why, how now, sirrah? What? Make mouths at me? Is your master grown your mirth? (*Beats him*) Ha, this will teach you 25
better; this will new-mould you. I'll fetch you out of your damned looks, i'fack. French grimaces,° rogue, French grimaces?

SPATTERDASH O Lord, what shall I do? Because he's deaf and cannot hear me, he thinks I mock him. (*Aloud*) Hold, sir, for heaven's sake. Upon my faith, I don't mock you. 'Tis all a mistake and, sir, you 30
have beaten me for nothing.

FUMBLE What a noise the rogue makes! Why, sirrah, cannot you speak temperately, but you must roar thus? I am not so deaf, but I can hear without this thunder-clap. But you do it in contempt, do you, sirrah? Bless us, to what an impudence this age is grown! But 35
I'll fetch the devil out, lest he should grow in ye. (*Beats him*) Thus. I should be loath to see thee hanged till you come to years of discretion.°

SPATTERDASH Mercy o' me, what a master have I. If I stay long here, I shall be beaten into mummy. 40

FUMBLE Come sir, now I have performed the part of a master and a friend in your castigation, I have now a word or two by way of instruction. Mark me, sirrah, nothing exasperates more than scorn, nor nothing pleases more than observance. A master should be strict in finding occasion to beat his servant, and a servant should 45
be careful in avoiding the beatings of his master.

SPATTERDASH So he has taught me; now I shall be careful of avoiding it hereafter if my legs will carry me.

FUMBLE What? Mouths again, sirrah, mouths again?

SPATTERDASH (*Makes a low congee; says nothing*) Umph. 50

FUMBLE O, this submission pacifies. Come hither. I have a message for ye, and let me see how you can behave yourself; 'tis a matter of moment.

SPATTERDASH I'll do my best to please ye, sir.

FUMBLE What dost thou say now? Look, look! Was ever such a rascal 55
as this? This rogue knows well enough that I cannot hear him. Sirrah, come and lay your mouth to my ear and then speak, if you would have me understand ye.

SPATTERDASH Yes, sir, I shall be very careful to remember it hereafter.

FUMBLE Rafters? What rafters, rogue? 60

SPATTERDASH (*aloud*) Sir, I shall be careful to remember it hereafter.

FUMBLE O, shall you so, sir? And 'twill become you, i'fack. For

look'ee, sirrah, 'tis my humour, as long as I am healthy and jovial, to
cover failings and imperfections in nature as well as I can. 'Tis a
wise man's virtue, and I have patterns° for't every day. Ah, here are   65
a sort of jolly, brisk, ingenious, old signiors about town that, with
false calves, false bellies, false teeth, false noses, and a false fleering
face upon the matter, fill up society as well as ere a masquerading
fop of 'em all. But to the matter. Sirrah, you must carry this ring to
Cordelia and possess her with my love° in an elegant manner.   70
Stand there and let me see how you can carry yourself in such a
business.

SPATTERDASH [bows low] Thus, sir. I had my honours° from the
dancing school.

FUMBLE O damned rogue! What a bow's there? 'Tis worse than a   75
country counsellor's to a client that has no money.° Sirrah, pull me
your hat off thus, with a grace. Ah, I could have done it rarely twenty
years ago, but, i'fack, time and gravity defaces all things. Come,
sirrah.

SPATTERDASH Madam, my master, too well knowing the charms of   80
your wit and beauty are too sharp at all times to be opposed, has by
me sent this ring and humbly desires—

FUMBLE Well, that last honour was pretty well. But come now, let's
hear what you can say.

SPATTERDASH 'Sdeath! He has not heard me all this while. What shall   85
I do?

Knocking offstage

O somebody knocks; this was happy. (*Aloud*) Sir, there's somebody
at door to speak with you.

FUMBLE Go see who 'tis. I'll follow.

[*Exit Spatterdash*]

This is a plaguy, dull rogue, but I must have patience and take pains   90
with him. Nor should he do anything in this business, had I not a
design in't, and, i'fack, I like the woman well. She's young and
plump, free in her nature, and of a sanguine complexion,° and, *bona
fide*, I never see her but some secret motions in my blood seem to
imply that she is the cause. What? I am not bedrid. I can dance yet,   95
ay, and run and jump too if occasion be—and why not t'other
thing?° Come, come; it must, it must. Mine was ever a stirring°
family. It must, I say; and she shall know it suddenly.

Exit

4.4

[Emilia's] bed-chamber

Enter Maria and Bubble

MARIA Come softly, sir, and plant yourself here at this back door. I have already made a discovery.

BUBBLE Are they together?

MARIA I believe so. They seldom miss such an opportunity, especially when they think you absent.   5

BUBBLE No. They are politic, with a pox to 'em. Sister, what revenge, ha? I am resolved to be a tyrant. 'Sbud, I'll pinch her to death with a pair of tongs.

MARIA O fie! That will be too cruel.

BUBBLE Cruel! By the Lord Harry, 'tis justice, palpable justice. Why,   10
should she live, she'd cuckold the whole nation.

MARIA Consider better on't. 'Tis but a venial crime° and deserves not such rigour. But come, meditate of no revenge till you are certain of the fault. Keep close° at that door. Be sure you discover not yourself till I come to you. I'll go and observe.   15

BUBBLE I'll try my patience, but 'tis a damned cause.

Exeunt Maria and Bubble. Enter Rashley and Emilia

EMILIA Our intrigue as yet goes well.

RASHLEY I swear, to admiration, and had I not seen each passage,° I should have thought 't had been impossible. (*Kisses her hand*) O, my dearest! How shall I gratify thee? My love's too poor and my desert   20
too mean ever to equal it.

Enter Ranger [unseen by Emilia and Rashley]

RANGER I am glad I've got air again. This damned old gib-cat has mewed me this half hour into such a hole that, had I stayed a minute longer I had certainly been smothered. It stinks worse than a pothecary's shop and is furnished with nothing but galley-pots   25
full of nasty oil, into which, groping about, I often thrust my fingers. Faugh! Assafœtida,° as I live! A most intolerable stink! Ah, the devil grind her old chops. Stay; this is sure Emilia's chamber and, if I am not mistaken, I heard a whispering here. It may be they're together. I'll be still and listen.   30

RASHLEY Our love shall last whole ages, and each kiss add new and fierce desires. Death shall want power to separate us, and envy droop and pine itself away to see its stratagem succeed no better.

RANGER [*aside*] By heaven, 'tis so. They are here. Blessed minute!   35
Now I shall make a rare discovery.

EMILIA I am confirmed and will proceed in loving. A husband is a
dull insipid thing, palled° and grown stale within a week; but a
lover appears still new and gay and is to perpetuity the same he was
at first—all mirth, all pleasure.   40

RANGER [*aside*] A most excellent theme. O, that that property, that
fool her husband, stood now to hear this devil of a wife make out
this free confession!

RASHLEY He, dull creature, heaven knows, is blind to all your charms.
Marriage acts only the decrees of duty; love has the least share in't.   45
In this age, a husband with a wife is like a bully in a church: the
only pleasure he takes is to sleep away the hours should be employed
in conjugal duty.

EMILIA Well, I am very glad our plots succeed so well. I swear I was
half-frighted t'other day when my sister-in-law Maria discovered   50
us. Was it not done subtly? Did I not fetch all off again with an
excellent invention?

RANGER [*aside*] Good? Rarely good! This devil cannot sure have so
much impudence to deny this again.

RASHLEY Ha, ha, ha! By heaven, I'm ready to die with laughing when   55
I think what asses we made of 'em. Ranger too, that busy coxcomb.
What a fretting and plotting and sweating did he make for nothing!
Alas, poor fool. Ha, ha, ha.

EMILIA Ha, ha, ha.

RANGER [*aside*] O, the devil fleer you. 'Sdeath, am I still their property?   60
I shall have a slice at your nose ere long. I doubt not, my young
gallant, I shall dash your mummery.

RASHLEY Come, we lose time. Let talk be our diversion when we are
old and can reap nothing else. Our minutes now should all be spent
in rapture. [*Embraces her*] Thus, thus, my sweet. O, that we could   65
live thus ever! How now, what noise is that?

BUBBLE (*offstage*) Bawds! Strumpets! Whores! Witches! Break open
the door there; break open the door.

MARIA (*offstage*) Fetch a lever° or call the smith° over the way presently.

EMILIA O heaven, my husband and Maria! We are undone.   70

RANGER [*aside*] 'Tis Bubble's voice sure. This completes my joy. Now
let Beelzebub, if he owes her any kindness, fetch her from hence.
I'll guard this passage.

RASHLEY What! What shall I do, madam?

EMILIA Here quickly. Run into this closet, sir, and jump out of   75 the window into the garden. If you were gone, let me alone for the rest.

RANGER Who steps a foot this way, steps on his death; his soul shall not be his a minute.

EMILIA Ha! Ranger here? I am lost in my amazement.   80

RASHLEY° Death and hell! And I defenceless too? O cursed minute!

RANGER No, madam, I'll secure you from this stratagem. This window shall be no bawd to th' intrigue now; that I'll be sure on.

    Exit Ranger into the closet

BUBBLE (*offstage*) Quickly, quickly. A lever, a lever!

RASHLEY No way t'escape? Can I not climb the chimney? Anything to   85
get free this once. O fate, taken i' th' midst of our security when we least thought of it! What shall we do?

EMILIA I have it. Come hither. Get ye under this table, and diligently listen to what I say. 'Tis ten to one he never searches here. Come, in, in, quickly, and pray the rest may prosper.   90

RASHLEY I never had more need of prayers. I'll try.

    Rashley goes under [the] table. Enter Ranger from the closet

RANGER So! That conveyance is fast enough. Now, madam, what think'ee of a fleering jest upon the fool Ranger; the coxcomb, the ass Ranger; and your jolly spleen to laugh? Ha ha! I think the dice are mine now. Now, devil, I have trapped ye.   95

    Knock offstage. Emilia takes out the key o' th' door

EMILIA [*aside*] This key may add to my design.

BUBBLE (*offstage*) Down, down with it. Break it open there.

RANGER What think you of that, madam? Does your husband's voice refresh you extremely?

EMILIA [*aside*] Now help me, wit, or I am lost.   100

    Emilia goes and puts the key into Ranger's coat pocket and then lays hold of him and cries out

Help, help there! For heaven's sake, I am undone, ruined forever. A rape, a rape! Help, help!

RANGER Hell and the devil. What does she mean?

EMILIA Ah, cruel man, cannot these tears prevail? Will nothing stop barbarity? What have I done that could deserve this usage? O, most   105
unfortunate of women.

RANGER Damn her. I shall be finely catched if this hold. I must get away.

    Ranger struggles. Emilia holds him

EMILIA A rape, a rape! Help there! For heaven's sake, help!

    Enter Bubble and Maria with a light. They stand amazed

RANGER [*aside*] By heaven, I am snapped again, catched in my own   110
    snare.

EMILIA Has my husband been so much thy friend, and wouldst abuse
    him thus, thou base man? But heaven forgive thee.

BUBBLE 'Sbud, what's this I see? Ranger?

MARIA [*aside*] Ranger here and Rashley absent? I have plotted finely.   115
    'Tis plain now that traitor loves her and has only made me an
    engine to work his design with more facility.

RANGER [*aside*] Rashley gone too? Now has the devil, to spite me,
    conveyed him away in a mist. Here's like to be fine work towards,
    but I must stand the brunt, now I am entered.   120

BUBBLE Now, sir, what a pox make you here with my wife? Ha?

RANGER [*aside*] So it begins rarely! O, this subtle devil! [*To Bubble*]
    Why, sir, as I am a gentleman, and upon my honour—

EMILIA O my dear, a thousand thanks for this deliverance; and by all
    our love, I charge thee, by our marriage vows, by all our pleasures   125
    since and joys to come, I charge you revenge me upon that traitor
    there. He would have ravished me! O heaven, that ever I should live
    to be so put to't!

BUBBLE 'Sbud! Ravish my chicken? Ranger, you are the son of a
    whore, and I shall presume to cut your throat.   130

RANGER Sir, do but hear me. Upon my honour, all this is false.

MARIA (*aside*) It must be true! What should he come hither for but
    upon some ill intent? I am resolved I'll be revenged on him, however.

RANGER [*overhearing Maria*] 'Sdeath! She against me too? This is
    worse and worse.   135

BUBBLE Discover the matter, that I may do justice on both sides.

EMILIA Sir, know then, Ranger long has loved me, often solicited me
    unlawfully. But, finding something in my virtue that shook his
    designs, his recourse was to make you jealous of me and Rashley,
    who, poor man, has often told me with sighs how deeply he has   140
    resented your unkind suspicions.

BUBBLE Alas, poor fellow!

RANGER [*aside*] O, confusion! He begins to believe her again.

EMILIA At last, sir, finding his suit to be too troublesome for me to
    bear, and being loath to vex you with such fooleries, I told Rashley,   145
    who promised all assistance imaginable. I desired him also to be
    careful and watch lest I should be surprised, as tonight, heaven
    knows, I was.

RANGER Damn her. What a lie is this! Pray, sir, let me speak.

BUBBLE Not in my house, sir. You have talked too much already and,   150 by the Lord Harry, I'll talk with you anon. But let that pass. [*To Emilia*] Go on, chicken.

EMILIA At last, sir, this unhappy night, coming hither as I used to do to my devotions, he, it seems, having corrupted some of my servants, got into the closet and thence came and surprised me, first locking the door and putting the key into his pocket.   155

RANGER I, a key? Sir, as I live, I saw none. This is the most notorious lie.

EMILIA O wretched man! Was it not crime enough to make such an attempt, but you must persist in falsehood? [*To Bubble*] Sir, he has it now about him there in that pocket. I saw him put it in.   160

RANGER This pocket? Why, thou devil! Ha!

    Ranger puts his hand in's pocket, pulls out a key

'Sdeath, how came it here? Magic, witchcraft, the devil, and all combine against me! Would I were well out. If ever I plot again—

MARIA [*aside*] 'Tis evident now he would have ravished her. Locked   165
her in for the purpose. [*Softly, to Ranger*] Perfidious traitor, see me no more.

RANGER A very fine business, this!

BUBBLE Is it so, sir? I'll do your business for you.

    Bubble goes to run° at Ranger and overthrows the table. [*Rashley is revealed*]

EMILIA [*aside*] Discovered? I am lost again.   170

BUBBLE 'Sbud, Rashley?

RASHLEY [*aside*] 'Sdeath and hell. What will become of me now?

RANGER How? Rashley under the table? Then fate is mine again. [*To Bubble*] Now, sir, do you perceive anything yet?

MARIA Stranger and stranger! What can this mean? Or what could   175
they both do here?

BUBBLE 'Sdeath! (*To Emilia*) How came he here? Huh?

RANGER Ay, examine that point closely. Sure this will make for me.

BUBBLE As Gad jidge me, and so I will. Speak, I say. How came he here?   180

EMILIA Nay, heaven knows, not I. I believe for the same design with Ranger.°

RASHLEY [*aside*] 'Sdeath, she'll betray me too.

EMILIA Tell him, tell him, sir. Speak for yourself. (*Softly*) Say anything.   185

RASHLEY Speak? Why, 'sbud, madam, have I not done as you commanded me? Have I not watched here this two hours to frustrate Ranger's design? What, d'ee think to make an ass of me?

RANGER How, sir? My design? Damn me, this must not pass upon
me, sir.   190

RASHLEY Nor you shall not pass upon my friend here neither, sir. I
heard you this evening when you corrupted one of the women to
get you into that closet, that you might accomplish with more
ease, sir. [*To Emilia*] But, madam, this is a little unnatural—to
make me suspected as his colleague when my design was so far   195
different.

BUBBLE 'Sbud, I cannot find the meaning of this.

RASHLEY The meaning! Why, sir, she hid me under the table as a
defence against Ranger's insolence. But when she heard you at the
door, and knew you were coming in, she conjured me by all the love   200
I bore her to sit still and not discover myself—and all her excuse
was your jealousy. Jealousy with a pox! A very fine slight for the
abuse she intended to me. [*To Emilia*] 'Sdeath, madam, my service
deserved a better reward, if you consider it. (*Aside*) Pray heaven this
lie prosper!   205

EMILIA Ha, ha, ha! I knew I should vex him, but I confess 'tis all true.
[*To Bubble*] For, my poor, dear rogue, I am so hourly tormented
with fear of thy naughty jealousy, that I dare not tell thee anything.
Prithee desert it; do, my dear sweet. I'fads, thou wouldst be the best
husband in the world if thou wouldst but leave it. (*Kisses him*)   210

BUBBLE Well, it must be so; this cannot be feigned. Come hither to
me; I will forsake it. By the Lord Harry, thou art the best wife in
Christendom, and I the most ungrateful husband; but forgive, my
dear, forgive. (*Kisses her*) We have all failings, thou knowest. Prithee
forgive me.   215

RANGER [*aside*] So! Now may I hang myself. 'Sdeath! All the fiends
are asses to her.° I'll be gone for shame, lest worse befall me.

Succubus, farewell;
There is not such a sorceress in hell.

Exit Ranger

BUBBLE Come. Hast thou sealed my pardon?   220

EMILIA You know the softness of my temper, but your unkind jealousy
will kill me one day.

BUBBLE Egad, I'll kill myself first. Come, prithee no more. [*To
Rashley*] Tom, thy hand too. Come, I know thou canst bear with my
frailty.   225

RASHLEY Ay, sir, I can bear well enough, but methought 'twas a little
strange to tax me.

BUBBLE Come, come, all shall be well. Faith, we'll go in and frolic.

[*To Emilia*] O, my dear. Suspect thee? Well, I am a fool, that's the
truth on't.   230

    Exeunt Bubble and Emilia

MARIA The devil helps her sure; for this was certainly an assignation.
I'll after Ranger and know the truth on't.

    Exit Maria

RASHLEY Ha, ha, ha! Was ever plot carried thus? Sure, never! Her wit
has more supplies than I have thoughts, and happily they end still;
and Gad, for my own part, I shall love lying the better as long as I   235
live for the success of this. Once more all is well, and he the cuckold
still. Ha, ha, ha. I must go in and laugh with her.

      Intrigue's her masterpiece, and all may see,
      A woman's wit's best in extremity.

    Exit

5.[1]

[A room in Bubble's house]

Enter Cordelia

CORDELIA Well, of all creatures that vex mortality, a superannuated lover is certainly the most troublesome, especially to one of my years. Our inequality is so preposterous, and his address so unnatural, that I always entertain rather hate for his person than compliance for his love. From fourscore and five,° heaven deliver me: 'tis an age of doting. Here he comes. I knew I could not be quiet one hour.   5

Enter Fumble

FUMBLE Sirrah, sirrah! Rogue, rogue! And how and how! Ha! Art thou jolly—blithe—like a bird in a tree? I'fack, I was impatient till I came to see thee. Well, and how fits the ring? Does it shine? Does it glitter? Ha, little black rogue! I'fack, I bought it of the best goldsmith in Cheapside,° a man of good reputation; a cuckold too, and they are always the honestest fellows.°   10

CORDELIA From henceforth let me desire you, sir, to bestow your presents on somebody else. I sent your ring back by your man. He can best give you an account of it.   15

FUMBLE Ha! What say'st thou? Counterfeit? I'fack, thou art mistaken, bird, thou art. *Bona fide*, they are as well cut as any in Christendom, and of the right black water.° What? Dost thou think I'll put any false stones upon thee,° i'fack? I am more civil, ecod. There! I was waggish. But she's a witty rogue. She'll apprehend the jest.   20

CORDELIA Was ever such an insipid piece of antiquity? Pray, sir, forbear these impertinences and assure yourself: I hate an old fellow for a husband as much as an old gown, or an old piece of wit, that, after forty years' oblivion, with a new name is published for a new Lenten play.°   25

FUMBLE What does she say now? But no matter; I'll go on. Well said, bird; well said. *Bona fide*, thou hast wit in abundance. That colour and such a sort of nose never fail. But come, we lose time. I know 'tis ordained I must marry thee. I am the man that must gather the rosebuds.° Ah, rogue! I'll warrant thou'rt a swinger, and, i'fack, that black a-top there fires me strangely. I am all flame and, *bona fide*, methinks as youthful and mercurial as any spark of 'em all. *(Sings)*   30

SONG   35

And he took her by the middle small,
And laid her on the plain;
With a hey down, derry down, come diddle,
With a ho down derry, etc.

What think you, madam? Am I old?   40

CORDELIA So old that your presence is more terrible than a death's
head at supper.° For my part, I tremble all over. There's a kind of
horror in all your antic gestures, especially those that you think
become you, that fright worse than the devil. (*Aloud*) Than the
devil, sir!   45

FUMBLE The devil! What of him, bird? Pish, the devil's an ass—I ha'
seen't in a play°—and, i'fack, we lose time in talking about so
worthless a matter. Lovers should ne'er be slow in their affairs. For,
as my good friend Randolph° tells me, nothing is like opportunity
taken in the nick, in the nick,° sweetheart. Ecod, I was waggish   50
again. I was waggish again, i'fack. Come, bird, come.

CORDELIA What will you do, sir? Heaven, how he tortures me!

FUMBLE Come along then. I have got a priest ready and paid for the
licence and all. Prithee let me kiss thee. I long to practise something
that might please thee. Never was man so altered, never! Come,   55
prithee, bird, come. I'fack, I have not patience.

    Enter Governess and Sir Roger

GOVERNESS Here's Sir Roger Petulant. My dear mouse desires to
speak a word or two with you.

CORDELIA O here's some hope of deliverance! [*Curtsies*] Sir Roger,
your humble servant. Come hither, Lettice, and stand just in my   60
place. I am so tortured with this old fellow! Prithee be kind to him,
and follow him whither he'd have thee; it may be a husband in thy
way and a good estate.

GOVERNESS A husband! Marry, that's fine. I warrant you, sweet
mouse, I'll be very punctual.   65

CORDELIA [*to Sir Roger*] So, now let us slip aside and observe.
'Twould be an excellent revenge if he should marry her. He's coming
to her already, and his eyes are so old and dim that he perceives not
his mistake.

    Cordelia and Sir Roger step aside°

FUMBLE Delays, sweetheart, are dangerous, i'fack. I have considered   70
it. The time I have lived in the world has given me the benefit of
knowing more than another of fewer minutes. Along, along, I say.

Thou shalt be my queen, my paramour, my Cleopatra, and I will
live another age in love and, then, farewell old Simon,° i'fack.
Come, come along.   75

GOVERNESS O sadness! What happy fortune's this? Well, I'll go with
him. Pray heaven he be blind enough; that's all I fear.

FUMBLE She seems kinder than usual. I'fack, I have wrought her
finely. Come poor rogue, come.

GOVERNESS I am ready, sir. [*Aside*]   80
This was a happy hour,
And if it hit but right, I'm made forever.
          Exeunt Governess and Fumble

          Sir Roger and Cordelia re-enter

CORDELIA Ha, ha. I am glad I am rid of him anyway. But now,
Sir Roger, to your business. I hear your nephew is sick.

SIR ROGER In verity, madam, most dangerously sick, and the cause of   85
my giving you this trouble was, in verity, to give you information of
it; for by his melancholy, I find love is the cause. Ah, madam, your
last indifference was very prejudicial to him. 'Tis true he denies it,
but I am old enough to judge of the contrary and therefore have
found out 'tis passion. Nay, passion for you has laid him thus   90
low, and nothing but your smiles can raise him, 'tis gone so far, in
verity.

CORDELIA I am sorry, sir, I have the misfortune to be th' occasion
of such a disaster. But is there any remedy? What would you have
me do?   95

SIR ROGER Madam, my suit to you is that you would be pleased to go
with me and give him a visit. The surprise of your presence, I am
confident, will dissipate his melancholy and perhaps totally banish
his distemper.
          Enter Maria
But I see we are interrupted. Let's retire, madam; and if you please,   100
now will be a very good time to visit him.

CORDELIA Softly, sir. I would not have my cousin Maria know anything of it, but if that can do him any good, I'll not be so cruel to
deny it; 'tis an act of charity. Come, sir, I'll go with you.

SIR ROGER Madam, you oblige us both.   105
          Exeunt Sir Roger and Cordelia

MARIA [*alone*] Still baffled! Sure this cannot last long; the devil will be
weary of obliging her in a little time. I have been yonder, sifting
Ranger about the last plot, and by all circumstances find what he
said was true. And shall I leave off thus poorly? Pish, I cannot for

shame. I have truth and honesty on my side. She's only cunning,   110
and 'tis impossible that should last ever. Once more then have at
'em. I have by several false messages buzzed it again into my
brother's ears. He believes and will once more follow my counsel.
Besides, I have here a false key to her chamber and can surprise 'em
when they least suspect. This, if Ranger be at all diligent, must   115
needs effect it; for I am resolved not to rest till 'tis done, for the
satisfaction of my revenge on that false man.
    Exit

5.[2]

    [*Sneak's chamber*]
    Enter Apothecary and Sneak in a nightgown

SNEAK Uh, uh!

APOTHECARY Nay, sir, if you would have the effects answer your
expectation, you must suffer, sir, and be patient.

SNEAK 'Oons! I cannot have patience. Sure a civil clap might be cured
without all this stir. 'Tis not a miracle in this age. O, Lord!   5
    Enter Sir Roger and Cordelia

SIR ROGER O horrible! What's this I see?

SNEAK My uncle! O, I am undone, lost forever.

APOTHECARY But, sir, your civil clap might ha' been an uncivil pox in
time.

CORDELIA How, Sir Roger? Was it fit to make me spectator of this   10
object?

SIR ROGER The pox? In verity, I have brought his mistress to fine
purpose. Ah, damned rascal! The pox? (*Aside*) What shall I do? I
am disgraced forever.
    [*Scene opens*]

CORDELIA Hark ye, sir. Pray what is that there? (*Pointing to a*   15
sweating-chair° within)

SIR ROGER [*aside*] What shall I say? Death, she has found out his
sweating-chair! [*To Cordelia*] Why, madam, 'tis—umph—'tis a
mathematical engine° they use at Cambridge. Cob was always
addicted to study.   20

CORDELIA 'Twere a fault to hinder him then, sir, being so well
employed. Farewell.
    Exit Cordelia

SIR ROGER She has found it out. Sirrah, see my face no more. From
this hour, I abhor thee. A damned rascal!

SNEAK [*pleading*] Good uncle!   25

SIR ROGER The pox! A sneaking, snivelling rogue! Heavens, was ever the like seen? But 'tis now a general maxim, and your sandy sheep's face, unthinking villain, is always the greatest whoremaster.

SNEAK Why, by Jericho, it was by chance, uncle. Hab-nab, as a man may say. As I hope to be saved, 'twas against my will.   30

APOTHECARY Sir, your anger makes an addition to his distemper.

SIR ROGER What? You are his pander, sir, are you? But I think you may be the devil for your honesty, so may ye all. Such as you soothe 'em in vices. I warrant you are tired with such customers. Ha, sir, are you not?   35

APOTHECARY In troth, sir, my rotten patients are so loath to die, and my sound ones, which, for my art's improvement, I would make rotten, so hasty to recover, that I confess I am often weary, but not tired, sir.

SIR ROGER So, sir, in verity you are all a company of rascals; and as for his part, I'll instantly write to his father to disinherit him, that I may revenge my disgrace and punish his folly. The pox! A son of a whore! The pox!   40

Exit Sir Roger

APOTHECARY A mad old fellow, but your penitence will recover all.

SNEAK Would you were hanged, by Jericho, for leaving the door open. O, what shall I do? This comes of learning the sciences in the devil's name.   45

APOTHECARY Patience, sir, have patience.

Scene shuts

Exeunt

5.[3]

[*Emilia's chamber*]

Enter Rashley, Emilia, and Betty

RASHLEY A trapdoor, say you, madam?

EMILIA Yes, we happily discovered it yesterday, looking for a ring accidentally dropped. It opens upon the stairs the backside of the kitchen. I am sure 'twill be very necessary in our intrigue. Here, take the candle, you, and go and watch, and when I give the sign, be sure be ready.   5

BETTY I'll not fail, madam.

[*Exit Betty*]

EMILIA 'Tis good to be secure. For I know Maria has still an eye over us, and my husband's new jealousy gives me fresh cause of doubt.°

RASHLEY Egad, 'tis unnecessary. This trapdoor must needs be very   10
useful. I see fortune is ours still and will not leave us. Let us doubt when we see danger. There is none now, nor can be whilst our love continues.

EMILIA Which I fear will be but a short time. For what is indirect is seldom permanent; therefore, let us consider on't.   15

RASHLEY Damn consideration! 'Tis a worse enemy to mankind than malice. Let impotent age consider, that is fit for nothing but dull, tame thoughts of what he has been formerly. Let the lawyer and physician consider what quibbles and what potions are most necessary. And let the sly fanatic think his time out and consider   20
how to be securely factious. But let the lover love on still transported, whilst all his thoughts and senses are employed in the dear joys of rapture, endless passion, without a grain of dull consideration.

EMILIA I swear the softness of our tempers abuses half our sex; we   25
should not else be won so easily. But we are such kind fools!

RASHLEY Ay, we are all fools, madam. That's the truth on't; but how shall we help it?

EMILIA Resolve upon a remedy: love no more.

RASHLEY Resolve upon the contrary: love forever. Gad, the world   30
would be at a fine pass if all were of your mind. (*Noise of a lock*) How now?

  Enter Maria with a light

MARIA [*to Bubble, who remains offstage*] Stand there till I fetch you in; I'm sure they're here.

EMILIA My sister, as I live! Malicious accident!   35

RASHLEY Ha! With a light too! How the devil got she in?

EMILIA Heaven knows, unless with a false key.

MARIA Nay, you are caught and finely too. I'm cozened else. What plot now, madam, to convey you hence? Now show your mighty skill; and if there is a devil at your service, employ him now. You   40
never had more cause. Methinks you are melancholy: why d'ee not laugh? Smile at your wit and great security? You, I know, have a thousand ways to get off still or, if you want, that gentleman can supply° you.

RASHLEY I, supply! A plague o' your damned jest!   45

EMILIA [*aside to Rashley*] Hush, and leave me to her. [*To Maria*] Nay, sister, this is barbarous to triumph o'er our misfortunes. You

235

know yourself what love is and what inconveniences it brings poor women to.

MARIA You can confess now; and here's a gentleman not far off, your 50 husband, madam. I know this cannot choose but be grateful to him; I'll call him to hear it.

EMILIA Ah, be not so cruel to undo me quite. I'll confess all to thee and from this minute be converted. Ah, had I taken thy counsel before, I had been happy. 55

MARIA Ay, but you would persist, and now see what comes on't.

EMILIA O, I am miserable! Forgive me, dear Maria! (*Weeps*)

MARIA Nay, heaven forgive you. But come, will you confess? (*Aside*) I have her at a rare advantage.

EMILIA Most faithfully; but let me do't i' th' dark. Let no light see my 60 guilty blushes; it is enough my tongue dares utter it. Dear sister, let me not be too much ashamed. O misery, misery. (*Weeps*)

MARIA Well, here is a light not far off, and thus much I'll comply with you. (*Puts out the light*) Now begin.

RASHLEY [*aside*] By heaven, I grow cheerful. We shall 'scape, I am 65 sure we shall. O this dear devil!

EMILIA My grief ties up my tongue.

MARIA 'Tis time to grieve. But, come, when d'ee begin?

EMILIA This cruel man seduced me, cruel Rashley. (*Aside*) Where are you, sir? 70

RASHLEY (*softly*) Here, sweet, here.

EMILIA First won upon me with his comely presence, handsome demeanour. Every several° grace my soul admired. (*To Rashley*) Give me your hand. [*To Maria*] But when he came to speak, his tongue, his charming tongue—O heaven, that I shall live to utter 75 it!—so ensnared me that I no longer knew my liberty, but as his victim, gloried in my passion.

MARIA With shame you live to speak it.

RASHLEY 'Twas my misfortune too. [*Aside*] But heaven forgive me, I shall laugh out. I am not able to hold. 80

EMILIA Down, quickly down.

Emilia and Rashley sink in the trap

MARIA Now could I laugh till my heart ached again to think how I have caught 'em. I knew 'twas impossible she should 'scape always, and I will tyrannize more than a Turk over his slave.° For my part, I am sorry for your infamy, and were it not that by the laws of nature 85 I have a great concern in any of my brother's injuries, you might

love on for me. But since my blood runs in his veins, I dare not see
his infamy and let it pass unquestioned. Therefore, either swear
from this hour to desert Rashley and never see him more, or your
disgrace I will this instant publish or call your husband to be spec-   90
tator of his shame and yours. What? Are ye dumb? Not answer me!
It seems you dislike this proposal, but do not provoke me. Not yet?
[*Calling to Bubble, offstage*] Nay then, within there? Brother, here
they are; a light, a light, quickly!

    Enter Bubble with a light and long sword

BUBBLE Where? Where is this traitor? This strumpet? By   95
'Scanderbeg,° I am ready for a charge. I'll push him with a
vengeance. Where is he?

MARIA Here, here! How now? What, are you got under the table again
or into a corner? Give me the candle, brother. I am sure I have 'em
fast.° (*Looks about*)   100

BUBBLE Here's nothing: another mistake, as Gad jidge me.

MARIA She is a devil, and I lose my labour. Gone? What, both gone?
O, I could tear myself! Which way? How? By what means could
they escape?

BUBBLE 'Scape? 'Sbud! 'Tis impossible they should escape if they   105
were here. Pish, this is only one of your maggots,° sister. You do
but fancy you saw 'em.

MARIA Fancy? Eternal light forsake me if I did not both see and speak
to 'em two minutes since—heard her confess the crime and vow
repentance—here, in this very place. But by what means they   110
'scaped, I only can admire, not imagine.

BUBBLE Prithee hold thy peace. I say once more 'tis only a maggot.
Sleep, fool, and purge thy head from fancies.

    Enter Ranger and Betty behind

How now, Ned?

RANGER Sir, I know not whether the news I bring may please you, but   115
I have made a strange discovery yonder.

BUBBLE Discovery! Of what, prithee?

RANGER Sir, I saw Rashley and your wife going laughing, arm in
arm, through the entry, the backside of the kitchen into the
parlour, where, if you please to give yourself the trouble, you may   120
find 'em.

BETTY [*aside*] This is as my mistress suspected, and I'll inform her
immediately.

    [*Exit Betty*]

BUBBLE Hey day! My wife and Rashley? Art sure on't, Ned?

RANGER As sure, sir, as I live. I saw 'em there. Nay, what's more, my   125
curiosity inducing me to peep through the key-hole, I saw his head
lie in her lap, whilst she, with a fond passion, stroked his cheeks and
dallied with his hair. Faith, sir, I could not see this and be silent, but
you, I fear, will think the worse of me for it.

BUBBLE In the parlour, say'st thou? 'Sbud, was ever such a confusion?   130
Why, my sister says that within these two minutes she saw and
spoke to 'em here in this chamber. They are here, and there, and
everywhere, and yet I can find 'em nowhere. What a pox should a
man think of this?

RANGER They are there this instant, sir, upon my honour.   135

MARIA Sure, I have not dreamt all this while! Did I not see her?° By
heaven, I saw the devil in her likeness then.

BUBBLE Why, peace, I say. If you are mad, offend no-one but yourself
with it. What a pox, shall I not believe my eyes? The house is not
haunted that I know of, unless it be with fools. There's a bob for   140
you by way of conclusion.

MARIA Yes, cuckolds too! There's a bob for you by way of repartee.

BUBBLE Cuckold? I'd have you to know I scorn your words; and were
you not my sister, I'd fetch you out° with your repartees. What?
Because you are a fool, you guess all persons are alike? Do you but   145
conceive me, Mrs Juniper?° I am a Turk at matter of fact when I
see occasion.

RANGER Good sir, no more of this; but go down and satisfy yourself
in the truth of my story. If I tell you a lie, call me fool, horse,
anything. Do but go and see.   150

BUBBLE 'Sbud, I know not what to do. One brings me up; another
carries me down. One jilts me; another abuses me. A third laughs at
me; and yet I find nothing, nor see nothing, nor know nothing, and
you are nothing but fools to make all this stir about nothing. But
come; I'll go with thee, Ned.   155

MARIA And I, that I may say once in my life I saw a miracle.

RANGER I have her once more in the noose of the slip;° now the
devil hold her fast in th' other world. 'Tis above mortal power!
Come, sir.

Exeunt

238

5.4

[*The parlour in Bubble's house*]

Enter Rashley and Emilia in nightgowns; Betty, Jeremy

EMILIA Here, here, quickly take my nightgown and put it on. You are sure they are coming?

BETTY Very sure, madam. I stood at the door and heard all.

RASHLEY What must I do, sweet? Prithee do not let us be surprised again.   5

EMILIA Uncase, uncase, sir; and let your man represent° you as Betty does me.

Betty and Jeremy put on the gowns

Jeremy, be sure you play your part well and court her to the life.

RASHLEY D'ee hear, sirrah?

JEREMY I'll warrant you, sir. Come, Mrs Betty.   10

EMILIA [*aside to Betty*] Stay, a word more in thy ear. I see this fellow is but a blockhead and therefore am afraid of trusting him too far. Keep him as ignorant of our intrigue as thou canst, and if my husband ask where I am, tell him I am gone to visit my Lady Courtly. I'll be in my chamber, and when they are all gone, bring   15
me word what Ranger and Maria are doing.

BETTY Yes, madam, I'll be very careful.

RASHLEY I will reward thy care, my pretty little—

Noise [*offstage*]

EMILIA Hark! I hear 'em coming. Now to your postures.

Exeunt Rashley and Emilia

JEREMY Now, Mrs Betty, we having so fit an occasion, let us make   20
love in some heroic vein.

BETTY No, I am for the plain-dealing° way.

JEREMY Pish! T'other's a great deal better, as thus:

  Your eyes with so bright charms are decked about,
  That I could kiss 'em till I kissed 'em out.   25

BETTY O I hate that. I vow 'tis very silly.

Enter Ranger, Bubble, and Maria

RANGER There, there, sir! D'ee see 'em now? Will you believe next time?

BUBBLE O dismal object! I am a cuckold then.

MARIA This is miraculous. How was it possible they could get hither?   30
But I am glad they are here, however.

BUBBLE Now for a good full blow at his head before he sees me. 'Tis a cuckold's way of revenge, I'm sure. (*Offers to strike*) Have at him!

JEREMY Oh Lord, what mean you, sir? What mean you?

BUBBLE Traitor! Rogue! Rascal! I'll—Ha, Jeremy?   35

JEREMY Ay, sir, 'tis I. Poor Jeremy, sir.

MARIA And Betty in her mistress's nightgown!

RANGER (*amazed*) Their old friend the devil has fetched 'em away again.

BUBBLE What make you here in their nightgowns?   40

BETTY Only, sir, through an ambition to make love as genteely as we could.

BUBBLE Go, go, and find your mistress out, and tell her, her humble servant and husband desires to speak with her. Look ye, Ned, you are a fool, I see.   45

RANGER I am so, sir. I acknowledge it.

BUBBLE And you, madam, are a little leaning that way, are ye not?

MARIA I can say nothing for myself, sir.

BUBBLE Then I can say y'are a couple of fools. Did I not tell you what all this would come to? Ha, ha, ha! It makes me laugh to think how   50
busy you two asses have been about nothing, and I am no better than a third fool for believing you. But from henceforth, he that speaks against my chicken's virtue is the son of a whore; for, 'udsblood, she's the honestest woman in Christendom, and he that denies it, I will immediately invade him with battle-axe, poniard,   55
and pistol.

RANGER She is a very saint, sir.

MARIA A very devil, sir! O death, is there no remedy?

BUBBLE I'll go instantly and reconcile myself to her with a strict vow never to doubt her more.   60
    Enter Sir Roger and Cordelia
Oh, Sir Roger! Welcome. Faith, I was wishing for some good company to be witness of my reconcilement to my dear chicken. You are melancholy, sir. I heard your nephew was sick; I suppose that's the cause.

SIR ROGER [*aside*] If he has heard of what, I am disgraced forever.   65

BUBBLE Come, sir, cheer up, cheer up. He will be well again, doubt not.

SIR ROGER I hope so, sir. [*Aside to Cordelia*] Madam, this generous act of concealing the infamy of our family has so wrought upon me, that if I could requite—

CORDELIA No more, sir. Your nephew's forbearance is all I desire.   70
You are sensible now that I have some reason to request that.

SIR ROGER I am, madam, and am extremely bound to your generosity, and, Gad, I have another nephew whom I'll make better by two hundred pounds a year to make you amends. Well, Mr Bubble, I am glad to come at so good a time when mirth is going forward. You are   75
a merry man, sir, and, in verity, I like your company.

BUBBLE And I yours, Sir Roger; for I am very merry, for some private reason best known to myself. We'll toss a bumper about by and by, faith!

Enter Fumble, pushing in Governess

FUMBLE An old crone, a sorceress! What, i'fack, and in the devil's   80
name, am I to be popped in the mouth° with fourscore and twelve? A beldame, a witch that expects next winter to be turned into a gib-cat, thought fit to be yoked with me? No, no, some wiser than some; and I'll have her know within this week that I am as fit for two-and-twenty as two-and-twenty is for me. In the meantime,   85
avaunt Jezebel!° I like thee not, ecod. Thou hast no black o' top, i'fack. Thou art not for my turn.

BUBBLE What, old Signior Fumble? What's the matter, man?

FUMBLE Yes, marry am I, sir, and choused damnably too, and some shall know't when I can find 'em.   90

CORDELIA He's groping for his spectacles, now I expected to be rated.°

FUMBLE Ah! Are you there, rogue? Are you there? Why, you very wag, would you offer to serve me so? But, hang thee thou'rt a rogue; and come, i'fack, though 'twas a knavish trick, I am pleased   95
with the wit on't. Give me thy hand, and come and kiss me, and all shall be well again.

CORDELIA Upon condition you never trouble me more. [*Kisses him on the cheek*] There 'tis.

FUMBLE Ecod, she has a pretty touch with her, she has, i'fack. I   100
forgive thee with all my heart. [*To Governess*] Well, old woman, depart in peace; old woman, I say, depart and trouble me no more. I am busy and can't dispense with° the fopperies of age now.

GOVERNESS [*aside*] Well, this comes of eating sweetmeats when I was   105
young. He had never found out the trick, if my want of teeth had not discovered me.

BUBBLE Ha, ha! Here had like to have been fine sport, i'faith. But would I knew where my wife is, that we might all go and address,°
now I am in this good humour.   110

GOVERNESS Sir, just as I came in, I saw her go up into her chamber.

BUBBLE Didst thou? I am glad on't, i'faith. Come, let's all go.
    Enter Betty

BETTY Sir, I cannot find her; but I heard her say about an hour since,
she intended to go and visit my Lady Courtly.

BUBBLE No, no. I know where she is now. Poor creature! I warrant she   115
sits so melancholy above now. Well, I dare proudly say I have the
best wife in Christendom. For, i'faith, I have been very jealous of
her, but I was wrought upon, when o' my conscience, the innocent
wretch would not hurt a worm. But come, we'll all go to her, and be
sure, Sir Roger, you plead for me. In troth, my heart aches to think   120
how I have used her.

BETTY [*aside*] I must prevent their going up, or we are undone.
    Betty is running; Maria stops her

MARIA Whither are you running? I have some business with you.

BETTY Good madam, I'll wait on you immediately.

MARIA Ye shall not stir till I have spoke to you. [*Aside*] Here must be   125
something in this, I find, by her eagerness to be gone.

SIR ROGER Well, Mr Bubble, in verity I'll do my best in your behalf;
my tongue is at your service at any time.

BUBBLE Sir Roger, you will oblige me in't. She is the most innocent,
sweetest, and most virtuous person in the whole world, and I shall   130
never be able to make her amends. Come, let us go.

RANGER [*aside*] Now will I see how she behaves herself and wonder at
the prosperous impudence hell has endowed her with, though it lies
not in my power to repel it.

MARIA [*to Betty*] Now I think better on't, I'll defer my business till   135
another time. You may go where you please.
    Exeunt Maria, Ranger, Bubble, Fumble, Governess, Sir Roger,
    and Cordelia

BETTY This cunning devil has undone 'em, nor lies it now in my
power to hinder it. O, I could curse!
    Exit

5.[5]

[Emilia's chamber]

Enter Rashley and Emilia

EMILIA The plague of living with such a husband, you must imagine,
is very disagreeable to my temper; and were it not for the happy

hours I have the good fortune to enjoy in thy society, my life would be
wholly uncomfortable. But, my dear, thou wilt forget me. One day I
shall grow cheap° to thee, shall I not?   5

RASHLEY No, never. Never, my sweet! Thou hast more charms each
hour added to thee, rather than one diminished. Forget thee! I
sooner shall forget to feed myself, or that the sun e'er shone in
midst of summer, than thy more precious favours. Thou bring'st
each hour new sweets and every minute a thousand thousand graces   10
throng about thee, my dear. (*Kisses her*) Dear, charming, sweet,
precious—

　　　Enter Bubble, Sir Roger, Fumble, Ranger, Maria, Cordelia

BUBBLE (*entering*) Softly, softly, Sir Roger. Poor soul. I warrant she's
at prayers. Ha! What's this I see? Gad jidge me—

RANGER By heaven, they're here a-kissing. O happy minute!   15

EMILIA [*to Rashley*] Ah, who could have the heart to leave thy blisses
for such a fool, such a beast, such a dull, sordid, filthy, insipid
creature as my husband?

BUBBLE How's that? O devil!

RASHLEY [*to Emilia*] I am smothered with thy charms. O for some air!   20
(*Starts*) Ha! O horror, cursed minute! Taken thus?

EMILIA My husband! Nay then, I am lost for ever.

BUBBLE Ah, cursed creature. Is this thy virtue? [*Bubble draws his
sword*] But I'll— (*Goes to wound her*)

SIR ROGER Hold, sir; in verity, that must not be. No swords against   25
women in my company.

BUBBLE [*turns to Rashley*] Then here let my vengeance light. Traitor!
Have I obliged thee so often for this? [*Lunges at him*] Have at thee!

RANGER [*stops Bubble*] Your pardon, sir. I must hinder dishonourable
proceedings; in the field you may do what you please.°   30

BUBBLE [*to Emilia*] Speak, witch, speak! What reason hadst thou to
use me thus? Thou limb of the devil, speak, I say.

EMILIA Use you thus? Why, sir, your rage makes you suggest strange
thoughts without cause. My kindness to Mr Rashley was only
because—he promised to be my friend in urging my reconcilement   35
with you. And because I knew he was your friend, I therefore—I
say, because I knew you loved him, I desired him to—to—I was
very urgent with him about—about—no, I mistake! 'Twas he was
urgent with me to entreat you to do me the favour—no—to do him
the favour. I mean, hum, to—to—   40

BUBBLE Pox! What a story's here? O strumpet! Witch!

MARIA To cuckold him, was that it, sister?

RANGER Madam, methinks your speech fails you exceedingly.

EMILIA All will not do. O spiteful minute! Taken thus at last? Shame ties my tongue, and absence is most necessary.

Exit Emilia

BUBBLE O farewell, in the devil's name! O horns, horns! Found a cuckold at last! I have spun a fair thread, by the Lord Harry. A cuckold at last!

RASHLEY A cuckold! Why, sir, have I done anything but by your directions? Why do you suggest such things to yourself? Well, sir, if I have injured you, I wear a sword, sir, and so, farewell.

Exit Rashley

SIR ROGER In verity, this° was a strange discovery, but such things will happen sometimes.

CORDELIA So it seems; yet this methinks is wonderful.°

BUBBLE O unfortunate husband! Well, I'll go instantly and get a divorce, and spend the remainder of my life in penning a satire against women. I'll call it *A Caution for Cuckolds*, where I will deplorably set down my own case and as a warning-piece for rash young men and for the benefit of my country. *Felix quem faciunt aliena cornua cautum.*°

Exit Bubble

FUMBLE [*aside*] Something is the matter now, if I could guess. But mum, I must not yet discover my failing.

RANGER Now the mighty sophistress is o'erthrown!

MARIA Thank chance for that, but no wit of our own.

RANGER Right, madam; and by this a man may see how unnecessary a thing it is to strive to turn the current of a woman's fancy, when it is bent to another. 'Tis a damned thing, this wenching, if a man considers seriously on it; and, yet, 'tis such a damnable age we live in that, Gad, he that does not follow it is either accounted sordidly unnatural or ridiculously impotent. Well, for my part, henceforward this shall be my resolution.

> I'll love for interest, court for recreation,
> Change still a mistress to be still in fashion.
> I'll aid all women in an amorous league,
> But from this hour ne'er baulk a love-intrigue.

Exeunt

Epilogue

Spoken by Fumble
[Mr Anthony Leigh]

Well, gentlemen, how d'ee? Ecod, you sit
As if you had no souls, no brains, no wit.
What, not a word now in the poet's praise?
Ha! Faith, I was a spark in my young days.
I clapped and clapped—nay, sometimes to my cost,   5
I clapped so long, Gad, I was clapped at last.°
There, I was waggish. You know what I mean;
The devil was in't, a plaguy Yorkshire quean.
But 'tis no matter, 'twas but thought a jest,
And, Gad, I was as brisk then as the best.   10
So I am now; for i'fack, I'd have you know,
Your old man, though he only serve for show,
Yet give him a young wench with black o' top,
And you shall see him frisk, and jump, and hop,
Ecod, and wriggle! Ha! Th' old bell will sound,   15
Though there is ne'er a clapper to be found.°
But let that pass. Now your applause disburse.
Why? What the devil makes you silent thus?
What say ye? The play does not deserve it? Ha!
Ecod, you are mistaken. For, I'll tell ye,   20
I once could write and judge and 'fack, did do
Very strange things, but I've forgot 'um now.
But I remember what a wag I was.
I had so many smutty jests those days,
I could get none but women to my plays.°   25
But that's all one. Ecod, the youth that writ
Does well, and—who knows?—may do better yet.
Therefore, you should encourage him, d'ee hear?
And he that fails, I wish this curse may bear:
That he be really my character,   30
Lascivious, deaf, and impotent as I;
And, Gad, that's plague enough, and so good-bye.

FRIENDSHIP IN FASHION

THOMAS OTWAY

Archilochum rabies armavit iambo°

To the Right Honourable Charles, Earl of Dorset and Middlesex, Gentleman of his Majesty's Bed-chamber, etc.°

My lord,

Your lordship has so often and so highly obliged me, that I cannot but condemn myself for giving you a trouble so impertinent as this is. Considering how remiss I have been in my respects to your lordship,° in that I have not waited on you so frequently as the duty I owe your lordship and my own inclinations required; but the circumstances of my condition,° whose daily business must be daily bread, have not, nor will, allow me that happiness. Be pleased then, my lord, to accept this humble dedication as an instance of his gratitude who, in a high measure, owes his well-being to you. I cannot doubt but your lordship will protect it, for nothing ever flew to you for succour unsuccessfully. I am sure I have reason to acknowledge it. As for the unlucky censures some have passed upon me for this play,° I hope your lordship will believe I hardly deserve 'em. For, to my best remembrance, when first I was accused of the thing° by some people of the world, who had perhaps as little reason to think I could be guilty of it as to believe themselves deserved it, I made it my business to clear myself to your lordship, whose good opinion is dearer to me than anything which my worst enemies can wrong me of else. I hope I convinced your lordship of my innocence in the matter, which I would not have endeavoured had it not been just. For I thank my stars I know myself better than (for all the threats some have been pleased to bestow upon me) to tell a lie to save my throat. Forgive me, my lord, this trouble; continue me in your lordship's favour and good opinion and accept of the prayers and well-wishes of

> Your most humble and
> most obliged servant,
> Thomas Otway

THE CHARACTERS OF THE PLAY°

Goodvile°	Mr Betterton
Truman	Mr Smith
Valentine	Mr Harris
Sir Noble Clumsy	Mr Underhill
Malagene	Mr Leigh
Caper	Mr Jevon
Saunter	Mr Bowman
Mrs Goodvile	Mrs Barry°
Victoria	Mrs Gibbs
Camilla	Mrs Price
Lady Squeamish	Mrs Quin
Lettice	Mrs Seymour
Bridget	Mrs ——

Prologue

Spoken by Mr Smith

How hard a task hath that poor drudge of stage
That strives to please in this fantastic age?
It is a thing so difficult to hit,
That he's a fool that thinks to do't by wit.
Therefore our author bade me plainly say,
You must not look for any in his play.
I' th' next place, ladies, there's no bawdy in't,
No, not so much as one well-meaning hint.
Nay more, 'twas written every word he says
On strictest vigils and on fasting days,°
When he his flesh to penance did enjoin—
Nay, took such care to work it chaste and fine,
He disciplined himself at every line.°
Then, gentlemen, no libel he intends,°
Though some have strove to wrong him with his friends;
And poets have so very few of those,
They'd need take care whose favour 'tis they lose.
Who'd be a poet? Parents all beware,
Cherish and educate your sons with care.
Breed 'em to wholesome law, or give 'em trades;
Let 'em not follow th' muses—they are jades.°
How many very hopeful rising cits
Have we of late known spoiled by turning wits?
Poets by critics are worse treated here,
Than on the Bankside butchers do a bear.°
Faith, sirs, be kind, since now his time is come,
When he must stand or fall as you shall doom.
Give him Bear Garden law; that's fair play for't,°
And he's content for one, to make you sport.

1.1

The Mall°

Truman, reading a billet, and Serving Boy

TRUMAN In a vizard, say you?

SERVANT Yes, sir, and as soon as she had delivered it, without anything more, gave the word to the coachman, drew up the tin lattice,° and away she hurried.

TRUMAN The meaning of a billet of this nature without a name is a   5
riddle to me. (*Reads*) 'You know me and see me often. I wish I may never see you more, except you knew better where to place your love, or I were abler to govern mine. As you are a gentleman, burn this so soon as it comes to your hands. *Adieu.*' Well, this can be no other than some staunch virtue of thirty-five that is just now fallen   10
under the temptation or, what is as bad, one of those cautious dealers that never venture but in masquerade, where they are sure to be wondrous kind, though they discover no more to the lover than he has just occasion to make use of.

Enter Goodvile and Valentine

VALENTINE Truman, good-morrow. Just out of your lodging? But   15
that I know thee better, I should swear thou hadst resolved to spend this day in humiliation and repentance for the sins of the last.

GOODVILE I beg your pardon! Some lady has taken up your time. Thou canst no more rise in a morning without a wench than thou canst go to bed at night without a bottle. Truman, wilt thou never   20
leave whoring?

TRUMAN Peace, matrimony, peace. Speak more reverently of your dearly beloved whoring. Valentine, he is the mere spirit of hypocrisy. He'd hardly been married ten days, but he left his wife to go home from the play alone in her coach, whilst he debauched me with two   25
vizards° in a hackney to supper.

VALENTINE Truly, Goodvile, that was very civil and may come to something. But, gentlemen, it begins to grow late. Where shall we dine?

TRUMAN Where you will. I am indifferent.   30

GOODVILE And I.

VALENTINE I had appointed° to meet at Chatelins,° but—

TRUMAN With whom?

VALENTINE Why, your cousin, Malagene, Goodvile.

GOODVILE Valentine, thou art too much with that fellow. 'Tis true   35
indeed he is some relation to me, but 'tis such a lying varlet, there is
no enduring of him.

VALENTINE But rogues and fools are so very plenty, 'tis hard always to
escape 'em.

TRUMAN Besides, he dares be no more a friend than a foe. He never   40
spoke well of any man behind his back, nor ill before his face. He is
a general disperser of nauseous scandal, though it be of his own
mother or sister. Prithee let's avoid him if we can today.

GOODVILE 'Twill be almost impossible, for he is as impudent as he is
troublesome. As there is no company so ill but he'll keep, so there is   45
none so good but he'll pretend to. If he has ever seen you once, he'll
be sure of you. And if he knows where you are, he's no more to be
kept out of your room than you can keep him out of your debt.

VALENTINE He came where I was last night roaring drunk. Swore,
damn him, he had been with my lord such a one, and had swallowed   50
three quarts of champagne for his share, said he had much ado° to
get away, but came then particularly to drink a bottle with me. I was
forced to promise him I would meet him today to get rid of him.

GOODVILE Faith, gentlemen, let us all go dine at my house. I have
snubbed him of late, and he'll hardly venture that way so soon   55
again. At night I'll promise you good company. My wife—for I
allow her for my own sake what freedom she pleases—has sent for
the fiddles to come.

TRUMAN Goodvile, if there be any such thing as ease in matrimony,
thou hast it. But methinks there's, as it were, a mark upon married   60
men that makes 'em as distinguishable from one of us as your Jews
are from the rest of mankind.°

GOODVILE O there are pleasures you dream not of. He is only confined
by it that will be so. A man may make his condition as easy as he
pleases. Mine is such a fond, wanton ape,° I never come home but   65
she entertains me with fresh kindness,° and, Jack, when I have been
hunting for game with you and missed of an opportunity, stops a
gap well enough.

TRUMAN There's no condition so wretched but has its reserve.° Your
spaniel turned out of doors goes contentedly to his kennel. Your   70
beggar, when he can get no better lodging, knows his old warm
bush. And your married whoremaster that misses of his wench goes
honestly home, and there's madam wife. But, Goodvile, who are to
be the company at night?

GOODVILE In the first place, my cousin Victoria, your idol, Jack   75

Truman; then, Mr Valentine, there will be the charming Camilla;
and another that never fails upon such an occasion, the unimitable
Lady Squeamish.

TRUMAN That indeed is a worthy person, a great critic forsooth;
one that censures° plays and takes it very ill she has none dedicated   80
to her yet,° a constant frequenter of all masquerades and public
meetings, a perfect coquette, very affected and something old.

VALENTINE Discourses readily of all the love intrigues of the court
and town, a strange admirer of accomplishments and good breeding,
as she calls it, a restless dancer. One that by her good will would   85
never be out of motion.

TRUMAN How, Valentine! You were once a great admirer there. Have
a care how you speak too harshly of your mistress, though the
business be over. You stand well with the ladies yet and are held a
man of principles.   90

GOODVILE That indeed is a fine creature. Your old harassed stager°
has always some such resty° whore-master or another, whom she
makes the best of her despair withal and, after being forsaken by
half the town besides, comforts herself in her man of principles.
But now I think on't, we delay too long. I'll go before and prepare.   95
Gentlemen, you'll be sure to follow?

TRUMAN Sir, we'll not fail to wait on you.

    Exit Goodvile

Boy, is the coach ready?

    [*Exit Serving Boy*]

Valentine, I have had the oddest adventure this morning

    Enter Malagene

Ha! Malagene! How came he hither?   100

MALAGENE Jack Truman, Monsieur Valentine, *bonjour*. Was not that
Goodvile I met coming in, ha?

VALENTINE Yes, he parted hence but now.

MALAGENE Faith, I'll tell ye what, gentlemen. Goodvile's a very honest
fellow as can be, but he and I are fallen out of late, though faith   105
'twas none of my seeking.

TRUMAN No, I'll be sworn for thee, thou lov'st thyself better.

VALENTINE Pray, what was the matter, Malagene?

MALAGENE Why, I was advising him to look after things better at
home. The fellow has married a young wife, and there he lets her   110
make balls and give entertainments. I was very free with him and
told him of it to the purpose. For faith, I should be sorry to see any
ill come on't, very sorry.

TRUMAN But, hark ye, Malagene, Goodvile's a sort of a surly companion and apt to have so good an opinion of himself that he is able° to manage affairs without your advice. He might have been very severe with you upon this occasion. 115

MALAGENE Severe with me! I thank you for that with all my heart. That had been the way to have made a fine piece of work on't indeed! Hark ye, under the rose,° he's sweetly fitted° with my cousin though. 120

VALENTINE Pray, sir, speak with more respect. We are his friends and not prepared to relish any of your satire at present.

MALAGENE O Lord, sir! I beg your pardon. You are a new acquaintance there, I remember, and may design an interest. Faith, Ned, if thou dost, I'll ne'er be thy hindrance, for all she's my kinswoman. 125

TRUMAN The rascal, if he had an opportunity, would pimp for his sister, though but for the bare pleasure of telling it himself.

MALAGENE Now, when he comes home, will she be hanging about his neck with, 'O Lord, dear, where have you been this morning? I can't abide you should go abroad so soon, that I can't. You are never well but when you are with that wicked, lewd Truman and his debauched companion, young Valentine. But that I know you are a good dear, I should be apt to be jealous of you, that I should'. Ha, ha. 130

135

TRUMAN Sir, you are very bold with our characters, methinks.

MALAGENE I? Pshaw! Your servant. Sure we that know one another may be free.° You may say as much of me, if you please. But no matter for that. Did you hear nothing of my business last night, ha?

TRUMAN Not a word, I assure you, sir. Pray, how was it? [Aside] 140 Prithee let him alone a little, Valentine.

MALAGENE Why, coming out of Chatelins last night—where it had cost me a guinea-club° with a right honourable° or two of this kingdom, which shall be nameless—just as I was getting into a coach, who should come by but a blustering fellow with a woman in 145 his hand and swore, damn him, the coach was for him. We had some words, and he drew. With that, I put by his pass, closed with him, and threw up his heels, took away Toledo,° gave him two or three good cuts over the face, seized upon damsel, carried her away with me to my chamber, managed her° all night, and just now sent 150 her off. Faith, amongst friends, she was a person of quality, I'll tell you that.

TRUMAN What? A person of quality at that time o' th' night, and on foot too?°

MALAGENE Ay, and one that you both know very well. But take no   155
notice on't.°

VALENTINE O, sir, you may be sure we shall be very cautious of
spreading any secrets of yours of this nature. [*Aside*] Lying rakehell!
The highest he ever arrived at was a bawd, and she too banished
him at last because he boasted of her favours.   160

MALAGENE Nay, not that I care very much neither. You may tell it if
you will, for I think it was no more than anyone would have done
upon the same occasion. Ha?

TRUMAN Doubtless, sir, you were much in the right. But, Valentine,
we shall stay too long. 'Tis time we were going.   165

MALAGENE What, to dinner? I'll make a third man. Where shall
it be?

TRUMAN Sir, I am sorry, we must beg your excuse this time, for we are
both engaged.

MALAGENE Whoo! Prithee, that's all one; I am sure I know the   170
company. I'll go along at a venture.

VALENTINE No. But, Malagene, to make short of the business, we are
going into company that are not very good friends of yours, and will
be very uneasy if you be there.

MALAGENE What's that to the purpose? I care as little for them as   175
they do for me, though, on my word, sparks, of honest fellows you
keep the oddest company sometimes that ever I knew!

TRUMAN But, sir, we are resolved to reform it and, in order thereunto,
desire you would leave us to ourselves today.

MALAGENE No. But I'll tell you, go along with me. I have discovered a   180
treasure of pale wine; I'll assure you 'tis the same the king drinks
of.° What say you, Jack? I am but for one bottle or two, for faith, I
have resolved to live sober for a week.

TRUMAN Prithee, tormentor, leave us! Do not I know the wine thou
drink'st is as base as the company thou keep'st? To be plain with   185
you, we will not go with you, nor must you go with us.

MALAGENE Why, if one should ask the question now: whither are you
going, ha?

VALENTINE How comes it, Malagene, you are not with your two
friends, Caper and Saunter? You may be sure of them; they'll eat   190
and drink and go all over the world with you.

MALAGENE How canst thou think that I would keep such loathsome
company? A brace of silly talking, dancing, singing rascals? 'Tis
true, I contracted an acquaintance with 'em, I know not how; and
now and then when I am out of humour, love to laugh at and abuse   195

'em for an hour or two, but, come what will on't, I am resolved to
go along with you today.

TRUMAN Upon my word, sir, you cannot. Why should you make so
many difficulties with your friends?

MALAGENE Whoo! Prithee leave fooling. You would shake me off   200
now, would you? But I know better things. The sham° won't pass
upon me, sir, it won't, look you.

TRUMAN [*aside to Valentine*] Death, we must use him ill, or there is no
getting rid of him. [*To Malagene*] Not pass, sir?

MALAGENE No, sir!   205

TRUMAN Pray, sir, leave us.

MALAGENE I shan't do't, sir.

TRUMAN But you must, sir.

MALAGENE Maybe not, sir.

TRUMAN I am going this way. (*Walking off*)   210

MALAGENE So am I. [*Following Truman*]

TRUMAN But, sir, I must stay here a little longer.

MALAGENE With all my heart! 'Tis the same thing; I am not in haste.

VALENTINE Have a care, Malagene, how you provoke Truman. You'll
run the hazard of a scurvy beating, my friend, if you do.   215

MALAGENE Beating! I am sorry, sir, you know no better. Pox, I am
used° to serve him so, man. Let me alone. You shall see how I'll
tease him. Hark you, Jack.

TRUMAN Sir, you are an impudent, troublesome coxcomb.

MALAGENE No matter for that; I shan't leave you.   220

TRUMAN Sir, I shall pull you by the nose then.

MALAGENE 'Tis all one to me. Do your worst.

TRUMAN Take that then, sir. (*Tweaks him by the nose*) Now d'ye hear:
go about your business.

MALAGENE Nay, faith, Jack, now you drive the jest too far. What a   225
pox, I know you are not in earnest. Prithee let's go.

TRUMAN Death, sir, you lie. Not in earnest? Let this convince you.
(*Kicks him*) How like you the jest now, sir?

MALAGENE Hark you, Truman, we shan't dine together then, shall we?

VALENTINE Faith, to tell you the truth of the matter, Truman had a   230
quarrel last night, and we are just now going to make an end on't.
'Tis that makes him so surly. Nevertheless, now I think on't better,
if you'll go, you shall. Perhaps we may have occasion for a third man.

MALAGENE No, no. If that be the business, I'll say no more, puh. I hate
to press into any man's company against his inclination. Truman,   235
upon my reputation, you are very uncivil now, that you are. But,

hark you, I ran to the groom-porter's° last night and lost my money. Prithee lend me two guineas till next time I see thee, child.

TRUMAN With all my heart, sir. I was sure 'twould come to this at last. 240
[*Produces the money*] 'Tis here. You may command what you please from your servant. Malagene, good-morrow.
      Enter Caper and Saunter

MALAGENE Dear Jack Truman, your humble—
      Exit Truman

VALENTINE Won't you go along with us then, Malagene?

MALAGENE No, here are two silly fellows coming. I'll go and divert 245
myself a little with them at present.

VALENTINE Why, those are the very people you railed at so but now. You will not leave us for them at a time when you may be so serviceable?

MALAGENE Hang 't, you'll have no occasion for me, man. Say no 250
more on't, but take my advice: be sure you stand fast. Don't give ground, d'ye hear? Push briskly, and I'll warrant you do your business.

VALENTINE Sir, I thank you for your counsel and am sorry we can't have your company, but you are engaged?   255

MALAGENE Are you sure, though, it will come to fighting? I have no mind to leave your company methinks.

VALENTINE Nay, nothing so certain as that we shall fight. I wish you would go, for I fancy there will be three in the field.

MALAGENE A pox on't, now I remember: I promised to meet these 260
people here and can't avoid 'em now. I'd go with you else with all my heart, faith and troth, but if you'd have me send a guard,° I'll do't.

VALENTINE No, sir; there's no danger. [*Aside*] Nothing but the rogue's cowardice could have rid us of him.   265
      Exit Valentine

MALAGENE How now, bullies,° whither so fast this morning? I parted just now with Jack Truman and Ned Valentine. They would fain have had me to dinner with 'em, but I was not in a humour of drinking, and to speak the truth on't, you are better company, ten to one. They engross still all the discourse to themselves, and a man 270
can never be free with them neither.

CAPER O Lord, Malagene, we met the delicatest creature but now as we came round. I am a rascal if I don't think her one of the finest women in the world. I shan't get her out of my mind this month.

SAUNTER 'Twas Victoria, my Lady Fairfield's daughter, that came to   275
town last summer when Goodvile was married. [*Aside to Malagene*]
He in love with her, poor soul! (*Sings*) '*I shall beg his pardon there, as
I take it.*'

MALAGENE That's Truman's blowing.° She's always lingering after
him here and at the playhouse. She heats herself here every morning   280
against the general course at night,° where she comes as constantly
as my Lady Squeamish herself.

SAUNTER I vow, that's a fine person too. Don't you think she has
abundance of wit, Malagene? She and I did so rally Caper t' other
day.   285

CAPER Ay, it may be so.

SAUNTER But did you never hear her sing? She made me sit with her
till two o'clock t' other morning to teach her an Italian song.° I
have, and I vow she sings it wonderfully.

MALAGENE Damn her. She's the most affected, amorous jilt and loves   290
young fellows more than an old kite does young chicken. There is
not a coxcomb of eighteen in town can escape her. We shall have her
draw one of you into matrimony within this fortnight.

CAPER Malagene, thou art the most satirical thief breathing. I'd give
anything thou didst but love dancing, that I might have thee on my   295
side sometimes.

SAUNTER Well, Malagene, I hope to see thee so in love one day as to
leave off drinking, as I have done, and set up for a shape and a face;
or, what is all one, write amorous sonnets and fight duels with all
that do but look like rivals. I would not be in love for all the world, I   300
vow and swear. (*Walks up and down with an affected motion*)

CAPER Nor I. (*Sings*) '*Ah Phyllis, if you would not love the Shepherd,
etc.*' But d'ye hear, Malagene, they say Goodvile gives a ball
tonight. Is it true?

MALAGENE Yes, I intend to be there, if I do not go to court.   305

CAPER I am glad of it with all my heart. [*Sees Lady Squeamish in the
distance*] Saunter, there's my lady. To be sure, she'll not fail.°

SAUNTER But will you go, Malagene? Goodvile and you are at a
distance.

MALAGENE Whoo! Pox, that's nothing, I'll go for all that. But, faith, I   310
should meet my Lord —— at court tonight.° Besides, I han't been
in the drawing-room these three days; the company will wonder
what's become of me.

    Enter Lady Squeamish
She here! Nay then.°

CAPER Madam, your ladyship's most humble servant. (*Congees* 315
  affectedly)

LADY SQUEAMISH [*curtsies*] Mr Caper, your most devoted. O dear
  Mr Saunter, a thousand thanks to you for my song.

SAUNTER Your ladyship does your servant too much honour. (*Sings*)
  'As Chloe full of, etc.'° 320

LADY SQUEAMISH Mr Caper, you are a stranger indeed. I have not
  seen you this two days. Lord, where d'ye live?

CAPER I should have waited on your ladyship but was so tired at the
  masquerade at my Lord Flutters t'other night. (*Dances and capers*)

SAUNTER Madam, madam, Mr Goodvile gives a ball tonight. Will 325
  your ladyship be there?

LADY SQUEAMISH Yes. I heard of it this morning; Victoria sent me
  word.

CAPER O, Madam, d'ye hear the news? Goodvile makes a ball tonight.
  I hope I shall have the honour of your ladyship's company. 330

LADY SQUEAMISH O, by all means. Mr Caper, pray don't you fail us.
  O Lord, Mr Malagene, I beg your pardon. Upon my honour, I did
  not see you, I was so engaged in the civilities of these gentlemen.

MALAGENE Your wit and beauty, madam, must command the honour
  and admiration of all the world. But when did your ladyship see 335
  Mr Valentine?

LADY SQUEAMISH O, name him not, Mr Malagene; he's the
  unworthiest, basest fellow. Besides, he has no principles nor
  breeding. I wonder you gentlemen will keep him company. I'll
  swear he's enough to bring an odium on the whole sex. 340

MALAGENE The truth on't is, madam, I do drink with him now and
  then because the fellow has some wit, but it is when better company
  is out of the way; and faith, he's always very civil to me as can be. I
  can rule him.

LADY SQUEAMISH O Lord, 'tis impossible. Wit! Why, he was abroad 345
  but two years and all that time too in an academy;° he knows nothing
  of the intrigues of the French court and has the worst mien in the
  world. He has a sort of an ill-natured way of talking indeed, and they
  say makes bold with me° sometimes, but I'll assure you, I scorn him.

MALAGENE Truly he has made very bold with you, or he is foully 350
  belied. Ha, ha, ha.

LADY SQUEAMISH They say, he's grown a great admirer of Madam
  Camilla of late, who passes for a wit forsooth. 'Tis true, she's well
  enough, but I suppose is not the first that has been troubled with
  his impertinent addresses. 355

MALAGENE Indeed, he would not let me alone till I brought him acquainted there. He owes that happiness to me. But methinks your ladyship speaks with something of heat. [*Aside*] By heaven, she's jealous!

LADY SQUEAMISH No, I assure you, sir, I am not concerned at it in the least. But did you ever hear 'em discourse anything of me?   360

MALAGENE Never any ill, madam, only a little idle raillery now and then; but Truman and he are wont to be something lavish when they have been drunk in my company. [*Aside*] 'Twill work.   365

LADY SQUEAMISH Nay, I know he has spoken dishonourably of me behind my back because he failed in his filthy designs. Madam Camilla may deserve better of him, I doubt not. (*Aside*) But if I am not revenged on his falsehood!—Mr Caper.

CAPER AND SAUNTER Madam   370

LADY SQUEAMISH Where do you go today?

CAPER Will your ladyship be at the new play?

LADY SQUEAMISH No, I saw it the first day and don't like it.

MALAGENE Madam, it has no ill character about the town.

LADY SQUEAMISH O Lord, sir, the town is no judge. 'Tis a tragedy,   375
and I'll assure you there's nothing in it that's moving. I love a tragedy that moves mightily.

SAUNTER Does your ladyship know who writ it?

LADY SQUEAMISH Yes, the poet came and read it to me at my lodgings.° He is but a young man, and I suppose he has not been a   380
writer long. Besides, he has had little or no conversation with the court, which has been the reason he has committed a great many indecorums in the conduct of it.°

SAUNTER I did not like it neither for my part. There was never a song in it, ha?   385

CAPER No, nor so much as a dance.

MALAGENE O, it's impossible it should take if there were neither song nor dance in it.°

LADY SQUEAMISH And then their comedies nowadays are the filthiest things, full of bawdy and nauseous doings, which they mistake for   390
raillery and intrigue. Besides, they have no wit in 'em neither, for all their gentlemen and men of wit, as they style 'em, are either silly, conceited, impudent coxcombs, or else rude, ill-mannerly, drunken fellows. Faugh. I am ashamed anyone should pretend to write a comedy that does not know the nicer rules of the court and all the   395
intrigues and gallantries that pass,° I vow.

MALAGENE Who would improve in those things must consult with your ladyship.

LADY SQUEAMISH I swear, Mr Malagene, you are an obliging person. I wonder the world should be so malicious to give you so undeserving a character as they do. I always found you extremely generous and a person of worth.

MALAGENE In troth, madam, your ladyship and myself are the subjects of abundance of envy. For I love to be malicious now and then, and faith, am the very scourge of the court; they all stand in awe of me, for I must speak what I know, though sometimes I am used a little scurvily for it. But, faith, I can't help it; 'tis my way.

LADY SQUEAMISH Ha, ha, ha. Really, I love scandal extremely too sometimes, so it be decently managed; but as I was saying, there is not a person in the world understands the intrigues of the court better than myself. I am the general confidante of the drawing room and know the loves of all the people of quality in town.

CAPER Dear madam, how stands the affair between my Lord Supple° and Madam Lofty?

LADY SQUEAMISH Worse than ever. 'Tis very provoking to see how she uses the poor creature. But, the truth is, she can never be at rest for him; he's more troublesome than an old husband, continually whispering his softnesses and making his vows, till at last she is forced to fly to me for shelter, and then we do so laugh, which the good-natured creature takes so patiently. I swear, I pity him.

SAUNTER But my Lady Colt,° they say, is kinder to the sparkish Mr Pruneit.°

LADY SQUEAMISH O Lord, Mr Saunter, that you should understand no better. To my knowledge, it is all false. I know all that intrigue from the beginning to the ending; it has been off this month. Besides, he keeps a player again.° O Mr Saunter, whatever you do, never concern yourself with those players.

SAUNTER Madam, I have left the folly long since. When first I came to town, I must confess I had a gallantry there. But since I have been acquainted with your ladyship's wit and beauty, I have learnt to lay out my heart to better advantage.° I think that was finely said!

LADY SQUEAMISH I'll swear, Mr Saunter, you have the most court-like way of expressing yourself.

SAUNTER (*bows and cringes*) O Lord, madam!

LADY SQUEAMISH Mr Malagene, these are both my intimate acquaintance, and I'll swear, I am proud of 'em. Here is Mr Saunter sings the French manner° better than ever I heard any English gentleman in my life. Besides, he pronounces his English in singing with a French kind of a tone or accent° that gives it a strange beauty. Sweet sir, do me the favour of the last new song. 440

SAUNTER Let me die! Your ladyship obliges me beyond expression. Malagene, thou shalt hear me. (*Sings a song in a French tone*)

MALAGENE [*aside*] What a devil was this? I understand not a word on't.

SAUNTER Ha, Malagene, ha? 445

LADY SQUEAMISH Did you ever hear anything so fine?

MALAGENE Never, madam, never. I swear, your ladyship is a great judge.

LADY SQUEAMISH But how plain and distinctly too every word was pronounced? 450

MALAGENE O, to admiration, to admiration. (*Makes mouths aside*)

LADY SQUEAMISH Well, Mr Saunter, you are a charming creature. O, sad Mr Caper, I long till night comes. I'll dance with nobody but you tonight, for I swear I believe I shall be out of humour.

MALAGENE [*aside*] That's more than she ever was in her life, so long 455
as she had a fool or a fiddle in her company.

LADY SQUEAMISH Though really I love dancing immoderately. But now you talk of intrigues, I am mistaken if you don't see something where we are going tonight.

MALAGENE What, Goodvile is to commence° cuckold, is it not so? 460

LADY SQUEAMISH O, fie, Mr Malagene, fie. I vow you'll make me hate you if you talk so strangely. But, let me die, I can't but laugh. Ha, ha, ha. Well, gentlemen, you shall dine with me today. What say you, Mr Malagene, will you go?

MALAGENE Your ladyship may be sure of me. I hate to break good 465
company.

LADY SQUEAMISH And pray now let us be very severe and talk maliciously of all the town. Mr Caper, your hand. O dear Mr Saunter, how shall I divide myself? I'll swear, I am strangely at a loss. Mr Malagene, you must be Mr Saunter's mistress, I think, at 470
present.

MALAGENE With all my heart, madam. Sweet Mr Saunter, your hand. I swear, you are a charming creature, and your courtship is as extraordinary as your voice. Let me die, and I vow I must have t' other song after dinner, for I am very humoursome and very 475
whimsical, I think. Ha, ha, ha.

    Exeunt

2.1

The ordinary°

Enter Mrs Goodvile and Lettice

MRS GOODVILE Did you deliver the billet?

LETTICE Yes, madam, faithfully.

MRS GOODVILE But are you sure you did?

LETTICE Can your ladyship think I would be guilty of the least
neglect in a concern of such moment?   5

MRS GOODVILE Are you sure he dines here today?

LETTICE Madam, they are now at dinner below. Mr Valentine's there
too. O, I'll swear he's a fine man, the most courteous person.

MRS GOODVILE What? Because he hunts and kisses you when he's
drunk? No, Lettice. Truman, Truman, O that Truman!   10

LETTICE I wonder your ladyship should be so taken with him. Were I
to choose, I should think my master the more agreeable man.

MRS GOODVILE And you may take him, if you will; he is as much a
husband as one would wish. I have not seen him this fortnight. He
never comes home till four in the morning, and then he sneaks to   15
his separate bed, where he lies till afternoon, then rises, and out
again upon his parole.° Flesh and blood can't endure it.

LETTICE But he always visits your ladyship first.

MRS GOODVILE That's his policy, as great debtors are always very
respectful and acknowledging where they never mean to pay.   20
'Tis true, he gives me what freedom I can desire, but God knows,
that's all.

LETTICE And where's the pleasure of going abroad and getting a
stomach° to return and starve at home?

MRS GOODVILE I laugh, though, to think what an easy fool he believes   25
me. He thinks me the most contented, innocent, harmless turtle°
breathing, the very pattern of patience.

LETTICE A jewel of a wife.

MRS GOODVILE And as blind with love as his own good opinion of
himself has made him.   30

LETTICE And can you find in your heart to wrong so good a natured,
complete, well-meaning, harmless husband that has so good an
opinion of you?

MRS GOODVILE Ha, wrong him? What you say, Lettice? I wrong my

husband! Such another word forfeits my good opinion of thee   35
forever.

LETTICE What meant the billet to Mr Truman then this morning?

MRS GOODVILE To make him my friend perhaps and discover, if I
can, who it is that wrongs me in my husband's affection. For I am
sure I have a rival. And I am apt to believe Victoria deserves no   40
better than ordinary of me, if the truth were known.

LETTICE Why, she is his near kinswoman and lives here in the house
with you. Besides, he would never dishonour his own family, surely.

MRS GOODVILE You are a fool, Lettice. The nearness of blood is the
least thing considered. Besides, as I have heard, 'tis almost the only   45
way relations care to be kind° to one another nowadays.

LETTICE Yet, madam, you never meet but you are as kind and fond of
him as if you had all the joys of love about you. Lord! How can you
dissemble with him so? Besides, Mr Truman, madam, you know is
his friend.   50

MRS GOODVILE O, if I would ever consent to wrong my husband—
which, heaven forbid, Lettice!—it should be to choose with his
friend. For such a one has a double obligation to secrecy, as well for
his own honour as mine. But, I'll swear, Lettice, you are an idle girl
for talking so much of this, that you are. 'Tis enough to put ill   55
thoughts into one's head, which I am the most averse to of all
things in the world.

LETTICE But, madam, thoughts are free, and it is as hard not to think
a little idly sometimes, as it is to be always in good humour. But it
would make anyone laugh to think Mr Truman should be in love   60
with Madam Victoria, if all be real which your ladyship suspects.

MRS GOODVILE Ay, and with a design of marriage too. But a ranging
gallant° thinks he fathoms all, and counts it as much beneath his
experience to doubt his security in a wife as success in a mistress.

LETTICE Besides, after a little time, he is so very industrious in   65
cuckolding others that he never dreams how swimmingly his own
affairs are managed at home.

Enter Victoria

MRS GOODVILE But, hush—she's here.

VICTORIA A happy day to you, madam.

MRS GOODVILE Dear cousin, your humble servant. Have you heard   70
who are below?

VICTORIA Yes, young Truman and his inseparable companion,
Valentine.

MRS GOODVILE Well, what will you do, cousin? Truman comes

resolved on conquest; for with the advantages he has in your heart   75
already, 'tis impossible you should be able to hold out against him.

VICTORIA Yes. Powerful champagne,° as they call it, may do much. A
spark can no more refrain running into love after a bottle than a
drunken country vicar can avoid disputing of religion when his
patron's ale grows stronger than his reason.°   80

MRS GOODVILE Come, come, dissemble your inclinations as artfully
as you please. I am sure they are not so indifferent, but they may be
easily discerned.

VICTORIA Truly, madam, you may be mistaken in your guess.

MRS GOODVILE How? I doubt° it is some other man then has caused   85
this alteration in you.° Lord, Lettice, is she not extremely altered?

VICTORIA Altered, madam, what do you mean?

MRS GOODVILE Nay, Lettice, fetch a glass, and let her see herself.
Lord, you are paler than you use to be.

LETTICE Ay, and then that blueness under the eyes.   90

MRS GOODVILE Besides, you are not so lively as I have known you.
Pardon me, cousin.

LETTICE Well, if there be a fault, marriage will cure all.°

VICTORIA I'll assure you, I have none that I know of stands in need of
so desperate a remedy. [*Aside*] Marriage! Fault! What can all this   95
tend to?

    Enter Page

MRS GOODVILE Well, what now?

PAGE Madam, Camilla is coming to wait upon your ladyship.

MRS GOODVILE Ha, Camilla! Tell her I'll attend her. Won't you go
with me, Victoria?   100

VICTORIA I'll but step into my chamber and follow you instantly.

    Exeunt Mrs Goodvile, [*Lettice*], *and the Page*

Whither can all this drive? Surely she has discovered something of
Goodvile's love and mine. If she has, I am ruined.

    Enter Goodvile

GOODVILE Victoria, your cousin is not here, is she? What, in clouds? I
stole this minute from my friends on purpose to see thee, and must   105
not I have a look? Not a word?

VICTORIA O, I am ruined and lost for ever. I fear your wife has had
some knowledge of our loves. And if it be so, what will then become
of me?

GOODVILE Prithee, no more. My wife! She has too good an opinion of   110
herself to have any ill one of me, and would as soon believe her glass
could flatter her, as I be false to her. My wife! Ha, ha.

VICTORIA Yes, I am sure it must be so; it can be no otherwise. But you are satisfied and now have nothing more to do but to leave me to be miserable.   115

GOODVILE Leave thee! By heaven, I'd sooner renounce my family and own myself the bastard of a rascal. Come, quiet thy doubts. Truman is here; and take my love for thy security, he shall be thine tonight.

VICTORIA I have great reason to expect it indeed: that you would hazard your interest in so good a friend for the reparation of my   120 honour that so little concerns you, and which you have already made your best of.

GOODVILE No more of that. Love's my province, and thine is too dear to me to be neglected. 'Tis true, I have made him my friend, and I hope he will deserve it by doing thee that justice which I am   125 incapable of.

VICTORIA You can promise easily.

GOODVILE Ay, and as resolutely perform. When I have heated him with wine, prepare to receive him.

    Enter Mrs Goodvile

Ha, she here!   130

MRS GOODVILE So, so, Mr Goodvile, are you there indeed? I thought I should catch you.

GOODVILE Faith, my dear, I have been speaking a good word for Jack Truman. My cousin Victoria's too cruel.

MRS GOODVILE O, fie, Victoria! Can you be so hard-hearted to deny   135 anything when Mr Goodvile is an advocate?

VICTORIA I must confess it is with some difficulty; but should I too easily comply upon Mr Goodvile's intercession, who knows but your ladyship might be jealous? For he that can prevail for another may presume there's hopes for himself.   140

MRS GOODVILE Ay, but cousin, I know you are my friend and would not, though but in regard of that, do me such injury. Besides, Mr Goodvile knows I dare trust him. Don't you, love?

GOODVILE Trust me! Yes, for if you don't, 'tis all one. (*Aside*) Credulous innocence! [*To Mrs Goodvile*] Alas, my dear, were I as   145 false as thou art good, thy generous confidence would shame me into honesty.

    Enter Camilla, running and squeaking; Truman and Valentine after her

CAMILLA For heaven's sake, madam, save me! Mr Goodvile, 'tis safer travelling through the deserts of Arabia than entering your house. Had I not ran hard for it, I had been devoured, that's certain.   150

VALENTINE O, madam, are you herded?° It will be to little purpose. I
am staunch and never change my game.

CAMILLA But when you have lost it, if fresh start up, you can be as
fully satisfied, who hunt more for the love of the sport than for the
sake of the prey.   155

VALENTINE But madam, should you chance to be taken, look to't; for
I shall touse and worry you most unmercifully, till I have revenged
myself severely for the pains you cost me catching.

CAMILLA Therefore I am resolved to keep out of your reach. Lord,
what would become of such a poor little creature as I am in the   160
paws of so ravenous an animal?

TRUMAN [to Victoria] But are you too, lady, so wild as Mrs Camilla?

VICTORIA O sir, to the full! But I hope you are not so unmerciful as
Mr Valentine.

TRUMAN No, madam, quite on the contrary: as soft and pliant as your   165
pillow. You may mould me to your own ease and pleasure, which
way you will.

VICTORIA 'Tis strange two of such different tempers should so well
agree. Methinks you look like two as roaring, ranting, tory-rory
sparks as one would wish to meet withal.   170

VALENTINE Yes, madam, at the playhouse in a vizard, when you come
dressed and prepared for the encounter; there indeed we can be as
unanimously modish and impertinent as the pertest coxcombs of
'em all, till like them too, we lose our hearts and never know what
becomes of 'em.   175

CAMILLA But the comfort is you are sure to find 'em again in the next
bottle.

MRS GOODVILE Then drink 'em down to the ladies' healths, and they
are as well at ease as ever they were.

TRUMAN Why, you would not be so unconscionable as to have us two   180
such whining, crop-sick lovers, as sigh away their hours and write
lamentable ditties to be sung about the town by fools and bullies in
taverns.

GOODVILE Till some Smithfield doggerel,° taking the hint, swells the
sonnet to a ballad, and Chloris dwindles into a kitchen-wench.°   185

VICTORIA 'Tis presumed then you are of that familiar tribe that never
make love but by contraries, and rally our faults when you pretend
to admire our perfections.

CAMILLA As if the only way to raise a good opinion of yourselves
were to let us know how ill a one you have of us.   190

TRUMAN Faith, madam, 'tis a hard world, and when beauty is held at so dear a rate,° 'tis the best way to beat down the market° as much as we can.

VALENTINE But you shall find, ladies, we'll bid like chapmen for all that.   195

VICTORIA You had best have a care, though, lest you overreach yourselves and repent of your purchase when 'tis too late.

CAMILLA Besides, I hate a Dutch bargain° that's made in heat of wine, for the love it raises is generally like the courage it gives: very extraordinary, but very short-lived.   200

GOODVILE How, madam? Have a care what you say. Wine is the prince of love, and all ladies that speak against it forfeit their charter. I must not have my favourite traduced. [*Calls to Serving Boy offstage*] Boy, bring some wine. You shall prove its good effects and then acknowledge it your friend. We'll drink—   205

CAMILLA Till your brains are afloat and all the rest sink.

VALENTINE I find then, ladies, you have the like opinion of our heads as you have of our hearts.

CAMILLA Really, sir, you are much in the right.

TRUMAN But if your ladyship should be in the wrong—though love,   210
like wine, be a good refresher, yet 'tis much more dangerous to be too busy withal. And, though now and then I may overheat my head with drinking, yet confound me, I think I shall have a care never to break my heart with loving.

MRS GOODVILE But, sir, if all men were of your cruel temper, what   215
would become of those tender-hearted creatures that cannot forbear saluting you with a billet in a morning, though it comes without a name, and makes you as unsatisfied as they, poor creatures, are themselves?

TRUMAN [*aside*] Ha, this concerns me! Blockhead, dull leaden sot that   220
I was, not to be sensible it must be she, and none but she, could send mine this morning. Well, poor Jack Truman, look to thyself; snares are laid for thee, but the virtuous must suffer temptation. And, heaven knows, all flesh is frail.

Enter Goodvile's Serving Boy with wine

GOODVILE Now, boy, fill the glasses. But before we proceed, one thing   225
is to be considered. [*To Mrs Goodvile*] My dear, you and I are to be no man and wife for this day, but be as indifferent, and take as little notice one of another, as we may chance to do seven years hence. But at night—

VALENTINE A very fair proposal.   230

MRS GOODVILE Agreed, sir, if you will have it so.

GOODVILE The wine.

    [Exit Goodvile's Serving Boy]

Now each man to his post.

    They separate: Goodvile to Camilla, Valentine to Victoria,
    Truman to Mrs Goodvile

The word.°

    All take glasses

TRUMAN Love and wine.   235

    Enter Lettice

GOODVILE Pass.°

    They drink

Now that nothing may be wanting, Lettice, you must sing the
song I brought home t' other morning, for music is as great an
encouragement to drinking as fighting.

LETTICE (*sings*)   240

          How blessed he appears,
     That revels and loves out his happy years,
     That fiercely spurs on till he finish his race,
     And, knowing life's short, chooses living apace.
  To cares we were born; 'twere a folly to doubt it.   245
  Then love and rejoice; there's no living without it.

          Each day we grow older,
     But as fate approaches, the brave still are bolder.
     The joys of love with our youth slide away,
     But yet there are pleasures that never decay.   250
  When beauty grows dull, and our passions grow cold,
  Wine still keeps its charms, and we drink when we're old.

    [Exit Lettice]

GOODVILE So, now show me an enemy to divine harmonious drinking!

    [Enter Goodvile's Serving Boy]

BOY Sir, my Lady Squeamish is below, just alighted out of her coach.

GOODVILE Nay, then drinking will have the major vote against it: she   255
is the most exact observer of decorums and decency alive. But she
is not alone, I hope?

BOY No, sir. There is Mr Malagene with her and three more gentlemen, one they call Sir Noble Clumsy, a full portly gentleman.

    [Exit Goodvile's Serving Boy]

TRUMAN That's a hopeful animal: an elder brother,° of a fair estate,   260
and her kinsman newly come up to town, whom her ladyship has
undertaken to polish and make a fine gentleman.

VALENTINE 'Tis such a fulsome overgrown rogue, yet hopes to be a
fine spark and a very courtly youth. He has been this half year
endeavouring at a shape, which he loves eating and drinking too   265
well ever to attain to. The others, I'll warrant you, are the nimble
Mr Caper and his polite companion Mr Saunter.

GOODVILE She's never without a kennel of fools at her heels, and we
may know as well when she is near by the noise her coxcombs make,
as we know when a certain spark of this town is at hand by the   270
new-fangled jingle of his coach. She comes—and woe be to the
wretch whom she first lights upon.

>   Enter Lady Squeamish, Sir Noble Clumsy, Malagene, Caper
>   and Saunter [with Serving Boy]

LADY SQUEAMISH Dear Madam Goodvile, ten thousand happinesses
wait on you. Fair madam Victoria, sweet, charming Camilla, which
way shall I express my service to you? [To Sir Noble Clumsy]   275
Cousin, your honour,° your honour to the ladies.

SIR NOBLE CLUMSY Ladies, as low as knee can bend or head can bow,
I salute you all. [Bows with an affected flourish] And gallants, I am
your most humble, most obliged, and most devoted servant. That I
learned at the end of an epistle dedicatory.°   280

GOODVILE Sir Noble Clumsy is too great a courtier.

SIR NOBLE CLUMSY Yes, sir, I can compliment upon an occasion; my
lady knows I am a pretty apt scholar.

LADY SQUEAMISH Gallants, you must pardon my cousin here. He is,
but as it were, a novice yet, and has had little conversation but what   285
I have had the honour to instruct him in.

MALAGENE But let me tell you, he is a man of parts, and one that I
respect and honour. Pray gentlemen, know my friend.

VALENTINE Hark you, Malagene. How durst you venture hither,
knowing that Goodvile and Truman care so little for your company?   290

MALAGENE O, sir, your servant. Your servant, sir. I guessed this was
the duel you were going about. I should not have left you else; faith,
Ned, I should not.

GOODVILE But, madam, can the worthy knight, your kinsman, drink?
What think you, Sir Noble, of the ladies' healths?   295

SIR NOBLE CLUMSY In a glass of small beer, if you please.

LADY SQUEAMISH O sweet Mr Goodvile, don't tempt him to drink,
don't! I'll swear, I am so afraid he should spoil himself with drinking.
Lord, how I should loathe a fellow with a red nose!

VALENTINE [indicating Caper and Saunter] See, Truman: the two   300
coxcombs are already boarding our mistresses.°

TRUMAN O, 'twere a pity to interrupt 'em. A woman loves to play and fondle with a coxcomb sometimes as naturally as with a lap-dog, and I could no more be jealous of one than of the other.

VALENTINE I am not of your opinion; they are too apt to love anything   305
that but makes 'em sport. And the familiarity of fools proceeds oftentimes from a privilege we are not aware of. For my part, I shall make bold to divert.—Mr Saunter, a word. Have you any pretences with that lady, ha?

SAUNTER Some small encouragement, I have had, sir, but I never   310
make my boast of those favours, never.

VALENTINE No, sir, 'twere not your best course.

SAUNTER O Lord, you are pleased to be merry. [*Aside*] Sure he takes me for a fool, but no matter for that. (*Sings*) '*Would Phyllis be mine, and for, etc.*'   315

      Enter Caper's Serving Boy

BOY Madam, the fiddles are below. Shall I call 'em up?

MRS GOODVILE No, let 'em stay a little; we'll dance below.

CAPER Ha, the fiddles! Boy, where are you?

      Caper capers

BOY Here, sir.

CAPER Have you brought my dancing-shoes?   320

BOY No, sir, you gave me no order. But your fiddle is below under the seat of the coach.

CAPER Rascal, dog, fool. When did you ever know me go abroad without my dancing-shoes? Sirrah, run home and fetch 'em quickly, or I'll cut off both your ears and have 'em fastened to the   325
heels of those I have on.

      [*Exit Caper's Serving Boy*]

TRUMAN It is an unpardonable fault, sir, that your boy should forget your dancing-shoes.

CAPER Ay, hang him, blockhead, he has no sense; I must get rid of him as soon as I can. I would no more dance in a pair of shoes that   330
we commonly wear than I would ride a race in a pair of gambados.°

LADY SQUEAMISH Mr Valentine, I hope, is a better-bred gentleman than to leave his mistress for wine. (*To Valentine*) I hear, sir, there is a love between you and madam Camilla, thou monster of perjury.

VALENTINE Faith, madam, you are much in the right; there is   335
abundance of love on my side, but I can find very little on hers. If your ladyship would but stand my friend° upon this occasion. [*Aside*] I think this is civil.

LADY SQUEAMISH I'll swear, sir, you are a most obliging person.

Ladies and gallants, poor Mr Valentine here is fallen in love and has   340
desired me to be his advocate. Who could withstand that eye, that
lip, that shape and mien, besides a thousand graces in everything he
does? O lovely Camilla, guard, guard your heart; but I'll swear, if it
were my own case, I doubt I should not. Ha, ha, ha.

VALENTINE Madam, what means all this?   345

GOODVILE Poor Ned Valentine!

TRUMAN 'Tis but what I told him he must look for. But, stay, there is
more yet coming.

LADY SQUEAMISH Nay, this is not half of what thou art to expect. I'll
haunt thee worse than thy ill genius, take all opportunities to   350
expose thy folly and falsehood everywhere, till I have made thee as
ridiculous to our whole sex as thou art odious to me.

VALENTINE But has your ladyship no mercy? Will nothing but my
ruin appease you? (*Approaches Lady Squeamish*) Why should you
choose by your malice to expose your decay of years and lay open   355
your poor lover's follies to all—because you could improve 'em to
your own use no longer?

LADY SQUEAMISH Come not near me, traitor. Lord, Madam Camilla,
how can you be so cruel? See, see, how wildly he looks. For heaven's
sake, have a care of him; I fear he is distempered in his mind. What   360
pity 'tis so hopeful a gentleman should run mad for love. Ha, ha, ha.

MRS GOODVILE Dear madam, how can you use Mr Valentine so? 'Tis
enough to put him out of humour and spoil him for being good
company all the day after it.

LADY SQUEAMISH O Lord, madam, 'tis the greatest pleasure to me in   365
the world. Let me die, but I love to rally a bashful young lover and
put him out of countenance, at my heart.°

SAUNTER Ha, ha, ha. And I'll swear the devil and all's in her wit when
she sets on't. Poor Ned Valentine! Lord, how sillily he looks!

CAPER Ay, and would fain be angry if he knew but how.   370

VALENTINE Hark you, coxcomb; I can be angry, very angry, d'ye mark
me?

SIR NOBLE CLUMSY No, but sir, don't be in a passion; my lady will
have her humour, but she's a very good woman at bottom.

VALENTINE Very likely, sir.   375

MRS GOODVILE Now, madam, if your ladyship thinks fit, we'll withdraw and leave the gentlemen to themselves a little; only Mr Caper
and Mr Saunter must do us the honour of their company.

SAUNTER Say you so, madam? I'faith, and you shall have it. Come,
Caper. We are the men for the ladies, I see that. Hey, boys!   380

LADY SQUEAMISH O dear and sweet Mr Saunter shall oblige us with a song.

SAUNTER O, Madam, ten thousand, ten thousand, if you please. I'll swear, I believe I could sing all day and all night and never be weary. (*Sings*) '*When Phyllis watched her harmless sheep, Not one poor* 385 *lamb etc.*'

> *Exeunt Saunter, Caper, Lady Squeamish, Mrs Goodvile, and Camilla*

GOODVILE A happy riddance, this. Now, gentlemen, for one bottle to entertain our noble friend and now acquaintance,° Sir Noble Clumsy.

SIR NOBLE CLUMSY Really, gallants, I must beg your pardon. I dare 390 not drink, for I have but a very weak brain, sir, and my head won't bear it.

TRUMAN O, surely that honourable bulk could never be maintained with thin regular diet and small beer.

SIR NOBLE CLUMSY I must confess, sir, I am something plump, but a 395 little fat is comely. I would not be too lean.

MALAGENE No, by no means, my dear. Thou hast an heroic face which well becomes the noble port° and fullness of thy body.

VALENTINE Goodvile, we have a suit to you. Here is Malagene has been sometime in a cloud; for this once, receive him into good grace 400 and favour again.

MALAGENE Faith, Goodvile, do. For, without any more words, I love thee with all my heart, faith and troth. Give me thy hand.

GOODVILE But sir, should I allow you my countenance, you would be very drunk, very rude, and very unmannerly, I fear. 405

MALAGENE Drunk, sir? I scorn your words. I'd have you know I han't been drunk this week; no, I am the son of a whore if I won't be very sober. This noble knight shall be security° for my good behaviour. Wilt thou not, knight?

SIR NOBLE CLUMSY Sir, you are a person altogether a stranger to me, 410 and I have sworn never to be bound for any man.

TRUMAN O but Sir Noble, you are obliged in honour to serve a gentleman and your friend.

SIR NOBLE CLUMSY Say you so, sir? Obliged in honour? I am satisfied. Sir, this gentleman is my friend and acquaintance, and whatsoever 415 he says, I'll stand to.

MALAGENE Hark thee, son of Mars:° thou art a knight already. I'll marry thee to a lady of my acquaintance and have thee made a lord.

GOODVILE Boy, the wine; give Sir Noble his glass. Gentlemen,   420
Sir Noble's lady's health.

SIR NOBLE CLUMSY Od's my life, I'll drink that, though I die for't.
Gallants, I have a lady in this head of mine, and that you shall find
anon. By my troth, I think this be a glass of good wine!

VALENTINE Say you so? Take the other glass° then, Sir Noble.   425

SIR NOBLE CLUMSY 'Fore George, and so I will. Pox on't, let it be a
brimmer. Gentlemen, God save the king.

MALAGENE Well said, my lovely man of might. His worship grows
good company.

TRUMAN Sir Noble, you are a great acquaintance with Mr Caper and   430
Mr Saunter; they are men of pretty parts.

SIR NOBLE CLUMSY O, sir, the finest persons, the most obliging,
well-bred, complaisant, modish gentlemen. They are acquainted
with all the ladies in town, and are men of fine estates.

TRUMAN [aside to Valentine and Goodvile] This rogue is one of those   435
earthy mongrels that knows the value of nothing but a good estate,
and loves a fellow with a great deal of land and a title, though his
grandfather were a blacksmith.

SIR NOBLE CLUMSY How say you, sir? A good estate? Od's heart, give
me the other glass. I have two thousand pounds a year.°   440

MALAGENE Say'st thou so? Boy, bring more wine. Wine in abundance,
sirrah, d' ye hear?
[Exit Goodvile's Serving Boy]
Frank Goodvile, thou see'st I am free, for faith, I hate ceremony and
would fain make the knight merry.

GOODVILE Malagene, it shall be your task. Drink him up lustily, and   445
when that's done, we'll bring him to my lady his cousin. It may
make some sport.

VALENTINE A very good proposal.
[Enter Goodvile's Serving Boy with wine]

MALAGENE Say no more. Thy word's a law, and it shall be done.
[To Malagene] Come, bear up, my lusty limb of honour, and hang   450
sobriety.

SIR NOBLE CLUMSY Ay, so say I. Hang sobriety! Drink, whore, rant,
roar, swear, make a noise, and all that. But be honest, dost hear? Be
honest.

TRUMAN [aside] I would very fain be so if I could, but the damned   455
billet this morning won't out of my head. Well, Madam Goodvile,
if any mischief comes on't, 'tis your own fault, not mine. I did not
strike first, and there's an end on't.

Music offstage. Enter Lettice

LETTICE Sir, the fiddles are ready, and the ladies desire your company. Mr Truman, my lady wants you.   460

TRUMAN Say'st thou so? I thank thee for thy news with all my heart. The devil, I see, will get the better on't, and there is no resisting.

LETTICE Sir Noble, my Lady Squeamish sent me to tell you she wants your company to dance.   465

SIR NOBLE CLUMSY Tell her, I am busy about a grand affair of the nation and cannot come. Dance? I look like a dancer indeed! But these women will be always putting us on more than we can do. Boy, give me more wine.

GOODVILE Malagene, remember and use expedition.°   470

Exeunt Goodvile, Truman, Valentine, Lettice

SIR NOBLE CLUMSY Sirrah, do you know me? I am a knight. And here's a health to all the whores in Christendom.

MALAGENE (*drinks*) Not forgetting all the ladies within. Now we are alone, I may talk.

SIR NOBLE CLUMSY (*breaks a glass*) So, there's for you, do you see?   475
Sirrah, don't look scurvily. I have money in my pocket, you must know that. [*To the boy*] Bring us more wine. Malagene, thou art a pretty fellow; dost thou love me? (*Staggers*) Give me thy hand. I will salute thy under-lip.°

MALAGENE [*aside*] Ha, what's the meaning of this? I doubt I shall   480
almost be drunk as soon as the knight. [*To Sir Noble Clumsy*] Sir Noble, canst thou whore?

SIR NOBLE CLUMSY How, whore? What a question's there! Thou shalt be my pimp, and I'll prefer° thee.

MALAGENE [*aside*] What a rascal this knight is. I have known as   485
worthy a person as himself a pimp, and one that thought it no blemish to his honour neither.

Enter Lady Squeamish at the door

SIR NOBLE CLUMSY Ha, my lady cousin? Faith, madam, you see I am at it.

MALAGENE [*aside*] The devil's in't, I think. We could no sooner talk   490
of whores, but she must come in, with a pox to her.—Madam, your ladyship's most humble servant.

LADY SQUEAMISH O, odious! Insufferable! Who would have thought, cousin, you would have served me so. Faugh! How he stinks of wine! I can smell him hither. How have you the patience to hear the   495
noise of fiddles and spend your time in nasty drinking?

SIR NOBLE CLUMSY Hum, 'tis a good creature. Lovely lady, thou shalt take thy glass.

LADY SQUEAMISH Ugh. Good murder, I had rather you had offered me a toad.   500

SIR NOBLE CLUMSY Then Malagene, here's a health to my lady cousin's Pelion upon Ossa.°

Drinks and breaks glass

LADY SQUEAMISH Lord, dear Mr Malagene, what's that?

MALAGENE A certain place, madam, in Greece much talked of by the ancients. The noble gentleman is well read.   505

LADY SQUEAMISH Nay, he is an ingenious person, I'll assure you.

SIR NOBLE CLUMSY Now, lady bright, I am wholly thy slave. Give me thy hand. I'll go straight and begin my grandmother's kissing dance,° but first design me the private honour of thy lip.

LADY SQUEAMISH Nay, fie, Sir Noble! How I hate you now! For   510 shame, be not so rude. I'll swear you are quite spoiled. Get you gone, you good-natured toad you.

Exeunt

3.1

[*The ordinary*]°

Enter Goodvile, a little heated

GOODVILE What a damned, chicken-brained fellow am I grown? If I
but dip my bill,° I am giddy. Now am I as hot-headed with my bare
two bottles as a drunken prentice on a holiday. Truman marries
Victoria—that's resolved on, and so one care is over. But then
Camilla: how I shall get possession of her? Well, my mind misgives   5
me I shall do something may call my discretion in question, and yet
I can't avoid it. Camilla I do love, and must have her, come what
will on't. And no time so fit to begin the enterprise as this; she may
make a good wife for Valentine, for all that.

    Music [offstage]. Enter Truman, Valentine

Fie, gentlemen! Without the ladies? Did you quit champagne for this?   10
Faith, I begin to despair of you and doubt you are grown as weak
lovers as drinkers.

TRUMAN Goodvile, thou hast no conscience. A decayed cavalier
captain° that drinks journey-work under a deputy lieutenant° in
the country is not able to keep thee company. Two bottles, as I take   15
it, is no such trifling matter.

GOODVILE O, but I hate to be baulked, and a friend that leaves me at
two bottles is as unkind as a mistress that jilts me when I thought I
had made sure of the business. But, gallants, how stand the affairs
of love? Truman, is Victoria kind? I question not your friendship in   20
the matter, but trust the honour of my family in your hands.

VALENTINE (*aside*) He little thinks Truman is informed of all, and no
longer a stranger on what score he is so wondrous civil. But I am
mistaken, if he be behind with him in kindness long.

TRUMAN A pox on't, I am afraid this marriage will never agree with   25
me; methinks the very thought on't goes a little against my stomach.
Like a young thief, though I have some itching to be at it, yet I am
loath to venture what may follow.

GOODVILE Well, I'll go in and better prepare Victoria; in the meantime,
believe it only my ambition to be as well allied in blood as friendship   30
to so good and generous a person as Truman.

    [*Exit Goodvile*]

TRUMAN What a damned creature man is! Valentine, didst thou
believe this fellow could be a villain?

VALENTINE I must confess, it something surprises me; he might have
found out a fitter person to put his mistress upon than his friend.   35
But how the devil got you the knowledge of it?

TRUMAN Faith, I'll tell thee; for I think I am no way obliged to
conceal it: his wife, even his very wife, told me all.

VALENTINE I begin to suspect that Mrs Goodvile has no ill opinion of
you. I observed something but now very obliging towards you.   40
Besides, when a woman begins to betray her husband's secrets, 'tis
a certain sign she has a mind to communicate very important ones
of her own.

TRUMAN Valentine, no more of that, though it would be a rare
revenge to make a cuckold of this smiling rogue.   45

VALENTINE 'Tis fifty times better than cutting his throat; that were to
do him more honour than he deserves.

     Enter Malagene

MALAGENE Ha, ha, ha, the rarest sport. Jack Truman, Ned Valentine.

TRUMAN Why, what's the matter? Where?

MALAGENE Yonder's my rogue of a knight, as drunk as a porter; and   50
faith, Jack, I am but little better.

VALENTINE Dear sir, and what of all this?

MALAGENE Why, with a bottle under his arm and a beer-glass in
his hand, I set him full drive at my Lady Squeamish, for nothing
else but to make mischief, Ned, nothing else in the world; for   55
everybody knows I am the worst-natured fellow breathing. 'Tis my
way of wit.

VALENTINE Do you love nobody then?

MALAGENE No, not I. Yes, a pox on't, I love you well enough because
ye are a rogue I have known a good while. Though, should I take   60
the least prejudice against you, I could not afford you a good word
behind your back, for my heart.

TRUMAN Sir, we are much obliged to you. [*Aside to Valentine*] 'Tis a
sign the rogue is drunk that he speaks truth.

MALAGENE I tell you what I did t'other day. Faith, 'tis as good a jest as   65
ever you heard.

VALENTINE Pray, sir, do.

MALAGENE Why, walking along, a lame fellow followed me and asked
my charity, which, by the way, was a pretty proposition to me.°
Being in one of my witty, merry fits, I asked him how long he had   70
been in that condition. The poor fellow shook his head and told me
he was born so. But how d'ye think I served him?

VALENTINE Nay, the devil knows.

MALAGENE I showed my parts, I think; for I tripped up both his wooden legs and walked off gravely about my business. 75

TRUMAN And this, you say, is your way of wit?

MALAGENE Ay, altogether this and mimicry. I am a very good mimic: I can act Punchinello, Scaramouchio, Harlequin, Prince Prettyman,° or anything. I can act the rumbling of a wheelbarrow.

VALENTINE The rumbling of a wheelbarrow? 80

MALAGENE Ay, the rumbling of a wheelbarrow, so I say. Nay, more than that, I can act a sow and pigs, sausages a-broiling, a shoulder of mutton a-roasting. I can act a fly in a honey-pot.

TRUMAN That indeed must be the effect of very curious observation.

MALAGENE No, hang it. I never make it my business to observe 85 anything. [*Disdainfully*] That is mechanic. But all this I do; you shall see me if you will. But here comes her ladyship and Sir Noble.

Enter Lady Squeamish and Sir Noble Clumsy

LADY SQUEAMISH O dear Mr Truman, rescue me. Nay, Sir Noble, for heaven's sake! 90

SIR NOBLE CLUMSY I tell thee, lady, I must embrace thy lovely body. [*To Valentine*] Sir, do you know me? I am Sir Noble Clumsy. I am a rogue of an estate and live I—do you want any money? I have fifty pound.

VALENTINE Nay, good Sir Noble, none of your generosity, we beseech 95 you. The lady, the lady, Sir Noble.

SIR NOBLE CLUMSY Nay, 'tis all one to me if you won't take it. There it is. Hang money; my father was an alderman.

MALAGENE 'Tis pity good guineas should be spoiled. Sir Noble, by your leave. (*Picks 'em up*) 100

SIR NOBLE CLUMSY But, sir, you will not keep my money?

MALAGENE O, hang money, sir. Your father was an alderman.

SIR NOBLE CLUMSY Well, get thee gone for an arch-wag. I do but sham all this while. But, by dad, he's pure company.

TRUMAN Was there ever such a blockhead! Now has he nevertheless 105 a mighty opinion of himself and thinks all this wit and pretty discourse.

SIR NOBLE CLUMSY Lady, once more I say be civil and come kiss me. I shall ravish else; I shall ravish mightily.

VALENTINE Well done, Sir Noble. To her, never spare. 110

LADY SQUEAMISH I may be even with you, though, for all this,

Mr Valentine.—Nay, dear Sir Noble. Mr Truman, I'll swear he'll
put me into fits.

SIR NOBLE CLUMSY No, but let me salute the hem of thy garment.
(*Kneels*) Wilt thou marry me?   115

MALAGENE Faith, madam, do. Let me make the match.

LADY SQUEAMISH Let me die, Mr Malagene, you are a strange man,
and I'll swear have a great deal of wit. Lord, why don't you write?

MALAGENE Write? I thank your ladyship for that with all my heart.
No, I have a finger in a lampoon or so sometimes; that's all.   120

TRUMAN But he can act.

LADY SQUEAMISH I'll swear and so he does, better than anyone
upon our theatres. I have seen him. O the English comedians are
nothing, not comparable to the French or Italian;° besides, we want
poets.°   125

SIR NOBLE CLUMSY Poets! Why, I am a poet. I have written three acts
of a play and have named it already. 'Tis to be a tragedy.

LADY SQUEAMISH O cousin, if you undertake to write a tragedy,
take my counsel. Be sure to say soft melting tender things in it
that may be moving, and make your ladies' characters virtuous,   130
whatever you do.

SIR NOBLE CLUMSY Moving? Why, I can never read it myself but it
makes me laugh; well, 'tis the prettiest plot and so full of waggery.

LADY SQUEAMISH O ridiculous!

MALAGENE But knight, the title; knight, the title.   135

SIR NOBLE CLUMSY Why let me see. 'Tis to be called *The Merry
Conceits of Love; or The Life and Death of the Emperor Charles the
Fifth, with the humours of his dog, Bobadillo.*°

MALAGENE Ha, ha, ha.

VALENTINE But Sir Noble, this sounds more like a comedy.   140

SIR NOBLE CLUMSY O, but I have resolved it shall be a tragedy
because Bobadillo's to be killed in the play. Comedy! No, I scorn to
write comedy. I know several that can squirt comedy.° I'll tell you
more of this when I am sober.

LADY SQUEAMISH But dear Mr Malagene, won't you let us see you   145
act a little something of Harlequin? I'll swear you do it so naturally,
it makes me think I am at the Louvre or Whitehall° all the time.
    Malagene acts
O Lord, don't; don't neither. I'll swear, you'll make me burst. Was
there ever anything so pleasant?

TRUMAN [*aside*] Was ever anything so affected and ridiculous? Her 150
whole life surely is a continued scene of impertinence. What a

damned creature is a decayed woman with all the exquisite silliness
and vanity of her sex, yet none of the charms!

    Malagene speaks in Punchinello's voice°

LADY SQUEAMISH O Lord, that, that—that is a pleasure intolerable.
Well, let me die if I can hold out any longer. Pray, Mr Malagene,   155
how long have you been in love with Mrs Tawdry the actress?

MALAGENE (*in his own voice aloud*) Ever since your ladyship has been
off from the hooks with Mr Valentine.

LADY SQUEAMISH Uh, Gud, I always thought Mr Malagene had been
better bred than to upbraid me with any such base thing to my face,   160
whatever he might say of me behind my back. But there is no
honour, no civility in the world; that I am satisfied of.

VALENTINE Can your ladyship take anything ill from Mr Malagene?
A woman should bear with the unlucky jerks° of her buffoon or
coxcomb as well as with the ill manners of her monkey sometimes.   165
The fools and rascals your sex delights in ought to have the privilege
of saying, as well as they have of doing, anything.

LADY SQUEAMISH Which you men of wit—as you think yourselves—
are very angry you should be debarred of. Lord, what pity 'tis your
good parts should be your misfortune.   170

VALENTINE Ay, madam; I feel the curse of it—I who had just sense
enough to fall in love with so much beauty and merit, yet could not
be able to keep the paradise I was so happily possessed of.

LADY SQUEAMISH This malice and ill-nature shall not serve your
turn. I shall know all your proceedings and intrigues with Camilla,   175
and be revenged on your love to her for all the affronts and injuries
you have done to mine.

    Enter Caper and Saunter

CAPER O dear madam, we're utterly undone for want of your
ladyship's company, I'll vow. Madam Goodvile is coming with the
fiddles to wait on you here. (*Cuts backward*)°   180

SIR NOBLE CLUMSY Sir, are you a dancing master?° You are very
nimble, methinks.

CAPER Ay, sir; I hate to stand still. But, Sir Noble, I thought you had
known me. I doubt you may be a little overtaken;° faith, dear heart,
I am glad to see thee so merry.   185

SIR NOBLE CLUMSY Yes, I do love dearly to be drunk once a year or
so; 'tis good for my bodily health. But do you never drink?

CAPER No, Sir Noble. That is not my province, you know. I mind
dancing altogether.°

SIR NOBLE CLUMSY [*to Saunter*] Nor you? Can't you drink, ha?   190

SAUNTER No, I make love and sing to ladies.

SIR NOBLE CLUMSY Whores to my knowledge, errant, rank, common whores. A pox on your woman of quality that you carried me to in the Mall.

TRUMAN Why, what was the matter, Sir Noble?   195

SIR NOBLE CLUMSY By yea and by nay,° a foul, overgrown strumpet, with a running bawd° instead of a waiting-woman, a great deal of paint, variety of old clothes, and nothing to eat. [*Lapses into a drunken stupor*]

LADY SQUEAMISH O dear, let me die if that was not extravagantly   200 pleasant.

    [*Exit Lady Squeamish*]

TRUMAN I believe Sir Noble is much in the right; for I never came near these giddy, intriguing blockheads, but they were talking of love and ladies, nor ever met with a hackney stripping whore° that did not know 'em.   205

CAPER Ned Valentine, I have a kindness to beg of you.

VALENTINE Sir, you may command me anything.

CAPER Why, you must know I am in love with Camilla.

VALENTINE Very good.

CAPER Now I would have you speak to Frank Goodvile not to make   210 love to her as he does; i' faith, I can't bear it. For, to tell you the truth on't, I intend to marry her. I catched him at it but now. Faith, it made my heart ache, never stir if it did not.

VALENTINE In troth, sir, 'tis very uncivil.

    Exit Caper and Saunter

Truman, this Goodvile has a mind to oblige us both: he's providing   215 a wife for me too as fast as he can. Camilla's his quarry now, I understand, and by that time he has played as fair a game with her as he has done with your mistress Victoria, I may stand fair to put in for the rubbers.°

TRUMAN Valentine, thou art upon too sure grounds for him there;   220 Camilla has both too much wit and virtue, and each with as little affectation as the other.

VALENTINE Jack, after this I cannot but be very free with you; I know there is some love hatching between you and his wife. Both our revenge lies in thy hands, and if thou dost not thyself and me   225 justice, I'll disown thee forever.

    Enter Goodvile

TRUMAN See where he comes with a heart as gay and light, as if there were nothing but honesty in it.

GOODVILE (*sings*)

>   *When Beauty can't move, and our passions grow cold,*
>   *Wine still keeps its charms, and we drink when we're cold.*   230

Jack Truman, yonder have I and Victoria been laughing at thee till
we were weary. She swears thou art so very modest, she would not
for all the world marry thee for fear of spoiling that virtue.

TRUMAN Nay, then I doubt I have lost her forever; for if she complains
of my modesty, she has found a fault which I never thought I had   235
been guilty of before.

GOODVILE But that is a quality which, though they hate never so
much in a gallant, they are apt for many reasons to value in a
husband. Fear not. Dissimulation is the natural adjunct of their
sex; and I would no more despair of a woman, though she swore she   240
hated me, than I would believe her though she swore she loved me.

>   *Enter Lady Squeamish, Caper, Saunter, Malagene,*
>   *Mrs Goodvile, Camilla, and Victoria with the fiddles*

LADY SQUEAMISH O a country dance, a country dance! Mr Caper,
where are you? You shall dance with madam Camilla. Mr Saunter,
wait on Victoria. [*Curtsies*] Mr Goodvile, your humble servant.
Dear Mr Truman, won't you oblige me? Madam Goodvile.° Ha,   245
ha, ha. I'll swear, I had utterly forgotten Mr Valentine.

VALENTINE Your ladyship knows me to be a civil person. If you
please, I'll keep good orders.°

>   *Caper, Saunter, Goodvile, and Truman take out the women*°

MALAGENE Faith, Ned, do, and I'll keep the music in tune. [*To the*
fiddlers] Away with it. [*Music and dancing begins*] Hold, hold! What   250
insufferable rascals are these? Why, ye scurvy, thrashing, scraping
mongrels; ye make a worse noise than cramped° hedge-hogs! An
old, gouty dancing master that teaches to dance with his spectacles
on makes better music on his cracked kit.° 'Sdeath, ye dogs, can't
you play now as a gentleman sings! Ha!   255

GOODVILE Sir, will you never leave this nauseous humour of yours? I
can never be with you, but I must be forced to use you ill or endure
the perpetual torment of your impertinence.

MALAGENE Well, sir; I ha' done, sir; I ha' done. But 'tis very hard a
man can't be permitted to show his parts. 'Sdeath, Frank, dost thou   260
think thou understand'st music?

GOODVILE Sir, I understand it so well, that I won't have it interrupted
in my company by you.

MALAGENE I am glad on't with all my heart; I never thought you

had understood anything before. I think there I was pretty even   265
with you.

GOODVILE Sauciness and ill manners are so much your province that
nothing but kicking is fit for you.

MALAGENE Sir, you may use your pleasure, but I care no more for
being kicked than you do for kicking. But prithee, Frank, why   270
should you be out of humour so? The devil take me if I shall not
give thee such a jerk presently will make thee angry indeed.

LADY SQUEAMISH Lord, Mr Goodvile, how can you be so ill-natured?
I'll swear Mr Malagene is in the right. These people have no
manners in the least; play not at all to dancing. But, I vow, he   275
himself sings a tune extreme prettily.

GOODVILE [aside] Death, hell, and the devil! How am I teased? I shall
have no opportunity to pursue my business with Camilla. I must
remove this troublesome coxcomb, and that perhaps may put stop
at least to her impertinence.   280

LADY SQUEAMISH Mr Truman, Mr Goodvile, and ladies, I beseech
you do me the favour to hear Mr Malagene sing a Scotch song. I'll
swear I am a strange admirer of Scotch songs. They are the prettiest,
soft, melting, gentle, harmless things.

SAUNTER By dad, and so they are. (Sings) 'In January last'° —   285

VALENTINE Deliver us! A Scotch song! I hate it worse than a Scotch
bagpipe, which even the bears are grown weary of and have better
music.° I wish I could see her ladyship dance a Scotch jig to one
of 'em.

MALAGENE I must needs beg your ladyship's pardon; I have forgotten   290
the last new Scotch song. But, if you please, I'll entertain you with
one of another nature, which I am apt to believe will be as pleasant.

LADY SQUEAMISH Let me die, Mr Malagene, you are eternally
obliging me.

           Malagene sings an Irish cronon°

MALAGENE Well, madam? How like you it, madam, ha?   295

LADY SQUEAMISH Really, it is very pretty now—the prettiest, odd,
out-of-the-way notes. Don't you admire it strangely?

MALAGENE I'll assure your ladyship, I learnt it of an Irish musician
that's lately come over,° and intend to present it to an author of my
acquaintance to put it in his next play.   300

LADY SQUEAMISH Ha, ha. Mr Valentine, I would have you learn it for
a serenade to your mistress. Ha, ha, ha.

VALENTINE My page, madam, is docible and has a pretty voice; he

shall learn it, if you please, and if your ladyship has any further
service for him°—   305

LADY SQUEAMISH Ah Lord, wit, wit, wit, as I live! Come, let's dance.

TRUMAN Valentine, thou art something too rough. I am afraid her
ladyship will be revenged. I see mischief in her eyes. 'Tis safer
provoking a Lancashire witch° than an old mistress, and she as
violent in her malice too.   310

GOODVILE Malagene, a word with you; hark ye, come hither. (*Goes to
the door*)

MALAGENE Well, Frank, what's the business now? I am clearly for
mischief; shall I break the fiddles and turn the rascals out of doors?

GOODVILE No, sir, but I'll be so civil to turn you out of doors. Nay,   315
sir, no struggling. I have footmen within.

MALAGENE Whoo, prithee what's all this for? What a pox, I know
my lady well enough for a silly, affected, fantastical gypsy.° I did
all this but o' purpose to show her.° Let me alone; I'll abuse her
worse.   320

GOODVILE No, sir; but I'll take more care of your reputation and turn
you out to learn better manners. No resistance, as you tender your
ears, but be gone.

    Exit Malagene

So, he's gone, and now I hope I may have some little time to myself.
Fiddles, strike up.   325

    *Truman and Mrs Goodvile, Saunter and Victoria, Goodvile and
    Camilla dance*

TRUMAN Thus, madam, you freely enjoy all the pleasures of a single
life, and ease yourself of that wretched formal austerity which
commonly attends a married one.

MRS GOODVILE Who would not hate to be one of those simpering
saints that enter into marriage as they would go into a nunnery,   330
where they keep very strict to their devotion for a while, but at last
turn as errant sinners as e'er they were?

TRUMAN Marriages indeed should be repaired to° as commonly
nunneries are: for handsome retreats and conveniences, not for
prisons, where those that cannot live without 'em may be safe, yet   335
sometimes venture too abroad a little.

MRS GOODVILE But never, sir, without a lady abbess or a confessor at
least.

TRUMAN Might I, madam, have the honour to be your confessor, I
should be very indulgent and lavish of absolution to so pretty a   340
sinner.

MRS GOODVILE See, Mr Goodvile and Madam Camilla, I believe, are
at shrift° already.

TRUMAN And poor Ned Valentine looks as pensively as if all the sins
of the company were his own.   345

MRS GOODVILE See, Mr Caper, your mistress.

CAPER Ha, Camilla! [*To Goodvile*] Sir, your servant. [*Bows*] May I
have the honour to lead this lady a coranto?

GOODVILE No, sir. [*Aside*] Death! Surely I have fools that rest and
harbour in my house, and they are a worse plague than bugs and   350
moths. Shall I never be quiet?

VALENTINE Sir Noble, Sir Noble, have a care of your mistress! Do
you see there?

SIR NOBLE CLUMSY (*wakes and rises*) Hum. Ha. Where? O!

SAUNTER [*to Victoria*] Nay, faith, madam, Harry Caper's as pretty 355
a fellow. 'Tis the wittiest rogue. He and I laugh at all the town.
[*To Caper*] Harry, I shall marry her.

SIR NOBLE CLUMSY Marry, sir! Whom will you marry, sir? You lie.
Sweetheart, come along with me; I'll marry thee myself presently.

VICTORIA You, Sir Noble! What d'ye mean? (*She squeaks*)   360

SIR NOBLE CLUMSY Mean? Honourably, honourably; I mean
honourably. These are rogues, my dear, arrant rogues. Come along.
        Exeunt Sir Noble Clumsy and Victoria

CAPER Ha, Saunter.

SAUNTER Ay, Caper. Ha! Let us follow this drunken knight.

CAPER I'faith, and so I will. I don't value him this. (*Cuts*)   365
        Exeunt Caper and Saunter

LADY SQUEAMISH Ha, ha, ha! Well, I'll swear, my cousin Sir Noble is
a strange pleasant creature. [*To Mrs Goodvile*] Dear madam, let us
follow and see the sport. Mr Truman, will you walk? O dear, 'tis
violent hot.
        Exeunt Lady Squeamish, Mrs Goodvile, and Truman

VALENTINE I'll withdraw too and at some distance observe how   370
matters are carried between Goodvile and Camilla.
        Exit Valentine

GOODVILE Are you then, madam, resolved to ruin me? Why should
all that stock of beauty be thrown away on one that can never be
able to deserve the gleanings of it? I love you—

CAMILLA And all the sex besides. That ever any man should take such 375
pains to forswear himself to no purpose!

GOODVILE Nay, then there's hopes yet. If you pretend to doubt the truth of my love, 'tis a sign you have some inclinations at least that are my friends.

CAMILLA [*aside*] This Goodvile, I see, is one of those spruce, polished fools, who have so good an opinion of themselves, that they think no woman can resist 'em, nor man of better sense despise 'em. I'll seem at present to comply and try how far 'twill pass upon him.

GOODVILE Well, madam, have you considered on't? Will the stone in your heart give way?

CAMILLA No, sir. 'Tis full as firm and hard as ever 'twas.

GOODVILE And I may then go hang, or drown, or do what I will with myself? Ha?

CAMILLA At your own discretion, sir, though I should be loath to see so proper a handsome gentleman come to an ill end.

GOODVILE Good, charitable creature! But, madam, know I can be revenged on you for this, and my revenge shall be to love you still; gloat° on and loll after you where ere I see you; in all public meetings haunt and vex you; write lamentable sonnets on you and so plain, that every fop that sings 'em shall know 'tis you I mean.

CAMILLA So, sir, this is something.° Could not you as well have told me you had been very ill-natured at first? You did not know how far° it might have wrought upon me; besides, 'tis a thousand times better than vowing and bowing, and making a deal of love and noise, and all to as little purpose as anything you say else.

GOODVILE Right exquisite tyrant! I'll set a watch and guard so strict upon you, you shall not entertain a well-dressed fool in private, but I'll know it; then, in a lewd lampoon, publish it to the town till you shall repent and curse the hour you ever saw me.

CAMILLA Ah, would I could, ill-natured, cruel man!

GOODVILE Ha, how's that? Am I then mistaken? And have I wronged you all this while? I ask ten thousand pardons, cursed, damned sot that I was! I have ruined myself now forever.

CAMILLA Well, sir, should I now forgive you all, could you consent to wrong your lady so far? You have not yet been married a full year. How must I then suspect your love to me that can so soon forget your faith to her?

GOODVILE O, Madam, what do you do? The name of a wife to a man in love is worse than cold water in a fever. 'Tis enough to strike the distemper to my heart and kill me quite. 'My lady', quoth a!

CAMILLA Besides, Valentine, you know, is your friend.

GOODVILE I grant it, he is so. A friend is a thing I love to eat and

drink and laugh withal. Nay more, I would on a good occasion lose
my life for my friend, but not my pleasure. Say where and when it
shall be.   420

CAMILLA Never. I dare not.

GOODVILE You must by and by when 'tis a little darker, in the left-hand
walk in the lowest garden.

CAMILLA I won't promise you; can't you trust my good nature?

GOODVILE Charming creature, I do. Now if I can but make up the   425
match between Truman and Victoria, my hopes are completed.

CAMILLA Haste, haste! Away, sir; I see Valentine coming.

Exit Goodvile. Enter Valentine

VALENTINE Madam, you are extremely merry; I am glad Mr Goodvile
has left you in so good a humour.

CAMILLA Ay sir, and what may please you more, he is parted hence in   430
as good a humour as he has left me here.

Enter Lady Squeamish, Bridget at the door [eavesdropping]

LADY SQUEAMISH [*aside*] Valentine and Camilla alone together! Now
for an opportunity to be revenged! Ah, how I love malice!

VALENTINE Ungratefullest of women!

CAMILLA Foolishest of men! Can you be so very silly to be jealous?   435
For I find you are so. What have you ever observed since first
your knowledge of me that might persuade you I should ever grow
fond of a man, as notoriously false to all women, as you are
unworthy of me?

LADY SQUEAMISH (*aside*) Has Valentine been false to her too? Nay,   440
then there is some pleasure left yet, to think I am not the only
woman that has suffered by his baseness.

VALENTINE What then, I'll warrant you were alone together
half-an-hour only for a little harmless raillery or so, an honour I
could never obtain without hard suit and humble supplication.   445

CAMILLA Alas, how very politic you are grown! You would pretend
displeasure to try your power. No, I shall henceforth think you
never had a good opinion of me, but that your love was at first as
ill-grounded as your fantastical jealousy is now.

VALENTINE What specious pretence can you urge? I know a woman   450
can never be without one. Come, I am easy and good-natured,
willing to believe and be deceived. What, not a word?

CAMILLA Though I can hardly descend to satisfy your distrust, for
which I hardly value you° and almost hate you; yet to torment you
farther, know I did discourse with him, and of love too; nay more,   455
granted him an appointment, but one I never meant to keep, and

promised it only to get rid of him. This is more than I am obliged to
tell you, but that I wanted such an opportunity as this to check your
pretences, which I found grew too unruly to be kept at a distance.

VALENTINE Though I had some reason to be in doubt, yet this true   460
resentment and just proceeding has convinced me. For Goodvile is
a man I have little reason to trust, as will appear hereafter, and 'twas
my knowledge of his baseness made me run into so mean a distrust
of you. But forgive me this, and when I fail again, discard me
forever.   465

CAMILLA Yes. But the next time I shall happen to discourse with a
gentleman in private, I shall have you listening at the door or
eavesdropping under the window. What, distrust your friend, the
honourable, worthy Mr Goodvile? Fie, how can you be so
ungenerous?   470

VALENTINE There is not such another hypocrite in the world. He
never made love but to delude, nor friendship but for his ends.
Even his own kinswoman and charge, Victoria, he has long since
corrupted, and now would put her on his best friend, Truman, for
a wife.   475

CAMILLA I cannot but laugh to think how easily he swallowed the
cheat. He could not be more transported at possession than he was
with expectation, and he went away in a greater triumph than if
he had conquered the Indies.

VALENTINE Where did you promise him?   480

CAMILLA In the left-hand walk in the lower garden.

LADY SQUEAMISH (*aside*) So, in the left-hand walk in the lower
garden. I heard that. But Mr Valentine, you may chance to meet
another there. Let me die, this is pleasant.

VALENTINE And when?   485

CAMILLA Anon, when it begins to grow dark.

LADY SQUEAMISH [*aside*] Enough. I know the time and place; and,
Madam Camilla, I shall make bold to cheat you of your lover
tonight. Alas, poor, inconsiderable creature. How this makes me
loathe her!   490

CAMILLA Now would this news be more welcome to her ladyship,
Madam Squeamish, than a new fashion, a new dance, or a new
song. How many visits would she make on the occasion! Not a
family in town would be at rest for her till she had made it a jest,
from the Mother of the Maids to the attorney's wife in Holborn.°   495

VALENTINE But for some private reasons I would have kept it from
her and from Madam Goodvile too. There are affairs to be carried

on tonight, which the least accident may interrupt. Besides, I have
thought upon't and will so contrive the matter that Goodvile shall
keep his assignation, and her ladyship herself supply the place of   500
the much expected charming Camilla.

CAMILLA But would you, sir, do me such an injury as to make me
break my word with Mr Goodvile? That were inhuman.

VALENTINE Good, conscionable creature, have patience, and don't
you think of paying debts too fast; there's an account yet between   505
you and I which must be made even, and I think I had best secure it
now I have you in my custody.

CAMILLA Ay, but sir, if I part with anything, I shall expect to have
something to show for't.

VALENTINE Nay, if I don't offer as lusty security and conditions as   510
any man, let me lose all I lay claim to; that's fair.
     Exeunt Valentine and Camilla

LADY SQUEAMISH So, are they gone? Now let me but live if this
intrigue be not extremely surprising. Bridget, go home and fetch
me the morning-gown I had last made in imitation of Camilla's, for
perhaps I shall go a-masquerading tonight, or it may be not, but   515
fetch it nevertheless.

BRIDGET Madam, won't the other serve? You may remember you left
it at my Lady Foplove's t'other night; that's nearer.

LADY SQUEAMISH Impertinent creature! And wouldst thou have me
appear in it twice? Do as I bid you, I say; andd'ye hear, bring me a   520
mask with an amber bead,° for I fear I may have fits tonight.

BRIDGET [*aside*] I never knew her without fantastical ones, I am sure,
for they cost me many a weary errand.
     Exit Bridget. Enter Victoria

LADY SQUEAMISH O my dear Victoria, the most unlooked-for
happiness! The pleasantest accident! The strangest discovery! The   525
very thought of it were enough to cure melancholy. Valentine and
Camilla, Camilla and Valentine. Ha, ha, ha.

VICTORIA Dear madam, what is it so transports you?

LADY SQUEAMISH Nay, 'tis too precious to be communicated. Hold
me, hold me, or I shall die with laughter. Ha, ha, ha. Camilla and   530
Valentine, Valentine and Camilla. Ha, ha, ha. O dear, my heart's
broke.

VICTORIA Good madam, refrain your mirth a little, and let me know
the story, that I may have a share in it.

LADY SQUEAMISH An assignation! An assignation tonight in the   535
lower garden. By strong good fortune, I overheard it all just now;

but to think on the pleasant consequence that will happen, drives
me into an excess of joy beyond all sufferance.

VICTORIA Madam, in all probability the pleasantest consequence is
like to be theirs, if anybody's, and I cannot guess how it should   540
touch your ladyship in the least.

LADY SQUEAMISH O Lord, how can you be so dull? Why, at the very
hour and place appointed will I meet Valentine in Camilla's stead
before she can be there herself; then when she comes, expose her
infamy to all the world, till I have thoroughly° revenged myself for   545
all the base injuries her lover has done to me.

VICTORIA But madam, can you endure to be so malicious?

LADY SQUEAMISH That, that's the dear pleasure of the thing; for, I
vow, I'd sooner die ten thousand deaths, if I thought I should
hazard the least temptation to the prejudice of my honour.   550

VICTORIA But why should your ladyship run into the mouth of danger?
Who knows what scurvy, lurking devil may stand in readiness and
seize your virtue before you are aware of him?

LADY SQUEAMISH Temptation? No, I'd have you know I scorn
temptation. I durst trust myself in a convent amongst a kennel of   555
crammed° friars. Besides, that ungrateful, ill-bred fellow, Valentine,
is my mortal aversion: more odious to me than foul weather on a
May day, or ill smell in a morning.

VICTORIA Nay, now madam, you are too violent.

LADY SQUEAMISH Too violent! I would not keep a waiting-woman   560
that should commend any one thing about him. Dear Victoria, urge
nothing in his behalf, for if you do, you lose my friendship
forever—though I swear he was a fine person once, before he was
spoiled.

VICTORIA (aside) I am sure your ladyship had the best share in his   565
spoiling then.

LADY SQUEAMISH No, were I inclined to entertain addresses, I assure
I need not want for servants. For, I swear, I am so perplexed with
billets-doux every day, I know not which way to turn myself.
Besides, there is no fidelity, no honour in mankind. O dear Victoria,   570
whatever you do, never let love come near your heart. Though
really I think true love is the greatest pleasure in the world.

VICTORIA Would I had never known love. My honour had not then
lain at the mercy of so ungrateful a wretch as Goodvile, who now
has certainly abandoned and forgotten me.   575

LADY SQUEAMISH Well, certainly I am the most unsteady, restless,
humoursome woman breathing. Now am I so transported at the

thoughts of what I have designed, that I long till the hour comes, with more impatience than—I'll swear I know not what to say. Dear Victoria, ten thousand adieus. Wish me good success. Yet, now I think on't, I'll stay a little longer—I'll swear I must not neither— well, I'll go—no, I'll stay—well, I am resolved neither to stand still, sit still, nor lie still, nor have one thought at rest till the business be over. I'll swear, I am a strange creature.   580

Exit Lady Squeamish

VICTORIA Farewell, whirligig.   585

Enter Goodvile

GOODVILE [*aside*] Victoria here! To meet with an old mistress when a man is in pursuit of a fresh one is a worse omen than a hare in a journey. I'll step aside this way till she's past me. So, farewell, fubb.° (*Makes mouths*)

Exit Victoria

Now for the lovely, kind, yielding Camilla! How I long for the happy   590
hour. Swelling burning breasts, dying eyes, balmy lips, trembling joints, millions of kisses, and unspeakable joys wait for me.

Enter Truman and Valentine

Well, gentlemen, now you have left the ladies, I hope there may be room near your hearts for a bottle or two.

TRUMAN Dear Goodvile, thou art too powerful to be denied anything.   595
'Tis a fine cool evening, and a swift glass or two now were seasonable and refreshing to wash away the toil and fatigue of the day.

VALENTINE After a man has been disturbed with the public impertinences and follies he meets withal abroad, he ought to recompense himself with a friend and a bottle in private at night.   600

GOODVILE Spoken like men that deserve the life you enjoy. I'll in before and put all things in readiness.

Exit Goodvile

VALENTINE This worthy person for his honesty and sobriety would have made a very good Dutch burgomaster.° But he is as damnable an English friend and gentleman as one would wish to meet withal.   605

TRUMAN Valentine, thou art too much concerned at him. Methinks Camilla's justice, and the pleasant cheat she has put upon him, should rather make thee despise and laugh at him as I do.

VALENTINE Truman, thou indeed hast reason. And when I shall know the happy success of the revenge thou hast in store for him,   610
I may do myself and him that justice as scorn him, but am too angry yet.

TRUMAN Then, to give thee ease—for I dare trust thee—know this

very night I also have an assignation with his wife in the grotto at
the upper end of the garden, the opposite walk to that where he 615
expects to meet Camilla.

VALENTINE Then I am at rest. Let's in. I have nothing else to do but
take care so to finish him, as that you shall fear no interruption. At
least he will be so full of his expectation of Camilla that he'll never
dream in what posture his own affairs stand in another place. 620

TRUMAN Away then. And may good luck attend us. Ere yet two hours
are past, his wife's my own methinks already in that secure, dark,
private grotto,

> Close in my arms, and languishing she lies,
> With dying looks, short breath, and wishing eyes; 625
> And the supine dull cuckold nothing spies.

Exeunt

4.1

Night-garden

Enter Goodvile at one door. Mrs Goodvile, and Lettice following her, at the other

GOODVILE So, I think I came off in good time. Hold! Now for Camilla. By Jove, I think I am little better than drunk. Ha! Who's there? Victoria, as I live; nay, it must be she, as I said before. The poor gypsy's jealous—has had some intimation of my appointment with Camilla. I'll loof° off and observe which way she steers.   5

MRS GOODVILE Lettice, I fear that's Mr Goodvile's voice. Whatever you do, if any cross accident happens, be sure you call me Victoria.

GOODVILE Ay, ay, 'tis Victoria. Vigilant devil! But I'll take this way and wait at the lower end of the walk.

　　　　[Exit Goodvile]

MRS GOODVILE Lettice, look well round you that nobody see us, and   10
then follow me.

　　　　[Exit Mrs Goodvile and Lettice]. Enter Truman

TRUMAN Thus far all is well. How I pity poor Valentine! Yonder is he plying bumpers, as they call 'em, more furiously than a foreign minister that comes into England to drink for the honour of his country. I have waited something long, though; who comes here?   15

　　　　Enter Lettice

LETTICE 'Tis I, sir, your servant, Lettice.

TRUMAN My little, good-natured agent, is it you? Where's thy lady? She's too cruel to let a poor lover languish here so long in expectation. It looks as if she rather meant to make a trial of my patience than my love. Is she coming?   20

LETTICE Well, I swear—as my Lady Squeamish says—you are a strange creature. But I'll go and tell her. Though I'll vow I utterly disown having any hand in this business; and if any ill comes of it, 'tis none of my fault.

TRUMAN No, no, not in the least. Prithee dispatch.   25

　　　　[Exit Lettice]

How's this! More company? Who comes there?

　　　　Enter Valentine

VALENTINE 'Tis I, Jack Truman, your friend Valentine.

TRUMAN My dear encourager of iniquity, what news? Where's Goodvile?

VALENTINE No matter for Goodvile; here comes your mistress.   30
　　　　Enter Mrs Goodvile [and Lettice]. Valentine retires

TRUMAN [*aside*] Now, now, now, what devil ails me? How I shall quake
and tremble.—Madam, dear madam, where are you?

MRS GOODVILE Mr Truman, is't your voice? Lettice, you may go in
again, if you will.
　　　　Exit Lettice
　Well, sir, I'll vow, sir, had it not been that I hate to break my word,   35
I would not have ventured abroad this cold damp evening for a
world.

TRUMAN I'll warrant you, madam, whilst you are in my possession,
no cold shall hurt you. Come, shall we withdraw to the grotto?

MRS GOODVILE Withdraw to the grotto? Bless me, sir! What do you   40
mean? I'll swear you make my heart ache.

TRUMAN O madam! I have the best cure for the passion of the heart in
the world. I have tried it, madam: 'tis *probatum.*° Come, come; let's
retire. [*She resists*] Do, make a disturbance and ruin yourself and
me, do!   45

MRS GOODVILE Nay, I'll swear, sir, you are insufferably rude. You had
best make a noise and alarm my husband, you had, for hang me, I
shall cry out.

TRUMAN No, no, I'm sure you won't complain before you are hurt,
and I'll use you so gently. Hark! Don't you hear? There's somebody   50
coming.

MRS GOODVILE Where, where, where? If we are seen, we are undone
forever. Well, I'll never give you such an advantage again.

TRUMAN I'm sure you would not, if I should let slip this. Come,
come; delays are dangerous, and I can endure 'em no longer.   55

MRS GOODVILE Ah Lord, you kill me! What will become of me?
Ah—
　　　　Truman carries her in. [Valentine comes forward]

VALENTINE Nay, faith, madam, your condition is something desperate, that's certain. 'Tis a pretty employment I am like to have here;
but it is for the fate of my friend and my revenge. And two dearer   60
arguments there cannot be to persuade me to anything.
　　　　Enter Malagene at some distance

MALAGENE So, Jack Truman and Madam Goodvile have ordered
matters pretty well; I'll say that for my kinswoman, she lays about
her handsomely, but certainly I hear another voice this way. I'll
withdraw once again; there may be more sport yet.   65
　　　　[*Exit Malagene*]

VALENTINE That should be Goodvile. I'll step behind this tree and
see how he and her ladyship behave themselves. This is like to be a
night of as civil business as I have known a great while.
  Enter Goodvile

GOODVILE Death and the devil! How that puny rogue Valentine has
soused me!° If I should have overstayed the time now and missed   70
of my appointment with Camilla. Truman is reeled home—that's
certain—and Valentine, I believe, has followed him by this time.
Camilla, dear, lovely, kind, tender, melting Camilla, where art thou?
  Enter Lady Squeamish

LADY SQUEAMISH That must be Valentine, nay, I am sure it is he.
How sneakingly will he look when he shall find his mistake; but I'll   75
take care, if possible, that no such thing shall happen, so mine be
the pleasure and Camilla's the scandal. I'll rush by him through the
walk into the wilderness. (*Runs across the walk*)

GOODVILE That must be she; how swiftly she flew along, as if she
feared to be too late, loosely attired and fit for joys! Now all the   80
power of love and good fortune direct me.
  Exit Goodvile

VALENTINE So, thanks to our stars, he is safe; though a pox on't,
methinks this dry pimping° is but a scurvy employment. Had I but
a sister or kinswoman of his to keep doing withal, there were some
comfort in it. But here comes Truman and the lady; I must not be   85
seen.
  Exit Valentine. Enter Truman and Mrs Goodvile

TRUMAN You shall not go. Come but back a little; I have something more to tell you that nearly concerns us both. Besides,
Mr Goodvile's in the garden, and if he should chance to meet us,
what excuse could we make to him?   90

MRS GOODVILE But will you promise me Victoria shall never rob me
of your heart? She does not deserve it, I am sure, half so well as I.

TRUMAN Kind, tender-hearted creature, I know it. Nor shall she
ever come so near it as to know that I have one. Alas, we talk too
long. (*Noise*) I hear company coming. We shall be surprised and   95
disappointed, and then I am undone.

MRS GOODVILE I'll swear you make me tremble—every joint of me.
What would you have me do?

TRUMAN See, see, who are yonder.
  *Exeunt Truman and Mrs Goodvile. Enter Goodvile and Lady
  Squeamish*

GOODVILE What a feast of delight have I had! Surely she was born   100 only to make me happy! Her natural and inexperienced tenderness exceeded practised charms. Dear, blest, lovely Camilla! O, my joys!

LADY SQUEAMISH Ha, ha, ha!

GOODVILE How's this? My Lady Squeamish? Death and the devil!

LADY SQUEAMISH Truly, sweet Mr Valentine, the same. Now, sir, I 105
hope—ugh, gad! Mr Goodvile!

GOODVILE Have I been mumbling° an old kite all this while instead of my young partridge? A pox o' my depraved palate that could distinguish no better.

LADY SQUEAMISH Lord, Mr Goodvile, what ails you? This was an 110
unexpected adventure; but, let me die, it is very pleasant. Ha, ha, ha.

GOODVILE A pox on the pleasures, and you too, I say.

LADY SQUEAMISH [aside] This malicious devil Camilla has over-reached me.—Well, Mr Goodvile, you are the worthiest person. Had I an only daughter, I durst trust her with you, you are so very 115
civil. Well, innocence is the greatest happiness in the world.

GOODVILE Right, madam, it is so, and you know we have been very innocent; done no harm in the world, not we.

LADY SQUEAMISH The censorious world, if they knew of this accident, I know would be apt enough to speak reproachfully; but so long as I 120
myself am satisfied in the integrity of my honour, the world is a thing I defy and scorn.

GOODVILE Very philosophically spoken. But madam, so long as the world is to be a stranger to our happiness, why should we deny ourselves the second pleasure of congratulation? 125

LADY SQUEAMISH Alas, alas, Mr Goodvile, you cannot say that you have had the least advantage over my frailty. Well, what might have happened if the strict severity of both our virtues had not secured us?

GOODVILE [aside] This affected impudence of hers is beyond all the 130
impertinence I ever knew her guilty of. Virtue with a pox! I think I have reason to know her pretty well, and the devil of any virtue found I about her.

LADY SQUEAMISH But dear sir, let us talk no more of it. Though I am extremely mistaken if I saw not Mr Valentine enter the garden 135
before me, and am as much mistaken if a lady was not with him too.

GOODVILE Hell and confusion! That must be Victoria. I thought indeed I saw her, but being hot-headed, and apprehending she came with a malicious design of discovering me, avoided her. False to me with Valentine? 140

LADY SQUEAMISH I'll swear, Mr Goodvile, I have long suspected an intrigue between you and Madam Victoria, and this jealousy has confirmed me, and I would not for all the world but have known it. Ha, ha, ha.

GOODVILE Death madam! This is beyond all sufferance. Disappointed and jilted by Camilla! Abused by Victoria—and with Valentine too, Truman's friend, whom I thought should have married her! Shame and infamy light upon the whole sex! May the best of 'em be ever suspected, and the most cautious always betrayed.

LADY SQUEAMISH Dear Mr Goodvile, be patient. Let me die, you are enough to frighten our whole sex from ever loving or trusting men again. Lord, I would not be poor Madam Victoria to gain an empire. I'll swear, if you are not more moderate, you'll discompose me strangely. How my heart beats!

GOODVILE Patience! Preach it to a galled lion. No, I am sure she is not far off, and I will find her—surprise her in the midst of her infamy and prostitution. 'Sdeath, madam, let me go.

LADY SQUEAMISH I will not part with you, you ill-natured creature. You shall not go. I vow, I'll cry a rape if you offer to stir. O my heart, here's Malagene.

Enter Malagene singing 'Frank, Frank, Frank, etc.'

MALAGENE Why, how now, Frank? What a pox, out of humour? Why, madam, what have you done to him; what have you done to him, madam? Lord, how he looks! Why Frank, I say, prithee bear up.

GOODVILE Hark, you dog, fool, coxcomb, hold that impertinent, impudent tongue of yours or I'll cut it out. 'Sdeath, you buffoon, I will.

MALAGENE No, but hark you, dear heart, good words, good words, do you hear, or I shall publish; by my soul, joy,° I shall.

GOODVILE How am I continually plagued with rogues and owls! I'll set my house o' fire rather than have it haunted and pestered by such vermin.

MALAGENE Faith, Frank, do. I have not seen a house o' fire this great while. It would be a pretty frolic. Prithee let us about it presently.

LADY SQUEAMISH Dear Mr Goodvile, you shall be persuaded. Don't run yourself into danger thus rashly.

GOODVILE Do you hear then, Monsieur Pimponio? As you expect to live a quiet hour, run in and call for some lights and return with 'em instantly.

MALAGENE Say no more, dear heart; I'll do't. If mischief comes not of this, the devil's in't. But dear Frank, stay till I come again; I'll be back in a trice. Take t'other turn with her ladyship into the wilderness°—or anything.

Exit Malagene

LADY SQUEAMISH Let me not live, this Mr Malagene is a very obliging person; and methinks, Mr Goodvile, you use him too severely.   185

GOODVILE I wish, madam, he may deserve that character of you. He is one of those worldlings you were speaking of, that are apt to talk reproachfully, and, I believe, knows all that has passed between us tonight, for he has a shrewd, discerning judgement in these matters.

LADY SQUEAMISH Lord, Mr Goodvile, what can he say of me? I defy   190
even envy itself to do me or my honour any prejudice, though I wish I had let this frolic alone tonight.

GOODVILE [*aside*] Frolic with a pox! If these be her frolics, what the devil is she when she is in earnest?

[*Enter Malagene with torch*]

O he returns with the lights. Look, who are these? By heaven, the   195
same.

Enter Truman and Mrs Goodvile

TRUMAN Gently, gently, madam, for fear of an ambuscade; I wonder I hear nothing from Ned Valentine since.

MRS GOODVILE See, see sir, here's Mr Goodvile. Haste, haste down the other walk, or we are ruined.   200

TRUMAN Fear not. Trust all to my conduct.

Exit Truman. As Mrs Goodvile is going away, Goodvile catches hold of her gown. She claps on her mask

GOODVILE Stay, Madam Victoria, nay you may stay; 'tis in vain to fly. I have discovered all your falsehood, I have. Was mine a passion to be thus abused? I, who have given you all my heart, perfidious, false woman! Is your lover too ashamed or afraid to show himself?   205
Where is he? Why comes he not forth?

Enter Truman

TRUMAN Here I am, sir.

GOODVILE Ha! Truman!

Mrs Goodvile gets loose and exits

TRUMAN Yes, sir, the same—ready both to acknowledge and justify my being here with Victoria, which I thought, sir, might have been   210
allowed without any offence to Mr Goodvile. That she is innocent as to anything on my part, I am ready with my sword to make good; but, sir, I wear it too to do my own honour justice, and to demand

of you on what grounds you appear so highly concerned for a woman you were pleased to commend to your friend for a wife.   215

GOODVILE Concerned, sir? Have I not reason to be concerned for the honour of my family? For a kinswoman under my charge to be abroad and alone with a gentleman at this unseasonable hour might alarm a man less tender of his reputation than I am.

TRUMAN Sir, this excuse won't serve my turn, nor am I so blind as not   220
to be sensible (which I before suspected) that Victoria has been long your mistress. A pox of the honour of your family. You had given her all your heart, you said, and your passion was not a thing to be thus abused. Nor, sir, is my honour.

GOODVILE No, but dear Jack Truman, thou art my friend.   225

TRUMAN You would have made me believe so indeed; but the daubing was too coarse and the artificial face appeared too plain.° One would have thought, sir, that you, who keep a general decoy° here for fools and coxcombs, might have found one to have recompensed a cast mistress withal, and not have endeavoured the betraying the   230
honour of a gentleman and your friend. But, sir, I am glad I have heard it from your own mouth. I hope it will not be esteemed much ill-nature in me, if worthy Mr Malagene and I join forces to publish a little, as he calls it.

MALAGENE Faith, Jack Truman, with all my heart. [*Aside*] Now I have   235
him on my side, I dare say anything. Frank Goodvile, pugh.

GOODVILE Sir, I shall require a better account of this hereafter.

LADY SQUEAMISH Lord, Mr Truman, what ails Mr Goodvile? How happened this difference? I'll swear, I am strangely surprised.

TRUMAN Your ladyship, I suppose, can best give an account how   240
matters are with him. I am apt to believe he has been very free with you.

LADY SQUEAMISH Dear sir, what do you mean? I'll swear, you are a scandalous person.

GOODVILE Sir, since you are so rough, be pleased not to concern   245
yourself with the honour of this lady; you may have enough to do if you dare justify your own tomorrow.

TRUMAN If I dare? Nay sir, since you question it, I'll convince you presently. Draw.

Goodvile and Truman fight. Enter Valentine

VALENTINE Hold, hold. What's the matter here? Jack Truman, Frank   250
Goodvile, for shame, put up.°

Enter Mrs Goodvile [followed by a Servant]

MRS GOODVILE Where is this perfidious, false man? Where is

Mr Goodvile? So, sir, I have found now the original of all my misfortunes. I have a rival, it seems; Victoria, the happy Victoria, possesses all my joys. What, have you been fighting too for the honour of your mistress? Here, come kill me. Would I had been lain in my grave ere I had known thy odious polluted bed.

GOODVILE [*aside*] 'Sdeath, I thought she had been in her chamber this hour at least. [*To Mrs Goodvile*] 'Tis true, my dear, I must own a kindness for Victoria as my kinswoman, but—

MRS GOODVILE How, dare you own it? And to my face too? Matchless impudence! Let me come at him, that I may tear out those hot, lascivious, glowing eyes that wander after every beauty in their way. O, that I could blast him with a look! Was my love so despicable to be abandoned for Victoria's? The thought of it makes me mad. I'll endure it no longer: I will have revenge, or I will die! O!

TRUMAN [*aside*] Delicate dissimulation! How I love her!

GOODVILE Dear madam, hear me speak. Madam, I say that—

MRS GOODVILE I know you cannot want an excuse; dissimulation and falsehood have been your practice. But that you should wrong me with Victoria, a woman that for the sake of your relation I had made my friend—for everything that was allied to you was dear to me—is an injury so great that it distracts my reason. I could pardon anything but my wronged love. Let me be gone; send me to a nunnery; confine me to a charnel house,° vile, ungrateful wretch— anything but thy presence I can endure.

GOODVILE Is there every way so damned a creature as a wife? Lord, madam, do you know what you do?

MRS GOODVILE I'll warrant it, you would persuade me I am mad. Would I had been born a fool! I might then have been happy. Patiently have passed over the many tedious nights I have endured in your absence. Contented myself with prayers for your safety—

MALAGENE O Lord, prayers!

MRS GOODVILE —when you in the very instant were languishing in the arms of a prostitute.

GOODVILE Lord, madam, I thought you had been in your chamber now. [*Aside*] Curse on her! What shall I do?

MRS GOODVILE 'Tis a sign you believed me safe enough; you would not certainly else have had the impudence to have brought a new mistress under my nose. I see there how guilty she stands; have you a stomach so hot that it can digest carrion that has been buzzed about and blown upon° by all the flies in the town? Or was it the fantasticalness of your appetite, to try how so coarse a dish would relish, after being cloyed with better feeding? Nay sir, I have been informed of all.   295

VALENTINE (*to Lady Squeamish*) Has then your virtuous ladyship been taking a little love and air with Mr Goodvile this evening?

GOODVILE (*aside*) Well, she has dealt with the devil, that's certain. A pox on't. I see there's no living for me in this side of the world. [*To the Servant*] Go, let the coach be made ready; I'll into the country.   300
      [*Exit Servant*]

MRS GOODVILE Nay, sir, I know my presence has always been uneasy to you. Day and night you are from me; or if ever you come home, 'tis with an aching head and heavy heart, which Victoria only has charms enough to cure. This in the first year of our marriage! Nay, and to own it! Proclaim your own falsehood and my disgraceful   305
injury in the face of the world when Malagene too, the trumpet of all the scandal in town, was by to be a witness! 'Twas very discreetly done, and doubtless will be a secret long.

GOODVILE Whirr!° Nay, since it is so, why the devil should I strive to smother my good actions? Well, if you will have it so, Madam   310
Victoria has been my mistress, is my mistress, and shall be my mistress, and what a pox would you have more? And so good-bye to you.

      Enter Sir Noble Clumsy, Caper, and Saunter

SIR NOBLE CLUMSY How's this? Who's that speaks dishonourably of my love and lady that shall be, Victoria? Before George, she's a   315
queen, and whoever says to the contrary, I'll first make him eat my sword, and then beat out his teeth with the hilts of it.

CAPER [*to Lady Squeamish*] O! Dear madam, yonder's all the town in masquerade. Won't you walk in? They'll be gone if they see no company. Jack Truman, dear Jack, prithee go and take one frisk.   320
As I hope to be saved, there are three or four the finest ladies, the delicatest-shaped women; I am sure I know 'em all.

TRUMAN Sir, I wish you good fortune, but I dare not venture. You know my temper; I shall be very boisterous and mistake 'em for whores, though if they be of your acquaintance, I know they must   325
be of quality.

CAPER Egad, and so they are, but mum for that. One of 'em is she that gave me this ring, and the other presented me with a gold enamelled watch could not cost less than thirty guineas. Trifles, Jack, which I have the fortune to meet withal sometimes.   330

SAUNTER Nay, sir, you must not come off so; Victoria your mistress!

GOODVILE Yes, sir, and how are you concerned at it?

SAUNTER Nay, sir, I can be as civil as anybody; Victoria your mistress!

GOODVILE 'Sdeath, you coxcomb, mind your singing, do you hear?
And play the fool by yourself or—   335

SAUNTER Sing, sir? So I can. [*Sings*] '*Fa, la, da, la, la, etc.*' Victoria
your mistress!

GOODVILE Yes, sir; I say, my mistress.

SIR NOBLE CLUMSY Oons, then draw.

VALENTINE Hold, Sir Noble; you are too furious. What's the matter?   340

CAPER Why, how now, Saunter? How dost do, dear heart? Sir, this
gentleman's my friend and—

GOODVILE Was ever man so overwhelmed with fools and blockheads?
Why, you ill-ordered, addle-pated, waddling brace of puppies!
[*To Saunter*] You fool, in the first place sing and be safe. [*To Caper*] 345
And you, slight grasshopper, dance and divert me. Dance, sirrah,
do you hear?

CAPER Dance, sir? And so I think I can, sir, and fence, and play at
tennis, and make love, and fold up a *billet-doux*, or anything better
than you, sir. Dance, quotha? There, sir!°   350

MRS GOODVILE Nay, Sir Noble, not only so, but owned and boasted
of it to my face. Told me—

SIR NOBLE CLUMSY Soul of my honour, 'tis unpardonable. And I'll
eat his heart for it.

GOODVILE [*to Sir Noble Clumsy*] Dear raw head and bloody bones,°   355
be patient a little. [*To Saunter and Caper*] See, see, you beagles.
Game for you, fresh game; that great towser° has started it already.
On, on, on. Halloo, halloo, halloo.

Thrusts Saunter and Caper at Mrs Goodvile and exits

LADY SQUEAMISH But dear Mr Caper, masqueraders, did you say?
I'll swear I'll among 'em; shall I not have your company? O, dear   360
masqueraders! I'll vow, I can stay no longer.

Exit Lady Squeamish hastily

VALENTINE Curse on her; she's gone and has prevented me. Caper,
Saunter, did you not hear my lady call you? She's gone to the
masqueraders; for shame, follow her. She'll take it ill you did not
wait on her.   365

SAUNTER Faith, Caper, and so she will. Well, I am resolved to marry
Victoria for fear of the worst.° [*To Mrs Goodvile*] Madam, your
most devoted servant. I hope our difference with Mr Goodvile
tonight—

MRS GOODVILE Dear sir, it needs no excuse.   370

CAPER My resentments,° madam—

TRUMAN You are too ceremonious, gentlemen, and my lady will fear she has lost you.

CAPER Dear Jack, as I told thee before, I must bring thee acquainted with those ladies.   375

SAUNTER Prithee put on a mask and come among us, Jack, faith, do.

TRUMAN Sirs, I'll wait on you in a moment.

SAUNTER AND CAPER (*embracing him*) Dear soul, adieu.

    Exeunt Saunter and Caper singing and dancing

TRUMAN These coxcombs, madam, came in a good time; they were never seasonable before.   380

MRS GOODVILE Diseases and visitations are necessary sometimes to sweep away the noisome crowds that infest and encumber the world.

MALAGENE As I have often said, I must publish, I must spread; and so good-bye to you.

    Exit Malagene. Enter Lettice

LETTICE O, madam! Yonder's my master raving for his coach. Says   385
he'll into the country presently—has given order to disperse the company. What will you do?

MRS GOODVILE Let him go. 'Twere pity to hinder him. Ha, ha, ha. Into the country? I'd as soon believe he would turn Capuchin.°

TRUMAN But, madam, 'twas inhumanly done, to come yourself upon   390
him. One would have thought that I had used him bad enough for the wise mistake he made of Victoria.

MRS GOODVILE I would not have missed it for the world. Now would he come on his knees for composition;° and if I do not bring him to it within these four hours—   395

TRUMAN Why, madam, what will you do?

MRS GOODVILE Put on all the notorious affectations and ridiculous impertinencies that ever the most eminent of our sex have studied, or the coxcombs of your sex admired; then, of a sudden, seem to grow fond of both those clinquant fools, which I am sure he, of all   400
things, loaths; yet do it too so forcedly that he himself shall find it only intended to give him vexation.

TRUMAN Have you then maliciously designed in spite of nature to keep me constant?

MRS GOODVILE Which you will be sure to be!   405

TRUMAN A dozen, new, fresh, young unseen beauties, and the devil himself in the rear of 'em, cannot make me otherwise. I never really loved or lived till now. There is nothing I'd not wish to be, except the very husband himself, rather than lose you.

    Enter Valentine and Camilla

VALENTINE Jack Truman!   410

TRUMAN Well, Ned, what's the matter?

VALENTINE Treason, Truman; your being here with Mrs Goodvile, I
fear, is discovered. I heard some such thing whispered among the
masqueraders, and Goodvile himself seems suddenly altered. I
would advise you to come and show yourself, and make the best on't.   415
　　[*Exeunt Valentine and Camilla*]

MRS GOODVILE Let me alone; I'll secure all, I'll warrant you. I'm sure
he can have no positive proofs. I'll instantly go and put all things in
a confusion, contradict all the orders he has given for going into the
country, shut up myself in my chamber, and not hear a word of him
till he comes upon submission. Lettice, follow me to my chamber   420
presently.
　　Exit Mrs Goodvile

TRUMAN Right exquisite woman and wife, good luck attend thee.
　　Exit Truman

LETTICE Well, my lady, certainly of a young lady, knows her business
and understands the managing of a husband the best of any woman
in the world. I'll swear she is an ingenious person. Forty ladies now   425
at such an accident would have been hurried and afraid, and the
poor waiting woman must have been sent forward and backward,
and backward and forward, to hearken and inquire; but she shows
all her changes in a motion.°
　　Enter Goodvile

GOODVILE How now, Lettice? Where's your lady?   430

LETTICE Within, sir, in her chamber.

GOODVILE Are you sure of it?

LETTICE Sir, she commanded me to follow her thither but now.

GOODVILE Is she alone there?

LETTICE Ay, sir, I'll assure you she seldom desires company. But I   435
must hasten and follow her.

GOODVILE Stay a little; are you sure she was in the house, before this
disturbance happened in the garden?

LETTICE Sure, sir, why, I myself was at the chamber window with her
when first she heard you exclaim against Madam Victoria. Poor   440
creature, I was afraid she would have fallen down dead on the floor.
I catched her in my arms, begged of her on my knees not to run
out; but she would hear nothing, but spite of force broke from me,
and came hither with all that impatience and rage the too sensible
resentment of your unkindness had raised in her.   445

GOODVILE Get you in presently, do you hear? And take no notice of
what I have said to you, as you tender your well-being.

LETTICE Yes, sir. [*Aside*] But if I conceal a word of it, may I never

serve London lady again, but be condemned to be a country
chambermaid and kill fleas as long as I live.   450

[*Exit Lettice*]

GOODVILE If I should have been in the wrong all this while, and
mistaken my own dear wife for Victoria! Ah, curse on this hot head
of mine! Pox on't, it is impossible! Yet that mischievous rogue
Malagene was all the while in the garden, and he has been at his
doubts, and ambiguities, and maybes with me. By this light, I am a   455
cuckold, an arrant, rank, stinking cuckold.

Enter Victoria

VICTORIA What will become of me! Whither shall I fly to hide my
misfortune? O, that I might never see the light again, but be forever
concealed in these shades!

GOODVILE Dear Victoria, is it you? Be free with me: were you really   460
in the garden before tonight, or no?

VICTORIA I have not been out of the house since it was dark, till this
minute; nor had I come hither now, but that I am destitute° where
to conceal myself from the malicious eyes and tongues of those, to
whom your baseness has given an opportunity of triumphing over   465
my misfortune and ruined honour.

GOODVILE Be not so outrageous;° I'll reconcile all yet.

VICTORIA Which way is it possible? By tomorrow morning your very
footmen will have it in their mouths; and Malagene, that keeps an
office of intelligence for all the scandal in town, will be spreading it   470
among his coffee-house companions,° and at the play whisper it to
the orange-women,° who shall make a fulsome jest of it to the next
coxcomb that comes in half drunk, to loll and play, and be nauseously
lewd with 'em in public.

GOODVILE I tell thee, it shall not be so; Malagene's my creature, or at   475
least, henceforth I'll make him so. I have reasons for it, and to
believe also that my wife, my own delicate, damned wife, was the
same I mistook for you in the garden tonight.

VICTORIA 'Tis true I was at the same time to see for her in her
chamber, and she was not there, but cannot believe her in the least   480
guilty of what you seem to accuse her of.

GOODVILE Confound her. She's an exquisite jilt, thorough paced and
practised in all the cunning arts and slights of falsehood. 'Sdeath,
how I could mince her! But here comes Malagene; he knows all,
and I'll make him confess all, or I'll murder him.   485

Enter Malagene

Well, sir, what say you to this matter?

MALAGENE Faith, bully, I think my dear kinswoman has mauled you
to some purpose. I'll say this for her: she has the true blood of the
Malagenes in her. [*Sings*] '*To lol dara lal, etc.*'

GOODVILE What is't you mean, fool? Be plain and unfold yourself.   490

MALAGENE Why, you must know, Frank, having a particular esteem
for my family—the nearest relation of which I would go fifty miles
to see hanged—I do think her as very a—but no more. Mum, dear
heart; mum, I say.

GOODVILE What's that you say, sir? What do you think my wife?   495

MALAGENE Ay, what, Frank? What now?

GOODVILE Nay, sir, that you must resolve me.

MALAGENE Why, then, I'll tell thee, Frank. Dost thou really think I
love thee?

GOODVILE I know you'll say so, sir, because you fear me.   500

MALAGENE Then prithee do so much as lend me ten guineas for a day
or two.

GOODVILE O sir, to the purpose, to the purpose. Be brief.

MALAGENE Nay, then, mum, I say again.

GOODVILE Will you never leave vexing me with your impertinence?   505
Must I be always forced to use you ill to bring you to good manners?

MALAGENE Faith, child, I am loath to make mischief; I have been a
very wicked, ill-natured, impudent fellow, that's the truth on't. But
I find I lose myself by it. The very poets themselves that were wont
to stand in awe of me, care not a louse for me now; and there's not a   510
common whore in town but calls me rogue and rascal to my face, as
impudently as if I were her pimp.

GOODVILE Therefore, sir, resolve to turn honest and be just to your
friend.

MALAGENE The devil take me, Frank, if thou art not a very impertinent   515
fellow. Know! Why, who should know better than yourself? Ha!

GOODVILE Here are five guineas for you, upon condition you make a
full and true relation of all you have discovered this night.

MALAGENE I'll do't. Down with your dust.°

GOODVILE [*aside*] What will not this rakehell do to borrow money? I   520
knew him make love to a chambermaid till he had borrowed five
pounds of her at half a crown a time.

MALAGENE Well, Frank Goodvile, you may think as you please of me,
but hang me like a dog if I am not a very honest fellow in my heart.
You would have me deal freely with you, you say, in this business?   525

GOODVILE I would so, sir, or I shall deal very roughly with you.

MALAGENE And you lent me these five guineas to that purpose?

GOODVILE You are much in the right, sir.

MALAGENE Then to make short of the matter, thou art as arrant a poor, silly cuckold as one would wish to drink withal, and confound me if I shall not be ashamed of thy company.   530

GOODVILE Confounded whore! O for a legion of devils to hurry her to hell, and that I had but the driving of 'em!

MALAGENE Nay, nay, man, since 'tis so, never be angry for the matter. What a pox, you thought to put the mistress upon Truman. Truman   535
has put the cuckold upon you; Valentine has been pimp in the business; and the devil take me if I don't think myself the honestest fellow amongst you.

VICTORIA Now, sir, consider what a wretched thing you have made me.

GOODVILE No more; I'm thine, and here I seal my heart to thee forever.   540

MALAGENE Well, Frank, can I serve thee any further in this business?

GOODVILE That, sir, is as time shall try. And, to convince you how fit I think you for my purpose, I know you are a rascal not to be trusted. Therefore observe it: if you offer to stir beyond the limits I set you, at that very instant I'll murder you.   545

MALAGENE Prithee talk not to me of limits and murdering; I hope you take me, sir, under the rose, for no fool. And what a pox do you think to make of me?

GOODVILE A spaniel to hunt and set the game I mean to take. O, Malagene, there will be mischief, Malagene, and new, ripe, fresh   550
scandal to treat of. I know it is an office thou lovest, and therefore do it to oblige thee.

MALAGENE I'faith, and so I do with all my heart. But, Frank, I don't know how this business will be brought about well. I have promised to meet two or three hearty old souls tomorrow at dinner, to swear   555
and drink and talk bawdy and treason together for an hour or two; they are all atheists and very honest fellows.

GOODVILE O, sir, you may be hanged in good time. But, for this present occasion, I must use you.—Victoria, do you with all your utmost art dissemble but the least knowledge of what has happened   560
tonight. And, sir, do you keep still that lying, sneering, ugly, merry face which you always wear when you design mischief. I'll pretend this morning to pursue my design of going into the country; then, when they are in the height of their pleasures and assurance of their safety, return and surprise 'em.   565

VICTORIA But do you believe, sir, that you can utterly abandon all sense of your past love and tenderness for a woman who has been so dear to you? You will be apt to relapse again.

GOODVILE I will sooner return to my vomit.° I am rather glad of the
occasion to be rid of so troublesome, uneasy a burden. A wife after a   570
year, like a garment that has been worn too long, hangs loose and
awkwardly on a man and grows a scandal to him that wears it.

VICTORIA But can you then resolve to quit and disown her forever?

GOODVILE Forever, my Victoria! No more, but straight go to thy
chamber and wait for the happy issue. You sir, keep close to me.   575
Quit her? As cheerfully as I would a shoe that wrings me. Then
how loosely shall I move,

> Free and unbounded, taste the sweets of life,
> Love where I please, and know no more the strife
> That's bred by that domestic plague called wife.   580

    Exeunt

5.1

Victoria's chamber

Enter Victoria

VICTORIA Now I am satisfied I must be wretched! O love! Unhappy
women's curse and men's slight game to pass their idle time at. I
find too in myself the common companion of infamy, malice. Has
Goodvile's wife ever wronged me? Never. Why then should I
conspire to betray her? No, let my revenge light wholly on that   5
false, perjured man. As he has deceived and ruined me, I'll play
false with him, make myself privy to his whole design of surprising
Truman and his wife together. Then, like a true mistress, betray his
counsels to her, that she, like a true wife, may spite of his teeth
deceive him quite; and so I have the pleasure of seeing him a sealed,   10
stigmatized, fond, believing cuckold. 'Twill at least be some ease
to me. Here he comes, equipped and prepared for the pretended
journey.

Enter Goodvile and Boy

GOODVILE Go bid the coachman hasten and get all things ready. I am
uneasy till I am gone. 'Tis time we were set out.   15

[*Exit Boy*]

> The wolves have preyed, and look the gentle day
> Before the wheels of Phoebus all about°
> Dapples the drowsy east with spots of gray.°

Wife! Adieu, dear wife. Ah, my Victoria, up already? So diligent
to wish me a happy journey? Certainly my good angel is like thee,   20
and whensoe'er I err, must meet me in thy shape. And with such
softness smile and direct me.

VICTORIA As those whom will-with-the-wisp bewitches
> Through bogs, through hedges and ditches.°

GOODVILE No. Thou hast led me out of the crooked, froward   25
road of matrimony into the pleasant, easy path of love, where I can
never leave my way and must be always happy. But where's
Malagene?

VICTORIA Below with Sir Noble. Whilst the butler was asleep, they
stole the key from him. And there they are with the fat, red-faced   30
fiddler that plays upon the bass, sitting cross-legged upon the
floor, stripped to their shirts, and drinking bawdy healths.

GOODVILE That fulsome rogue will ruin all our business. See here what I have discovered just now in the private corner of a window, a place I supposed appointed for the purpose. I found this billet to my sweet wife. (*Reads*) 'If Goodvile goes out of town this morning, let me know it, that I may wait on you, and tell you the rest of my heart, for you do not know how much I love you yet. Truman.' Now if I am not a cuckold, let any honest wittol° judge. Ha, ha, ha. How it pleases me! Blood, fire, and daggers!

VICTORIA But, sir, what do you resolve on?

GOODVILE As I told thee, instantly to pretend a journey out of town and return and surprise 'em, for I am sure they'll not be long asunder when I am out of the way. O, this billet is a very honest billet, and I know won't lie. But why should I spend my time in talking of what but vexes me, when pleasures are so near me? Come my Victoria, take me to thy arms; a moment's joy with thee would sweeten years of cares. The devil—

Enter Mrs Goodvile and Lettice

MRS GOODVILE Good morning to you, sir.

GOODVILE Goodnight to you, madam.

MRS GOODVILE How so, sir?

GOODVILE Why, goodnight or good-morrow, 'tis all one. Ceremony is the least thing I take care of. You see I am busy.

MRS GOODVILE I must confess, considering the humble duty of a wife, 'tis something rude in me to interrupt you, but I hope when you know my intentions, you'll pardon me. They were only to take a civil leave of you. I find you are preparing for the country, sir.

GOODVILE Ay. A little air will be very seasonable at present, madam; I shall grow rank° else, and all the company I keep will smell me out.

MRS GOODVILE O what joy will fill each neighbouring village, to hear our landlord's honour's coming down. The bells shall jangle out of tune all day; and at night the curate of the hamlet comes in the name of the whole parish to bid his patron welcome into the country, and invite himself the next Lord's day° to dinner.

GOODVILE I am glad to see you so pleasant, madam.

MRS GOODVILE Then, the next morning, our tenant's dainty daughter is sent with a present of pippins of the largest size, culled by the good old drudge her mother, which she delivers with a curtsy, and blushes in expectation of what his worship will bestow upon her.

GOODVILE O madam, let not any thoughts of that nature disturb you; I shall leave all my wanton inclinations here, and only please myself when I am there sometimes to contemplate your ladyship's picture in the gallery.

MRS GOODVILE Then come the country squires and their dogs, the
cleanlier sort of creatures of the two. Straight w' are invited to the   75
noble hunt, and not a deer in all the forest's safe.

GOODVILE No, madam. No horned beast shall suffer for my pleasure.
I am lately grown a philosopher, madam, and find we ought not
hurt our fellow creatures.

MRS GOODVILE What is the reason that you use me thus?   80

GOODVILE What is't I would not do to purchase quietness? Your
injurious suspicions of me were tolerable, but the wrongs your
jealousy has done Victoria—

MRS GOODVILE I jealous of Victoria! No. Though my passion last
night made me extravagant when I discovered you with that naughty   85
Lady Squeamish, which I can easily forgive, if you'll but promise to
forget her. For I am confident it was your first transgression.

GOODVILE Very quaint and pretty.

MRS GOODVILE Yet I am too well satisfied of Victoria's virtue, for
she's my friend, and though I should see her in your arms, I could   90
not harbour such a thought.—No, Victoria, you must love me, and
I'll love you; you shall call me your love, and I'll call you my dear;
and we'll always go to the play together, and to the park together,
and everywhere together; and when Mr Goodvile's out of town,
we'll lie together.°   95

    Enter Servant

SERVANT Sir, the coach is ready.

GOODVILE You think, madam, you have a fine, easy fool to play
withal, but the gayness of your face is too thin to hide the rancour
of your heart; and so, my dear, jocund, witty devil wife, I take my
leave of you, never more from this minute to look on you.   100

MRS GOODVILE Are you then inexorable? Relentless, cruel man!

GOODVILE Good, easy, melting, kind-hearted woman, farewell.

    Exit Goodvile

MRS GOODVILE Ah, wretched me.

LETTICE My lady swoons. Dear madam Victoria, hasten and bring my
master back again; you can do anything with him.   105

    Exit Victoria

MRS GOODVILE No, no, Lettice. Let him alone; art thou sure he's
gone?

LETTICE I hope so,° madam.

MRS GOODVILE Then so soon as I am returned to my chamber, be
sure you go yourself to Mr Truman, and tell him if he has nothing   110
else to do he may come hither today.

Enter Victoria

VICTORIA There is no prevailing with him; he cries aloud his house is infected, and that no man that values his health will stay in it. My Lady Squeamish too is arrived just as he left the door. I am sure she'll come in; will you see her, madam? 115

MRS GOODVILE O I am sick at the very name of her. Let all the doors be barred against her, and gun powder under each threshold-place, ready to blow her up, if she but offer an entrance. Lettice, lend me your hand a little. I'll to my chamber instantly. O my head!

Exit Mrs Goodvile with Lettice

VICTORIA This management of hers so charms me, that I can almost 120 forget all the mischief she has done me. 'Tis true she reproached me, but 'twas done so handsomely that I had doubly deserved it to have taken notice of it.

Enter Lady Squeamish

LADY SQUEAMISH O dear Victoria, what will become of me? I am lost and undone forever. O I shall die, I shall die; the lord of my heart, 125 the jewel of my soul, is false to me.

VICTORIA What ails your ladyship? Surely she's distracted!

LADY SQUEAMISH O Goodvile, Goodvile! The false, cruel, remorseless Goodvile! I came just as his coach was parting from the door, yet he would not speak to me, would hardly see me, but away he drove, 130 and smiling mocked my sorrows.

VICTORIA Alas, her ladyship is passionate, as I live, very passionate.

LADY SQUEAMISH So Theseus left the wretched Ariadne on the shore, so fled the false Æneas from his Dido.°

VICTORIA What could you expect less of him, madam? Falsehood is his 135 province. Your ladyship should have made choice of a civil, sober, discreet person, but Goodvile, you know, is a spark, a very spark.

LADY SQUEAMISH That, that has been my ruin; it was therefore I adored him. What woman would dote on a dull, melancholy ass? Because she might be sure of him? No, a spark is my life, my darling, 140 the joy of my soul. O how I dote on a spark! I could live and die with a spark. Victoria, I make you a confidante, and you must pardon me for robbing you of Mr Goodvile. Come, come. I know all.

VICTORIA Your ladyship knows more than all the world besides.

LADY SQUEAMISH And as I was saying, a spark is the dearest thing to 145 me in the world; I have had acquaintance, I think, with all the sparks. Well, one of 'em that you know was a sweet person. O he danced and sung and dressed to a miracle, and then he spoke French as if he had been bred all his lifetime at Paris, and admired

everything that was French. Besides, he would look so languishingly   150
and lisp so prettily when he talked, and then never wanted discourse.
I'll swear, he has entertained me two hours together with the
description of an equipage.

VICTORIA That must needs be very charming.

LADY SQUEAMISH But Mr Goodvile was a wit too. O, I never had a   155
wit before, for, to speak the truth, now I think on't better, all my
lovers have been a little foolish, I'll swear. Ha, ha, ha.

MALAGENE (*at the door, drunk*) Scour, scour, scour.°

SIR NOBLE CLUMSY (*at the door, drunk*) Down goes the main mast,
down, down, down.   160

    Enter Malagene and Sir Noble Clumsy

Malagene, roar, roar, and ravish; here are punks in beaten satin,°
sirrah, termagant, triumphant, first-rate punks, you rogue.

VICTORIA How came these ruffians here?

SIR NOBLE CLUMSY Ruffians! Do you know who you talk to, madam?
I am a civil, sober, discreet person and come particularly to   165
embrace thy lovely body.

MALAGENE Look you, madam, make no noise about this matter. This
is a person of quality and a friend of mine; therefore, pray be civil.

LADY SQUEAMISH Has Mr Goodvile left no footmen at home to
cudgel such fops? Faugh! How like drunken, journeymen tailors°   170
they look!

MALAGENE Journeymen, madam! Hold there! None of your ladyship's
journeymen, that's one comfort! Woe to the poor devil that is, I say.

LADY SQUEAMISH Were Mr Goodvile at home you durst not talk
thus, you scandalous fellow.   175

MALAGENE Goodvile, you say. Hark you, my dear, were he here in
person, I would first of all decently kick him out of doors, then turn
up thy keel and discover here to thy kinsman what a leaky vessel
thou art!

SIR NOBLE CLUMSY Why, what is that Goodvile? Will he wrestle? Or   180
will he box for 50 pounds? Look you, this fellow is my pimp. 'Tis
true his countance is none of the best. But he's a neat° lad and
keeps good company.

MALAGENE Hark you, knight! You'll bear me out° in this business,
knight? For, under the rose, I have apprehension that this carcass of   185
mine may suffer else.

SIR NOBLE CLUMSY No more of that, rogue, no more. Take notice,
good people. [*Indicates Malagene*] This civil person shall marry my

sister; she is a pretty, hopeful lady. Truly, she is not full thirteen, but she has had two children already, od's heart.   190

VICTORIA Ridiculous oaf!

SIR NOBLE CLUMSY Come, let us talk bawdy.

VICTORIA I'll call those shall talk with you presently.

> *Exit Victoria*

SIR NOBLE CLUMSY Whew! She's gone.

LADY SQUEAMISH Beast! Brute! Barbarian! Sot!   195

SIR NOBLE CLUMSY O law! My aunt! What have I done now? Madam, as I hope to be—(*Runs against her and almost beats her backward*)°

LADY SQUEAMISH O help! I am murdered! O my head!

SIR NOBLE CLUMSY Nay, lady, that was no fault of mine. You shall   200
see I'll keep my distance and, as I was saying, if I have offended— (*Reels against a table and throws down a china jar and several little china dishes*)

LADY SQUEAMISH O insufferable! Quickly, quickly, a porter and basket to carry out this swine to a dunghill.   205

SIR NOBLE CLUMSY Look you, madam, no harm, no harm! You shall see me behave myself notably yet—as, for example, suppose now, suppose this the door. (*Goes to the door*) Very well. Thus then I move— (*Steps forward and leaves his peruke on one of the hinges*) Ha! Who was that? Rogues! Dogs! Sons of whores!   210

> *Enter Servants*

FIRST SERVANT Such as we are, sir, you shall find us at your service.

SIR NOBLE CLUMSY Murder, murder, murder.

> [*Exit Servants*]

MALAGENE [*aside*] Where there is such odds, a man may with honour retire and steal off.

> *Exit Malagene. Enter Caper and Saunter*

CAPER Where is this rascal? This coxcomb? This fop? How dare you   215
come hither, sir, to affront ladies and persons of quality!

SIR NOBLE CLUMSY Sir, your humble servant. Did you see my periwig?

CAPER Sir, you are an ass and never wore periwig in your life. [*Looks at Sir Noble Clumsy's peruke*] Jerniè,° what a bush of briars and   220
thorns is here! The mane of my Lady Squeamish's shock° is a *chedreux* to it.

SIR NOBLE CLUMSY Why, sir, I know who made it. He was an honest fellow and a barber, and one that loved music and poetry.

SAUNTER How, sir!   225

CAPER But, sir, come close to the business. How durst you treat ladies
so rudely as we saw you but now? Answer to that, and tell not us of
music and poetry.

SIR NOBLE CLUMSY Why, he had all *Westminster Drollery*° and
Oxford Jests° at his fingers' ends. And, for the cittern,° if ever *Troy*   230
Town° were a tune, he mastered it upon that instrument, when he
was our butler in the country. An old maid of my grandmother's
took great delight in him for it.

SAUNTER But, sir, this is nothing to our business.

SIR NOBLE CLUMSY Business! Hang business! I hate a man of business.   235
If you'll drink or whore, break windows, or commit murder, I am
for you.

CAPER Sir, will you fight?

SIR NOBLE CLUMSY Fight! With whom? For what?

CAPER With me.   240

SAUNTER With me.

SIR NOBLE CLUMSY Ay, sir, with all my heart; I love fighting, sir.

SAUNTER But will you, sir? Dare you?

CAPER Ay, sir, will you fight? Do you think you dare fight?

SIR NOBLE CLUMSY Why, you sweet-perfumed, jessamine° knaves!   245
You rogues in buckram!° Were there a dozen of you, I'd beat you
out of your artificial sweetness into your own natural rankness, you
stinkards! Shall I draw my *Cerberus*° and cut you off, you gaudy
popinjays?°

CAPER This fellow's mad, Saunter, stark mad, by Jericho. Dear   250
knight, how long hast thou been in this pickle, this condition,
knight. Ha?

SIR NOBLE CLUMSY What pickle, what conditions, you worms?

SAUNTER Ay, ay, 'tis so. The poor devil must to Bedlam—Bedlam,°
knight, the madman's hospital.   255

SIR NOBLE CLUMSY What will become of you then, you vermin?
There's never a hospital for fools yet; mercy on me if there were!
How many handsome fellows in this town might be provided for?
          Fiddles play offstage

CAPER Hey-day! Fiddles!

SAUNTER Madam Goodvile, hearing we were here, hath sent for 'em   260
on purpose to regale us.

          Enter Mrs Goodvile, Lettice, Lady Squeamish, with the fiddles
          playing. Saunter falls to sing the tune with 'em and Caper dances
          to it

MRS GOODVILE Let my servants take care that all the doors stand open. I'll have entrance denied to no one fool in town. Mr Caper and Mr Saunter here? Then we can never want company. [*To Lady Squeamish*] Come, madam, let us begin the revels of the day; I long to enjoy the freedom I am mistress of. Lettice, try your voice.° 265

LADY SQUEAMISH O madam, this gallant spirit ravishes me! Dear Mr Caper, you and Mr Saunter were born to be happy. Madam Goodvile has resolved to sacrifice this day to pleasure. What shall we do with ourselves? 270

CAPER Do, madam! We'll dance forever.

LADY SQUEAMISH O ay, dance.

SAUNTER And sing.

LADY SQUEAMISH And sing. 275

CAPER AND SAUNTER And love.

LADY SQUEAMISH O ay, love! But, Madam Goodvile, have you resolved to wear the willow° and be very melancholy? Ha, ha, ha. Fiddles, where are you? I cannot endure you out of my sight.

MRS GOODVILE Willow! Hang it; give it to country girls that sigh for 280 clowns, and melancholy is a disease for bankrupt beauty. I have yet a stock of youth and charms,

> Unsullied by the hands of age or care,
> And whilst that lasts, what woman would despair?

SIR NOBLE CLUMSY In the meantime, I'll scout out for a doxy of my 285 acquaintance hard by, return in triumph, and let Victoria go hang and despair. (*Sings*)

> *To love is a pleasure divine;*
> *Yet I'll never sigh or be sad.*
> *They are coxcombs that languish and pine,* 290
> *So long as whores are to be had.*
> *To daroll, darolda.*

LADY SQUEAMISH O secure that deformed monster, that rebel of mine. Fellows take care of him, and keep him up till I talk with him and make him sensible of his enormities. 295

SIR NOBLE CLUMSY Slaves, avaunt! If my lady will have it so, I'll walk soberly into the garden and consider of what is past. [*Sings*] '*To love is a pleasure, etc.*'

> *Exit Sir Noble Clumsy*

MRS GOODVILE Lettice!

LETTICE Madam. 300

MRS GOODVILE Is Mr Truman come?

LETTICE He'll be here presently, madam.

Enter Page with a letter

PAGE A letter for your ladyship.

MRS GOODVILE Who brought it?

PAGE A porter brought it to the door, madam, but said he had no   305
orders to stay for an answer.

Exit Page

MRS GOODVILE [*aside*] A woman's hand! (*Reads*) 'Mr Goodvile's
journey out of town is but a pretence. He is jealous of you and
Mr Truman; you will find him anon, returned in hopes to surprise
you together. Though he has trusted me with the secret and obliged   310
me to assist him in it, yet I would endeavour by this discovery
to persuade you that I am your real servant. Victoria. Postscript.
Beware of Malagene, for he's appointed the spy to betray you.'
This is generously done, Victoria, and I'll study to deserve it of
thee. Now, if I plague not this wise, jealous husband of mine, let   315
all wives curse me and cuckolds laugh at me.—Fiddles, lead in!
Mr Caper and Mr Saunter, pray wait on my lady and entertain her
a little. I'll follow you presently.

LADY SQUEAMISH Come, Mr Caper, will you walk?

CAPER A coranto, madam?   320

LADY SQUEAMISH Ay, ten thousand, ten thousand. Mr Saunter, I
would be always near you two. O for a grove now and a purling
brook with that delightful, charming voice of yours! Come, let us
walk and study which way to divert ourselves.

CAPER *Allons*, for love and pleasure! By these hands—   325

SAUNTER By those eyes—

LADY SQUEAMISH O, no more, no more! I shall be lost in happiness!

Exeunt Lady Squeamish, Caper, and Saunter

MRS GOODVILE So. This consort of fools shall be the chorus to my
farce. Now all the malice, ill-nature, falsehood, and hypocrisy of
my sex inspire me! Lettice, see Camilla be sent for instantly; she   330
shall join with me in my revenge—she has reason. Mr Valentine, I
suppose, will be here with Mr Truman.

Enter Truman

TRUMAN And think you, madam, he durst not answer a fair lady's
challenge without a second?

MRS GOODVILE You would pretend, I'll warrant you, to be very   335
stout. You hectors in love are as errant cheats as hectors in fighting that bluster, rant, and make a noise for the present, but, when

they come to the business, prove errant dastards and good for nothing.

TRUMAN But madam, you should find I dare do something, would   340
you but be civil and stand your ground.

MRS GOODVILE What think you, though, of a cutthroat husband now behind the hangings? What would become of you then?

TRUMAN Whilst I have such beauty on my side, nothing can hurt me.

MRS GOODVILE Then, sir, prepare yourself; Mr Goodvile is really   345
jealous and mistrusts all or more than has passed between us. His journey out of town was but a pretence, but we shall see him instantly in expectation to catch us together.

TRUMAN Fear him not, madam; these moles that work underground are as blind as they are busy. Let him run on in his dull jealousy,   350
whilst we still find new windings out and lose him in the maze.

MRS GOODVILE Then if you wish to preserve me yours, join with me today in my design, which is, if possible, to make him mad, work him up to the height of furious suspicion, and, at that moment when he thinks his jealousy most just, baffle him out of it. And let   355
the world know how dull a tool a husband is, compared with that triumphant thing, a wife, and her guardian angel lover.

TRUMAN But Mr Goodvile, madam, has wit, and so good an opinion of it too.

MRS GOODVILE 'Tis that shall be his ruin. Were he a fool, he were not   360
worth the trouble of deceiving.

TRUMAN Dear jewel of my soul, proceed then and prosper. But what must be my part?

MRS GOODVILE To secure Malagene. That ill-natured villain has betrayed us and is appointed by Goodvile chief instrument in the   365
discovery. He has cowardice enough to sell his soul to buy off a beating. He never told truth enough to be believed once so long as he lives. Get him but in your power, and he shall own more villainies than ever were in his thoughts to commit, or the necessity of our affair can invent to put upon him.   370

TRUMAN And I'll be sure of him, or may I never taste those lips again, but be condemned to cast mistresses in the side-box at the playhouse,° or, what is worse, take up with a seamstress and drudge° for cuffs and cravats.

Enter Malagene

MRS GOODVILE Here he comes!   375

TRUMAN O Monsieur Malagene, welcome.

MALAGENE [*bows*] Jack Truman, your humble servant.

TRUMAN Whither so fast, I beseech you, sir? A word with you, a word
with you.

MALAGENE Why? Can I do anything for thee? Hast thou any business   380
for me? Prithee what is it?

TRUMAN Sir, you must lie for me.

MALAGENE Ha, ha, ha. Is that all?

TRUMAN Nay, sir, you must!

MALAGENE Anything in a civil way or so, Jack, but nothing upon   385
compulsion,° lad. Prithee let me do nothing upon compulsion,
prithee now!

TRUMAN Then, sir, to be brief, this is the business: Goodvile, I hear,
has been informed by you of what passed in the garden last night.
How durst you be so impudent as to pry into my secrets, where I   390
was concerned?

MALAGENE Why, look you, Jack, curiosity, you know, and a natural
inclination which I have—

TRUMAN To pimping.

MALAGENE Confound me, Jack, thou art much in the right. I believe   395
thou art a witch. I knew as well, man—

TRUMAN What did you know?

MALAGENE Why, I knew thee to be an arch wag and an honest fellow.
Ah, rogue, prithee kiss me. [*Truman refuses*] The rogue's out of
humour!   400

TRUMAN No, sir. I dare not use you so like a friend; you must deserve
it better first.

MALAGENE Look you, Jack, the truth of the business is, I am bespoke.
But the love I have to see the business go forward may persuade me
to much.   405

TRUMAN Then presently resolve entirely to disown and abjure all
the intelligence you gave Goodvile, or promise to yourself that
wherever next I meet you, I'll cut your throat upon the spot.

MALAGENE But hark you, Jack, how shall I come off with the
business? I shall be kicked and used very scurvily. For the truth is, I   410
did tell—

TRUMAN What did you tell?

MALAGENE Why, I told him, you knave—I won't tell! You little,
cunning cur, I told him all, man!

TRUMAN All, sir!   415

MALAGENE Ay, hang me like a dog, all. But madam, you must pardon
me; there was not a word of it true.

TRUMAN And what do you think to do with yourself?

MALAGENE Do? Why, I'll deny it all again, man, every word of it, as
impudently as ever I at first affirmed it. Maybe he'll kick me, and   420
beat me, and use me like a dog, man. That's nothing, nothing at all,
man. I do not value it this! (*Pulls out a Jew's trump° and plays*)

TRUMAN And this, sir, you'll stand to.

MALAGENE If I do not, hang me up for a sign at a bawdy house door.
In the meantime, I'll retire and peruse a young lampoon, which I   425
am lately the happy father of.

TRUMAN Nay, sir, you are not to stir from me!

    Enter Lettice

LETTICE O, madam, shift for yourself. Madam Victoria sent me to tell
you that my master is returned, and that he pretends to come as a
masquerader.   430

MALAGENE Well, since it must be so, I'll deny all indeed. What an
excellent fellow might I have been. Some men now with my stock
of honesty and a little more gravity would have made a fortune.
Well, I have been a lazy rogue and never knew till now that I was fit
for business.   435

MRS GOODVILE Mr Goodvile in masquerade, say you?

LETTICE Yes, madam, and two women with him, madam; they are
just now alighted.

MRS GOODVILE Women with him! Nay, then he comes triumphantly
indeed. Mr Truman, do you retire with Malagene.   440

    [*Exeunt Truman and Malagene*]

I'll stay here and receive this Machiavel° in disguise. Now, once more
let me invoke all the arts of affectation, all the revenge, the counterfeit passions, pretended love, pretended jealousy, pretended rage,
and, in sum, the very genius of my sex to my assistance.

    Enter Goodvile, First Woman, and Second Woman, masked

So here they come. Now, this throw for all my future peace.° Who   445
waits there?

    Enter Servants

GOODVILE Madam, you'll excuse this freedom.

MRS GOODVILE You oblige me by using it. [*To the Servants*] Let all
the company know that these noble persons of quality have honoured me with their presence. Let the fiddles be ready and see the   450
banquet prepared, and let Mr Truman come to me instantly; I
cannot live a minute, a moment without him!

    [*Exit Servants*]

GOODVILE [*aside*] Delicate devil!

MRS GOODVILE Sir, let me beg your patience for a moment, whilst I
go and put things in order fit for your reception.   455

Exit Mrs Goodvile

GOODVILE Footmen, take care that the engines which I have
ordered be ready when I call for 'em. Truman, I see, is a man of
punctual assignation, and my wife is a person very adroit at these
matters; some hot-brained, horn-mad cuckold now would be for
cutting of throats; but I am resolved to turn a civil, sober, dis-   460
creet person and hate bloodshed. No. I'll manage the matter so
temperately that I'll catch her in his very arms, then civilly discard her, bag and baggage, whilst you, my dainty doxies, take
possession of her privileges and enter the territories with colours
flying.   465

FIRST WOMAN And shall I keep my coach, Mr Goodvile?

GOODVILE Ay, and six,° my lovely Rampant.° Nay, thou shalt every
morning swoop the Exchange in triumph to see what gaudy bauble
thou canst first grow fond of. And, after noon at the theatre, exalted
in a box, give audience to every trim, amorous, twiring fop of the   470
corner° that comes thither to make a noise, hear no play, and show
himself, thou shalt, my *bona roba*.

SECOND WOMAN But Mr Goodvile, what shall I do then?

GOODVILE O, thou! Thou shalt be my more peculiar punk,° my
housekeeper, my necessary sin; manage all th'affairs of my estate   475
and family; ride up and down in my own coach, attended by my
own footmen; nose° my wife where ere you meet; and, if I had any,
breed my children. O, what a delicious life will this be!

Fiddles offstage

FIRST WOMAN Hear you, sir, the fiddles?

GOODVILE O the procession's coming; put on your vizards and   480
observe the ceremony.

Enter Truman, with a letter, Mrs Goodvile, Caper, Saunter,
Lady Squeamish, Camilla, and fiddles

MRS GOODVILE Mr Caper, Mr Saunter, you are the life and soul of all
good company. Command me anything; command my house, that,
and all freedom are yours.

CAPER Masks, my life, my joy, my top of happiness! [*To Goodvile*] Sir,   485
your humble servant. [*To First Woman*] By your leave, madam, shall
you and I touse and tumble together in the drawing room hard by
for half an hour or so? Ha? (*Cuts*)

SAUNTER [*sings*] 'Fa toldara, toldara, etc.' [*To Second Woman*] Ah, madam, what do you wear a mask for? Have you never a nose, or but one eye? Let me see how you are furnished. 490

SECOND WOMAN Sir, if I want anything, 'tis to be doubted you cannot supply me.

GOODVILE So! Sure, this must come to something anon!

MRS GOODVILE Ah, were but Mr Goodvile here now, what a happy 495 day might this be! But he is melancholy and forlorn in the country, summoning in his tenants and their rents, that shining pelf° that must support me in my pleasures.

GOODVILE Is he then, madam, so kind a husband?

MRS GOODVILE O the most indulgent creature in the world! What 500 husband but he, Mr Truman, would have so seasonably withdrawn and left me mistress of such freedom? To spend my days in triumph as I do; to sacrifice myself, my soul, and all my sense to you, the lord of all my joys, my conqueror and protector?

CAMILLA Heavens, madam, you'll provoke him beyond all patience. 505

MRS GOODVILE Who, Mr Goodvile? Which way shall it reach his knowledge? No, we'll be as secret—

TRUMAN As we are happy. So subtly lay the scene of all our joys that envy or malice—nay, the very husband himself, and Malagene to boot, well hired to the business—shall ne'er discover us. 510

MRS GOODVILE O discover us! A husband discover us? Were he indeed as jealous as he has reason, I could no more apprehend discovery than a kindness from him.

GOODVILE This impudence is so rank that I can hold no longer. (*He unmasks*) Say you so, madam? 515

MRS GOODVILE O, a ghost, a ghost! Save me, save me. Mr Truman, see, see Mr Goodvile's spirit! Sure some base villain has murdered him, and his angry ghost is come to revenge it on me.

GOODVILE No, madam, fear nothing. I am a very harmless goblin, though you are a little shocked at the sight of me. 520

CAPER Ha, ha, ha. Goodvile returned? Dear Frank!

SAUNTER Honest Goodvile, thou see'st, dear soul, we are free here in thy absence.

GOODVILE I see you are, gentlemen, and shall take an opportunity to return the favour. Footmen, be ready. 525

MRS GOODVILE But is it really Mr Goodvile then? Let me receive him to my arms. Welcome ten thousand, thousand, thousand times. Dear sir, how does my picture in the gallery do?

GOODVILE O Madam, it looked so very charmingly that I had no power to stay longer from the dear, loving original. 530

MRS GOODVILE So now begins the battle.

GOODVILE Well, madam, and for your set of fools here: to what end and purpose have you decreed them in this new model of your family? I hope you have not designed 'em for your own use?

MRS GOODVILE Why, sir, methinks you should not grudge me a   535
coxcomb or two to pass away the time withal, since you had taken your dearer conversation from me.

GOODVILE No, madam, I understand your diet better. A fool is too squab° and tender a bit for your fierce appetite. You are for a substantial dish, a man of heat and honour, such as Mr Truman I   540
know is, and I doubt not will do me reason.°

TRUMAN Ay, sir, whenever you'll demand it.

MRS GOODVILE Nay, sirs, no quarrelling, I beseech you; what would you be at, sir?

GOODVILE At rest, madam; like an honest snail, shrink up my horns   545
into my shell and, if possible, hold a quiet possession of it.

MRS GOODVILE I hope I have done nothing that may disturb your quiet, sir.

GOODVILE Nothing, madam, nothing in the least; how is it possible that anything should disturb me? A sot, a beetle, a drone of a   550
husband, a mere utensil, a block for you to fashion° all your false-hood on, whilst I must still be stupid, bear my office, and never be disturbed, I.

MRS GOODVILE So, now your heart is opening; and for your ease, I'll give it a little vent myself. You are jealous, alas, jealous of Truman,   555
are you?

GOODVILE And I have no reason, madam, though I come and catch you in his arms, rolling and throwing your wanton eyes like fire-balls at his heart; oh, what an indulgent creature's Mr Goodvile, so season-ably to withdraw and leave you mistress of such freedom! To spend   560
your days in triumph as you do, to sacrifice yourself, your soul and sense to him, the lord of all your joys, your conqueror and protector.

MRS GOODVILE I am glad to find my plot so well succeed. I knew of your jealousy last night, knew too your journey out of town was but a pretence in hope to return and surprise me with Truman. I was   565
informed too of your return but now; and your disguise, I knew you through it so soon as I saw you, and therefore I acted all that fondness to Truman before your face. It was all the revenge I had within my power.

GOODVILE Can you deny your being with Truman in the garden last   570

night? Were you not there so openly, that even the broad eyes of
fools might see?

MRS GOODVILE What fool? What villain have you dares accuse me?

GOODVILE One who, though he rarely told truth before, will be sure
to do it now: Malagene, your kinsman; Malagene, a hopeful branch   575
of your own stock.

TRUMAN The rascal dares not own it.

GOODVILE But he shall, sir, though you protect him.

TRUMAN 'Twas basely done to set a spy upon your friend, after the
trick you had played me with Victoria.   580

GOODVILE Basely done!

TRUMAN Yes, basely, sir.

GOODVILE Death, you lie, sir! Why do I trifle thus when I have a
sword by my side? [*Draws his sword*]

CAPER Nay, look you, Frank, you had better be patient. Here shall be   585
nothing done; therefore, pray put up.

Enter Valentine

VALENTINE What, again quarrelling? Goodvile, this must not be;
Truman is my friend and, if he has done you wrong, I'll engage,
shall make you satisfaction.°

SAUNTER Ay, ay. Prithee, man, take some other time, and don't quarrel   590
now and spoil good company.

GOODVILE Death! You dancing, talking, mettled, frisking rogues,
stand off! O I had forgot. [*Calls offstage*] Footmen, where are ye?

Enter Footmen

Here, take away these butterflies, and do speedy execution upon 'em as
I ordered; do it instantly.   595

Footmen seize Caper and Saunter

CAPER Nay, Frank, what's all this for?

SAUNTER Nay, Goodvile, prithee now, as I hope to live.

Enter Malagene

GOODVILE Away with 'em!

Exeunt Footmen with Caper and Saunter

Now for Malagene. O, here he comes, madam, who will refresh your
memory. Speak, sir, as you tender life and limb; whom did you see   600
together in the garden last night?

MALAGENE Ha! Nobody.

GOODVILE Were not Truman and my wife there to your knowledge
privately?

MALAGENE Ha, ha, ha. Child, no.   605

GOODVILE Did you not tell me that you overheard 'em whispering in
the grotto together?

MALAGENE No.

GOODVILE Hell and devils, this fellow has been tampered withal and
instructed to abuse me. This is all contrivance, a studied scene to   610
fool me of my reason.

Enter Footmen

Here, take him hence, and harness him with the other two, till he
confess the truth.

MRS GOODVILE He shall not go, touch him who dares. Must people
then be forced and tortured to accuse me falsely? Ah, Mr Goodvile,   615
how have I deserved this at your hands? Let not my good name be
ravished from me. If you have resolved to break my heart, kill me
now quickly and put me out of pain.

Malagene runs away

GOODVILE Nay, madam, here is that shall yet convince.° See here a
letter from your lover left for you in a private corner; hear me read   620
it. And if you have modesty enough left, blush. (*Reads*) 'If Goodvile
goes out of town this morning, let me know of it that I may wait on
you and tell you the rest of my heart. For you do not know how
much I love you yet. Truman.'

MRS GOODVILE Death and destruction! It was all my own contriv-   625
ance; madded with your jealousy, I sought all ways to vex you. I
counterfeited it with my own hand, and left it in a place where you
might be sure to find it. To convince you farther, see here a caution
sent me just before by one whom you have trusted and loved too
much for my quiet. (*Gives Victoria's letter*) Peruse it, and when   630
you have done, consider how you have used me and how I have
deserved it. O!

GOODVILE (*reads*) 'Journey out of town—is a pretence—return
and surprise—believe by this discovery—your servant, Victoria.'
Victoria. Has she betrayed me? Nay then, I pronounce there is no   635
trust nor faith in the sex. By heaven, in every condition they are all
jilts, all false, from the bawd to the babe.

MRS GOODVILE Now sir, I hope I may withdraw; from this minute
never expect I'll see your face again. No, I'll leave you to be
happy at your own choice. Love where you please, and be as free   640
as if I ne'er had had relation to you. I shall take care to trouble
you no more, but wish you may be happier than ever yet I made
you.

GOODVILE Stay, madam.

MRS GOODVILE No, sir, I'll be gone; I will not stay a moment longer.   645
Inhuman, cruel, false traitor, wert thou now languishing on thy
knees, prostrate at my feet, ready to grow mad with thy own guilt, I
would not stop nor turn my face to save thee from despair.

GOODVILE You shall.

MRS GOODVILE For what?   650

GOODVILE To let the world see how much a fool I can be. Art thou
innocent?

MRS GOODVILE By my love, I am; I never wronged you, but you have
undone me, ruined my fame and quiet. What mouth will not be full
of my dishonour? Henceforth let all my sex remember me when   655
they'd upbraid mankind for baseness. O that I could dissemble
longer with you, that I might to your torment persuade you still all
your jealousies were just, and I as infamous as you are cruel.

Exit Mrs Goodvile in a rage

GOODVILE Get thee in then and talk to me no more; there's something in thy face will make a fool of me, and there's a devil in this   660
business which yet I cannot discover. Truman, if thou hast enjoyed
her, I beg thee keep it close;° and, if it be possible, let us yet be
friends.

TRUMAN 'Tis not my fault if we be foes.

[Exit Truman]

GOODVILE But now to my fools; bring 'em forth and let us see how   665
their new equipage becomes 'em.

[Exit Footmen]

O dear Valentine, how does the fair Camilla?

VALENTINE Faith, sir, she and I have been dispatching a trifling affair
this morning, commonly called matrimony.

GOODVILE Married! Nay, then there is some comfort yet, that thou°   670
art fallen into the snare. Valentine, look to her, keep her as secret
as thou wouldst a murder, hadst thou committed one. Trust her
not with thy dearest friend; she has beauty enough to corrupt
him.

*Enter [Footmen with] Caper and Saunter, their hands tied
behind 'em, fools' caps° on their heads. Caper with one leg tied
up, and Saunter gagged.*

See here these rogues, how like themselves they look! Now, you paltry   675
vermin, you rats that run squeaking from house to house, up and

down the town, that no man can eat his bread in quiet for you: take
warning of what° you feel, and come not near these doors again on
peril of hanging. [*To the Footmen*] Here, discharge them of their
punishment and see 'em forth the gates.   680

> [*Exit Footmen with Caper and Saunter.*] *Enter Lady Squeamish,*
> *Sir Noble Clumsy, and Victoria*

LADY SQUEAMISH [*curtsies*] O gallants, your humble servant. Dear
Mr Goodvile, be pleased to give my kinsman Sir Noble joy.° He has
done himself the honour to marry your cousin Victoria, whom now
I must be proud to call my relation, since she has accepted of the
title of my lady Clumsy.   685

SIR NOBLE CLUMSY Ay, sir, I am married, and will be drunk again too
before night, as simply as I stand here.°

GOODVILE Sir Noble married? To Victoria too? Nay then, in spite of
misfortunes

> This Day shall be a day of jubilee.   690

But first

> Good people, all that my sad fortune see,°
> I beg you to take warning here by me:
> Marriage and hanging go by destiny.

Especially you gay young married blades,
Beware and keep your wives from balls and masquerades.

> *Exeunt*

Epilogue

Spoken by Mrs Barry

Well, sirs, if now my spouse and I should part,
To which kind critic shall I give my heart?
Stay, let me look; not one in all the place
But has a scurvy, froward, damning face.
Have you resolved then on the poet's fall?   5
Go, you're ill-natured, ugly devils all.
The married sparks, I know this play will curse
For the wife's sake, but some of 'em have worse.
Poets themselves their own ill luck have wrought;
You ne'er had learnt, had not their quarrels taught.°   10
But, as in the disturbance of a state,
Each factious maggot thinks of growing great,
So when the poets first had jarring fits,
You all set up for critics and for wits.
Then straight there came, which cost you mothers' pains,   15
Songs and lampoons in litters from your brains.
Libels like spurious brats run up and down,
Which their dull parents were ashamed to own,
But vented 'em in other's names, like whores
That lay their bastards down at honest doors.   20
For shame, leave off this higgling way of wit,°
Railing abroad and roaring in the pit.
Let poets live in peace, in quiet write;
Else may they all to punish you unite,
Join in one force to study to abuse ye,   25
And teach your wives and misses how to use ye.°

EXPLANATORY NOTES

Abbreviations

Barnard	*The Man of Mode*, ed. John Barnard (London, 1979)
Brett-Smith	*The Dramatic Works of Sir George Etherege*, ed. H. F. B. Brett-Smith (Oxford, 1927), 2 vols.
Carnochan	*The Man of Mode*, ed. W. B. Carnochan (Lincoln, Neb., 1966)
Cordner	*The Plays of Sir George Etherege*, ed. Michael Cordner (Cambridge, 1982)
Downes	John Downes, *Roscius Anglicanus*, ed. Judith Milhous and Robert D. Hume (London, 1987)
FF	*Friendship in Fashion*
FH	*A Fond Husband*
Ghosh	Thomas Otway, *Works*, ed. J. C. Ghosh (Oxford, 1932), 2 vols.
MM	*The Man of Mode*
OED	*Oxford English Dictionary*
Pellegrin	Helen Pellegrin, *Thomas Shadwell's* The Libertine: *A Critical Edition* (New York, 1987)
Price	Curtis Alexander Price, *Henry Purcell and the London Stage* (Cambridge, 1984)
SEL	*Studies in English Literature*
SP	*Studies in Philology*
Summers, *Shadwell*	*The Complete Works of Thomas Shadwell*, ed. Montague Summers (London, 1927), 4 vols.
Summers, *Otway*	*The Complete Works of Thomas Otway*, ed. Montague Summers (London, 1926), 2 vols.
Tilley	M. P. Tilley, *A Dictionary of Proverbs in England in the Sixteenth and Seventeenth Centuries* (Ann Arbor, 1950)
Van Lennep	*The London Stage, Part 1: 1660–1800*, ed. William Van Lennep (Carbondale, Ill., 1965), 5 vols.
Vaughn	*Two Comedies by Thomas D'Urfey*, ed. Jack A. Vaughn (Rutherford, NJ, 1976)

The Libertine

2 *William, Duke . . . of Newcastle*: a distinguished courtier, equestrian, and minor playwright, Newcastle was one of the most munificent patrons during the seventeenth century. Before the Civil War, Newcastle supported dramatists such as Jonson, Brome, and Shirley. During the Restoration, he assisted Dryden, with whom he collaborated on the comedy, *Sir Martin Mar-all* (1667), but it was Shadwell, the self-professed follower of Jonsonian humours comedy, who earned Newcastle's deepest friendship. Sixty-seven at the outset of the Restoration, Newcastle and his wife Margaret, also a noteworthy amateur writer, were figures from an older Caroline age, quaint and eccentric to onlookers like Pepys. Newcastle supported the king during the Civil War, commanding the royalist armies in the north of England. After their defeat, he followed the court into exile abroad for sixteen years and drained his estates on Prince Charles's behalf. Margaret estimated their losses at roughly £1 million. After the Restoration, Charles II failed to recompense Newcastle adequately for his loyalty. *The Libertine* would be the last literary work dedicated to Newcastle, who died on Christmas day of 1676. For additional information, see Geoffrey Trease, *Portrait of a Cavalier: William Cavendish, First Duke of Newcastle* (New York, 1979).

5 *your grace's unwearied bounty*: Shadwell mentions visiting Welbeck, one of Newcastle's country seats, and benefiting from the peer's comments on a play. Shadwell dedicated four plays to William, one to Margaret, and another to his son. Like Dryden, Shadwell collaborated on a joint venture with Newcastle, *The Triumphant Widow*, which was performed in 1674 and published after Newcastle's death in 1676.

19 *your quality*: suitable to rank or social station.

26 *wait upon your grace*: pay a respectful visit to; call upon with the intention of showing respect or admiration.

28 *Welbeck*: the family acquired Welbeck, a former Premonstratensian abbey in Sherwood Forest, in 1597. Much beloved by Newcastle, Welbeck was decimated during the Civil War. Upon returning to the estate after his long exile abroad, Newcastle found it bereft of woods and wildlife. He set about rebuilding the estate, no small feat given his straitened circumstances.

33 *worship*: respect.

56 *as any return*: compensation.

THE CHARACTERS OF THE PLAY

As Montague Summers points out in his edition of Shadwell's plays, there are several errors in the original *dramatis personae*. Don Octavio is not 'Brother to Maria'; he is her lover. Maria is not the maid of Leonora; rather, an important character in her own right, Maria follows Don John, attempting to exact revenge for his murder of her father and brother. These and other errors—an unusual number for a Restoration script— suggest that Shadwell, perhaps buoyed by the success of the play, hurried it into print without producing fair copy for the publisher. Although the first edition does not list the cast, we know from the prompter John Downes that the great Thomas Betterton played the title role of Don John.

PREFACE

2 *The story from which I took . . . Spain, Italy, and France*: according to a French nineteenth-century scholar, the story of Don Juan was based on an actual event described in the chronicles of Seville. Louis Viardot claims that Don Juan Tenorio, part of a distinguished family in Seville, killed the Commander de Ulloa, whose daughter he had abducted. Franciscan monks lured Don Juan into a trap and killed him. Later, hoping to make an example of Don Juan, they circulated the story that he had gone into the chapel housing the memorial statue of the Commander to insult him, only to be cast down into Hell by the statue. To this story Viardot attributes the origins of the Don Juan myth. See Louis Viardot, *Études sur l'histoire des institutions, de la littérature, du théâtre et des beaux-arts en Espagne* (Paris, 1835).

6 *It was first put into a Spanish play . . . were made upon the story*: Shadwell gives an accurate summary of the earlier versions of this play. The Spanish dramatist Tirso de Molina wrote *El Burlador de Sevilla* (1630) which became the basis for several Italian versions of the play: one by Jacinto Andrea Cicognini, *Convitato di pietra* (*c.*1650); another by Onofrio Giliberto under the same title, now lost (1652); and then the *commedia* version introduced by the Italian troupes into France (1658). The success of the *commedia* Don Juan play inspired two French playwrights, Dorimon (1658) and Villiers (1659) to produce their own versions, both entitled *Le Festin de Pierre ou le fils criminel*. Molière's own *Festin de Pierre* appeared in 1665, the best known of the French plays on the subject. Four years later in 1669, the French actor Rosimond borrowed heavily from Dorimon, Villiers, and Molière to produce *Le Nouveau Festin de Pierre*. It is this version of the story—a series of pastiches—that provided Shadwell with the basis for *The Libertine* in 1676.

10 *And all the rest . . . which has been done upon the subject*: the first three acts, which include a shipwreck, rapes, abandoned wives, and multiple

murders (including parricide), create a Don Juan figure who is far more dissolute and violent than his predecessors, someone who is monstrous and inhuman, as his victims allege throughout the play. Shadwell has indeed 'varied' the story considerably from Molière and the other dramatists who have written on the Don Juan myth.

11 *the irregularities of the play*: Shadwell appears to be quite aware of the unusual nature of this play which, as several critics have observed, veers wildly in tone from horror to comedy. The play is also 'irregular' in ignoring the classical unities, a dramatic convention Shadwell knew as evinced in his preface to *The Sullen Lovers* (1668): 'I have in this Play, as neer as I could, observ'd the three Unities, of Time, Place, and Action' (*Shadwell*, i. 10).

17 *ago*: 'agon' (1676).

19 *Atheisto Fulminato . . . as a part of devotion*: Shadwell here refers to *auto sacramentals*, verse plays on religious themes performed in convents and monasteries during the fifteenth and sixteenth centuries. The story of a morally bankrupt atheist, the *Atheisto Fulminato* was among the stories told in these plays and may have provided a basis for subsequent dramas about Don Juan.

22 *the success of this play*: according to the prompter John Downes, '*The Libertine* and *Virtuoso*: Both Wrote by Mr. *Shadwell*; they were both very well Acted, and got the Company great Reputation. The *Libertine* perform'd by Mr. *Betterton* Crown'd the Play' (Downes, 78).

24 *town*: the urban elite; those with sufficient cultural capital to be the opinion makers of the town.

26 *above five days writing*: dramatists during this period aspired to compositional celerity; slow writing was considered a mark of intellectual dullness, as lampoons and satires from the period make apparent. Shadwell was especially sensitive to accusations of 'slowness'. Large and bulky, his physical appearance was taken as a visual sign—a metonymy— of his mental dullness, as was his habit of using opium to relieve pain. See, for instance, Dryden's portrait of Shadwell in *MacFlecknoe*.

32 *Love and Revenge*: Shadwell here refers to a play by Elkanah Settle, with whom he conducted a war of words for several years. The quarrel began when Shadwell, Dryden, and Crowne published a pamphlet in 1674 attacking Settle's play, *The Empress of Morocco* (1674). In the postscript to *Love and Revenge* (1674), Settle retaliated, disparaging the members of 'our Impertinent Tribe' who claim to write plays in 'Three Weeks, or a Months time', a direct hit against Shadwell. He further asserted Shadwell was 'Lazy, if not Dull' (M2ᵛ), thus originating a character of the dramatist that would persist for years. Worst of all, Settle poached on Shadwell's territory: *Love and Revenge* is dedicated to the duke of Newcastle, Shadwell's adored patron; and Settle's plays were being

produced by the Duke's Company, the same company to which Shadwell had moved, as had Dryden, in the mid-seventies. The feud continued for another year. Settle, infuriated by Shadwell's remarks in *The Libertine*, wrote his sharpest attack yet in the preface to *Ibrahim the Illustrious Bassa* (1677).

33 *I having before publicly owned the writing two plays in so short a time*: actually, Shadwell had made this statement three times previously. In the preface to *The Sullen Lovers*, Shadwell said he 'wrote in haste' (Summers, *Shadwell*, i. 12). Of *The Miser* (1672), Shadwell's adaptation of Molière's *L'Avare*, he claims to have written it 'in less than a moneth' (Summers, *Shadwell*, ii. 16). And in the preface to *Psyche* (1673), Shadwell declares that the opera was 'a thing written in five weeks' (ibid., ii. 279).

38 *The Conquest of China*: a popular play by Settle, produced at Dorset Garden by the Duke's Company in late spring of 1675. The success of this and other plays by Settle threatened the authorial dominance of Dryden and Shadwell.

45 *servant to his majesty*: on the title-page to *The Conquest of China* (London, 1676), Settle signs himself 'Servant to His Majesty', a fictitious honorific that clearly rankled Shadwell no end.

48 *he is sworn into in Extraordinary*: in royal households, a rank just below those styled 'in ordinary'; again, Shadwell emphasizes the fictitious nature of these honorary titles that Settle claims for himself.

54 *that will not own him*: gentlemen who will not profess fellowship or fraternity with him.

56 *to tax them*: censure, reprove.

61 *for the good of the Duke's Theatre*: as mentioned previously, the Duke's Theatre employed both dramatists; here Shadwell snidely insinuates that Settle's 'fustian', the deprecatory term often levelled against his florid tragic style, has lost the players money. The Duke's Company actually did quite well by Settle.

PROLOGUE

2 *bloody*: blood-stained.

   critics: complaints about critics were legend. Not to be confused with the professionals who write for newspapers and magazines—a later development—these critics were young men of fashion who sat in the pit and made loud, often unpleasant, remarks about the playwright and the production.

3 *picaroons*: pirates; can also refer to pirate ships.

   road: sheltered area of water near the shore where vessels may lie in safety; a roadstead.

4 *snap*: catch or seize quickly or by surprise.

6 *Ostend privateers*: also Oostende; a Flemish port town, Ostend was a favourite haunt of pirates because of its strategic position on the English channel coast.

15 *The most irregular play upon the stage*: Shadwell comments on the 'irregular' nature of the play in the Preface. See also the note to the Preface, l. 11

25 *predestination*: in theological terms, predestination is the act of God fore-ordaining the fate of humans, both in this and the afterlife. Here Shadwell jokes that the critics have damned the play, foreordaining its fate before anyone has seen the performance.

28 *Our scarcity of plays*: although performance records for this period remain sketchy, it appears that the preceding two months before the première of *The Libertine* saw few new plays. Shadwell's semi-opera *Psyche* was produced at Dorset Garden on 27 February; Lee's florid tragedy *Sophonisba* premièred at the rival Drury Lane Theatre at the end of April; and Settle's *The Conquest of China* took the boards at Dorset Garden at the end of May. Several revivals of 'old stock' plays (plays written before the Civil War) took place, but overall it seems to have been a 'thin' period for the companies, perhaps because they were both coming toward the end of the theatre season.

33 *Caesar*: Pellegrin takes this as an allusion to Charles II, 'known for his interest in all aspects of the drama' (p. 143).

1.1 s.d. *A street in Seville*: the first edition, hereafter referred to as Q1, does not indicate the location of this scene, but subsequent action reveals that it takes place out of doors.

4 *fantastic*: Don John uses this word in the seventeenth-century sense of bizarre or fanciful, not, as in our modern sense, as a superlative.

11 *infallible nature*: in their discussion, the three men have inverted the common ethical formula prevalent in the seventeenth century whereby one was to follow conscience or the dictates of 'right reason'. Here, the Dons maintain that conscience obfuscates the animal passions which alone should inform our actions.

19 *wantonly they roll*: wanton or luxuriate in.

23 *pupillage*: the condition of being a pupil or scholar; also, a minor or ward.

31 *Nature gave us our senses . . . all objects sense conveys*: Don John employs bad logic here, arguing for the primacy of the five senses since they convey all objects to the mind. The philosopher John Locke, who in all likelihood was writing *An Essay upon Human Understanding* during this period, systematized the apprehension of external objects by the mind; however, he drew a sharp distinction between *primary* and *secondary* sense perception. As Locke observed, the mind, once it is full of images, must still perform an operation that *does something* with these data.

Clearly, a human being must deploy reason, judgement, conscience, and a host of other mental operations in order to arrive at meaningful conclusions. Don John's illogical syllogism would have been evident to the better educated members of the audience.

35 *cholic*: i.e. thou illness of the mind.

41 *phlegmatic*: according to humours theory, phlegm was one of the four fluids in the body that, if unchecked, had the potential to dominate one's personality. A phlegmatic personality was marked by sluggishness and lethargy.

45 *keep'st the door*: a cant set-phrase for 'acts as a pimp or bawd'. See the epilogue to Shakespeare's *The History of Troilus and Cressida* where Pandarus refers to the 'Brethren and sisters of the hold-door trade' (5.10.50).

48 *halters and axes*: standard instruments of dispatch—the hangman's noose and the executioner's axe.

49 *men of as pretty parts*: i.e. men of as genteel appearances. The expression also connotes gentlemen who possess striking talents and capacities.

56 *like master, like man*: an old aphorism, according to Summers. He cites Porter's *The Two Angry Women of Abingdon* (1599): 'like tutor like scholar'.

76 *to my hopeful master*: i.e. in comparison to my hopeful master.

turn: 'turu' (1676). Jacomo uses 'turn loose' in the sense of unleashing a hunting dog or another animal of prey.

Beelzebub: the Hebrew means 'fly-lord'; by the time of the New Testament, it meant 'prince of demons'. In *Paradise Lost*, Milton ranks Beelzebub just below Satan in the hierarchy of fallen angels.

78 *rascal*: a rebuke to Jacomo. Don John is putting him firmly in his place. Between social equals, 'rascal' was a deliberate insult, a term of provocation

85 *whither*: 'whether' (1676).

95 *insipid*: devoid of taste or judgement; foolish, dull, stupid. As Pellegrin points out, Shadwell habitually uses this word in the seventeenth-century sense throughout the play (p. 145).

109 *decently*: suitably, fittingly.

110 *jealous coxcomb*: suspicious fool.

127 *carbonado*: a piece of meat, scored and grilled; thus, to 'carbonado' someone meant to slash or score his body with a sword.

136 *save the pox a labour*: in its advanced stages, syphilis—known during the period as 'the pox'—attacks the cartilage of the nose, resulting sometimes in grotesque disfigurement. In effect, Don John says he will chop off Jacomo's nose, thereby saving the disease the labour of rotting it off.

136 *sirrah*: a term of address to men or boys expressing contempt or authority on the part of the speaker.

145 *formal fops*: prudish fools.

154 *the devil and the witch*: Summers thinks this expression alludes to an incident in Lille in 1661 when the students of a woman accused of witchcraft confessed to receiving 'Marks' from the devil (iii. 381). The allusion might not be that specific: nervous jokes about concourse between witches and the devil were common in the seventeenth century.

156 *would be free . . . durst not venture*: i.e. would be free from further contact with the devil if it were not for fear of what he might do in the present.

190 *but have bowels for you*: have pity for you.

201 *earnest*: a pledge or foretaste.

212 *receipt*: recipe.

215 *A deuce*: 'misfortune, mischief; the Devil' (*OED*). Frequently used in exclamatory or imprecatory phrases (in which 'the devil' can be substituted).

217 *Inhuman*: 'Inhumane' (1676); note, I have regularized to 'inhuman' throughout the text. The early modern use of the word collapses together both meanings, 'inhuman' and 'inhumane'.

235 *another-guess man*: another kind of man.

243 *His nose . . . is somewhat short*: the snub nose was typical of servants in classical comedy. Jacomo inadvertently advertises to Leonora his low status, as well as his sexual insufficiency, given the traditional association between noses and genitals, what John Kerrigan calls the 'genital nose'. See 'A Complete History of Comic Noses', in Michael Corder, Peter Holland, and John Kerrigan (eds), *English Comedy* (Cambridge, 1994), 241–66.

282 *she's another woman*: 'she's a woman' (1697).

292 *served her in her kind*: i.e. treated her according to her social position as a mistress (possessed her sexually).

302 *upon my clavis*: in Latin, *clavis* means key. Don John could be punning on the standard joke about locks and keys (i.e. female and male genitalia), swearing, in effect, upon his penis. Clavis could also be a synonym for clavicle, the collar bone. The former meaning makes more sense given Don Antonio's libidinous nature.

329 S.D. *Window opens*: it is not entirely clear how this would have been staged. The Restoration theatre, as Jocelyn Powell notes, retained some aspects of the earlier Elizabethan playhouse, including a closed gallery over the stage that normally housed the musicians. Maria could throw

open one of the windows in this gallery, speak her line, and then descend stairs to the main level.

333 S.D. *Reads by a dark lantern*: a lantern containing a sliding device to conceal the light; thus it functions as Maria's 'false light'.

351 *Cloris or a Phyllis*: standard female names in pastoral and erotic poetry (see, for instance, Rochester's lyrics).

354 *clear*: splendid, brilliant; of women, beautiful or fair.

401 *she'll*: 'he'll' (1676).

410 *blackamoor*: a black-skinned African or Ethiopian; any dark-skinned person.

416 *bustle*: conflict; a struggle or scuffle.

424 S.D. *going the round*: making the nightly watch.

427 S.D. *Offers to run*: i.e. tries or attempts to run.

429 *bilbow*: a sword; more specifically, a sword from Bilbao in Spain, which was known throughout Europe for its fine quality.

440 *I'll swear the murder against you*: i.e. I'll swear you committed the murder.

445 *pinked*: stabbed; pierced.

1.2 S.D.: stage directions in the first edition, which indicate that the action has moved from the street to Maria's chamber, call for a new scene division.

18 *Your heroes in plays beat five times as many*: heroic plays, especially those written by Dryden in the 1660s, featured protagonists like Almanzor in *The Conquest of Granada* (1670) who were given to florid speeches and unrealistic feats of daring. Shadwell's enemy, Elkanah Settle (see the Preface), also included super-heroes in his plays of spectacle and horror.

2.1 S.D. *Don John's lodging in Seville*: the locale is not specified; however, Jacomo at the end of this scene declares that 'the house is beset', suggesting that the action occurs within Don John's lodging.

12 *You oblige me extremely*: i.e. you place me under extreme obligation (by what you are doing for me).

14 *in exchange of certainty that*: i.e. even though what replaces doubt is a certainty which.

20 *buffle*: fool; simpleton.

27 *ride post*: ride with speed or haste.

58 *hemp*: fibre used in the making of rope; also, slang for a hangman's rope.

68 *I can hold no longer*: i.e. I can restrain myself no longer.

107 *What a devil would you have more*: Don John uses 'devil' here as a blasphemous intensifier, a gasp of emphasis and interjection.

23 *rook*: cheat, swindle.

123 *play upon the square*: to play fairly ('fair and square').

144 *of course*: conventional; formulaic; demanded by the situation.

159 S.D. *Enter six Women*: as Summers notes, Shadwell in all likelihood borrowed this device from James Howard's popular comedy, *All's Mistaken; or, The Mad Couple* (1667). Philador, the madcap rake, promises marriage to half-a-dozen women in order to win sexual favours from them. The women then dog him continually throughout the play. See Summers, *Shadwell*, iii. 381.

179 *If you go to that*: i.e. if you come to that.

206 *fleas in their ears*: proverbial, from the French *avoir la puce en l'oreille*; to be tormented by the cares and desires of love.

230 *repair*: return; come.

247 *Grand Signior*: the Sultan of Turkey; the possessor of a harem of wives and concubines.

255 *Don Lopez*: Q1 assigns this and the preceding speech to Don Antonio, a clear error. The subsequent exchange, especially Don Lopez's statement 'poor harlots', suggests that he should also utter 'use your ladies civilly, for shame'.

266 *several and respective*: separate, distinct.

271 *epithalamium*: verses composed for the occasion of a wedding.

286 *chew the cud*: reflect on things done or said; therefore, the singer says he will not waste time reflecting after love-making but move on to the next woman.

289 *stomach*: appetite.

310 S.D. *Dance*: Q1 does not make apparent the identity of the dancers. From the dialogue, it would appear that Don John dances with the Fourth Woman, to whom he has just spoken. It is also possible that Don John dances with all of his 'wives'.

323 *Lucrece*: the story of Lucrece (also Lucretia) and Tarquin has figured in art and poetry, including a long poem by Shakespeare. According to the legend, the chaste Roman matron Lucrece was raped by Sextus Tarquinius, son of the tyrannical Tarquinius Superbus, king of Rome. Initially she resisted Tarquin's demands, but he threatened to murder her and a slave, leaving both of their bodies to be found together. Fear of dishonour induced Lucrece to submit. Afterwards, she summoned her husband and father to her tent, told of the deed, and then killed herself rather than bring dishonour to the family. Her family and friends, headed by Lucius Junius Brutus, overthrew the Tarquins, thus eliminating the monarchy and ushering in the Roman republic. The story, a parable of female chastity, also served as an allegory for freedom against tyranny. Nathaniel Lee, a contemporary of the dramatists in this volume, wrote a

tragedy, *Lucius Junius Brutus* (1680) upon the subject. The play was banned for its 'Scandalous Expressions & Reflections upon ye Government'. Lee's version of the story, according to Susan J. Owen, 'celebrates parliamentary institutions, the rule of law, and the ability to put political obligations before personal ones'. See 'Drama and Political Crisis', in Deborah Payne Fisk (ed.), *The Cambridge Companion to English Restoration Theatre* (Cambridge, 2000), 170.

351   *providence*: foresight; also a blasphemous variation on the notion of divine providence.

361   *re infecta*: with the matter unfinished (i.e. without having been ravished).

370   *horrid fact*: horrid deed or crime.

382   *meddle*: have sexual intercourse with.

396   *beldam*: a grandmother; more generally, a woman of advanced years.

399   *Shift for yourself*: look after yourself, take care of yourself.

405   *fast*: secured.

2.2   Q1 does not indicate a change of location, but the stage directions and dialogue suggest that the scene has shifted back to Maria's chamber or to a street near her house.

     s.d.: '*In Man's habit, Enter* Maria, *and her Maid* Flora' (1676).

2   *Thus I have abandoned . . . for thee*: the punctuation in Q1 appears to be confused here ('Thus I have abandon'd all my Fortune, and laid by My Sex. Revenge for thee'). Q1 sets the dialogue in this scene as verse, but the punctuation and lineation argue for prose, which I have produced.

4   *bravos*: hired murderers or assassins.

5   *beset*: assailed; attacked.

18   *engine*: engine of torture, in this case, the rack.

31   *wracked*: ruined or destroyed.

32   *enow*: plural form of 'enough'.

40   *man's innocent nature*: a popular sentiment in verse about the 'golden age', the period before man's 'innocent nature' was corrupted by social conventions; ironically, Maria's position is not too far from Don John's. Both uphold idealized notions of natural states of being that existed prior to fallen civilization.

42   *complain*: lament.

2.3   s.d. *Bravos watch at Don John's house*: again, Q1 does not specify a location change; however, the stage direction clearly indicates the new scene.

12   *van*: the foremost position in a group of men moving forward, usually in military formation.

16 *take place of*: take precedence over; go before.

27 *fall on*: a command to begin fighting.

29 S.D. '*They fight, and are driven off, but* Maria *and* Flora *remain*' (1676). Maria's exclamation two lines later ('O cowardly villains!') expresses her dismay at the Bravos' cowardice, thus suggesting that the Dons are successful in driving her hired assassins offstage.

49 *a stag at bay*: a male deer that, unable to flee further, turns and defends itself from the hunters and hounds.

54 *laid horses*: prepared and/or saddled horses.

73 S.D. *Ghost of Don John's father rises*: Dorset Garden, where *The Libertine* was first mounted, certainly had the technical capacity for this sort of special effect. The Ghost most likely rose slowly through a trap in the stage floor. Clinking chains or rumbling thunder might have provided a suitable aural accompaniment.

112 *bugbears*: a goblin in the shape of a bear that is supposed to devour children; more generally, an imaginary fear or terror.

113 *urge on*: push forward; hasten along.

3.1.2 *Luff, luff*: in nautical language, to luff means to turn the bow of the ship into the wind to empty the sails. In a storm, such as the one represented in this scene, luffing is essential: it allows the sailors to furl the sails and also minimizes the possibility of capsizing. A lightning strike to the forecastle (see below), not poor handling, eventually sinks this ship.

9 *squibs and crackers*: these are different kinds of firecrackers. The squib, cylindrical in shape, explodes lightly, while the cracker explodes in a sharp succession of reports.

23 *Your drowning will prepare you for burning*: in other words, your drowning will prepare you for burning eternally in hell.

24 *forecastle*: the fore part of the ship; more specifically, a short, raised deck at the fore end of a sailing vessel.

32 *unmanned*: deprived of courage by extraordinary circumstances, as occurs to the Captain here.

58 S.D. *A great shriek . . . all leap overboard*: '*A great shriek, they all leap overboard*' (1676). The stage direction in Q1 does not make apparent the identity of the 'leapers'. The dialogue, however, suggests that the Dons have grabbed the sole lifeboat for themselves, leaving Jacomo and the hapless crew little choice but to abandon the burning ship.

3.2 As often happens with Q1, scene changes are not indicated, but the action here and the Hermit's reference to 'these dreadful Cliffs' and 'this neighbouring Cave' clearly indicate that the scene has shifted from the storm at sea to the shore.

24 *it*: the neuter pronoun was sometimes used for children and servants, as in 'it was a sweet child'. Don John's use of the pronoun reinforces Jacomo's subservience, as well as his childishness.

38 *ever a*: any.

48 *physic*: medicine; the profession of medicine.

49 *cordials*: medicines that stimulate the circulation.

51 *nastiness*: as Michael Cordner points out, by the Restoration 'nasty' and its derivatives designated that which is low-class or demeaning. Don John is most likely referring to the 'nasty' (i.e. plain or even ragged) ecclesiastical robe worn by the Hermit as part of his vow of poverty.

67 *salacious*: lustful, lecherous; provocative of lust.

74 *necessitated*: preordained, predetermined; beyond our wills. Don Lopez thus articulates once again the libertine belief that appetite, not reason, governs human action.

77 *that*: i.e. heaven.

101 *as those represent them, this*: 'this' refers to the understanding, which Don John ranks below apprehension since, for him, it is a secondary function of the mind.

130 *cavaliers*: in general terms, courtly gentlemen; more specifically, 'cavaliers' refers to the royalists who supported Charles I during the Civil War. Don Francisco judges the Dons on their courtly manners and genteel appearance and assumes they are cavaliers. By associating the libertine Dons with cavalier behaviour, Shadwell is also making a sly comment on the libertine royalists who surrounded the hedonistic Charles II.

135 *You pose us with this kindness*: i.e. you overwhelm us with your kindness.

142 *adventure*: piece of good fortune; chance occurrence.

143 *toys*: trifles.

151 S.D. *in man's habit*: Q1 in an earlier stage direction suggests that both Maria and Flora are disguised as men (see the beginning of 2.1); here, however, 'in man's habit' appears to apply to Maria only.

207 S.D. *extends ... stage floor*: Jacomo must appear in such a way as to suggest his emergence from the sea. Given the capabilities of Dorset Garden, it is likely that Jacomo gradually comes into view through one of the traps in the stage floor.

250 *a Spanish wife*: Restoration plays frequently contrast the freedom enjoyed by Englishwomen with the restrictions visited upon Spanish women. Unlike their fathers, brothers, and husbands, Spanish women were expected to stay at home and entertain themselves with innocent pastimes, such as needlework.

259 *one throw*: i.e. of the dice.

343

264 *ramble*: in the Restoration, this word has a sexual overtone. To 'ramble' is to break out and have a good time, perhaps even a sexual escapade. See, for instance, Hellena's declaration to her sister Florinda in Aphra Behn's *The Rover* (1677), 'let's ramble' (1.1.187).

267 *wittol*: a contented cuckold; a man complaisant about the infidelity of his wife.

273 *indifferent*: impartial, fair, even-handed.

284 *treats*: entertains.

  glass-coach: a recent and expensive innovation.

285 *hackney*: another type of coach popular in the period.

286 *gallant*: lover; an attractive gentleman of fashion.

293 *none will into*: none will enter into.

296 *never unhooded . . . just upon the quarry*: i.e. the hawks are not released until the quarry is in sight.

318 *'for better, for worse'*: the famous phrase from the marriage service in the Book of Common Prayer.

350 *proper*: genuine, true; excellent, admirable; good-looking, handsome.

371 *sneaking*: mean, contemptible; petty, paltry.

393 *generous*: having the qualities and virtues appropriate to a gentleman; Jacomo is being sarcastic here.

395 *serve you not in your kind*: i.e. if I don't do the same to you.

399 *What makes him here?*: what brings him here? What is he doing here?

424 *improve*: take advantage of, derive benefit from, make best use of.

446 *dispense with*: i.e. absolve or release himself from fulfilling his promise.

477 *Victoria, victoria*: Latin; an exclamation of triumph.

478 *hopeful*: inspiring hope; promising. Jacomo is being ironic here.

556 *use you kindly*: i.e. use you fittingly. The implication here is sexual.

571 *sower cudgels*: 'sower' here most likely indicates a country pronunciation of 'sour' (in the sense of something that is unpleasant or disagreeable)

  wasler: to waste (dialect).

595 *spaniel love*: it was a commonplace that spaniels, even when beaten, never forsook their masters, so fawning was their nature. Cf. the proverbs, 'Spaniels that fawn when beaten, will never forsake their masters', or 'A spaniel, a woman, and a walnut-tree, the more they're beaten the better they be'.

601 *not such a woman*: no other such woman.

609 *subtlest*: working secretly, taking effect imperceptibly; cleverly designed or contrived.

627 *object*: sight.

4.1.2 *several*: different.

9 *shall to pot*: be 'bagged' as hunted game. Don Lopez could also be using 'pot' in a horticultural sense, whereby the maids are receptacles (or 'pots') for the 'seed' of the two men.

30 *tickles my spleen*: spleen in this sense means ill temper or spite; therefore, the mere thought of deceiving the bridegrooms provokes Don John's gleeful spite.

48 *beam*: i.e. to hang yourself from.

122 *perfected*: completed, brought to fruition.

123 *duccatoon*: in the seventeenth and eighteenth centuries, a silver coin found in Italy and some other European countries, worth from five to six shillings sterling.

126 *have a vein opened*: letting blood was a common treatment for madness or frenzy.

127 *impostor*: cheat.

133 *lay . . . by the heels*: arrest or confine; put in stocks or irons.

146 *wonderful*: marvellous or astonishing.

194 *by your favour*: i.e. your kind indulgence or leave. Jacomo is being sarcastic.

4.2.18 *Saturn's happy days*: in some mythological accounts, Saturn's reign ushered in a golden age of civilization.

19 *luxury*: lasciviousness; indulgence in food, drink, or dress

20 *homely*: simple; unsophisticated.

26 *riot*: indulgence, revelry.

39 *grievance*: 'gievance' (1676)

77 *jugging*: the nightingale was thought to make a warbling sound of 'jug jug'.

119 *as the Romans did the Sabines*: Don John invokes another famous story of rape from antiquity. The Sabines, one of the Sabelli group, lived in the hills north-east of Rome. According to legend, they were known for the simplicity and virtue of their lives. The story of the rape of the Sabine women by the single followers of Romulus might be an attempt to explain the assimilation of the Sabines into the Roman population; they were admitted to full Roman citizenship in 268 BC.

129 *Shall I keep a rascal for a cipher*: a cipher in this sense means an arithmetical figure of no value; hence Don John asks rhetorically if his 'rascal' Jacomo is merely a zero, a nothing. This remark follows upon the heels of his previous threat to cut Jacomo 'into so many pieces, it shall pose a mathematician to sum up the fractions of thy body'.

153 *a very Tarquin*: see note to 2.1. 328.

159 *hot*: lustful, lecherous.

161 *the sign's in Scorpio*: in astrology a sign of fertility; in man it rules his penis and scrotum.

165 *my representers*: i.e. my testicles. Jacomo suggests that his testicles represent or symbolize his future progeny.

176 *when we have housed 'em*: followed them to their house or abode.

4.4.9 *look to yourself*: i.e. take care of yourself; mind your own business.

37 S.D. *salute*: greet, usually with a flourish.

47 *put it about*: Don John asks each of them to echo his toast to the Ghost's 'health'.

48 *cher entire*: 'Don John tells his guest that he would rather have served *cher entire*, that is, an entire roast rather than the less desirable cuts of meat used in a "ragoust" (ragout = stew). The punning here turns on the French for meat: *chair*, food in general; and the term of endearment: *cher* or *chère*. By extension, then, Don John is suggesting that he would have produced young women for the statue's delectation, rather than leftover or inferior fare, "but the Women care not for Marble"' (Pellegrin, 149–50).

67 S.D. *Devils rise*: Restoration playhouses such as Dorset Garden were well equipped for these sorts of special effects. The devils would 'rise' through a trap in the stage floor, slowly appearing to the audience.

85 *burnt brandy . . . drink fit for devils*: Don John associates 'burnt' brandy with the fires of hell the devils presumably inhabit.

5.1 S.D. *back, breast, and headpiece*: Jacomo wears partial armour consisting of a metal sheath covering his torso and a helmet.

2 *one day with another*: one day after another; in perpetuity.

6 *tierce*: the third position in fencing for guard, parry, or thrust; also the third of the eight parries in swordplay.

29 *placed there for probation*: she has been enrolled as a novice in the convent.

51 *fired the temple at Ephesus*: built in the latter half of the sixth century BC by the architect Chersiphron, this temple was burnt down by an Ephesian named Herostatus on the night Alexander the Great was born, 13–14 October 356 BC. Under torture, Herostatus confessed that he had done the deed to immortalize his name; in retaliation, the Ephesians passed a decree condemning him to everlasting oblivion. History, nevertheless, took notice of his name.

61 *Alexander the Great*: born in 356 BC, the son of Philip II of Macedon. By the age of 32, he had founded an empire stretching from the Adriatic to

India. Exhausted and wounded from his many battles, he died at 33. Alexander figures in the legends of many nations. The Egyptians considered him a god, while the Arabo-Persian tradition represented him as a heroic saint. Israelite lore associated Alexander with the house of David as a precursor to the Messiah. Christian tales from the Middle Ages told of how *Alexandre le Grant* searched for paradise.

89   *a piece of eight*: the Spanish dollar or peso, worth the value of eight *reals*. It was marked with the figure 8.

116   *dark-lantern*: see note to 333.

119   *at a fault*: loss of scent; to be off track.

130   *There lie*: not entirely clear. Jacomo could be addressing himself or his armour.

154   S.D. *probationers*: novices.

205   *mobile*: rabble; mob.

5.2.14   S.D.   *Ghost descends*: presumably through the trap in the stage floor.

69   S.D.   *flourish*: although Q1 does not specify a locale, it seems likely that the music would first sound offstage, the devils entering and thus inspiring Don Lopez to say, 'What's here? Music to treat us with?'

112   *former chaos*: Don John alludes to Greek mythology here, particularly the notion that the universe was created by the gods out of chaos.

121   S.D.   *Scene shuts*: Restoration playhouses deployed movable scenery. Flats or shutters, which ran along grooves in the stage floor, could be opened or closed to reveal successive scenes.

EPILOGUE

9   *solemn leagues and covenants*: a phrase rich with political and religious associations for Restoration audiences. The Solemn League and Covenant of 1643 banded together the Scots against attempts by Charles I to impose an episcopal system of church government, including the use of the Book of Common Prayer. The so-called Covenanters were instrumental in the events leading up to the Civil War. Later, after the Restoration, all judges and office-holders were compelled to sign a document pledging that they would not enter into 'leagues and covenants'. The phrase also has clear biblical overtones: the Pentateuch, the first five books of the Old Testament, are largely concerned with establishing the covenant between God and his chosen people, the Jews. In more general terms, the phrase 'solemn leagues and covenants' would have conjured up to contemporary audiences political and religious opposition to Royalist rule—it smacked of the Interregnum.

22   *Angling for single money with a shoe*: it was common for debtors in prison to hold a shoe outside the grate or window of their cell (which sometimes

faced the street) in order to beg for coins ('single money') from people passing by.

29 *within the pit*: critics, those self-styled 'men of wit', usually sat in the pit, the benches that faced the stage (and therefore put them within hearing range of the hapless actors who were forced to listen to disparaging comments).

31 *to fright the city*: shorthand for the citizens, the tradesmen and their wives who were often the butt of jokes because of their supposed naivety.

35 *machines*: by the mid-1670s, stage machinery was increasingly used by the companies to produce special effects. Dorset Garden, where this play was produced, was especially well equipped for descents and movable scenery. Shadwell's previous play *Psyche* (which premièred two months earlier) drew heavily upon spectacle; by contrast, *The Libertine*, despite the presence of ghosts and devils, was fairly simple.

36 *behind our scenes*: as we know from Pepys's *Diary*, it was common for visitors to go backstage and visit the actors and actresses. The Lord Chamberlain's records make numerous mention of complaints lodged by the players against these visitors—who could be a nuisance, especially to the actresses—but the custom persisted.

37 *guineas*: first struck in 1663, the guinea had a nominal value of 21*s*. Much of the gold used for making these coins was imported from Guinea by the Africa Company, hence the name.

40 *free ingress and egress*: this epilogue, one of the more salacious examples of the form, plays upon the sexual availability of the actresses. The epilogue suggests the actresses shall be 'kind' (a euphemism for sexually compliant) to visitors and give them free 'ingress and egress' (i.e. the visitors can come and go at will). Clearly, the allusion is sexual as well, hinting that privileged visitors will have free entrance to the bodies of the actresses, not merely to the stage space behind the scenery (the painted shutters that ran along grooves in the stage). The 'sweet chink of guineas' will ease access; moreover, if none of the actresses pleases, Jacomo promises to procure a girl of 'sixteen'.

The Man of Mode

DEDICATION

1 *To Her Royal Highness the Duchess*: married to the king's brother, James, Mary of Modena became duchess of York in 1673 and queen upon her husband's accession to the throne in 1685. James's first wife Anne Hyde, daughter of Sir Edward Hyde, the earl of Clarendon, had died on 31 March 1671, and in the summer of 1672 negotiations ensued for a new

marriage. James during this period converted to Roman Catholicism; and Louis XIV, eager to encourage the prince's new religion, proposed a match with one of the two princesses of Modena. James wed Mary Beatrice by proxy on 30 September, and the House of Commons denounced the marriage shortly thereafter. Although Mary was welcomed by the court poets Dryden and Waller, her life in England was difficult. She lost several babies to death, and her religion made her unpopular with parliament and the population at large. Mary also had to contend with her husband's chronic philandering; most hurtful was his infatuation with Catherine Sedley, daughter of Sir Charles Sedley, court wit, poet, and dramatist. The Duke's Company, which produced this play, was so named after Mary's husband. Although not avid theatregoers in the manner of the king and his various mistresses, the duke and duchess of York did attend plays frequently. Etherege appears to have benefited from some sort of relationship with the duke who granted him a pension in 1682 and later (after he became king) sent him as envoy to Ratisbon in 1685.

11 *the success it had in the acting*: the prompter John Downes claimed that the comedy, 'being well Cloath'd and well Acted, got a great deal of Money'. In 1722, the critic John Dennis, recalling the original production, said 'that all the World was charm'd with Dorimont' (Van Lennep, i. 243). From these contemporary accounts it appears that Etherege's inimitable characters and sparkling dialogue enjoyed high production values.

21 *are never wanting to publish a particular*: i.e. eager to publish the singular and noteworthy 'virtues and perfections' of their patron.

THE CHARACTERS OF THE PLAY

The quarto of 1676 does not list the names of actors, an unusual omission for a Restoration play. Fortunately, the prompter John Downes noted down the cast list: Dorimant was played by Thomas Betterton, Medley by Henry Harris, Sir Fopling Flutter by William Smith, Old Bellair by Anthony Leigh, Bellair by Thomas Jevon, Mrs Loveit by Elizabeth Barry, Bellinda by Mrs Betterton, Lady Woodvill by Mrs Leigh, and Emilia by Mrs Twyford. The editors of *Roscius Anglicanus*, Judith Milhous and Robert D. Hume, unlike the editor of *The London Stage*, feel strongly that Mrs Barry originated the role of Loveit. They point out she was already performing by autumn of 1675. See Downes, 76.

PROLOGUE

Sir Car Scroope: (1649–80) a minor poet and member of the circle of court wits who congregated around Charles II. There are many references to Scroope in lampoons from the period; he was frequently ridiculed for his short stature. A member of the Green Ribbon Club, a notable Whig watering hole, Scroope never married, although at one point he courted a lady-in-waiting to the duchess of York. The baronetcy became extinct upon his death.

1 *dancers on the ropes*: an increasingly popular form of dancing after the Restoration. Although most commonly seen at fairs, rope dancers performed at Whitehall in August of 1660, again on 25 October 1667, and in the Banqueting Hall on 19 September 1671 (see Van Lennep, i. cviii). Rope dancing entailed combining conventional dancing with rope skipping and twirling. The most famous rope dancer of the period was Jacob Hall, who performed at Bartholomew and Southwark Fairs.

6 *cannot leave play*: the pun here on 'play' encompasses gambling as well as writing for the theatre, another form of 'play'.

9 *good will*: a pun meaning (1) her consent, and (2) sexual appetite (in the seventeenth century 'will' could signify carnal desire).

13 *dirty drabs*: prostitutes.

19 *while to France we go*: French theatrical practice heavily influenced the Restoration stage, sometimes to the chagrin of English dramatists, especially by the 1670s, who wanted to promote their own native tradition.

25 *your own follies may supply the stage*: a common sentiment in prologues and epilogues from the period, that the comedies merely reflect back to the audience their own follies and shortcomings.

1.1 S.D. *A dressing room ... clothes laid ready*: the stage directions for this and subsequent scenes in Dorimant's lodging are unusually detailed, suggesting Etherege's effort to individualize this character. A 'toilet' is a cloth cover, often sumptuous in material, which is draped over the dressing table.

1 *Now for some ... the world in vain*: the opening couplet of Edmund Waller's 'Of a War with Spain, and a Fight at Sea'. See *Poems*, ii, ed. Thorn Drury (London, 1901), 23.

6 *fanatic*: religious extremist. This sense of the word was fairly recent (1640s), and during the Restoration applied to Quakers, Anabaptists, and other 'nonconformists'. A 'fanatic' would thus have particular 'regret' paying taxes to the Church of England (see the next note).

Royal Aid or church duties: 'Royal Aid' was a special tax passed by parliament to raise revenue for the king. 'Church duties' were levied locally for the services of the established church (the Church of England).

11 *Who waits*: i.e. who waits on me?

17 *poaching*: carries the usual meaning of hunting game illegally, but Barnard also considers this a sexual pun on 'poke' (from the Old French *pocher*, to thrust or dig out with fingers).

21 *Foggy*: bloated, puffy; a comment on her appearance.

23 *flasket*: 'a long shallow basket' (Samuel Johnson, *Dictionary*).

26 *It is not . . . your feet I lay*: the first two lines of Waller's poem, 'The Self-Banished' (*Poems*, ed. Drury, i. 101).

27 *double-tripe*: someone so fat that she has a double stomach.

33 *culled*: selected or chosen.

35 *Tottenham*: about 7 miles to the north-east of central London. Originally a forested area, it was cleared in the seventeenth century for development. Cordner notes that Tottenham became a fashionable holiday resort for the citizens who worked in the city.

39 *angel*: a gold coin, originally known as an angel-noble, imprinted with the archangel Michael and the dragon. It was worth from 6*s.* 8*d.* to 10*s.*

48 *comes from the stone*: perhaps a freestone peach, so-called because the flesh parts easily from the stone.

Newington: a 'town in Kent from which some varieties of peach took their name' (Carnochan, 9).

52 *fruz*: a wig of short, curled—perhaps frizzy—hair.

sparkishly: when applied to a woman, it indicated an elegant or smart appearance; for a man, the connotation was more foppish.

53 *the King's box at an old play*: the connotation here is pejorative. 'Old plays' (that is, plays written before the Civil War) were often considered insufficiently modern for Restoration tastes: even plays by Jonson, Beaumont, and Shakespeare were updated and revised to appease playgoers. The king's private box would be empty and therefore available to a 'country toad' such as the one described here precisely because the king would not bother attending a performance of an 'old play'.

57 *Change*: slang for the New Exchange (1608–9), a building containing two long double galleries that housed fashionable shops and continued to be a major attraction until the eighteenth century. References to the New Exchange and the Strand abound in Restoration plays.

59 *mask*: metonymy for woman. Women of fashion, as well as prostitutes, wore masks during the period.

65 *kissing one another*: from sarcastic references here and in other plays, for instance Shadwell's *The Sullen Lovers* (1668), it can be deduced that most people considered this practice another new-fangled French importation.

69 *Good now*: interjection expressing acquiescence, surprise, or entreaty.

73 *gentlemen ushers*: men who attended upon a person of rank; by the Restoration, considered an outmoded practice.

74 *old stagers*: old hands.

75 *brandy bottle*: although cognac, a French export, was enjoyed at the

Restoration court, cheap brandy—essentially burnt wine—was consumed by people of lesser means. Medley's remark figures the Orange-Woman as an empty vessel, a mere container for the cheap brandy she consumes in prodigious quantities (see Dorimant's following rejoinder).

76 *canary*: a sweet wine from the Canary Islands. Cordner points out that 'canary' was also slang for (1) a whore and (2) a jail-bird. 'Dorimant's choice of intoxicant may hint at the orange-woman's characteristic habitat' (Cordner, 223).

85 *crudities may breed diseases*: it was commonly thought that undigested matter in the stomach caused all sorts of diseases, thus the early modern obsession with purgatives and emetics.

90 *honest*: chaste.

93 *resty*: intractable, stubborn.

94 *jade's*: commonly applied to a broken-down horse but also used for women. 'Jade' picks up on 'resty bawd' in the previous line since horses were also known to be 'resty' or difficult.

101 *a hopeful way*: perhaps pregnant. Young women in this condition were often whisked off to live in boarding houses until they could be delivered of their child (who was often dispatched to an indifferent wet nurse). The young woman could also be in 'a hopeful way' because the Orange-Woman's influence will soon make her sexually available—for a price.

126 *fine, easy, clean shape*: a graceful, attractive figure, one free from any imperfection or blemish (i.e. 'clean').

131 *Provence rose*: Carnochan emends this to 'Provins', a town near Paris known for its rose industry. As Cordner observes, there existed a Provence rose, a red rose with large round flowers, as well as a Provins rose, the *rosa gallica*. 'Provence' makes more sense in this context.

134 *delicate*: 'delicate' here encompasses a range of meanings now lost to us: lovely, graceful, elegant. The Orange-Woman could also be hinting at another connotation—that Harriet possesses a sensuous, perhaps even voluptuous nature (thus making her a fit libertine companion for Dorimant).

146 *saluted*: greeted formally, often with a bow or some other stately flourish. It can also include a kiss.

smacked: kissed with gusto; smooched loudly.

152 *trappings*: clothing.

163 *bog*: by this word Medley again emphasizes the fat, puffy appearance of the Orange-Woman.

164 *your pis aller*: literally, your last resort.

183 *vizard*: women of fashion, as well as prostitutes, often wore masks in public to disguise their identity. Medley here uses 'vizard' as an instance

of metonymy, associating Dorimant's new *amour* with the mask she wears to the playhouse.

198 *fit o' the mother*: a hysterical fit.

201 *address*: courteous approach or manner of speaking; it also connotes dexterity and adroitness, both of which are necessary in the business Dorimant describes.

210 *tenders*: has regard for; wants to protect.

226 *fop*: in general terms, a fool. Sir Fopling Flutter, the resident fop in *The Man of Mode*, is a gentleman with excessive fashion sense. In Restoration comedies, the fop is usually indicated by his outlandish appearance: an overly large wig, brightly coloured fabrics, and numerous bows and buckles. Invariably the fop is the butt of jokes.

234 *uncase*: strip of livery; dismiss from employment.

236 S.D. *Exit Handy and Footman*: previous editors note that Handy re-enters during the ensuing conversation, as Dorimant's command makes evident. I have placed his re-entry shortly before Dorimant's address to him.

241 *sack*: white wines imported from Spain and the Canary Islands.

251 *engross*: monopolize.

257 *journeymen ... lampoons*: Cordner glosses this thoroughly. 'The city journeymen's taste has turned from their traditional liking for ballads to an enthusiasm for the scurrilous and lubricious verse satires (often against named individuals) which were produced in large quantities in the 1660s and 1670s. The Shoemaker (in many ways aptly) associates the production of the latter with such gentlemen as Dorimant . . .' (p. 229).

260 *your own commentaries as well as Caesar*: there are two meanings of 'commentary' here: (1) a memoir in the manner of Caesar's writings on his own life, and (2) a satiric comment or gloss.

262 *ale and history*: Tilley records this as a proverb but, as Barnard notes, some commentators question its status as such. Barnard points out the currency of the phrase in the seventeenth century (p. 21).

271 *coxcombs*: fools, also, as Barnard observes, a possible pun on 'cockscombs', which were used as a garnish in stews or ragouts. I have followed Q1 in retaining 'coxcombs'.

273 *caterpillars*: slang for parasites or extortionists; people who prey upon society.

275 *your health ... my heart now*: 'the shoemaker asks Dorimant for money to drink his health; *next my heart* may refer to a toast drunk with hand on heart' (Carnochan, 19).

282 *soak together*: drink together.

353

283 *several*: separate.

settle-bed: a long wooden bench that could also function as a bed.

286 *Tope's the word*: perhaps the Shoemaker gently rebukes Medley for using the phrase 'bloody drunk' (a recent colloquialism) by responding with the more gentlemanly 'tope'. Barnard observes that 'tope' also functions as an exclamation, as in 'I pledge you' (p. 23). This meaning sets up the ensuing sentence, which appears to be directed at Handy.

295 *answer*: justify.

297 *men of sense*: libertines such as Dorimant and himself. Presumably, the 'reason' they advocate concerns the libertine lifestyle they want Medley to emulate.

311 *the mad fanatic . . . in Bethlem*: a reference to Oliver Cromwell's porter, Daniel, who was imprisoned in Bethlehem Hospital, the lunatic asylum known popularly as 'Bedlam'. There are other contemporary references to him.

316 *deal with Jews . . . give judgements*: depictions of Jews in seventeenth- and eighteenth-century literature drew upon ethnic stereotypes (and were therefore frequently anti-Semitic). Usury, or moneylending, was one of the few professions permitted to Jews living in the urban centres of Europe, who then found themselves in the unenviable position of being maligned for the very occupation they were forced to practise. The stereotype of the greedy or flint-hearted Jew—see Shylock, for instance—gave rise to the commonplace that a Jewish moneylender would demand especially harsh conditions for a loan, e.g. demand chattels for security ('give judgements').

322 *just*: exactly; in the correct manner.

325 *essence*: perfume.

orange-flower water: scent extracted from the orange-flower.

330 *necessary coxcombs*: fools (especially conceited or vain fools) essential to the amusement of others.

333 *fancy*: taste or critical judgement in the matter of fashion.

362 *an agreeable voice for a chamber*: a voice sufficiently melodious to entertain a lady in her chamber.

377 *jilting baggage*: originally a strumpet or loose woman, but as Barnard notes, by the 1670s it could be applied playfully to any young woman.

392 *complaisant*: deferential; eager to please.

439 *galoshes*: 'goloshoes' (1676). Clogs or rustic shoes; it could also refer to a slipper that was worn over the shoe for protection.

449 *Long's or Lockett's*: fashionable taverns in London. Lockett's, located at Charing Cross, is frequently mentioned in Restoration comedies; indeed, Etherege himself dined at the tavern. Long's was one of two taverns, one

in Covent Garden and the other in the Haymarket, operated by the Long brothers.

465 *perk up*: behave with a conceited, bold air before well-to-do people.

475 *chair*: enclosed chair or covered sedan for one person, carried on poles by two men.

477 *ride the elephant*: as Barnard notes, there are several contemporary references to elephants that were exhibited in London between 1675 and 1682. The *City Mercury* advertised in its issue dated 11–18 November 1675 an elephant 'to be seen at the *White Horse* Inn over against *Salisbury Court* in Fleet-Street' (Barnard, 31).

479 s.d. *Be calm ye great parents, etc.*: from the song 'My Lord: Great *Neptune*, for my Sake' featured in the final scene of Shadwell's operatic version of *The Tempest* (1674?).

2.1 s.d. *Lady Townley's house*: Etherege does not indicate a scene change here, but the action of 2.1 clearly unfolds in Lady Townley's London house.

40 *Mr Fourbe's*: a cheat or imposter; from the French.

the Temple: the Inner and Middle Temple of the Inns of Court, originally the property of the Knights Templars. Since the fourteenth century, this has been the centre for the legal profession in London.

52 *changeable colours*: like a silken fabric that changes colours when viewed from different angles.

57 *mum*: two meanings are possible: (1) hush or silence and (2) a colloquial variant of 'madam'.

59 *slip*: release a hunting-dog to race after its prey.

64 *flirt*: a woman of giddy, flighty character; a loose woman; a fickle, inconstant person. Old Bellair's use of the term could encompass all meanings.

crazy: broken down, ruined.

68 *a pize*: an imprecation of uncertain meaning.

keeping fools: fools who keep mistresses.

81 *pleasant*: amusing, witty. It can also during this period describe someone who is ridiculous, a meaning that might also apply to Medley.

83 *not scandalous i' the least*: Lady Townley uses 'scandalous' here in a very particular seventeenth-century sense of the word, to mean someone sufficiently offensive as to disgrace his class or social position. In the modern sense of the word, Medley is indubitably 'scandalous' insofar as he gossips with avid glee. Lady Townley, however, praises Medley for his gentility: possessing good manners, he will never offend the assembled guests and thereby prove 'scandalous'.

355

84 *ombre*: a very popular card game in the seventeenth and eighteenth centuries. Three players used forty cards, with the eights, nines, and tens thrown out of the pack.

86 *intrigues*: a recent word, 'intrigues' carried a wide range of meanings, from political schemes to romantic liaisons to literary plots. Given the political tenor of the Restoration, with its dark murmurings of plots and schemes (which were intensifying at this time), it is likely that Emilia wants Medley to describe the latest political shenanigans, in addition to the usual gossip about love affairs among the high and mighty.

98 *gleeker*: someone who plays gleek, a relatively rare card game. Like ombre, it was played by three people.

100 *tour*: a crescent of false hair. As Barnard notes, another word of French extraction newly imported into English.

105 *matador*: in ombre, the principle cards (the black aces and a variable third card).

109 *Soliciting his affairs*: Medley's pun yokes together legal and sexual connotations.

110 *depending*: pending; awaiting settlement.

111 *causes*: legal cases or briefs.

118 *points*: pieces of lace or cord for fastening clothes.

knots: bows made out of ribbons.

122 *Danish serenade*: 'serenade' is another recent word imported from the French language. Medley's remark indicates that by 1676 French wind instruments were a standard feature of a serenade. Dorimant's 'serenade', by contrast, is a barbarous cacophony of kettledrums and trumpets. Carnochan cites *Hamlet*, 1.4.8–12: 'The King doth wake tonight and takes his rouse, | Keeps wassail, and the swaggering upspring reels; | And as he drains his draughts of Rhenish down, | The kettledrum and trumpet thus bray out | The triumph of his pledge' (p. 35).

126 *flûtes douces*: 'flute doux' (1676); a recorder, a recent arrival in England.

French hautboys: oboes.

130 *The Diversions of Bruxelles*: 'Bruxells' (1676). Carnochan emends this to 'Brussels'. R. S. Cox, Jr., thinks the title parodies Richard Flecknoe's *A Treatise of the Sports of Wit* (1675). See 'Richard Flecknoe and *The Man of Mode*', *Modern Language Quarterly*, 29 (1968), 183–9.

132 *questions and commands*: a game, considered unfashionable by wits such as Medley, in which one person addressed ludicrous questions and commands to the participants.

134 *The Art of Affectation*: evidently Medley is mocking Hannah Woolley's *The Gentlewoman's Companion* (1675). It recommends that women

practise the sort of behaviour ridiculed by Medley and later parodied by Harriet and Bellair.

141 *wash and paint*: i.e. apply a liquid cosmetic (what we now call 'foundation') to the complexion, followed by the application of rouge or other forms of coloured 'paint'.

146 *baladines*: ballet dancers; originally referred to mountebanks or fools.

147 *Bear Garden*: bear and bull baiting had taken place in the Bear Garden on the Bankside of London (in Southwark) since 1546. Henry VIII and Elizabeth I attended this barbaric sport, which persisted well into the Restoration. Both Pepys and Evelyn record attending the Bear Garden but were repulsed by the spectacle. Pepys thought it a 'very rude and nasty pleasure' and Evelyn a 'rude and dirty pastime'. As Medley's remark makes apparent, by the Restoration, the Bear Garden was also being used by visiting troupes of foreign players.

151 *chopping and changing*: 'the phrase meant, originally, "bartering with, trading"; here it keeps something of that meaning' (Carnochan, 36).

2.2 S.D. *A room in Mrs Loveit's house*: again, Etherege does not indicate a scene change, but the action indicates a shift to the dwelling of Mrs Loveit.

 16 *something of the angel . . . never so wicked*: although now disputed, this line has been taken as evidence for the earl of Rochester being the original for Dorimant. The earl, while dissolute, was uncommonly handsome, attractive both to men and women.

 36 *Caperwell*: i.e. dances well; someone who 'cuts a caper'. Given the name, dancing may very well be Caperwell's sole attribute.

 56 *St Winifred's*: 'The Welsh town of Holywell takes its name from St Winifred's well, believed to have risen where the head of St Winifred fell, cut off by a pagan prince she had rejected' (Carnochan, 39)

 66 *the man at Westminster does the dead*: the guide at Westminster Abbey, then as now, showed the tombs and effigies to tourists.

 74 *déshabillé*: 'dishabillié' (1676). A lady 'in *déshabillé*' wore a loose-fitting, relaxed dress, thought to be very sexy because of the lack of stays.

 91 *person of condition*: person of means and status.

120 *They taste of death . . . approach alive*: the first two lines of Waller's 'Of her Chamber' (*Works*, ed. Drury, i. 26). Previous editors note that Dorimant substitutes 'who' for Waller's 'that'.

121 *Dancing the galloping nag without a fiddle*: as Cordner observes, although this has been glossed by Carnochan as a country dance, there is no evidence to substantiate this identification (p. 249).

138 *alarm*: a call to arms or summons to battle.

154 *So thunder . . . for the rain*: R. G. Howarth identifies these lines from Matthew Roydon's 'An Elegie, or Friend's Passion, for his Astrophill'

(1593). Dorimant substitutes 'breaks' for 'rends'. See R. G. Howarth, 'Untraced Quotations in Etherege', *Notes and Queries*, 188 (1945), 281.

161 *the Mall*: Etherege uses the variant spelling 'Mail' which I have regularized throughout to 'Mall'. The Mall was created as part of the post-Restoration improvements to St James's Park. A path along which the fashionable citizens of London could promenade, 'Mall' also referred to the early seventeenth-century game (entailing a staff and a ball) played on an alley or 'mall'.

163 *the drawing room*: not, as in current usage, a formal reception room in a house, but, rather, a reception at court with the king present.

172 *There's one made jealous already*: as Cordner notes, the first edition of 1676 does not mark this as an aside, a practice he follows. Although Dorimant might want to hurt Mrs Loveit further by letting her overhear the remark, the content of his line argues against it. He has at this point in the play gone to great pains to orchestrate Loveit's jealousy, and having her overhear his remark too boldly reveals his machinations. Thus I have marked this line as an aside.

177 *set up my rest*: lodged for a long period.

216 *cock-fool*: according to Barnard, 'a nonce formation' (p. 48).

229 *enter*: initiate.

239 *much good may do you*: sometimes emended to 'much good may it do you' but, as Cordner points out, the phrase is common in the seventeenth century.

3.1.14 *patching*: women sometimes wore a small patch, usually of black silk, on the face as a fake 'beauty mark'. Often patches were used to disguise blemishes or visible evidence of a diseased constitution.

33 *fetches*: tricks, stratagems.

46 *Merab*: Merab was the eldest daughter of Saul who was promised to David but then married to Adriel (1 Samuel 18: 19).

48 *which*: as Cordner notes, 'which' was printed in the 1676 quarto as a catchword at the bottom of p. 32 but omitted from its proper place at the head of p. 33.

49 *Find much aversion . . . promised and designed*: Harriet invokes Abraham Cowley's description of Merab in his *Davideis* (1656): 'And much aversion in her stubborn mind | Was bred by being *promis'd* and *design'd*' (*Poems*, ed. A. R. Waller (Cambridge, 1905), 341).

64 *purchase*: prize, reward.

83 *Bart'lomew*: a reference to the character Bartholomew Cokes in Ben Jonson's *Bartholomew Fair* (1614). A gull, he is robbed of the possessions he brought into the fair, including his intended, a rich heiress.

85 *gingerbread*: a popular snack at fairs, often sold in the shape of human

figures. Harriet's quip alludes again to Jonson's play: unlike Bartholomew (who counted the theft of his gingerbread his greatest loss), she does not hanker for the sweet in Bellair's possession, his heart.

87 *a day after the fair*: a day too late (proverbial).

90 *the confidence*: i.e. your confiding in me.

94 *landscapes and . . . hangings*: paintings and tapestries. Country scenes were a staple of seventeenth-century art.

96 *Hampshire*: a county in the south of England, known for sheep-farming and other rural delights. It is not the sort of landscape to attract Harriet, who several times in the play proclaims her love of urban pastimes.

103 *playing it on booty*: in a card game, joining with someone else to spoil the chances of another player.

109 *pretty*: ingenious, artful, clever.

120 *Quality*: people of social rank and/or high birth.

124 *Exchange women*: women who work in the shops of the New Exchange.

146 *tell*: count.

151 *etc.*: there is some editorial difference here. Carnochan regards this as a stage direction telling the actors to improvise. Cordner, however, sees the 'etc.' as Bellair's permission to Harriet to improvise his 'good instructions'. Cordner's gloss makes far more sense given the nature of the exchange between Bellair and Harriet.

157 *i' th' Circle*: generally agreed to be the circle in Hyde Park, used by fashionable people for riding and walking. Carnochan mentions the assembly at court, an unlikely reference.

162 *Take up*: stop, cease.

169 *game-cocks*: roosters bred for cock fights; typically, they begin sparring the moment they are released into the ring.

172 *sirrah*: 'applied to a woman seriously or in jest up to 1711, but almost certainly used here to indicate Old Bellair's old-fashioned vulgarity' (Barnard, 58).

3.2 S.D. *Lady Townley's house*: again, Etherege does not provide a setting, but the ensuing dialogue places the action in Lady Townley's house.

6 *a living libel, a breathing lampoon*: a broadsheet or manuscript poem, usually one that attacked a person's character. They were often pinned to the doors of victims. Medley here is likened to one of these scurrilous pieces, and therefore can be 'torn in pieces', an image supported by his gossipy invective throughout the play.

11 *Muddiman*: Henry Muddiman, the first editor of the *London Gazette*, by far the best-known and most widely circulated of Restoration newspapers.

80 *prettily over*: almost over, nearly finished.

81 *defying you and all your works*: Cordner thinks this alludes ironically to the promise made by godparents in the Anglican baptismal service 'to renounce the devil and all his works', a likely allusion given the many theological puns in this play (p. 264).

96 *play*: gambling.

99 *play in public places*: the extended pun here is between gambling and love. Medley advises Dorimant to 'play' (i.e. engage in amours) in public places, presumably with a prostitute, where he can dispense with 'complaisance'.

100 *Ordinaries*: taverns.

102 *deep play is now in private houses*: serious love affairs, like intense gambling, now occur in private homes.

104 *the Park*: most likely Hyde or St James's Park, both fashionable retreats.

105 *confidence*: see note to 3.1.90. Here Lady Townley refers to Medley and Dorimant's bald disclosure about the reality of sexual relationships among the fashionable denizens of London.

111 *an embarras*: a crush of chairs and coaches. From the French *embarras de voitures*.

125 *delicate*: fastidious, fussy.

138 *belles assemblees*: fashionable gatherings or events.

142 *Tuileries*: the garden of the Palais de Tuileries in Paris.

143 *'Hey, Chevalier'*: I am following Cordner's practice in not emending this expression to 'Hé, chevalier!' Given Sir Fopling's many gaffes, it stands to reason that he would misconstrue this as well.

162 *due of course*: customary

164 *brillant*: glitter.

166 *high work*: a type of raised needlework.

167 *point d'Espagne*: Spanish lacework.

168 *point de Venise*: Venetian lace.

174 *equipage*: in this context, apparel or high fashion.

180 *gallesh*: from the French '*calèche*'. Another fashion imported across the Channel, the gallesh was a light carriage with low wheels and a removable folded hood, sort of a seventeenth-century version of a convertible.

182 *tumbril*: a two-wheeled cart which tips to empty its load; also used as a dung cart.

183 *Inns of Court man*: attorney.

184 *bel air*: an elegant or beautiful style.

186 *grossier*: crude, coarse.

188 *proper*: excellent, commendable, fine; of high quality. One assumes some sarcasm here on Emilia's part.

191 *pantaloon*: skirt-like breeches popular during the Restoration; they hung wide down to the knee. Barnard points out that Dorimant uses the singular form, perhaps an allusion to Pantaloon, the doddering old man in the *commedia dell'arte* (p. 67).

201 *bien ganté*: well gloved.

206 *Barroy*: most editors think that the Parisian merchants itemized here by Sir Fopling are authentic; nonetheless, Chedreux, a famous maker of wigs, is the only one identified with any certainty.

207 *garniture*: ornamentation, such as ribbons and jewellery, added to clothing.

214 *Orangerie*: orange scent extracted from the orange-flower. Interestingly, Dorimant also mentions using orange-flower water in the opening act, yet another instance of the parallel between him and Sir Fopling.

225 *a rest of reputation enough*: enough reputation left.

232 *St James's*: the oldest of London's royal parks, it extends to about 90 acres with the Mall as the northern boundary and Birdcage Walk as the southern. It went through significant improvements at the Restoration. Charles II laid out the park anew, advised (so it is said) by André Le Nôtre, the great landscape architect who designed the parks and gardens at Versailles. It was stocked with deer, planted with fruit trees, and covered with powdered cockleshells where the king could play pall-mall. The Canal, a constellation of several small ponds, became a favourite haunt of the monarch. Because of the king's frequent appearances, St James's Park was one of the most fashionable sites in London.

236 *Ring*: a circular road in St James's Park used by men and women of fashion. One could promenade by foot or coach.

239 *à revoir*: several editors have noted the unusual spelling here, which presumably underscores Sir Fopling's affected pronunciation (see also Dorimant's sarcastic mimicry at the end of the scene).

240 *fine mettled*: sometimes emended to 'fine-mettled'.

245 *stums*: a way of renewing wine by mixing it with stum (must) to raise a new fermentation.

246 *sophisticate*: adulterated, impure; mixed with a foreign substance.

3.3 S.D. *The Mall*: comedies from the period frequently set scenes in the Mall or one of the fashionable parks.

  6 *freak*: whim.

  9 *the last king's time*: the period of Charles I, a good forty years earlier.

 11 *in a fine taking*: in an agitated state; excited or impassioned.

34 *lottery*: as previous editors note, in the seventeenth century, a common way of raising money, both for individuals and the state.

37 *In love the victors . . . pursue that die*: the final lines of Waller's poem, 'To a Friend, of the Different Success of their Loves' (*Poems*, ed. Drury, i. 103).

38 *High Park*: variant of Hyde Park.

45 *temper*: self-control.

56 *I am not mistaken; she's handsome*: as Cordner observes, although some editors print this line as an aside, it is perfectly playable as part of the dialogue between Dorimant and Bellair; indeed, Bellair's response that Harriet's 'wit is better than her face' makes sense only if he has overheard Dorimant's exclamation about her appearance.

65 *stint*: upper limit for gambling; here, clearly for love.

70 *make one at*: be part of; form part of a group.

86 *begin to be particular*: begin to be personal or private.

110 *high Mall*: the busiest and most fashionable hour for visiting the Mall.

113 *you so cry out of for:* proclaim, call.

122 s.d. *equipage*: in this usage, Sir Fopling's retinue of servants.

124 *Champagne . . . La Verdure*: some time ago, Arthur Sherbo pointed out that Sir Fopling's entry here follows scene 11 of Molière's *Les Précieuses Ridicules* (1659). See *Modern Language Notes*, 64 (1949), 343–4.

132 *Snatched from myself . . . behold the shore*: yet again, Dorimant quotes from Waller, in this instance, lines 3–4 from 'Of Loving at First Sight' (*Works*, ed. Drury, i. 100).

146 *St James's*: Carnochan thinks this refers to St James's Palace, opposite the park to the west end of the Mall.

151 *the next turn*: 'next circuit of the Mall' (Barnard, 77).

167 *rencounter*: also rancounter (see Cordner, 277). A skirmish, a duel, or verbal contest.

174 *See how unregarded . . . Beauty passes*: the opening lines of Sir John Suckling's 'Sonnet I' (*Non-Dramatic Works*, ed. Thomas Clayton (Oxford, 1971), 47). Dorimant substitutes 'See' for the original 'Do'st see'.

179 *unlucky*: malicious.

188 *hulched up*: hunched up; cramped.

200 *temper*: character.

207 *Whitehall*: royal palace, located across the park from the Mall. It was destroyed in a fire in 1698.

217 *beau monde*: fashionable society.

219 s.d. *Enter four*: as previous editors observe, there is some confusion

about the number of 'ill-fashioned fellows' who actually enter here. The *dramatis personae* lists only three. Barnard reiterates John Conaghan's observation (in his 1973 edition of the play) about the theatrical effectiveness of having 'nasty fellows' outnumber people of fashion on the stage; but he also thinks the reduction to three actors might reflect a need for economy (p. 80). Both points seem unlikely to me. According to the prompter John Downes, the original production was 'well Cloath'd'; and costumes in the seventeenth century consumed far more of the production budget than did labour costs (which were relatively low). See Downes, 77. Also, it is not clear that Sir Fopling and Mrs Loveit *are* outnumbered, given that his command to have the 'coachman send home four of his horses' would have been directed to the head servant, not to all six. There is no evidence that the entire equipage exits. In all likelihood, the difference between the stage direction and the *dramatis personae* derives from a printer's error: these sorts of mistake are common in original editions of Restoration plays.

219 S.D. *"Tis not for kisses alone etc.'*: Carnochan identifies these as lines 5–8 of an anonymous song, 'Tell me no more you love', published in *A New Collection of the Choicest Songs* (1676): 'Tis not for kisses alone | So long I have made my address. | There's something else to be done, | Which you cannot choose but guess.'

224 *convenient*: mistress, concubine.

225 *oily buttock*: smooth whore.

226 *spruce prig*: fop.

227 *caravan*: object for plunder (thieves' cant).

228 *smoke*: notice (us).

228 S.D. *'There's something else to be done, etc.'*: the nasty fellows exit, singing the final two lines of the song. Notice that the stage direction here does not specify their number.

234 *insulting:* gloating, exulting contemptuously.

239 *cordovan gloves*: a Spanish leather, originally made from tanned goatskins, later from split horse-hides. From Sir Fopling's comment, it appears they gave off a strong odour.

246 *flageolets*: 'a relation of the recorder with six fingerholes, invented in France'. As Barnard notes, Pepys played the flageolet (p. 82).

248 *hollow tooth*: a rotten tooth and therefore 'hollow' from decay.

251 *dainty pair of boxes*: wooden overshoes or clogs; some sort of cheap, ungainly footware.

256 *Holborn equipage*: a snobbish putdown. Mrs Loveit sniffs at the sort of retinue a citizen's wife might parade in Holborn, an area known for merchants and lawyers.

256 *Gray's Inn Walks*: the gardens of Gray's Inn, one of the two Inns of Court in Holborn. According to Barnard, it was a place notorious for assignations (p. 82).

259 *jealous*: suspicious.

271 *What countryman are you*: i.e. what county or district do you come from?

273 *Then Hampshire be your name*: Brett-Smith cites Congreve on this passage: 'The Ancients us'd to call their Servants by the names of the Countries from whence they came ... The French to this Day do the same, and call their Footmen *Champagne le Picard, le Gascon, le Bourgignon, &c.* And Sir *George Etheridge* in his *Fopling Flutter*, the *Hampshire, &c.* speaking to his Valet, imitates this Custom' (p. 320).

295 *hankering*: hanging about.

301 *engage*: take part.

303 *No, no! Exceptions*: as Cordner points out, most modern texts emend this line to 'No! No exceptions', following the 1693 text. I have followed Cordner's lead and retained the form used in 1676.

319 *last*: latest.

341 *And you and Loveit ... depths of Womankind*: Brett-Smith hears an echo here of Waller's 'Of the Danger his Majesty (Being Prince) Escaped in the Road at Saint Andrews', ll. 13–14: 'Of the Fourth Edward was his noble song, | Fierce, goodly, valiant, beautiful, and young.' See *Works*, ed. Drury, i. 1.

4.1 s.d. *scene opens*: a common stage direction in Restoration plays. Literally, the shutters 'open' (i.e. slide apart) to reveal another location. In this instance, the scene opens to reveal the interior of Lady Townley's house.

1 *bout*: a 'round' at any kind of exercise, in this instance a dance.

21 *tumbling*: disordering, rumpling, tousling.

22 *handkercher*: a kerchief for the neck or head.

30 *kissing dance*: a dance popular at weddings in which the men and women knelt alternately upon a cushion to be kissed; it was also known as the cushion dance. This traditional round dance was already considered quaint by the Restoration.

44 *tastes*: has a taste for.

    kindly: naturally, slowly.

60 *gorget*: a gorget covered a woman's neck and shoulders; thus, Old Bellair boasts of having once been able to caper as high as his partner's neck.

91 *bare*: mere.

116 *point and rebate*: sharpen and blunt, like knives.

119 *makes the doux yeux*: makes eyes at; flirts.

120 *her monkey*: exotic pets for women of fashion. Cordner cites the poem by John Wilmot, earl of Rochester, 'A Letter from Artemisia in the Town to Chloe in the Country', lines 135 ff. See *Complete Poems*, ed. David M. Vieth (New Haven, 1968), 106.

127 *critics of the circle*: either the inner circle at court or, more generally, the fashionable set in London.

136 *risk*: 'risque' (1676).

139 *has an ascendant*: has an advantage; possesses the upper hand.

140 *making a party*: making good one's cause or position; as Barnard points out, Harriet should take the side of beauty against the 'ugly and foolish'.

144 *settled ague*: chronic or wasting fever.

155 *use to*: you are accustomed to, it is your habit to.

167 *Masquerades*: Barnard notes the popularity of masquerades during the period, especially among the court who would, according to Bishop Burnet, go 'about masked, and came into houses unknown, and danced. People were so disguised, that without being in the secret none could distinguish them' (Barnard, 93).

190 *the king's couchée*: the king's evening reception.

201 *take my measures*: set my plans.

202 *faux-prude*: false prude.

      demi-prude: half-prude.

206 *coq-à-l'âne*: piece of foolishness; string of nonsense.

214 *La Corneus and Sallyes*: previous editors cite Verity's suggestion that this refers to Mesdames Cornuel and Selles, minor literary figures of the day mentioned in works by Bussy.

      habitudes: acquaintances.

215 *A comedian would have been a bonne fortune*: even a lowly actor would have been welcome. Carnochan thinks Sir Fopling shows his ignorance here since Madame Cornuel was known for her wit (p. 95).

222 *mechanic*: vulgar, base.

227 *Bussy . . . Rabutin*: Sir Fopling confuses Bussy d'Ambois, the sixteenth-century French adventurer (and the subject of a play by George Chapman) with Roger de Rabutin, comte de Bussy (1618–93), author of the *Histoire amoureuse des Gaules* (see Harriet's rejoinder, 'He who writ the *Loves of France*').

238 *my court within*: i.e., when I had paid court to the king.

239 *under the state*: under the canopy.

240 *jeèr*: evidently, Sir Fopling pronounces this word affectedly, in the French manner.

248 *to your power*: to the extent of your power.

250 *birthday*: the king's birthday celebration.

255 *sifted 'em*: questioned them; examined them.

256 *Ah, filthy!*: tallow candles, made from the fat of animals, were notorious for emitting foul-smelling smoke. Wax candles, however, were still a considerable luxury, even for the likes of Lady Townley; thus her decision to retain tallow candles for everyday use.

286 *a courante, a bourrée, or a menuet*: all 'low' dances because they do not require high kicks or leaps.

    St. André: 'a French choreographer brought over with a troup to stage the dances in the opera *Psyche* which (after long preparation) had been finally produced on 27 February 1675' (Cordner, 294).

291 *the Basque*: previous editors take this as an allusion to 'le Basque sauteur', a French dancer whose affair with Madame de Berthillac was recounted in *La France Galante*. More likely, however, is that Sir Fopling refers either to a particular Spanish dance popular during the period (which entailed more 'capers' than 'low dancing') or to a troupe of Basque dancers who would have performed this particular dance. A 'basque' dance is indicated in the stage directions to the Purcell opera, *Dido and Aeneas*.

    entry: dance performed as an interlude to an entertainment.

297 *At your feet . . . No matter*: in terms of staging, it is possible to construe this exchange literally, with Sir Fopling seating himself at the 'feet' of Harriet and Emilia, thus provoking their horrified response that he will 'spoil it' (i.e. their dresses). Sir Fopling, self-absorbed as always, thinks their outburst indicates *his* clothing ('No matter. My clothes are my creatures'), a humorous and revealing response.

299 *Qu'on commence*: begin! As Cordner points out, the quarto of 1676 exists in corrected and uncorrected forms, and there is some confusion about this particular line, which reads 'Quon Comencè, English motions' in the uncorrected version and 'Quon Comencè to an English Dancer English motions' in the corrected version. I have followed the practice of Cordner, Brett-Smith, and Carnochan in treating 'to an English dancer, English motions' as dialogue, not a stage direction.

300 *entertain*: hire, employ.

303 *not a*: 'not had a' (1676).

305 *mumming*: elaborately costumed folk play.

319 *perfect day*: broad daylight.

323 *sensible*: i.e., conscious of your courtesy.

371 *I know you well*: Carnochan and Barnard emend to 'I know you will', but Cordner retains the spelling of 1676. Given the dialogue, either spelling makes sense.

373 *bachique*: a drinking song. The word appears to be a neologism, perhaps another instance of Sir Fopling's obsession with all things French.

374 *hard*: in the usual sense of 'difficult'; it also functions as a canting word (which would underscore Sir Fopling's use of the new-fangled 'bachique').

378 S.D. *Musicians sing*: Etherege does not specify the singers here, but Sir Fopling's declaration ('Let us have the new bachique'), followed by Old Bellair's agreement ('Let us have it then') suggests that they expect to be entertained rather than do the singing themselves.

379 *The pleasures of love . . .*: evidently an original song by Etherege, although Carnochan notes the similarity to two songs in Thomas Shadwell's opera *Psyche* (p. 103). This song went through several reprintings.

388 *champagne*: a new word (also used in *FF*) and a new import, although champagne had been available in France for some time.

400 *Present all together*: raise your weapons (i.e. your drinks) and 'aim'.

414 *flambeaux*: torches.

4.2 S.D. *Dorimant's lodging*: once again, Etherege provides the most detailed stage directions for the scenes in Dorimant's lodging. The direction, 'Handy tying up linen', is singular insofar as Restoration plays usually refrain from specifying stage business that entails the handling of props, such as the bed linen here.

9 *sleeveless errands*: trifling errands; inconsequential chores.

24 *By all the joys . . . never did before*: Brett-Smith observes that 'Dorimant may or may not have intended his asseveration to take the form of an Alexandrine, but [Harriet] is quick to interrupt his heroics with her rhyming reply' (p. 321).

65 *an irregular fit*: Medley sarcastically reminds Dorimant of his previous remark at 3.3.286 when he claimed 'the fit has long been over'.

71 *make us a confidence*: i.e. tell us the truth; share with us your secret.

73 *Le sage*: the prudent or circumspect one.

75 *pay parish duties*: (1) a luxury tax on the coach or, perhaps, (2) a fine levied on a woman who gave birth out of wedlock. The latter meaning sets up Medley's rejoinder.

89 *the saying . . . study yourself*: 'the injunction "Know thyself" was inscribed on the temple of Apollo; Plato (*Protagoras*, 343B) ascribes the saying to the Seven Wise Men' (Cordner, 303).

98 *Mérille*: the *premier valet de chambre* to the duc de Candale.
   genie: genius.

101 *Duke of Candale*: Louis-Charles-Gaston de Nogaret de Foix (1627–58), a

French general. In Bussy's *Histoire amoureuse des Gaules* he is touted as a leader of fashion; thus, Sir Fopling's interest in him.

103 *brandenburgh*: a morning gown made of wool.

105 *periwig tied up*: to save combing.

107 *en cavalier*: dashing.

déshabillé: when used by a man, as here, it indicated informal or relaxed dress.

113 *coup d'essai*: first attempt.

121 *Lambert*: Michel Lambert (1610–96), master of chamber music to Louis XIV; he was also a singer, composer, and teacher to fashionable students.

123 *ruelle*: a lady's bedroom, where morning receptions were sometimes held.

133 *Still as*: whenever.

135 *Baptiste*: 'Baptist' (1676). Jean-Baptiste Lully (1633–87), composer, director of opera, and master of court music to Louis XIV.

143 *Slap down goes the glass*: of the coach window.

146 *La Tour*: 'La Tower' (1676).

148 *Adieu donc, mes chers*: goodbye then, my friends.

150 *change my linen*: outer garments, especially if they were made out of costly fabrics, were changed rarely in the seventeenth century; instead, people of means changed their 'linen' (i.e. shirts or clothing worn next to the body) daily. Dorimant has already given proof of his fastidious nature in the opening act.

157 *an't*: if it. Medley may be mimicking the speech of lower-class characters here. See, for instance, the use of 'an't' by the first chairman in 4.3.

177 *give you joy*: congratulate you (on your betrothal).

179 *Without church security*: i.e. without a marriage licence.

taking up there: (1) possessing her; or (2) borrowing at interest (playing on 'church security').

4.3 S.D. *The Mall, near Mrs Loveit's lodging*: Mrs Loveit's house must be near the Mall since in this scene Bellinda discharges her chair and walks to her house, something ladies of fashion usually avoided because of the muddy condition of the streets and the ever-present danger of crime.

20 *the Strand*: the street, just over three-quarters of a mile long, which extends from Charing Cross to the law courts and thus links Westminster to the City. The Strand was known for its large mansions occupied originally by bishops and then by a succession of courtiers and nobleman. By the early seventeenth century these mansions were increasingly being replaced by smaller houses designed for prosperous citizens. Shops also began to appear in the area.

5.1.29 *nosegays*: small bouquets of sweet-smelling flowers.

33 *sweet waters*: perfume or scent.

35 *narolii*: also 'neroli' or 'neroly'. Oil distilled from the flowers of the bitter orange and used as perfume.

39 *stock-gillyflowers*: a flower with a clove-like smell that blooms in July.

41 *tuberose*: a plant with white, lily-like flowers. Barnard notes that, like the orange-flower, this was an exotic plant recently imported from Italy. He also claims that 'in the language of flowers, tuberose signifies dangerous pleasures' (p. 117).

46 *crowded out*: pushed out by force, largely because of the press of the crowd.

66 *What makes him here?*: What is he doing here? or Why is he here?

70 *oppression*: bodily or mental distress or uneasiness; Bellinda may very well be experiencing both symptoms.

74 *surfeit water*: a medicinal drink.

76 *strange*: unusual, immoderate.

82 *canaille*: rabble.

85 *I that I may . . . to what you love*: Waller again. 'To the Mutable Fair', ll. 5–6 in *Works*, ed. Drury (i. 106). Dorimant substitutes 'I' for the original 'And'.

98 *brisk-insipid*: Cordner retains the hyphen from 1676 to underscore the paradox of yoking these two disparate qualities side-by-side.

127 *implicit faith*: Mrs Loveit's remark here alludes to the theological notion of 'subjective' or 'implicit' faith, an act of the will in response to divine truth. As a supernatural act, faith is a higher faculty than reason. Mrs Loveit likens the faith fools have in their mistresses' fidelity to the faith Christians have in their deity: both demand a conscious act of the will. This remark also prefigures the theological allusions and puns dotting the exchange between Dorimant and Harriet in 5.2.

137 *properties*: mere instruments, tools; again, a word that figures prominently in *FH*.

138 *indifferent*: moderate amount; fairly large.

139 *frank*: liberal, generous, lavish.

on the square: in a fair, honest, or straightforward fashion; without artifice or trickery.

140 *turn rook*: sharper; cheat.

141 *bubble*: dupe, gull; see Emilia's husband in *FH*.

241 *mirabilis*: aqua mirabilis, a medicinal drink of wine and spices.

283 *heaviness*: torpor, want of animation.

5.2.10 *closet*: not, in the modern sense, a place to store clothing, but a small room, usually within a bedchamber, that could be used for reading, devotions, or even tea. Customarily, a closet could not accommodate more than two people.

19 *huddle up*: hasten along unceremoniously.

26 *go to*: express disapproval.

28 *writings*: legal documents.

55 *well-fashioned*: stylishly dressed; fashionably genteel in his behaviour.

56 *apish*: foolishly imitative, like an ape. In effect, Harriet accuses Dorimant of being a slave to fashion in much the same manner as Sir Fopling.

58 *rallied*: accused.

69 *cat-call*: 'a kind of whistle, used to express disapproval or impatience (later in the century, if not already, in the play-houses)' (Cordner, 320, n. 83).

71 S.D. *sings*: 'song by C.S.' (1676). In the 1722 edition of Etherege's *Works*, this song was attributed to Sir Charles Sedley; most editors think it was written by Sir Car Scroope (see the first note to the Prologue).

89 *Music so softens . . . does resistance find*: the sixth couplet of Waller's 'Of my Lady Isabella, Playing on the Lute' (*Works*, ed. Drury, i. 90). Dorimant substitutes 'one' for the original 'an'.

94 *celebrated Beauty*: often in modern editions emended to 'a celebrated beauty'. Cordner follows the practice of 1676, reasoning that Etherege may have intended personification rather than one particular, beautiful lady, a likely choice.

99 *a suit of hangings*: see note on to 3.1.94.

146 *talk thus in Hampshire*: earlier (see 3.1.96) Harriet made evident to Bellair her horror of returning to Hampshire; here she first suggests the sort of rural trial she will impose on Dorimant.

147 *little*: the uncorrected 1676 quarto omits this adjective.

some little truth enlarged upon: i.e. something believable in what you say; some degree of truth.

174 *the canonical hour*: the hours during which a marriage could be legally performed, 8 a.m. to noon.

227 *The devil owes . . . done paying it*: Carnochan points out that Dorimant varies the proverb 'the devil owed (one) a shame and now has paid it' (p. 137).

293 *prevailing faction*: references to political and literary 'factions' abound in the Restoration. Both Cordner and Barnard mention Dryden's dedication to *The Assignation* (1673) as a possible source for this line, but I think the sense is far more general.

325 *antechamber*: a small waiting room just outside the main apartment; in the

palace, the room outside the royal apartments in which one could adjust appearances before paying court to the monarch.

341 *fière*: haughty.

Serviteur: 'your servant, madam'.

353 *a cut*: the movement Caper performs in *FF* when he leaps into the air and twiddles his feet one in front of the other with great rapidity.

384 *Hartley*: unfortunately, there are three towns in Hampshire that feature the name 'Hartley', Hartley Wespall, Hartley Mauditt, and Hartley Wintney (Barnard, 142).

406 s.d. *Harriet . . . dance*: Q1 does not specify the dancers; however, it is customary to have all of the characters in the concluding scene participate. In this instance, I have refrained from including Sir Fopling and Medley on the grounds that the former would be staring at himself in the mirror or making a 'ballet' to himself and the latter would be on the sidelines, silently making notes for the next gossip session.

EPILOGUE

By Mr Dryden: the poet laureate John Dryden was much sought after as a composer of prologues and epilogues. As Cordner notes, Dryden sent an amiable verse letter to Etherege while the latter was in Ratisbon, and he also paid him tribute in the mock-heroic *MacFlecknoe*, ll. 151–4.

3 *harlequins*: the harlequin, a fool or buffoon, was featured originally in the *commedia dell'arte* but then migrated to the farces that were increasingly popular on the English and French stage. Serious playwrights frequently levelled complaints against farce and the accompanying character types.

9 *cocks*: (1) struts; (2) cocks his hat.

16 *knight o' th' shire*: parliamentary representative of a shire (county).

22 *the new French wallow*: evidently a kind of walk—a rolling gait—that originated in France.

23 *sword knot*: a ribbon or tassel tied to the hilt of a sword.

24 *snake*: a long curl or tail attached to a wig.

28 *shog*: shake.

A Fond Husband; or, The Plotting Sisters

EPIGRAPH

Hæc, dum . . . cognôris, facilia: 'these things, when you are ignorant and just starting out, are difficult; when you understand them, they are easy' (Terence, 'The Self Tormentor').

DEDICATION

1 *To His Grace, the Duke of Ormond*: James Butler (1610–88), soldier, statesman, and consummate Royalist, was appointed lieutenant-general of the army by Charles I in 1641. Three years later he was made lord-lieutenant in recognition for his service in battle. Ormonde fought hard for the Royalist cause throughout the Civil War, and his personal losses were said to number over £1,000,000, even though he recovered his Irish estates after 1660. Ormonde enjoyed many honours after the Restoration: he was on the commission for the treasury and navy, made lord steward of the household and privy councillor, and created Baron Butler of Llanthony, and earl of Brecknock in the English peerage. On 30 March 1661 he was made duke of Ormonde in the Irish peerage. Ormonde earned the enmity of many at court, largely for his unyielding principles. He was also singular for maintaining an old-fashioned, moral lifestyle in the midst of Charles II's dissolute court. Having lost favour with the king—Ormonde was removed from the lord-lieutenancy in March of 1669—he returned to Ireland. Charles II called Ormonde back to London in April 1675. Reinstated into princely favour, Ormonde was given rule of Ireland and another dukedom. Ormonde's last act was to have James II proclaimed in Dublin. Although not a gentleman writer himself, Ormonde acquired a notable collection of manuscripts at his house in Kilkenny. Durfey came to Ormonde's attention at the première of *Madam Fickle*, which was produced by the Duke's Company the previous year. In the dedication to that play, Durfey mentions that Charles II gave 'it a particular applause, which was seconded by your Grace'. Subsequently, Durfey was invited to wait upon Ormonde at his estate. Durfey, of Huguenot descent, may have been attracted to Ormonde's rabidly anti-Catholic policies in Ireland.

13 *indifferently passed*: impartially passed; in other words, the play did not receive condemnation or praise from the 'town'. The play actually proved to be very popular with audiences and went through a series of revivals in the Restoration and well into the eighteenth century.

18 *address*: application, courteous approach.

23 *for your grace's departure from England*: Roger L'Estrange licensed the play on 15 June 1676, when Ormonde was still in London (and back in the favour of Charles II). News of Ormonde's appointment to Ireland had become public that spring.

29 *which relation*: the recounting of which.

38 *only that it was my own*: Durfey was frequently accused of plagiarism. Gerard Langbaine, in *An Account of the English Dramatick Poets* (1691), declared that 'Mr. *Durfey* like the *Cuckow*, makes it his business to suck other Birds Eggs' (i. 179).

THE CHARACTERS OF THE PLAY

Rashley: the name suggests someone who is nimble, vigorous, and quick, as well as someone who disregards consequences.

Ranger: commonly in the seventeenth century, a rake or rover, but it also signifies a sieve. Both meanings illuminate Ranger's character. A rake, he wants Emilia for himself, but he also acts like a sieve in leaking information of her sexual exploits to her husband. 'Ranger' has additional associations with gaming—a 'ranger' was a forester or gamekeeper—that explain the comedy's many references to hunting.

Peregrine Bubble: 'Perrgrine' (1677). Typically a dupe or gull, but peregrine also signifies someone who is 'foreign, belonging to another country; outlandish, strange' (*OED*).

fond: foolish, credulous, idiotic; over-affectionate, doting. All of these meanings apply equally to Bubble.

Old Fumble: in addition to the usual sense of someone who gropes objects awkwardly, 'fumble' also refers to a man who cannot perform sexually. The suggestion of impotence is particularly humorous since the aged Fumble announces his virility to the world at large.

alderman: next in dignity to a mayor, the alderman in English and Irish boroughs was a magistrate. In London, the alderman was usually the chief officer of a ward.

black women: not, in the modern sense, a woman of African or Indian origin, but a brunette (see Old Fumble's later reference at 2.3.101 to 'black o' th' top'). Dark-haired women were preferred during the Restoration; blondes were tolerated and redheads pitied.

Mr Jevon: 'Mr Jevan' (1677).

Emilia: 'Emillia' (1677).

Mrs Barry: 'Mr Barrer' (1677).

Mrs Knapper: 'Mrs Napper' (1677).

Mrs Norris: 'Mrs Norrice' (1677).

Mrs Snare: omitted from all editions.

PROLOGUE

2 *the critics that sit here to view*: see the note on critics for the Prologue of *The Libertine*, l. 2.

7 *design no praise . . . dull grimace and repartee*: Durfey preferred to write fast-paced comedies of action that featured physical business rather than witty language. These lines might also allude to Etherege's *The Man of Mode*, a play of elegant conversation that won the approbation of court and town alike. Etherege's comedy premièred the previous season; and

Durfey here distinguishes between his own brand of comedy and Etherege's.

10 *hardly*: not easily; with difficulty.

36 *though your faction . . . our endeavours crown*: prologues and epilogues invoke factions and cabals as frequently as they do the dreaded critics. Powerful cliques, especially of fashionable nobility, could ruin or ensure the fortunes of a production.

38 *bays*: a crown of laurels, the customary emblem of the poet.

1.1 S.D. *shuttlecock, and battledores*: 'shuttlecock' was an early version of badminton in which two players hit a shuttlecock back and forth with a battledore, a small racket.

1 S.D. *sings*: Durfey wrote the song, which later appeared in his *New Collection of Songs and Poems* (1683), 47.

7 *amour*: love affair; courtship; also by the seventeenth century, an intrigue or illicit affair.

10 *Elysium*: the resting place of the dead in Greek mythology; also, more generally, a blessed state of being.

12 *my sceptre*: penis; jokes were rife during the period about Charles II's 'sceptre'.

20 *a horse race a mile beyond Highgate*: during the Restoration, Highgate was still a village just north of the city. Its slight elevation made it a welcome retreat for Londoners seeking fresh air and grassy walks. Horse races were increasingly popular by the Restoration.

21 *resentment*: appreciation, understanding.

26 *indirect*: corrupt, deceitful.

30 *clog*: block, lump; impediment, hindrance.

45 *invading her propriety in your heart*: i.e. overthrowing her dominance in your affections.

47 *design*: plot, intention.

49 *to possess him*: to convince him.

54 *to colour my design and divert you*: to lend plausibility to my plot and entertain you.

have feigned: 'have I feign'd' (1685).

69 *turn thee . . . Lapland*: i.e. match you in combat against any witch or fiend, the fabled inhabitants of Lapland.

75 *Besides, our love . . . by the by*: Rashley invokes the idea of a golden age when men and women loved freely without worrying about social conventions. Love becomes a 'second-rate innocence' (that is, once removed from the original innocence of Adam and Eve and therefore 'second-rate' or second in quality) when affection outweighs money and ambition. In

this prelapsarian state, men and women can love openly without studying motives or scrutinizing reactions. This nostalgic yearning for a golden age of unfettered love is common in libertine writings of the period; see, for instance, Aphra Behn's poem, 'The Golden Age' (1684).

79 *Mrs Jilt*: not a common streetwalker, but a prostitute who has acquired her own premises or works for a madam. Ranger insults both Betty and Emilia in suggesting they are little better than prostitute and madam (with a clear pun on 'madam').

80 *door-keeping*: see note to *The Libertine*, 1.1.45.

84 *horns*: symbol of the cuckolded male.

85 *hawthorn-bush*: a small tree or bush well known for its thorniness.

86 *commodious*: opportune, accommodating.

94 *surprise*: sudden attack.

127 *perspective*: a telescope; also refers to a magnifying glass or spy-glass.

134 *in the mumps*: a fit of melancholy; sulks.

pop: short for poppet; a term of endearment for a girl or woman.

140 *brave*: fine.

141 *clowns*: peasants.

150 *'Tis a raging Turk at repartee*: seventeenth-century Englishmen both feared and admired the Ottoman Empire, which had expanded its territories steadily since the fourteenth century. Vienna nearly fell to the Ottomans in 1669—there would be another siege in 1683—and Europeans felt increasingly vulnerable. Sir Henry Blount, whose *A Voyage into the Levant* (1636) went through multiple printings during the Restoration, was fairly typical in his reaction: 'Thus if ever any race of men were born with Spirits able to bear down the world before them, I think it to be the *Turks*' (1671 edn., p. 127). Thus the 'rage' Bubble mentions has to do with martial disposition, not anger, and he compliments Emilia for her ability to argue fiercely.

Invent: Bubble uses this in the sense of classical rhetoric—to 'invent' a rebuttal or a topic for argument.

151 *strike her home*: unwittingly Bubble applies the expression 'strike home' (to make an effective thrust with a weapon) to his wife, blithely ignorant of the sexual connotation; effectively, he asks Ranger to penetrate her with his 'weapon'.

156 *hold*: wager, bet.

guinea: See note to *The Libertine*, Epilogue, l. 37.

157 *fleering'st quean*: to 'fleer' is to grimace or grin, often in a coarse or impudent manner. A 'quean' is a bold or ill-behaved woman; by the seventeenth century it designated a harlot.

160 *has more tropes and figures*: i.e. *if* you take her, you will find she has more tropes and figures than any orator. In classical rhetoric, these are the two major divisions of figures of speech. 'Trope' comes from the Greek word for 'turning'; thus, a trope is a turn or a twist of a word to make it mean something else. By contrast, a 'figure' uses a word in some special way to create unexpected effects—but without altering the basic meaning of the word.

Take her when her hand's in: i.e. try her when she is in practice or on top form.

162 *non parelio*: a woman without equal; a paragon.

166 *caress*: fondle, embrace tenderly; treat kindly or affectionately.

179 *a-fowling*: bird-hunting.

180 *Holloway*: this northern stretch of Islington—now a London borough—was still rural at the time of the Restoration and therefore rich with fowl and game (Henry VIII supposedly hunted in the area). Whether by coach or horse, a day trip to Holloway from the Strand or the area around St James's Park, both fashionable neighbourhoods during the Restoration, would have been a time-consuming venture.

199 *grinning like a monkey eating of chestnuts*: sweet chestnuts, which had been grown in England since the thirteenth century, were prized as delicacies and therefore likely to induce smiles, whether in humans or simians.

204 *quirks and quiddits*: subtle niceties in arguments; also, obscure scholastic arguments on the nature or essence of things.

205 *Cambridge puns and Westminster quibbles*: universities and courts, then as now, were notorious for fostering obscure language; 'Westminster' most likely refers to Westminster Hall, a court of justice.

208 *Beelzebub*: see note to *The Libertine*, 1.1.76.

212 *sensible*: Rashley here means physical senses or sensation. He implies that Emilia has 'obliged' him physically.

222 *much good ... warrant it right*: i.e. don't worry, I'll guarantee its authenticity.

224 *square*: setting.

236 *posted*: positioned or pasted in a public place, as a public notice.

241 *instant satisfaction*: Ranger here demands a duel, the usual recourse of the affronted gentleman. Duels were outlawed in 1666, but they still occurred.

so clearly: without serious or effective opposition.

250 *Hard*: angry, quarrelsome.

256 *huff*: scold, rebuke; also, speak arrogantly or bluster.

268 *powdering-tub*: (i) tub used to salt and pickle meat; also (ii) sweating-tub used to treat those afflicted with venereal disease.

283 *wait on 'em up*: London homes, especially after the Great Fire of 1666, were narrow buildings that featured several levels. The first act occurs in the dining room, which was situated at least one, if not two, floors above the kitchen (usually on the bottom level of the house). Since guests entered on the street level, the footman would need to escort them upstairs to the dining room. Cordelia's chamber is probably on the uppermost level of the house; thus, she needs to be called 'down' to the dining room.

298 *Venetian spectacles*: in 1275 Marco Polo reported seeing people in China wearing spectacles; Europeans began wearing them in the 1400s, and demand increased as printed materials became more widely available. Venetians were known for their skill in working with glass, including the making of spectacles.

300 *Cob*: a large, lumpish person; also a short, stout horse—both perhaps comments on Sneak's appearance.

307 *Yours, good Mr Peregrine*: i.e. 'and your most humble servant, Mr Peregrine'.

309 *salute her*: kiss her.

348 *catches*: musical rounds in which one singer 'catches' at the words of another, producing a humorous effect.

Sawny Brome: Alexander Brome (1620–66), a poet and songwriter who supported the Royalist cause during the Civil War. Brome was the leading composer of Cavalier lyrics prior to the Restoration; he may also have edited two collections of Rump songs, one in 1660 and the other in 1662. Sir Roger reminisces over the time spent carousing with Brome and other Royalists.

349 *Royalists*: supporters of the king during the Civil War (1642–49). Sir Roger expresses nostalgia for the fervent royalism of the 1640s and 1650s.

the Mitre under the rose: two associations come together in this expression: (i) the Mitre, the name of a tavern in London, and (ii) 'sub rosa' (literally, 'under the rose'), a phrase that designates concealment and secrecy. Royalist cadres frequently met at taverns 'sub rosa' to plot against the Parliamentarians. In this instance, Sir Roger may very well be referring to a particular Mitre tavern where they met 'sub rosa'; however, given the number of Mitre taverns in London during the seventeenth century, it is impossible to determine the exact one.

350 *the leveller*: (i) the tankard which 'levels' to the ground those who drink from it, and (ii) the political party (the 'Levellers') during the reign of Charles I who placed political principles before social rank; thus, they would 'level' all arbitrary social distinctions between men. Both meanings are possible here given the context.

353 *Scotch song*: Scotch songs became very popular on the Restoration stage

during the 1670s. In the epistle dedicatory, Durfey says of the Scotch song that 'a part of which was not mine, nor do I desire any reputation from it'. His collaborator on the song remains unknown. The song was reprinted in *Choice Ayres and Songs* (1679), 46.

356 *Munnonday*: Monday.

358 *leaked*: looked.

 knough: knoll; small hill or mound.

359 *Yen glenting*: one moving.

 brent: smooth.

361 *Bekt lew*: curtseyed low.

 sine: also 'syne'; then; thereupon.

362 *speard*: variant of 'speered'; to ask or enquire.

 quo: quoth; said.

363 *twa*: two.

 brough: 'brow' (of hill).

364 *sike*: such.

365 *ganging*: going; specifically, travelling on foot.

366 *dow*: dove; dear.

367 *light*: probably to lighten in the sense of removing or lifting an object (in this case, a woman's apron).

368 *Nea*: 'nay'.

 mistean: mistaken.

 nean: none.

371 *my*: 'your' (1677).

372 *gif*: if.

374 *rew*: more commonly 'rue'; to change one's mind or to go back on a bargain.

376 *leath*: loathe; reluctant.

377 *tall*: contraction of t'all (at all).

 eaght: aught; anything.

378 *knaw*: know.

 wemun: women.

 boo: bow.

2.1.33 *hand-granado*: variant of 'hand grenade'. First developed in the 1400s, grenades were a standard feature of warfare by the Restoration. Grenadiers, three or four men attached to each company, were the only soldiers authorized to use them.

37 *obscure*: hidden, not manifest.

39 *shall make his gall flow upwards*: gall, also known as bile, is the secretion produced by the liver. During the sixteenth and seventeenth centuries, people believed that too much gall would create a surly, embittered personality. Maria hopes to torment Bubble to the point where his gall, which normally would flow downward, will back up, producing a rancorous disposition.

2.2.27 *thee*: 'the' (1677).

28 *gammon*: the bottom piece of bacon, including the hind or haunch of the swine. Gammon could also refer to talk that was considered rubbish, a sort of ridiculous nonsense. This second meaning reinforces 'a-mort' and 'foppery'.

37 *cause*: (i) reason for; (ii) legal action, brief.

45 *too positive*: too assertive or opinionated; dictatorial.

54 *a Leviathan . . . a whale*: someone who possesses vast or formidable powers; it also refers to an aquatic animal of enormous size, commonly a whale. Bubble's remark encompasses both meanings.

69 *Tom*: 'Dom' (1677).

71 *with a vengeance*: with a curse or malediction.

82 *to give her a squirrel . . . and she loves squirrels passionately*: another double entendre missed by the oblivious Bubble. Emilia's complaint—that Rashley did not 'give her a squirrel'—refers to a failed sexual encounter.

85 *from thence sprung this fatal consequence*: Rashley's seemingly innocuous explanation is actually quite louche. Too much alcohol caused the 'fatal consequence' of his inability to perform sexually.

87 *ne'er*: 'near' (1677).

98 *petty*: inconsiderable, of little importance; inferior, subordinate.

2.3.15 *from the college*: i.e. at the University of Cambridge.

24 *address*: courteous approach to anyone; in this instance, courteous courtship to a lady.

29 *Jericho*: in the Old Testament, the Palestinian town where David ordered his servants to wait until they had grown beards.

38 *Plato's great year*: the year (*c.*25800) when all the planets were supposed to return to their original positions.

44 *court-cabal*: clique or junta. More specifically, during the 1670s it referred to the five ministers of the Privy Council who signed the Treaty of Alliance with France (1672) that declared war on Holland. In contemporary writings the names of the ministers were arranged to create the acronym, CABAL: Clifford, Arlington, Buckingham, Ashley (Anthony Ashley Cooper, earl of Shaftesbury), and Lauderdale. In effect,

Sneak says that if one discounts the cabal, known for their wit, he doesn't look too bad by comparison.

52 *period*: a complete sentence, usually one with several clauses.

62 *the round cap*: worn by Sneak as a Cambridge undergraduate.

71 *chops of rotten mutton*: a pun on 'rotten' (syphilitic) and 'mutton' (prostitute).

fellow-commoners: class of undergraduates at Oxford and Cambridge also known as 'gentlemen-commoners', so called because they were privileged to dine in common with the fellows of the college.

76 *prigs*: dandies, coxcombs, or fops.

79 *proctor*: one of two officers appointed annually to discharge particular functions at the university having to do with meetings, boards, examinations, and degrees. Proctors were also responsible for the discipline of undergraduates; thus, Sneak, having abused the proctor 'damnably', has been expelled from his college.

82 *professors of debauchery*: those who espouse debauchery as a way of life.

83 *shift him off*: get rid of him.

84 *put up to her*: incite or induce her (to respond to his courtship).

101 *black o' th' top there*: Fumble refers to Cordelia's brunette hair, a sign of sexual alacrity; hence, his enthusiasm and resolve to 'say no more'.

104 *patch or two ... tissues and embroideries*: despite his resolve to 'say no more' (see previous entry), Fumble enumerates Cordelia's more sensual features, stopping just short of mentioning her genitals ('and a black—'). Michael Cordner suggests that Fumble may be suppressing the phrase 'black mark' (i.e. the female genitalia, fringed with black hair, as a 'mark' for the male member). Fumble recovers quickly enough to substitute the word 'patch', which is both (i) a beauty-spot and (ii) another possible euphemism for the genitalia. In effect, he claims that a 'patch or two' promote pregnancy—presumably by enflaming male desire—more effectively than expensive clothing decorated with gold or silver thread.

106 *rotten in his minority*: disgusted by Fumble's lubricious speech (see preceding entry), Sneak avers that the old man was rotten before he was ever ripe (i.e. diseased while still a minor).

116 *baboon in his age*: a fool in his old age. Baboons are also known for their lechery.

118 *knows a hawk from a handsaw*: proverbial; handsaw is probably a corruption of 'hernsew', a dialectical form of 'heron'.

127 *reverend*: normally a courteous mode of address, acknowledging superiority of rank and age; in Sneak's sarcastic usage, it comes to mean (i) ancient; and (ii) gross and libidinous.

134 *She'll make ... a pint of ale*: Fumble's granddaughter will produce a

pottle (equivalent to two quarts or a half-gallon) of urine from a pint of ale, a feat in accordance with Fumble's claim that 'she's a juicy, spritely girl'.

134 *turn her back to*: turn away from; refuse.

135 *of her inches*: of her stature; more specifically, of her height; someone tall.

160 *swinger*: a forceful personality; a 'whopper'. Undoubtedly, Fumble implies sexual overtones here, suggesting that Cordelia has an abundance of libidinous energy.

2.4 s.d. *severally*: separately; individually.

22 *fitted me*: matched, countered, checkmated.

28 *Rare*: (i) uncommon, exceptional; also (ii) splendid, excellent (ironic in this context).

40 *methinks this is so strange a design*: i.e. it seems to me this is an odd plot.

56 *basilisk*: in mythology and classical writings, a reptile whose hissing supposedly drove away all other creatures. Its look and breath were said to be fatal.

69 *policy*: crafty device, plot, stratagem.

3.1.8 *devil's pater noster*: 'pater noster' refers to the 'Our Father', the prayer Christians say before taking Holy Communion. It was thought that witches in their ceremonies followed the basic format of the Christian mass (thus the term 'Black Mass'), only inverting the standard prayers and rituals.

10 *charge*: expense.

15 *make me thankful*: i.e. may God make me thankful.

16 *snapped*: tricked, deceived.

45 *makes Ranger here*: i.e. what is Ranger doing here?

63 *distastes*: offence given or taken; mutual estrangement or aversion.

94 *I'll turn you away like a vagabond for contempt of my government*: vagabonds, or vagrants, were an increasing problem in early modern England. The economy could not absorb the increase in workers resulting from the population boom, with the result that many unemployed men and women wandered along roads and highways. Petty crime was often blamed on these homeless people; moreover, parishes turned away vagabonds claiming residency in an attempt to avoid paying support. Bubble uses this simile, likening Emilia to a vagabond and himself to a government authority, to assert his dominance. See J. A. Sharpe, *Crime in Early Modern England 1550–1750* (London, 1984), 141–6.

95 *had liked to have spoiled*: came very close to spoiling.

Scoggin: Ned Scoggin was court jester to Edward IV; the phrase, 'by Scoggin' or 'what says Scoggin', came to mean, 'what says the fool?'

106 *horse-pox*: a severe pox (a pustular disease) associated with cow-pox; basically, Sir Roger says that in his prime he could have fought other young men with a force equivalent to this disease.

120 *presently*: be one of the players immediately.

123 *So Paris stole . . . grew bright with fire*: according to classical mythology, Paris abducted the beautiful Helen from her husband, Menelaus, and took her back with him to Troy. Menelaus' brother, Agamemnon, headed an army of Greek heroes on a quest to retrieve Helen and destroy Troy, which, after ten years of warfare, they accomplished.

126 *your reputation . . . will grow nauseous*: Maria's metaphor implicitly likens Bubble's reputation to dead game; both, suspended for an hour or more, will emit a 'nauseous' smell.

130 *cuckold-buzz*: to 'buzz' was to whisper or gossip; it could also mean a tale or story. Both senses combine here to suggest that Bubble will become a living tale of cuckoldry to the town.

136 *your want of sense has taken from you*: 'your want of sence taken from you' (1677).

147 *designed*: mere deceit, a plot between them.

159 *clap*: pat or caress fondly.

178 *with eagle-aspect*: with the fierce demeanour of an eagle.

186 *a precedent of excellent nature*: as an example or model of good nature.

193 *crush him into mummy*: into a pulpy substance or mass.

195 *succubus*: a female demon who has sexual intercourse with a man while he sleeps; by the Restoration, it was often used for a whore or loose woman.

208 *I'll cut off her nose*: Bubble's threat does not accord with any known judicial punishment of adulteresses in England. Sometimes women were whipped or pilloried, and the Rump Parliament made adultery a capital crime (although this was rarely enforced). In earlier plays, the threat of nose-slitting as a punishment for adultery is usually uttered by an Italian. In Jonson's *Volpone* (1606), for instance, Corvino warns Celia that he will 'slit thy nose, | Like a raw rotchet' (3.7.98–9).

210 *handsomely*: skilfully; carefully.

212 *in the Strand*: see note to *MM*, 4.3.20.

259 *wonder*: act amazed; bewildered.

Let me alone: rely on me.

260 *after-plot*: after-game.

295 *Your song of . . . brave old fellows*: a song pillorying Sir Thomas Fairfax and his comrades, undoubtedly a 'Rump' song of the sort described below. Fairfax was the most beloved and respected of the military leaders in the Parliamentary army. He became a general as the result of his many

victories against the king's forces. Evidence suggests that he did not approve of the execution of Charles I, and he subsequently tempered his support for the new Commonwealth, even though he was reappointed commander-in-chief of all the forces in England and Ireland (30 March 1649). Fairfax was instrumental in bringing about the Restoration, perhaps one of the reasons he does not figure prominently in the miscellanies of 'Rump' songs published after 1660 (see below). Although Fumble waxes nostalgic about these songs and the good old days of the Civil War, his declaration that they have 'a great deal of judgement and sheer wit' is hardly the case. Most were little more than heavy-handed propaganda for the Royalist cause, dressed up in doggerel verse set to well-known tunes.

297   *Rump songs*: pro-Royalist ballads and poems. Although composed and circulated from 1639 onwards, these works became especially popular in the wake of pro-Royalist fervour after the Restoration. Sometimes they were published as individual broadsides, as with *Arsy versy; or, the second martyrdom of the Rump. To the tune of, The blind beggar of Bednall-green* (London, 1660), or *The Rump serv'd in with a grand sallet. Or, A new ballad, to the tune of the Blacksmith* (London, 1660). More commonly, they were published in miscellanies such as *The Rump, or A collection of songs and ballads made upon those who would be a Parliament, and were but the rump of an House of Commons, five times dissolv'd* (London, 1660). Anti-Rump sentiment made its way into the theatre: John Tatham's comedy, *The Rump: or the mirrour of the late times* (London, 1660), proved an early hit with Restoration audiences.

300   *you had been hanged . . . the Rump*: the Rump Parliament, which numbered only a fifth of the usual number of members, held power from 1648 until 1653. In effect, the Rump was a remnant of the so-called Long Parliament, the session of the English Parliament that lasted without a break from 1640 to 1653. Although the Long Parliament entered into conflict with Charles I and made several political reforms, it remained seriously divided along religious lines. In 1648, an army detachment under Colonel Thomas Pride ('Pride's Purge') prevented the Presbyterian majority from entering the House. The remaining members, all of them Independents, comprised the new Rump Parliament. The Rump executed Charles I and made England a Commonwealth. In 1653, Oliver Cromwell, finding the Rump Parliament unruly, suppressed them. When Oliver died in 1658, his son Richard attempted to sustain the Protectorate. When that coalition collapsed a few months later, he recalled the Rump Parliament in 1659, before resigning as Lord Protector. In September the Republican John Lambert, following the example of Oliver Cromwell, dissolved them. In 1660, two years after Cromwell's death, General George Monck officially dissolved the Long Parliament and ordered new elections. Members of the Rump Parliament directly responsible for the

execution of Charles I were, after the restoration of Charles II, hanged, drawn, and quartered. The heads of several of the regicides were still adorning City gates seven years later. Feelings about the 'Rump' ran high during the early days of the Restoration. On 11 February 1660 Samuel Pepys saw 'rumps tied upon sticks and carried up and down. The butchers at the maypole in the Strand rang a peal with their knifes when they were going to sacrifice their rump. On Ludgate-hill there was one turning of the spit, that had a rump tied upon it, and another basting of it' (i. 52).

303 *Chevy Chase*: an old-fashioned, popular ballad about the Battle of Otterburn (1388) that had a reputation for being 'the favorite ballad of the common people of England' (see Addison's *Spectator*, 70 and 74).

304 *Hunting of the Hare*: 'the title for a number of popular hunting songs' (see Vaughn, 256, nn. 385–6).

310 *animal of her magnitude*: of her small size.

315 *disaffected persons*: undoubtedly the religious 'fanatics' and Quakers mentioned below.

319 *dogs were hieroglyphic characters . . . of the Quakers*: i.e. the dogs represented Puritan extremists while the hare signified equally zealous Quakers. The word 'fanatic' as a designation for a religious or political zealot emerged in 1659–60. Much to the impatience of Sir Roger (who by this point has exited unobserved), Fumble treats this rather innocuous hunting song as a beast fable, a literary form that was popular from the mid-century onwards. Beast fables were often written as religious and/or political polemics, in the manner of Dryden's *The Hind and the Panther* (1687).

320 *sisters*: female separatists and religious dissenters.

323 *cony-Quaker*: i.e. rabbit-Quaker. Fumble continues here to interpret hares and rabbits as 'hieroglyphs' of Quakers.

324 *vacuity*: empty or vacant space.

329 *sensibly obliged*: i.e. Betty, having received bribes from Ranger, is obligated to him; however, by mentioning the fact, she also prompts him to continue their mutually advantageous relationship.

347 *penny-pot poets*: the penny pot was a small box for change; it was also a pimple on the face. Both meanings point to writers who barely eke out a living in penning ballads, lampoons, and other forms of 'cheap print' and manuscript in the period.

361 *than pristine ages*: i.e. than the delight experienced in ancient (and presumably) prelapsarian times.

364 *Charon's boat*: in classical mythology, Charon is the old boatman who ferries the spirits of the dead across the river Styx to their eventual resting place in the underworld.

364 *mongrel love*: a love of a mixed and debased nature; not a pure love.

380 *moonshine in the water*: pursuing an objective they can and will never achieve (proverbial).

383 *were the diet*: i.e. would eating it (the heart) be.

404 *at my devotion*: praying.

415 *Hercules*: mythological hero of prodigious strength, who performed twelve immense labours.

429 S.D. *Gapes*: yawns.

434 *wedding day*: anniversary.

441 *you shall hear from me*: i.e. Bubble threatens legal action or a challenge should Ranger persist in slandering Emilia.

4.[1].5 *bastards—birds of night*: certain species, such as the cuckoo, were thought to lay their eggs in the nests of other birds under the cover of night, thus producing bastard offspring. 'Birds' here also signifies prostitutes who move around under cover of darkness because their trade requires concealment.

15 *we cannot appoint our own destinies*: proverbial.

19 *a natural*: someone mentally handicapped from birth.

20 *I'd beg thee . . . to inherit thy estate*: Sir Roger's threat to disinherit Sneak and petition the Court of Wards for custody of another child in his place reveals the depth of his rage, given early modern attitudes towards adoption. From the sixteenth century, 'the notion of the family became increasingly based on the dual criteria of blood and marriage, [and] the adopted child—tied to the family through a legal fiction rather than through biological ties—threatened to violate the sanctioned ordering of the domestic sphere'. See Kristin Elizabeth Gager, *Blood Ties and Fictive Ties* (Princeton, 1996), 19.

21 *go to that*: go to that topic; bring that up.

37 *country*: neighbourhood, district.

38 *the rogue has me upon the hip*: at a disadvantage.

72 *cock o' th' game*: a cock bred to fight in games; also, a man adept at playing sexual games.

77 *I shall be a by-word to th' town*: an object of contempt back home.

4.2.2 *wet through*: totally inebriated, completely drunk.

9 *been bumping it*: i.e. been passing the bumpers around, getting drunk.

dipped: thoroughly suffused with moisture (in this case, wine).

20 *soop*: probably from the Irish 'supeen'. A drink.

22 *dust*: drink quickly; 'toss' it back.

23 *cherishes*: nourishes, cheers.

27 *'Tis in praise . . . not one ready-made of 'em in town*: an allusion to the anti-marriage polemics written by libertine authors in the 1670s (see the general introduction to this volume). So prevalent are these publications that Bubble cannot find a 'ready-made' song in praise of marriage.

28 *the poets' lodging*: book publishers would house and feed writers in exchange for their labour, a practice that eventually resulted in the Grub Street phenomenon of the eighteenth century. Exploited writers would pen poems, lampoons, and songs on speculation.

30 *not take*: not be popular.

31 *getting plays up for the next term*: the theatre season ran from October to June, with intermittent performances given over the summer months. Bubble's comment suggests that *A Fond Husband* is set in the summer since the poets are busy preparing new plays for the upcoming autumn season. The theatre 'term' deliberately overlapped with the law terms at the nearby Inns of Court in the hope of attracting law students.

33 *vein that way*: talent for that kind of writing.

35 *Tom Farthing*: probably a folk song or ballad. Unidentified.

  Colly my Cow: a folk song.

41 *drowsy*: sluggish, lethargic.

47 s.d. *Song*: written by Durfey and set to music by William Turner, the singer and composer (1651–1740). Turner, a chorister at Christ Church, Oxford, became master of the choristers at Lincoln Cathedral in 1667. He served as a member of the King's Private Musick from 1672, and was later employed at St Paul's Cathedral (1683) and Westminster Abbey (1699). Turner appeared in Shadwell's operatic version of *The Tempest* in 1674. His compositions include forty anthems, odes, a cantata, a motet, services, hymns, and chants, in addition to over fifty songs. This particular song also appears in Durfey's *New Collection of Songs and Poems* (1683), 31.

84 *tongue*: meat, specifically, the tongue of a cow, considered a delicacy.

92 *character*: style of writing; handwriting.

114 *Westminster Hall*: see note to 1.1.205.

138 *closet*: see note to *MM*, 5.2.10.

4.3.5 *nine-holes*: a game in which the players endeavour to roll small balls into nine holes in the ground. Each hole is worth a different value.

  6 *spends me three-pence a day*: given that Fumble, an alderman, probably enjoys a good income, his grumbling at the threepence his servant costs him daily points to his cheapness. Complaints about the profligacy of servants were a commonplace.

  9 *desolate*: alone.

9 *I have not the plague, I think*: victims of the plague were locked in their homes and isolated.

15 *Mr Little-Pox*: smallpox was sometimes referred to as 'little-pox'.

16 *stinted at nurse*: premature cessation of breastfeeding means that the boy has stunted growth.

18 *know a bailey . . . by her buttocks*: a bailey is a bailiff, a kind of sheriff, someone who 'sniffs out crime'. Thus the nose would be the distinguishing feature of a bailey and a plump bottom that of a wench.

20 *can hold the door with a steady hand*: the boy, a 'pretty pimp', can function as the door-keeper to a brothel.

27 *French grimaces*: the French were often mocked by the English for their airs and manners; thus 'French grimaces' came to signify affectation.

38 *years of discretion*: the age at which a person is supposedly capable of exercising good judgement; in English common law, the age of 14.

65 *patterns*: models; precedents.

70 *possess her with my love*: persuade her of my love.

73 *honours*: bows.

76 *'Tis worse than . . . has no money*: that bow is worse than a country lawyer's to his penniless client.

93 *sanguine complexion*: someone with a sanguine disposition—caused by a predominance of blood, according to humours physiology—had a ruddy face and a courageous, cheerful, and amorous nature. Fumble often fantasizes about Cordelia's sanguine and therefore passionate nature.

97 *and why not t'other thing*: Fumble suggests he is still capable of sexual activity, 'the other thing'. 'Another thing' also in Shakespeare refers to a woman's genitals.

stirring: (i) active, energetic; (ii) easily aroused, swiftly erect.

4.4.12 *venial crime*: Christianity traditionally classified sins as venial or mortal. Venial sins, such as lust, result from our human nature (with its accompanying appetites) and therefore are of a less serious nature. Mortal sins since they are acts of volition—of deliberate action—incur a much harsher penalty. Maria follows traditional thought in considering Emilia's adultery a 'venial crime'.

14 *close*: secretly, hidden.

18 *passage*: exchange; segment of the action or story.

27 *Assafœtida*: a resinous gum with a strong odour; it was used as a flavouring in cooking and as an antispasmodic drug.

38 *palled*: become flat and stale; become unattractive and uninteresting.

69 *lever*: a bar of iron used to dislodge a heavy or fixed object. It is similar to the modern crowbar.

69 *smith*: someone who works in iron or some other metal; a blacksmith or farrier.

81 S.D. *Rashley*: 'Ranger' (1677).

169 S.D. *run*: Bubble attacks Ranger with a sword.

182 *with Ranger*: i.e. as Ranger came to execute.

217 *All the fiends are asses to her*: she is so great a devil herself, that she makes fiends look like mere asses by comparison.

5.[1].5 *fourscore and five*: 85; Fumble's given age varies at different places.

12 *best goldsmith in Cheapside*: the chief market place of medieval London. All of the craft guilds worked in nearby streets, a practice that continued well into the eighteenth century. Fumble would have found the 'best goldsmith' in Goldsmiths Row in Cheapside.

13 *a cuckold too ... the honestest fellows*: presumably because they are so naive.

19 *of the right black water*: 'water' in this context indicates the limpidity and lustre of a precious stone, especially a diamond. The 'first water' describes a diamond of perfect translucency; second and third water indicate stones of less perfection. 'Black water' is ironic insofar as Fumble apparently recommends to Cordelia a dark, murky stone. See Harold Newman, *An Illustrated Dictionary of Jewelry* (1981), 325.

20 *put any false stones upon thee*: as Fumble indicates a couple of lines later, he is being 'waggish' with Cordelia in punning upon 'stones' (testicles).

26 *with a new name ... a new Lenten play*: normally the theatre companies did not perform on Wednesdays and Fridays during the Lenten season. Court performances were suspended entirely between Shrove Tuesday and Easter Sunday. In general, this was considered a dry period for the theatres, and, rather than première a new play to small or indifferent audiences, the companies recycled pre-Commonwealth plays instead. Vaughn thinks Durfey alludes to Aphra Behn's *The Debauchee; or, the Credulous Cuckold*, an adaptation of a pre-Commonwealth play, *Mad Couple Well Matched*, by Richard Brome. Behn's play premièred during Lent, shortly before *A Fond Husband* came to the stage. See Vaughn, 257, nn. 34–6.

31 *I am the man ... the rosebuds*: ironic given Fumble's age. Customarily, invocations of *carpe diem* are uttered by young lovers, not old men.

41 *a death's head at supper*: 'referring to the ancient Egyptian custom of placing a skull on the dining table, as a remembrance of mortality. According to Herodotus (Book II, chapter 78), it was not a skull, however, but a small carved mummy, which was carried about by a slave' (Vaughn, 257–58, n. 53).

47 *the devil's an ass ... in a play*: an allusion to Ben Jonson's play, *The Devil*

is an Ass (1616). Although no performance records exist for this play, it was in all likelihood revived, given Jonson's popularity on the Restoration stage.

49 *Randolph*: most likely Thomas Randolph (1605–35), the Caroline poet who was one of the famed 'sons' (followers) of Ben Jonson. Randolph wrote six racy, witty plays that typified 'college drama' of the period. Among his best-known poems are 'A Gratulatory to Ben Jonson' and 'On the Death of a Nightingale'. Randolph also penned several *carpe diem* poems, including 'An Ode to Master Anthony Stafford to hasten Him into the Country', that urge seizing an 'opportunity taken in the nick' (see note below). Fumble's literary tastes would seem rather antiquated to Restoration audiences.

50 *in the nick, in the nick*: an obscene pun on 'nick', which means a woman's genitals, as well as the more conventional meaning of 'the exact moment'.

69 S.D. *Cordelia and Sir Roger step aside*: this stage direction from Q1 indicates the actors should 'step aside' to overhear the exchange between Fumble and the Governess, while still being visible to the audience. The subsequent direction, however, has them 're-enter' on the next page, suggesting that the actors have completely exited the scene. In performance, the director would clearly have to choose between these two possibilities.

74 *farewell old Simon*: i.e. goodbye life. Fumble imagines living 'another age' (another lifetime) with Cordelia and *then* dying.

5.2.16 *sweating-chair*: similar to the sweating-tub used to cure venereal disease. There are two possibilities for staging here. In scripts written after 1660, 'within' usually meant 'offstage'; indeed, as the introductory 'Note on the Texts' indicates, it is editorial practice within this series to emend such stage directions accordingly. If 'within' is taken here in the customary sense, then it follows that Cordelia points to an offstage object in the characters' imagined line of vision. Durfey, however, could be making excellent comic use of the wings and shutters that opened and closed either to shift locales or to produce revelatory moments. Indeed, the stage direction at the end of this scene specifying 'Scene shuts' suggests that he has used Restoration staging for just such a revelation, thereby showing Sneak's sweating-chair to the characters *and* the audience.

9 *mathematical engine*: machine for doing computations.

5.[3].9 *doubt*: fear.

44 *supply*: aid, assist (sexual innuendo).

73 *several*: distinct, separate.

84 *I will tyrannize ... over his slave*: Turks enslaved large numbers of Europeans captured during the height of Ottoman rule. Although reputed

to be tyrannical, in actual practice Turkish masters were often quite clement. Indeed, memoirs and captivity narratives indicate that many Europeans preferred life under their Ottoman masters to life back home.

96 *By 'Scanderbeg*: i.e. by Jove (or a comparable expression). Bubble uses the proper name Scanderbeg allusively as an exclamation; comparable usage can be found in some of Ben Jonson's plays, such as *Every Man in his Humour* (1598). Scanderbeg (also Skanderbeg) was a fifteenth-century Albanian national hero who, with backing from Venice, Naples, and the papacy, fought against the Ottomans. His life became the source for many Albanian tales.

100 *I am sure I have 'em fast*: 'I am sure have em fast' (1677).

106 *maggots*: whims; fancies.

136 *her*: 'here' (1677).

144 *fetch you out*: draw you out; make or impart clarity to your repartees.

146 *Mrs Juniper*: juniper shrubs have prickly leaves and pungent, almost bitter, purple berries, attributes Bubble perhaps associates with his sister.

157 *noose of the slip*: noose of the cord or leash.

5.4.6 *represent*: impersonate.

22 *plain-dealing*: straightforward; plain talking. Proverbs about plain dealing date from the 1580s. William Wycherley's play, *The Plain-Dealer*, premiered in December of 1676, just five months before *A Fond Husband*, making the phrase newly fashionable again.

81 *popped in the mouth*: smacked on the mouth; kissed.

86 *avaunt Jezebel*: begone Jezebel! In the Old Testament, Jezebel was the infamous wife of Ahab, the king of Israel. The term 'Jezebel' came to mean a wicked, immodest, or impudent woman.

92 *rated*: scolded; reproved.

103 *dispense with*: spend time; forgo, do without.

109 *address*: put things right; redress this wrong.

5.[5].5 *cheap*: lightly esteemed through familiarity.

30 *I must hinder . . . do what you please*: it was considered dishonourable for a man to draw a sword upon an unarmed gentleman; also, Ranger stops Bubble since it was unmannerly for gentlemen to fight before guests, especially ladies. As Ranger reminds Bubble, 'in the field you may do what you please'.

52 *this*: 'his' (1677).

54 *wonderful*: to be wondered at.

60 *Felix quem faciunt aliena cornua cautum*: 'happy is he who is made cautious by the horns of another man'.

EPILOGUE

6 *clapped so long . . . clapped at last*: i.e. I fornicated so much, I got venereal disease ('the clap') at last.

16 *a clapper to be found*: the tongue of a bell which strikes on the inside and creates a ringing sound. Here it is used sexually. Fumble says that an old man will 'peal' with excitement over a young wench, even though he lacks a 'clapper' (a functioning penis).

25 *none but women to my plays*: a fairly standard joke by the mid-1670s. Prologues and epilogues frequently depict women feigning embarrassment or incomprehension at the smutty jokes, implying, of course, that despite this hypocritical display of modesty, they understood and took pleasure in the louche humour. It appears, however, that some women were truly offended by the more ribald plays. William Wycherley's *The Country Wife* (1675) occasioned an outcry that he bitterly acknowledged in his subsequent comedy, *The Plain-Dealer* (1676). For more information, see David Roberts's *The Ladies: Female Patronage of Restoration Drama 1660–1700* (Oxford, 1989).

Friendship in Fashion

EPIGRAPH

Archilochum rabies armavit iambo: 'Rage armed Archilochus with an iambic poem' (Horace, *Ars Poetica*). Archilochus of Paros had a reputation for being the most bitter of the satirists. This quotation stresses the harsh nature of Otway's comedy.

DEDICATION

2 Charles Sackville, Lord Buckhurst, earl of Middlesex and Dorset. Otway also dedicated *Alcibiades* (1675) to him. The Maecenas of the Restoration, Dorset was patron to a host of playwrights and poets. He entertained writers at both of his country seats, but Knole House became associated with Dryden and Durfey, while writers such as Shadwell, Etherege, and Prior frequented Copt Hall. Knole House featured a Poet's Parlour which displayed portraits of contemporary actors and writers, including one of Otway commissioned shortly before the painter Gerard Soest died in 1681. Dorset's generosity was legend; often he would leave a £50 or £100 note under the dinner plate of a writer. He also read drafts of plays and used his influence with the playhouses. In the dedications to *Friendship in Fashion* and *Alcibiades*, Otway expressed gratitude for Dorset's generosity, a munificence that included an appointment as tutor to Nell

Gwyn's eldest son by Charles II. Dorset was himself an accomplished poet and a member of the court wits who surrounded Charles II. He specialized in the satiric lyric, a brief poem in ballad stanzas mocking a person or event. Along with Sir Charles Sedley, Edward Filmer, Sidney Godolphin, and Charles Sackville, Dorset assisted Edmund Waller in putting together *Pompey the Great* (1664), a translation of Corneille's *La mort de Pompée*. This translation rivalled Katherine Phillips's version, produced the previous year in Dublin. For additional information on Dorset, see Brice Harris, *Charles Sackville, Sixth Earl of Dorset: Patron and Poet of the Restoration* (Urbana, Ill., 1940).

6 *in my respects to your lordship*: i.e. in making visits to your lordship.

9 *the circumstances of my condition*: Otway frequently complained in print about his penurious circumstances; his bitter poem, *The Poet's Complaint of His Muse* (1680), describes in great detail the indignities facing any writer during the Restoration whose 'daily business must be daily bread'.

15 *As for the unlucky censures . . . for this play*: the defensive tone of Otway's dedication suggests an embattled stance against the audience; certainly, the sole known performance and the meagre printing history indicate that the play was unpopular with spectators and readers alike.

17 *accused of the thing*: the language here reveals that 'some people of the world' took the satire personally ('as to believe themselves deserved it'). That Otway appealed to Dorset for assistance further suggests that the complaints pre-dated the first performance; in all likelihood, he needed the peer's help to ensure the play's appearance on the stage. The conciliatory language of the Prologue also hints at the hostility Otway and the players expected to encounter from factions in the audience.

THE CHARACTERS OF THE PLAY

Like many Restoration dramatists, Otway gives his characters humorous yet revelatory names. The romantic young blades, Truman and Valentine, are marked by their names, as are the musically inclined fops, Caper and Saunter. 'Goodvile' functions as a kind of oxymoron, as might befit an unhappy marriage between a good wife and a vile husband. Less apparent are the names Otway assigns to Malagene and Lady Squeamish. 'Malagene' implies an innately bad nature ('mal' = bad and 'gen' = condition), while 'Squeamish' suggests someone who is both excessively fastidious and coyly sexual.

Goodvile: 1678 fluctuates between 'Goodvile' and 'Goodvil'. I have regularized the name throughout.

Mrs Barry: 'Mrs. Barrey' (1678).

THE PROLOGUE

10 *fasting days*: the Christian calendar designated certain days during the year for fasting or abstinence, including the Lenten season and the Wednesday, Friday, and Saturday of Ember weeks. The allusion to 'strictest vigils and fasting days' suggests that Otway composed the play during Lent, which began on 13 February in 1677/8. The only known performance took place after Easter of that year.

13 *disciplined*: in both the religious and artistic sense.

14 *libel*: a piece of writing, usually brief in nature, defaming the character of someone.

21 *jades*: hussies or trollops; also applied commonly to Fortune. Otway appears to be using it in this latter sense—of the Muses as capricious hussies.

25 *Bankside butchers do a bear*: see note to *MM*, 2.1.147.

28 *Bear Garden law*: the animals were expected to fight until death; thus, the reference to 'stand or fall' in the preceding line.

1.1 s.d. *The Mall*: see note to *MM*, 2.1.161.

3 *tin lattice*: a lattice is a gate, screen, or window; here it clearly designates the tin window—so-called because of the lattice design—in the coach.

26 *two vizards*: see note to *MM*, 2.1.183.

32 *appointed*: make an appointment.

Chatelins: 'Chatolins' (1678). A famous ordinary in London, frequently referred to in the plays of the period. Pepys mentions it twice in his diary.

51 *had much ado*: had much trouble or ceremony.

62 *as your Jews are from the rest of mankind*: an allusion to the Jewish practice of circumcision, a procedure that renders Jews 'distinguishable from one of us' (i.e. Christians or gentiles).

65 *fond, wanton ape*: (i) natural-born fool, a naïf; (ii) lascivious, abandoned lover; a woman who has 'apish' (and therefore highly sexual) characteristics.

66 *fresh kindness*: 'kindness' in Restoration plays and poetry is frequently a code word for sexual favours.

69 *reserve:* something to fall back upon, solace oneself with, when need arises.

79 *censures*: passes judgement on, estimates, criticizes.

80 *none dedicated to her yet*: as the plays in this volume indicate, it was common for dramatists during the Restoration to dedicate their plays to patrons, largely in the hopes of receiving a cash gift. For the patron, a dedication acknowledged social status, as well as aesthetic authority.

91 *stager*: one qualified by long experience; a veteran or old hand.

92 *resty*: also reasty; here, stale or rancid.

116 *that he is able*: i.e. as to think that he is able.

120 *under the rose*: see note to *FH*, 1.1.349.

sweetly fitted: nicely joined; sexually connected or fitted.

138 *free*: frank in what we say.

143 *guinea-club*: during this time, a 'club' designated one's share of the bill; thus, Malagene claims that his share of the evening's expenses cost one guinea, a not inconsiderable sum.

a right honourable: applies to peers below the rank of marquess; applies also to privy councillors and to certain civil functionaries. Malagene boasts that he keeps only the most select of company, a snobbery based entirely upon titles.

148 *Toledo*: a generic name for a Spanish blade of superb quality.

150 *managed her*: Malagene plays upon the early modern sense of 'manage' (handle, train, or direct a horse in its paces); thus, he has put this woman through her sexual paces. He also implies he has commanded her for his pleasure with total authority and control.

154 *person of quality . . . on foot too?*: urban violence discouraged people of means, especially women, from walking around the city at night. Not until the mid-eighteenth century would a police force be established.

156 *take no notice on't*: don't reveal her identity.

182 *I have discovered . . . drinks of*: Malagene's claim that Charles II drank 'pale wine' has some basis in fact. Although the monarch preferred French wine, by 1673 he was drinking wine from the Rhine region—undoubtedly the 'pale wine' mentioned by Malagene—in sufficient quantities to justify a purchase of 100 vats.

201 *sham*: ruse, trick; according to Ghosh, a word that had just entered the language the previous year, in 1677.

217 *am used*: am accustomed.

237 *the groom-porter's*: the gambling hall. It was managed by the groom-porter, originally a member of the royal household but later authorized to oversee gambling within the precincts of the court. He was also empowered to decide gambling disputes and settle wagers.

262 *send a guard*: Malagene offers to send one of his own household guards to adjudicate the duel. Guards from the royal household were expected to prevent duels, which were outlawed (but nonetheless occurred frequently).

266 *bullies*: good friends, fine fellows.

279 *blowing*: whore.

281 *heats herself . . . course at night*: i.e. in the morning, she limbers up sexually in St James's Park to prepare for the truly serious erotic activities

that will occur there later under cover of darkness. See Rochester's poem, *A Ramble in St James's Park*.

288 *an Italian song:* Italian composers and musicians who worked in London during the Restoration—men such as Nicola Matteis, Pietro Reggio, and Giovanni Battista Draghi—popularized Italian song and singing.

307 *not fail:* i.e. not fail to attend Goodvile's ball.

311 *my Lord —— at court tonight:* there are a couple of possibilities here for performance. Malagene could be teasing Saunter and Caper with the identity of the nobleman by almost naming him—and then not doing so. The line could also be delivered absent-mindedly insofar as Malagene nearly blurts out the nobleman's name and then catches himself.

314 *Nay then:* i.e. let's be on our guard; or, wait for it; or, a show's about to happen.

320 *'As Chloe full of, etc.':* a song by Rochester, at one point a patron of Otway's. The song actually begins *'As Chloris, full of harmless thoughts . . .'*

346 *abroad but two years . . . in an academy:* 'abroad' makes it apparent that Valentine has spent two years in a Parisian academy. An institution of learning halfway between a preparatory school and a university, the academy functioned as a finishing school for privileged young men and women.

349 *makes bold with me:* speaks satirically or mockingly about me. Malagene in his next speech puns on 'bold' to indicate a sexual relationship has taken place between Lady Squeamish and Valentine.

380 *the poet came . . . my lodgings:* it was customary for the poet to read his play to a patron for approval; Lady Squeamish clearly fancies herself a patron of the arts despite Truman's claim on at 1.1.80–1 that she has never had a play dedicated to her.

383 *the reason he . . . the conduct of it:* debates raged during the Restoration over the proper composition of plays. French neoclassical precepts dictated strict adherence to rules for action and language; but English writers, well aware of the idiosyncratic practice of dramatists like Shakespeare, vacillated between their own native tradition and that of the continent. The court, much influenced by French fashion, was commonly thought to promote decorous speech and writing. See e.g. Dryden's compliment to the earl of Rochester in the dedication to *Marriage A-la-Mode*.

398 *neither song nor dance in it:* to attract audiences, the theatres often included songs and/or dances in plays, always sure crowd-pleasers. See, for instance, the many songs in *FH*. Some dramatists dismissed these more popular aspects of the drama.

396 *pass:* happen, are current.

413 *Supple*: in addition to its still current meanings, 'supple' signified someone who was servilely submissive or ingratiatingly accommodating.

421 *Colt*: both an awkward young person who needs to be 'broken in', as well as a wanton, lascivious person.

422 *Pruneit*: 'prune' describes someone who plumes himself—who decks himself out in fancy dress; it also signified the conventional meaning of lopping off superfluous branches or shoots. Both meanings operate here, as Mr Pruneit preens while 'pruning' the sexually the inexperienced (but eager) Lady Colt.

426 *he keeps a player again*: references in the period abound to the practice of 'keeping' an actress for a mistress. Charles II took the actresses Moll Davis and Nell Gwyn for mistresses, and several of the nobility, including the earls of Oxford and Rochester, followed suit.

431 *lay out . . . to better advantage*: (i) exhibit or display my romantic inclinations in a more advantageous light; (ii) spend my affections on someone more worthy (i.e. possessing more wealth and status).

437 *Mr Saunter sings the French manner*: years of exile in Paris and elsewhere on the continent had formed Charles II's predilection for French music. French musicians such as Louis Grabu, Robert Cambert, and Jacques Paisible popularized the 'French manner' of music, as did performances in England of works by the great composer Jean-Baptiste Lully. The French influence, however, was not to last: increasingly Italian music replaced French; and even Louis Grabu, who in 1674 was replaced by a native Englishman, Nicholas Staggins, as Master of the King's Musick, saw himself removed from royal favour. Much like the remark about continental actors surpassing their English counterparts (see below), this comment reveals the extent of Lady Squeamish's ignorance. For all of her professions of being *au courant*, she is actually quite passé.

439 *he pronounces . . . a tone or accent*: it appears that Mr Saunter applies a French accent to English verses, with the end result that no one can understand him, as evidenced by Malagene's irritable aside.

460 *commence*: grow into, become.

2.1 S.D. *The ordinary*: a public house or tavern where meals could be had for a fixed price. In keeping with fashionable practices during the Restoration, the Goodviles have taken over a dining room for eating and dancing. Mrs Goodvile and the other women appear to be using a chamber off the dining room (cf. Victoria's comment, 'I'll but step into my chamber and follow you instantly').

17 *parole*: release from prison on condition not to do certain things. Goodvile is 'paroled' from the prison of marriage, having promised (ineffectually) not to repeat the sins of the previous night.

24 *getting a stomach*: acquiring an appetite, in this instance, sexual appetite.

26 *turtle*: shortened form of turtle-dove, a bird known for its affection for its mate; term of endearment.

46 *kind*: see Goodvile's sardonic remark on receiving a 'fresh kindness' from his wife, 1.1.66.

63 *ranging gallant*: hunts sexual partners everywhere.

77 *champagne*: see note to *MM*, 4.1.388.

80 *a drunken country vicar . . . stronger than his reason*: nobility and powerful politicians in the seventeenth and eighteenth centuries dispensed ecclesiastical positions as part of the privilege of patronage.

85 *doubt*: fear.

88 *has caused this alteration in you*: both Mrs Goodvile and Lettice claim to observe the signs of pregnancy that have caused an alteration in Victoria's appearance, including pale skin and dark circles under the eyes.

93 *if there . . . will cure all*: in other words, if Victoria is indeed pregnant out of wedlock, a hastily arranged marriage will 'cure all'.

151 *herded*: joined the party, become part of the crowd.

184 *Smithfield doggerel*: a form of low, popular verse sung by the clowns and 'Merry Andrews' in Smithfield Market, the site of the annual Bartholomew Fair.

185 *Chloris dwindles into a kitchen-wench*: 'Chloris' was one of the stock names used for the young woman who functioned as the object of love in pastoral poetry. Customarily a shepherdess or a nymph, Chloris has here 'dwindled' into a scullery-maid.

192 *held at so dear a rate*: offered at such a high price.

     beat down the market: reduce the going rate (of beauty—see above).

198 *Dutch bargain*: bargain concluded with a drink and therefore unlikely to last.

234 *the word*: Goodvile invites a toast.

236 *Pass*: proceed, go.

260 *an elder brother*: because of primogeniture—which ensured that estates passed intact into the hands of the first son—'elder brothers' were much coveted as marriage prospects.

276 *honour*: respect or deferential admiration paid to ladies.

280 *And, gallants, I am . . . epistle dedicatory*: Sir Noble Clumsy recites the standard closing address at the end of an epistle dedicated to the poet's patron.

301 *boarding our mistresses*: making advances to our mistresses.

331 *gambados*: boots—almost a kind of leather shield—that were attached to the saddle to protect the rider's legs and feet from the elements. Because they were cumbersome, gambados were not used by riders during horse races (thus Caper's remark).

337 *stand my friend*: intercede with her on my behalf.

367 *at my heart*: at bottom; in reality.

388 *now acquaintance*: present or recent acquaintance.

398 *port*: deportment, carriage, bearing.

408 *shall be security*: Malagene speaks metaphorically here, but Sir Noble Clumsy takes his pledge of security literally ('I have sworn never to be bound for any man').

417 *son of Mars*: in Roman mythology, Mars was the god of war. Malagene uses this epithet sarcastically, not taking Sir Noble Clumsy seriously as a swordsman or fighter.

425 *Take the other glass*: let me have your glass refilled.

440 *I have two thousand pounds a year*: by late seventeenth-century standards, Sir Noble Clumsy is quite well off. In 1688 the demographer Gregory King estimated the annual income for a successful merchant at £400; Sir Noble Clumsy's income is five times that amount.

470 *expedition*: speed.

479 *I will salute thy under-lip*: kiss thy lower lip.

484 *prefer*: promote or advance in status.

502 *Pelion upon Ossa*: Pelion is the name of a mountain in Thessaly; the common phrase—to pile Pelion upon Ossa—means to add to what is already great. The phrase comes from Virgil's *Georgics* i. 281 (*imponere Pelio Ossam*).

508 *my grandmother's kissing dance*: see note to *MM*, 4.1.30.

3.1 S.D. *The ordinary*: a setting is not indicated in the first edition; the ensuing action, however, argues for this locale.

  2 *dip my bill*: Goodvile continues the metaphor from the first sentence, likening himself to a bird that dips its bill into water (i.e. sips delicately). The two bottles of wine he has consumed, as the subsequent sentence makes clear, belie the image.

14 *a decayed cavalier captain*: a captain who served with Royalist forces during the Civil War; he is now 'decayed' (i.e. impoverished) because he was never adequately compensated under the Restoration Settlement, a chronic complaint of the times.

  drinks journey-work under a deputy lieutenant: journey-work is work of an inferior or servile nature; hackwork. Truman jokes that the impoverished cavalier captain now ekes out a living by functioning as a hanger-on in a household of rank and means.

69 *a pretty proposition to me*: a pretty offering for me to consider.

78 *Punchinello ... Prince Prettyman*: Punchinello, Scaramouchio, and Harlequin were all stock characters from the Italian *commedia dell'arte*, an

improvisational form of drama. *Commedia* troupes performed in London immediately at the Restoration and proved very popular with audiences, much to the chagrin of the English theatre managers. Prince Prettyman is a mock-heroic character from the duke of Buckingham's *The Rehearsal* (1672), his hilarious send-up of Dryden's penchant for writing bombastic heroic tragedies.

124 *O the English comedians . . . the French or Italian*: 'Comedian' was still used in the Elizabethan sense (for actor) until the end of the Restoration. This comment reveals the ignorance of Lady Squeamish; generally, English actors were regarded as being far superior to their continental brethren. A letter from John Verney written a year before *Friendship in Fashion* was produced is fairly typical in its assessment of French actors: 'a French opera, but most pitifully done, so ill that the King was aweary on't, and some say it was not well contrived to entertain the English gentry, who came that night in honour to their King, with a lamentable ill-acted French play, when our English actors so much surpass . . .' (as cited in Van Lennep, i. 257).

125 *we want poets*: we lack good dramatists; 'poet' designated all manner of literary endeavour, from the writing of verses to the composition of plays.

138 *The Merry Conceits . . . his dog, Bobadillo*: a hit against Dryden. The play *Sir Noble Clumsy* has undertaken to write mixes genres, as is evident from its title. Throughout the period, critics attacked Dryden for writing tragicomedies that juxtaposed heroic scenes written in verse against comic scenes written in prose. These plays were not always happy inventions. 'Bobadillo' is most likely a variation on 'Drybob', a character in Shadwell's *The Humorists* (1670) clearly modelled on Dryden. Shadwell, according to James Anderson, 'creates a spoken idiom for Drybob by repeating two phrases he had first used against Dryden in 1668, when he accused him of "imagining that all the Wit in *Playes* consisted in bringing two persons upon the Stage to break Jests, and to bob one another, which they call Repartie" '. A dry bob, more vulgarly, was also slang for sex without ejaculation. See James Anderson Winn's *John Dryden and His World* (New Haven, 1987), 222.

143 *squirt comedy*: the *OED* cites this particular usage in the play. Normally, to squirt is to eject or spew a stream of liquid; it was also used to describe diarrhoea. Sir Noble Clumsy, who looks down on comedy, implicitly likens this form of literary output to the alimentary kind.

147 *Louvre or Whitehall*: a fortress built at the beginning of the thirteenth century, the Louvre had, by the sixteenth, become a palace for monarchs. During the Restoration period, Louis XIV added classical colonnades and had the apartments decorated by the painter Charles Le Brun. Whitehall—originally known as York House—was purchased by the archbishop of York in 1298 and became the London palace for his successors. Seized by Henry VIII and renamed Whitehall, the palace

subsequently became a royal residence. Troupes of *commedia* players frequently performed at the Louvre and Whitehall, the reason why Lady Squeamish associates Malagene's imitation of Harlequin with these abodes.

153 S.D. *Punchinello's voice*: one of the comic servants in the *commedia dell'arte*. In his original Italian form, he represented the Neapolitan area. Malagene could be using a Neapolitan accent, or he could be imitating Punchinello in his more Anglicized form: as a rough-hewn, doltish fellow.

164 *unlucky jerks*: mischievous jibes.

180 *Cuts backward*: in dance, to execute a 'cut' one sprang from the ground and, while in mid-air, twiddled the feet one in front of the other with great rapidity. The prodigious Caper manages to perform this feat *backwards*.

181 *are you a dancing master?*: Thomas Jevon, who played the part of Caper, had taught dancing and singing before he joined the Duke's Company.

184 *overtaken*: inebriated.

189 *I mind dancing altogether*: I only care for dancing.

196 *By yea and by nay*: phrase attributed to certain kinds of religious separatists, especially Quakers, and cited in mockery of them. Sir Noble Clumsy, however, appears to use the phrase earnestly to express moral revulsion at the 'foul' strumpet.

197 *a running bawd*: (i) a street prostitute who 'runs' from street to street in search of business; and (ii) a diseased prostitute with 'running' sores or suppurations.

204 *hackney stripping whore*: almost a redundancy. A hackney is a common drudge or prostitute. Truman appears to be describing the lowest sort of whore.

219 *to put in for the rubbers*: in games of chance, a set of three games, the last of which decides the winner. Goodvile has won the first two rounds with his wife and Victoria, but Valentine hopes to win the final decisive round with Camilla as his prize.

245 *Madam Goodvile*: it is not entirely clear how Lady Squeamish is pairing off these three remaining characters. 'Dear Mr Truman, won't you oblige me?' indicates that she has taken Truman for her dancing partner, thus forcing the Goodviles—who are left without partners—to dance together. She could also be offering herself to Goodvile as a dancing partner ('your humble servant'), thereby asking Truman to 'oblige' her by dancing with Mrs Goodvile.

248 *I'll keep good orders*: keep the dancers in orderly formation.

248 S.D. *take out the women*: i.e. the men join the women and take them to the place onstage where they will begin the dance.

252 *cramped*: forcibly or unnaturally compressed; constrained (*OED*).

254 *kit*: also kitt. A small fiddle, often preferred by dancing masters during the period.

285 *'In January last'*: Ghosh thinks this is the song beginning 'In January last, on Munnonday at Morn' in Durfey's *Wit and Mirth; or, Pills to Purge Melancholy* (1719).

288 *a Scotch bagpipe . . . have better music*: musical instruments dating back perhaps as far as the second or fifth centuries, bagpipes continued to be played widely in the less Anglicized regions of north and west Scotland. 'Scotch songs' and bagpipes became part of the ballad revival of the seventeenth century, expressing in part an urban longing for rustic innocence. Trained bears often danced to the accompaniment of bagpipes. Despite the popularity of Scottish music, some urban dwellers looked down upon its 'rude' origins and 'barbaric' tones.

294 S.D. *Irish cronon*: also 'cronane'; a monotonous chant or drone; a song without words.

299 *an Irish musician that's lately come over*: perhaps a reference to an actual musician. His identity remains unknown.

305 *if your ladyship has any further service for him*: service of a clearly sexual nature. During the period, libertine poetry often joked about the sexual use of pages and boys 'in service'.

309 *Lancashire witch*: Lancashire was known for its large number of witches. In 1612 nine witches were hanged; and in 1633 seventeen were sentenced but not executed. Thomas Heywood and Richard Brome wrote a play called *The Lancashire Witches* (1634), inspired in part by this second wave of witchcraft. By the Restoration, the expression 'a Lancashire witch' had become proverbial.

318 *gypsy*: contemptuous term for a woman, someone who is cunning, deceitful, or fickle; a 'baggage'.

319 *show her*: put her on display, expose her folly.

333 *repaired to*: retreated to; escaped to.

343 *shrift*: confession, admission. The connotation here is sexual, as Mrs Goodvile suggests that her husband and Camilla are 'confessing' mutually sinful desires.

393 *gloat*: look amorously or longingly upon someone.

396 *this is something*: this is of some consideration.

398 *far*: 'fat' (1678).

454 *hardly value you*: judge you severely, condemn you.

495 *the Mother of . . . wife in Holborn*: the Mother of the Maids, an official position in the queen's household, oversaw the maids of honour. Holborn was known for its thoroughly middle-class, unsophisticated denizens.

Camilla suggests that Lady Squeamish, armed with the latest gossip about Victoria's condition, would spread rumours from the highest to the lowest ranks of town.

521   *a mask with an amber bead*: ladies' masks had beads inside which could be held in the mouth to keep the mask secure; that way, a lady could use her hands freely. Amber was thought to have medicinal qualities, perhaps the reason why Lady Squeamish specifically requests a mask with amber beads to forestall any fits (e.g. spells of fainting) she might have.

545   *thoroughly*: 'throughly' (1678).

556   *crammed*: confined.

589   *fubb*: a small, chubby person, perhaps here an allusion to Victoria's 'altered' condition.

604   *a very good Dutch burgomaster*: the burgomaster was the chief magistrate in a Dutch or Flemish town. Valentine expresses the standard English view of the Dutch—that they were dishonest drunkards.

4.[1].5   *loof*: see note to *The Libertine*, 3.1.2.

43   *probatum*: a proven thing; an approved remedy.

70   *soused me*: soaked me in drink.

83   *dry pimping*: 'dry' because Valentine himself cannot enjoy the sexual fruits of pimping. 'Dry' in the period often connoted incomplete sexual pleasure (e.g. sex without ejaculation was known as a 'dry bob'). See note to 138.

107   *mumbling*: literally, to chew softly; the meaning here is sexual, of course. Goodvile complains that he has been consuming sexually a tough old bird instead of a nice, young partridge.

168   *joy*: sweetheart.

182   *wilderness*: 'piece of ground in a large garden or park, planted with trees, and laid out in an ornamental or fantastic style, often in the form of a maze or labyrinth' (*OED*).

227   *the daubing . . . appeared too plain*: 'daubing' during the period connoted coarse painting and hypocritical flattery. Truman pulls both meanings together, suggesting that the pretence of Goodvile's friendship is as obvious as heavily applied make-up: both appear 'too plain'.

228   *decoy*: brothel.

251   *put up*: sheathe your swords.

275   *charnel house*: a house for dead bodies; also, a vault in which human bones are piled up.

292   *blown upon*: had eggs deposited on it; tainted.

309   *Whirr*: Goodvile is making a snarling or growling sound.

350 *There, sir*: Caper appears to make a dismissive gesture at this point.

355 *raw head and bloody bones*: a huge mastiff given to eating raw meat and bones; in Goodvile's mind, Sir Noble Clumsy qualifies himself as such when he declares 'I'll eat his heart for it'.

357 *towser*: a large guard dog, sometimes used in bear or bull baiting. Truman here is the 'great towser' who has already 'started' on the 'fresh game' (i.e. Mrs Goodvile).

367 *I am resolved . . . of the worst*: there are two possibilities here. Saunter, in a show of generosity, could be pledging to save Victoria's reputation by marriage if the 'worst' should come to light—i.e. that she's pregnant by Goodvile. Victoria's unavailability could also constitute Saunter's 'worst' fear, if she returns to Goodvile or marries Sir Noble Clumsy.

371 *resentments*: thanks, gratitude.

389 *Capuchin*: in 1528 the Capuchins, a monastic order, received papal authority to become an autonomous branch of the Franciscans. They were known as Capuchins because of their practice of wearing a long hood (or *capuche*) attached to the standard issue Franciscan robe.

394 *for composition*: for the settling of differences.

429 *she shows all her changes in a motion*: she focuses all her emotions in a specific plan.

463 *destitute*: without power; without resources.

467 *outrageous*: excessively emotional, extravagant.

471 *coffee-house companions*: coffee houses were notorious for fostering scandal and sedition. The government tried, albeit unsuccessfully, to shut down coffee houses in London for these very reasons.

472 *orange-women*: the women who sold oranges, at the time, a costly delicacy, at the playhouse. Orange-women were reputed to be purveyors of gossip; in Wycherley's *The Country Wife*, Horner orders Quack in the opening scene to tell the orange-women in the playhouse about his condition in the hope it will circulate around town more quickly. See also the Orange-Woman in *MM* 1.1.

519 *Down with your dust*: hand over your money.

569 *I will sooner return to my vomit*: proverbial; perhaps a paraphrase of Proverbs 26: 11: 'As a dog returneth to his vomit, so a fool returneth to his folly.'

5.1.17 *Phoebus*: also Apollo, the Greek god associated with music, archery, prophecy, and medicine. He was also during the Hellenistic and Roman periods thought to be the sun god.

18 *The wolves have preyed . . . spots of gray*: Goodvile quotes several lines from *Much Ado About Nothing*. The lines actually read: 'The wolves have prey'd; and look, the gentle day, | Before the wheels of Phœbus,

round about | Dapples the drowsy east with spots of grey' (5.3.25–7). Otway frequently quotes from Shakespeare in his plays and emulates several of his dramatic techniques, including the use of blank verse in the tragedies.

24 *As those whom . . . hedges and ditches*: Summers (*Otway*) thinks this is an intentional misquotation from Samuel Butler's *Hudibras*: 'An *ignis fatuus*, that bewitches | And leads men into Pools and Ditches' (1.1). It could also be an allusion to the earl of Rochester's *Satyr against Reason and Mankind*: 'Reason, an *ignis fatuus*, in the mind, | Which leaving light of Nature, sense behind; | Pathless and dangerous wandering ways it takes, | Through errors, fenny bogs, and thorny brakes' (12–15).

39 *wittol*: a contented cuckold; a man complaisant about the infidelity of his wife.

59 *rank*: offensive, rancid.

64 *Lord's day*: Sunday.

95 *And when Mr Goodvile's . . . lie together*: Mrs Goodvile implies nothing sexual by this remark. Women during the seventeenth and eighteenth centuries often slept together, in part for protection and in part for warmth. Good friends, sisters, and cousins frequently shared beds.

108 *I hope so*: I believe so.

134 *So Theseus left . . . Æneas from his Dido*: in Book IV of The Aeneid, Aeneas abandons Queen Dido in Carthage, sailing off with his men to found Rome. Theseus and Ariadne inhabit another tale of abandonment: Theseus, in exchange for Ariadne's assistance in slaying the Minotaur, promises to marry her. Instead, on his voyage home, he abandons Ariadne and marries her sister Phaedra. Otway treats the final segment of this story in *Phaedra to Hippolytus*, which tells of the queen's illicit love for her stepson.

158 *Scour, scour, scour*: 'scourers' (or scowrers) were violent young men who rampaged drunkenly through streets, breaking windows and causing fights; thus, to scour is to cause mayhem.

161 *punks in beaten satin*: whores in expensive dresses; satin was still a fairly new fabric for the period and quite costly.

170 *journeymen tailors*: tailors who do poor quality work.

182 *neat*: elegant, smartly dressed.

184 *bear me out*: support me.

198 S.D. *beats her backward*: knocks her to the ground.

220 *Jerniè*: from the French '*je renie Dieu*' ('I renounce God'); clearly, a blasphemous expression.

221 *shock*: slang for a gentlewoman's lap dog. See Pope, *The Rape of the Lock*: 'He said; when *Shock*, who thought she slept too long, | Leapt up, and wak'd his Mistress with his Tongue' (i. 114–16).

229 *Westminster Drollery*: first published in 1671, this miscellany included some of the most popular songs, poems, prologues and epilogues of the day ('both at Court and Theatres'). Subsequent volumes were published in 1672, 1673, and 1674. Miscellanies or 'drolleries' were extremely popular after the Restoration.

230 *Oxford Jests*: another popular collection, this one of 'Witty Jests, merry Tales, and pleasant Joques' (1669). Like *Westminster Drollery*, it went through subsequent printings and volumes. These were far from being highbrow works of art; thus, when Sir Noble Clumsy brags about the barber, the creator of his periwig, having drolleries 'at his fingers' ends' (i.e. memorized), his audience is hardly to be impressed.

230 *cittern*: an instrument somewhat like a guitar, only strung with wire and played with a quill. According to Summers (*Otway*), it was commonly kept in barber shops for the customers to play. The modern zither is a descendant of the cittern.

231 *Troy Town*: a popular ballad, already old by the Restoration. It was much reprinted.

245 *jessamine*: variant of 'jasmine'; perfume made from jasmine flowers.

246 *rogues in buckram*: an allusion to Falstaff's 'two rogues in buckram suits . . . four rogues in buckram' (*1 Henry IV*, 2.4). Buckram was a kind of coarse linen stiffened with paste. The expression 'men in buckram' or 'rogues in buckram' came to refer proverbially to non-existent persons; thus, Sir Noble Clumsy's application of the expression to Caper and Saunter suggests they are men without substance, hollow men.

248 *Cerberus*: in Roman and Greek mythology, the three-headed dog who guards the entrance to the infernal regions.

249 *popinjays*: vain, conceited persons.

254 *Bedlam*: the abbreviated term for the Hospital of St Mary of Bethlehem in London. Founded as a priory in 1247, it became a hospital for the insane by 1402. Originally outside Bishopsgate, the asylum was moved during the Restoration to a building in Moorfields which was designed by Robert Hooke and said by Evelyn to be very beautiful.

267 *your voice*: 'your vow' (1678). Summers emends 'vow' to 'voice', a reasonable change given that Saunter has just begun singing, and it appears that Mrs Goodvile is urging her maid to join in the song.

277 *wear the willow*: proverbial; the willow symbolized grief for unrequited love or the death of a mate; thus, 'to wear the willow' was to don the visible sign of mourning.

373 *cast mistresses . . . at the playhouse*: it is not entirely clear whether 'cast' is being used as a verb or an adjective. If the former, Truman must resort to 'cast' for mistresses at the playhouse in the manner one might angle for trout. If the latter, then he is condemned to cast-off (abandoned) mistresses. Parallel structure suggests that 'cast' is the first in a succession of verbs ('take up' and 'drudge') in the sentence.

374 *drudge*: perform sexually.

386 *nothing upon compulsion*: Malagene teasingly echoes Falstaff's outraged response to Prince Hal's interrogation ('What, upon compulsion? Zounds, an I were at the strappado or all the racks in the world, I would not tell you on compulsion. Give you a reason on compulsion? If reasons were as plentiful as blackberries, I would give no man a reason upon compulsion, I'). See *1 Henry IV*, 2.4.224–8.

422 S.D. *Jew's trump*: also known as a Jew's harp; 'a musical instrument of simple construction, consisting of an elastic steel tongue fixed at one end to a small lyre-shaped frame of brass or iron, and bent at the other end at right angles; it is played by holding the frame between the teeth and striking the free end of the metal tongue with the finger' (*OED*).

441 *Machiavel*: Anglicized name of Niccolo Machiavelli, the Florentine political philosopher who wrote *The Prince* (1513). The term 'Machiavel' signified an unscrupulous nature, someone who plots and schemes against others for his own amoral or selfish ends (which is how Mrs Goodvile uses it). The stage Machiavel was a stock character in the Renaissance theatre: Iago and Richard III certainly qualify as prototypes.

445 *this throw for all my future peace*: this final throw of the dice will decide my future.

467 *Ay, and six*: a coach and six horses was a much coveted status symbol of the period.

Rampant: someone extravagant in action or opinion; it could also describe someone lustful or vicious. Otway might be alluding here to Madame Rampant, the whore we never actually see, in Etherege's *She Would If She Could*.

471 *fop of the corner*: fop's corner was a section of the pit near the stage where the most foppish of critics issued (frequently loud) pronouncements on the play.

474 *my more peculiar punk:* my special strumpet.

477 *nose*: confront, reproach.

497 *pelf*: money or riches, but with a depreciatory connotation. It could also mean booty or stolen property. Mrs Goodvile appears to acknowledge here that her London lifestyle is supported by ill gain, namely, the exploitation of the tenants (peasants) on their country estate.

539 *squab*: also 'squobb'; young, tender game, not quite old enough to eat. Goodvile accuses his wife of having a fierce sexual appetite, one which requires 'a substantial dish'.

541 *do me reason*: (1) justify by his behaviour what I say of him; (2) grant me a duel. It is to this latter meaning that Truman responds.

551 *block . . . to fashion*: piece of wood on which you can carve (or shape) your lies.

589 *I'll engage, shall make you satisfaction*: Valentine urges Goodvile to save his energy for the duelling field, where Truman can be relied upon to oblige him.

619 *convince*: accomplish my victory; establish your guilt.

662 *close*: secret.

670 *that thou*: in the fact that you.

674 S.D. *fools' caps*: caps of fantastic shape, often large, cone-like structures, formerly worn by fools or jesters.

678 *warning of what*: warning from what.

682 *give my kinsman Sir Noble joy*: congratulate my kinsman Sir Noble on his marriage.

687 *as simply as I stand here*: (1) as plainly as I stand here; (2) as I stand here, a fool or simpleton. Sir Noble's response clearly encompasses both meanings.

692 *Good people*: Goodvile sardonically invokes the mode of address typical of the condemned criminal making his final speech before the gallows.

EPILOGUE

10 *Poets themselves . . . quarrels taught*: Otway here suggests that in-fighting among dramatists has taught others savagery in their criticism of plays. Historically, there may be something to this comment. By the 1670s, the theatre witnessed far more competition, as the gentleman poets of the 1660s were increasingly replaced by ambitious—and hungry—professional writers, such as Otway, Behn, Shadwell, Lee, and Durfey.

21 *higgling*: wrangling, cavilling. *OED* cites this particular use of the word by Otway.

26 *misses*: shorthand for mistress, a kept woman.

GLOSSARY

abroad out of doors, away from home

acquired to be come to be

addle-pated stupid; muddled

address courteous approach or conversation; courtship

admirable wondrous; amazing

admire wonder

adod interjection; abbreviated form of 'Ah God!'

ague fever, fit

air expression, demeanour; melody or tune

alderman governor or warden of a guild

allons 'let us go' (French)

ambuscade ambush

amiss untowardly

a-mort lifeless, dejected (from the French *à mort*)

amour love affair; courtship; also by the seventeenth century, an intrigue or illicit affair

anon (adv.) soon; presently

antic grotesque, bizarre, ludicrous

apace swiftly, quickly

apprehend understand; fear

arch-wag an extreme joker

artificially ingeniously, artfully; feigned skilfully

aspect facial expression

assignation secret meeting, usually between lovers

baffle foil, frustrate the intentions of; treat with scorn, reduce to mockery

baulk thwart, disappoint

bawd procurer; woman keeping a house of prostitution

bawdy (n.) smutty language

bedrid confined to bed

begetting procreating

begone be gone; get out of here

beldame an aged woman; specifically, a hag, witch, or virago

belle passion violent passion

bepat to pat frequently

betimes quickly

betwixt between

billet letter

billet-doux love letter

blackamoor dark-skinned person

blade a gallant or beau

blast ruin, discredit

bob taunt, bitter jest

bobbed tricked, deceived

boggle start with fright, shy away

bona fide literally, 'with good faith'; more generally, with sincerity, truly

bona roba a wench; a lustful woman

bonjour good day

brimmer full cup

bring about come about, make a complete revolution; reverse, convert

brisk full of mettle, high-spirited

bubble cheat

bud form of 'sbud (q.v.)

buffle fool; simpleton

bumper a glass filled to the brim

buzz whisper, murmur

by dad a mild oath; a variant of 'by God'

by Jericho exclamation

by the Lord Harry a mild oath

by-words proverbs; pat expressions

caper (n.) dance

carder card player

carriage conduct, behaviour

chaffering haggling, bargaining

chalks out sketch out; plan

chapmen merchants; retail dealers

charge (n.) ward

chedreux expensive, fashionable periwig (q.v.), named after its creator

choused cheated, duped, gulled

cit (abbrev.) citizen; normally a term of contempt

civil polite, modest, refined; can also mean sexually compliant

clack loud chatter, noise

clap venereal disease, usually syphilis

clinquant glittering; tinselled

collation a light meal, often taken in the evening

collop a slice or piece of flesh

comedians actors

compass (vb.) accomplish

complaisance eagerness to please, civility

confidence impudence

confound (vb.) curse; confuse, perplex, amaze

congee courteous or obeisant bow

conjure constrain by oath; conspire

conjuror sorcerer

contribution fee levied for support of the army in the field

coranto a brisk lively dance of French origin

cordial medicine

countenance face; patronage, appearance of favour

counterfeit (vb.) feign, pretend

coxcomb fool; simpleton

cozened defrauded, tricked

cravat a neck cloth or tie

crop-sick having an upset stomach, especially through effeminate lovesickness

cross-grained contrary; perverse; difficult to deal with

cudgel (vb.) beat

cum privilegio with privilege, with impunity

curate assistant to parish priest

curious careful

daggled bespattered, filthy

dastard (adj.) cowardly, meek

dastard (n.) dullard, sot; despicable coward

d'ee do you

delicate delightful, charming, pleasant; lovely, graceful, elegant

derogate detract from, lessen

desert worthiness; deserving of recompense

design plot, intention

devotions prayers; religious observances

disburse defray a charge; spend, give away

discourse conversation

discover reveal, unmask

discovery revelation, unmasking

dispatch (intr. vb.) hasten; be quick to conclude a business; be done with

distance, at a at an impasse; feuding

distemper illness of the body or mind

distracted insane

diversion entertainment, pleasure

divert entertain

divertive producing diversion; entertaining

docible teachable

dogged followed, trailed

doggerel trivial, coarse verse

doom (vb.) determine, decree

doubloons a Spanish gold coin worth a double pistole

doubt (vb.) fear

doxy strumpet, whore

draw cuts draw lots

drone idler, sluggard

due of course customary

dumps melancholy, low spirits

durst dare

easy compliant; something done with ease

éclaircissement the clearing up of a misunderstanding

éclat brilliance

e'er contraction of 'ever'

egad an interjection used as a softened oath; probably a form of 'A God' or 'By God'

equipage carriage and horses with attendant servants; can also refer to a retinue of retainers

ere at a former time; before

errant arrant, erring

eternized made eternal

éveillée sprightly, lively

exact precise; formal

except object

excepted excluded

exception objection

extravagant immoderate; beyond reason

fact deed

faculty aptitude

fain willing under the circumstances

fain (adv.) gladly

farthing a quarter of a penny

faugh exclamation of disgust

fleering jeering, mocking

fond foolish, excessively amorous

fop (n.) a pretender to wit; more generally, a fool

foppery foolishness, stupidity

forage (n.) food (especially for horses in army)

forbear (vb.) abstain or refrain from

'fore George a mild oath

formal prudish; rigid

forsooth truly, in truth

fourscore eighty

freshman newcomer, novice

frisk jig or dance

frolic (adj.) free, joyous, mirthful

froward adverse, unfavourable

frustrated thwarted

fulsome repulsive, coarse, nauseating

fustian bombastic or turgid speech

gad an asseveration; a milder form of 'God'

gadso variant of 'Catso', an interjection based on the Italian *cazzo* ('penis')

gallantry (n.) amorous intrigue; polite or courteous attention to ladies

galled vexed

galley-pots jars used by apothecaries to store ointments and salves

game-mistress a woman addicted to amorous 'play'

gamester gambler; someone addicted to amorous sport

geld castrate

generation the manner of begetting; generating progeny

generous having the qualities and virtues appropriate to a gentleman

gentlemen of the long robe judges, magistrates

gib-cat castrated male cat; also, an insulting name for an old woman

give over give up

give the go-by pass without being noticed, slip away unperceived

glass mirror

God a mercy used in the sense of 'God reward you', as an exclamation of thanks

goodly comely; also generous or gracious

grimace pretence

hab-nab hit or miss; succeed or fail; anyhow

habit dress

hale (vb.) drag; draw forcibly

hand handwriting

handsomely properly, favourably

hangings tapestries, wall hangings

hard by close by; near

hark listen

harkee hark ye ('listen, you')

hast have

hazard (vb.) risk, gamble

heart, in secretly, in one's innermost thoughts

hector bully

hen-hearted timorous or cowardly

hey-day exclamation denoting gaiety, high spirits, or wonder

hobbling a halting rhythm in verse

hoiting giddy

horrid offensive, disagreeable; very bad or objectionable

horrid fact horrid deed or crime

hugger mugger in secret; clandestinely

humour temperament, character; inclination, frame of mind

huswife housewife

idle insignificant, frivolous; useless

i'fack parallel form of 'i'fads' ('in faith')

i'fads parallel form to 'i'fack', a perversion of 'i'faith' (in faith; by my faith)

ill-favoured ugly

imbrued stained with, soaked in

immoderately excessively, beyond bounds

impertinent impudent, pert

inapprehensive not apprehensive, without apprehension

infernal (n.) devil, fiend

injurious hurtful, deleterious

interest self-interest

interior existing in the mind or soul

intrigue secret love affair

in troth truly, verily, indeed

issue outcome

jade derogatory term for a woman

jeer mock, deride

jerk blow, slash of the whip; jibe

jidge judge

jilt (n.) strumpet

jilt (vb.) trick, deceive

jocose playful, humorous

jubilee day of rejoicing, a holiday

kinswoman female relative

knight-errant knight in medieval romance who wandered in search of acts of chivalry; sometimes used in ridicule (as an allusion to Don Quixote)

lampoon scurrilous satirical poem, usually directed against an individual

lately recently

law exclamation of astonishment or admiration

legions vast host; multitude of spirits

light off get off; dismount

light on come upon; run into

lightsome nimble; lively.

loll (vb.) saunter, follow

lovesome lovable, worthy of love; lovely, beautiful

maidenhead state of virginity

make mouths make faces

marry exclamation of surprise or indignation

meanness lowness or humbleness of rank; insignificance or inferiority

mechanic vulgar, base; belonging to the 'lower orders'

mercy o' me may God have mercy on me; interjection expressing surprise or fear

methinks it seems to me

methoughts it seemed to me

mettle spirit

mettled spirited, courageous

mewed up enclosed, imprisoned

mien bearing, air

miscarry to go wrong; to fail or come to nothing

misgive suggest doubts or apprehensions; suggest the fear of

mobile angry mob

modishly fashionably

mum silence!

mummery ridiculous play-acting or an absurd ceremonial

mump (vb.) disappoint; overreach, cheat

ne'er never

nice fastidious

nick critical moment; exact point aimed at

nigh (adv.) near; next

ninny simpleton; fool

noisome noxious, harmful

noodle brain

nose (vb.) make faces, grimace

not without not lacking; with or having some

nuncle uncle

object sight

observance respectful attention; dutifulness

od's heart shortening of 'God's heart', an earlier version of 'God bless your heart'

od's my life variation of 'God's my life', an exclamation of surprise

o'er over

of course routine; formulaic; demanded by the situation

offers attempts, tries

ombre popular card game

oons softened form of 'God's wounds'

or . . . or either . . . or

original source

ought anything

out exclamation expressing abhorrence or indignation

out on't expel, reject; put a thing out

overreach outwit, outmanoeuvre

overture discovery, declaration; negotiations towards a proposal

own admit to

pander a bawd; a go–between in an intrigue or amour

paramour lady-love of a knight, lover; illicit lover or clandestine mistress

pattern model

periwig wig worn as fashionable headdress

peruke another term for periwig (q.v.)

phlegmatic sluggish; apathetic

pickle sorry plight or predicament

pippins variety of apple

pish exclamation of contempt or disgust

pitch on select; choose

pize an imprecation, perhaps a variant on 'pox' as in 'what a pox!'

plaguy (adj.) troublesome; annoying

pleasant amusing, humorous

poltroon spiritless coward

poniard dagger

positive absolute; dogmatic or opinionated

postures poses, tricks

pothecary apothecary (dialectal)

pother disturbance or commotion

practic practical, not theoretical

practice artful dealing, contrivance; pertaining to practice or action

prating foolish talk; inconsequential chatter

prentice abbreviated form of apprentice

presented given a present

presently immediately

pristine ancient, good old (as in a golden age)

prithee pray thee; please

privy private; pertaining to a person in his private capacity; possessing knowledge of

property tool, instrument

protest declare, assert

publish declare, make known

pudding-bag bag in which pudding is boiled

pugh exclamation of disgust

pulvilio scented powder

punk whore, prostitute

quality rank; social station

qualm sudden feeling of illness or faintness

quean jade, hussy; prostitute

quondam former

quoth said he

quoth a also 'quotha'; a variant of 'quoth' (said he). Sometimes used sarcastically after repeating a word or phrase uttered by someone else

ragout a stewed dish of meat and vegetables

railing against using abusive or foul language

raillery ridicule, rallying

rakehell scoundrel; immoral or dissolute person

rally (vb.) tease; banter with

ranging roving, wandering

rebate (vb.) blunt, dull; reduce the effect of

refractory stubborn, rebellious

regale entertain handsomely with food and/or conversation

remiss negligent, careless of duty

rencounter duel

repartees answers wittily, responds pertly

repast food eaten at a meal

repel drive back an attack

repose rest; sit or lie down

revel (vb.) carouse

rhymer poet; writer (also a dramatist who writes in verse)

riding cross riding in a contrary way; passing or intersecting each other

rotten diseased

rout (n.) assembly of rioters or revellers

sally sortie; an outburst of activity

saucy impudent, bold

'sbud contraction of 'God's blood'

Scotch song song sung on the Restoration stage in a Scottish dialect

scurvy worthless; contemptible

'sdeath contraction of 'God's death'

sensible perceptible by the senses

serviceable willing to be of service; diligent in service; profitable, useful

shift (vb.) bestir oneself; change (as in clothing)

sifting questioning, interrogating

signor sir; person of distinction or rank

siren mythological creature, often half-woman and half-bird, who lured unwary sailors to their death with enchanted music; temptress

smack an agreeable taste or flavour

small beer weak beer

sneaking petty, paltry; mean, contemptible

society companionship

solemnity wedding ceremony

something (adv.) rather, quite

sot fool or idiot; also a drunkard

soused soaked in liquor; drunk

sovereign (adj.) very good

spark (n.) a fashionable young man or woman about town

spark (vb.) to make a display; show off

spleen(s) ill-humour; peevishness; abdominal organ regarded as the source of laughter or mirth

spruce smartly dressed, nice in appearance

start (vb.) jump up suddenly; react with astonishment

staunch airtight, impervious; resolute

stinkard term of abuse; one who stinks

straight (adv.) immediately

strumpet harlot, unchaste woman

style (vb.) call; characterize

subtle cunning, acute

suddenly shortly, very soon

suffer (vb.) permit me

suit petition, appeal

superscription address on a letter

surfeit (vb.) overeat, satiate ourselves

swain a shepherd; a country gallant or lover

sweetmeats confections, especially candied fruits or sugared nuts

swimmingly smoothly and without impediment

swinge (vb.) beat, hit; scold, castigate

swinger rogue, rascal

swoons faints

tender (vb.) value, have a regard for

termagant (n.) a scold, a brawling woman

termagant (adj.) violent, truculent, quarrelsome

thither to that place; there

thorough paced skilled, accomplished

threshold-place storage area located beneath the threshold

'tis it is

to boot in addition; as well

tory-rory behave uproariously; also, sing a rowdy drinking song

touse pull roughly about; to engage roughly in horseplay with a woman

towards imminent

town London

transports (n.) raptures; outbursts

transports (vb.) moves to a state of emotional outburst, carries away

treat of negotiate about

trice, in a in a moment

trig walk quickly

troth truth; upon my word

tumble engage in sexual play

tweers lascivious glances; leers

'twere it were

'twill it will

twiring leering; giving amorous glances

'twould it would

'udsblood God's blood

uncase strip, undress

unconscionable unscrupulous, having no conscience; unreasonably harsh

undertaking energetic, enterprising

unsensible variant of 'insensible'

untoward perverse, intractable, uncooperative

vacuity absence, a vacuum

valet de chambre manservant, especially one who attends to his master's person

variance lack of harmony, being at odds

varlet someone of knavish disposition; a rascal or rogue

vent publish

venture, at a by chance, at a risk

verity truth

virago a heroic woman; a female warrior

vizard mask

volary a large birdcage; an aviary

wag (n.) joker; mischievous person

waggery drollery; a mischievous action or piece of business

waggish jocular, teasing in manner, mischievous

want lack

wanton (vb.) sport; gambol; behave lasciviously

warrant (vb.) promise, assure; authorize (to do something)

well-favoured handsome, comely

wenching consorting with 'common' or 'loose' women

wert were

wheedle persuade through the use of flattery; cajole

whirligig an inconstant or flighty person

whither where; wherever

whoop exclamation or shout indicating surprise, derision, or exultation

whoremaster procurer or pimp

withal with; in addition, moreover; at the same time

without outside

wont habitual, usual

wordling worldly person

worry (vb.) harass; tease

wot know

wrack damage, destruction; also, an instance of suffering

wrought created, fashioned

yonder over there; within view but distant

GEORGE ELIOT	Daniel Deronda
	The Lifted Veil and Brother Jacob
	Middlemarch
	The Mill on the Floss
	Silas Marner
SUSAN FERRIER	Marriage
ELIZABETH GASKELL	Cranford
	The Life of Charlotte Brontë
	Mary Barton
	North and South
	Wives and Daughters
GEORGE GISSING	New Grub Street
	The Odd Woman
THOMAS HARDY	Far from the Madding Crowd
	Jude the Obscure
	The Mayor of Casterbridge
	The Return of the Native
	Tess of the d'Urbervilles
	The Woodlanders
WILLIAM HAZLITT	Selected Writings
JAMES HOGG	The Private Memoirs and Confessions of a Justified Sinner
JOHN KEATS	The Major Works
	Selected Letters
CHARLES MATURIN	Melmoth the Wanderer
WALTER SCOTT	The Antiquary
	Ivanhoe
	Rob Roy
MARY SHELLEY	Frankenstein
	The Last Man

American Literature

British and Irish Literature

Children's Literature

Classics and Ancient Literature

Colonial Literature

Eastern Literature

European Literature

History

Medieval Literature

Oxford English Drama

Poetry

Philosophy

Politics

Religion

The Oxford Shakespeare

A complete list of Oxford Paperbacks, including Oxford World's Classics, Oxford Shakespeare, Oxford Drama, and Oxford Paperback Reference, is available in the UK from the Academic Division Publicity Department, Oxford University Press, Great Clarendon Street, Oxford OX2 6DP.

In the USA, complete lists are available from the Paperbacks Marketing Manager, Oxford University Press, 198 Madison Avenue, New York, NY 10016.

Oxford Paperbacks are available from all good bookshops. In case of difficulty, customers in the UK can order direct from Oxford University Press Bookshop, Freepost, 116 High Street, Oxford OX1 4BR, enclosing full payment. Please add 10 per cent of published price for postage and packing.